ALL MUSIC GUIDE REQUIRED LISTENING

CLASSIC ROCK

All Music Guide Required Listening Series, No. 1

ALL MUSIC GUIDE REQUIRED LISTENING

CLASSIC ROCK

Edited by

Chris Woodstra
John Bush
Stephen Thomas Erlewine

Backbeat
Books

An Imprint of Hal Leonard Corporation
New York

Published in 2007 by Backbeat Books
An Imprint of Hal Leonard Corporation
19 West 21st Street, New York, NY 10010

Printed in the United States of America

Book design by Snow Creative Services

Library of Congress Cataloging-in-Publication Data is available upon request.

All Media Guide has created the world's largest and most comprehensive information databases for music, videos, DVDs, and video games. With coverage of both in-print and out-of-print titles, the massive AMG archive includes reviews, plot synopses, biographies, ratings, images, titles, credits, essays, and thousands of descriptive categories. All content is original, written expressly for AMG by a worldwide network of professional staff and freelance writers specializing in music, movies, and games. The AMG databases—**All Music Guide®**, **All Movie Guide®**, and **All Game Guide**™—are licensed by major retailers, Internet sites, and other entertainment media providers and are available to the public through its websites (www.allmusic.com, www.allmovie.com, www.allgame.com) and through its published works: *All Music Guide, All Music Guide to Rock, All Music Guide to Country, All Music Guide to Jazz, All Music Guide to the Blues, All Music Guide to Electronica, All Music Guide to Soul, All Music Guide to Hip-Hop,* and *All Music Guide to Classical Music.*

All Media Guide, LLC, 1168 Oak Valley Drive, Ann Arbor, MI 48108
T: 734/887-5600. F: 734/827-2492
www.allmediaguide.com, www.allmusic.com, www.allgame.com

ISBN-10: 0-87930-917-2
ISBN-13: 978-0-87930-917-6

www.backbeatbooks.com

CONTENTS

INTRODUCTION

What is classic rock? Unlike the British invasion, psychedelia, punk, or alternative rock, it's not a description that was applied to the music during its heyday; it's a classification bestowed in retrospect, as listeners look back at the past through rose-colored glasses. The genre's congratulatory name conveys that this music wasn't only great, it was *classic*, nearly timeless. It's no surprise the term originated in marketing. It was used to describe a radio format developed in the '80s as a way to play all those favorites from the '60s and '70s that were being pushed aside by metalheads with makeup or pale guys with angular haircuts. Rooted in marketing it may have been, but "classic rock," like so much other terminology from the corporate world, transcended its origins and took on a life of its own. It was a name that was needed—not just by the baby boomers raised on this music, but by the generations who picked up on this stuff later. "Classic rock" came to be known as shorthand for the peak of the rock & roll era, the time when the music was at its greatest popularity and creativity, and the whole rock & roll lifestyle essentially came into being.

Of course, rock & roll was around long before classic rock. It came crashing into existence in the mid-50s, as the music of Elvis Presley, Chuck Berry, Jerry Lee Lewis, Little Richard, Buddy Holly, Bo Diddley, Gene Vincent, Fats Domino, the Everly Brothers, and so many others created shock waves in pop culture, inspiring the musicians that became the classic rock generation. Classic rockers grew up on Elvis and Chuck, or perhaps Muddy Waters and Robert Johnson, or any number of blues, folk, and country singers. Classic rock artists started synthesizing these styles into their own sounds sometime in the early '60s, after the Beatles spearheaded the British invasion. This invasion kick-started a renaissance in rock, an era in which musicians invented and reinvented rock & roll at a delirious pace. The Beatles mark the start of the classic rock era, but their first records were more closely aligned to the reckless energy and enthusiasm of early rock & roll. It wasn't until the mid-60s, as they—along with almost all their peers—started to experiment, that the classic rock era began.

Arguably, the true beginning of the classic rock era was the Beatles' 1967 LP *Sgt. Pepper's Lonely Hearts Club Band*, the record that established the shift from single to album as the primary rock & roll method of expression. Singles, addictive rushes of rhythm and hooks, were all about the moment. Albums lingered longer, as bands could explore different ideas on different tracks, creating their own worlds through the course of two sides of a vinyl LP. On no album was this truer than on *Sgt. Pepper*, where the Beatles not only tried different sounds, but acted as if they were a different band altogether, giving themselves freedom to explore things that were unimaginable just a few short years before. Inspired by *Sgt. Pepper*, other bands took this freedom to new heights almost immediately, sometimes replicating its carnivalesque sound, other times running away from it. Regardless, there was no denying that after 1967, music was no longer the same. This was largely due to *Pepper*, but also other seminal '67 albums like the Jimi Hendrix Experience's *Are You Experienced?*; Pink Floyd's *Piper at the Gates of Dawn*; the Who's *Who Sell Out*; The Doors' self-titled debut, *The Doors*; Cream's *Disraeli Gears*; and Jefferson Airplane's *Surrealistic Pillow*. All these albums suggested new worlds, and provided a foundation for classic rock.

For the next 15 years or so following 1967, rock music was at its peak as a cultural force. It was the time when bands were turning into global superstars, as all the cornerstones of rock culture began to fall into place: albums that were popular without a hit single, guitarists who became heroes, and bands that treated stadiums like territories to be conquered. This was the time that rock stars became larger-than-life figures who drove Cadillacs into swimming pools and had groupies in every port. They seemed like golden gods—maybe because their faces weren't seen on MTV and their music wasn't immediately available on the Internet, or perhaps because the music really was that powerful. Certainly, it can be argued that during the years that followed, most rock & roll was either a reaction or an expansion on classic rock—either building upon it, or spitting in its face.

It may sound as if classic rock was monolithic, but it was not. Much of it was hard rock, powered by the blues. However, Aerosmith's greasy boogie did not sound like Lynyrd Skynyrd's gutsy Southern rock, and neither band sounded like their forefathers, the Rolling Stones. Although they built upon the orchestral pop of *Sgt. Pepper*, Electric Light Orchestra were also a far cry from their heroes, the Beatles, and their artiness was quite different from that of Pink Floyd or Yes. All these bands created their own sounds, and while some of these sounds could be called "dated" (it's hard to deny that much of classic rock is of a particular time or place), there's an inventiveness and fearlessness to the music that continues to be compelling decades after its recording. With the benefit of hindsight, it's easy to see how once derided bands like Genesis and Queen were utterly original in their approaches, or how Led Zeppelin's roots were almost as deep in British folk as they were in the blues. This variety is what has kept classic rock vital, even for listeners who weren't yet born when *Sgt. Pepper*, *Exile on Mainstreet*, *Dark Side of the Moon*, *Physical Grafitti*, or *Eliminator* were released. There's a reason why kids wear shirts bearing the logo of dead bands or play games called Guitar Hero—because the music still captures the imagination.

This volume of *All Music Guide Required Listening* provides a roadmap to all the noteworthy albums within the classic rock era. With a book like this, intended to showcase the best albums, some limits have to be set. So, we stick to the prime years of the genre, starting with the rise of album-oriented rock and stretching until the dawn of MTV's popularity, which undercut album-oriented radio and its stars like Styx and REO Speedwagon (who weren't as photogenic as Duran Duran or even ZZ Top, with their beards and babes). Generally, we cover the time frame of 1967–1982, but since music never quite fits into such tidy guidelines, some albums fall just outside the reach of this span. Because classic rock is album-oriented, we're album-oriented too, downplaying compilations for proper LPs and including records that may not be perfect, but are interesting; some capture the era perfectly.

The heart of this book is built upon album reviews, but we've added several supplements to the back to bring it up to the MP3 era. These include playlists of songs featuring classic riffs and guitar solos, and songs about love and rock & roll itself. We've also provided a timeline of the noteworthy albums for each year of the classic rock era, along with a list of artist debuts and our choices for the Basic 50—the albums that you need to hear to understand classic rock. But then again, why stop at 50? As this book shows, there are far more than 50 classic rock albums that you should hear. This volume will guide you through the good stuff, whether you're looking to replace your tattered old vinyl or starting to discover this music for the first time. And if you should ever need further guidance, turn to www.allmusic.com, where we provide detailed reviews and biographies of all the artists covered in these pages, plus much, much more.

ALL MUSIC GUIDE REQUIRED LISTENING

CLASSIC ROCK

CLASSIC ROCK ALBUM DIRECTORY

AC/DC

High Voltage
October 1976, Epic

One of the perennial complaints about AC/DC is that they've never changed—and if that's true, *High Voltage* is the blueprint they've followed all their career. Comprised of highlights from their first two Australian albums—1975's *TNT* and its '76 follow-up, also entitled *High Voltage*—the album has every single one of AC/DC's archetypes. There are songs about rock & roll, slow sleazy blues, high-voltage boogie, double entendres so obvious they qualify as single-entendres and, of course, the monster riffs of Angus Young, so big and bold they bruise the listener upon contact. It's those riffs—so catchy, they sound lifted when they're original, so simple they're often wrongly dismissed as easy—that give the music its backbone, the foundation for Bon Scott to get dirty, and rockers never got quite as dirty as Bon Scott. Scott sounded as if you could catch a disease by listening to him. He sounded like the gateman at hell, somebody that never hid the notion that lurking behind the door are some bad, dangerous things, but they're also *fun*, too, and he made no apologies for that. But for as primal as *High Voltage* is, it's also a lot weirder and funnier than it's given credit for, too—those are bagpipes that solo on "It's a Long Way to the Top (If You Want to Rock & Roll)" and "She's Got Balls" is a perversely funny dirty joke. This is music so primal that it's enduring—it feels like it existed before AC/DC got there, and it will exist long afterward. And if AC/DC did wind up bettering this blueprint in the future, there's no question that this original is still potent, even thrilling no matter how many times they returned to the well, or how many times this record is played.

Stephen Thomas Erlewine

Dirty Deeds Done Dirt Cheap
1976, Epic

There's a real sense of menace to "Dirty Deeds Done Dirt Cheap," the title song of AC/DC's third album. More than most of their songs to date, it captured the seething malevolence of Bon Scott, the sense that he *reveled* in doing bad things, encouraged by the maniacal riffs of Angus and Malcolm Young who provided him with their most brutish rock & roll yet. But for as glorious as the title track was, the entire album served as a call to arms from a group that wanted nothing more than to celebrate the dirtiest, nastiest instincts humans could have, right down to the insurgent anti-authority vibe that runs throughout the record. Take "Big Balls"—sure, it's a dirty joke, but it's a dirty joke with class overthrow in mind. There's a sense on *Dirty Deeds* that AC/DC is storming the gates—they're problem children sick of waiting around to be a millionaire, so they're gonna make their own money, even if they take down others as they go. That's what gives *Dirty Deeds Done Dirt Cheap* its supercharged, nervy pulse; there's a real sense of danger to this record, something that can't be hidden beneath the jokes. Maybe that's why the album wasn't released in the US until 1981, after Bon's death, after AC/DC had become millionaires—if it arrived any earlier, it would have been too insurrectionist for the common good.

Stephen Thomas Erlewine

Let There Be Rock
June 1977, Epic

Let There Be Rock, the fourth AC/DC album—and first to see simultaneous international release—is as lean and mean as the original lineup ever got. Shaved down to the bone—there are only eight tracks, giving this a lethal efficiency even with a couple of meandering jams—this is a high-voltage, brutal record, filled with "Bad Boy Boogie." It has a bit of a bluesier edge than other AC/DC records, but this is truly the sound of the band reaching its peak. There's the near majesty of "Let There Be Rock," there's Bon Scott acknowledging with a wink that "Hell Ain't a Bad Place to Be," and then there's the monumental "Whole Lotta Rosie." Which gets down to a key thing about AC/DC. If Led Zeppelin were celebrating a "Whole Lotta Love," AC/DC got down to the grimy details in their leering tribute to the joys of sex with a plus-sized woman. And that's AC/DC's allure in a nutshell—it's sweaty, dirty, nasty rock, music that is played to the last call and beyond, and they've rarely done that kind of rock better than they did here.

Stephen Thomas Erlewine

Powerage
May 1978, Epic

Powerage was a first in the sense that it debuted bassist Cliff Williams, but it really is more of a final curtain to the band's early years. It would be the last produced by Vanda & Young, the legendary Australian production team who also helmed hits by the Easybeats, and it was the last before AC/DC became superstars. As such, it's perhaps the most overlooked of their '70s records, also because, frankly, it is the most uneven of them. Not that it's a bad record—far from it, actually. There are a few genuine classics here, most notably "Down Payment Blues" and "Up to My Neck in You," and there's a real appeal in how Bon Scott's gutter poems of excess are reaching a mythic level; there's a real sense that he truly does believe that rock & roll leads straight to hell on "Rock 'n' Roll Damnation." But overall, the record is just a bit too wobbly, one where the parts don't add up to a record as hard and addictive as before—but there's still plenty worth hearing here.

Stephen Thomas Erlewine

Highway to Hell
August 1979, Epic

Of course, *Highway to Hell* is the final album AC/DC recorded with Bon Scott, the lead singer who provided the group with a fair share of its signature sleaze. Just months after its release, Scott literally partied himself to death, dying of alcohol poisoning after a night of drinking, a rock & roll fatality that took no imagination to predict. In light of his passing, it's hard not to see *Highway to Hell* as a last testament of sorts, being that it was his last work and all, and if Scott was going to go out in a blaze of glory, this certainly was the way to do it. This is a veritable rogue's gallery of deviance, from cheerfully clumsy sex talk and drinking anthems to general outlandish behavior. It's tempting to say that Scott might have been prescient about his end—or to see the title track as ominous in the wake of his death—trying to spill it all out on paper, but it's more accurate to say that the ride had just gotten very fast and very wild for AC/DC, and he was simply flying high. After all, it wasn't just Scott who reached a new peak on *Highway to Hell*; so did the Young brothers, crafting their monster riffs into full-fledged, undeniable songs. This is their best set of songs yet, from the incessant, intoxicating boogie of "Girls Got Rhythm" to "If You Want Blood (You've Got It)." Some of the credit should also go to Robert John "Mutt" Lange, who gives the album a precision and magnitude that the Vanda & Young LPs lacked in their grimy charm. Filtered through Mutt's mixing board, AC/DC has never sounded so enormous, and they've never had such great songs, and they had never delivered an album as singularly bone-crunching or classic as this until now.

Stephen Thomas Erlewine

Back in Black
August 1980, Epic

The first sound on *Back in Black* is the deep, ominous drone of church bells—or "Hell's Bells," as it were, opening the album and AC/DC's next era with a fanfare while ringing a fond farewell to Bon Scott, their late lead singer who partied himself straight to hell. But this implies that *Back in Black* is some kind of tribute to Scott, which may be true on a superficial level—black is a funeral cover, hell's bells certainly signify death—but this isn't filled with mournful songs about the departed. It's a more fitting tribute, actually, since AC/DC not only carried on without him, but they delivered a record that to the casual ear sounds like the seamless successor to *Highway to Hell*, right down to how Brian Johnson's screech is a dead ringer for Scott's growl. Most listeners could be forgiven for thinking that Johnson was Scott, but Johnson is different than Bon. He's driven by the same obsessions—sex and drink and rock & roll, basically—but there isn't nearly as much malevolence in his words or attitude as there was with Scott. Bon sounded like a criminal, Brian sounds like a rowdy scamp throughout *Back in Black*, which helps give it a real party atmosphere. Of course, Johnson shouldn't be given all the credit for *Back in Black*, since Angus and Malcolm carry on with the song-oriented riffing that made *Highway to Hell* close to divine. Song for song, they deliver not just mammoth riffs but songs that are anthems, from the greasy "Shoot to Thrill" to the pummeling "Back in Black," which pales only next to "You Shook Me All Night Long," the greatest one-night-stand anthem in rock history. That tawdry celebration of sex is what made AC/DC different from all other metal bands—there was no sword & sorcery, no darkness, just a rowdy party, and they never held a bigger, better party than they did on *Back in Black*.

Stephen Thomas Erlewine

Aerosmith

Aerosmith
January 1973, Columbia

In retrospect, it's a bit shocking how fully formed the signature Aerosmith sound was on their self-titled 1973 debut—which may not be the same thing as best-executed, because this album still sounds like a first album, complete with the typical stumbles and haziness that comes with a debut. Despite all this, *Aerosmith* clearly showcases all the attributes of the band that would become the defining American hard rock band of the '70s. Here, the Stones influences are readily apparent, from the Jagger-esque phrasing of Steven Tyler to the group's high-octane boogie, but the group displays little of the Stones' deep love of blues here. Instead, Aerosmith is bloozy—their riffs don't swing, they slide. They borrow liberally from Led Zeppelin's hybridization of Chess and Sun riffs without ever sounding much like Zep. They are never as British as Zeppelin—they lack the delicate folky preciousness, they lack the obsession with blues authenticity, they lack the larger-than-life persona of so many Brit bands. They are truly an American band, sounding as though they were the best bar band in your local town, cranking out nasty hard-edged rock, best heard on "Mama Kin," the best rocker here, one that's so greasy it nearly slips through their fingers. But the early masterpiece is, of course, "Dream On," the first full-fledged power ballad. There was nothing quite like it in 1973, and it remains the blueprint for all power ballads since. The rest of the record contains the seeds of Aerosmith's sleazoid blues-rock, but they wouldn't quite perfect that sound until the next time around.

Stephen Thomas Erlewine

Get Your Wings
March 1974, Columbia

Often overshadowed by the subsequent twin highlights of *Toys in the Attic* and *Rocks*, Aerosmith's 1974 second album, *Get Your Wings*, is where Aerosmith became Aerosmith—it's where they teamed up with producer Jack Douglas, it's 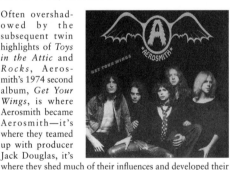 where they shed much of their influences and developed their own trademark sound, it's where they turned into songwriters, it's where Steven Tyler unveiled his signature obsessions with sex and sleaze. Chief among these attributes may be Douglas, who either helped the band ease into the studio or captured their sound in a way their debut never did. This is a leaner, harder album, bathed in grease and layered in grit, but it's not just down to Douglas. The band itself sounds more distinctive. There are blues in Joe Perry and Joey Kramer's interplay, but this leapfrogs over blues-rock; it turns into slippery hard rock. To be sure, it's still easy to hear the Stones here, but they never really sound Stonesy; there's almost more of the Yardbirds to the way the group works the riffs, particularly evident on the cover of the early 'Birds classic "The Train Kept a Rollin'." But if the Yardbirds were tight and nervy, Aerosmith is blown out and loose, the sound of excess incarnate—that is, in every way but the writing itself which is confident and strong, fueled by Tyler's gonzo sex drive. He is the "Lord of the Thighs," playing that "Same, Old Song and Dance," but he also slows down enough for the eerie "Seasons of Wither," a powerful slow-churning ballad whose mastery of atmosphere is a good indication of how far the band has grown. They never attempted anything quite so creepy on their debut, but it isn't just that Aerosmith is trying newer things on *Get Your Wings*, it's that they're doing their bloozy bluster better and bolder, which is what turns this sophomore effort into their first classic.

Stephen Thomas Erlewine

Toys in the Attic
April 1975, Sony

After nearly getting off the ground with *Get Your Wings*, Aerosmith finally perfected their mix of Stonesy raunch and Zeppelin-esque riffing with their third album, *Toys in the Attic*. The success of the album derives from a combination of an increased sense of songwriting skills and purpose. Not only does Joe Perry turn out indelible riffs like "Walk This Way," "Toys in the Attic," and "Sweet Emotion," but Steven Tyler has fully embraced sleaziness as his artistic muse. Taking his cue from the old dirty blues "Big Ten Inch Record," Tyler writes with a gleeful impishness about sex throughout *Toys in the Attic*, whether it's the teenage heavy petting of "Walk This Way," the promiscuous "Sweet Emotion," or the double-entendres of "Uncle Salty" and "Adam's Apple." The rest of Aerosmith, led by Perry's dirty, exaggerated riffing, provide an appropriately greasy backing. Before *Toys in the Attic*, no other hard rock band sounded like this. Sure, Aerosmith cribbed heavily from the records of the Rolling Stones, New York Dolls, and Led Zeppelin, but they didn't have any of the menace of their influences, nor any of their mystique. Aerosmith was a gritty, street-wise hard rock band who played their blues as blooze and were in it for a good time; *Toys in the Attic* crystallizes that attitude.

Stephen Thomas Erlewine

Rocks
May 1976, Columbia

Few albums have been so appropriately named as Aerosmith's 1976 classic *Rocks*. Despite hard drug use escalating among bandmembers, Aerosmith produced a superb follow-up to their masterwork *Toys in the Attic*, nearly topping it in the process. Many Aero fans will point to *Toys* as the band's quintessential album (it contained two radio/concert standards after all, "Walk This Way" and "Sweet Emotion"), but out of all their albums, *Rocks* did the best job of capturing Aerosmith at their most raw and rocking. Like its predecessor, a pair of songs have become their most renowned—the menacing, hard rock, cowboy-stomper "Back in the Saddle," as well as the downright viscous funk groove of "Last Child." Again, even the lesser-known tracks prove essential to the makeup of the album, such as the stimulated "Rats in the Cellar" (a response of sorts to "Toys in the Attic"), the Stonesy "Combination," and the forgotten riff-rocker "Get the Lead Out." Also included is the apocalyptic "Nobody's Fault," the up-and-coming rock star tale of "Lick and a Promise," and the album-closing ballad "Home Tonight."

With *Rocks*, Aerosmith appeared to be indestructible.

Greg Prato

Draw the Line
December 1977, Columbia

Renting out an abandoned convent on the outskirts of New York City to record the follow-up to the hellacious *Rocks* may not have been the best idea, but 1977's *Draw the Line* still managed to be another down-and-dirty Aerosmith release. While it wasn't as awe-inspiring as their last two albums—the members have said that the music suddenly got "cloudy" around this time (due to in-band fighting/ego clashes, excessive living, etc.), *Draw the Line* catches fire more times than not. Unlike their most recent album successes, the band shies away from studio experimenting and dabbling in different styles; instead they return to simple, straight-ahead hard rock. The album-opening title track features a gloriously abrasive Joe Perry slide guitar riff and has been featured in concert ever since, while the punk-esque "Bright Light Fright" featured Perry's first ever lead vocal spot on an Aerosmith record. Other highlights include a reworking of the blues obscurity "Milk Cow Blues," which Perry's pre-Aerosmith group, the Jam Band, played live, as well as "I Wanna Know Why," "Critical Mass," "Get It Up," "Kings and Queens," and "Sight for Sore Eyes." *Draw the Line* would turn out to be the last true studio album from Aerosmith's original lineup for nearly a decade.

Greg Prato

Permanent Vacation
August 1987, Geffen

The much-ballyhooed reunion of the original Aerosmith lineup had pretty much fallen flat on its face after 1985's hit-and-miss *Done With Mirrors*. Realizing that the band simply couldn't do it alone, A&R guru John Kalodner capitalized on the runaway success of Run-D.M.C.'s cover of "Walk This Way" and decided to draft in the day's top hired hands, including knob-twiddler extraordinaire Bruce Fairbairn and career-revitalizing song doctors Desmond Child and Jim Vallance. Together, they would help craft *Permanent Vacation*, the album which would reinvent Aerosmith as '80s and '90s superstars. Yet, despite the mostly stellar songwriting, which makes it a strong effort overall, some of the album's nooks and crannies haven't aged all that well because of Fairbairn's overwrought production, featuring an exaggerated sleekness typical of most mid-'80s pop-metal albums. Furthermore, Desmond Child's pedantic writing often compromises the timeliness of even the best material. On the other hand, prefab radio gems like "Rag Doll" and "Dude (Looks Like a Lady)" remain largely unassailable from a "delivering the goods" perspective. But remember kids, this *is* Aerosmith, so that can only mean one thing: a guaranteed number of incredible tracks for any time and place. These include the earthy voodoo blues of "St. John" and the excellent hobo-harmonica fable of "Hangman Jury." And, although some of the remaining cuts lean to the filler side, both the awkwardly Caribbean title track and the cover of the Beatles' "I'm Down" are well executed. Finally, the crowd-pleasing schmaltz of "Angel" showcases the band at the peak of its power ballad cheese. A valiant effort, this album proved to be the crucial catalyst in reintroducing Aerosmith to the masses, but if you're looking for an even better example of the band's renewed strength, check out *Pump* first.

John Franck & Ed Rivadavia

Pump
September 1989, Geffen

Where *Permanent Vacation* seemed a little overwhelmed by its pop concessions, *Pump* revels in them without ever losing sight of Aerosmith's dirty hard rock core. Which doesn't mean the record is a sellout—"What It Takes" has more emotion and grit than any of their other power ballads; "Janie's Got a Gun" tackles more complex territory than most previous songs; and "The Other Side" and "Love in an Elevator" rock relentlessly, no matter how many horns and synths fight with the guitars. Such ambition and successful musical eclecticism make *Pump* rank with *Rocks* and *Toys in the Attic*.

Stephen Thomas Erlewine

The Allman Brothers Band

The Allman Brothers Band
1969, Polydor

This might be the best debut album ever delivered by an American blues band, a bold, powerful, hard-edged, soulful essay in electric blues with a native Southern ambience. Some lingering elements of the psychedelic era then drawing to a close can be found in "Dreams," along with the template for the group's on-stage workouts with "Whipping Post," and a solid cover of Muddy Waters' "Trouble No More." There isn't a bad song here, and only the fact that the group did even better the next time out keeps this from getting the highest possible rating.

Bruce Eder

Idlewild South
1970, Polydor

The best studio album in the group's history, electric blues with an acoustic texture, virtuoso lead, slide, and organ playing, and a killer selection of songs, including "Midnight Rider," "Revival," "Don't Keep Me Wonderin'," and "In Memory of Elizabeth Reed" in its embryonic studio version, which is pretty impressive even at a mere six minutes and change. They also do the best white cover of Willie Dixon's "Hoochie Coochie Man" anyone's ever likely to hear.

Bruce Eder

At Fillmore East
July 1971, Polydor

Whereas most great live rock albums are about energy, *At Fillmore East* is like a great live jazz session, where the pleasure comes from the musicians' interaction and playing. The great thing about that is, the original album that brought the Allmans so much acclaim is as notable for its clever studio editing as it is for its performances. Producer Tom Dowd skillfully trimmed some of the performances down to relatively concise running time (edits later restored on the double-disc set *The Fillmore Concerts*), at times condensing several performances into one track. Far from being a sacrilege, this tactic helps present the Allmans in their best light, since even if the music isn't necessarily concise (three tracks run over ten minutes, with two in the 20-minute range), it does showcase the group's terrific instrumental interplay, letting each member (but particularly guitarist Duane and keyboardist/vocalist Gregg) shine. Even after the release of the unedited concerts, this original double album (single CD) remains the pinnacle of the Allmans and Southern rock at its most elastic, bluesy, and jazzy. [In 2004, Mercury reissued *At Fillmore East* as a hybrid SACD, playable in both regular CD players and Super Audio CD players. On each of the layers, the remastered sound is spectacular, a considerable upgrade from the initial CD pressings.]

Stephen Thomas Erlewine

Eat a Peach
1972, Polydor

A tribute to the dearly departed Duane, *Eat a Peach* rambles through two albums, running through a side of new songs, recorded post-Duane, spending a full album on live cuts from the *Fillmore East* sessions, then offering a round of studio tracks Duane completed before his death. On the first side, they do suggest the mellowness of the Dickey Betts-led *Brothers and Sisters*, particularly on the lovely "Melissa," and this stands in direct contrast with the monumental live cuts that dominate the album. They're at their best on the punchier covers of "One Way Out" and "Trouble No More," both proof of the group's exceptional talents as a roadhouse blues-rock band, but Duane does get his needed showcase on "Mountain Jam," a sprawling 33-minute jam that may feature a lot of great playing, but is certainly a little hard for anyone outside of diehards to sit through. Apart from that cut, the record showcases the Allmans at their peak, and it's hard not to feel sad as the acoustic guitars of "Little Martha" conclude the record, since this tribute isn't just heartfelt, it offers proof of Duane Allman's immense talents and contribution to the band.

Stephen Thomas Erlewine

Brothers and Sisters
1973, Polydor

Brothers and Sisters, the Allman Brothers Band's first new studio album in two years, shows off a leaner brand of musicianship, which, coupled with a pair of serious crowd-pleasers, "Ramblin' Man" and "Jessica," helped drive it to the top of the charts for a month and a half and to platinum record sales. This was the first album to feature the group's new lineup, with Chuck Leavell on keyboards and Lamar Williams on bass, as well as Dickey Betts' emergence as a singer alongside Gregg Allman. The tracks appear on the album in the order in which they were recorded, and the first three, up through "Ramblin' Man," feature Berry Oakley—their sound is rock-hard and crisp. The subsequent songs with Williams have the bass buried in the mix, and an overall muddier sound. The interplay between Leavell and Betts is beautiful on some songs, and Betts' slide on "Pony Boy" is a dazzling showcase that surprised everybody. Despite its sales, *Brothers and Sisters* is not quite a classic album (although it was their best for the next 17 years), especially in the wake of the four that had appeared previously, but it served as a template for some killer stage performances, and it proved that the band could survive the deaths of two key members.

Bruce Eder

America

History: America's Greatest Hits
1975, Warner Bros.

Mirroring the cover art depiction of America's dual life in England and the U.S., *History: America's Greatest Hits* perfectly spotlights both the polished and layered production of British studio legend George Martin and the West Coast tones of the band's folk-pop style. Featuring the group's many chart toppers from the first half of the '70s, this definitive roundup includes Neil Young-style acoustic sides like "Lonely People," the hippie MOR of "Muskrat Love," and breezy acid rock like "Sandman." And even though Martin didn't produce the entire lot of songs here, his sophisticated and mostly subtle way with strings, keyboards, and multi-track guitars is in evidence throughout. Adding to the fun are additional highlights like the updated surf cut "Sister Golden Hair" and ingenious McCartney-esque pop like "Only in Your Heart" and "Daisy Jane." An essential collection for fans who like their '70s folk with a pop sheen, loads of hooks, and top-drawer arrangements.

Stephen Cook

The Animals

Animalism
December 1966, MGM

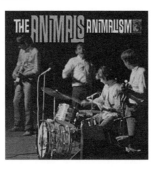

If the Animals had never recorded another album except for *Animalism*, their musical reputation would have been assured—none of the participants ever participated on, or would ever work on, a better long-player. The irony was that *Animalism* (not to be confused with the group's earlier, British-issued *Animalisms*, or its American counterpart, *Animalization*) was only ever issued in America, and came out after the group had ceased to exist and, thus, was scarcely noticed by anybody (which made it a choice occupant of cut-out bins for decades). Recorded mostly during the spring and summer of 1966 by the lineup of Eric Burdon, Hilton Valentine, Chas Chandler, Dave Rowberry, and Barry Jenkins, *Animalism* proved to be a glorious musical high point, as well as an end point for the band. Even as they were playing out their string, all of the members had begun growing in their musicianship, with guitarist Hilton Valentine taking on a much bolder, bluesier voice on his instrument and keyboardist Dave Rowberry developing a sound as distinctive as that of his predecessor, Alan Price. Part of *Animalism* was cut in Los Angeles under the aegis of Frank Zappa, who arranged (and probably played on) the opening number, "All Night Long," a surging traditional blues song, and who also worked on the album's ominous rendition of "The Other Side of This Life." Sam Cooke's "Shake" is treated to a restrained Burdon vocal and superb musical acrobatics by Valentine and Rowberry, and B.B. King's "Rock Me Baby" becomes the vehicle for a virtuoso workout by Valentine, and a thunderous performance by

Chandler and Jenkins. "Smokestack Lightning" is the most successful cover the group ever did of a Chicago blues number (unless you count their version of Donovan's "Hey Gyp," which is also here in all of its Bo Diddley-inspired glory), and "Hit the Road, Jack" represents the best work that Burdon ever did with a Ray Charles number. After years of languishing out of print—with many vinyl junkies hunting down treasured copies—*Animalism* was finally issued on CD in January of 2006 by Hip-O Select for a limited Internet-only purchase. For the uninitiated, *Animalism* is the place to start.

Thom Jurek

Absolute Animals 1964–1968
October 2003, Raven

As hard as it is to believe, there was no single-disc collection that contained all of the Animals' greatest hits until Raven Records released *Absolute Animals 1964-1968* in 2003. Prior to this, compilations were devoted to one of three distinct eras. First, there were the first recordings that they made with producer Mickie Most, which included "House of the Rising Sun," "I'm Crying," "Don't Let Me Be Misunderstood," "We Gotta Get Out of This Place," and "It's My Life." Then, they severed ties with Most, recording the acclaimed *Animalisms* album and having hits with "Inside, Looking Out," "Help Me Girl," and "Don't Bring Me Down" before imploding. Lead singer Eric Burdon then assembled a new version of the group, putting his name above the Animals in their official billing, and cut several psychedelic recordings and singles, including "San Franciscan Nights," "Monterey," and "Sky Pilot." Since each of these three eras were owned by different labels, there were many legal obstacles to assembling a definitive comp with all three eras being represented equally, but Raven managed to do an excellent job with the 20-track *Absolute Animals* (note: the final track is four minutes of interviews, bringing the total songs to 19). All of the singles mentioned above are featured here, along with other highlights like "Boom Boom," "Bring It on Home to Me," "See See Rider," and "When I Was Young." Perhaps some of the early recordings are glossed over—"Gonna Send You Back to Walker," "Story of Bo Diddley," and "Bury My Body" all arguably hold up better than some of the later psychedelicized tracks—but frankly, it's a relief to have one compilation that has all the hits from all the incarnations on one disc. Not only that, but it's hard to imagine a single-disc that would tell a complete Animals history as succinctly as this essential disc.

Stephen Thomas Erlewine

Bachman-Turner Overdrive

The Best of B.T.O. (So Far)
July 1976, Mercury

This nine-song collection released in 1976 was the first of close to two dozen "Best Of," "Greatest Hits," and "Greatest Hits Live" collections by the Guess Who's major competition when Randy Bachman left that venerable Canadian band. If you add "Free Wheelin'" (not included on this initial compilation), Bachman-Turner Overdrive equaled the seven hits the Guess Who had after Bachman bolted from them and they entered their "Hand Me Down World" phase. "Roll on Down the Highway" has a great riff, a sparkling neo-Led Zeppelin vamp, mutating "Black Dog" somewhat, slowed up and made commercial—it's an almost forgotten rock & roll call to arms that doesn't get the airplay it deserves years later—and it's the biggest hit they had that was not written by Randy Bachman. "Hey You," a reworking of the "You Ain't Seen Nothing Yet" chord changes and perhaps a dig at

Burton Cummings in the same way that Lennon gave "How Do You Sleep?" to McCartney, clocks in at five seconds less than "Roll on Down the Highway," and is as equally forgotten years later, classics hits radio stations opting for B.T.O.'s first three hits for the narrow rotation that is that format. These songs are culled from the group's first five albums, 1973's *Bachman Turner Overdrive* debut up to 1975's *Head On*. They ruled the charts as a North American counterpart to the British Bad Company, whose first version charted during the same time period with almost the same amount of hits. Five of the nine songs were composed all or in part by Randy Bachman, including the song that didn't break the Top 40 but should have, "Looking Out for #1." Its "Girl From Ipanema" riff and majestic performance was touted by Mercury in the trades as their next number one, but for some inexplicable reason, it fizzled. This album has been re-mastered and refined over the years, but it is what it is, a compact collection of their hits released over a two-year period.

Joe Viglione

Bad Company

Bad Company
June 1974, Swan Song

Bad Company's 1974 self-titled re-lease stands as one of the most important and accomplished debut hard rock albums from the '70s. Though hardly visionary, it was one of the most successful steps in the continuing evolution of rock & roll, riding on the coattails of achievement from artists like the Eagles and Crosby, Stills, Nash and Young. From the simple electric guitar lick on "Can't Get Enough" to the haunting bassline in "Bad Company" and the fast beats of "Movin' On," *Bad Company* exemplified raw rock & roll at its best. Erupting out of an experimental period created by the likes of Pink Floyd, Bad Company signified a return to more primal, stripped-down rock & roll. Even while labelmates Led Zeppelin's *Houses of the Holy* and *IV* featured highly acclaimed, colorful album artwork, *Bad Company*'s austere black and white record cover stood out in stark contrast. Six years later, AC/DC used the same idea on their smash *Back in Black*. Throughout the 35-minute album, Paul Rodgers' mesmerizing and gritty vocals hardly vary in tonal quality, offering a perfect complement to Mick Ralphs' blues-based guitar work. Several songs include three-chord verses offset by unembellished, distorted choruses, filled rich with Rodgers' cries. *Bad Company* is an essential addition to the rock & roll library; clearly influential to '70s and '80s hard rock bands like Tom Petty, Lynyrd Skynyrd, and Boston.

Gautam Baksi

Original Bad Company Anthology
March 1999, Elektra

Somehow or other, Bad Company got lumped in with other '70s rock dinosaurs. In a way they were—not because their music was excessive or dated, but because when Bad Company walked the earth, the ground shook. Featuring the voice of Paul Rodgers, one of rock's greatest singers, the thoroughly excellent *Original Bad Company Anthology* re-establishes Bad Company as a force in the music world. The 33-song, two-CD set contains all the classic songs that made the band a top-selling recording and concert attraction, as well as four brand new songs and six B-sides and outtakes. The new songs are (surprise!) awesome. All four tracks (two by Mick Ralphs, two by Paul Rodgers) sound like they could be on the band's classic early albums. The first single, "Hey Hey," is a blustery rocker; "Tracking Down a Runaway," a totally exhilarating number, sounds like a future hit. The rarities include "Easy on My Soul," a remade Free song from the *Straight Shooter* sessions—complete with Paul Rodgers' signature piano—that blows the Free version out of the water, and might just be the best track Bad Company has ever done. Other highlights include "Superstar Woman," a soulful outtake from the first LP sessions, and "Smokin' 45" from the *Burnin' Sky* sessions. "Little Miss Fortune," with its cool lyrics and groove, is a former B-side finally seeing the light of day in the CD age. The set draws from all of their albums, emphasizing the first two, but the band even found two good tracks from the utterly pathetic *Rough Diamonds*; if those songs are good you can be sure the rest kick some serious butt as well.

Geoff Ginsberg

Badfinger

No Dice
November 1970, Capitol

Badfinger's second album *No Dice* kicks off with "I Can't Take It," a rocker that signaled even if Badfinger still played pop and sang ballads, they considered themselves a rock band. What gave Badfinger character is they blended their desire to rock with their sensitive side instead of compartmentalizing. Even when they rock on *No Dice*, it's never earthy, like, say, the Stones. Badfinger's very sensibility and sound is modeled after the early British Invasion, where bands sang catchy, concise love songs. Yet there's a worldliness to their music absent from that of their forefathers, partially because Badfinger styled themselves as classicists, adapting the sound of their idols and striving to create a similar body of work. *No Dice* bears this out, boasting old-fashioned rockers, catchy pop tunes, and acoustic ballads. On the surface, there's nothing special about such a well-crafted, sharply produced, straight-ahead pop record, but the pleasure of a power pop album is in the craft. *No Dice* is not without flaws—a byproduct of an all-writing, all-singing band is that some songs don't measure up—but it does achieve the right balance of craft, fun, and emotion, due in no small part to Pete Ham's songwriting. Ham dominates the record, providing note-perfect openers and closers, along with the centerpiece singles "No Matter What" and "Without You," the latter a yearning, painful ballad co-written with Tom Evans. Collaborating with new guitarist Joey Molland, Evans wrote two other excellent songs ("I Don't Mind," "Better Days"), while Molland's own "Love Me Do" chugs along with nice momentum. Still, the heart of the album lies in Ham's work. He proves that songcraft is what separates great power-pop from good, and it's what makes *No Dice* a superb pop record.

Stephen Thomas Erlewine

Straight Up
December 1971, Capitol

Straight Up winds up somewhat less dynamic than *No Dice*, largely because that record alternated its rockers, pop tunes, and ballads. Here, everything is at a similar level, as the ballads are made grander and the rockers have their melodic side emphasized. Consequently, the record sounds more unified than *No Dice*, which had a bit of a split personality. Todd Rundgren's warm, detailed production makes each songwriter sound as if he was on the same page, although the bonus tracks—revealing the abandoned original Geoff Emerick productions—prove that the distinctive voices on *No Dice* were still present. Frankly, the increased production is for the best, since Badfinger sounds best when there's as much craft in the production as there is in the writing. Here, there's absolutely no filler and everybody is in top form. Pete Ham's "Baby Blue" is textbook power-pop—irresistibly catchy fuzz riffs and sighing melodies—and with its Harrison-esque slide guitars, "Day After Day" is so gorgeous it practically aches. "Perfection" is an unheralded gem, while "Name of the Game" and "Take It All" are note-perfect pop ballads. Tom Evans isn't as prolific here, but the one-two punch of "Money" and "Flying" is the closest *Straight Up* gets to *Abbey Road*, and "It's Over" is a fine closer. Still, what holds the record together is Joey Molland's emergence as a songwriter. His work on *No Dice* is enjoyable, but here, he comes into his own with a set of well-constructed songs. This fine songwriting, combined with sharp performances and exquisite studio craft, make *Straight Up* one of the cornerstones of power-pop, a record that proved that it was possible to make classic guitar-pop after its golden era had passed.

Stephen Thomas Erlewine

The Band

Music from Big Pink
July 1968, Capitol

None of the Band's previous work gave much of a clue about how they would sound when they released their first album in July 1968. As it was, *Music from Big Pink* came as a surprise. At first blush, the group seemed to affect the sound of a loose jam session,  alternating emphasis on different instruments, while the lead and harmony vocals passed back and forth as if the singers were making up their blend on the spot. In retrospect, especially as the lyrics sank in, the arrangements seemed far more considered and crafted to support a group of songs that took family, faith, and rural life as their subjects and proceeded to imbue their values with uncertainty. Some songs took on the theme of declining institutions less clearly than others, but the points were made musically as much as lyrically. Tenor Richard Manuel's haunting, lonely voice gave the album much of its frightening aspect, while Rick Danko's and Levon Helm's rough-hewn styles reinforced the songs' rustic fervor. The dominant instrument was Garth Hudson's often icy and majestic organ, while Robbie Robertson's unusual guitar work further destabilized the sound. The result was an album that reflected the turmoil of the late '60s in a way that emphasized the tragedy inherent in the conflicts. *Music from Big Pink* came off as a shockingly divergent musical statement only a year after the ornate productions of *Sgt. Pepper*, and initially attracted attention because of the three songs Bob Dylan had either written or co-written. However, as soon as "The Weight" became a minor singles chart entry, the album and the group made their own impact, influencing a movement toward roots styles and country elements in rock. Over time, *Music from Big Pink* came to be regarded as a watershed work in the history of rock, one that introduced new tones and approaches to the constantly evolving genre.

William Ruhlmann

The Band
September 1969, Capitol

The Band's first album, *Music from Big Pink*, seemed to come out of nowhere, with its ramshackle musical blend and songs of rural tragedy. *The Band*, the group's second album, was a more deliberate and even more accomplished effort, partially because the players had become a more cohesive unit and partially because guitarist Robbie Robertson had taken over the songwriting, writing or co-writing all 12 songs. Though a Canadian, Robertson focused on a series of American archetypes from the union worker in "King Harvest (Has Surely Come)" and the retired sailor in "Rockin' Chair" to, most famously, the Confederate Civil War observer Virgil Cane in "The Night They Drove Old Dixie Down." The album effectively mixed the kind of mournful songs that had dominated *Music from Big Pink*, here including "Whispering Pines" and "When You Awake" (both co-written by Richard Manuel), with rollicking uptempo numbers like "Rag Mama Rag" and "Up on Cripple Creek" (both sung by Levon Helm and released as singles, with "Up on Cripple Creek" making the Top 40). As had been true of the first album, it was the Band's sound that stood out the most, from Helm's (and occasionally Manuel's) propulsive drumming to Robertson's distinctive guitar fills and the endlessly inventive keyboard textures of Garth Hudson, all topped by the rough, expressive singing of Manuel, Helm, and Rick Danko that mixed leads with harmonies. The arrangements were simultaneously loose and assured, giving the songs a timeless appeal, while the lyrics continued to paint portraits of 19th century rural life (especially Southern life, as references to Tennessee and Virginia made clear), its sometimes less savory aspects treated with warmth and humor.

William Ruhlmann

Stage Fright
August 1970, EMI-Capitol Special Markets

Stage Fright, the Band's third album, sounded on its surface like the group's first two releases, *Music From Big Pink* and *The Band*, employing the same dense arrangements, with their mixture of a deep bottom formed by drummer Levon Helm and bassist Rick Danko, penetrating guitar work by Robbie Robertson, and the varied keyboard work of pianist Richard Manuel and organist Garth Hudson, with Helm, Danko, and Manuel's vocals on top. But the songs this time around were far more personal, and, despite a nominal complacency, quite troubling. Only "All La Glory," Robertson's song about the birth of his daughter, was fully positive. "Strawberry Wine" and "Sleeping" were celebrations of indolence, while "Time to Kill," as its title implied, revealed boredom while claiming romantic contentment. Several of the album's later songs seemed to be metaphors for trouble the group was encountering, with "The W.S. Walcott Medicine Show" commenting on the falseness of show business, "Daniel and the

Sacred Harp" worrying about a loss of integrity, and the title song talking about the pitfalls of fortune and fame. "The Shape I'm In" was perhaps the album's most blatant statement of panic. The Band was widely acclaimed after its first two albums; *Stage Fright* seemed to be the group's alarmed response, which made it their most nakedly confessional. It was certainly different from their previous work, which had tended toward story songs set in earlier times, but it was hardly less compelling for that.

The album was reissued on CD more than once, but it was not until the expanded edition released on August 29, 2000, that the reissuers got it right and released the mixes that had been used on the original LP. This version also included revealing liner notes by Rob Bowman and a few alternate versions of the songs as bonus tracks, making this the configuration of the album to buy.

William Ruhlmann

Rock of Ages
November 1972, Capitol

Recorded on New Year's Eve 1971, *Rock of Ages* was the Band's last gig for a year-and-a-half. Allen Toussaint was brought in again to write horn arrangements for many of their classics. The results were inspired. Highlights are many, but of particular note are a cover of Marvin Gaye's "Baby Don't Do It" and a live recording of a track that had earlier been relegated to B-side status only, "Get Up Jake." [The deluxe edition consolidates the double-disc standard edition onto one disc and also includes a ten-track bonus disc that features Bob Dylan performing on several songs ("Down in the Flood," "When I Paint My Masterpiece," "Don't Ya Tell Henry," and "Like a Rolling Stone").]

Rob Bowman

Northern Lights–Southern Cross
November 1975, Capitol

The first studio album of Band originals in four years; in many respects *Northern Lights-Southern Cross* was viewed as a comeback. It also can be seen as a swan song, in that its recording marked the last time the five members would work together in the studio as a permanent group, with a commitment to making a record that they would tour behind and build on as a working band. The album was also, ironically enough, the Band's finest since their self-titled sophomore effort, even outdoing *Stage Fright*. It was spawned after a series of battery-recharging events—the move of all five members out of Woodstock, New York and to Malibu, California, and to a new, state-of-the-art 24-track studio that not only felt right but offered them (especially Garth Hudson, working with Moog synthesizers and other new instruments, as well as brass and reeds) a bigger creative and sonic canvas than they'd ever known before; and the decision to finally let the other shoe drop on their early career, accompanying Bob Dylan on their first-ever studio album together (*Planet Waves*) which, in turn, had led to an eight-week tour together, this time captured for posterity and, unlike their mid-'60s Dylan tour, rushed out midway through the work on the album at hand. Between all of that, their own live album (*Rock of Ages*), and the *Moondog Matinee* album of rock & roll and R&B covers, the group found itself with more music in print at one time than they'd ever dreamed possible, despite the four-year gap in new material, and in several genres and modes, and blossoming in some unexpected directions—just prior to the start of the sessions for this album, Levon Helm and Garth Hudson had fulfilled another milestone, the goal of doing an honest-to-God blues album (which dated from the group's tragically brief liaison with Sonny Boy Williamson in 1965), producing and/or playing on what ended up being a Grammy-winning LP by Muddy Waters, the *Woodstock Album*. It was time to make some of their own music again, and Robbie Robertson obliged by showing up with a bumper crop of great new compositions. *Northern Lights-Southern Cross* totals eight songs in all, and he and the rest of the group rose to the occasion, luxuriating in the range afforded by the studio (christened Shangri-La, a reference to the idyllic haven for art and civilization in James Hilton's novel *Lost Horizon*—the vibes were that good). On this album the Band explore new timbres, utilizing 24 tracks and what was (then) new synthesizer technology, and also opening out their sound in some unexpected ways. After years of restrained, economical playing Robbie Robertson—who was practically the Count Basie of rock guitarists in terms of following a less-is-more philosophy—stepped out in front with flashy, extroverted playing on "Forbidden Fruit," a semi-autobiographical (about the group) cautionary rock ballad; his elegant trills and flourishes on "Hobo Jungle"; his twanging and twisting away behind Hudson's beautiful, complex brass and horn parts on "Ophelia," a close relative of "W.S. Walcott Medicine Show" from *Stage Fright*, which captured the kind of old-timey New Orleans sound that the group had also embraced, in the form of covers, on *Moondog Matinee*. Robertson and Hudson seem to feed off one another's presence throughout, perhaps best of all on "Ring Your Bell," which also restores the group's trademarked shared vocals. "It Makes No Difference" might be the best romantic ballad ever done by the group, while the ebullient "Jupiter Hollow" is an exceptional track three times over, a brilliant showcase for keyboards (and not just by Hudson—Robertson forsakes the guitar here for a clavinet), as well as offering Levon Helm and Richard Manuel tripling up on percussion with a drum machine. "Rags and Bones" is one of Robertson's most deceptively personal songs, and features the most elaborate keyboard sounds of any recording in the group's history. "Acadian Driftwood" stands out as one of Robertson's finest compositions, equal to anything else the Band ever recorded, and a slightly more complex and ambitious (and successful) down-north analog to "The Night They Drove Old Dixie Down." The vocals by Helm, Manuel, and Rick Danko were all spot-on as well, on this last great musical statement from the group, and the fact that it only made number 26 on the charts is much more indicative of the state of music radio and Capitol's marketing department (which was only really good at selling Beatles and Beach Boys reissues at the time), than any flaws in the record. [The 2001 reissue offers exceptional sound, upgraded to 24-bit mastering, and extends the running time by seven delightful minutes with the addition of a pair of bonus tracks, an early run-through of "Twilight," which was released as a single in the wake of the LP, and a stripped down, upbeat rehearsal version of "Christmas Must Be Tonight"; but either version one gets of *Northern Lights-Southern Cross*, is worth owning].

Rob Bowman & Bruce Eder

A Musical History
September 2005, Capitol

Given the countless Band compilations released over the years, plus the exhaustive bonus-track-laden reissues of the proper albums in 2000 and 2001, it's easy to be suspicious of the six-disc *A Musical History*, especially since it's the *third* Band box set released in the CD era. It would seem that all the worthwhile previously unreleased music has been excavated and that the Band's career has been anthologized in every possible way, but *A Musical History* proves that's not true. As its title implies, the set is a biography, tracing the group's career from their early days as the Hawks supporting Ronnie Hawkins, through their stint as Levon & the Hawks, through their time as Bob Dylan's backing band in 1966, through their emergence as the Band in 1968, then through their years of stardom in the early '70s, leading up to their departure at *The Last Waltz* in 1976. No previous compilation has done this—they've either picked up the story with *Music from Big Pink* or offered up the greatest hits, and they've never weaved Ronnie Hawkins or Bob Dylan tracks into the story line—and this thorough, all-encompassing approach does result in an absorbing narrative that does provide some revelations, most arriving on the spectacular, necessary first disc that traces the evolution of the band before they were the Band. Here, for the first time on a Band album, you get to hear the group's beginning as a rough rock & roll and blues combo, and while some of this material is a bit generic (albeit in the best possible sense, since they were a lean, tough, straight-ahead rock & roll group), this music echoes throughout the four CDs that follow, whether it's in the muscular R&B grooves of Levon Helm and Rick Danko, Robbie Robertson's tight, squealing guitar, or Richard Manual's piano chord clusters, or how the group touched on rockabilly, Motown, New Orleans R&B, country, and folk even on their earliest recordings. In this context, their teaming with Dylan not only seems like a natural outgrowth of their work as the struggling Levon & the Hawks, but it's clear that Dylan helped give the band focus and ideas, inspiring not just the songs that the group wrote for *Music from Big Pink*, but the whole Americana aesthetic that came to define the Band and made them separate from their rock & roll peers of the late '60s. Once *A Musical History* hits the second disc, the Band's story enters familiar territory and the revelations start drying up even if the unreleased material doesn't (there are a whopping 32 unreleased tracks on this 102-song set, and there's about ten or so other cuts that could qualify as rarities, as well). All the same, the conventional story line carries more weight here, since the first disc not only provides context, but because the sequencing and song selection are excellent, helping to drive the Band's story in addition to just being flat-out entertaining. Plus, there are some great rarities scattered throughout here, including an exciting, careening live version of Woody Guthrie's "I Ain't Got No Home" with Bob Dylan that was only released on a Woody tribute album, the funky, gritty "Baby Lou," a raucous "Slippin' & Slidin'" from the Festival Express tour in 1970, hard-rocking live versions of "Strawberry Wine" and "Look out Cleveland" from Royal Albert Hall in 1971, a live "Highway 61 Revisited" with Bob Dylan from a 1974 Madison Square Garden show, and Rick Danko's sweet, lazy unreleased "Home Cookin'" from 1976. These not only help keep a familiar story interesting to the hardcore fans (who, after all, are the primary audience for such a lavish set as this), but help fill little details within that story, along with illustrating how good the Band could sound as a band right up until the very end of their career. Despite all this, the arc of their career—the sudden, glorious beginning and the slow descent into equal parts pretension

and lethargy—can't help but shine through in a biography such as this. No amount of well-chosen rarities and expert song sequencing (all the group's major songs, along with all of their noteworthy minor tunes, are here in some incarnation or another) can hide the downward turn in the Band's fortunes. There was a pretty steep decline in quality material after their third album, *Stage Fright*, in 1970, and while the next four studio albums, plus the live *Rock of Ages* and *The Last Waltz*, are summarized on the final two discs of the set, it's hard to ignore how covers keep popping up or how numerous songs are repeated in different versions (no matter how good the alternate versions are, it's clear that the group was running out of strong new songs), nor is it easy to ignore that the rest of the Band, for whatever reason, simply stopped writing, transferring the burden to Robbie Robertson, who struggled to come up with songs that seemed as effortless and graceful as his early songs, despite a slight rejuvenation on *Northern Lights-Southern Cross*. That doesn't mean these last two discs are bad—far from it, they put the best spin on an uneven era—but they do make it clear that the Band were caught at an awkward spot and were unable to successfully move forward, no matter how much Robertson prodded. As the accompanying DVD, which has nine live performances beginning with a 1970 clip from Woodstock and ending with three spots from *Saturday Night Live* in 1976, illustrates, Robertson had his mind elsewhere, but the rest of the guys were happy to simply be in a band. Being the one with ambitions, Robertson made the move and brought the curtains down on their career when the rest of the Band weren't necessarily ready to call it quits, as evidenced by their ongoing reunions in the '80s and '90s. Despite the existence of a touring Band minus their guitarist and songwriter, Robertson wound up as the member who was generally acknowledged as the one who kept the spirit of the group alive, at least according to the mainstream rock press. He also shepherded nearly all of the official Band reissues, including this one, where he acts as executive producer and the main interview for Rob Bowman's detail-heavy, perhaps too affectionate liner notes. Bowman's long piece ends abruptly when Robertson leaves the group; it's acknowledged that the Band soldiered on, but this fact is dismissed quickly, since it doesn't fit the romanticized notion of the Band's career that Robertson has been selling since Martin Scorsese's *The Last Waltz*. The bad blood between Robertson and Levon Helm runs too deep for them to make friends over this project (Garth Hudson is credited as an archival producer), but that acrimony is only noticeable within the liner notes to this beautiful hardcover book-styled box set. The five discs captures the Band at their peak as a band, containing their very best music. *Music from Big Pink* and *The Band* remain the essential, definitive albums, the records that not only capture their essence but have a nearly mythical grandeur. This box is for those who already know and love the group, who know their ups and downs, and who want to hear them in all their glory—and, as this proves, the Band were glorious indeed.

Stephen Thomas Erlewine

Syd Barrett

The Madcap Laughs
January 1970, Capitol

Wisely, *The Madcap Laughs* doesn't even try to sound like a consistent record. Half the album was recorded by Barrett's former bandmates Roger Waters and Dave Gilmour, and the other half by Harvest Records head Malcolm Jones.

Surprisingly, Jones' tracks are song for song much stronger than the more-lauded Floyd entries. The opening "Terrapin" seems to go on three times as long as its five-minute length, creating a hypnotic effect through Barrett's simple, repetitive guitar figure and stream of consciousness lyrics. The much bouncier "Love You" sounds like a sunny little Carnaby Street pop song along the lines of an early Move single, complete with music hall piano, until the listener tries to parse the lyrics and realizes that they make no sense at all. The downright Kinksy"Here I Go" is in the same style, although it's both more lyrically direct and musically freaky, speeding up and slowing down seemingly at random. Like many of the "band" tracks, "Here I Go" is a Barrett solo performance with overdubs by Mike Ratledge, Hugh Hopper, and Robert Wyatt of the Soft Machine; the combination doesn't always particularly work, as the Softs' jazzy, improvisational style is hemmed in by having to follow Barrett's predetermined lead, so on several tracks, like "No Good Trying," they content themselves with simply making weird noises in the background. The solo tracks are what made the album's reputation, though, particularly the horrifying "Dark Globe," a first-person portrait of schizophrenia that's seemingly the most self-aware song this normally whimsical songwriter ever created. Honestly, however, the other solo tracks are the album's weakest tracks, with the exception of the plain gorgeous "Golden Hair," a musical setting of a James Joyce poem that's simply spellbinding. The album falls apart with the appalling "Feel." Frankly, the inclusion of false starts and studio chatter, not to mention some simply horrible off-key singing by Barrett, makes this already marginal track feel disgustingly exploitative. But for that misstep, however, *The Madcap Laughs* is a surprisingly effective record that holds up better than its "ooh, lookit the scary crazy person" reputation suggests.

Stewart Mason

Barrett
November 1970, Capitol

On his second solo album, Barrett was joined by Humble Pie drummer Jerry Shirley and Pink Floyd members Rick Wright (organ) and Dave Gilmour (guitar). Gilmour and Wright acted as producers as well. Instrumentally, the result is a bit fuller and smoother than the first album, although it's since been revealed that Gilmour and Wright embellished these songs as best they could without much involvement from Barrett, who was often unable or unwilling to perfect his performance. The songs, however, are just as fractured as on his debut, if not more so. "Baby Lemonade," "Gigolo Aunt," and the nursery rhyming "Effervescing Elephant" rank among his peppiest and best-loved tunes. Elsewhere, the tone is darker and more meandering. It was regarded as something of a charming but unfocused throwaway at the time of its release, but Barrett's singularly whimsical and unsettling vision holds up well.

Richie Unterberger

The Beach Boys

Pet Sounds
May 1966, Capitol

The best Beach Boys album, and one of the best of the 1960s. The group here reached a whole new level in terms of both composition and production, layering tracks upon tracks of vocals and instruments to create a richly symphonic sound. Conventional keyboards and guitars were combined with exotic touches of orchestrated strings, bicycle bells, buzzing organs, harpsichords, flutes, theremin, Hawaiian-sounding

string instruments, Coca-Cola cans, barking dogs, and more. It wouldn't have been a classic without great songs, and this has some of the group's most stunning melodies, as well as lyrical themes which evoke both the intensity of newly born love affairs and the disappointment of failed romance (add in some general statements about loss of innocence and modern-day confusion as well). The spiritual quality of the material is enhanced by some of the most gorgeous upper-register male vocals (especially by Brian  and Carl Wilson) ever heard on a rock record. "Wouldn't It Be Nice," "God Only Knows," "Caroline No," and "Sloop John B" (the last of which wasn't originally intended to go on the album) are the well-known hits, but equally worthy are such cuts as "You Still Believe in Me," "Don't Talk," "I Know There's an Answer," and "I Just Wasn't Made for These Times." It's often said that this is more of a Brian Wilson album than a Beach Boys recording (session musicians played most of the parts), but it should be noted that the harmonies are pure Beach Boys (and some of their best). Massively influential upon its release (although it was a relatively low seller compared to their previous LPs), it immediately vaunted the band into the top level of rock innovators among the intelligentsia, especially in Britain, where it was a much bigger hit.

Richie Unterberger

Sounds of Summer: The Very Best of the Beach Boys
June 2003, Capitol

After gaining control of the Beach Boys' entire catalog (including all the band's post-1969 material), Capitol released two-fers covering their out of print '70s records and a Brian Wilson-selected compilation titled *Classics*, then later, this hits compilation—the longest single-disc American collection ever seen. With all but five tracks coming from their 1962-1969 peak, and every one a Top 40 hit, *Sounds of Summer: The Very Best of the Beach Boys* is also the best, a worthy digital-age successor to previous classics like *Endless Summer* and *Greatest Hits, Vol. 1.* Though the songs don't appear in chronological order, the compilers improved the concept of a hits compilation by bunching the disc into minisets—one of classic adolescence songs ("Be True to Your School," "When I Grow Up [To Be a Man]," "In My Room"), one of surfing songs ("Surfin' Safari," "Surfin' U.S.A.," "Surfer Girl"), one of frat-boy classics ("Dance, Dance, Dance," "Barbara Ann"), and another including selections from their masterpiece *Pet Sounds* ("God Only Knows," "Sloop John B.," "Wouldn't It Be Nice"). Nearly any compilation on an important artist can be argued, but it's the rare one that covers as many bases and leaves out so few classics as *Sounds of Summer: The Very Best of the Beach Boys.*

John Bush

The Beatles

Please Please Me
March 1963, Capitol

Once "Please Please Me" rocketed to number one, the Beatles

rushed to deliver a debut album, bashing out *Please Please Me* in a day. Decades after its release, the album still sounds fresh, precisely because of its intense origins. As the songs rush past, it's easy to get wrapped up in the sound of the record itself without realizing how the album effectively summarizes the band's eclectic influences. Naturally, the influences shine through their covers, all of which are unconventional and illustrate the group's superior taste. There's a love of girl groups, vocal harmonies, sophisticated popcraft, schmaltz, R&B, and hard-driving rock & roll, which is enough to make *Please Please Me* impressive, but what makes it astonishing is how these elements converge in the originals. "I Saw Here Standing There" is one of their best rockers, yet it has surprising harmonies and melodic progressions. "Misery" and "There's a Place" grow out of the girl group tradition without being tied to it. A few of their originals, such as "Do You Want to Know a Secret" and the pleasantly light "P.S. I Love You," have dated slightly, but endearingly so, since they're infused with cheerful innocence and enthusiasm. And there is an innocence to *Please Please Me*. The Beatles may have played notoriously rough dives in Hamburg, but the only way you could tell that on their first album was how the constant gigging turned the group into a tight, professional band that could run through their set list at the drop of a hat with boundless energy. It's no surprise that Lennon had shouted himself hoarse by the end of the session, barely getting through "Twist and Shout," the most famous single take in rock history. He simply got caught up in the music, just like generations of listeners did.

Stephen Thomas Erlewine

With the Beatles
November 1963, Capitol

With the Beatles is a sequel of the highest order—one that betters the original by developing its own tone and adding depth. While it may share several similarities with its predecessor—there is an equal ratio of covers-to-originals, a familiar blend of girl group, Motown, R&B, pop, and rock, and a show tune that interrupts the flow of the album—*With the Beatles* is a better record that not only rocks harder, it's considerably more sophisticated. They could deliver rock & roll straight ("I Wanna Be Your Man") or twist it around with a little Latin lilt ("Little Child," one of their most underrated early rockers); Lennon and McCartney wrote sweet ballads (the achingly gorgeous "All I've Got to Do") and sprightly pop/rockers ("All My Loving") with equal aplomb; and the propulsive rockers ("It Won't Be Long") were as richly melodic as slower songs ("Not a Second Time"). Even George Harrison's first recorded song, "Don't Bother Me," is a standout, with its wonderfully foreboding minor-key melody. Since the Beatles covered so much ground with their originals, their covers pale slightly in comparison, particularly since they rely on familiar hits (only "Devil in Her Heart" qualifies as a forgotten gem). But for every "Roll Over Beethoven," a surprisingly stiff reading of the Chuck Berry standard, there is a sublime moment, such as Lennon's soaring interpretation of "You Really Got a Hold on Me," and the group always turns in thoroughly enjoyable performances. Still, the heart of *With the Beatles* lies not in the covers, but the originals, where it was clear that, even at this early stage, the Beatles were rapidly maturing and changing, turning into expert craftsmen and musical innovators.

Stephen Thomas Erlewine

A Hard Day's Night [UK]
July 1964, Capitol

A Hard Day's Night not only was the de facto soundtrack for their movie, not only was it filled with nothing but Lennon-McCartney originals, but it found the Beatles truly coming into their own as a band. All of the disparate influences on their first two albums had coalesced into a bright, joyous, original sound, filled with ringing guitars and irresistible melodies. *A Hard Day's Night* is where the Beatles became mythical, but this is the sound of Beatlemania in all of its giddy glory. Decades after its original release, its punchy blend of propulsive rhythms, jangly guitars, and infectious, singalong melodies is remarkably fresh. There's something intrinsically exciting in the *sound* of the album itself, something to keep the record vital years after it was recorded. Even more impressive

are the songs themselves. Not only are the melodies forceful and memorable, but Lennon and McCartney have found a number of variations to their basic Merseybeat sound, from the brash "Can't Buy Me Love" and "Any Time at All" through the gentle "If I Fell" to the tough folk-rock of "I'll Cry Instead." It's possible to hear both songwriters develop their own distinctive voices on the album, but, overall, *A Hard Day's Night* stands as a testament to their collaborative powers—never again did they write together so well or so easily, choosing to pursue their own routes. John and Paul must have known how strong the material is—they threw the pleasant trifle "I'm Happy Just to Dance With You" to George and didn't give anything to Ringo to sing. That may have been a little selfish, but it hardly hurts the album, since everything on the record is performed with genuine glee and excitement. It's the pinnacle of their early years.

Stephen Thomas Erlewine

Beatles for Sale
December 1964, Capitol

It was inevitable that the constant grind of touring, writing, promoting, and recording would grate on the Beatles, but the weariness of *Beatles for Sale* comes as something of a shock. Only five months before, the group released the joyous *A Hard Day's Night*. Now, they sound beaten, worn, and, in Lennon's case, bitter and self-loathing. His opening trilogy ("No Reply," "I'm a Loser," "Baby's in Black") is the darkest sequence on any Beatles record, setting the tone for the album. Moments of joy pop up now and again, mainly in the forms of covers and the dynamic "Eight Days a Week," but the very presence of six covers after the triumphant all-original *A Hard Day's Night* feels like an admission of defeat or at least a regression. (It doesn't help that Lennon's cover of his beloved obscurity "Mr. Moonlight" winds up as arguably the worst thing the group ever recorded.) Beneath those surface suspicions, however, there are some important changes on *Beatles for Sale*, most notably Lennon's discovery of Bob Dylan and folk-rock. The opening three songs, along with "I Don't Want to Spoil the Party," are implicitly confessional and all quite bleak, which is a new development. This spirit winds up overshadowing McCartney's cheery "I'll Follow the Sun" or the thundering covers of "Rock & Roll Music," "Honey Don't," and "Kansas City/Hey-Hey-Hey-Hey!," and the weariness creeps up in unexpected places—"Every Little Thing," "What You're Doing," even George's cover of Carl Perkins' "Everybody's Trying to Be My Baby"—leaving the impression that Beatlemania may have been fun but now the group is exhausted. That exhaustion results in the group's most uneven album, but its best moments find them moving from Merseybeat to the sophisticated pop/rock they developed in mid-career.

Stephen Thomas Erlewine

Help! [UK]
August 1965, Capitol

Considering that *Help!* functions as the Beatles' fifth album and as the soundtrack to their second film—while filming, they continued to release non-LP singles on a regular basis—it's not entirely surprising that it still has some of the weariness of *Beatles for Sale*. Again, they pad the album with covers, but the Bakersfield bounce of "Act Naturally" adds new flavor (along with an ideal showcase for Ringo's amiable vocals) and "Dizzy Miss Lizzy" gives John an opportunity to flex his rock & roll muscle. George is writing again and if his two contributions don't touch Lennon and McCartney's originals, they hold their own against much of their British pop peers. Since Lennon wrote *a third* more songs than McCartney, it's easy to forgive a pair of minor numbers ("It's Only Love," "Tell Me What You See"), especially since they're overshadowed by four great songs. His Dylan infatuation holds strong, particularly on the plaintive "You've Got to Hide Your Love Away" and the title track, where the brash arrangement disguises Lennon's desperation. Driven by an indelible 12-string guitar, "Ticket to Ride" is another masterpiece and "You're Going to Lose That Girl" is the kind of song McCartney effortlessly tosses off—which he does with the jaunty "The Night Before" and "Another Girl," two very fine tunes that simply update his melodic signature. He did much better with "I've Just Seen a Face," an irresistible folk-rock gem, and "Yesterday," a simple, beautiful ballad whose arrangement—an acoustic guitar supported by a string quartet—and composition suggested much more sophisticated and adventurous musical territory, which the group immediately began exploring with *Rubber Soul*.

Stephen Thomas Erlewine

Rubber Soul [UK]
December 1965, Capitol

While the Beatles still largely stuck to love songs on *Rubber Soul*, the lyrics represented a quantum leap in terms of thoughtfulness, maturity, and complex ambiguities. Musically, too, it was a substantial leap forward, with intricate folk-rock arrangements that reflected the increasing influence of Dylan and the Byrds. The group and George Martin were also beginning to expand the conventional instrumental parameters of the rock group, using a sitar on "Norwegian Wood (This Bird Has Flown)," Greek-like guitar lines on "Michelle" and "Girl," fuzz bass on "Think for Yourself," and a piano made to sound like a harpsichord on the instrumental break of "In My Life." While John and Paul were beginning to carve separate songwriting identities at this point, the album is full of great tunes, from "Norwegian Wood (This Bird Has Flown)" and "Michelle" to "Girl," "I'm Looking Through You," "You Won't See Me," "Drive My Car," and "Nowhere Man" (the last of which was the first Beatle song to move beyond

romantic themes entirely). George Harrison was also developing into a fine songwriter with his two contributions, "Think for Yourself" and the Byrds-ish "If I Needed Someone."

Richie Unterberger

Revolver [UK]
August 1966, Capitol

All the rules fell by the wayside with *Revolver*, as the Beatles began exploring new sonic territory, lyrical subjects, and styles of composition. It wasn't just Lennon and McCartney, either—Harrison staked out his own dark territory with the tightly wound, cynical rocker "Taxman"; the jaunty yet dissonant "I Want to Tell You"; and "Love You To," George's first and best foray into Indian music. Such explorations were bold, yet they were eclipsed by Lennon's trippy kaleidoscopes of sound. His most straightforward number was "Doctor Robert," an ode to his dealer, and things just got stranger from there as he buried "And Your Bird Can Sing" in a maze of multi-tracked guitars, gave Ringo a charmingly hallucinogenic slice of childhood whimsy in "Yellow Submarine," and then capped it off with a triptych of bad trips: the spiraling "She Said She Said"; the crawling, druggy "I'm Only Sleeping"; and "Tomorrow Never Knows," a pure nightmare where John sang portions of the *Tibetan Book of the Dead* into a suspended microphone over Ringo's thundering, menacing drumbeats and layers of overdubbed, phased guitars and tape loops. McCartney's experiments were formal, as he tried on every pop style from chamber pop to soul, and when placed alongside Lennon's and Harrison's outright experimentations, McCartney's songcraft becomes all the more impressive. The biggest miracle of *Revolver* may be that the Beatles covered so much new stylistic ground and executed it perfectly on one record, or it may be that all of it holds together perfectly. Either way, its daring sonic adventures and consistently stunning songcraft set the standard for what pop/rock could achieve. Even after *Sgt. Pepper*, *Revolver* stands as the ultimate modern pop album and it's still as emulated as it was upon its original release.

Stephen Thomas Erlewine

Sgt. Pepper's Lonely Hearts Club Band
June 1967, Capitol

With *Revolver*, the Beatles made the Great Leap Forward, reaching a previously unheard-of level of sophistication and fearless experimentation. *Sgt. Pepper*, in many ways, refines that breakthrough, as the Beatles consciously synthesized such disparate influences as psychedelia, art-song, classical music, rock & roll, and music hall, often in the course of one song. Not once does the diversity seem forced—the genius of the record is how the vaudevillian "When I'm 64" seems like a logical extension of "Within You Without You" and how it provides a gateway to the chiming guitars of "Lovely Rita." There's no discounting the individual contributions of each member or their producer, George Martin, but the preponderance of whimsy and self-conscious art gives the impression that Paul McCartney is the leader of the Lonely Hearts Club Band. He dominates the album in terms of compositions, setting the tone for the album with his unabashed melodicism and deviously clever arrangements. In comparison, Lennon's contributions seem fewer, and a couple of them are a little slight but his major statements are stunning. "With a Little Help From My Friends" is the ideal Ringo tune, a rolling, friendly pop song that hides genuine Lennon anguish, à la "Help!"; "Lucy in the Sky With Diamonds" remains one of the touchstones of British psychedelia; and he's the mastermind behind the bulk of "A Day in the Life," a haunting number that skillfully blends Lennon's verse and chorus with McCartney's bridge. It's possible to argue that there are better Beatles albums, yet no album is as historically important as this. After *Sgt. Pepper*, there were no rules to follow—rock and pop bands could try anything, for better or worse. Ironically, few tried to achieve the sweeping, all-encompassing embrace of music as the Beatles did here.

Stephen Thomas Erlewine

Magical Mystery Tour
November 1967, Capitol

The U.S. version of the soundtrack for the Beatles' ill-fated British television special embellished the six songs that were found on the British *Magical Mystery Tour* double EP with five other cuts from their 1967 singles. (The CD version of the record has now been standardized worldwide as the 11 tracks found on the American version.) The psychedelic sound is very much in the vein of *Sgt. Pepper*, and even spacier in parts (especially the sound collages of "I Am the Walrus"). Unlike *Sgt. Pepper*, there's no vague overall conceptual/thematic unity to the material, which has made *Magical Mystery Tour* suffer slightly in comparison. Still, the music is mostly great, and "Penny Lane," "Strawberry Fields Forever," "All You Need Is Love," and "Hello Goodbye" were all huge, glorious, and innovative singles. The ballad "The Fool on the Hill," though only a part of the *Magical Mystery Tour* soundtrack, is also one of the most popular Beatle tunes from the era.

Richie Unterberger

The Beatles [White Album]
November 1968, Capitol

Each song on the sprawling double album *The Beatles* is an entity to itself, as the band touches on anything and everything it can. This makes for a frustratingly scattershot record or a singularly gripping musical experience, depending on your view, but what makes the so-called *White Album* interesting is its mess. Never before had a rock record been so self-reflective, or so ironic; the Beach Boys send-up "Back in the U.S.S.R." and the British blooze parody "Yer Blues" are delivered straight-faced, so it's never clear if these are affectionate tributes or wicked satires. Lennon turns in two of his best ballads with "Dear Prudence" and "Julia"; scours the Abbey Road vaults for the musique concrète collage "Revolution 9"; pours on the schmaltz for Ringo's closing number, "Good Night"; celebrates the Beatles cult with "Glass Onion"; and, with "Cry Baby Cry," rivals Syd Barrett. McCartney doesn't reach quite as far, yet his songs are stunning—the music hall romp "Honey Pie," the mock country of "Rocky Raccoon," the ska-inflected "Ob-La-Di, Ob-La-Da," and the proto-metal roar of "Helter Skelter." Clearly, the Beatles' two main songwriting forces were no longer on the same page, but neither were George and Ringo. Harrison still had just two songs per LP, but it's clear from "While My Guitar Gently Weeps," the canned soul of "Savoy Truffle," the haunting "Long, Long, Long," and even the silly "Piggies" that he had developed into a songwriter who deserved wider exposure. And Ringo turns in a delight with his first original, the lumbering country-carnival stomp "Don't Pass Me By." None of it sounds like it was meant to share album space

together, but somehow *The Beatles* creates its own style and sound through its mess.

Stephen Thomas Erlewine

Abbey Road
September 1969, Capitol

The last Beatles album to be recorded (although *Let It Be* was the last to be released), *Abbey Road* was a fitting swan song for the group, echoing some of the faux-conceptual forms of *Sgt. Pepper*, but featuring stronger compositions and more rock-oriented ensemble work. The group was still pushing forward in all facets of its art, whether devising some of the greatest harmonies to be heard on any rock record (especially on "Because"), constructing a medley of songs/vignettes that covered much of side two, adding subtle touches of Moog synthesizer, or crafting furious guitar-heavy rock ("The End," "I Want You (She's So Heavy)," "Come Together"). George Harrison also blossomed into a major songwriter, contributing the buoyant "Here Comes the Sun" and the supremely melodic ballad "Something," the latter of which became the first Harrison-penned Beatles hit. Whether *Abbey Road* is the Beatles' best work is debatable, but it's certainly the most immaculately produced (with the possible exception of *Sgt. Pepper*) and most tightly constructed.

Richie Unterberger

Let It Be
May 1970, Capitol

The only Beatles album to occasion negative, even hostile reviews, there are few other rock records as controversial as *Let It Be*. First off, several facts need to be explained: although released in May 1970, this was *not* their final album, but largely recorded in early 1969, way before *Abbey Road*. Phil Spector was enlisted in early 1970 to do some post-production mixing and overdubs, but he did *not* work with the band as a unit. And, although his use of strings has generated much criticism, by and large he left the original performances to stand as is: only "The Long and Winding Road" and (to a lesser degree) "Across the Universe" and "I Me Mine" get the Wall of Sound treatment. The main problem was that the material wasn't uniformly strong, and that the Beatles themselves were in fairly lousy moods due to intergroup tension. All that said, the album is on the whole underrated, even discounting the fact that a substandard Beatles record is better than almost any other group's best work. McCartney in particular offers several gems: the gospel-ish "Let It Be," which has some of his best lyrics; "Get Back," one of his hardest rockers; and the melodic "The Long and Winding Road," ruined by Spector's heavy-handed overdubs. The folky "Two of Us," with John and Paul harmonizing together, was also a highlight. Most of the rest of the material, by contrast, was going through the motions to some degree, although there are some good moments of straight hard rock in "I've Got a Feeling" and "Dig a Pony." As flawed and bumpy as it is, it's an album well worth having, as when the Beatles were in top form here, they were as good as ever. [In November 2003, the Beatles released an alternate version of *Let It Be* called *Let*

It Be... Naked, which mixed out Spector's contributions and deleted snippets of conversation scattered throughout the album. "Dig It" and "Maggie Mae" were cut from the record in favor of "Don't Let Me Down," which was placed in the middle of an album that now had a considerably different sequencing than the originally released version of *Let It Be*.]

Richie Unterberger

Past Masters, Vol. 1
March 1988, Capitol

When Capitol decided to release the original British editions of the Beatles' albums instead of the bastardized American versions, they were left with a bit of a quandary. Since the Beatles had an enormous number of non-LP singles, some of their greatest hits—from "I Want to Hold Your Hand" through "Hey Jude"—would not be included on disc if Capitol simply served up straight reissues. They had two options: they could add the singles as bonus tracks to the appropriate CDs, or they could release a compilation of all the non-LP tracks. It should come as no surprise that they chose the latter. In fact, they took it one further, issuing two separate compilations of non-LP tracks, which is fairly appropriate since the Beatles released far more singles and EPs in the first two years of their recording career than they did in the last five. *Past Masters, Vol. 1* covers those first two years and, to be fair, there are some cuts that are unnecessary for anyone outside of the hardcore—only a handful of people will be able to spot the difference in the alternate "Love Me Do," while German versions of "I Want to Hold Your Hand" and "She Loves You" aren't even good for a chuckle. Still, the sheer number of astounding singles makes this essential, even with its faults. These 17 songs capture the exuberance of Beatlemania while confirming their talents as popcraftsmen ("This Boy," "Yes It Is") and proving that they could rock really, really hard ("I Feel Fine," "She's a Woman," the peerless "I'm Down"). Apart from the cuts that are merely rarities, this is a near-perfect compilation that captures the energy and spirit of the Beatles' early years.

Stephen Thomas Erlewine

Past Masters, Vol. 2
March 1988, Capitol

Picking up in 1965 where *Past Masters, Vol. 1* left off, *Past Masters, Vol. 2* collects the 15 non-LP tracks that the Beatles released in the last five years of their career (not counting the singles that were released on *Magical Mystery Tour*). If *Vol. 2* is more eclectic than its predecessor, it isn't quite as thematically consistent, but it does hit greater highs with a greater frequency. Indeed, some of the greatest singles in pop history are here: "Day Tripper," "We Can Work It Out," "Paperback Writer," "Rain," "Lady Madonna," "Hey Jude," "Revolution," "Don't Let Me Down," and "The Ballad of John and Yoko." All of the aforementioned are staples in the Lennon/McCartney canon, and while George Harrison's two contributions aren't as familiar, "The Inner Light" is arguably his best Indian excursion and "Old Brown Shoe" is a charmingly jaunty tune that points toward his solo career. In the middle of all this, single versions of "Get Back" and "Let It Be" appear (the former is stiffer than the LP version, the latter is better than its counterpart), along with the alternate (and superior) "Across the Universe" and the silly yet strangely irresistible "You Know My Name (Look Up the Number)." Overall, the compilation feels a little disjointed, mainly because it covers so much ground so quickly, but that takes nothing away from the quality of the music, since many of these songs rank among the best, most inventive recordings of the pop/rock era.

Stephen Thomas Erlewine

Jeff Beck

Truth
August 1968, Epic/Legacy

Jeff Beck's *Truth*—which was already regarded as the pioneering heavy metal blues album of its era, beating Led Zeppelin to the punch by about six months—got a lot better with this British import remastered reissue, which puts all prior or editions of the CD to shame. EMI Records have remastered the original LP in 24-bit digital, which puts Beck's guitar and John Paul Jones' organ on "You Shook Me" practically in your lap, and the amp on the former almost up against your ear, and Mickey Waller's drums and Ron Wood's bass on "Shapes of Things" into a position of similar intimacy, so you can almost hear the action on the bass strings. And Rod Stewart's voice is not only close but flows out with a resonance that can't entirely be covered by his rasping delivery—"Ol' Man River" now seems like an ideal choice for him (as well as a distant precursor to his later recordings of standards), and Keith Moon's timpani performance is totally larger-than-life here. Beck's guitar sounds like it's in the room with you on "Rock My Plimsoul," and Stewart's singing is presented in such detail, that his nuances now seem fine and intimate. There are so many details revealed in the playing here in this remastering, that even longtime listeners are certain to find nuances in the playing and the different parts that are new to them—and that's just the established album. The original ten songs have been very judiciously augmented with a brace of killer bonus tracks, starting with "I've Been Drinking," where Rod Stewart first treaded into Sam Cooke territory stylistically, which somehow never got included on the LP and ended up relegated to the B-side of the Beck single "Love Is Blue" in mono (it's in stereo here, natch); there's also the undubbed, stripped-down first take of "You Shook Me," filled with instruments that are nice and close and crunchy (especially the guitar); the early, single-take of "Rock My Plimsoul," remixed to stereo here; "Beck's Bolero" in its original mono single version; the previously unissued first take of the shattering "Blues De Luxe"; and the early single A-sides "Tallyman," "Love Is Blue," and "Hi Ho Silver Lining," the first and last featuring Beck's own singing (a decision imposed by producer Mickie Most over the guitarist's vociferous objections) the latter in its unedited form with a "wee surprise" at the very end. It's worth the upgrade—you may well find yourself practically getting high off the raw invention and passions oozing from virtually all of the music, and even playing it once for some younger friends who've heard it before will make a few converts to its cause.

Bruce Eder

Beck-Ola
June 1969, Epic/Legacy

When it was originally released in June 1969, *Beck-Ola*, the Jeff Beck Group's second album, featured a famous sleeve note on its back cover: "Today, with all the hard competition in the music business, it's almost impossible to come up with anything totally original. So we haven't. However, this disc was made with the accent on heavy music. So sit back and listen and try and decide if you can find a small place in your heads for it." Beck was reacting to the success of peers and competitors like Cream and Led Zeppelin here, bands that had been all over the charts with a hard rock sound soon to be dubbed heavy metal, and indeed, his sound employs much the same brand of "heavy music" as theirs, with deliberate rhythms anchoring the beat, over which the guitar solos fiercely and the lead singer emotes. But he was also preparing listeners for the weakness of the material on an album that sounds somewhat thrown together. Two songs are rehauls of Elvis Presley standards ("All Shook Up" and "Jailhouse Rock") and one is an instrumental interlude contributed by pianist Nicky Hopkins, promoted from sideman to group member, with the rest being band-written songs that serve basically as platforms for Beck's improvisations. But that doesn't detract from the album's overall quality, due both to the guitar work and the distinctive vocals of Rod Stewart, and *Beck-Ola* easily could have been the album to establish the Jeff Beck Group as the equal of the other heavy bands of the day. Unfortunately, a series of misfortunes occurred. Beck canceled out of a scheduled appearance at Woodstock; he was in a car accident that sidelined him for over a year; and Stewart and bass player Ron Wood decamped to join Faces, breaking up the group. Nevertheless, *Beck-Ola* stands as a prime example of late-'60s British blues-rock and one of Beck's best records. [In June 2004 EMI released a digitally remastered edition of *Beck-Ola* featuring four previously unreleased bonus tracks: "Sweet Little Angel," "Throw Down a Line," and early versions of "All Shook Up" and "Jailhouse Rock."]

William Ruhlmann

Beck, Bogert & Appice
1973, Epic

One of the great things about Jeff Beck is his utter unpredictability. It's also one of the most maddening things about him, too, since it's as likely to lead to flights of genius as it is to weird detours like *Beck, Bogert & Appice*. It's hard to tell what exactly attracted Beck to the rhythm section of Vanilla Fudge and Cactus—perhaps he just wanted to rock really loud and really hard, beating Led Zeppelin at their own game. Whatever the motivation, the end result was the same—a leaden album, with occasional interesting guitar work smothered by heavy riffs and rhythms that don't succeed on a visceral level. It's a loud, lumbering record that may be of interest for Beck archivists, provided they want to hear absolutely everything he did.

Stephen Thomas Erlewine

Blow by Blow
March 1975, Epic

Blow by Blow typifies Jeff Beck's wonderfully unpredictable career. Released in 1975, Beck's fifth effort as a leader and first instrumental album was a marked departure from its more rock-based predecessors. Only composer/keyboardist Max Middleton returned

from Beck's previous lineups. To Beck's credit, *Blow by Blow* features a tremendous supporting cast. Middleton's tasteful use of the Fender Rhodes, clavinet, and analog synthesizers leaves a soulful imprint. Drummer Richard Bailey is in equal measure supportive and propulsive as he deftly combines elements of jazz and funk with contemporary mixed meters. Much of the album's success is also attributable to the excellent material, which includes Middleton's two originals and two collaborations with Beck, a clever arrangement of Lennon and McCartney's "She's a Woman," and two originals by Stevie Wonder. George Martin's ingenious production and string arrangements rival his greatest work. Beck's versatile soloing and diverse tones are clearly the album's focus, and he proves to be an adept rhythm player. *Blow by Blow* is balanced by open-ended jamming and crisp ensemble interaction as it sidesteps the bombast that sank much of the jazz-rock fusion of the period. One of the album's unique qualities is the sense of fun that permeates the performances. On the opening "You Know What I Mean," Beck's stinging, blues-based soloing is full of imaginative shapes and daring leaps. On "Air Blower," elaborate layers of rhythm, duel lead, and solo guitars find their place in the mix. Propelled by the galvanic rhythm section, Beck slashes his way into "Scatterbrain," where a dizzying keyboard and guitar line leads to more energetic soloing from Beck and Middleton. In Stevie Wonder's ballad "Cause We've Ended as Lovers," Beck variously coaxes and unleashes sighs and screams from his guitar in an aching dedication to Roy Buchanan. Middleton's aptly titled "Freeway Jam" best exemplifies the album's loose and fun-loving qualities, with Beck again riding high atop the rhythm section's wave. As with "Scatterbrain," Martin's impeccable string arrangements enhance the subtle harmonic shades of the closing "Diamond Dust." *Blow by Blow* signaled a new creative peak for Beck, and it proved to be a difficult act to follow. It is a testament to the power of effective collaboration and, given the circumstances, Beck clearly rose to the occasion. In addition to being a personal milestone, *Blow by Blow* ranks as one of the premiere recordings in the canon of instrumental rock music.

Mark Kirschenmann

Wired
May 1976, Epic

Released in 1976, Jeff Beck's *Wired* contains some of the best jazz-rock fusion of the period. *Wired* is generally more muscular, albeit less-unique than its predecessor, *Blow by Blow*. Joining keyboardist Max Middleton, drummer Richard Bailey,

and producer George Martin from the *Blow by Blow* sessions are drummer Narada Michael Walden, bassist Wilbur Bascomb, and keyboardist Jan Hammer. Beck contributed no original material to *Wired*, instead relying on the considerable talents of his supporting cast. Perhaps this explains why *Wired* is not as cohesive as *Blow by Blow*, seemingly more assembled from component parts. Walden's powerful drumming propels much of *Wired*, particularly Middleton's explosive opener, "Led Boots," where Beck erupts into a stunning solo of volcanic intensity. Walden also contributes four compositions, including the funk-infused "Come Dancing," which adds an unnamed horn section. While Walden's

"Sophie" is overly long and marred by Hammer's arena rock clichés, his "Play With Me" is spirited and Hammer's soloing more melodic. Acoustic guitar and piano predominate the closing ballad, "Love Is Green"; Beck's electric solo gracefully massages the quiet timbres. *Wired* is well balanced by looser, riff-oriented material and Walden's more intricate compositions. Walden and Hammer give *Wired* a '70s-era jazz-rock flavor that is indicative of their work with the Mahavishnu Orchestra. Bascomb's throw-down, "Head for Backstage Pass," finds Bailey skillfully navigating the mixed meters while Beck counters with a dazzling, gritty solo. Hammer's "Blue Wind" features an infectious riff over which Beck and Hammer trade heated salvos. As good as "Blue Wind" is, it would have benefited from the Walden/Bascomb rhythm section and a horn arrangement by Martin. One of *Wired's* finest tracks is an arrangement of Charles Mingus' "Goodbye Pork Pie Hat." Beck's playing is particularly alluring: cleanly ringing tones, weeping bends, and sculpted feedback form a resonant palette. Bailey and Middleton lend supple support. Within a two-year span, the twin towers *Blow by Blow* and *Wired* set a standard for instrumental rock that even Beck has found difficult to match. On *Wired,* with first-rate material and collaborators on hand, one of rock's most compelling guitarists is in top form.

Mark Kirschenmann

Beckology
November 1991, Epic/Legacy

This triple-CD set—obviously modeled after the four-CD Eric Clapton *Crossroads* box—was the first attempt to survey Jeff Beck's entire career. In actual fact, that would be a hopeless task, given the amount of anonymous session work that the guitarist did circa 1964-1966, but *Beckology* still manages to touch a few unexpected bases, even as it strings together all of the obvious and most of the important sides in Beck's output. Disc one opens with the most alluring part of the entire set, three demo tracks left behind by Beck's 1963-1965 group, the Tridents; the first official releases by this band are of far more than academic interest, presenting a first-rate blues/R&B outfit supercharged by Beck's guitar and Ray Cook's drumming, doing killer Jimmy Reed and Bo Diddley material, and even showing off Beck's prowess as a singer. The next 15 tracks represent the core of the Yardbirds' output during Beck's tenure, which lasted from March of 1965 through the summer of 1966—anything here could justify a place on a Yardbirds best-of set; the makers have rounded this disc out with four live cuts by the band from the BBC archives, including Beck's extraordinary homage to Elmore James' guitar playing on "The Sun Is Shining" and the unheralded group original "Love Me Like I Love You", and finish the platter with Beck's first three solo single sides, two of which, "Hi Ho Silver Lining" and "Tally Man," comprise the guitarist's brief, achingly beautiful virtuoso digression into trippy psychedelic pop, before he broke through to the more fertile field of what came to be known as heavy metal. Disc two is all of that, made up of the core of his output with the Jeff Beck Group and Beck Bogert & Appice, the latter filled out with a pair of previously unissued tracks: a live version of "Blues Deluxe/BBA Boogie" and "Jizz Whizz." Disc three skips across Beck's instrumental sides off of *Blow by Blow*, *Wired*, and *There and Back* and his tour with the Jan Hammer Group from the later 1970s, and wraps up with ten songs from *Flash* and *Jeff Beck's Guitar Shop*, sandwiching some key odd singles and Beck's contributions to the soundtracks of the movies *Twins* and *Porky's Revenge*. There are flaws in this set, to be sure; originally conceived as a four-disc retrospective, it was reduced to three, over Beck's wishes that some proposed cuts be omitted and Sony Music's

timidity over the sales prospect of the four-CD set. But it is a good package within those boundaries, with fairly thorough annotation accompanied by great photos and a Pete Frame family tree, and, above all, excellent tape research—not only were the right masters (i.e., the mono masters) used on "Hot House of Omagarashid" and "Lost Woman," but this is also the only CD package to combine the Yardbirds' 1965 catalog material with their 1966 tracks (owned by separate parties who will not get together). The mastering of it all is so clean that it put most of the older versions of this material to shame at the time.

Bruce Eder

Pat Benatar

Greatest Hits
June 2005, Capitol

The liner notes to Capitol's 20-track retrospective of rock goddess Pat Benatar's golden years are filled with testimonials from some of the genre's queens, both reigning (Sarah McLachlan, Tori Amos) and retired (Jane Wiedlin, Martha Davis). It's a fitting tribute to the artist, as her four-and-a-half-octave vocal range spewing arena-sized anthems has yet to be matched by anyone with as much rock & roll panache. "We Belong," "Shadows of the Night," "Promises in the Dark," and "Love Is a Battlefield" are all certifiable '80s classics—not just guilty pleasures—and even later semi-hits like "Sex as a Weapon" and "All Fired Up" don't sound as overwrought as one would imagine, having not heard them in some time. *Greatest Hits* is just five songs longer than 1989's *Best Shots*—reissued in 2003 with an accompanying DVD—but the inclusion of fan favorites such as "Little Too Late" and "Le Bel Age" make this collection the most effective to date. Fair is fair.

James Christopher Monger

Big Brother & the Holding Company

Cheap Thrills
August 1968, Columbia

Cheap Thrills, the major-label debut of Janis Joplin, was one of the most eagerly anticipated, and one of the most successful, albums of 1968. Joplin and Big Brother had earned extensive press notice ever since they played the Monterey Pop Festival in June 1967, but their only recorded work was a poorly produced, self-titled Mainstream album, and they spent a year getting out of their contract with Mainstream in order to sign with Columbia while demand built. When *Cheap Thrills* appeared in August 1968, it shot into the charts, reaching number one and going gold within a couple of months, and "Piece of My Heart" became a Top 40 hit. Joplin, with her ear- (and vocal cord-) shredding voice, was the obvious standout. Nobody had ever heard singing as emotional, as desperate, as determined, as loud as Joplin's, and *Cheap Thrills* was her greatest moment. Big Brother's backup, typical of the guitar-dominated sound of San Francisco psychedelia, made up in enthusiasm what it lacked in precision. But everybody knew who the real star was, and Joplin played her last gig with Big Brother while the album was still on top of the charts. Neither she nor the band would ever equal it. Heard today, *Cheap Thrills* is a musical time capsule and remains a showcase for one of rock's most distinctive singers.

William Ruhlmann

Black Oak Arkansas

Raunch 'N' Roll Live
March 1973, Atco

In the '70s, Black Oak Arkansas' albums could be uneven and inconsistent; many of their releases weren't without their share of mediocre filler. But when the Southern rockers soared, they *really* soared. Arguably, Black Oak's best and most consistent release is *Raunch 'N' Roll Live*. Recorded at 1973 concerts in Portland, OR, and Seattle, this LP is without a dull moment. The colorful, hell-raising lead singer Jim Dandy is inspired and focused throughout the album, excelling on inspired performances of Southern-fried gems like "Hot and Nasty," "Mutants of the Monster," "Gigolo," and "Hot Rod." One of Black Oak's big problems was the fact that they went through so many personnel changes in the '70s; when a band is such a revolving door, their albums can easily become erratic—and unfortunately, that was sometimes the case with Black Oak. Some of Black Oak's lineups were more successful than others; the 1973 lineup heard on *Raunch 'N' Roll Live* was among their more productive ones. On this LP, Dandy is well-served by a lineup who includes bassist Pat Daugherty, drummer Tommy Aldrige, and no less than three guitarists: Rick Reynolds, Stanley Knight, and Harvey Jett. *Raunch 'N' Roll Live* wasn't the only live album that Black Oak provided in the '70s; in 1975—only two years after the release of this LP—the band recorded *Live! Mutha* at a Long Beach, CA, show. While that release is enjoyable, *Raunch 'N' Roll Live* remains the most exciting and vital document of Black Oak on-stage. Without a doubt, *Raunch 'N' Roll Live* is essential listening for those who have even a casual interest in the rowdy Southern rockers.

Alex Henderson

Black Sabbath

Black Sabbath
May 1970, Warner Bros.

Black Sabbath's debut album is given over to lengthy songs and suite-like pieces where individual songs blur together and riffs pound away one after another, frequently under extended jams. There isn't much variety in tempo, mood, or the band's simple, blues-derived musical vocabulary, but that's not the point; Sabbath's slowed-down, murky guitar rock bludgeons the listener in an almost hallucinatory fashion, reveling in its own dazed, druggy state of consciousness. Songs like the apocalyptic title track, "N.I.B.," and "The Wizard" make their obsessions with evil and black magic seem like more than just stereotypical heavy metal posturing because of the dim, suffocating musical atmosphere the band frames them in. This blueprint would be refined and

occasionally elaborated upon over the band's next few albums, but there are plenty of metal classics already here.

Steve Huey

Paranoid
January 1971, Warner Bros.

Paranoid was not only Black Sabbath's most popular record (it was a number one smash in the U.K., and "Paranoid" and "Iron Man" both scraped the U.S. charts despite virtually nonexistent radio play), it also stands as one of the greatest and most influential heavy metal albums of all time. *Paranoid* refined Black Sabbath's signature sound—crushingly loud, minor-key dirges loosely based on heavy blues-rock—and applied it to a newly consistent set of songs with utterly memorable riffs, most of which now rank as all-time metal classics. Where the extended, multi-sectioned songs on the debut sometimes felt like aimless jams, their counterparts on *Paranoid* have been given focus and direction, lending an epic drama to now-standards like "War Pigs" and "Iron Man" (which sports one of the most immediately identifiable riffs in metal history). The subject matter is unrelentingly, obsessively dark, covering both supernatural/sci-fi horrors and the real-life traumas of death, war, nuclear annihilation, mental illness, drug hallucinations, and narcotic abuse. Yet Sabbath makes it totally convincing, thanks to the crawling, muddled bleakness and bad-trip depression evoked so frighteningly well by their music. Even the qualities that made critics deplore the album (and the group) for years increase the overall effect—the technical simplicity of Ozzy Osbourne's vocals and Tony Iommi's lead guitar vocabulary; the spots when the lyrics sink into melodrama or awkwardness; the lack of subtlety and the infrequent dynamic contrast. Everything adds up to more than the sum of its parts, as though the music simply demanded that the band achieve catharsis by steamrolling everything in its path, including its own limitations. Monolithic and primally powerful, *Paranoid* defined the sound and style of heavy metal more than any other record in rock history.

Steve Huey

Master of Reality
August 1971, Warner Bros.

With *Paranoid*, Black Sabbath perfected the formula for their lumbering heavy metal. On its follow-up, *Master of Reality*, the group merely repeated the formula, setting the stage for a career of recycling the same sounds and riffs. But on *Master of Reality* Sabbath still were fresh and had a seemingly endless supply of crushingly heavy riffs to bludgeon their audiences into sweet, willing oblivion. If the album is a showcase for anyone, it is Tony Iommi, who keeps the album afloat with a series of slow, loud riffs, the best of which—"Sweet Leaf" and "Children of the Grave" among them—rank among his finest playing. Taken in tandem with the more consistent *Paranoid*, *Master of Reality* forms the core of Sabbath's canon. There are a few stray necessary tracks scattered throughout the group's other early-'70s albums, but *Master of Reality* is the last time they delivered a consistent album and its influence can be heard throughout the generations of heavy metal bands that followed.

Stephen Thomas Erlewine

Black Sabbath, Vol. 4
September 1972, Warner Bros.

Black Sabbath, Vol. 4 is just a cut below its two indisputably classic predecessors, as it begins to run out of steam—and memorable riffs—toward the end. However, it finds Sabbath beginning to experiment successfully with their trademark sound on tracks like the ambitious, psychedelic-tinged, multi-part "Wheels of Confusion," the concise, textured "Tomorrow's Dream," and the orchestrated piano ballad "Changes" (even if the latter's lyrics cross the line into triteness). But the classic Sabbath sound is still very much in evidence; the crushing "Supernaut" is one of the heaviest tracks the band ever recorded.

Steve Huey

Sabbath Bloody Sabbath
December 1973, Castle

With 1973's *Sabbath Bloody Sabbath* (their fifth masterpiece in four years), Black Sabbath made a concerted effort to raise their creative stakes and dispensed unprecedented attention to the album's production, arrangements, and even  the cover artwork. While faithful to the band's signature compositional style and sound, brilliant songs such as the title track, "A National Acrobat," and "Killing Yourself to Live" also displayed a newfound sense of finesse and maturity. The introduction of keyboards and synthesizers, on the other hand, meets with mixed results. Erstwhile Yes keyboard wizard Rick Wakeman makes a positive contribution to "Sabbra Cadabra," but "Who Are You" definitely suffers from synth overkill. Still, "Spiral Architect" benefits from its tasteful background orchestration, and the gentle "Fluff" is the first truly memorable solo instrumental from guitarist Tony Iommi, whose previous attempts often seemed pointless and haphazard. Simply put, this album is essential to any heavy metal collection.

Ed Rivadavia

Heaven & Hell
May 1980, Warner Bros.

Many had left Black Sabbath for dead at the dawn of the '80s, and with good reason—the band's last few albums were not even close to their early classics, and original singer Ozzy Osbourne had just split from the band. But the Sabs had found a worthy replacement in former Elf and Rainbow singer Ronnie James Dio, and bounced back to issue their finest album since the early '70s, 1980's *Heaven and Hell*. The band sounds reborn and re-energized throughout. Several tracks easily rank among Sabbath's all-time best, such as the vicious album opener, "Neon Knights," the moody, mid-paced epic "Children of the Sea," and the title track, which features one of

Tony Iommi's best guitar riffs. With *Heaven and Hell*, Black Sabbath were obviously back in business. Unfortunately, the Dio-led version of the band would only record one more studio album before splitting up (although Dio would return briefly in the early '90s). One of Sabbath's finest records.

Greg Prato

Blind Faith

Blind Faith
July 1969, Polydor

Blind Faith's first and last album, more than 30 years old and counting, remains one of the jewels of the Eric Clapton, Steve Winwood, and Ginger Baker catalogs, despite the crash-and-burn history of the band itself, which scarcely lasted six months. As much a follow-up to Traffic's self-titled second album as it is to Cream's final output, it merges the soulful blues of the former with the heavy riffing and outsized song lengths of the latter for a very compelling sound unique to this band. Not all of it works—between the virtuoso electric blues of "Had to Cry Today," the acoustic-textured "Can't Find My Way Home," the soaring "Presence of the Lord" (Eric Clapton's one contribution here as a songwriter, and the first great song he ever authored) and "Sea of Joy," the band doesn't do much with the Buddy Holly song "Well All Right"; and Ginger Baker's "Do What You Like" was a little weak to take up 15 minutes of space on an LP that might have been better used for a shorter drum solo and more songs. Unfortunately, the group was never *that* together as a band and evidently had just the 42 minutes of new music here ready to tour behind.

Bruce Eder

Blodwyn Pig

Ahead Rings Out
August 1969, BGO

None of Jethro Tull's progressive rock tendencies or classical influences followed Mick Abrahams into his creation of Blodwyn Pig, even with the inclusion Jack Lancaster's sax- and flute-playing prowess. Instead, Abrahams built up a sturdy British blues-rock sound and used Lancaster's horn work to add some fire to the band's jazzy repertoire. *Ahead Rings Out* is a stellar concoction of gritty yet flamboyant blues-rock tunes and open-ended jazz centered around Mick Abrahams' cool-handed guitar playing, but it's the nonstop infusion of the other styles that makes the album such a solid listen. After only one album with Jethro Tull, Abrahams left to form this band, and it's evident that he had a lot of pent-up energy inside him when he recorded each of the album's tracks. With a barrage of electrifying rhythms and fleeting saxophone and woodwind excursions, cuts like "Sing Me a Song That I Know," "Up and Coming," and "Backwash" whip up highly energetic sprees of rock and blues. Most of the tracks have a hearty shot of rock up the middle, but in cuts like "The Change Song" and "Backwash," the explosive riffs are accompanied by a big band style of enthusiasm, adding even more depth to the material. Andy Pyle's bass playing is definitely distinct throughout each track and is used for anything but a steady background, while labeling Ron Berg's drumming as freewheeling and intemperate would be an understatement. It's apparent that Blodwyn Pig's style is indeed distinct, releasing a liberated and devil-may-care intensity while still managing to stay on track, but the fact that each cut convokes a different type of instrumental spiritedness is where the album really gains its reputation. Wonderfully busy and even a tad motley in some places, *Ahead Rings Out* shows off the power and vitality that can be channeled by combining a number of classic styles without sounding pretentious or overly inflated. A year later, Blodwyn Pig recorded *Getting to This* before Abrahams left the band, and although it's a solid effort, it falls just a smidgen short of *Ahead Rings Out*'s bluesy dynamism.

Mike DeGagne

Blood, Sweat & Tears

Child Is Father to the Man
February 1968, Columbia/Legacy

Child Is Father to the Man is keyboard player/singer/arranger Al Kooper's finest work, an album on which he moves the folk-blues-rock amalgamation of the Blues Project into even wider pastures, taking in classical and jazz elements (including strings and horns), all without losing the pop essence that makes the hybrid work. This is one of the great albums of the eclectic post-*Sgt. Pepper* era of the late '60s, a time when you could borrow styles from Greenwich Village contemporary folk to San Francisco acid rock and mix them into what seemed to have the potential to become a new American musical form. It's Kooper's bluesy songs, such as "I Love You More Than You'll Ever Know" and "I Can't Quit Her," and his singing that are the primary focus, but the album is an aural delight; listen to the way the bass guitar interacts with the horns on "My Days Are Numbered" or the charming arrangement and Steve Katz's vocal on Tim Buckley's "Morning Glory." Then Kooper sings Harry Nilsson's "Without Her" over a delicate, jazzy backing with flügelhorn/alto saxophone interplay by Randy Brecker and Fred Lipsius. This is the sound of a group of virtuosos enjoying itself in the newly open possibilities of pop music. Maybe it couldn't have lasted; anyway, it didn't.

William Ruhlmann

Blood, Sweat & Tears
January 1969, Columbia/Legacy

The difference between *Blood, Sweat & Tears* and the group's preceding long-player, *Child Is Father to the Man*, is the difference between a monumental seller and a record that was "merely" a huge critical success. Arguably, the Blood, Sweat & Tears that made this self-titled second album—consisting of five of the eight original members and four newcomers, including singer David Clayton-Thomas—was really a different group from the one that made *Child Is Father to the Man*, which was done largely under the direction of singer/songwriter/keyboard player/arranger Al Kooper. They had certain similarities to the original: the musical mixture of classical, jazz, and rock elements was still apparent, and

the interplay between the horns and the keyboards was still occurring, even if those instruments were being played by different people. Kooper was even still present as an arranger on two tracks, notably the initial hit "You've Made Me So Very Happy." But the second BS&T, under the aegis of producer James William Guercio, was a less adventurous unit, and, as fronted by Clayton-Thomas, a far more commercial one. Not only did the album contain three songs that neared the top of the charts as singles—"Happy," "Spinning Wheel," and "And When I Die"—but the whole album, including an arrangement of "God Bless the Child" and the radical rewrite of Traffic's "Smiling Phases," was wonderfully accessible. It was a repertoire to build a career on, and Blood, Sweat & Tears did exactly that, although they never came close to equaling this album.

William Ruhlmann & Bruce Eder

Blue Cheer

Vincebus Eruptum
January 1968, Polygram

Had "Summertime Blues" not gone Top 15 in the spring of 1968, Blue Cheer might not have had the opportunity to unleash their expression over numerous albums through multiple personnel changes. *Vincebus Eruptum* sports a serious silver/off-purple cover wrapped around the punk-metal fury. Leigh Stephens is nowhere near Hendrix, Beck, Clapton, or Jimmy Page, the skill of a Yardbirds replaced by a thud of bass/drums/low-end guitar. Vocalist Dickie Peterson takes almost six minutes on Allison's "Parchment Farm" [sic] to talk about shooting his arm, shooting his wife, picking cotton, and having sex. Definitely more risqué than Grand Funk Railroad's "T.N.U.C.," Abe "Voco" Kesh's production is almost nonexistent. They certainly influenced the way Grand Funk would take the power trio; you can hear in Peterson's voice that tonal quality Mark Farner had to employ as well to get the lyrics over the morass of sound. It's interesting that the Velvet Underground's classic *White Light/White Heat* took this attitude up a notch at this exact point in time, going in to the studio and unleashing "Sister Ray," the almost 20-minute scream that was the result of Lou Reed's shock treatment therapy as a teen. Both bands were influenced heavily by drugs, heroin appearing to be the culprit, and while "Second Time Around," which closes this album, came in from the West Coast, the Velvet Underground blasted with even higher intensity from the East. Also interesting that "Doctor Please" on *Vincebus Eruptum* doesn't have the crunch West/Bruce and Laing would insert into their own "The Doctor" four years later on *Why Dontcha*. That power trio showed off their chops while Blue Cheer was looking for their chops on this record. *Vincebus Eruptum* is a dark power trio recording with punk attitude exploring blues through heavy metal. That later version of the band would go on to produce "I'm the Light," a spacy cosmic anthem as delicate as Grand Funk's "Closer to Home," says a lot about the musical journey initiated by *Vincebus Eruptum*. The album is an underappreciated classic with "Rock Me Baby" leaning more toward Ten Years After than Steppenwolf, without Alvin Lee's technical expertise. Guitar that quivers and roars with a heavy dependence on rhythm à la the Who, Blue Cheer knows that attitude is as important as musicianship in rock, and they exploit that virtue for all it is worth here.

Joe Viglione

Blue Öyster Cult

Blue Öyster Cult
January 1972, Columbia

Two years before Kiss roared out of Long Island with its self-titled debut, Blue Öyster Cult, the latest incarnation of a band assembled by guitarist Donald "Buck Dharma" Roeser and drummer Albert Bouchard in 1967, issued its dark, eponymously-titled heavy rock monolith. Managed and produced by the astronomically minded and conspiratorially haunted Sandy Pearlman, BÖC rode the hot, hellbound rails of blistering hard rock as pioneered by Steppenwolf, fierce mutated biker blues, and a kind of dark psychedelia that could have only come out New York. The band's debut relied heavily on the lyrics of Pearlman and rock critic Richard Meltzer, as well as Pearlman's pioneering production that layered guitars in staggered sheets of sound over a muddy mix that kept Eric Bloom's delivery in the middle of the mix and made it tough to decipher. This was on purpose—to draw the listener into the songs cryptically and ambiguously. From the opener, "Transmaniacon MC," the listener knew something very different was afoot. This is dark, amphetamine-fueled occult music that relied on not one, but *three* guitars—Bloom and keyboardist Allen Lanier added their own parts to Roeser's incessant riffing: a barely audible upright piano keeping the changes rooted in early rock and the blues, and a rhythm attack by Bouchard and his brother Joe on bass that was barely contained inside the tune's time signature. From the next track on "I'm on the Lamb But I Ain't No Sheep," elliptical lyrics talked about "the red and the black," while darkening themselves with stunning riffs and crescendos that were as theatrical as they were musical, and insured the Cult notice among the other acts bursting out of the seams of post-'60's rock. Other standouts include the cosmic "Stairway to the Stars," the boogie rave-up "Before the Kiss, a Redcap," that sounded like a mutant Savoy Brown meeting Canned Heat at Altamont. But it is on "Cities on Flame With Rock & Roll," that the Cult's sinister plan for world domination is best displayed. From it's knotty, overdriven riff to its rhythm guitar vamp, Vox organ shimmer, its crash cymbal ride and plodding bass and drum slog through the changes—not to mention it's title—it is the ultimate in early metal anthems. Add to this the swirling quizzicality of "Workshop of the Telescopes" that lent the band an air of image cred. The 2001 remastered edition by Legacy gives punters four bonus tracks in the form of demos recorded by the band's first incarnation as "Soft White Underbelly." These are not merely throwaways: it is readily apparent that by 1969, BÖC was well on their way to creating something new and menacingly different. The only questionable item is the last track: a cover version of Bobby Freeman's "Betty Lou's Got a New Pair of Shoes," that is utterly devoid of interest.

Thom Jurek

Tyranny and Mutation
February 1973, Columbia/Legacy

On *Tyranny and Mutation*, the Blue Öyster Cult achieved the seemingly impossible: They brightened their sound and deepened their mystique. The band picked up its tempos considerably on this sophomore effort, and producers Sandy Pearlman and Murray Krugman added a lightning bolt of high-end sonics to their frequency range. Add to this the starling lyrical contributions of Pearlman, rock critic Richard Meltzer, and poet cum rocker Patti Smith (who was keyboardist Allen Lanier's girlfriend at the time), the split

imagery of Side One's thematic, The Red and Side Two's The Black, and the flip-to-wig-city, dark conspiracy of Gawlik's cover art, and an entire concept was not only born and executed, it was received. The Red side of *Tyranny and Mutation* is its reliance on speed, punched-up big guitars, and throbbing riffs such as in "The Red and the Black," "O.D'd on Life Itself," "Hot Rails to Hell," and "7 Screaming Diz-Busters," all of which showcased the biker boogie taken to a dizzingly extreme boundary; one where everything flies by in a dark blur, and  the articulations of that worldview are informed as much by atmosphere as idea. This is screaming, methamphetamine-fueled rock and roll that was all about attitude, mystery, and a sense of nihilistic humor that was deep in the cuff. Here was the crossroads: the middle of rock's Bermuda triangle where BÖC marked the black cross of the intersection between New York's *other* reigning kings of mystery theater and absurd excess: the Velvet Underground and Kiss—two years before their first album—and the "it's all F#$&%* so who gives a rat's ass" attitude that embodied the City's punk chic half-a-decade later. On the Red Side, beginning with the syncopated striations of "Baby Ice Dog," in which Allen Lanier's piano was as important as Buck Dharma's guitar throb, elements of ambiguity and bluesy swagger enter into the mix. Eric Bloom was the perfect frontman: he twirled the words around in his mouth before spitting them out with requisite piss-and-vinegar, and a sense of decadent dandy that underscored the music's elegance, as well as its power. He was at ease whether the topic was necromancy, S&M, apocalyptic warfare, or cultural dissolution. By the LP's end, on "Mistress of the Salmon Salt," Bloom was being covered over by a kind of aggressively architected psychedelia that kept the '60s at bay while embracing the more aggressive, tenser nature of the times. While BÖC's *Secret Treaties* is widely recognized as the Cult's classic album, one would do well to consider *Tyranny and Mutation* in the same light. On the 2001 remastered version, Legacy added live versions of "Cities on Flame With Rock & Roll," "7 Screaming Diz-Busters," and "O.D.'d on Life Itself," as well as a studio read of Buck Dharma's "Buck's Boogie," but they add little to the power and sinister majesty of the original album.

Thom Jurek

Secret Treaties
April 1974, Columbia

While the speed-freak adrenaline heaviness and shrouded occult mystery of *Tyranny and Mutation* is the watermark for Blue Öyster Cult's creative invention, it is *Secret Treaties* that is widely and critically regarded as the band's classic. Issued in 1974, *Secret Treaties* is the purest distillation of all of BÖC's strengths. Here the songs are expansive, and lush in their textures. The flamboyance is all here, and so are the overdriven guitar riffs provided by Buck Dharma and Eric Bloom. But there is something else, texturally, that moves these songs out from the blackness and into the shadows. Perhaps it's the bottom-heavy mix by producer and lyricist Sandy Pearlman, with Allen Lanier's electric piano and Joe

Bouchard's bass coming to rest in an uneasy balance with the twin-guitar attack. Perhaps it's in the tautness of songwriting and instrumental architectures created by drummer Albert Bouchard, Bloom, and Don Roeser (Buck Dharma). Whatever it is, it offers the Cult a new depth and breadth. While elements of psychedelia have always been a part of the band's sound, it was always enfolded in proto-metal heaviness and biker boogie. Here, BÖC created their own brand of heavy psychedelic noir to diversify their considerably aggressive attack. Listen to "Subhuman" or "Dominance and Submission." Their minor chord flourishes and multi-tracked layered guitars and Bouchard's constantly shimmering cymbals and snare work (he is the most underrated drummer in rock history) and elliptical lyrics—that Pearlman put out in front of the mix for a change—added to the fathomless dread and mystery at the heart of the music. Elsewhere, on "Cagey Cretins" and "Harvester of Eyes" (both with lyrics by critic Richard Meltzer), the razor-wire guitar riffs were underscored by Lanier's organ, and their sci-fi urgency heightened by vocal harmonies. But it is on "Flaming Telepaths," with its single-chord hypnotic piano line that brings the lyric "Well, I've opened up my veins too many times/And the poison's in my heart in my heart and in my mind/Poison's in my bloodstream/Poison's in my pride/I'm after rebellion/I'll settle for lives/Is it any wonder that my mind is on fire?" down into the maelstrom and wreaks havoc on the listener. It's a stunner, full of crossing guitar lines and an insistent, demanding rhythmic throb. The set closes with the quark strangeness of "Astronomy," full of melancholy, dread, and loss that leaves the listener unsettled and in an entirely new terrain, having traveled a long way from the boasting rockery of "Career of Evil" that began the journey. It's a breathless rock monolith that is all dark delight and sinister pleasure. While the Cult went on to well-deserved commercial success with *Agents of Fortune* an album later, the freaky inspiration that was offered on their debut, and brought to shine like a black jewel on *Tyranny and Mutation*, was fully articulated as visionary on *Secret Treaties*.

Thom Jurek

Agents of Fortune
May 1976, Columbia

If ever there were a manifesto for 1970s rock, one that prefigured both the decadence of the decade's burgeoning heavy metal and prog rock excesses and the rage of punk rock, "This Ain't the Summer of Love," the opening track from *Agents of Fortune*, Blue Öyster Cult's fourth album, was it. The irony was that while the cut itself came down firmly on the hard rock side of the fence, most of the rest of the album didn't. *Agents of Fortune* was co-produced by longtime Cult record boss Sandy Pearlman, Murray Krugman, and newcomer David Lucas, and in addition, the band's lyric writing was being done internally with help from poet-cum-rocker Patti Smith (who also sings on "The Revenge of Vera Gemini"). Pearlman, a major contributor to the band's songwriting output, received a solitary credit while critic Richard Meltzer, whose words were prevalent on the Cult's previous outings, was absent. The album yielded the band's biggest single with "(Don't Fear) The Reaper," a multi-textured, deeply melodic soft rock song with psychedelic overtones, written by guitarist Donald "Buck Dharma" Roeser. The rest of the album is ambitious in that it all but tosses aside the Cult's proto-metal stance and instead recontextualizes their entire stance. It's still dark, mysterious, and creepy, and perhaps even more so, it's still rooted in rock posturing and excess, but gone is the nihilistic biker boogie in favor of a more tempered—indeed, nearly pop arena rock—sound that gave Allen Lanier's keyboards

parity with Dharma's guitar roar, as evidenced by "E.T.I.," "Debbie Denise," and "True Confessions." This is not to say that the Cult abandoned their adrenaline rock sound entirely. Cuts like "Tattoo Vampire" and "Sinful Love" have plenty of feral wail in them. Ultimately, *Agents of Fortune* is a solid record, albeit a startling one for fans of the band's earlier sound. It also sounds like one of restless inspiration, which is, in fact, what it turned out to be given the recordings that came after. It turned out to be the Cult's last consistent effort until they released *Fire of Unknown Origin* in 1981.

Thom Jurek

Some Enchanted Evening
September 1978, Columbia/Legacy

According to Lenny Kaye—a rock hero and historian who gets his facts ruler straight—*Some Enchanted Evening* is the mighty beast that is Blue Öyster Cult's best-selling record, with numbers signifying double platinum. Yeah, small potatoes by today's standards, but then the music industry is self-destructing anyway; these totals sum up not only the BÖC faithful, but those who were initially turned onto the band through this wonder of a cut-up live record. And the reason? Because it kicks serious rock & roll ass, that's why. This new deluxe edition from Legacy restores *Some Enchanted Evening* to its intended double-LP length. The Cult had released its first live record, *On Your Feet or on Your Knees* in 1975, just three years earlier with only two studio offerings in between. Wondering why? There were two absolute smashes— *Agents of Fortune* (1976) and *Spectres* (1977)—in between. The grueling touring they took on in support of these albums dictated a rest, and thus *Some Enchanted Evening* was assembled and released. This restored version contains 14 cuts—doubling the length of the original—and includes a full-length, wild and wooly DVD of a BÖC performance of the band playing live in Maryland that same year (some rest—they toured to support the live record, too). The DVD is worth it because BÖC were as much about giving a show as Kiss; they just didn't need to be corny about it because they were all great musicians. The lasers alone are worth the price of admission here, and to see the interaction of the band with their show's pyrotechnics is anything but studied. It was instinctive and led to a performance captured on film that was actually typical in terms of its intensity, focus, professional '70s work ethic, and sheer rock & roll abandon. The CD bonus tracks include the classic "ME 262," "Hot Rails to Hell" "(This Ain't The) Summer of Love," and the climax of the *Some Enchanted Evening* show "5 Guitars." Staples in the band's covers stable include "Born to Be Wild" and an alternate of "We Gotta Get Out of This Place." In other words, this new edition, apart from the absolutely glorious DVD, puts back all the early classics that appeared and were left off for marketing reasons—the biz thinking that folks wouldn't plunk down the cash for another live double with songs that repeated. The Deluxe Edition of *Some Enchanted Evening* lifts the album's original profile in stellar sound and excellent video production. It can't be recommended highly enough.

Thom Jurek

Fire of Unknown Origin
June 1981, Columbia

Who would have thought that in 1981, after a pair of limp, unfocused studio offerings, and two mixed—at best—live outings, that the once mighty Blue Öyster Cult would come back with such a fierce, creative, and uncompromising effort as *Fire of Unknown Origin*. Here was their finest moment since *Agents of Fortune* five years earlier, and one of their finest ever. Bringing back into the fold the faithful team who helped articulate their earlier vision, producer Sandy Pearlman, Richard Meltzer, and Patti Smith all helped in the lyric department, as did science fiction and dark fantasy writer Michael Moorcock. The band's sound was augmented by a plethora of keyboards courtesy of Allen Lanier, but nonetheless retained a modicum of its heaviness, and the sheer songwriting craft that had helped separate the band form its peers early on was everywhere evident here—especially the gloriously noir-ish Top 40 single "Burning for You," written by Meltzer and guitarist Buck Dharma. Other standouts on the set include the plodding, über-riff pyrotechnics of "Heavy Metal: The Black and the Silver," and the Mott the Hoople- and Queen-influenced glammed up roots rock of "Joan Crawford." The terrifying images of desecration and apocalyptic war in "Veteran of Psychic Wars," with words by Moorcock, feature huge synth lines, dual leads by Dharma and Eric Bloom—as well as a tom-tom orgy from Albert Bouchard—offered a new pathway through the eternal night of the Cult's best work. *Fire of Unknown Origin* has aged well, and deserves to be remastered in the 21st century.

Thom Jurek

Tommy Bolin

Teaser
1975, Columbia

After performing in a variety of bands since the late '60s, Bolin finally released his first solo album in 1975. *Teaser* is an impressive display of the guitarist's prowess and range, and is a natural progression from the previous Bolin-dominated James Gang albums *Bang* and *Miami* and his work with drummer Billy Cobham. The album features heavy doses of jazz-rock fusion (furthered by guests Jan Hammer, Dave Sanborn, and Michael Walden) in the instrumentals "Homeward Strut" and "Marching Powder," and straight-ahead rock in tracks like "The Grind." Bolin was always equally adept at subtleties, and the ballad "Dreamer" and the exotic "Savannah Woman" (with percussion from Phil Collins) represent this stylistic range here. Overshadowed historically by his guitar dynamics, Bolin's understated yet strong vocals are another selling point. *Teaser* is a stronger album than its one successor, the uneven *Private Eyes*, and survives as Bolin's signature work.

Rob Caldwell

Private Eyes
1976, Columbia

After the breakup of Deep Purple in 1976, guitarist Tommy Bolin wasted little time beginning work on his second solo album, *Private Eyes*. While it was more of a conventional rock album than its predecessor, *Teaser* (which served primarily as a showcase for his guitar skills and contained several jazz/rock instrumentals), it was not as potent. The performances aren't as inspired as those on *Teaser* or even

those on Bolin's lone album with Deep Purple, *Come Taste the Band*, although there a few highlights could be found. The nine-minute rocker "Post Toastee" merges a long jam section with lyrics concerning the dangers of drug addiction, while "Shake the Devil" is similar stylistically. But Bolin wasn't simply a hard-rocker; he was extremely talented with other kinds of music: the quiet, acoustic-based compositions "Hello, Again" and "Gypsy Soul," and the heartbroken ballad "Sweet Burgundy." With his solo career starting to take shape (after the album's release, he opened for some of rock's biggest names: Peter Frampton, Jeff Beck, Rush, ZZ Top, etc.), Bolin's life was tragically cut short at the end of the year due to a drug overdose in Miami, FL.

Greg Prato

Boston

Boston
September 1976, Epic

Boston is one of the best-selling albums of all time, and deservedly so. Because of the rise of disco and punk, FM rock radio seemed all but dead until the rise of acts like Boston, Tom Petty, and Bruce Springsteen. Nearly every song on Boston's debut album can still be heard on classic rock radio today due to the strong vocals of Brad Delp and unique guitar sound of Tom Scholz. Tom Scholz, who wrote most of the songs, was a studio wizard and used self-designed equipment such as 12-track recording devices to come up with an anthemic "arena rock" sound before the term was even coined. The sound was hard rock, but the layered melodies and harmonics reveal the work of a master craftsman. While much has been written about the sound of the album, the lyrics are often overlooked. There are songs about their rise from a bar band ("Rock and Roll Band") as well as fond remembrances of summers gone by ("More Than a Feeling"). *Boston* is essential for any fan of classic rock, and the album marks the re-emergence of the genre in the 1970s.

Vik Iyengar

Don't Look Back
August 1978, Epic

The follow-up to Boston's mega-hit first album, *Boston*, *Don't Look Back* took two long years to complete and it's hard to figure out why it took so long because it is almost exactly the same as their debut. The guitars still sound like they are being fed through computers and stacked into great walls of sound by robots, lead singer Brad Delp still sounds like he is ripping his throat out and the harmony vocals still sound like a choir of androids warbling angelically. Most importantly, the songs are overflowing with hooks, there are plenty of riffs to air guitar to, and the songs stick in your head like dirt on a dog. The main difference lies in the semi-melancholy tone of the record. *Boston* was a nonstop party of a record but one look at the song titles lets you know that *Don't Look*

Back is a little different: "A Man I'll Never Be," "Used to Bad News," "Don't Be Afraid." These songs reveal a reflective side that was nowhere to be found on *Boston*. Not to say the record doesn't rock because it does mightily. "Don't Look Back" has a killer riff that's very similar to the timeless riff in "More Than a Feeling," "Party" is a storming rocker much like "Smokin'" and "It's Easy" is mellow 70's AOR at its absolute best. *Don't Look Back* is basically *Boston*, Pt. 2, but don't let that put you off because even though the band was treading water they were treading like Esther Williams. This record is better than 96.7% of the AOR records released in the 1970s, combine it with *Boston* and you are looking at two tickets to AOR paradise.

Tim Sendra

David Bowie

The Man Who Sold the World
1970, Virgin

Even though it contained no hits, *The Man Who Sold the World*, for most intents and purposes, is the beginning of David Bowie's classic period. Working with guitarist Mick Ronson and producer Tony Visconti for the first time, Bowie developed a tight, twisted heavy guitar rock that appears simple on the surface but sounds more gnarled upon each listen. The mix is off-center, with the fuzz-bass dominating the compressed, razor-thin guitars and Bowie's strangled, affected voice. The sound of *The Man Who Sold the World* is odd, but the music is bizarre itself, with Bowie's bizarre, paranoid futuristic tales melded to Ronson's riffing and the band's relentless attack. Musically, there isn't much innovation on *The Man Who Sold the World*—it's almost all hard blues-rock or psychedelic folk-rock—but there's an unsettling edge to the band's performance, which makes the record one of Bowie's best albums. [Rykodisc's 1990 CD reissue includes four bonus tracks, including the previously unreleased "Lightning Frightening," and the single "Holy Holy," and both sides of the 1971 "Arnold Corns" single, "Moonage Daydream" and "Hang On to Yourself," which are early and inferior versions of songs that would later appear on *Ziggy Stardust*.]

Stephen Thomas Erlewine

Hunky Dory
1971, Virgin

After the freakish hard rock of *The Man Who Sold the World*, David Bowie returned to singer/songwriter territory on *Hunky Dory*. Not only did the album boast more folky songs ("Song for Bob Dylan," "The Bewlay Brothers"), but he again flirted with Anthony Newley-esque dancehall music ("Kooks," "Fill Your Heart"), seemingly leaving heavy metal behind. As a result, *Hunky Dory* is a kaleidoscopic array of pop styles, tied together only by Bowie's sense of vision: a sweeping, cinematic mélange of high and low art, ambiguous sexuality, kitsch, and class. Mick Ronson's guitar is pushed to the back, leaving Rick Wakeman's cabaret piano to dominate the sound of the album. The subdued support accentuates the depth of Bowie's material, whether it's the revamped Tin Pan Alley of "Changes," the Neil Young homage "Quicksand," the soaring "Life on Mars?," the rolling, vaguely homosexual anthem "Oh! You Pretty Things," or the dark acoustic rocker "Andy Warhol." On the surface, such a wide range of styles and sounds would make an album incoherent, but Bowie's improved songwriting and determined sense of style instead

made *Hunky Dory* a touchstone for reinterpreting pop's traditions into fresh, postmodern pop music.

Stephen Thomas Erlewine

Ziggy Stardust
1972, Virgin

Borrowing heavily from Marc Bolan's glam rock and the future shock of *A Clockwork Orange*, David Bowie reached back to the heavy rock of *The Man Who Sold the World* for *The Rise & Fall of Ziggy Stardust and the Spiders From Mars*. Constructed as a loose concept album about an androgynous alien rock star named Ziggy Stardust, the story falls apart quickly, yet Bowie's fractured, paranoid lyrics are evocative of a decadent, decaying future, and the music echoes an apocalyptic, nuclear dread. Fleshing out the off-kilter metallic mix with fatter guitars, genuine pop songs, string sections, keyboards, and a cinematic flourish, *Ziggy Stardust* is a glitzy array of riffs, hooks, melodrama, and style and the logical culmination of glam. Mick Ronson plays with a maverick flair that invigorates rockers like "Suffragette City," "Moonage Daydream," and "Hang Onto Yourself," while "Lady Stardust," "Five Years," and "Rock 'n' Roll Suicide" have a grand sense of staged drama previously unheard of in rock & roll. And that self-conscious sense of theater is part of the reason why *Ziggy Stardust* sounds so foreign. Bowie succeeds not in spite of his pretensions but because of them, and *Ziggy Stardust*—familiar in structure, but alien in performance—is the first time his vision and execution met in such a grand, sweeping fashion.

Stephen Thomas Erlewine

Aladdin Sane
1973, Virgin

Ziggy Stardust wrote the blueprint for David Bowie's hard-rocking glam, and *Aladdin Sane* essentially follows the pattern, for both better and worse. A lighter affair than *Ziggy Stardust*, *Aladdin Sane* is actually a stranger album than its predecessor, buoyed by bizarre lounge-jazz flourishes from pianist Mick Garson and a handful of winding, vaguely experimental songs. Bowie abandons his futuristic obsessions to concentrate on the detached cool of New York and London hipsters, as on the compressed rockers "Watch That Man," "Cracked Actor," and "The Jean Genie." Bowie follows the hard stuff with the jazzy, dissonant sprawls of "Lady Grinning Soul," "Aladdin Sane," and "Time," all of which manage to be both campy and avant-garde simultaneously, while the sweepingly cinematic "Drive-In Saturday" is a soaring fusion of sci-fi doo wop and melodramatic teenage glam. He lets his paranoia slip through in the clenched rhythms of "Panic in Detroit," as well as on his oddly clueless cover of "Let's Spend the Night Together." For all the pleasures on *Aladdin Sane*, there's no distinctive sound or theme to make the album cohesive; it's Bowie riding the wake of *Ziggy Stardust*, which means there's a wealth of classic material here, but not enough focus to make the album itself a classic.

Stephen Thomas Erlewine

Young Americans
1975, Virgin

David Bowie had dropped hints during the *Diamond Dogs* tour that he was moving toward R&B, but the full-blown blue-eyed soul of *Young Americans* came as a shock. Surrounding himself with first-rate sessionmen, Bowie comes up with a set of songs that approximate the sound of Philly soul and disco, yet remain detached from their inspirations; even at his most passionate, Bowie sounds like a commentator, as if the entire album was a genre exercise. Nevertheless, the distance doesn't hurt the album—it gives the record its own distinctive flavor, and its plastic, robotic soul helped inform generations of synthetic British soul. What does hurt the record is a lack of strong songwriting. "Young Americans" is a masterpiece, and "Fame" had a beat funky enough that James Brown ripped it off, but only a handful of cuts ("Win," "Fascination," "Somebody up There Likes Me") comes close to matching their quality. As a result, *Young Americans* is more enjoyable as a stylistic adventure than as a substantive record.

Stephen Thomas Erlewine

Station to Station
1976, Virgin

Taking the detached plastic soul of *Young Americans* to an elegant, robotic extreme, *Station to Station* is a transitional album that creates its own distinctive style. Abandoning any pretense of being a soulman, yet keeping rhythmic elements of soul, David Bowie positions himself as a cold, clinical crooner and explores a variety of styles. Everything from epic ballads and disco to synthesized avant pop is present on *Station to Station*, but what ties it together is Bowie's cocaine-induced paranoia and detached musical persona. At its heart, *Station to Station* is an avant-garde art-rock album, most explicitly on "TVC 15" and the epic sprawl of the title track, but also on the cool crooning of "Wild Is the Wind" and "Word on a Wing," as well as the disco stylings of "Golden Years." It's not an easy album to warm to, but its epic structure and clinical sound were an impressive, individualistic achievement, as well as a style that would prove enormously influential on post-punk.

Stephen Thomas Erlewine

Low
January 1977, Virgin

Following through with the avant-garde inclinations of *Station to Station*, yet explicitly breaking with David Bowie's past, *Low* is a dense, challenging album that confirmed his place at rock's cutting edge. Driven by dissonant synthesizers and electronics, *Low* is divided between brief, angular songs and atmospheric instrumentals. Throughout the record's first half, the guitars are jagged and the synthesizers drone with a menacing robotic pulse, while Bowie's vocals are unnaturally layered and overdubbed. During the instrumental half, the electronics turn cool, which is a relief after the intensity of the preceding avant pop. Half the credit for *Low*'s success

goes to Brian Eno, who explored similar ambient territory on his own releases. Eno functioned as a conduit for Bowie's ideas, and in turn Bowie made the experimentalism of not only Eno but of the German synth group Kraftwerk and the post-punk group Wire respectable, if not quite mainstream. Though a handful of the vocal pieces on *Low* are accessible— "Sound and Vision" has a shimmering guitar hook, and "Be My Wife" subverts soul structure in a surprisingly catchy fashion—the record is defiantly experimental and dense with detail, providing a new direction for the avant-garde in rock & roll.

Stephen Thomas Erlewine

Heroes
October 1977, Virgin

Repeating the formula of *Low*'s half-vocal/half-instrumental structure, *Heroes* develops and strengthens the sonic innovations David Bowie and Brian Eno explored on their first collaboration. The vocal songs are fuller, boasting harder rhythms and deeper layers of sound. Much of the harder-edged sound of *Heroes* is due to Robert Fripp's guitar, which provides a muscular foundation for the electronics, especially on the relatively conventional rock songs. Similarly, the instrumentals on *Heroes* are more detailed, this time showing a more explicit debt to German synth pop and European experimental rock. Essentially, the difference between *Low* and *Heroes* lies in the details, but the record is equally challenging and groundbreaking.

Stephen Thomas Erlewine

Lodger
1979, Virgin

On the surface, *Lodger* is the most accessible of the three Berlin-era records David Bowie made with Brian Eno, simply because there are no instrumentals and there are a handful of concise pop songs. Nevertheless, *Lodger* is still gnarled and twisted avant pop; what makes it different is how it incorporates such experimental tendencies into genuine songs, something that *Low* and *Heroes* purposely avoided. "D.J.," "Look Back in Anger," and "Boys Keep Swinging" have strong melodic hooks that are subverted and strengthened by the layered, dissonant productions, while the remainder of the record is divided between similarly effective avant pop and ambient instrumentals. *Lodger* has an edgier, more minimalistic bent than its two predecessors, which makes it more accessible for rock fans, as well as giving it a more immediate, emotional impact. It might not stretch the boundaries of rock like *Low* and *Heroes*, but it arguably utilizes those ideas in a more effective fashion.

Stephen Thomas Erlewine

Scary Monsters
1980, Virgin

David Bowie returned to relatively conventional rock & roll with *Scary Monsters*, an album that effectively acts as an encapsulation of all his '70s experiments. Reworking glam rock themes with avant-garde synth flourishes, and reversing the process as well, Bowie creates dense but accessible music throughout *Scary Monsters*. Though it doesn't have the vision of his other classic records, it wasn't designed to break new ground—it was created as the culmination of Bowie's experimental genre-shifting of the '70s. As a result, *Scary Monsters* is Bowie's last great album. While the music isn't far removed from the post-punk of the early '80s, it does sound fresh, hip, and contemporary, which is something Bowie lost over the course of the '80s. [Rykodisc's 1992 reissue includes re-recorded versions of "Space Oddity" and "Panic in Detroit," the Japanese single "Crystal Japan," and the British single "Alabama Song."]

Stephen Thomas Erlewine

Arthur Brown

The Crazy World of Arthur Brown
1968, Polydor

Though a bit over-the-top, this album was still powerful and surprisingly melodic, and managed to be quite bluesy and soulful even as the band overhauled chestnuts by James Brown and Screamin' Jay Hawkins. "Spontaneous Apple Creation" is a willfully histrionic, atonal song that gives Captain Beefheart a run for his money. Though this one-shot was not (and perhaps could not ever be) repeated, it remains an exhilaratingly reckless slice of psychedelia. The CD reissue includes both mono and stereo versions of five of the songs. Although the mono mixes lack the full-bodied power of the stereo ones, they're marked by some interesting differences, especially in the brief spoken and instrumental links between tracks.

Richie Unterberger

Jackson Browne

Jackson Browne
January 1972, Asylum

An auspicious debut that doesn't sound like a debut: although only 23, Jackson Browne had kicked around the music business for several years and developed an unusual use of language, studiedly casual yet full of striking imagery, and a post-apocalyptic viewpoint to go with it. He sang with a calm certainty over spare, discretely placed backup that highlighted the songs and always seemed about to disappear. In song after song, Browne described the world as a desert in need of moisture: in "Doctor My Eyes," the album's most propulsive song and a Top Ten hit, he sang, "Doctor, my eyes/Cannot see the sky/Is this the prize/For having learned how not to cry?" If Browne's outlook was cautious, its expression was original. His conditional optimism seemed to reflect hard experience, and in the early '70s, a lot of his listeners shared that perspective. Like any great artist, Browne articulated the tenor of his times. But the album has long since come to seem a timeless collection of reflective ballads touching on still-difficult subjects—suicide (explicitly), depression and drug use (probably), spiritual uncertainty and desperate hope—all in calm, reasoned tones, and all with an amazingly eloquent sense of language. *Jackson Browne*'s greater triumph is that, having perfectly expressed its times, it transcended them as well.

William Ruhlmann

For Everyman
October 1973, Asylum

Jackson Browne faced the nearly insurmountable task of following a masterpiece in making his second album. Having cherry-picked years of songwriting the first time around, he turned to some of his secondary older material, which was still better than most people's best and, ironically, more accessible—notably such songs as "These Days," which had been covered six times already, dating back to Nico's *Chelsea Girl* album in 1967, and "Take It Easy," a co-composition with the Eagles' Glenn Frey that had been a Top 40 hit for the group in 1972. Browne unsuccessfully looked for another hit single with the up-tempo "Red Neck Friend," reminisced about meeting his wife and starting a family in the coy "Ready or Not," and, at the end, finally came up with a new song to rank with those on the first album in the philosophical title track, which reportedly was his more positive reply to Crosby, Stills, Nash & Young's "Wooden Ships." (David Crosby sang harmony.) Musically, the album was still restrained, but not as austere as *Jackson Browne*, as the singer had hooked up with multi-instrumentalist David Lindley, who would introduce interesting textures in his music on a variety of stringed instruments for the next several years. All of which is to say that *For Everyman* was a less consistent collection than Browne's debut album. But Browne's songwriting ability remained impressive.

William Ruhlmann

Late for the Sky
September 1974, Asylum

On his third album, Jackson Browne returned to the themes of his debut record (love, loss, identity, apocalypse) and, amazingly, delved even deeper into them. "For a Dancer," a meditation on death like the first album's "Song for Adam," is a more eloquent eulogy; "Farther On" extends the "moving on" point of "Looking Into You"; "Before the Deluge" is a glimpse beyond the apocalypse evoked on "My Opening Farewell" and the second album's "For Everyman." If Browne had seemed to question everything in his first records, here he even questioned himself. "For me some words come easy, but I know that they don't mean that much," he sang on the opening track, "Late for the Sky," and added in "Farther On," "I'm not sure what I'm trying to say." Yet his seeming uncertainty and self-doubt reflected the size and complexity of the problems he was addressing in these songs, and few had ever explored such territory, much less mapped it so well. "The Late Show," the album's thematic center, doubted but ultimately affirmed the nature of relationships, while by the end, "After the Deluge," if "only a few survived," the human race continued nonetheless. It was a lot to put into a pop music album, but Browne stretched the limits of what could be found in what he called "the beauty in songs," just as Bob Dylan had a decade before.

William Ruhlmann

The Pretender
November 1976, Asylum

On *The Pretender*, Jackson Browne took a step back from the precipice so well defined on his first three albums, but doing so didn't seem to make him feel any better. Employing a real producer, Jon Landau, for the first time, Browne made what sounded like a real contemporary rock record, but this made his songs less effective; the ersatz Mexican arrangement of "Linda Paloma" and the bouncy second half of "Daddy's Tune," with its horn charts and guitar solo, undercut the lyrics. The man who had delved so deeply into life's abyss on his earlier albums was in search of escape this time around, whether by crying ("Here Come Those Tears Again"), sleeping ("Sleep's Dark and Silent Gate"), or making peace with estranged love ones ("The Only Child," "Daddy's Tune"). None of it worked, however, and when Browne came to the final track—traditionally the place on his albums where he summed up his current philosophical stance—he delivered "The Pretender," a cynical, sarcastic treatise on moneygrubbing and the shallow life of the suburbs. Primarily inner-directed, the song's defeatist tone demands rejection, but it is also a quintessential statement of its time, the post-Watergate '70s; dire as that might be, you had to admire that kind of honesty, even as it made you wince.

William Ruhlmann

Running on Empty
1977, Asylum

Having acknowledged a certain creative desperation on *The Pretender*, Jackson Browne lowered his sights (and raised his commercial appeal) considerably with *Running on Empty*, which was more a concept album about the road than an actual live album, even though its songs were sometimes recorded on-stage (and sometimes on the bus or in the hotel). Unlike most live albums, though, it consisted of previously unrecorded songs. Browne had less creative participation on this album than on any he ever made, solely composing only two songs, co-writing four others, and covering another four. And he had less to say—the title song and leadoff track neatly conjoined his artistic and escapist themes. Figuratively and creatively, he was out of gas, but like "the pretender," he still had to make a living. The songs covered all aspects of touring, from Danny O'Keefe's "The Road," which detailed romantic encounters, and "Rosie" (co-written by Browne and his manager Donald Miller), in which a soundman pays tribute to auto-eroticism, to, well, "Cocaine," to the travails of being a roadie ("The Load-Out"). Audience noises, humorous asides, loose playing—they were all part of a rough-around-the-edges musical evocation of the rock & roll touring life. It was not what fans had come to expect from Browne, of course, but the disaffected were more than outnumbered by the newly converted. (It didn't hurt that "Running on Empty" and "The Load-Out"/"Stay" both became Top 40 hits.) As a result, Browne's least ambitious, but perhaps most accessible, album ironically became his biggest seller. But it is not characteristic of his other work: for many, it will be the only Browne album they will want to own, just as others always will regard it disdainfully as "Jackson Browne lite."

William Ruhlmann

Brownsville Station

Yeah!
1973, Wounded Bird

With ten great songs, *Yeah!* is an album that lives up to its name—quite possibly the only fully realized LP the band ever made. Eight covers, all given the treatment, and two originals—one of which sold two million copies. *Yeah!* is the quintessential "nice little record"—it won't take up a lot of your time, and it's got a very friendly vibe to it. The cover songs span a wide variety of musical styles, which isn't that surprising, considering that guitarist/vocalist Cub Koda has a deep knowledge of music history. From Hoyt Axton's "Lightning Bar Blues" to then-unknown Jimmy Cliff's "Let Your Yeah Be Yeah" to Lou Reed's "Sweet Jane," the band pumps out all of its songs in a chugging, lighthearted

manner that ends up being nothing but fun. Lead vocals were previously the exclusive domain of bassist Michael Lutz, but Koda emerges as a singer as well; Lutz may have been the more prototypical rock singer, but it was Koda's sleazy, nasal snarl that worked to perfection on the classic hit single "Smokin' In the Boys Room."

While the success of "Smokin" opened a lot of doors for the band, it also pigeonholed them in such a way as to render them almost un-arrestable only a couple of years later. Between their wild onstage antics and the fact that the follow-up album, *School Punks*, was a blatant attempt at cashing in, the band lost a lot of the credibility they had earned by playing straight-ahead rock & roll. Although Brownsville Station would never again capture the magic here, *Yeah!* easily stands the test of time—it's truly delightful.

Geoff Ginsberg

Smokin' in the Boy's Room: The Best of Brownsville Station
December 1993, Rhino

A roaring romp through Brownsville Station's back pages compiled by Cub Koda himself, *Smokin' in the Boy's Room: The Best of Brownsville Station* makes a convincing case that these Ann Arbor, MI, garage punks were one of the most underrated rock & roll bands of the 1970s.

Stephen Thomas Erlewine

Jack Bruce

Songs for a Tailor
1969, Universal International

After nearly a decade as a primary fixture on London's seminal electric R&B scene in groups such as Blues Incorporated, John Mayall & the Bluesbreakers, and Cream, Jack Bruce (bass/keyboards/vocals) commenced his solo career with the release of *Songs for a Tailor* (1969). Bruce's decision to temporarily can the decidedly jazzier tunes that he had recorded the previous year with John McLaughlin (guitar), Jon Hiseman (drums), and Dick Heckstall-Smith (brass/woodwinds) proved to be a shrewd artistic decision. After having recently exited Cream, Bruce establishes his own identity with this collection of more inclusive songs, rather than the instrumentally intensive sides that would eventually come out as *Things We Like* (1970). Bruce exhibits his versatility as a multi-instrumentalist and, along with collaborator Pete Brown (lyrics), his prowess as a songwriter. Interestingly, a majority of the titles are executed by compact power trios. The personnel includes Chris Spedding (guitar), Hiseman, and Felix Pappalardi (vocals/guitar). Although comparisons to Cream are perhaps inevitable, the diversity of musicians as well as the strong arrangements of equally inspired material give these a distinct feel. From right off the bat, Bruce's inimitable and undulating basslines thrust the groove on the cryptically titled lead track, "Never Tell Your Mother She's Out of Tune." The lineup is of considerable note here, as a subdued George Harrison, under the alias of L'Angelo Misterioso, joins Bruce, Hiseman, Harry Beckett (trumpet), Henry Lowther (trumpet), Heckstall-Smith, and Art Theman (sax). The off-kilter intro lands into a heavy rocker with prominent brass augmentation, recalling the punctuation of Chicago's fusion of jazz and straight-ahead rock & roll. This directly contrasts the other two cuts with the horn section. The R&B vibe on "Ministry of Bag" is agile and funky, much like the bluesy Bay Area blend from the Electric Flag or Cold Blood. In the same vein, "Boston Ball Game 1967" is another inspired brief flash of jazzy rock—clocking in at under two minutes. One obvious standout from the respective three-piece combos is Bruce's definitive reading of "Theme from an Imaginary Western." The song's earthy quality is not unlike that which permeates the Band's debut, *Music from Big Pink* (1968). "Weird of Hermiston" and the uptempo and trippy "Tickets to Waterfalls" both feature Bruce on organ, providing a slightly psychedelic feel à la Traffic. [In 2003 *Songs for a Tailor* was issued with digitally remastered sound and four previously unreleased supplementary sides: demo and alternate mix versions of "Ministry of Bag" as well as alternate mixes of both "Weird of Hermiston" and "The Clearout."]

Lindsay Planer

against the nimble melody. While Hiseman's style is decidedly less aggressive than that of Ginger Baker, his drumming helps to amalgamate the song's various sections. McLaughlin's unmistakable sinuous leads are commanding throughout the "Sam Enchanted Dick" medley, with a cover of Milt Jackson's "Sam's Sack" and a Heckstall-Smith original titled "Rills Thrills." The tempo is slowed on the smoky cover of Mel Tormé's "Born to Be Blue." This interpretation is part West Coast cool and part Chicago-style blues. McLaughlin's contributions to "HCKHH Blues" is similar to that of Robert Fripp's jazzy fretwork throughout the *Islands* (1971) era King Crimson. While it was the first of Bruce's solo records to be recorded, he chose to issue the more rock-oriented *Songs for a Tailor* (1969) prior to *Things We Like*, which was perhaps considered an indulgent side project rather than a permanent musical diversion. [The 2003 CD reissue contains the previously unissued track "Ageing, Jack Bruce, Three, from Scotland, England," which is another brilliant Heckstall-Smith piece with all four musicians in top form—especially McLaughlin, who provokes a variety of sonic imagery, ranging from intense fingerpicking to chiming notes and chord augmentations.]

Lindsay Planer

Things We Like
1970, Polydor

Enthusiasts expecting to hear a continuation of the type of material that Jack Bruce (bass) had been responsible for during his tenure(s) with Cream or the Graham Bond Organisation might be in for quite a shock when spinning *Things We Like* (1970) for the first time. Instead of an album's worth of blues-based rockers, the seven instrumentals feature Bruce with other former Graham Bond stablemates John McLaughlin (guitar), Jon Hiseman (drums), and Dick Heckstall-Smith (sax) performing post-bop and free jazz. A majority of the compositions were penned by Bruce in his preteen days of formal scholarship at the Royal Scottish Academy of Music, where he also mastered the cello and composed a string quartet at the age of 11. After having gained significant clout from Cream, Bruce assembled what was initially a trio. However, after a chance meeting with McLaughlin—who was so broke he had to refuse an offer to fly stateside to join the newly formed Tony Williams Lifetime—Bruce incorporated the guitarist into the fold in order to help him finance his journey, which was ultimately successful. The entire effort was recorded and mixed in less than a week during August of 1968—less than three months prior to the infamous *Farewell Concert of Cream* at the Royal Albert Hall on November 26, 1968.

As a testament to Bruce's expansive musical tastes, capabilities, and horizons, this disc sounds more like a collection of Rahsaan Roland Kirk sides than anything even remotely connected with Cream. This is especially true of the frenetic pacing of the brief opener, "Over the Cliff." Heckstall-Smith's ability to perform alto and soprano saxophone *simultaneously* likewise lends itself to Kirk's distinct reed polyphony. "Statues" is an interesting exercise, again with Heckstall-Smith providing some excellent extemporaneous blows during the darkly toned introduction working well

Harmony Row
1971, Polydor

Named after a street in Jack Bruce's childhood home of Glasgow, Scotland, *Harmony Row* (1971) was the bassist's third solo long-player, returning him to his blues-infused rock & roll roots. The disc boasts collaborative efforts from Pete Brown (lyrics), Chris Spedding (guitar), and Soft Machine/Nucleus drummer John Marshall, replacing Jon Hiseman (drums). As Bruce recalls in the liner notes to the 2003 CD reissue, much of "the album was recorded with me [read: Bruce] playing the piano, guitar and drums [and] also playing live in the studio." Bruce adds, "I'd do overdubs later and sometimes the live vocal that I recorded ended up as the finished vocal." In the absence of the horn section featured on *Songs for a Tailor* (1969), these sides are much more compact and instrumentally sparse. It also gives an opportunity for Bruce—as a multi-instrumentalist—to temporarily break away from his regular electric bass duties. A case in point is the plaintively poignant opener, "Can You Follow?," with Bruce accompanying himself with some well-crafted piano lines and interesting modal chord progressions. It perfectly preludes the nimble rocker "Escape to the Royal Wood (On Ice)." The words were a reflection of Bruce's marriage, with distinctly regal imagery inspired by a "couple of pantomimes staged on ice and [they] hit me emotionally," Brown comments in the notes of the 2003 CD reissue. The raucous "You Burned the Tables on Me" could have easily been a contender for Cream, as it sports a strong vocal presence and catchy frenetic tempo, much in the same way that "Swlabr" had on *Disraeli Gears* (1967) or "N.S.U." did as far back as *Fresh Cream* (1966). "Morning Story" is slightly progressive with a driving rhythm and intricately layered arrangement. The pastoral "Folk Song" has an organic acoustic quality that would not have been out of place from Procol Harum or any number of Canterbury prog rock groups such as Caravan or Matching Mole. Emerson, Lake & Palmer could have done significant damage to "Smiles and Grins" with its aggressive attitude and prominent swirling keyboards. [There are five recently unearthed bonus tracks included on the 2003 CD reissue. Among them are early stabs at "You Burned the Tables on Me" with Bruce on electric piano and a demo of "Escape to the Royal Wood (On Ice)" without lyrics, as well as both an incipient reading and first take of "Can You Follow?," which was initially titled "Green Hills."]

Lindsay Planer

27

How's Tricks
1977, Polydor

A wonderfully tortured Jack Bruce vocal on the song "Without a Word" opens up *How's Tricks*, the second LP for RSO records by the journeyman bassist/vocalist. Produced by Bill Halverson, who engineered Cream as well as solo Eric Clapton recordings, the material further fuses the all out jazz of *Things We Like* with the pop found on "Songs for a Taylor." "Johnny B'77" has the quartet driving the melody onto the fringes of rock, while "Time" bares elements Bruce brought to *Disraeli Gears*, defining his third of the Cream saga. As former bandmate Leslie West had his Leslie West Band out and about in the mid-70s, this quartet is listed as the Jack Bruce Band. It is yet another about-face for Bruce, singing nine more sets of lyrics by Peter Brown, with guitarist Hughie Burns and keyboardist Tony Hymas getting their chance to participate in the songwriting; it's basically well-performed pop with jazz overtones that has the voice of Jack Bruce adding the blues. The reggae of the title track, and the accompanying album art, may have made for some marketing confusion. There's a magician with cards and old-world glitz permeating this show, the band holding a crystal ball on the back-cover photograph. Having left Atlantic for Robert Stigwood's imprint, a bit more direction could have been in store for this important artist. The packaging doesn't have the elegance of *Harmony Row*, nor does it show respect for the music inside the package. Hughie Burns takes the lead vocal on "Baby Jane," his own composition, and it sounds out of place, disrupting the flow which returns on the exquisite "Lost Inside a Song," where Jack Bruce picks up where he left off. The Steely Dan comparisons are harder to make here, songs like "Madhouse" more hardcore jazz-rock than Fagen and Becker would care to indulge in. "Waiting for the Call" is perhaps the album's blusiest track, with magnificent harmonica-playing by the vocalist/rock legend. "Outsiders" sounds like Roxy Music gone jazz, while the final track, written by keyboardist Tony Hymas and lyricist Peter Brown, is a nice melodic vehicle for Jack Bruce's voice to conclude the album with. Simon Phillips provides solid drumming throughout, and the well-crafted lyrics are included on the inner sleeve. A strange but highly musical and important outing in the Jack Bruce catalog.

Joe Viglione

Buffalo Springfield

Buffalo Springfield
1966, Atco

The band themselves were displeased with this record, feeling that the production did not capture their on-stage energy and excitement. Yet to most ears, this debut sounds pretty great, featuring some of their most melodic and accomplished songwriting and harmonies, delivered with a hard-rocking punch. "For What It's Worth" was the hit single, but there are several other equally stunning treasures. Stephen Stills' "Go and Say Goodbye" was a pioneering country-rock fusion; his "Sit Down I Think I Love You" was the band at their poppiest and most early Beatlesque; and his "Everybody's Wrong" and "Pay the Price" were tough rockers. Although Neil Young has only two lead vocals on the record (Richie Furay sang three other Young compositions), he's already a songwriter of great talent and enigmatic lyricism, particularly on "Nowadays Clancy Can't Even Sing," "Out of My Mind," and "Flying on the Ground Is Wrong." The entire album bursts with thrilling guitar and vocal interplay, with a bright exuberance that would tone down considerably by their second record. [A 1997 CD reissue presents both mono and stereo mixes of the album, and includes "Baby Don't Scold Me" (which was on the first pressing of the record, but was soon replaced by "For What It's Worth").]

Richie Unterberger

Buffalo Springfield Again
1967, Atco

Due in part to personnel problems which saw Bruce Palmer and Neil Young in and out of the group, Buffalo Springfield's second album did not have as unified an approach as their debut. Yet it doesn't suffer for that in the least—indeed, the group continued to make major strides in both their songwriting and arranging, and this record stands as their greatest triumph. Stephen Stills' "Bluebird" and "Rock & Roll Woman" were masterful folk-rockers that should have been big hits (although they did manage to become small ones); his lesser-known contributions "Hung Upside Down" and the jazz-flavored "Everydays" were also first-rate. Young contributed the Rolling Stones-derived "Mr. Soul," as well as the brilliant "Expecting to Fly" and "Broken Arrow," both of which employed lush psychedelic textures and brooding, surrealistic lyrics that stretched rock conventions to their breaking point. Richie Furay (who had not written any of the songs on the debut) takes tentative songwriting steps with three compositions, although only "A Child's Claim to Fame," with its memorable dobro hooks by James Burton, meets the standards of the material by Stills and Young; the cut also anticipates the country-rock direction of Furay's post-Springfield band, Poco. Although a slightly uneven record that did not feature the entire band on several cuts, the high points were so high and plentiful that its classic status cannot be denied.

Richie Unterberger

Box Set
July 2001, Rhino

The plainly named *Box Set*—that's the actual title—contains four CDs by a band that made only three albums in their brief lifetime. It goes without saying that this has a lot of great music, and is an essential purchase for fans of this phenomenal 1960s folk-rock-psychedelic band, containing no less than 36 previously unreleased demos, outtakes, and previously unissued mixes. It's the unreleased stuff that holds the most interest, especially since even on their outtakes, Buffalo Springfield were often superb. Songs like "Neighbor Don't You Worry," "Down Down Down" (which contains seeds of both "Broken Arrow" and the Neil Young solo standout "Country Girl"), "We'll See," and "My Kind of Love" are actually up to the standard of many of the songs that made it onto the official albums. Although acoustic demos of various Young, Stills, and Furay songs are not as strong, they are always at the least pleasant, and often show intriguing, unsuspected sentimental pop and folk leanings.

Alternate versions of great songs, such as "Hung Upside Down" and a piano-only "Four Days Gone," are substantially different from the fully arranged familiar versions, yet worthwhile performances in their own right. At the same time, this box—which, other than the last disc, sequences the material in the chronological order it was recorded—is not all it could have been. First of all, for some reason, this does *not* have everything the band ever released. Not only are a few songs from *Last Time Around* missing (including one of Richie Furay's best moments, "In the Hour of Not Quite Rain"), but the nine-minute version of "Bluebird" (available on the two-LP *Buffalo Springfield* compilation) and the Neil Young-sung take of "Down to the Wire" (which came out on his *Decade* collection) are also absent. First-rate songs from *Last Time Around*, including "On the Way Home," "Pretty Girl Why," and "Four Days Gone," are represented by different demos and remixes, though it would have been easily possible to include the official final versions too. Worst of all, disc four is comprised solely of all the material from the group's brilliant first two albums—which would not be cause for criticism, except that identical versions of every one of them (except for "Mr. Soul" and "Baby Don't Scold Me") also appear at some point in the course of the preceding three discs. This bizarre repetition is doubly galling both because that space could have been used for remaining *Last Time Around* absentees, and because other quality unreleased material, both studio and live, is known to exist, and is far more hungrily desired by fans eager to purchase a box set in the first place. Fortunately you can still (almost) complete the Springfield discography by buying *Last Time Around* itself. The sound is very good, and on the rarities, notably superior to bootlegs (such as the famous *Stampede*) on which some of the songs have previously surfaced. The 82-page booklet, primarily comprised of vintage clippings, is nice too, even if specific details and anecdotes about the unreleased songs in particular would have been good. As good as it is, though, this could have been one of the greatest rock box sets of all time, if only a saner approach to presenting the band's complete official albums, and more rarities, in one place had been employed.

Richie Unterberger

Jimmy Buffett

Songs You Know by Heart
October 1985, MCA

Combining aloof humor with a laid-back, devil-may-care island attitude, Jimmy Buffett sang songs about alcohol consumption, lazing around in the sun, and the freedom of not having to work for a living. *Songs You Know By Heart* is a solid offering of Buffett's greatest hits, pulling together his truly strongest material and avoiding the unnecessary filler that appears on his albums. His claim to fame, "Margaritaville," is the jewel in the crown here, which still harbors that tropical feel thanks to its Caribbean-styled rhythm and relaxed flow. "Come Monday" picks up where "Margaritaville" leaves off, only this ballad plays out with subdued sincerity and has Buffett sounding strangely serious, and romantic. Most of the songs from Buffett are centered around his frolicking lifestyle, like the comical "Cheeseburger in Paradise" or the naughtiness of "Why Don't We Get Drunk," an ode to his party-filled outlook on life. Buffett's voice shines on the clever "Changes in Latitudes, Changes in Attitudes," which again spotlights his love of living without concern, especially in someplace warm. The catchy and whimsical

"Fins" is lifted by a contagious pace with a smart chorus and serves as one of the highlights of this collection. As a compilation, this bunch of Jimmy Buffett's most famous tunes contains just the right amount of tracks. Any less would be inconsistent and any more would be deemed as overkill.

Mike DeGagne

The Byrds

Mr. Tambourine Man
June 1965, Columbia/Legacy

One of the greatest debuts in the history of rock, *Mr. Tambourine Man* was nothing less than a significant step in the evolution of rock & roll itself, demonstrating that intelligent lyrical content could be wedded to compelling electric guitar riffs and a solid backbeat. It was also the album that was most responsible for establishing folk-rock as a popular phenomenon, its most alluring traits being Roger McGuinn's immediately distinctive 12-string Rickenbacker jangle and the band's beautiful harmonies. The material was uniformly strong, whether they were interpreting Bob Dylan (on the title cut and three other songs, including the hit single "All I Really Want to Do"), Pete Seeger ("The Bells of Rhymney"), or Jackie DeShannon ("Don't Doubt Yourself, Babe"). The originals were lyrically less challenging, but equally powerful musically, especially Gene Clark's "I Knew I'd Want You," "I'll Feel a Whole Lot Better," and "Here Without You"; "It's No Use" showed a tougher, harder-rocking side and a guitar solo with hints of psychedelia. [The CD reissue adds six less impressive (but still satisfying) bonus tracks and alternate takes from the same era.]

Richie Unterberger

Turn! Turn! Turn!
December 1965, Columbia/Legacy

The Byrds' second album was only a disappointment in comparison with *Mr. Tambourine Man*. They couldn't maintain such a level of consistent magnificence, and the follow-up was not quite as powerful or impressive. It was still quite good, however, particularly the ringing number one title cut, a classic on par with the "Mr. Tambourine Man" single. Elsewhere they concentrated more on original material, Gene Clark in particular offering some strong compositions with "Set You Free This Time," "The World Turns All Around Her," and "If You're Gone." A couple more Dylan covers were included as well, and "Satisfied Mind" was their first foray into country-rock, a direction they would explore in much greater depth throughout the rest of the '60s. [The reissue adds seven decent alternate takes and bonus tracks, the most interesting being a version of Dylan's "It's All Over Now, Baby Blue," and an enigmatic Gene Clark song, "The Day Walk (Never Before)."]

Richie Unterberger

Fifth Dimension
July 1966, Columbia/Legacy

Although the Byrds' *Fifth Dimension* was wildly uneven, its high points were as innovative as any rock music being recorded in 1966. Immaculate folk-rock was still present in their superb arrangements of the traditional songs "Wild Mountain Thyme" and "John Riley." For the originals, they devised some of the first and best psychedelic rock, often drawing from the influence of Indian raga in the guitar arrangements. "Eight Miles High," with its astral lyrics, pumping bassline, and fractured guitar solo, was a Top 20 hit, and one of the greatest singles of the '60s. The minor hit title track and the country-rock-tinged "Mr. Spaceman" are among their best songs; "I See You" has great 12-string psychedelic guitar solos; and "I Come and Stand at Every Door" is an unusual and moving update of a traditional rock tune, with new lyrics pleading for peace in the nuclear age. At the same time, the R&B instrumental "Captain Soul" was a throwaway, "Hey Joe" not nearly as good as the versions by the Leaves or Jimi Hendrix, and "What's Happening?!?!" the earliest example of David Crosby's disagreeably vapid hippie ethos. These weak spots keep *Fifth Dimension* from attaining truly classic status. [The CD reissue has six notable bonus tracks, including the single version of the early psychedelic cut "Why" (the B-side to "Eight Miles High"), a significantly different alternate take of "Eight Miles High," "I Know My Rider" (with some fine Roger McGuinn 12-string workouts), and a much jazzier, faster instrumental version of "John Riley."]

Richie Unterberger

The Byrds' Greatest Hits
1967, Columbia/Legacy

Without question, the Byrds were one of the great bands of the '60s and one of the few American bands of their time to continually turn out inventive, compelling albums. As they were recording a series of fine records, they released a number of classic singles that defined their era. *The Byrds' Greatest Hits* does an excellent job of chronicling the peak years of their popularity before they went country-rock on 1968's *Sweetheart of the Rodeo*. Columbia/Legacy's expanded 1999 reissue added the three minor hits missing from the original collection, which means that *Greatest Hits* now contains all of the group's hit singles—from 1965's "Mr. Tambourine Man" to 1967's "Have You Seen Her Face." That's an impressive collection indeed, and it also includes "All I Really Want to Do," "Turn! Turn! Turn! (To Everything There Is a Season)," "It Won't Be Wrong," "Set You Free This Time," "Eight Miles High," "5D (Fifth Dimension)," "Mr. Spaceman," "So You Want to Be a Rock N' Roll Star," and "My Back Pages." Yes, some great songs were left behind on the albums, but important cuts like "I'll Feel a Whole Lot Better," "The Bells of Rhymney," and "Chimes of Freedom" are included, making this pretty close to a definitive single-disc summary of the Byrds' prime.

Stephen Thomas Erlewine

Younger Than Yesterday
February 1967, Columbia

Younger Than Yesterday was somewhat overlooked at the time of its release during an intensely competitive era that found the Byrds on a commercial downslide. However, time has shown it to be the most durable of the Byrds' albums, with the exception of *Mr. Tambourine Man*. David Crosby, Roger McGuinn, and especially Chris Hillman come into their own as songwriters on an eclectic but focused set blending folk-rock, psychedelia, and early country-rock. The sardonic "So You Want to Be a Rock & Roll Star" was a terrific single; "My Back Pages," also a small hit, was the last of their classic Dylan covers; "Thoughts and Words," the flower-power anthem "Renaissance Fair," "Have You Seen Her Face," and the bluegrass-tinged "Time Between" are all among their best songs. The jazzy "Everybody's Been Burned" may be Crosby's best composition, although his "Mind Gardens" is one of his most excessive. [The CD reissue has six bonus tracks, including the fine Crosby-penned single "Lady Friend," and notably different alternate versions of "Mind Gardens" and "My Back Pages."]

Richie Unterberger

The Notorious Byrd Brothers
January 1968, Columbia

The recording sessions for the Byrds' fifth album, *The Notorious Byrd Brothers*, were conducted in the midst of internal turmoil that found them reduced to a duo by the time the record was completed. That wasn't evident from listening to the results, which showed the group continuing to expand the parameters of their eclecticism while retaining their hallmark guitar jangle and harmonies. With assistance from producer Gary Usher, they took more chances in the studio, enhancing the spacy quality of tracks like "Natural Harmony" and Goffin & King's "Wasn't Born to Follow" with electronic phasing. Washes of Moog synthesizer formed the eerie backdrop for "Space Odyssey," and the songs were craftily and unobtrusively linked with segues and fades. But the Byrds did not bury the essential strengths of their tunes in effects: "Goin' Back" (also written by Goffin & King) was a magnificent and melodic cover with the expected tasteful 12-string guitar runs that should have been a big hit. "Tribal Gathering" has some of the band's most effervescent harmonies; "Draft Morning" is a subtle and effective reflection of the horrors of the Vietnam War; and "Old John Robertson" looks forward to the country-rock that would soon dominate their repertoire. [The CD reissue adds six bonus tracks, including different versions of "Goin' Back" and "Draft Morning," a few instrumentals, and David Crosby's controversial "Triad"; unlisted on the sleeve is a rehearsal outtake which captures comically vitriolic arguments among the band.]

Richie Unterberger

Sweetheart of the Rodeo
August 1968, Columbia/Legacy

The Byrds' *Sweetheart of the Rodeo* was not the first important country-rock album (Gram Parsons managed that feat with the International Submarine Band's debut *Safe at Home*), and the Byrds were hardly strangers to country music, dipping their toes in the twangy stuff as early as their second album. But no major band had gone so deep into the sound and feeling of classic country (without parody or condescension) as the Byrds did on *Sweetheart*; at a time when most rock fans viewed country as a musical "L'il Abner" routine, the Byrds dared to declare that C&W could be hip, cool, and heartfelt. Though Gram Parsons had joined the band as a pianist and lead guitarist, his deep love of C&W soon took hold, and Roger McGuinn and Chris Hillman followed his lead; significantly, the only two original songs on the album were both written by Parsons (the achingly beautiful "Hickory Wind" and "One Hundred Years from Now"), while on the rest of the set classic tunes by Merle Haggard, the Louvin Brothers, and Woody Guthrie were sandwiched between a pair of twanged-up Bob Dylan compositions. While many cite this as more of a Gram Parsons album than a Byrds set, given the strong country influence of McGuinn's and Hillman's later work, it's obvious Parsons didn't impose a style upon this band so much as he tapped into a sound that was already there, waiting to be released. If the Byrds didn't do country-rock first, they did it brilliantly, and few albums in the style are as beautiful and emotionally affecting as this. [Columbia's 1997 CD reissue of the album improves on the masterpiece by adding eight strong bonus tracks, including four cuts with Gram Parsons singing lead trimmed from the original release for legal reasons.]

Mark Deming

Ballad of Easy Rider
October 1969, Columbia

If *Dr. Byrds & Mr. Hyde* found Roger McGuinn having to re-create the Byrds after massive personnel turnovers (and not having an easy time of it), *Ballad of Easy Rider* was the album where the new lineup really hit its stride. Gracefully moving back and forth between serene folk-rock (the title cut, still one of McGuinn's most beautiful melodies), sure-footed rock & roll ("Jesus Is Just All Right"), heartfelt country-rock ("Oil In My Lamp" and "Tulsa County"), and even a dash of R&B (the unexpectedly funky "Fido," which even features a percussion solo), *Ballad of Easy Rider* sounds confident and committed where *Dr. Byrds & Mr. Hyde* often seemed tentative. The band sounds tight, self-assured, and fully in touch with the music's emotional palette, and Clarence White's guitar work is truly a pleasure to hear (if Roger McGuinn's fabled 12-string work seems to take a back seat to White's superb string bends, it is doubtful that any but the most fanatical fans would think to object). While not generally regarded as one of the group's major works, in retrospect this release stands alongside *Untitled* as the finest work of the Byrds' final period.

Mark Deming

Untitled
October 1970, Sony International

Among the later Byrds albums, *Untitled* was always the one to own, even if you weren't a huge fan. Issued back in 1970 as a two-priced-as-one LP, *Untitled* was one of the few modest commercial successes for the latter-day group. "Eight Miles High" is the high point, a 15-minute jam that showcases this band's prowess. The studio sides aren't to be overlooked, however—the group by this time was modifying its established sound into more of a '70s mode, and the influence

of new members Gene Parsons and Skip Battin was showing up, pushing aside the familiar timbre of Roger McGuinn's 12-string Rickenbacker in favor of a leaner country-rock orientation. On some of this material (especially the Parsons-Battin "Yesterday's Train" and Battin's "Well Come Back Home"), they sound more like Crosby, Stills, Nash & Young. The only song on the album to get heard by people other than serious Byrds fanatics was McGuinn's "Chestnut Mare," but "Truck Stop Girl," "All the Things," the group's version of Leadbelly's "Take a Whiff on Me," and, especially, "Just a Season" (maybe the prettiest song McGuinn has ever written) also hold up very well. Other numbers, like the environmental ode "Hungry Planet," are more of an acquired taste.

Bruce Eder

J.J. Cale

Troubadour
September 1976, Mercury

Producer Audie Ashworth introduced some different instruments, notably vibes and what sound like horns (although none are credited), for a slightly altered sound on *Troubadour*. But J.J. Cale's albums are so steeped in his introspective style that they become interchangeable. If you like one of them, chances are you'll want to have them all. This one is notable for introducing "Cocaine," which Eric Clapton covered on his *Slowhand* album a year later.

William Ruhlmann

Canned Heat

Canned Heat
1967, Liberty

This debut long-player from Canned Heat was issued shortly after their appearance at the Monterey International Pop Music Festival. That performance, for all intents and purposes, was not only the combo's entrée into the burgeoning underground rock & roll scene, but was also among the first high-profile showcases to garner national and international attention. The quartet featured on *Canned Heat* (1967) includes the unique personnel of Alan "Blind Owl" Wilson (guitar/vocals), Larry "The Mole" Taylor (bass), Henry "Sunflower" Vestine (guitar), Bob "The Bear" Hite (vocals), and Frank Cook (drums). Cook's tenure with the Heat would be exceedingly brief, however, as he was replaced by Aldolfo "Fido" Dela Parra (drums) a few months later. Although their blues might have suggested that the aggregate hailed from the likes of Chicago or Memphis, Canned Heat actually formed in the Los Angeles suburb of Topanga Canyon, where they were contemporaries of other up-and-coming rockers Spirit and Kaleidoscope. Wilson and Hite's almost scholarly approach created a unique synthesis when blended with the band's amplified rock & roll. After their initial studio sessions in April of 1967 produced favorable demos, they returned several weeks later to begin work in earnest on this platter. The dearth of original material on *Canned Heat* was less of a result of any songwriting deficiencies, but rather exemplifies their authentic renderings of traditionals such as the open-throttled boogie of "Rollin' and Tumblin'"—which is rightfully recognized as having been derived from the Muddy Waters arrangement. Similarly, a rousing reading of Robert Johnson's "Dust My Broom" is co-credited to Elmore James. Blues aficionados will undoubtedly notice references to a pair of Howlin' Wolf classics—"Smokestack Lightning" as well as "I Asked for Water (She Gave Me Gasoline)"—as part of the rambling "Road Song." While decidedly more obscure to the casual listener, Eddie "Guitar Slim" Jones's "Story of My Life" is both a high point on this recording, as well as one of the fiercest renditions ever committed to tape. Until a thorough overhaul of Canned Heat's catalog materializes, this title can be found on the *Canned Heat/Boogie With Canned Heat* (2003) two-fer that couples this title with their 1968 follow-up.

Lindsay Planer

Hooker 'n' Heat
1971, EMI

Canned Heat brought a fresh personnel to this confab with blues legend John Lee Hooker (guitar/vocals). Likewise, Larry "The Mole" Taylor (bass) and Harvey Mandel (guitar) linked up with John Mayall & the Bluesbreakers during the spring of 1970. In their stead, Henry "Sunflower" Vestine (guitar) returned from a failed outing as "The Sun" with Antonio "Tony" de la Barreda (bass) replacing Taylor. *Hooker 'n' Heat* (1971) would be the last release to include contributions from co-founder and blues scholar Alan "Blind Owl" Wilson (piano/guitar/harmonica), as he overdosed in September of the same year. Although Canned Heat got top bill—as the band's record company issued the two-LP package—this project is uncategorically a John Lee Hooker outlet, and a fine one at that. The contents commence with a bevy of solo Hooker pieces, a few collaborations between Hooker and Wilson, and then the full integration of the entire quartet on the final five sides. While the collection features no real bombs, per se, the results range from the aimlessness of "Send Me Your Pillow" and the appropriately titled "Drifter," to the emotive "Sittin' Here Thinkin'" or the vigorous workout on the indispensable and classic "Burning Hell" and "Bottle Up and Go." "I Got My Eyes on You"—an unabashed take-off of Hooker's "Dimples"—is also a keeper. This is also true of "Boogie Chillen No. 2," which rambles, ambles, and shakes for nearly 12 glorious minutes. Audiophiles seeking Mobile Fidelity Lab's gold disc version of *Hooker 'n' Heat* (1996) should take note of the 24-bit remaster from the French Magic Records label, which equals those efforts and adds "It's All Right," with the single edit of "Whiskey and Wimmen'" added in the process.

Lindsay Planer

The Cars

The Cars
May 1978, Elektra

The Cars' 1978 self-titled debut, issued on the Elektra label, is a genuine rock masterpiece. The band jokingly referred to the album as their "true greatest-hits album," but it's no exaggeration—all nine tracks are new wave/rock classics, still in rotation on rock radio. Whereas most bands of the late '70s embraced either punk/new wave or hard rock, the Cars were one of the first bands to do the unthinkable—merge the two styles together. Add to it bandleader/songwriter Ric Ocasek's supreme pop sensibilities, and you had an album that appealed to new wavers, rockers, and Top 40 fans. One of the most popular new wave songs ever, "Just What I Needed," is an obvious highlight, as are such familiar hits as "Good Times Roll," "My Best Friend's Girl," and "You're All I've Got Tonight." But like most consummate rock albums, the lesser-known compositions are just as exhilarating: "Don't Cha Stop," "Bye Bye Love," "All Mixed Up," and "Moving in Stereo," the latter featured as an instrumental during a steamy scene in the popular movie *Fast Times at Ridgemont High*. With flawless performances, songwriting, and production (courtesy of Queen alumni Roy Thomas Baker), the Cars' debut remains one of rock's all-time classics.

Greg Prato

Candy-O
June 1979, Elektra

Since the Cars had created a perfect album with their 1978 self-titled debut, it would be nearly impossible to top it. Instead of laboring long and hard over a follow-up like many '70s bands did after a huge commercial success, the band cranked out their sophomore effort, *Candy-O*, almost exactly one year later from the first LP. And while the album was not as stellar as its predecessor was, it did contain several classics, resulting in another smash album that solidified the band's standing as one of the most promising new bands of the late '70s. The first single, the Top 20 anthem "Let's Go," proves to be the best track, but plenty of other standouts can be found as well. The title track remains one of the band's best rockers, while the gentle "It's All I Can Do" also deserved to be a hit. The band pays tribute to T. Rex on "Dangerous Type" (the main guitar riff resembles "Bang a Gong"), rocks out on "Got a Lot on My Head" and "Night Spots," shows their softer side on "Since I Held You," and embraces modern pop on "Double Life" and "Lust for Kicks." Their second strong release in a row, *Candy-O* proved that the Cars were not one-hit wonders, like so many other bands from the same era.

Greg Prato

Shake It Up
November 1981, Elektra

By augmenting their sound with more synthesizers, electronics, and drum machines, the Cars' fourth release, *Shake It Up*, helped bridge their hard rock-based early work (1978's *The Cars*) with the futuristic-pop direction of 1984's *Heartbeat City*. The band's sound may have been evolving with each succeeding album, but Ric Ocasek was still writing compelling new wave compositions despite all the change, many of which would ultimately become rock & roll standards. The up-tempo title track remains a party favorite to this day (reaching number four on the singles charts), while the melancholic "Since You're Gone" remains one of Ocasek's best-ever tales of heartbreak. Intriguing videos were made for both songs, officially introducing the band to the MTV age. Like its predecessor, 1980's *Panorama*, filler is present ("This Could Be Love," "Maybe Baby"), but many lesser-known album tracks prove to be highlights: the almost entirely synth-oriented tracks "Think It Over" and "A Dream Away," the rocking "Cruiser," plus the more pop-oriented "I'm Not the One" and "Victim of Love." Although *Shake It Up* was another resounding commercial success, their next album would be the one that made the Cars one of rock's quintessential acts of the '80s.

Greg Prato

Heartbeat City
March 1984, Elektra

MTV had become a major marketing tool by 1984, and the Cars were one of the first bands to use the new video medium to their advantage. The band's fifth album, *Heartbeat City* (Elektra), spawned several imaginative and memorable videos, which translated into massive chart and commercial success, making it one of the biggest releases of the year. Produced by hitmaker John "Mutt" Lange (AC/DC, Def Leppard), the album included two Top Ten singles—the ballad "Drive" and the charismatic "You Might Think"—plus an additional two that landed in the Top 20: the summer anthem "Magic" and the eccentric "Hello Again." But it didn't just stop there, plenty of other tracks could have been hits as well, such as the sparse rocker "It's Not the Night" and the breezy pop of "Looking for Love." Other highlights included the ethereal title track, the melodic rocker "Stranger Eyes," and the moderately paced love song "Why Can't I Have You." Although the Cars experienced their greatest success yet with *Heartbeat City*, it would unfortunately not last for long—after just one more studio album (1987's spotty *Door to Door*), the band split up.

Greg Prato

Complete Greatest Hits
February 2002, Rhino

When the Cars released their first greatest-hits album in 1985, it was capping a golden run that culminated in 1984's *Heartbeat City*, their biggest hit yet. They lasted one more album, 1987's abysmal *Door to Door*. So, technically, there isn't that much new territory covered by *Complete Greatest Hits*, especially since there's only one song—the only good one, "You Are the Girl"—from *Door to Door*, but it's nevertheless a substantial improvement over that initial hits collection, while being easier to digest for most listeners than the exhaustive 1995 anthology *Just What I Needed*. Essentially, the title explains it all, since it has all of the hits, which also means many are AOR staples. This approach means that nearly all of their debut and half of *Heartbeat City* is on this disc, but it also means that there's essentially nothing missing (apart from perhaps "Candy-O") that casual fans would

want. Also, this approach confirms that the Cars were a sexy, stylish new wave singles band on the order of Blondie—sure, they had one classic album in their canon (the debut), along with some very good follow-ups, but they made the most sense song by song on the radio, even years after their prime. To hear why, this is the disc to get.

Stephen Thomas Erlewine

Cheap Trick

Cheap Trick
1977, Epic/Legacy

Cheap Trick's eponymous debut is an explosive fusion of Beatlesque melodic hooks, Who-styled power, and a twisted sense of humor partially borrowed from the Move. But that only begins to scratch the surface of what makes *Cheap Trick* a dynamic record. Guitarist Rick Nielsen has a powerful sense of dynamics and arrangements, which gives the music an extra kick, but he also can write exceptionally melodic and subversive songs. Nothing on *Cheap Trick* is quite what it seems. While the songs have hooks and attitude that arena rock was sorely lacking in the late '70s, they are also informed by a bizarre sensibility, whether it's the driving "He's a Whore," the dreamy "Mandocello," or the thumping Gary Glitter perversion "ELO Kiddies." "The Ballad of TV Violence" is about mass murder, while "Daddy Should Have Stayed in High School" concerns pedophiles. All of it is told with a sense of humor, but it doesn't come off as cheap or smirking because of the group's hard-rocking drive and Rob-in Zander's pop-idol vocals. Even "Oh, Candy," apparently a love song on first listen, is an affecting tribute to a friend who committed suicide. In short, Cheap Trick revel in taboo subjects with abandon, devoting themselves to the power of the hook, as well as sheer volume and gut-wrenching rock & roll—though the record is more musically accomplished than punk rock, it shares the same aesthetic. The combination of off-kilter humor, bizarre subjects, and blissful power pop made *Cheap Trick* one of the defining albums of its era, as well as one of the most influential. [The 1998 Epic/Legacy reissue of *Cheap Trick* features a different track sequence than the original and also adds several bonus tracks, many of which are previously unreleased.]

Stephen Thomas Erlewine

In Color
1977, Epic

Though Cheap Trick's second album, *In Color*, draws from the same stockpile of Midwestern barroom favorites as their debut album, it was produced by Tom Werman, who had the band strip away their raw attack and replace it with a shiny, radio-ready sound. Consequently, *In Color* doesn't have the visceral attack of its predecessor, but it still has the same sensibility and a similar set of spectacular songs. From the druggy psychedelia of "Downed" and the bubblegum sing-along "I Want You to Want Me" to the "California Girls" homage of "Southern Girls," the album has the same encyclopedic knowledge of rock & roll, as well as the good sense to subvert it with a perverse sense of humor. Portions of the album haven't dated well, simply due to the glossy production, but the songs and music on *In Color* are as splendid as the band's debut. [The 1998 Epic/Legacy reissue of *In Color* adds several bonus tracks, including previously unreleased demos and live recordings.]

Stephen Thomas Erlewine

Heaven Tonight
1978, Epic

Heaven Tonight, like *In Color*, was produced by Tom Werman, but the difference between the two records is substantial. Where *In Color* often sounded emasculated, *Heaven Tonight* regains the powerful, arena-ready punch of *Cheap Trick*, but crosses it with a clever radio-friendly production that relies both on synthesizers and studio effects. Even with the fairly slick production, Cheap Trick sound ferocious throughout the album, slamming heavy metal, power pop, and hard rock together in a humongous sound. "Surrender," the definitive Cheap Trick song, opens the album with a tale about a kid whose parents are hipper than himself, and the remainder of the record is a roller coaster ride, peaking with the sneering "Auf Wiedersehen," the dreamily psychedelic title track, the roaring rocker "On Top of the World," the high-stepping, tongue-in-cheek "How Are You," and the pulverizing cover of the Move's "California Man." *Heaven Tonight* is the culmination of the group's dizzying early career, summing up the strengths of their first two albums, their live show, and their talent for inverting pop conventions. They were never quite as consistently thrilling on record ever again.

Stephen Thomas Erlewine

At Budokan
February 1979, Epic

While their records were entertaining and full of skillful pop, it wasn't until *At Budokan* that Cheap Trick's vision truly gelled. Many of these songs, like "I Want You to Want Me" and "Big Eyes," were pleasant in their original form, but seemed more like sketches compared to the roaring versions on this album. With their ear-shatteringly loud guitars and sweet melodies, Cheap Trick unwittingly paved the way for much of the hard rock of the next decade, as well as a surprising amount of alternative rock of the 1990s, and it was *At Budokan* that captured the band in all of its power.

Stephen Thomas Erlewine

Dream Police
October 1979, Epic

At Budokan unexpectedly made Cheap Trick stars, largely because "I Want You to Want Me" had a tougher sound than its original studio incarnation. Perversely—and most things Cheap Trick have done are somehow perverse—the band decided *not* to continue with the direct, stripped-down sound of *At Budokan*, which would have been a return to their debut. Instead, the group went for their biggest, most elaborate production to date, taking the synthesized flourishes of *Heaven Tonight* to extremes. While it kept the group in the charts, it lessened the impact of the music. Underneath the gloss, there are a number of songs that rank among Cheap Trick's finest, particularly the paranoid title track, the epic rocker "Gonna Raise Hell," the tough "I Know What I Want," the simple pop of "Voices," and the closer, "Need Your Love." Still, *Dream Police* feels like a letdown in comparison to its predecessors,

even though it would later feel like one of the group's last high-water marks. [An expanded edition of *Dream Police* was released in 2006 with four bonus tracks.]

Stephen Thomas Erlewine

Chicago

Chicago Transit Authority
April 1969, Chicago

Few debut albums can boast as consistently solid an effort as the self-titled *Chicago Transit Authority* (1969). Even fewer can claim to have enough material to fill out a double-disc affair. Although this long-player was ultimately the septet's first national exposure, the group was far from the proverbial "overnight sensation." Under the guise of the Big Thing, the group soon to be known as CTA had been honing its eclectic blend of jazz, classical, and straight-ahead rock & roll in and around the Windy City for several years. Their initial non-musical meeting occurred during a mid-February 1967 confab between the original combo at Walter Parazaider's apartment on the north side of Chi Town. Over a year later, Columbia Records staff producer James Guercio became a key supporter of the group, which he rechristened Chicago Transit Authority. In fairly short order the band relocated to the West Coast and began woodshedding the material that would comprise this title. In April of 1969, the dozen sides of *Chicago Transit Authority* unleashed a formidable and ultimately American musical experience. This included an unheralded synthesis of electric guitar wailin' rock & roll to more deeply rooted jazz influences and arrangements. This approach economized the finest of what the band had to offer—actually two highly stylized units that coexisted with remarkable singularity. On the one hand, listeners were presented with an incendiary rock & roll quartet of Terry Kath (lead guitar/vocals), Robert Lamm (keyboards/vocals), Peter Cetera (bass/vocals), and Danny Seraphine (drums). They were augmented by the equally aggressive power brass trio that included Lee Loughnane (trumpet/vocals), James Pankow (trombone), and the aforementioned Parazaider (woodwind/vocals). This fusion of rock with jazz would also yield some memorable pop sides and enthusiasts' favorites as well. Most notably, a quarter of the material on the double album—"Does Anybody Really Know What Time It Is?," "Beginnings," "Questions 67 and 68," and the only cover on the project, Steve Winwood's "I'm a Man"—also scored as respective entries on the singles chart. The tight, infectious, and decidedly pop arrangements contrast with the piledriving blues-based rock of "Introduction" and "South California Purples" as well as the 15-plus minute extemporaneous free for all "Liberation." Even farther left of center are the experimental avant-garde "Free Form Guitar" and the politically intoned and emotive "Prologue, August 29, 1968" and "Someday (August 29, 1968)." The 2003 remastered edition of *Chicago Transit Authority* offers a marked sonic improvement over all previous pressings—including the pricey gold disc incarnation.

Lindsay Planer

Chicago II
January 1970, Chicago

The Chicago Transit Authority recorded this double-barreled follow-up to their eponymously titled 1969 debut effort. The contents of *Chicago II* (1970) underscore the solid foundation of complex jazz changes with heavy electric rock & roll that the band so brazenly forged on the first set. The septet also continued its ability to blend the seemingly divergent musical styles into some of the best and most effective pop music of the era. One thing that *had* changed was the band's name, which was shortened to simply Chicago to avoid any potential litigious situations from the city of Chicago's transportation department—which claimed the name as proprietary property. Musically, James Pankow (trombone) was about to further cross-pollinate the band's sound with the multifaceted six-song "Ballet for a Girl in Buchannon." The classically inspired suite also garnered the band two of its most beloved hits—the upbeat pop opener "Make Me Smile" as well as the achingly poignant "Color My World"—both of which remained at the center of the group's live sets. Chicago had certainly not abandoned its active pursuit of blending high-octane electric rockers such as "25 or 6 to 4" to the progressive jazz inflections heard in the breezy syncopation of "The Road." Adding further depth of field is the darker "Poem for the People" as well as the politically charged five-song set titled "It Better End Soon." These selections feature the band driving home its formidable musicality and uncanny ability to coalesce styles telepathically and at a moment's notice. The contributions of Terry Kath (guitar/vocals) stand out as he unleashes some of his most pungent and sinuous leads, which contrast with the tight brass and woodwind trio of Lee Loughnane (trumpet/vocals), Walter Parazaider (woodwinds/vocals), and the aforementioned Pankow. Peter Cetera (bass/vocals) also marks his songwriting debut—on the final cut of both the suite and the album—with "Where Do We Go from Here." It bookends both with at the very least the anticipation and projection of a positive and optimistic future. Potential consumers should note the unsurpassed sound quality and deluxe packaging of the 2002 CD remaster.

Lindsay Planer

Chicago V
July 1972, Chicago

With four gold multi-disc LPs and twice as many hit singles to its credit, Chicago issued its fifth effort, the first to clock in at under an hour. What they lack in quantity, they more than make up for in the wide range of quality of material. The disc quite literally erupts with the progressive free-form "A Hit By Varese"—which seems to have been inspired as much by Emerson, Lake & Palmer's *Tarkus* (1971) or Yes circa *Close to the Edge* (1972) as by the Parisian composer for whom it is named. Fully 80 percent of the material on *Chicago V* (1972) is also a spotlight for the prolific songwriting of Robert Lamm (keyboards/vocals). In addition to penning the opening rocker, he is also responsible for the easy and airy "All Is Well," which is particularly notable for its lush Beach Boys-esque harmonies. However, Lamm's most memorable contributions are undoubtedly the Top Ten sunshine power pop anthem "Saturday in the Park" and the equally upbeat and buoyant "Dialogue, Pt. 1" and "Dialogue, Pt. 2." Those more accessible tracks are contrasted by James Pankow's (trombone/percussion) aggressive jazz fusion "Now That You've Gone." Although somewhat dark and brooding, it recalls the bittersweet "So Much to Say, So Much to Give" and "Anxiety's Moment" movements of "Ballet for a Girl in Buchannon" found on *Chicago II* (1970).

Terry Kath's (guitar/vocals) heartfelt ballad "Alma Mater" seems to be influenced by a Randy Newman sensibility. Lyrically, it could be interpreted as an open letter to his generation. Lines such as "Looking back a few short years/When we made our plans and played the cards/The way they fell/Clinging to our confidence/We stood on the threshold of the goal/That we knew, dear" affectively recall the monumental world events that had taken place during the late '60s and early '70s. Likewise, there is an undeniable one-on-one intimated in the verse "And though we had our fights/Had our short tempered nights/It couldn't pull our dreams apart/All our needs and all our wants/Drawn together in our heart/We felt it from the very start." This is a fitting way to conclude both the original album, if not the entire troubled era. Due to the time constraints of a single-disc LP, Chicago never issued a studio version of the mini political epic "A Song for Richard and His Friends." It had been worked on and performed live while touring behind *Chicago III* (1971), and appears as a standout on the much maligned *At Carnegie Hall, Vols. 1-4 (Chicago IV)* four-disc concert package (1971). The 2002 CD reissue of *Chicago V* includes among its supplemental materials an eight-plus minute instrumental studio version of the track. Also featured as "bonus selections" are a seminal rendering of Kath's powerhouse "Mississippi Delta City Blues"—which would be shelved for nearly five years before turning up on *Chicago XI* (1977)—and the 45 rpm edit of "Dialogue, Pts. 1-2."

Lindsay Planer

Chicago VI
June 1973, Chicago

This is the sixth album from the jazz/pop/rock combo Chicago, and was likewise the first to be recorded at the plush, well-lit, and custom-built Caribou Studios in Nederland, CO. The facility was owned and operated by the band's manager and producer, James William Guercio, and eventually became the group's retreat for their next five (non-compilation) longplayers. Another and perhaps more significant change was the incorporation of several "outside" additional musicians—most notably Laudir De Oliveira (percussion), who would remain with the band for the next seven years and eight LPs. Although Chicago had begun as a harder-edged rock & roll band, popular music styles were undergoing a shift during the mid-'70s into a decidedly more middle-of-the-road (MOR) and less-aggressive sound. This is reflected in the succinct pop and light rock efforts, contrasting the earlier lengthy and multi-movement epics that filled their earlier works. Nowhere is this more evident than on *Chicago VI's* (1973) two Top Ten singles: the easygoing James Pankow (trombone) ballad "Just You & Me" as well as the up-tempo rocker "Feelin' Stronger Every Day," which Pankow co-wrote with Peter Cetera (vocal/bass). This more melodic and introverted sensibility pervades the rest of the disc as well—especially from Robert Lamm (keyboard/vocals), who is particularly prolific, penning half of the material on the disc. Even his sardonically titled "Critics' Choice"—which is undoubtedly a musical rebuttal to Chicago's increasingly negative critical assessment—is a languid and delicate response, rather than a full-force confutation. "Darlin' Dear"—another Lamm contribution—on the other hand, is a horn-fuelled rocker that actually recalls Little Feat more than it does most of Chicago's previous sides. Compositions from other band-members include the heartfelt Terry Kath (guitar/vocals) ballad "Jenny," which features some fluid fretwork much in the same vein as that of Jimi Hendrix's "Angel" or "Castles Made of Sand." Additionally, Peter Cetera's (bass/vocals) "In Terms of Two" includes a more down-home and countrified acoustic vibe. While *Chicago VI* is an undeniably strong effort—supported at the time by its chart-topping status—many bandmembers and longtime enthusiasts were beginning to grow apart from the lighter, pop-oriented material.

Lindsay Planer

Chicago IX: Greatest Hits
November 1975, Chicago

Does anyone need another Chicago album besides this one? For the casual fan, the answer is definitely no. The 1975 blockbuster includes all the band's hits from its prime. And while tracks like "Wishing You Were Here" and "Feelin' Stronger Every Day" have worn a wee thin over the years, most of the cuts here are still topnotch. Standouts include the incomparable "Saturday in the Park," "Beginnings," and "Does Anybody Really Know What Time It Is?" When rock grew up with horns, jazz charts, and chops. Not as snide as Steely Dan or as soulful as Blood, Sweat & Tears, Chicago still delivered with the 11 fine sides heard here.

Stephen Cook

Eric Clapton

Eric Clapton
July 1970, Polydor

Eric Clapton's eponymous solo debut was re-corded after he completed a tour with Delaney & Bonnie. Clapton used the core of the duo's backing band and co-wrote the majority of the songs with Delaney Bramlett—accord-ingly, *Eric Clapton* sounds more laid-back and straightforward than any of the guitarist's previous recordings. There are still elements of blues and rock & roll, but they're hidden beneath layers of gospel, R&B, country, and pop flourishes. And the pop element of the record is the strongest of the album's many elements—"Blues Power" isn't a blues song and only "Let It Rain," the album's closer, features extended solos. Throughout the album, Clapton turns out concise solos that de-emphasize his status as guitar god, even when they display astonishing musicality and technique. That is both a good and a bad thing—it's encouraging to hear him grow and become a more fully rounded musician, but too often the album needs the spark that some long guitar solos would have given it. In short, it needs a little more of Clapton's personality.

Stephen Thomas Erlewine

461 Ocean Boulevard
July 1974, Polydor

461 Ocean Boulevard is Eric Clapton's second studio solo album, arriving after his side project of Derek and the Dominos and a long struggle with heroin addiction. Although there are some new reggae influences, the album doesn't sound all that different from the rock, pop, blues, country, and R&B amalgam of *Eric Clapton*. However, *461 Ocean Boulevard* is a tighter, more focused outing that enables Clapton to stretch out instrumentally. Furthermore, the pop concessions on the album—the sleek production, the concise running times—don't detract from the rootsy origins of the material, whether it's Johnny Otis' "Willie and the Hand Jive," the traditional blues "Motherless Children," Bob Marley's "I Shot the Sheriff," or Clapton's emotional original "Let It Grow." With its relaxed, friendly atmosphere and strong bluesy roots, *461 Ocean Boulevard* set the template for Clapton's '70s albums. Though he tried hard to make an album exactly like it, he never quite managed to replicate its charms.

Stephen Thomas Erlewine

E.C. Was Here
August 1975, Polydor

Following Eric Clapton's recovery from heroin addition in 1974 and subsequent comeback (announced by *461 Ocean Boulevard*), the guitar legend retained his fine band and toured extensively, and this live album is a souvenir of that period. Despite having such pop-oriented hits as "I Shot the Sheriff," *E.C. Was Here* makes it clear that Clapton was and always would be a blues man. The opening cut, "Have You Ever Loved a Woman," clearly illustrates this, and underlines the fact that Clapton had a firm grasp on his blues guitar ability, with some sterling, emotionally charged and sustained lines and riffs. A short version of "Drifting Blues" also drives the point home, with a lazy, Delta blues feel that is intoxicating. Aside from these standout blues workouts, Clapton provides a surprise with two songs from his Blind Faith period. "Presence of the Lord" and Steve Winwood's classic "Can't Find My Way Home" are given great readings here and highlight Clapton's fine touring band, particularly co-vocalist Yvonne Elliman, whose singing adds a mellifluousness to Clapton's blues vocal inflections. The market was a bit oversaturated with Clapton and Cream reissue products at the time, and this fine record got lost in the shuffle, but it remains an excellent document of the period.

Matthew Greenwald

Slowhand
November 1977, Polydor

After the guest-star-drenched *No Reason to Cry* failed to make much of an impact commerically, Eric Clapton returned to using his own band for *Slowhand*. The difference is substantial—where *No Reason to Cry* struggled hard to find the right tone, *Slowhand* opens with the relaxed, bluesy shuffle of J.J. Cale's "Cocaine" and sustains it throughout the course of the album. Alternating between straight blues ("Mean Old Frisco"), country ("Lay Down Sally"), mainstream rock ("Cocaine," "The Core"), and pop ("Wonderful Tonight"), *Slowhand* doesn't sound schizophrenic because of the band's grasp of the material. This is laid-back virtuosity—although Clapton and his band are never flashy, their playing is masterful and assured. That assurance and the album's eclectic material make *Slowhand* rank with *461 Ocean Boulevard* as Eric Clapton's best albums.

Stephen Thomas Erlewine

Backless
November 1978, Polydor

Having made his best album since *461 Ocean Boulevard* with *Slowhand*, Eric Clapton followed with *Backless*, which took the same authoritative, no-nonsense approach. If it wasn't quite the masterpiece, or the sales monster, that *Slowhand* had been, this probably was because of that usual Clapton problem—material. Once again, he returned to those Oklahoma hills for another song from J.J. Cale, but "I'll Make Love to You Anytime" wasn't quite up to "Cocaine" or "After Midnight." Bob Dylan contributed two songs, but you could see why he hadn't saved them for his own album, and Clapton's own writing contributions were mediocre. Clapton did earn a Top Ten hit with Richard Feldman and Roger Linn's understated pop shuffle "Promises," but it was not one of his more memorable recordings. Of course, Clapton's blues playing on the lone obligatory blues cut, "Early in the Morning" (presented in its full eight-minute version on the CD reissue), was stellar. (*Backless* was his last album to feature the backup group that had been with him since 1974.)

William Ruhlmann

Crossroads
April 1988, Polydor

A four-disc box set spanning Eric Clapton's entire career—running from the Yardbirds to his '80s solo recordings—*Crossroads* not only revitalized Clapton's commercial standing, but it established the rock & roll multi-disc box set retrospective as a commercially viable proposition. Bob Dylan's *Biograph* was successful two years before the release of *Crossroads*, but Clapton's set was a bona fide blockbuster. And it's easy to see why. *Crossroads* manages to sum up Clapton's career succinctly and thoroughly, touching upon all of his hits and adding a bevy of first-rate unreleased material (most notably selections from the scrapped second Derek and the Dominos album). Although not all of his greatest performances are included on the set—none of his work as a session musician or guest artist is included, for instance—every truly essential item he recorded is present on these four discs. No other Clapton album accurately explains why the guitarist was so influential, or demonstrates exactly what he accomplished.

Stephen Thomas Erlewine

Joe Cocker

With a Little Help from My Friends
April 1969, A&M

Joe Cocker's debut album holds up extraordinarily well across four decades, the singer's performance bolstered by some very sharp playing, not only by his established sideman/collaborator Chris Stainton, but also some top-notch session musicians, among them drummer Clem Cattini, Steve

Winwood on organ, and guitarists Jimmy Page and Albert Lee, all sitting in. It's Cocker's voice, a soulful rasp of an instrument backed up by Madeline Bell, Sunny Weetman and Rossetta Hightower that carries this album and makes "Change in Louise," "Feeling Alright," "Just Like a Woman," "I Shall Be Released," and even "Bye Bye Blackbird" into profound listening experiences. But the surprises in the arrangements, tempo, and approaches taken help make this an exceptional album. Tracks like "Just Like a Woman," with its soaring gospel organ above a lean textured acoustic and light electric accompaniment, and the guitar-dominated rendition of "Don't Let Me Be Misunderstood"—the formal debut of the Grease Band on record—all help make this an exceptional listening experience. The 1999 A&M reissue not only includes new notes and audiophile-quality sound, but also a pair of bonus tracks, the previously unanthologized B-sides "The New Age of Lily" and "Something Coming On," deserved better than the obscurity in which they previously dwelt.

Bruce Eder

Joe Cocker!
November 1969, A&M

Joe Cocker's first three A&M albums form the bedrock of a career that spans over three decades. While Cocker certainly wasn't always in top form during this stretch—thanks to alcohol problems and questionable comeback moves in the '80s and '90s—his early records did inform the classic pub rock sound later credited to proto-punk figures like Graham Parker and Brinsley Schwarz. On those early records, Cocker mixed elements of late-'60s English blues revival recordings (John Mayall, et al.) with the more contemporary sounds of soul and pop; a sound fused in no small part by producer and arranger Leon Russell, whose gumbo mix figures prominently on this eponymous release and the infamous *Mad Dogs & Englishmen* live set. Russell's sophisticated swamp blues aesthetic is felt directly with versions of his gospel ballad "Hello, Little Friend" and Beatles-inspired bit of New Orleans pop—and one of Cocker's biggest hits—"Delta Lady." Following up on the huge success of an earlier cover of "With a Little Help From My Friends," Cocker mines more Beatles gold with very respectable renditions of "She Came in Through the Bathroom Window" and "Something." And rounding out this impressive set are equally astute takes on Dylan's "Dear Landlord," Leonard Cohen's "Bird on the Wire," and John Sebastian's "Darling Be Home Soon." Throughout, Cocker gets superb support from his regular backing group of the time, the Grease Band. A fine introduction to the singer's classic, late-'60s and early-'70s period.

Stephen Cook

Mad Dogs & Englishmen
August 1970, A&M

Listening to this CD brings back a lot of memories. *Mad Dogs & Englishmen* was just about the most elaborate album that A&M Records had ever released, back in 1971, a double LP in a three-panel, fold-out, gatefold sleeve, with almost 80 minutes of music inside and a ton of photos, graphics, and annotation wrapping around it. A live recording done in tandem with a killer documentary film of the same U.S. tour, it was recorded at the Fillmore East, where the movie was a cross-country affair, and the two were, thus, completely separate entities—also, as people couldn't "buy" the film in those days, the double LP has lingered longer in the memory, by virtue of its being on shelves, and also being taken off those shelves to be played. Unlike a lot of other "coffee table"-type rock releases of the era, such as *Woodstock* and *The Concert for Bangladesh*, people actually listened to *Mad Dogs & Englishmen*—most of its content was exciting, and its sound, a veritable definition of big-band rock with three dozen players working behind the singer, was unique. The CD offers a seriously good sound, whether it's just Joe Cocker and a pianist and organist in the opening of "Bird on a Wire," or the entire band going full-tilt on "Cry Me a River"; the remastering was set at a high volume level and there was a decent amount of care taken to get the detail right, so you can appreciate the presence of the multiple drummers, and the legion of guitarists and singers, plus the multiple keyboard players. The lead guitar and solo piano on "Feelin' Alright," for example, come through, but so do the 34 other players and singers behind the lead. This record was also just as much a showcase for Leon Russell as it was for Joe Cocker, which A&M probably didn't mind a bit, as Russell was selling millions of records at the time. As is now known, and it's recounted in the new notes, the tour from which this album was drawn all but wiped out Joe Cocker—on a psychic level—because the music was presented on such a vast scale (and there is a moment in the movie where he mentions breaking up his former backing group, the Grease Band, with a hint of regret in his voice) and his own contribution was so muted by Russell's work as arranger and bandleader. He may well have been the "victim" of a "hijacking" of sorts, but the musical results, apart from the dubious "Give Peace a Chance," are difficult to argue about upon hearing this record anew, decades after the fact—it's almost all bracing and beautiful.

Bruce Eder

Commander Cody and His Lost Planet Airmen

Tales from the Ozone
1975, Warner Bros.

Tales from the Ozone was the second album Commander Cody & His Lost Planet Airmen cut for Warner Bros. in 1975. It was to be their last studio effort with the label, but what a way to go out. Like their eponymously titled set earlier in 1975, *Tales from the Ozone* featured a plethora of great songs, from writers as diverse as Cab Calloway ("Minnie the Moocher,"

which opens the set) to Billy Joe Shaver ("I Been to Georgia on a Fast Train") to Hoyt Axton ("Lightning Bar Blues" and "Paid in Advance"), who produced the band here, to Leiber & Stoller ("The Shadow Knows") to Blackie Farrell ("Tina Louise"), Mel McDaniel ("Roll Your Own"), George Hawke ("Honky Tonk Music"), and Hank Williams ("Cajun Baby"). There was also room for a couple of group originals, the swinging rockabilly of "It's Gonna Be One of Those Nights" and the stomping "Gypsy Fiddle." Critics have been critical of the production on this set in the past, but Axton knew exactly what he was doing in the studio. The "flat" sound is the dynamic the band had live, with everything up in the mix. Check out the country subtleties in "Connie," where the story comes across full and plain despite the outrageous chops of this very large-voiced octet. The Shaver tune rocks far harder than it ever did in either its original or Waylon Jennings' versions, especially with the Commander (George Frayne) riding the upper register with Bobby Black's steel and Billy Kitchen's Telecaster struggling for dominance against the horn section—provided courtesy of Tower of Power. There is care and delicacy put into country songs like "Honky Tonk Music" and "Lightning Bar Blues." The latter is one of the great party songs ever put on wax, and equals Jerry Jeff Walker's "Pick Up the Tempo" in singalong quotient. The Williams tune, "Roll Your Own," and "Tina Louise" are equally driven country gems, rounding out one of the most consistent and live sounding records the Lost Planet Airmen ever cut.

Thom Jurek

Ry Cooder

Ry Cooder
1970, Reprise

Already a seasoned music business veteran at the age of 22, Ry Cooder stepped out from behind the shadows of the likes of Jackie DeShannon, Taj Mahal, the Rolling Stones, and Captain Beefheart, signing his own deal with Warner Brothers records in 1969. Released the following year, Cooder's eponymous debut creates an intriguing fusion of blues, folk, rock & roll, and pop, filtered through his own intricate, syncopated guitar; Van Dyke Parks and Lenny Waronker's idiosyncratic production; and Parks and Kirby Johnson's string arrangements. And while he's still finding his feet as a singer, Cooder puts this unique blend across with a combination of terrific songs, virtuosic playing, and quirky, yet imaginative, arrangements. For material, Cooder, the son of folklorist parents, unearths ten gems—spanning six decades dating back to the 1920s—by legends such as Woody Guthrie, Blind Blake, Sleepy John Estes, and Leadbelly, as well as a current Randy Newman composition. Still, as great as his outside choices are, it's the exuberant charm of his own instrumental "Available Space" that nearly steals the show. Its joyful interplay between Cooder's slide, Van Dyke Parks' music hall piano, and the street-corner drumming creates a piece that is both loose and sophisticated. If "Available Space" is the record's most playful moment, its closer, "Dark Is the Night," is the converse, with Cooder's stark, acoustic slide extracting every ounce of torment from Blind Willie Johnson's mournful masterpiece. Some of the eccentric arrangements may prove to be a bit much for both purists and pop audiences alike, but still, Cooder's need to stretch, tempered with a reverence for the past, helps to create a completely original work that should reward adventurous listeners.

Brett Hartenbach

Into the Purple Valley
1971, Reprise

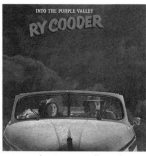

Ry Cooder is known as a virtuoso on almost every stringed instrument, and on *Into the Purple Valley*, he demonstrates this ability on a wide variety of instruments. The main focus of the music here is on the era of the Dust Bowl, and what was happening in America at the time, socially and musically. Songs by Woody Guthrie, Leadbelly, and a variety of others show Cooder's encyclopedic knowledge of the music of this time, combined with an instinctive feel for the songs. 'Phenomenal' is the descriptive word to describe his playing, whether it is on guitar, Hawaiian "slack key" guitar, mandolin, or the more arcane instruments he has found. This is a must for those who love instrumental virtuosity, authentic reworkings of an era, or just plain good music.

Bob Gottlieb

Boomer's Story
1972, Reprise

Boomer's Story, Ry Cooder's third record, continues his archeological dig through music's familiar and forgotten past. As was the case with his previous recordings, he not only looks to the masters—including blues legend Sleepy John Estes, songwriter Dan Penn (both of whom appear here) and the great Skip James—for material, but to lost and neglected pieces of American folk and blues, as well. Cooder adds the traditional title-track, which opens the album, and Lawrence Wilson's "Crow Black Chicken," which dates back to the late 1920s, to this collection of discoveries—both of which are handled with just the right balance of personality and reverence. Elsewhere, he injects a dark irony into the jingoistic "Rally 'Round the Flag," with its slow, mournful piano (played by Randy Newman) and slide guitar, while the Joseph Spence-style guitar arrangement of the World War II standard "Comin' in on a Wing and a Prayer" has a sense of hope and conviction. Often criticized for possessing a less than commanding voice, Cooder steps back from the microphone for four of the album's ten tracks—three instrumentals and one featuring Sleepy John Estes on his own "President Kennedy." And while all of the instrumentals presented here are fine renditions of great tunes, it's "Dark End of the Street" which truly stands out. Here, Cooder realizes that the only thing in his arsenal that can do justice to James Carr's definitive version is his own remorseful slide guitar. Without uttering a single lyric, he's able to convey the shame and deep regret of the Dan Penn/Chips Moman classic. Thanks to moments like this, along with Cooder's consistently strong choice of material and brilliant guitar work, *Boomer's Story*—less eccentric than his first, and less eclectic than *Into the Purple Valley*—ranks among his best work

Brett Hartenbach

Paradise and Lunch
1974, Reprise

Ry Cooder understands that a great song is a great song,

whether it was written before the Depression or last week. Still, at the same time he isn't afraid to explore new avenues and possibilities for the material. Like his three previous records, *Paradise and Lunch* is filled with treasures which become part of a world where eras and styles converge without ever sounding forced or contrived. One may think that an album that contains a traditional railroad song, tunes by assorted blues greats, and a Negro spiritual alongside selections by the likes of Bobby Womack, Burt Bacharach, and Little Milton may lack cohesiveness or merely come across as a history lesson, but to Cooder this music is all part of the same fabric and is as relevant and accessible as anything else that may be happening at the time. No matter when it was written or how it may have been done in the past, the tracks, led by Cooder's brilliant guitar, are taken to new territory where they can coexist. It's as if Washington Phillips' "Tattler" could have shared a place on the charts with Womack's "It's All Over Now" or Little Milton's "If Walls Could Talk." That he's successful on these, as well as the Salvation Army march of "Jesus on the Mainline" or the funky, gospel feel of Blind Willie McTell's "Married Man's a Fool," is not only a credit to Cooder's talent and ingenuity as an arranger and bandleader, but also to the songs themselves. The album closes with its most stripped-down track, an acoustic guitar and piano duet with jazz legend Earl "Fatha" Hines on the Blind Blake classic "Ditty Wah Ditty." Here both musicians are given plenty of room to showcase their instrumental prowess, and the results are nothing short of stunning. Eclectic, intelligent, and thoroughly entertaining, *Paradise and Lunch* remains Ry Cooder's masterpiece.

Brett Hartenbach

Alice Cooper

Love It to Death
January 1971, Warner Bros.

Alice Cooper's third album, *Love It to Death*, can be pinpointed as the release when everything began to come together for the band. Their first couple of albums (*Pretties for You* and *Easy Action*) were both largely psychedelic/acid rock affairs and bore little comparison to the band's eventual rip-roaring, teenage-anthem direction. The main reason for the quintet's change was that the eventually legendary producer Bob Ezrin was on board for the first time and helped the Coopers focus their songwriting and sound, while they also perfected their trashy, violent, and theatrical stage show and image. One of the band's most instantly identifiable anthems, "I'm Eighteen," was what made the album a hit, as well as another classic, "Is It My Body." But like Alice Cooper's other albums from the early '70s, it was an incredibly consistent listen from beginning to end. The garage rocker "Caught in a Dream" as well as the ass-kicking "Long Way to Go" and a pair of epics—the Doors-esque "Black Juju" and the eerie "Ballad of Dwight Fry"—showed that Alice was easily in league with other high-energy Detroit bands of the era (MC5, Stooges). *Love It to Death* was the first of a string of classic releases from the original Alice Cooper group.

Greg Prato

Killer
February 1971, Warner Bros.

Alice Cooper wasted little time following up the breakthrough success of *Love It to Death* with another album released the same year, *Killer*. Again, producer Bob Ezrin was on board and helps the group solidify their heavy rock (yet wide-ranging)  style even further. The band's stage show dealt with the macabre, and such disturbing tracks as "Dead Babies" and the title track fit in perfectly. Other songs were even more exceptional, such as the perennial barnstorming concert standard "Under My Wheels," the melodic yet gritty "Be My Lover," and the tribute to their fallen friend Jim Morrison, "Desperado." The long and winding "Halo of Flies" correctly hinted that the band would be tackling more complex song structures on future albums, while "You Drive Me Nervous" and "Yeah, Yeah, Yeah" showed that Alice Cooper hadn't completely abandoned their early garage rock direction. With *Killer*, they became one of the world's top rock bands and concert attractions; it rewarded them as being among the most notorious and misunderstood entertainers, thoroughly despised by grownups.

Greg Prato

School's Out
1972, Warner Bros.

School's Out catapulted Alice Cooper into the hard rock stratosphere, largely due to its timeless, all-time classic title track. But while the song became Alice's highest-charting single ever (reaching number seven on the U.S. charts) and recalled the brash, three-and-a-half-minute garage rock of yore, the majority of the album signaled a more complex compositional directional for the band. Unlike Cooper's previous releases (*Love It to Death*, *Killer*), which contained several instantly identifiable hard rock classics, *School's Out* appears to be a concept album, and aside from the aforementioned title track anthem, few of the other tracks have ever popped up in concert. That's not to say they weren't still strong and memorable; while such cuts as "Gutter Cat vs. the Jets," "Street Fight," "My Stars," and "Grande Finale" came off like mini-epics with a slightly progressive edge, Alice Cooper still managed to maintain their raw, unrefined punk edges, regardless. Other highlights included the rowdy "Public Animal #9," the mid-paced "Luney Tune," and the sinister, cabaret-esque "Blue Turk."

Greg Prato

Billion Dollar Babies
1973, Warner Bros.

With *Billion Dollar Babies*, Alice Cooper refined the raw grit of their earlier work in favor of a slightly more polished sound (courtesy of super-producer Bob Ezrin), resulting in a mega-hit album that reached the top of the U.S. album charts.

Song for song, *Billion Dollar Babies* is probably the original Alice Cooper group's finest and strongest. Such tracks as "Hello Hooray," the lethal stomp of the title track, the defiant "Elected" (a rewrite of an earlier song, "Reflected"), and the poison-laced pop candy of "No More Mr. Nice Guy" remain among Cooper's greatest achievements. Also included are a pair of perennial concert standards—the disturbing necrophilia ditty "I Love the Dead" and the chilling macabre of "Sick Things"—as well as such strong, lesser-known selections as "Raped and Freezin'," "Unfinished Sweet," and perhaps Cooper's most overlooked gem, "Generation Landslide." Nothing seemed like it could stop this great hard rock band from overtaking the universe, but tensions between the members behind the scenes would force the stellar original AC band to split up after just one more album. Not only is *Billion Dollar Babies* one of Cooper's very best; it remains one of rock's all-time, quintessential classics.

Greg Prato

Alice Cooper's Greatest Hits
1974, Warner Bros.

With the future of the original Alice Cooper band in doubt by mid-1974 (they would soon break up for good with Alice going solo), Warner Bros. decided to issue a best-of compilation entitled *Greatest Hits*. If you're a newcomer to Alice, this 12-track compilation is a must-hear—all the selections are exceptional. While many have chosen to focus primarily on Cooper's theatrics over the years, the original bandmembers were indeed supreme rock songwriters; such anthems as "I'm Eighteen," "Under My Wheels," "School's Out," and "No More Mr. Nice Guy" are unquestionably among the finest hard rock tracks of all time. And the other selections prove to be just as strong—"Is It My Body," "Desperado," "Be My Lover," "Elected," "Billion Dollar Babies," and "Muscle of Love" are all outstanding as well. The only criticism of the original release is that the collection overlooked the band's key album tracks never issued as singles.

Greg Prato

Crazy Horse

Gone Dead Train: Best of Crazy Horse
November 2005, Raven

While Crazy Horse have often been praised as one of America's great rock & roll bands, that's usually when they've been working in collaboration with fan, friend, and frequent patron Neil Young. On their own, Crazy Horse have recorded a handful of worth-  while albums, but they've never connected with audiences the same way they have when working with Young. Of course, it doesn't help that the band has never had a consistent frontman, guitarist, or songwriter of their own, with bassist Billy Talbot and drummer Ralph Molina the only musicians to play on every Crazy Horse album. (Original guitarist Danny Whitten died of a drug overdose in 1972, while Frank "Poncho" Sampedro has often drifted out of the group, usually to work with Young.) Crazy Horse's career has followed a strange and crooked path, but they've also made some fine music along the way, and *Gone Dead Train* is a compilation which attempts to make sense of the band's checkered recording history outside of their work with Neil Young (though his unmistakable guitar tone is apparent on several tracks here). *Gone Dead Train* features material from four of Crazy Horse's five albums (the band's wildly disappointing second album, *Loose*, has thankfully been ignored), and while each record has a distinct personality of its own, the sequence gives the material an admirable flow, from the gutbucket country-rock stomp of their self-titled 1971 debut to the "Neil Young without Neil Young" fury of 1989's *Left for Dead*. The disc also includes two cuts from the first and only album (released in 1968) by the Rockets, which featured Talbot, Molina, and Whitten before they formed Crazy Horse (and the woozy "Pills Blues" sounds like an uncomfortable foreshadowing of the drug problems that would take Whitten's life four years later). *Gone Dead Train* shows that Crazy Horse don't have to have Neil Young around to make great rock & roll records, and makes you wish they'd head into the studio on their own a bit more often.

Mark Deming

The Complete Reprise Recordings 1971–'73
May 2006, Warner Bros. UK

In 2005, Rhino Handmade, the Internet-only mail-order specialty label dedicated to limited-edition reissues from the vaults of Warner Bros. Records, released *Scratchy: The Complete Reprise Recordings*, by Crazy Horse. The two-disc set contained Crazy Horse's two albums for the Warner subsidiary Reprise Records, *Crazy Horse* (1971) and *Loose* (1972), on the first CD, with the second CD containing rehearsals and outtakes, plus two tracks recorded by the group in its '60s doo wop days as Danny & the Memories. Only 2500 copies of the set were printed, and they sold out quickly. So, the British branch of Warner Bros. decided to re-create the album for conventional retail, minus the Danny & the Memories tracks, as *The Complete Reprise Recordings 1971-'73*. Crazy Horse went on to make several additional albums for other labels over its career while, of course, gaining its greatest recognition as a backup band for Neil Young. But even on the material heard here, the group's essential nature is clear, confusing as it is. In essence, the history of Crazy Horse, not unlike the history of Fleetwood Mac, is one of a rhythm section, in this case bassist Billy Talbot and drummer Ralph Molina, backing a changing population of singer/songwriter/guitarist frontmen (and that's even leaving Young out of the discussion). It didn't look like that would be the story at first, however, as Talbot, Molina, and singer/songwriter/guitarist Danny Whitten made up the core of the initial group, as they had Danny & the Memories and the Rockets, another early configuration. Adding two talented journeymen, veteran pianist/arranger Jack Nitzsche and young guitarist Nils Lofgren, as quasi-members, they made *Crazy Horse*, a highly regarded country-rock effort in the style of the Young/Crazy Horse albums *Everybody Knows This Is Nowhere* and *After the Gold Rush*. Whitten, with his singing and playing, and with standout songs like the future Rod Stewart hit "I Don't Want to Talk About It," was the obvious star, but he was also the band's first casualty, suffering from a heroin addiction that caused him to be dismissed from the group shortly after the LP was released. That sabotaged promotion for the album, and it never found the audience it deserved. Nitzsche and Lofgren went back to their other activities, and Talbot and Molina were forced to recruit three new members to make *Loose*, which, not surprisingly, sounds like the work of an entirely different, and vastly inferior, band. This means the first 11 tracks on the first disc here are the only essential ones, although some of the playing in the outtakes is powerful. Even two tracks shorter, the package is an important one for fans of '70s country-rock.

William Ruhlmann

Cream

Fresh Cream
December 1966, Polydor

Fresh Cream represents so many different firsts, it's difficult to keep count. Cream, of course, was the first supergroup, but their first album not only gave birth to the power trio, it also was instrumental in the birth of heavy metal and the birth of jam rock. That's a lot of weight for one record and, like a lot of pioneering records, *Fresh Cream* doesn't seem quite as mighty as what would come later, both from the group and its acolytes. In retrospect, the moments on the LP that are a bit unformed—in particular, the halting waltz of "Dreaming" never achieves the sweet ethereal atmosphere it aspires to—stand out more than the innovations, which have been so thoroughly assimilated into the vocabulary of rock & roll, but *Fresh Cream* was a remarkable shift forward in rock upon its 1966 release and it remains quite potent. Certainly at this early stage the trio was still grounded heavily in blues, only fitting given guitarist Eric Clapton's stint in John Mayall's Bluesbreakers, which is where he first played with bassist Jack Bruce, but Cream never had the purist bent of Mayall, and not just because they dabbled heavily in psychedelia. The rhythm section of Bruce and Ginger Baker had a distinct jazzy bent to their beat; this isn't hard and pure, it's spongy and elastic, giving the musicians plenty of room to roam. This fluidity is most apparent on the blues covers that take up nearly half the record, especially on "Spoonful," where the swirling instrumental interplay, echo, fuzz tones, and overwhelming volume constitute true psychedelic music, and also points strongly toward the guitar worship of heavy metal. Almost all the second side of *Fresh Cream* is devoted to this, closing with Baker's showcase "Toad," but for as hard and restless as this half of the album is, there is some lightness on the first portion of the record where Bruce reveals himself as an inventive psychedelic pop songwriter with the tense, colorful "N.S.U." and the hook- and harmony-laden "I Feel Free." Cream shows as much force and mastery on these tighter, poppier tunes as they do on the free-flowing jams, yet they show a clear bias toward the long-form blues numbers, which makes sense: they formed to be able to pursue this freedom, which they do so without restraint. If at times that does make the album indulgent or lopsided, this is nevertheless where Cream was feeling their way forward, creating their heavy psychedelic jazz-blues and, in the process, opening the door to all kinds of serious rock music that may have happened without *Fresh Cream*, but it just would not have happened in the same fashion as it did with this record as precedent.

Stephen Thomas Erlewine

Disraeli Gears
November 1967, Polydor

Cream teamed up with producer Felix Pappalardi for their second album, *Disraeli Gears*, a move that helped push the power trio toward psychedelia and also helped give the album a thematic coherence missing from the debut. This, of course, means that *Disraeli Gears* gets further away from the pure blues improvisatory troupe they were intended to be, but it does get them to be who they truly are: a massive, innovative power trio. The blues still courses throughout *Disraeli Gears*—the swirling kaleidoscopic "Strange Brew" is built upon a riff lifted from Albert King—but it's filtered into saturated colors, as it is on "Sunshine of Your Love," or it's slowed down and blurred out as it is on the ominous murk of "Tales of Brave Ulysses." It's a pure psychedelic move that's spurred along by Jack Bruce's flourishing collaboration with Pete Brown. Together, this pair steers this album away from recycled blues-rock and toward its eccentric British core, for with the fuzzy freak-out "Swlabr," the music hall flourishes of "Dance the Night Away," the swinging "Take It Back," and of course, the schoolboy singalong "Monther's Lament," this is a very British record. Even so, this crossed the ocean and became a major hit in America as well, because for no matter how whimsical certain segments are, Cream is still a heavy rock trio and *Disraeli Gears* is a quintessential heavy rock album of the '60s. Yes, its psychedelic trappings tie it forever to 1967, but the imagination of the arrangements, the strength of the compositions, and especially the force of the musicianship make this album transcend its time as well.

Stephen Thomas Erlewine

Wheels of Fire
June 1968, Polydor

If *Disraeli Gears* was the album where Cream came into their own, its successor, *Wheels of Fire*, finds the trio in full fight, capturing every side of their multifaceted personality, even hinting at the internal pressures that soon would tear the band asunder. A dense, unwieldy double album split into an LP of new studio material and an LP of live material, it's sprawling and scattered, at once awesome in its achievement and maddening in how it falls just short of greatness. It misses its goal not because one LP works and the other doesn't, but because both the live and studio sets suffer from strikingly similar flaws, deriving from the constant power struggle between the trio. Of the three, Ginger Baker comes up short, contributing the passable "Passing the Time" and "Those Were the

Days," which are overshadowed by how he extends his solo drum showcase "Toad" to a numbing quarter of an hour and trips upon the *Wind & the Willows* whimsy of "Pressed Rat and Warthog," whose studied eccentricity pales next to Eric Clapton's nimble, eerily cheerful "Anyone for Tennis." In almost every regard, *Wheels of Fire* is a terrific showcase for Clapton as a guitarist, especially on the first side of the live album with "Crossroads," a mighty encapsulation of all of his strengths. Some of that is studio trickery, as producer Felix Pappalardi cut together the best bits of a winding improvisation to a tight four minutes, giving this track a relentless momentum that's exceptionally exciting, but there's no denying that Clapton is at a peak here, whether he's tearing off solos on a 17-minute "Spoonful" or goosing "White Room" toward the heights of madness. But it's the architect of "White Room," bassist Jack Bruce, who, along with his collaborator Peter Brown, reaches a peak as a songwriter. Aside from the monumental "White Room," he has the lovely, wistful "As You Said," the cinematic "Deserted Cities of the Heart," and the slow, cynical blues "Politician," all among Cream's very best work. And in many ways *Wheels of Fire* is indeed filled with Cream's very best work, since it also captures the fury and invention (and indulgence) of the band at its peak on the stage and in the studio, but as it tries to find a delicate balance between these three titanic egos, it doesn't quite add up to something greater than the sum of its parts. But taken alone, those individual parts are often quite tremendous.

Stephen Thomas Erlewine

Goodbye
January 1969, Polydor

After a mere three albums in just under three years, Cream called it quits in 1969. Being proper gentlemen, they said their formal goodbyes with a tour and a farewell album called—what else?—*Goodbye*. As a slim, six-song single LP, it's far shorter than the rambling, out-of-control *Wheels of Fire*, but it boasts the same structure, evenly dividing its time between tracks cut on-stage and in the studio. While the live side contains nothing as indelible as "Crossroads," the live music on the whole is better than that on *Wheels of Fire*, capturing the trio at an empathetic peak as a band. It's hard, heavy rock, with Cream digging deep into their original "Politician" with the same intensity as they do on "Sitting on Top of the World," but it's the rampaging "I'm So Glad" that illustrates how far they've come; compare it to the original studio version on *Fresh Cream* and it's easy to see just how much further they're stretching their improvisation. The studio side also finds them at something of a peak. Boasting a song apiece from each member, it opens with the majestic classic "Badge," co-written by Eric Clapton and George Harrison and ranking among both of their best work. It's followed by Jack Bruce's "Doing That Scrapyard Thing," an overstuffed near-masterpiece filled with wonderful, imaginative eccentricities, and finally, there's Ginger Baker's tense, dramatic "What a Bringdown," easily the best original he contributed to the group. Like all of Cream's albums outside *Disraeli Gears*, *Goodbye* is an album of moments, not a tight cohesive work, but those moments are all quite strong on their own terms, making this a good and appropriate final bow.

Stephen Thomas Erlewine

BBC Sessions
March 2003, Polydor

This compilation of 22 Cream BBC tracks from 1966-1968 marked a major addition to the group's discography, particularly as they released relatively little product during their actual lifetime. All of but two of these cuts ("Lawdy Mama" and the 1968 version of "Steppin' Out," which had appeared on Eric Clapton's *Crossroads* box) were previously unreleased, and although many of these had made the round on bootlegs, the sound and presentation here is unsurprisingly preferable. As for actual surprises, there aren't many. It's a good cross section of songs from their studio records, though a couple, "Steppin' Out" and "Traintime," only appeared on live releases, and some of these BBC takes actually predate the release and recording of the album versions, which makes them of historical interest for intense Cream fans. (There are also four brief interviews with Eric Clapton from the original broadcasts.) There's a mild surprise in the absence of a version of "White Room," but otherwise many of the group's better compositions and covers are here, including "I Feel Free," "N.S.U.," "Strange Brew," "Tales of Brave Ulysses," "Sunshine of Your Love," "Born Under a Bad Sign," "Outside Woman Blues," "Crossroads," "We're Going Wrong," "I'm So Glad," "SWLABR," and "Politician." Cream took better advantage of the live-in-the-studio BBC format than some groups of similar stature. There's a lean urgency to most of the performances that, while not necessarily superior to the more fully realized and polished studio renditions, do vary notably in ambience from the more familiar versions. The sound quality is good but not perfect, and variable; sometimes it's excellent, yet at other times there seem to be imperfections in the tapes sourced, with "Sunshine of Your Love" suffering from a (not grievously) hollow, muffled quality. If there's any other slight criticism of this set, it's that a handful of BBC tracks don't appear, including some that don't make it onto this CD in any version, like "Sleepy Time Time," "Toad," and "Sitting on Top of the World." Given Cream's tendency to over-improvise on the band's live concert recordings, however, the concise nature of these BBC tracks (none of which exceed five minutes) makes them preferable listening in some respects.

Richie Unterberger

Creedence Clearwater Revival

Creedence Clearwater Revival
July 1968, Fantasy

Released in the summer of 1968—a year after the summer of love, but still in the thick of the Age of Aquarius— Creedence Clearwater Revival's self-titled debut album was gloriously out-of-step with the times, teeming with John Fogerty's Americana fascinations. While many of Fogerty's obsessions and CCR's signatures are in place— weird blues ("I Put a Spell on You"), Stax R&B (Wilson Pickett's "Ninety-Nine and a Half"), rockabilly ("Susie Q"), winding instrumental interplay, the swamp sound, and songs for "The Working Man"—the band was still finding their way. Out of all their records (discounting *Mardi Gras*), this is the one that sounds the most like its era, thanks to the wordless vocal harmonies toward the end of "Susie Q,"

the backward guitars on "Gloomy," and the directionless, awkward jamming that concludes "Walking on the Water." Still, the band's sound is vibrant, with gutsy arrangements that borrow equally from Sun, Stax, and the swamp. Fogerty's songwriting is a little tentative. Not for nothing were two of the three singles pulled from the album covers (Dale Hawkins' "Susie Q," Screamin' Jay Hawkins' "I Put a Spell on You")—he wasn't an accomplished tunesmith yet. Though "The Working Man" isn't bad, the true exception is that third single, "Porterville," an exceptional song with great hooks, an underlying sense of menace, and the first inkling of the working-class rage that fueled such landmarks as "Fortunate Son." It's the song that points the way to the breakthrough of *Bayou Country*, but the rest of the album shouldn't be dismissed, because judged simply against the rock & roll of its time, it rises above its peers.

Stephen Thomas Erlewine

Bayou Country
January 1969, Fantasy

Opening slowly with the dark, swampy "Born on the Bayou," *Bayou Country* reveals an assured Creedence Clearwater Revival, a band that has found its voice between their first and second album. It's not just that "Born on the Bayou" announces that CCR has discovered its sound—it reveals the extent of John Fogerty's myth-making. With this song, he sketches out his persona; it makes him sound as if he crawled out of the backwoods of Louisiana instead of being a native San Franciscan. He carries this illusion throughout the record, through the ominous meanderings of "Graveyard Train" through the stoked cover of "Good Golly Miss Molly" to "Keep on Chooglin'," which rides out a southern-fried groove for nearly eight minutes. At the heart of *Bayou Country*, as well as Fogerty's myth and Creedence's entire career, is "Proud Mary." A riverboat tale where the narrator leaves a good job in the city for a life rolling down the river, the song is filled with details that ring so true that it feels autobiographical. The lyric is married to music that is utterly unique yet curiously timeless, blending rockabilly, country, and Stax R&B into something utterly distinctive and addictive. "Proud Mary" is the emotional fulcrum at the center of Fogerty's seductive imaginary Americana, and while it's the best song here, his other songs are no slouch, either. "Born on the Bayou" is a magnificent piece of swamp-rock, "Penthouse Pauper" is a first-rate rocker with the angry undertow apparent on "Porterville" and "Bootleg" is a minor masterpiece, thanks to its tough acoustic foundation, sterling guitar work, and clever story. All the songs add up to a superb statement of purpose, a record that captures Creedence Clearwater Revival's muscular, spare, deceptively simple sound as an evocative portrait of America.

Stephen Thomas Erlewine

Green River
August 1969, Fantasy

If anything, CCR's third album *Green River* represents the full flower of their classic sound initially essayed on its predecessor, *Bayou Country*. One of the differences between the two albums is that *Green River* is tighter, with none of the five-minute-plus jams that filled out both their debut and *Bayou Country*, but the true key to its success is a peak in John Fogerty's creativity. Although CCR had at least one cover on each album, they relied on Fogerty to crank out new material every month. He was writing so frequently that the craft became second-nature and he laid his emotions and fears bare, perhaps unintentionally. Perhaps that's why

Green River has fear, anger, dread, and weariness creeping on the edges of gleeful music. This was a band that played rock & roll so joyously that they masked the, well, "sinister" undercurrents in Fogerty's songs. "Bad Moon Rising" has the famous line "Hope you've got your things together/ Hope you're quite prepared to die," but that was only the most obvious indication of Fogerty's gloom. Consider all the other dark touches: the "Sinister purpose knocking at your door"; the chaos of "Commotion"; the threat of death in "Tombstone Shadow"; you only return to the idyllic "Green River" once you get lost and realize the "world is smolderin'." Even the ballads have a strong melancholy undercurrent, highlighted by "Lodi," where Fogerty imagines himself stuck playing in dead-end towns for the rest of his life. Not the typical thoughts of a newly famous rock & roller, but certainly an indication of Fogerty's inner tumult. For all its darkness, *Green River* is ultimately welcoming music, since the band rocks hard and bright and the melancholy feels comforting, not alienating.

Stephen Thomas Erlewine

Willy and the Poor Boys
November 1969, Fantasy

Make no mistake, *Willie & the Poor Boys* is a *fun* record, perhaps the breeziest album CCR ever made. Apart from the eerie minor-key closer "Effigy" (one of John Fogerty's most haunting numbers), there is little of the doom that colored *Green River*. Fogerty's rage remains, blazing to the forefront on "Fortunate Son," a working-class protest song that cuts harder than any of the explicit Vietnam protest songs of the era, which is one of the reasons that it hasn't aged where its peers have. Also, there's that unbridled vocal from Fogerty and the ferocious playing on *CCR*, which both sound fresh as they did upon release. "Fortunate Son" is one of the greatest, hardest rock & rollers ever cut, so it might seem to be out of step with an album that is pretty laid-back and friendly, but there's that elemental joy that by late '69 was one of CCR's main trademarks. That joy runs throughout the album, from the gleeful single "Down on the Corner" and the lazy jugband blues of "Poorboy Shuffle" through the great slow blues jam "Feelin' Blue" to the great rockabilly spiritual "Don't Look Now," one of Fogerty's overlooked gems. The covers don't feel like throwaways, either, since both "Cotton Fields" and "The Midnight Special" have been overhauled to feel like genuine CCR songs. It all adds up to one of the greatest pure rock & roll records ever cut.

Stephen Thomas Erlewine

Cosmo's Factory
July 1970, Fantasy

Throughout 1969 and into 1970, CCR toured incessantly and recorded nearly as much. Appropriately, *Cosmo's Factory*'s first single was the working band's anthem "Travelin' Band," a funny, piledriving rocker with a blaring horn section—the first indication their sonic palette was broadening. Two more singles appeared prior to the album's release, backed by John Fogerty originals that rivaled the A-side or

paled just slightly. When it came time to assemble a full album, Fogerty had only one original left, the claustrophobic, paranoid rocker "Ramble Tamble." Unlike some extended instrumentals, this was dramatic and had a direction—a distinction made clear by the meandering jam that brings CCR's version of "I Heard It Through the Grapevine" to 11 minutes. Even if it wanders, their take on the Marvin Gaye classic isn't unpleasant, and their faithful, exuberant takes on the Sun classics "Ooby Dooby" and "My Baby Left Me" are joyous tributes. Still, the heart of the album lays in those six fantastic songs released on singles. "Up Around the Bend" is a searing rocker, one of their best, balanced by the menacing murkiness of "Run Through the Jungle." "Who'll Stop the Rain"'s poignant melody and melancholy undertow has a counterpart in Fogerty's dope song, "Lookin' out My Back Door," a charming, bright shuffle, filled with dancing animals and domestic bliss—he had never been as sweet and silly as he is here. On "Long as I Can See the Light," the record's final song, he again finds solace in home, anchored by a soulful, laid-back groove. It hits a comforting, elegiac note, the perfect way to draw *Cosmo's Factory*—an album made during stress and chaos, filled with raging rockers, covers, and intense jams—to a close.

Stephen Thomas Erlewine

Pendulum
December 1970, Fantasy

During 1969 and 1970, CCR was dismissed by hipsters as a bubblegum pop band and the sniping had grown intolerable, at least to John Fogerty, who designed *Pendulum* as a rebuke to critics. He spent time polishing the production, bringing in keyboards, horns, even a vocal choir. His songs became self-consciously serious and tighter, working with the aesthetic of the rock underground—*Pendulum* was constructed as a proper album, contrasting dramatically with CCR's previous records, all throwbacks to joyous early rock records where covers sat nicely next to hits and overlooked gems tucked away at the end of the second side. To some fans of classic CCR, this approach may feel a little odd since only "Have You Ever Seen the Rain" and maybe its B-side "Hey Tonight" sound undeniably like prime Creedence. But, given time, the album is a real grower, revealing many overlooked Fogerty gems. Yes, it isn't transcendent like the albums they made from *Bayou Country* through *Cosmo's Factory*, but most bands never even come close to that kind of hot streak. Instead, *Pendulum* finds a first-class songwriter and craftsman pushing himself and his band to try new sounds, styles, and textures. His ambition results in a stumble—"Rude Awakening 2" portentously teeters on the verge of prog-rock, something CCR just can't pull off—but the rest of the record is excellent, with such great numbers as the bluesy groove "Pagan Baby," the soulful vamp "Chameleon," the moody "It's Just a Thought," and the raver "Molina." Most bands would kill for this to be their best stuff, and the fact that it's tucked away on an album that even some fans forget illustrates what a tremendous band Creedence Clearwater Revival was.

Stephen Thomas Erlewine

Creedence Clearwater Revival [Box Set]
October 2001, Fantasy

In 2000, Fantasy finally treated the Creedence Clearwater Revival catalog with the respect it deserved, remastering the entire catalog and issuing them in lavish editions with rich liner notes and slipcases. So, when they decided to release a "complete recorded works" box set a year later, the results weren't quite as revelatory as they may have been, since even if this was remastered again, it's hard for most listeners to notice the difference between this and the previous material, and all the liner notes—from such luminaries as Dave Marsh, Ben Fong-Torres, Ed Ward, Stanley Booth, and Robert Christgau—are printed as the liners here, meaning that for the hardcore who bought the whole catalog a year before, this is almost anti-climatic. That is the operative word here, since there is one thing that makes this set essential for the fanatics, even if they bought the remasters, and that's the first disc, which contains all known pre-CCR recordings by the Golliwogs and Tommy Fogerty & the Blue Velvets. These aren't really stunning recordings; they're very much within the style and sound of the time, borrowing from Richie Valens, Buddy Holly, and the Beach Boys, all twisted to something much sweeter than what CCR came to be known for. This may not be as musically satisfying as the other five discs—which, after all, comprise perhaps the greatest body of work by an American rock band—but it's necessary for any true fan, since this stuff is not only rare, but there's a lot of stuff that hasn't even been bootlegged, particularly on the Golliwogs' material on the first disc. But this box really kicks into full gear on the second disc, with the rare single "Call It Pretending"—a dynamite slice of Stax-styled R&B rock—before heading into that remarkable set of albums, running through each album in order, with only a promotional single to break up the flow of the albums (each record is presented uninterrupted except for *Pendulum*, which is split between two discs: nine cuts on one disc, two on another), before it winds up with the two live albums (including cuts that didn't make it on *The Concert*). Again, this extra material isn't essential for anyone but collectors (with the exception of "Call It Pretending"), but the music is so good that anybody looking to get everything the great American rock & roll band recorded in one fell swoop would be encouraged to take this route. After all, after you memorize the proper albums, the live cuts and pre-CCR material will be necessary.

Stephen Thomas Erlewine

David Crosby

Crosby, Stills & Nash
May 1969, Atlantic

The Crosby, Stills & Nash triumvirate shot to immediate superstardom with the release of its self-titled debut LP, a sparkling set immortalizing the group's amazingly close, high harmonies. While elements of the record haven't dated well—Nash's Eastern-influenced musings on the hit "Marrakesh Express" now seem more than a little silly, while the antiwar sentiments of "Wooden Ships," though well-intentioned, are rather hokey—the harmonies are absolutely timeless, and the best material remains rock-solid. Stills' gorgeous opener, "Suite: Judy Blue Eyes," in particular, is an epic love song remarkable in its musical and emotional intricacy, Nash's "Pre-Road Downs" is buoyant folk-pop underpinned by light psychedelic textures, and Crosby's "Long Time Gone" remains a potent indictment of the assassination of Robert Kennedy. A definitive document of its era.

Jason Ankeny

Déjà Vu
March 1970, Atlantic

One of the most hotly awaited second albums in history—right up there with those by the Beatles and the Band—*Déjà Vu* lived up to its expectations and rose to number one on the charts. Those achievements are all the more astonishing given the fact that the group barely held together through the estimated 800 hours it took to record *Déjà Vu* and scarcely functioned as a group for most of that time. *Déjà Vu* worked

as an album, a product of four potent musical talents who were all ascending to the top of their game coupled with some very skilled production, engineering, and editing. There were also some obvious virtues in evidence—the addition of Neil Young to the Crosby, Stills & Nash lineup added to the level of virtuosity, with Young and Stephen Stills rising to new levels of complexity and volume on their guitars. Young's presence also ratcheted up the range of available voices one notch and added a uniquely idiosyncratic songwriter to the fold, though most of Young's contributions in this area were confined to the second side of the LP. Most of the music, apart from the quartet's version of Joni Mitchell's "Woodstock," was done as individual sessions by each of the members when they turned up (which was seldom together), contributing whatever was needed that could be agreed upon. "Carry On" worked as the album's opener when Stills "sacrificed" another copyright, "Questions," which comprised the second half of the track and made it more substantial. "Woodstock" and "Carry On" represented the group as a whole, while the rest of the record was a showcase for the individual members. David Crosby's "Almost Cut My Hair" was a piece of high-energy hippie-era paranoia not too far removed in subject from the Byrds' "Drug Store Truck Drivin' Man," only angrier in mood and texture (especially amid the pumping organ and slashing guitars); the title track, also by Crosby, took 100 hours to work out and was a better-received successor to such experimental works as "Mind Gardens," out of his earlier career with the Byrds, showing his occasional abandonment of a rock beat, or any fixed rhythm at all, in favor of washing over the listener with tones and moods. "Teach Your Children," the major hit off the album, was a reflection of the hippie-era idealism that still filled Graham Nash's life, while "Our House" was his stylistic paean to the late-era Beatles and "4+20" was a gorgeous Stephen Stills blues excursion that was a precursor to the material he would explore on the solo album that followed. And then there were Neil Young's pieces, the exquisitely harmonized "Helpless" (which took many hours to get to the slow version finally used) and the roaring country-ish rockers that ended side two, which underwent a lot of tinkering by Young—even his seeming throwaway finale, "Everybody I Love You," was a bone thrown to longtime fans as perhaps the greatest Buffalo Springfield song that they didn't record. All of this variety made *Déjà Vu* a rich musical banquet for the most serious and personal listeners, while mass audiences reveled in the glorious harmonies and the thundering electric guitars, which were presented in even more dramatic and expansive fashion on the tour that followed.

Bruce Eder

If I Could Only Remember My Name
February 1971, Rhino

David Crosby's debut solo album, *If I Could Only Remember My Name* is a one-shot wonder of dreamy but ominous California ambience. The songs range from brief snapshots of inspiration (the angelic chorale-vocal showcase on "Orleans" and the a cappella closer, "I'd Swear There Was Somebody Here") to the full-blown, rambling western epic "Cowboy Movie," and there are absolutely no false notes struck or missteps taken. No one before or since has gotten as much mileage out of a wordless vocal as Crosby does on "Tamalpais High (At About 3)" and "Song with No Words (Tree with No Leaves)," and because the music is so relaxed, each song turns into its own panoramic vista. Those who don't go for trippy Aquarian sentiment, however, may be slightly put off by the obscure, cosmic storytelling of the gorgeous "Laughing," or the ambiguous (but pointed) social questioning of "What Are Their Names," but in actuality it is an incredibly focused album. Even when a song as pretty as "Traction in the Rain" shimmers with its picked guitars and autoharp, the album is coated in a distinct, persistent menace that is impossible to shake. It is a shame that Crosby would continue to descend throughout the remainder of the decade and the beginning of the next into aimless drug addiction, and that he would not issue another solo album until 18 years later. As it is, *If I Could Only Remember My Name* is a shambolic masterpiece, meandering but transcendentally so, full of frayed threads. Not only is it among the finest splinter albums out of the CSN&Y diaspora, it is one of the defining moments of hungover spirituality from the era. [In 2006, Rhino reissued the album with a bonus track (the seven-minute instrumental "Kids and Dogs," on which the singing is wordless scatting); historical liner notes, including comments on individual tracks by Crosby himself; and a DVD that included a Surround Sound mix, a stereo Dolby Digital mix, photos, and lyrics. The DVD also included a lengthy interview—with only printed content, and no video or audio component—about the recording of the album with Stephen Barncard, who recorded and mixed the original LP.]

Stanton Swihart

4 Way Street
April 1971, Atlantic

This 1992 expanded version of the original double live album (originally released on April 7, 1971) by CSN&Y is now an indispensable part of any collection, with additional Neil Young and Graham Nash material (and even a version of "King Midas in Reverse," the old Hollies tune) that any serious listener will want. Some of the extended guitar jams between Stills and Young ("Southern Man") go on longer than strict musical sense would dictate, but it seemed right at the time, and they capture a form that was far more abused in other hands after this group broke up.

Bruce Eder

So Far
August 1974, Atlantic

Unbeknown to most fans, *So Far* was a stopgap release, undertaken by Atlantic Records in the absence of a new Crosby, Stills, Nash & Young album to accompany the reunited quartet's summer 1974 tour. At the time, the members thought it was ridiculous to release a greatest-hits/best-of compilation distilled down from two in-print LPs plus the single sides "Ohio" and "Find the Cost of Freedom"; but propelled by the publicity surrounding the group's massive stadium tour (the first exclusive stadium tour ever done in rock), *So Far* topped the charts and sold hundreds of thousands of copies, all without containing so much as a single new note of music. Ironically, the quartet had been working on what would have been, by all accounts, the best album in their history; as with so many other projects attempted by the four-man lineup, however, that album fell apart halfway through, amid clashes of egos and creative differences, and so there was *So Far*. Taken on its own terms, the album manages to be both enjoyable and frustrating, as well as virtually obsolete in the 21st century—the Joni Mitchell cover art is cool, and the presence of "Ohio" and "Find the Cost of Freedom" makes

it attractive (until the 1990s, *So Far* was the only album to contain both songs); and a case can be made that it contains some of the better moments from *Crosby, Stills & Nash* and *Déjà Vu*. The problem is that those were two virtually perfect albums, and the idea of excerpting parts of them for a compilation makes no more sense than, say, excerpting the first two Beatles albums for a "best of" on that band. Further, it's not even a true greatest-hits or best-of compilation, with "Marrakesh Express" not present. And it is difficult to imagine anyone who enjoys this disc not enjoying the two complete albums even more. So, essentially, owning *So Far* serves no purpose except to get "Ohio" and "Find the Cost of Freedom," which are also on *Carry On* and the *Crosby, Stills & Nash* box, both of which offer a lot more, dollar for dollar and song for song. For those inclined to buy it, however, the 1994 reissue (Atlantic 82648) of *So Far* is to be preferred for sound quality over the earlier edition.

Bruce Eder

CSN
June 1977, Atlantic

The times had certainly changed since *Déjà Vu*'s release in 1970. Nevertheless, there was a hunger in audiences for a return to the harmony-soaked idealism with which the trio had been catapulted to popularity, and *CSN* consequently reached number two on the charts, behind Fleetwood Mac's megasuccessful *Rumours*. The music here is very good, though probably not up to the hard-to-match level of *Crosby, Stills & Nash* or *Déjà Vu*. Still, the songs showed a great deal of lyrical maturity and compositional complexity compared to those earlier albums (from a far more innocent time). "Just a Song Before I Go" was the latest of Graham Nash's radio-friendly acoustic numbers, and a Top Ten single. "See the Changes" and "Dark Star" ranked with the best of Stephen Stills' work, while David Crosby contributed three classics from his distinctive oeuvre: "Shadow Captain," "Anything at All," and the beautiful "In My Dreams." Nash's multi-part "Cathedral," a recollection of an acid trip taken in Winchester Cathedral on his 32nd birthday, became a staple of the group's live repertoire. *CSN* was the trio's last fully realized album, and also the last recording on which the three principals handled all the vocal parts without the sweetening of additional voices. It has held up remarkably well, both as a memento of its time and as a thoroughly enjoyable musical work.

Jim Newsom

Crosby, Stills & Nash
October 1991, Atlantic

This 77-track, four-CD set remains one of the best boxes devoted to a single music act that one can buy, covering the output of Crosby, Stills, Nash & Young across 22 years, from 1968 until 1990. The first thing that becomes apparent, beyond the excellent sound (which was a revelation at the time, when only extant editions of the group's work were the early, substandard CD editions), is the sheer worth of the material. Crosby, Stills & Nash's reputation, based on their first four albums, can be taken as a given for anyone who would think of buying this set, and it does cover virtually every base that one could involving the trio, with an occasional Crosby, Stills, Nash & Young cut included for completeness' sake. Disc one by itself should be worth the price of the set to serious fans, eight of its 18 tracks being previously unissued songs (including a version of the Beatles' "Blackbird") and unissued early demos, alternate takes, or variant mixes on songs from the *Crosby, Stills & Nash* or *Déjà Vu* albums, along with one *Crosby & Nash* outtake. Disc two is similarly filled with previously unheard songs and versions of songs, although here the rarities are more focused on material by Stephen Stills (including a Crosby, Stills & Young version of "Black Queen"), Graham Nash solo, and the Crosby & Nash duo. Disc three is devoted more to Manassas and Crosby & Nash, but does work in Crosby, Stills, Nash & Young's "Taken at All" and "See the Changes" from various attempts at doing albums. Disc four takes listeners up to 1990, with Stills, Nash, and Crosby solo material (including unissued live and studio cuts) of the '80s interspersed with released Crosby, Stills & Nash tracks and previously unissued Crosby, Stills, Nash & Young tracks. The accompanying booklet includes a sessionography and reminiscence about each track, and as most of this set is presented in chronological order, one not only gets a dazzling four-hour-plus song-by-song listening experience, but also what amounts to a montage/history of the group and their members across more than two decades.

Bruce Eder

Jesse Ed Davis

Jesse Davis/Ululu
November 2004, Wounded Bird

Wounded Bird is a label that has been dredging the depths of the record company catalogs and issuing a slew of outings from the sublime—the MJQ's 1957 *Modern Jazz Quartet* album—to the ridiculous—Fiona's two albums—on CD. Here they do the rock & roll world a great service by reissuing the first two albums by the brilliant late guitarist Jesse Ed Davis, who recorded for Atlantic in the early '70s. *Jesse Davis* was originally released in 1971 and cut haphazardly over a weekend. It has the same loose feel that Delaney & Bonnie's *Motel Shot* does, though it does not reach the same staggering heights. This is a star-studded affair that includes Eric Clapton, Ben Sidran, Leon Russell, Joel Scott Hill, Alan White, and a dozen others, along with a horn section. The backing vocalists are a who's who as well: Gloria Jones, Venetta Fields, Clydie King, Merry Clayton, Bobby Jones, Maxine Willard, and some kid named Gram Parsons (also present on the *Motel Shot* session in the same capacity). Davis' songwriting wasn't quite there, but 30 years later, its raw immediacy and good-time feel hold up and deserve another listen. In contrast, *Ululu*, released in 1973, is a monster. It's swampy, greasy, nocturnal blues and roll of the highest order. The cast this time out is no less stellar, though there are a lot fewer people in the mix. Russell is back, as are most of the background singers, but added to the fold are Dr. John, Donald "Duck" Dunn, and drummer Jim Keltner. This time out, Davis' guitar playing, particularly

his slide work, is front and center, and the overall approach is tighter, more focused. The album's first cut, Davis' "Red Dirt Boogie, Brother," is spooky, dirty, and nasty, and the next track, a cover of Merle Haggard's "White Line Fever," transforms the tune from a hillbilly anthem into a barroom singalong with killer guitar fills. Other remakes include a beautiful version of George Harrison's "Sue Me, Sue You Blues," the Band's "Strawberry Wine," and Leon Russell's "Alcatraz," which closes the set. The finest moment here, however, is in "Farther On Down the Road (You Will Accompany Me)," co-written with Taj Mahal and first recorded when Davis was playing with the bluesman. It's grittier than the original, more desperate, forlorn, and shambolic, with Davis' vocal stretched to its limit buoyed by his weeping guitar. No doubt about it, everyone is richer for having these recordings available on CD domestically, and '70s rock fans would do well to check this disc out.

Thom Jurek

Deep Purple

Deep Purple
1969, Tetragrammaton

This is a record that this even those who aren't Deep Purple fans can listen to two or three times in one sitting—but then, this wasn't much like any other album that the group ever issued. Actually, *Deep Purple* was highly prized for many years by fans of progressive rock, and for good reason. The group was going through a transition—original lead singer Rod Evans and bassist Nick Simper would be voted out of the lineup soon after the album was finished (although they weren't told about it until three months later), organist Jon Lord and guitarist Ritchie Blackmore having perceived limitations in their work in terms of where each wanted to take the band. And between Lord's ever-greater ambitions toward fusing classical and rock and Blackmore's ever-bolder guitar attack, both of which began to coalesce with the session for *Deep Purple* in early 1969, the group managed to create an LP that combined heavy metal's early, raw excitement, intensity, and boldness with progressive rock's complexity and intellectual scope, and virtuosity on both levels. On "The Painter," "Why Didn't Rosemary?," and, especially, "Bird Has Flown," they strike a spellbinding balance between all of those elements, and Evans' work on the latter is one of the landmark vocal performances in progressive rock. "April," a three-part suite with orchestral accompaniment, is overall a match for such similar efforts by the Nice as the "Five Bridges Suite," and gets extra points for crediting its audience with the patience for a relatively long, moody developmental section and for including a serious orchestral interlude that does more than feature a pretty tune, exploiting the timbre of various instruments as well as the characteristics of the full ensemble. Additionally, the band turns in a very successful stripped-down, hard rock version of Donovan's "Lalena," with an organ break that shows Lord's debt to modern jazz as well as classical training. In all, amid all of those elements—the orchestral accompaniment, harpsichord embellishments, and backward organ and drum tracks—*Deep Purple* holds together astonishingly well as a great body of music. This is one of the most bracing progressive rock albums ever, and a successful vision of a musical path that the group might have taken but didn't. Ironically, the group's American label, Tetragrammaton Records, which was rapidly approaching bankruptcy, released this album a lot sooner than EMI did in England, but ran into trouble over the use of the Heironymus Bosch painting "The Garden of Earthly Delights" on the cover; although it has been on display at the Vatican, the work was wrongly perceived as containing profane images and never stocked as widely in stores as it might've been. [The 2000 remastered edition on the Spitfire label, by way of EMI, sounds magnificent and offers five bonus tracks: a killer hard rock B-side, "Emmaretta," showcasing a slashing Ritchie Blackmore guitar break, and a looser, more flowing BBC-recorded version of the latter song, plus "Lalena" and "The Painter" and a harder alternate take of "The Bird Has Flown."]

Bruce Eder

Deep Purple in Rock
1970, Warner Bros.

After satisfying all of their classical music kinks with keyboard player Jon Lord's overblown *Concerto for Group and Orchestra*, Deep Purple's soon to be classic Mark II version made its proper debut and established the sonic blueprint that would immortalize this lineup of the band on 1970's awesome *In Rock*. The cacophony of sound (spearheaded by Ritchie Blackmore's blistering guitar solo) introducing opener "Speed King" made it immediately obvious that the band was no longer fooling around, but the slightly less intense "Bloodsucker" did afford stunned listeners a chance to catch their breaths before the band launched into the album's epic, ten-minute *tour de force*, "Child in Time." In what still stands as arguably his single greatest performance, singer Ian Gillan led his bandmates on a series of hypnotizing crescendos, from the song's gentle beginning through to its ear-shattering climax and then back again for an even more intense encore that brought the original vinyl album's seismic first side to a close. Side two opened with the searing power chords of "Flight of the Rat"—another example of the band's new take-no-prisoners hard rock stance, though at nearly eight minutes, it too found room for some extended soloing from Blackmore and Lord. Next, "Into the Fire" and "Living Wreck" proved more concise but equally appealing, and though closer "Hard Lovin' Man" finally saw the new-look Deep Purple waffling on a bit too long before descending into feedback, the die was cast for one of heavy metal's defining albums.

Eduardo Rivadavia

Fireball
1971, Warner Bros.

One of Deep Purple's four indispensable albums (the others being *In Rock*, *Machine Head*, and *Burn*), 1971's *Fireball* saw the band broadening out from the no-holds-barred hard rock direction of the previous year's cacophonous *In Rock*. Metal machine noises introduced the sizzling title track—an unusually compact but explosively tight group effort on which Jon Lord's organ truly shined. The somewhat tiring repetitions of "No No No" actually threatened to drop the ball next, but the fantastic single "Strange Kind of Woman" nimbly caught and set it rolling again, just in time for the innuendo-encrusted hilarity of "Anyone's Daughter," featuring one of singer Ian Gillan's first (and still best) humorous storylines to go with one of guitarist Ritchie Blackmore's

most uncharacteristic, bluesiest performances ever. "The Mule" opened the vinyl album's second side with what is perhaps Purple's finest instrumental, and on the hyper-extended "Fools," the bandmembers proved they could flirt with progressive rock without plunging off its cliff (although the song could probably have done without its drawn-out middle section). And closing the album was the exceptional "No One Came," where intertwining instrumental lines locked together beautifully, Gillan wove another entertaining yarn that was part autobiography and part Monty Python, and the often underrated skills of drummer Ian Paice helped the song sound so unreservedly fresh and intuitive that one could almost be convinced the band had winged it on the spot. Sure, the following year's *Machine Head* would provide Deep Purple with their commercial peak, but on *Fireball*, the formidable quintet was already firing on all cylinders.

Eduardo Rivadavia

Machine Head
1972, Warner Bros.

Led Zeppelin's fourth album, Black Sabbath's *Paranoid*, and Deep Purple's *Machine Head* have stood the test of time as the Holy Trinity of English hard rock and heavy metal, serving as the fundamental blueprints followed by virtually every heavy rock & roll band since the early '70s. And, though it is probably the least celebrated of the three, *Machine Head* contains the "mother of all guitar riffs"—and one of the first learned by every beginning guitarist—in "Smoke on the Water." Inspired by real life events in Montreux, Switzerland, where Deep Purple were recording the album when the Grand Hotel was burned to the ground during a Frank Zappa concert, neither the song, nor its timeless riff, should need any further description. However, *Machine Head* was anything but a one-trick pony, introducing the bona fide classic opener "Highway Star," which epitomized all of Deep Purple's intensity and versatility while featuring perhaps the greatest soloing duel ever between guitarist Ritchie Blackmore and organist Jon Lord. Also in top form was singer Ian Gillan, who crooned and exploded with amazing power and range throughout to establish himself once and for all as one of the finest voices of his generation, bar none. His presence was certainly missed on the album's requisite instrumental, "Lazy," but the track would nonetheless evolve and expand into an incredible live jam for the band in years to come. Yes, the plodding shuffle of "Maybe I'm a Leo" shows some signs of age, but punchy singles "Pictures of Home" and "Never Before" remain as vital as ever, displaying Purple at their melodic best. And finally, the spectacular "Space Truckin'" drove *Machine Head* home with yet another tremendous Blackmore riff, providing a fitting conclusion to one of the essential hard rock albums of all time.

Eduardo Rivadavia

Shades 1968–1998
March 1999, Rhino

A lot of care went into the track selection and mastering on this four-CD set, devoted to 30 years in the history of Deep Purple—though for most listeners, discs one through three, devoted to the band's first eight years, are what will really count. Deep Purple recorded significant bodies of work in several styles, but the years 1968 through 1974, when they evolved out of psychedelia and into heavy metal, are the vitally important ones. The first disc is a treat not only for Deep Purple fans but '60s British rock completists, highlighted by two previously unissued tracks dating from a time when the band was apparently still known officially as Roundabout.

The band's chart singles and a beautifully lyrical and reflective version of the Beatles' "Help" open the first disk, and it's hard not to love those early singles. And then comes "Hallelujah (I Am the Preacher)," which opens the group's classic heavy metal era and heralds the arrival of Ian Gillan on lead vocals and Roger Glover on bass. From there on, and for most of the next two-and-a-half CDs, this set threatens to fry any speakers or ears in its presence. Disc two is from the core of the group's prime years, from the spring of 1971 through the end of that year. The *Fireball* and *Machine Head* albums are well represented, and some of this music is surprisingly durable. Disc three covers the peak years, closing out in 1975 at the end of the Tommy Bolin/Glenn Hughes lineup, and disc four picks up with the 1984 reunion. The packaging is slightly awkward, but it comes with a 55-page booklet giving just about the fullest easily available account of the band's impact and importance.

Bruce Eder

Delaney & Bonnie

To Bonnie from Delaney
1970, Atco

Delaney and Bonnie hit their pop-soul prime on this, their first Atlantic Records album. Buoyed by their acclaim from their first Elektra album, as well as their association with Eric Clapton, the group switched record labels and recorded this, probably their most definitive album. Backed by an awesome cast of musicians which included Jim Gordon (drums), Kenny Gradney (bass—later of Little Feat), and many others, this record shows why anyone connected with the band became a tambourine-shaking convert to soul-based rhythm & blues rock. Some great vocal performances by Bonnie Bramlett, especially the low-down "The Love of My Man," show why she was put in the same league as Janis Joplin. One of the more definitive albums of the period.

Matthew Greenwald

On Tour with Eric Clapton
June 1970, Atco

This 42-minute, eight-song live album, cut at Croydon late in 1969, is not only the peak of Delaney & Bonnie's output, but also the nexus in the recording and performing careers of Eric Clapton and George Harrison. *On Tour With Eric Clapton* features the guitarist performing the same blend of country, blues, and gospel that would characterize his own early solo ventures in 1970. He rises to the occasion with dazzling displays of virtuosity throughout, highlighted by a dizzying solo on "I Don't Want to Discuss," a long, languid part on "Only You Know and I Know," and searing, soulful lead on the beautifully harmonized "Coming Home." Vocally, Delaney & Bonnie were never better than they come off on this live set, and the 11-piece band sounds tighter musically than a lot of quartets that were working at the time, whether they're playing extended blues or ripping through a medley of Little Richard songs. It's no accident that the band featured here would become Clapton's own studio outfit for his debut solo LP, or that the core of this group—Bobby Whitlock, Carl Radle, and Jim Gordon—would transform itself into Derek & the Dominoes as well; or that most of the full band here would also comprise the group that played with George Harrison on *All Things Must Pass* and at the Concert for Bangladesh, except that the playing here (not to mention the recording) is better. Half the musicians on this record achieved near-superstar status less than a year later, and although the reasons behind their fame didn't last, listening to their work decades later, it all seems justified. One only wishes that Atlantic Records might check their vaults for any unreleased numbers from these shows that could fit on an extended CD.

Bruce Eder

Motel Shot
1971, Atco

Decades before the MTV Unplugged phenomenon took off, Delaney and Bonnie recorded an album's worth of tunes in just that acoustic fashion. Rounding up a cast of "friends" for the event (including Joe Cocker, Leon Russell, and Duane Allman, to name a few "friends"), *Motel Shot* tries to show how musicians on the road unwind after concerts and get back to the basics. Delaney and Bonnie even had a hit single here, with "Never Ending Song of Love." This is a refreshing record, and one that should not be missed. It includes strains of gospel, country, blues, folk, and R&B, while never straying from the acoustic trail.

James Chrispell

Derek & the Dominos

Layla and Other Assorted Love Songs
November 1970, Polydor

Wishing to escape the superstar expectations that sank Blind Faith before it was launched, Eric Clapton retreated with several sidemen from Delaney & Bonnie to record the material that would form *Layla and Other Assorted Love Songs*. From these meager beginnings grew his greatest album. Duane Allman joined the band shortly after recording began, and his spectacular slide guitar pushed Clapton to new heights. Then again, Clapton may have gotten there without him, considering the emotional turmoil he was in during the recording. He was in hopeless, unrequited love with Patti Boyd, the wife of his best friend, George Harrison, and that pain surges throughout *Layla*, especially on its epic title track. But what really makes *Layla* such a powerful record is that Clapton, ignoring the traditions that occasionally painted him into a corner, simply tears through these songs with burning, intense emotion. He makes standards like "Have You Ever Loved a Woman" and "Nobody Knows You (When You're Down and Out)" into his own, while his collaborations with Bobby Whitlock—including "Any Day" and "Why Does Love Got to Be So Sad?"—teem with passion. And, considering what a personal album *Layla* is, it's somewhat ironic that the lovely coda "Thorn Tree in the Garden" is a solo performance by Whitlock, and that the song sums up the entire album as well as "Layla" itself.

Stephen Thomas Erlewine

Rick Derringer

All American Boy
1974, Blue Sky

Fresh from stints in the McCoys and Johnny Winter Band, *All American Boy* was supposed to be Rick Derringer's breakthrough solo album. For years, it was argued that the frightfully touched-up cover photo of Derringer sank the album before anyone heard it. If that's true, it's a shame, because this is simply Rick Derringer's most focused and cohesive album, a marvelous blend of rockers, ballads, and atmospheric instrumentals. Joe Walsh helps out on a couple of tracks, but mostly it's Derringer's show—multi-instrumental virtuosity in a number of styles. Consider this one of the great albums of the '70s that fell between the cracks.

Cub Koda

Dire Straits

Dire Straits
October 1978, Warner Bros.

Dire Straits' minimalist interpretation of pub rock had already crystallized by the time they released their eponymous debut. Driven by Mark Knopfler's spare, tasteful guitar lines and his husky warbling, the album is a set of bluesy rockers. And while the bar band mentality of pub-rock is at the core of Dire Straits—even the group's breakthrough single, "Sultans of Swing," offered a lament for a neglected pub rock band—their music is already beyond the simple boogies and shuffles of their forefathers, occasionally dipping into jazz and country. Knopfler also shows an inclination toward Dylanesque imagery, which enhances the smoky, low-key atmosphere of the album. While a few of the songs fall flat, the album is remarkably accomplished for a debut, and Dire Straits had difficulty surpassing it throughout their career.

Stephen Thomas Erlewine

Making Movies
October 1980, Warner Bros.

Without second guitarist David Knopfler, Dire Straits began to move away from its roots rock origins into a jazzier variation of country-rock and singer/songwriter folk-rock. Naturally, this means that Mark Knopfler's ambitions as a songwriter are growing, as the storytelling pretensions of *Making Movies* indicate. Fortunately, his skills are increasing, as the lovely "Romeo and Juliet," "Tunnel of Love," and "Skateaway" indicate. And *Making Movies* is helped by a new wave-tinged pop production, which actually helps Knopfler's jazzy inclinations take hold. The record runs out of steam toward the end, closing with the borderline offensive "Les Boys," but the remainder of *Making Movies* ranks among the band's finest work.

Stephen Thomas Erlewine

Love over Gold
September 1982, Warner Bros.

Adding a new rhythm guitarist, Dire Straits expands its sounds and ambitions on the sprawling *Love Over Gold*. In a sense, the album is their prog rock effort, containing only five songs, including the 14-minute opener "Telegraph Road." Since Mark Knopfler is a skilled, tasteful guitarist, he can sustain interest even throughout the languid stretches, but the long, atmospheric, instrumental passages aren't as effective as the group's tight blues-rock, leaving *Love Over Gold* only a fitfully engaging listen.

Stephen Thomas Erlewine

Brothers in Arms
May 1985, Warner Bros.

Brothers in Arms brought the atmospheric, jazz-rock inclinations of *Love Over Gold* into a pop setting, resulting in a surprise international best-seller. Of course, the success of *Brothers in Arms* was helped considerably by the clever computer-animated video for "Money for Nothing," a sardonic attack on MTV. But what kept the record selling was Mark Knopfler's increased sense of pop songcraft—"Money for Nothing" had an indelible guitar riff, "Walk of Life" is a catchy up-tempo boogie variation on "Sultans of Swing," and the melodies of the bluesy "So Far Away" and the down-tempo, Everly Brothers-style "Why Worry" were wistful and lovely. Dire Straits had never been so concise or pop-oriented, and it wore well on them. Though they couldn't maintain that consistency through the rest of the album—only the jazzy "Your Latest Trick" and the flinty "Ride Across the River" make an impact—*Brothers in Arms* remains one of their most focused and accomplished albums, and in its succinct pop sense, it's distinctive within their catalog. [In 2005 Mercury released a 20th anniversary limited edition version of *Brothers in Arms* in the Hybrid/SACD format.]

Stephen Thomas Erlewine

Dr. Hook & the Medicine Show

Dr. Hook & the Medicine Show
1971, Columbia

When "Sylvia's Mother" went to number five in 1972, Dr. Hook & the Medicine Show sold over three and a half million copies of this, their debut album. The bulk of the songs were written by children's author and *Playboy* cartoonist Shel Silverstein, who moved between shady comedy and serious heart songs with ease. Many album purchasers were perplexed to hear "Makin' It Natural" and "Marie Lavaux" on the same record with the lump-in-the-throat tune "Sylvia's Mother." Complicating things further, the public, for the most part, was taken aback once again when Dr. Hook began showing up as an unkempt, high-as-a-kite rock & roll troupe on television shows like *American Bandstand* and *The Midnight Special*. Still, their first album serves as very good documentation of a band that would one day produce a handful of Top Ten dance songs.

Michael B. Smith

Sloppy Seconds
1972, Columbia

Sloppy Seconds began to unveil Dr. Hook's crude brand of humor, with its only saving grace coming from "Cover of the Rolling Stone," the band's second Top Ten hit which followed the insipid "Sylvia's Mother" from a year before. Although a feel for the band and Ray Sawyer's slackened vocal style can be attained throughout the tracks, there isn't much substance filtering through the songs, as cuts like "Looking for Pussy," "If I'd Only Come and Gone," and "Get My Rocks Off" sound more like lewd jottings from a teenager than they do rock & roll tunes. "Carry Me Carrie" and "The Things I Didn't Say" come off as facetious attempts to rekindle *some* of the charm that came with their first single, but the band's efforts fall way short. "Queen of the Silver Dollar" is the album's only other redeemable track, but it's best heard in amongst a compilation along with "Cover of the Rolling Stone" than it is here, which means, for the most part, *Sloppy Seconds* can be deemed inessential. After this album, Dr. Hook added the Medicine Show to their name and, throughout the rest of the '70s and the early '70s, they garnered eight more Top 40 hits. Every one of them was of the mawkish, eased-back love song type though, a style the band wisely took advantage of.

Mike DeGagne

Dr. John

Gris-Gris
1968, Collectors' Choice Music

The most exploratory and psychedelic outing of Dr. John's career, a one-of-a-kind fusion of New Orleans Mardi Gras R&B and voodoo mysticism. Great rasping, bluesy vocals, soulful backup singers, and eerie melodies on flute, sax, and clarinet, as well as odd Middle Eastern-like chanting and mandolin runs. It's got the setting of a strange religious ritual, but the mood is far more joyous than solemn.

Richie Unterberger

In the Right Place
March 1973, Atco

Dr. John finally struck paydirt here and was certainly *In the Right Place*. With the hit single "Right Place Wrong Time" bounding up the charts, this fine collection saw many unaware listeners being initiated into New Orleans-style rock. Also including Allen Toussaint's "Life," and a funky little number entitled "Traveling Mood," which shows off the good doctor's fine piano styling, and with able help from the Meters as backup group, *In the Right Place* is still a fine collection to own.

James Chrispell

Mos' Scocious: Anthology
October 1993, Rhino

Over his 35 years of recording, Mac "Dr. John" Rebennack has worn many hats, from '50s greasy rock & roller to psychedelic '70s weirdo to keeper of the New Orleans music flame. All of these modes, plus more, are excellently served up on this two-disc anthology. From the early New Orleans sides featuring Rebennack's blistering guitar work ("Storm

Warning" and "Morgus the Magnificent") to the fabled '70s sides as the Night Tripper to his present-day status as repository of the Crescent City's noble musical tradition, this is the one you want to have for the collection.

Cub Koda

Donovan

Donovan's Greatest Hits
January 1969, Epic/Legacy

Epic/Legacy's 1999 reissue of *Greatest Hits* improves on the original 1969 collection in a number of ways. First of all, the original Hickory versions of "Catch the Wind" and "Colours" are included instead of re-recordings, which is enough to make this new edition preferable, but the compilers have also chosen to include the original mono version of these hits instead of the stereo cuts that were on the first edition. Plus, they've added four excellent bonus tracks: "Atlantis," "To Susan on the West Coast Waiting," "Barabajagal," and "Riki Tiki Tavi." All of that means that this expanded and updated *Greatest Hits* is a near-perfect single-disc summary of Donovan's most popular material and hit singles. As these songs prove, Donovan and producer Mickie Most could craft irresistible folk-rock and psychedelic pop singles. Some of the sounds and sentiments may sound a little dated, but the productions and the songs—"Sunshine Superman," "Jennifer Juniper," "Wear Your Love Like Heaven," "Season of the Witch," "Mellow Yellow," "Hurdy Gurdy Man," "Epistle to Dippy," "There Is a Mountain," "Lalena," plus the aforementioned bonus tracks—have proven to be classics of the era, and this is the best place to get them all on one collection.

Stephen Thomas Erlewine

The Doobie Brothers

Toulouse Street
July 1972, Warner Bros.

This was the album by which most of their fans began discovering the Doobie Brothers, and it has retained a lot of its freshness over the decades. Producer Ted Templeman was attuned to the slightly heavier and more Southern style the band wanted to work toward on this, their second album, and the results were not only profitable—including a platinum record award—but artistically impeccable. *Toulouse Street* is actually pretty close in style and sound at various points to what the Eagles were doing during the same period, except that the Doobies threw jazz and R&B into the mix, as well as country, folk, and bluegrass elements, and (surprise!) ended up just about as ubiquitous as the Eagles in peoples' record collections, especially in the wake of the singles "Listen to the Music" and "Jesus Is Just Alright." But those two singles represented only the tip of the iceberg in terms of what this group had to offer, as purchasers of the album discovered even on the singles—both songs appear here in distinctly longer versions, with more exposition and development, and in keeping with the ambitions that album cuts (even of popular numbers) were supposed to display in those days. Actually, "Listen to the Music" (written by Tom Johnston) offers subtle use of phasing and other studio tricks that make its seemingly earthy, laid-back approach some of the most complex and contrived of the period. Johnston's "Rockin' Down the Highway" shows the band working at a higher wattage and moving into Creedence Clearwater Revival territory, while "Mamaloi" was Patrick Simmons' laid-back Caribbean idyll, and the title tune (also by Simmons) is a hauntingly beautiful ballad. The band then switches gears into swamp rock for "Cotton Mouth" and takes a left turn into the Mississippi Delta for a version of Sonny Boy Williamson II's "Don't Start Me Talkin'" before shifting into a gospel mode with "Jesus Is Just Alright." Johnston's nearly seven-minute "Disciple" was the sort of soaring, bluesy hard rock workout that led to the group's comparison to the Allman Brothers Band, though their interlocking vocals were nearly as prominent as their crunching, surging double lead guitars and paired drummers. And it all still sounds astonishingly bracing decades later; it's still a keeper, and one of the most inviting and alluring albums of its era.

Bruce Eder

The Captain and Me
March 1973, Warner Bros.

The Doobie Brothers' third long-player was the charm, their most substantial and consistent album to date, and one that rode the charts for a year. It was also a study in contrasts, Tom Johnston's harder-edged, bolder rocking numbers balanced by Patrick Simmons' more laid-back country-rock ballad style. The leadoff track, Johnston's "Natural Thing," melded the two, opening with interlocking guitars and showcasing the band's exquisite soaring harmonies around a beautiful melody, all wrapped up in a midtempo beat—the result was somewhere midway between Allman Brothers-style virtuosity and Eagles/Crosby & Nash-type lyricism, which defined this period in the Doobies' history and gave them a well-deserved lock on the top of the charts. Next up was the punchy, catchy "Long Train Runnin'," a piece they'd been playing for years as an instrumental—a reluctant Johnston was persuaded by producer Ted Templeman to write lyrics to it and record the song, and the resulting track became the group's next hit. The slashing, fast-tempo "China Grove" and "Without You" represented the harder side of the Doobies' sound, and were juxtaposed with Simmons' romantic country-rock ballads "Dark Eyed Cajun Woman," "Clear as the Driven Snow," and "South City Midnight Lady." Simmons also showed off his louder side with "Evil Woman," while Johnston showed his more reflective side with "Ukiah" and "The Captain and Me"—the latter, a soaring rocker clocking in at nearly five minutes, features radiant guitars and harmonies, soaring ever higher and faster to a triumphant finish.

Bruce Eder

What Were Once Vices Are Now Habits
February 1974, Warner Bros.

The Doobies team up with the Memphis Horns for an even more Southern-flavored album than usual, although also a more uneven one. By this time, Tom Johnston, Patrick Simmons, and company had pretty well inherited the mantle and the core (and then some) of the audience left behind by Creedence Clearwater Revival and John Fogerty, with Johnston songs like "Pursuit on 53rd Street," "Down in the Track," and "Road Angel" recalling pieces like "Travelin' Band," while Simmons' "Black Water" (their first number one hit) evoked the softer side of the "swamp rock" popularized by CCR. Actually, in some respects, given the range of instruments employed here, including an autoharp (courtesy of Arlo Guthrie) and viola, the songs on the original LP's first side suffer somewhat from a sameness that makes *What Were Once Vices Are Now Habits* a little less interesting than the albums that preceded it. The original side two had a lot more variety, which is as good as any full album the band ever recorded: Simmons' "Tell Me What You Want (And I'll Give You What You Need)" and Johnston's "Another Park, Another Sunday," which both outdo the Eagles and Poco at their respective country-rock games (and keep a certain soulful edge, too), Simmons' lyrical, ethereal, slightly spacy "Daughters of the Sea," and the very spacy, shimmering instrumental "Flying Cloud" (written by bassist Tiran Porter). In all, despite the weakness of its original first side, it's got a lot more to offer than the single hit, and has at least six numbers (out of 12) that rate with the better album tracks the group has ever done.

Bruce Eder

Stampede
May 1975, Warner Bros.

Talk about greatness—the Doobie Brothers, with Jeff "Skunk" Baxter added to their lineup, delivered their best album to date helped by a fairly big hit, though "Take Me in Your Arms" never did anything close to its predecessors despite some chords and modulations that recalled "Black Water" ever so slightly. *Stampede*'s virtue was its musicianship, which, in addition to new member Baxter, was also showcased in the guises of some impressive guests. The Doobie Brothers' rootsiest album to date, *Stampede* was virtuoso soulful countrified rock of a gritty nature, crossing over into blues as well as reaching back to a raw, traditional rock & roll sound that wouldn't have sounded too out of place 20 years earlier. That was the opener, the searing "Sweet Maxine," which just might've made a good single with an edit or two to bring it down to three and a half minutes; the record gets better with the bouncing "Neal's Fandango," which is highlighted by lyrical as well as instrumental acrobatics on the verses and a delicious guitar and piano break. "Texas Lullaby" is one of the prettiest pieces of country rock (though it's a little more "Western rock") to come out of the genre since the Byrds and the Beau Brummels trod into it eight years earlier, and gets a magnificently soulful performance from Tom Johnston. And speaking of soul, Curtis Mayfield is the arranger on Johnston's hard-driving "Music Man." The group strips down to its acoustic basics for "Slat Key Soquel Rag," which could have been an outtake from the group's self-titled debut album; Maria Muldaur is the guest vocalist on "I Cheat the Hangman," representing Patrick Simmons' songwriting at its most ethereal. Baxter's "Précis" was the group's nod to classical and Spanish guitar technique, and "Rainy Day Crossroad Blues" provides guest artist Ry Cooder with a gorgeous canvas on which to paint his slide guitar licks. And the album lands with its feet firmly in 1970s-style roots rock on "I've Been Workin' on You" and "Double Dealin' Four Flusher."

Bruce Eder

Takin' It to the Streets
March 1976, Warner Bros.

The group's first album with Michael McDonald marked a shift to a more mellow and self-consciously soulful sound for the Doobies, not all that different from what happened to Steely Dan—whence McDonald (and Jeff Baxter) had come—between, say, *Can't Buy a Thrill* and *Pretzel Logic*. They showed an ability to expand on the lyricism of Patrick Simmons and Baxter's writing on "Wheels of Fortune," while the title track introduced McDonald's white funk sound cold to their output, successfully. Simmons' "8th Avenue Shuffle" vaguely recalled "Black Water," only with an urban theme and a more self-consciously soul sound (with extraordinarily beautiful choruses and a thick, rippling guitar break). "Rio" and "It Keeps You Runnin'" both manage to sound like Steely Dan tracks—and that's a compliment—while Tiran Porter's hauntingly beautiful "For Someone Special" was a pure soul classic right in the midst of all of these higher-energy pieces. Tom Johnston's "Turn It Loose" is a last look back to their earlier sound, while Simmons' "Carry Me Away" shows off the new interplay and sounds that were to carry the group into the 1980s, with gorgeous playing and singing all around.

Bruce Eder

Minute by Minute
December 1978, Warner Bros.

With Tom Johnston gone from the lineup because of health problems, this is where the "new" Doobie Brothers really make their debut, with a richly soulful sound throughout and emphasis on horns and Michael McDonald's piano more than on Patrick Simmons' or Jeff Baxter's guitars. Not that they were absent entirely, or weren't sometimes right up front in the mix, as the rocking, slashing "Don't Stop to Watch the Wheels" and the bluegrass-influenced "Steamer Lane Breakdown" demonstrate. But given the keyboards, the funky rhythms, and McDonald's soaring tenor (showcased best on "What a Fool Believes"), it's almost difficult to believe that this is the hippie bar band that came out of California in 1970. There's less virtuosity here than on the group's first half-dozen albums, but overall a more commercial sound steeped in white funk. It's still all pretty compelling even if its appeal couldn't be more different from the group's earlier work (i.e., *The Captain and Me*, etc.). The public loved it, buying something like three million copies, and the recording establishment gave *Minute by Minute* four Grammy Awards, propelling the group to its biggest success ever.

Bruce Eder

The Doors

The Doors
January 1967, Elektra

A tremendous debut album, and indeed one of the best first-time outings in rock history, introducing the band's fusion of rock, blues, classical, jazz, and poetry with a knockout punch. The lean, spidery guitar and organ riffs interweave with a hypnotic menace, providing a seductive backdrop for Jim Morrison's captivating vocals and probing prose. "Light My Fire" was the cut that topped the charts and established the group as stars, but most of the rest of the album is just as impressive, including some of their best songs: the propulsive "Break On Through" (their first single), the beguiling Oriental mystery of "The Crystal Ship," the mysterious "End of the Night," "Take It as It Comes" (one of several tunes besides "Light My Fire" that also had hit potential), and the stomping rock of "Soul Kitchen" and "Twentieth Century Fox." The 11-minute Oedipal drama "The End" was the group at its most daring and, some would contend, overambitious. It was nonetheless a haunting cap to an album whose nonstop melodicism and dynamic tension would never be equaled by the group again, let alone bettered.

Richie Unterberger

Strange Days
October 1967, Elektra

Many of the songs on *Strange Days* had been written around the same time as the ones that appeared on *The Doors*, and with hindsight one has the sense that the best of the batch had already been cherry picked for the debut album. For that reason, the band's second effort isn't as consistently stunning as their debut, though overall it's a very successful continuation of the themes of their classic album. Besides the hit "Strange Days," highlights included the funky "Moonlight Drive," the eerie "You're Lost Little Girl," and the jerkily rhythmic "Love Me Two Times," which gave the band a small chart single. "My Eyes Have Seen You" and "I Can't See Your Face in My Mind" are minor but pleasing entries in the group's repertoire that share a subdued Eastern psychedelic air. The 11-minute "When the Music's Over" would often be featured as a live showstopper, yet it also illustrated their tendency to occasionally slip into drawn-out bombast.

Richie Unterberger

Waiting for the Sun
July 1968, Elektra

The Doors' 1967 albums had raised expectations so high that their third effort was greeted as a major disappointment. With a few exceptions, the material was much mellower, and while this yielded some fine melodic ballad rock in "Love

Street," "Wintertime Love," "Summer's Almost Gone," and "Yes, the River Knows," there was no denying that the songwriting was not as impressive as it had been on the first two records. On the other hand, there were first-rate tunes such as the spooky "The Unknown Soldier," with antiwar lyrics as uncompromisingly forceful as anything the band did, and the compulsively riff-driven "Hello, I Love You," which nonetheless bore an uncomfortably close resemblance to the Kinks' "All Day and All of the Night." The flamenco guitar of "Spanish Caravan," the all-out weirdness of "Not to Touch the Earth" (which was a snippet of a legendary abandoned opus, "The Celebration of the Lizard"), and the menacing closer "Five to One" were also interesting. In fact, time's been fairly kind to the record, which is quite enjoyable and diverse, just not as powerful a full-length statement as the group's best albums.

Richie Unterberger

The Soft Parade
July 1969, Elektra

The weakest studio album recorded with Jim Morrison in the group, partially because their experiments with brass and strings on about half the tracks weren't entirely successful. More to the point, though, this was their weakest set of material, low lights including filler like "Do It" and "Runnin' Blue," a strange bluegrass-soul blend that was a small hit. On the other hand, about half the record is quite good, especially the huge hit "Touch Me" (their most successful integration of orchestration), the vicious hard rock riffs of "Wild Child," the overlooked "Shaman's Blues," and the lengthy title track, a multi-part suite that was one of the band's best attempts to mix rock with poetry. "Tell All the People" and "Wishful Sinful," both penned by Robbie Krieger, were uncharacteristically wistful tunes that became small hits but were not all that good, and not sung very convincingly by Morrison.

Richie Unterberger

Morrison Hotel
1970, Elektra

The Doors returned to crunching, straightforward hard rock on *Morrison Hotel*, an album that, despite yielding no major hit singles, returned them to critical favor with hip listeners. An increasingly bluesy flavor began to color the songwriting and arrangements, especially on the party'n'booze anthem "Roadhouse Blues." Airy mysticism was still present on "Waiting for the Sun," "Queen of the Highway," and "Indian Summer"; "Ship of Fools" and "Land Ho!" struck effective balances between the hard rock arrangements and the narrative reach of the lyrics. "Peace Frog" was the most political and controversial track, documenting the domestic unrest of late-'60s America before unexpectedly segueing into the restful ballad "Blue Sunday." "The Spy," by contrast, was a slow blues that pointed to the direction that would fully blossom on *L.A. Woman*.

Richie Unterberger

L.A. Woman
April 1971, Elektra

The final album with Jim Morrison in the lineup is by far their most blues-oriented, and the singer's poetic ardor is undiminished, though his voice sounds increasingly worn and craggy on some numbers. Actually, some of the straight blues items sound kind of turgid, but that's more than made up for by several cuts that rate among their finest and most disturbing work. The seven-minute title track was a car-chasing classic that celebrated both the glamour and seediness of Los Angeles; the other long cut, the brooding, jazzy "Riders on the Storm," was the group at its most melodic and ominous. It and the far bouncier "Love Her Madly" were hit singles, and "The Changeling" and "L'America" count as some of their better little-heeded album tracks. An uneven but worthy finale from the original quartet.

Richie Unterberger

Perception
November 2006, Rhino

It's hard not to look at the 2006 box set *Perception* without a skeptical eye, since it is not only the third box set of the Doors studio recordings to be released within the course of a decade, it is the second in a row to purport to house the "complete studio recordings" of a group that released six studio albums—and this doesn't count the live sets and hits comps that have appeared during that decade, either. Needless to say, the band has been packaged, repackaged, and reissued more than most, but just because there has been more Doors boxes than necessary doesn't mean that *Perception* lacks value. Indeed, it trumps the 1999 box *The Complete Studio Recordings* in every sense, since it covers the same territory in a set that is better packaged and better-sounding while also offering many more rarities. It also offers brand-new remasters supervised by the surviving band and their original producer Bruce Botnick, highlighted by the first-ever release of the classic debut album at its proper speed; apart from that, the improvements are by and large marginal in terms of the CD audio, but there are also 5.1 surround mixes of each of the albums on the DVD-Audios that accompany each album in this set, which are the primary sonic enticements to those who have already purchased these albums two, three, four times on CD. The bonus material—and each of the albums has bonus tracks, ranging from two cuts on *L.A. Woman* to ten on *Morrison Hotel*—by and large presents songs that have been official releases before (including much of the music from the *Essential Rarities* disc that was included in the 1999 box), but there have been a handful of rarities excavated for this set, including the unheard "Push Push" which has been added to *The Soft Parade*. All this makes *Perception* into what the 1999 box promised to be in its title: the complete recorded works, more or less, and it's better-looking and better-sounding, too. Even so, any fan who has purchased the prior sets would be forgiven if they passed on this otherwise excellent box: no matter how well-done it is, it's hard not to shake the perception that you've bought this all before.

Stephen Thomas Erlewine

Bob Dylan

Bringing It All Back Home
March 1965, Columbia

With *Another Side of Bob Dylan*, Dylan had begun pushing

past folk, and with *Bringing It All Back Home*, he exploded the boundaries, producing an album of boundless imagination and skill. And it's not just that he went electric, either, rocking hard on "Subterranean Homesick Blues," "Maggie's Farm," and "Outlaw Blues"; it's that he's exploding with imagination throughout the record. After all, the music on its second side—the nominal folk songs—derive from the same van-

tage point as the rockers, leaving traditional folk concerns behind and delving deep into the personal. And this isn't just introspection, either, since the surreal paranoia on "It's Alright, Ma (I'm Only Bleeding)" and the whimsical poetry of "Mr. Tambourine Man" are individual, yet not personal. And that's just the tip of the iceberg, really, as he writes uncommonly beautiful love songs ("She Belongs to Me," "Love Minus Zero/No Limit") that sit alongside uncommonly funny fantasias ("On the Road Again," "Bob Dylan's 115th Dream"). This is the point where Dylan eclipses any conventional sense of folk and rewrites the rules of rock, making it safe for personal expression and poetry, not only making words mean as much as the music, but making the music an extension of the words. A truly remarkable album.

Stephen Thomas Erlewine

Highway 61 Revisited
August 1965, Columbia

Taking the first, electric side of *Bringing It All Back Home* to its logical conclusion, Bob Dylan hired a full rock & roll band, featuring guitarist Michael Bloomfield, for *Highway 61 Revisited*. Opening with the epic "Like a Rolling Stone," *Highway 61 Revisited* careens through nine songs that range from reflective folk-rock ("Desolation Row") and blues ("It Takes a Lot to Laugh, It Takes a Train to Cry") to flat-out garage rock ("Tombstone Blues," "From a Buick 6," "Highway 61 Revisited"). Dylan had not only changed his sound, but his persona, trading the folk troubadour for a streetwise, cynical hipster. Throughout the album, he embraces druggy, surreal imagery, which can either have a sense of menace or beauty, and the music reflects that, jumping between soothing melodies to hard, bluesy rock. And that is the most revolutionary thing about *Highway 61 Revisited*—it proved that rock & roll needn't be collegiate and tame in order to be literate, poetic, and complex.

Stephen Thomas Erlewine

Blonde on Blonde
May 1966, Columbia

If *Highway 61 Revisited* played as a garage rock record, the double album *Blonde on Blonde* inverted that sound, blending blues, country, rock, and folk into a wild, careening, and dense sound. Replacing the fiery Michael Bloomfield with the intense, weaving guitar of Robbie Robertson, Bob Dylan led a group comprised of his touring band the Hawks and session musicians through his richest set of songs. *Blonde on Blonde* is an album of enormous depth, providing endless lyrical and musical revelations on each play. Leavening the edginess of *Highway 61* with a sense of the absurd, *Blonde*

on Blonde is comprised entirely of songs driven by inventive, surreal, and witty wordplay, not only on the rockers but also on winding, moving ballads like "Visions of Johanna," "Just Like a Woman," and "Sad Eyed Lady of the Lowlands." Throughout the record, the music matches the inventiveness of the songs, filled with cutting guitar riffs, liquid organ riffs, crisp pianos, and even woozy brass bands ("Rainy Day Women #12 & 35"). It's the culmination of Dylan's electric rock & roll period—he would never release a studio record that rocked this hard, or had such bizarre imagery, ever again.

Stephen Thomas Erlewine

Bob Dylan's Greatest Hits
March 1967, Columbia

Arriving in 1967, *Greatest Hits* does an excellent job of summarizing Dylan's best-known songs from his first seven albums. At just ten songs, it's a little brief, and the song selection may be a little predictable, but that's actually not a bad thing, since this provides a nice sampler for the curious and casual listener, as it boasts standards from "Blowin' in the Wind" to "Like a Rolling Stone." And, for collectors, the brilliant non-LP single "Positively Fourth Street" was added, which provided reason enough for anybody that already owned the original records to pick this up. This has since been supplanted by more exhaustive collections, but as a sampler of Dylan at his absolute peak, this is first-rate.

Stephen Thomas Erlewine

John Wesley Harding
December 1967, Columbia

Bob Dylan returned from exile with *John Wesley Harding*, a quiet, country-tinged album that split dramatically from his previous three. A calm, reflective album, *John Wesley Harding* strips away all of the wilder tendencies of Dylan's rock albums—even

the then-unreleased *Basement Tapes* he made the previous year—but it isn't a return to his folk roots. If anything, the album is his first serious foray into country, but only a handful of songs, such as "I'll Be Your Baby Tonight," are straight country songs. Instead, *John Wesley Harding* is informed by the rustic sound of country, as well as many rural myths, with seemingly simple songs like "All Along the Watchtower," "I Dreamed I Saw St. Augustine," and "The Wicked Messenger" revealing several layers of meaning with repeated plays. Although the lyrics are somewhat enigmatic, the music is simple, direct, and melodic, providing a touchstone for the country-rock revolution that swept through rock in the late '60s.

Stephen Thomas Erlewine

Nashville Skyline
April 1969, Columbia

John Wesley Harding suggested country with its textures and structures, but *Nashville Skyline* was a full-fledged country album, complete with steel guitars and brief, direct songs. It's a warm, friendly album, particularly since Bob Dylan is singing in a previously unheard gentle croon—the sound of his voice is so different it may be disarming upon first listen, but it suits the songs. While there are a handful of lightweight numbers on the record, at its core are several excellent songs—"Lay Lady Lay," "To Be Alone With You," "I Threw It All Away," "Tonight I'll Be Staying Here With You," as well as a duet with Johnny Cash on "Girl From the North Country"—that have become country-rock standards. And there's no discounting that *Nashville Skyline*, arriving in the spring of 1969, established country-rock as a vital force in pop music, as well as a commercially viable genre.

Stephen Thomas Erlewine

New Morning
October 1970, Columbia

Dylan rushed out *New Morning* in the wake of the commercial and critical disaster *Self Portrait*, and the difference between the two albums suggests that its legendary failed predecessor was intentionally flawed. *New Morning* expands on the laid-back country-rock of *John Wesley Harding* and *Nashville Skyline* by adding a more pronounced rock & roll edge. While there are only a couple of genuine classics on the record ("If Not for You," "One More Weekend"), the overall quality is quite high, and many of the songs explore idiosyncratic routes Dylan had previously left untouched, whether it's the jazzy experiments of "Sign on the Window" and "Winterlude," the rambling spoken word piece "If Dogs Run Free" or the Elvis parable "Went to See the Gypsy." Such offbeat songs make *New Morning* a charming, endearing record.

Stephen Thomas Erlewine

Bob Dylan's Greatest Hits, Vol. 2
November 1971, Columbia

Where Dylan's first *Greatest Hits* took its title literally, *Greatest Hits, Vol. 2* is a greatest-hits album only in the loosest sense of the term. While the double album does contain several genuine hits—"Lay Lady Lay," "Tonight I'll Be Staying Here With You," the non-LP "Watching the River Flow"—it is largely comprised of album tracks which became classics, either through Dylan's own version or through covers. These include "Don't Think Twice, It's All Right," "All I Really Want to Do," "My Back Pages," "Maggie's Farm," "She Belongs to Me," "If Not for You," and "Just Like Tom Thumb's Blues," among many others. There are also a number of rarities scattered throughout the 21 songs, including a live version of "Tomorrow Is a Long Time" from 1963, a live take of "The Mighty Quinn (Quinn, the Eskimo)," and the *Basement Tapes* songs "I Shall Be Released," "Down in the Flood," and "You Ain't Goin' Nowhere." While some of the cuts may not be immediately familiar to some listeners, *Greatest Hits, Vol. 2* in many ways is a more accurate picture of the depth and breadth of Dylan's talents, making it an excellent introduction. And it's not just for casual fans, because the rarities and sequencing are revealing for even devoted

Dylan fans. [*Greatest Hits, Vol. 2* was reissued with 24-bit remastering in the summer of 1999.]

Stephen Thomas Erlewine

Planet Waves
January 1974, Columbia

Reteaming with the Band, Bob Dylan winds up with an album that recalls *New Morning* more than *The Basement Tapes*, since *Planet Waves* is given to a relaxed intimate tone—all the more appropriate for a collection of modest songs about domestic life. As such, it may seem a little anticlimactic since it has none of the wildness of the best Dylan and Band music of the '60s—just an approximation of the homespun rusticness. Considering that the record was knocked out in the course of three days, its unassuming nature shouldn't be a surprise, and sometimes it's as much a flaw as a virtue, since there are several cuts that float into the ether. Still, it is a virtue in places, as there are moments—"On a Night Like This," "Something There Is About You," the lovely "Forever Young"—where it just gels, almost making the diffuse nature of the rest of the record acceptable.

Stephen Thomas Erlewine

Before the Flood
June 1974, Columbia

Bob Dylan and the Band both needed the celebrated reunion tour of 1974, since Dylan's fortunes had been floundering since *Self Portrait* and the Band stumbled with 1971's *Cahoots*. The tour, with its attendant publicity, definitely returned both artists to center stage, and it definitely succeeded, breaking box office records and earning great reviews. *Before the Flood*, a double-album souvenir of the tour, suggests that these were generally dynamic shows, but not because they were reveling in the past, but because Dylan was fighting the nostalgia of his audience—nostalgia, it must be noted, that was promoted as the very reason behind these shows. Yet that's what gives this music such kick—Dylan reworks, rearranges, reinterprets these songs in ways that are still disarming, years after its initial release. He could only have performed interpretations this radical with a group as sympathetic, knowing of his traits as the band, whose own recordings here are respites from the storm. And this is a storm—the sound of a great rocker, surprising his band and audience by tearing through his greatest songs in a manner that might not be comforting, but it guarantees it to be one of the best live albums of its time. Ever, maybe.

Stephen Thomas Erlewine

Blood on the Tracks
January 1975, Columbia

Following on the heels of an album where he repudiated his past with his greatest backing band, *Blood on the Tracks* finds Bob Dylan, in a way, retreating to the past, recording a largely quiet, acoustic-based album. But this is hardly nostalgia—this is the sound of an artist returning to his strengths, what feels most familiar, as he accepts a traumatic situation, namely the breakdown of his marriage. This is an album alternately bitter, sorrowful, regretful, and peaceful, easily the closest he ever came to wearing his emotions on his sleeve. That's not to say that it's an explicitly confessional record, since many songs are riddles or allegories, yet the warmth of the music makes it feel that way. The original version of the album was even quieter—first takes of "Idiot Wind" and "Tangled Up in Blue," available on *The Bootleg Series, Vols. 1-3*, are hushed and quiet (excised verses are quoted in the liner notes, but not heard on the record)—but *Blood on the Tracks* remains an intimate, revealing affair since these harsher takes let his anger surface the way his sadness does elsewhere. As such, it's an affecting, unbearably poignant record, not because it's a glimpse into his soul, but because the songs are remarkably clear-eyed *and* sentimental, lovely and melancholy at once. And, in a way, it's best that he was backed with studio musicians here, since the professional, understated backing lets the songs and emotion stand at the forefront. Dylan made albums more influential than this, but he never made one better.

Stephen Thomas Erlewine

The Basement Tapes
June 1975, Columbia

The official release of *The Basement Tapes*—which were first heard on a 1968 bootleg called *The Great White Wonder*—plays with history somewhat, as Robbie Robertson overemphasizes the Band's status in the sessions, making them out to be equally active to Dylan, adding in demos not cut at the sessions and overdubbing their recordings to flesh them out. As many bootlegs (most notably the complete five-disc series) reveal, this isn't entirely true and that the Band were nowhere near as active as Dylan, but that ultimately is a bit like nit-picking, since the music here (including the Band's) is astonishingly good. The party line on *The Basement Tapes* is that it is Americana, as Dylan and the Band pick up the weirdness inherent in old folk, country, and blues tunes, but it transcends mere historical arcana by being lively, humorous, full-bodied performances. Dylan never sounded as loose, nor was he ever as funny as he is here, and this positively revels in its weird, wild character. For all the apparent antecedents—and the allusions are sly and obvious in equal measures—this is truly Dylan's show, as he majestically evokes old myths and creates new ones, resulting in a crazy quilt of blues, humor, folk, tall tales, inside jokes, and rock. The Band pretty much pick up where Dylan left off, even singing a couple of his tunes, but they play it a little straight, on both their rockers and ballads. Not a bad thing at all, since this actually winds up providing context for the wild, mercurial brilliance of Dylan's work—and, taken together, the results (especially in this judiciously compiled form; expert song selection, even if there's a bit too much Band) rank among the greatest American music ever made.

Stephen Thomas Erlewine

Desire
January 1976, Columbia

If *Blood on the Tracks* was an unapologetically intimate affair, *Desire* is unwieldy and messy, the deliberate work of a collective. And while Bob Dylan directly addresses his crumbling relationship with his wife, Sara, on the final track, *Desire* is hardly as personal as its predecessor, finding Dylan returning to topical songwriting and folk tales for the core of the record. It's all over the map, as far as songwriting goes, and so is it musically, capturing

Dylan at the beginning of the Rolling Thunder Revue era, which was more notable for its chaos than its music. And, so it's only fitting that *Desire* fits that description as well, as it careens between surging folk-rock, Mideastern dirges, skipping pop, and epic narratives. It's little surprise that *Desire* doesn't quite gel, yet it retains its own character—really, there's no other place where Dylan tried as many different styles, as many weird detours, as he does here. And, there's something to be said for its rambling, sprawling character, which has a charm of its own. Even so, the record would have been assisted by a more consistent set of songs; there are some masterpieces here, though: "Hurricane" is the best-known, but the effervescent "Mozambique" is Dylan at his breeziest, "Sara" at his most nakedly emotional, and "Isis" is one of his very best songs of the '70s, a hypnotic, contemporized spin on a classic fable. This may not add up to a masterpiece, but it does result in one of his most fascinating records of the '70s and '80s—more intriguing, lyrically and musically, than most of his latter-day affairs.

Stephen Thomas Erlewine

Street Legal
June 1978, Columbia

Arriving after the twin peaks of *Blood on the Tracks* and *Desire*, *Street Legal* seemed like a disappointment upon its 1978 release, and it still seems a little subpar, years after its release. Perhaps that's because Bob Dylan was uncertain himself, not just writing a set of songs with no connecting themes, but replacing the sprawl of the Rolling Thunder Revue with a slick, professional big band, featuring a horn section and several backing vocalists. The interesting thing about this is that the music and slick production don't jibe with the songs, which are as dense as anything Dylan had written since before his motorcycle accident. So, *Street Legal* becomes an interesting dichotomy, filled with songs that deserve close attention but recorded in arrangements that discourage such listening. As such, *Street Legal* is fascinating just for that reason—in another setting, these are songs that would have been hailed as near-masterpieces, but covered in gloss, they seem strange. Consequentially, it's not surprising that there are factions of Dylanphiles that find this worth the time, while just as many consider it a missed opportunity.

Stephen Thomas Erlewine

Eagles

Eagles
June 1972, Asylum

Balance is the key element of the Eagles' self-titled debut album, a collection that contains elements of rock & roll, folk, and country, overlaid by vocal harmonies alternately suggestive of doo wop, the Beach Boys, and the Everly Brothers. If the group kicks up its heels on rockers like "Chug All Night," "Nightingale," and "Tryin'," it is equally convincing on ballads like "Most of Us Are Sad" and "Train Leaves Here This Morning." The album is also balanced among its members, who trade off on lead vocal chores and divide the songwriting such that Glenn Frey, Bernie Leadon, and Randy Meisner all get three writing or co-writing credits. (Fourth member Don Henley, with only one co-writing credit and two lead vocals, falls a little behind, while Jackson Browne, Gene Clark, and Jack Tempchin also figure in the writing credits.) The album's overall balance is worth keeping in mind because it produced three Top 40 hit singles (all of which turned up on the massively popular *Eagles: Their Greatest Hits 1971-1975)* that do not reflect that balance. "Take It Easy" and "Peaceful Easy Feeling" are similar-sounding mid-tempo folk-rock tunes sung by Frey that express the same sort of laid-back philosophy, as indicated by the word "easy" in both titles, while "Witchy Woman," a Henley vocal and co-composition, initiates the band's career-long examination of supernatural evil females. These are the songs one remembers from *Eagles*, and they look forward to the eventual dominance of the band by Frey and Henley. But the complete album from which they come belongs as much to Leadon's country-steeped playing and singing and to Meisner's melodic rock & roll feel, which, on the release date, made it seem a more varied and consistent effort than it did later, when the singles had become overly familiar.

William Ruhlmann

Desperado
April 1973, Asylum

If Don Henley was the sole member of the Eagles underrepresented on their debut album, *Eagles*, with only two lead vocals and one co-songwriting credit, he made up for it on their follow-up, the "concept" album *Desperado*. The concept had to do with Old West outlaws, but it had no specific narrative. On *Eagles*, the group had already begun to marry itself to a Southwest sound and lyrical references, from the Indian-style introduction of "Witchy Woman" to the Winslow, AZ, address in "Take It Easy." All of this became more overt on *Desperado*, and it may be that Henley, who hailed from Northeast Texas, had the greatest affinity for the subject matter. In any case, he had co-writing credits on eight of the 11 selections and sang such key tracks as "Doolin-Dalton" and the title song. What would become recognizable as Henley's lyrical touch was apparent on those songs, which bore a serious, world-weary tone. Henley had begun co-writing with Glenn Frey, and they contributed the album's strongest material, which included the first single, "Tequila Sunrise," and "Desperado" (strangely never released as a single). But where *Eagles* seemed deliberately to balance the band's many musical styles and the talents of the band's members, *Desperado*, despite its overarching theme, often seemed a collection of disparate tracks—"Out of Control" was a raucous rocker, while "Desperado" was a painfully slow ballad backed by strings—with other bandmembers' contributions tacked on rather than integrated. Randy Meisner was down to two co-writing credits and one lead vocal ("Certain Kind of Fool"), while Bernie Leadon's two songs, "Twenty-One" and "Bitter Creek," seemed to come from a different record entirely. The result was an album that was simultaneously more ambitious and serious-minded than its predecessor and also slighter and less consistent.

William Ruhlmann

On the Border
March 1974, Asylum

The Eagles began recording their third album in England with producer Glyn Johns, as they had their first two albums, but abandoned the sessions after completing two acceptable tracks. Johns, it is said, tended to emphasize the group's country elements and its harmonies, while the band, in particular Glenn Frey and Don Henley, wanted to take more of a hard rock direction. They reconvened with a new producer, Bill Szymczyk, who had produced artists like B.B. King and, more significantly, Joe Walsh. But the resulting album is not an outright rock effort by any means. Certainly, Frey and Henley got what they wanted with "Already Gone," the lead-off track, which introduces new band member Don Felder as one part of the twin guitar solo that recalls the Allman Brothers Band; "James Dean," a rock & roll song on the order of "Your Mama Don't Dance"; and "Good Day in Hell," which is strongly reminiscent of Joe Walsh songs like "Rocky Mountain Way." But the album also features the usual mixture of styles typical of an Eagles album. For example, "Midnight Flyer," sung by Randy Meisner, is modern bluegrass; "My Man" is Bernie Leadon's country-rock tribute to the recently deceased Gram Parsons; and "Ol' 55" is one of the group's well-done covers of a tune by a singer-songwriter labelmate, in this case Tom Waits. The title track, meanwhile, points the band in a new R&B direction that was later pursued more fully. Like most successful groups, the Eagles combined many different elements, and their third album, which looked back to their earlier work and anticipated their later work, was a transitional effort that combined even more styles than most of their records did.

William Ruhlmann

One of These Nights
June 1975, Asylum

The Eagles recorded their albums relatively quickly in their first years of existence, their albums succeeding each other by less than a year. *One of These Nights*, their fourth album, was released in June 1975, more than 14 months after its predecessor. Anticipation had been heightened by the belated chart-topping success of the third album's "The Best of My Love"; taking a little more time, the band generated more original material, and that material was more polished. More than ever, the Eagles seemed to be a vehicle for Don Henley (six co-writing credits) and Glenn Frey (five), but at the same time Randy Meisner was more audible than ever, his two lead vocals including one of the album's three hit singles, "Take It to the Limit," and Bernie Leadon had two showcases, among them the cosmic-cowboy instrumental "Journey of the Sorcerer" (later used as the theme music for the British television series *The Hitchhiker's Guide to the Galaxy*). Nevertheless, it was the team of Henley and Frey that stood out, starting with the title track, a number one single, which had more of an R&B—even disco—sound than anything the band had attempted previously, and continuing through the band's Western swing of "Hollywood Waltz" to "Lyin' Eyes," one of Frey's patented folk-rock shuffles, which became another major hit. *One of These Nights* was the culmination of the blend of rock, country, and folk styles the Eagles had been making since their start; there wasn't much that was new, just the same sorts of things done better than they had been before. In particular, a lyrical stance—knowing and disillusioned, but desperately hopeful—had evolved, and the musical arrangements were tighter and more purposeful. The result was the Eagles' best-realized and most popular album so far.

William Ruhlmann

Their Greatest Hits (1971–1975)
February 1976, Elektra

On their first four albums, the Eagles were at pains to demonstrate that they were a group of at least near-equals, each getting a share of the songwriting credits and lead vocals. But this compilation drawn from those albums, comprising the group's nine Top 40 hits plus "Desperado," demonstrates that this evenhandedness did not extend to singles—as far as those go, the Eagles belong to Glenn Frey and Don Henley. The tunes are melodic, and the arrangements—full of strummed acoustic guitars over a rock rhythm section often playing a shuffle beat, topped by tenor-dominated harmonies—are immediately engaging. There is also a lyrical consistency to the songs, which often concern romantic uncertainties in an atmosphere soaked in intoxicants. The narrators of the songs usually seem exhausted, if not satiated, and the loping rhythms are appropriate to these impressions. All of which means that, unlike the albums from which they come, these songs make up a collection consistent in mood and identity, which may help explain why *Their Greatest Hits (1971-1975)* works so much better than the band's previous discs and practically makes them redundant. No wonder it was such a big hit out of the box, topping the charts and becoming the first album ever certified platinum. Still, there must be more to it, since the album wasn't just a big hit, but one of the biggest ever, becoming one of the very few discs to cross the threshold of 20 million copies and competing for the title of best-selling album of all time. There may be no explaining that, really, except to note that this was the pervasive music of the first half of the 1970s, and somehow it never went away.

William Ruhlmann

Hotel California
December 1976, Asylum

The Eagles took 18 months between their fourth and fifth albums, reportedly spending eight months in the studio recording *Hotel California*. The album was also their first to be made without Bernie Leadon, who had given the band much of its country flavor, and with rock guitarist Joe Walsh. As a result, the album marks a major leap for the Eagles from their earlier work, as well as a stylistic shift toward mainstream rock. An even more important aspect, however, is the emergence of Don Henley as the band's dominant voice, both as a singer and a lyricist. On the six songs to which he contributes, Henley sketches a thematic statement that begins by using California as a metaphor for a dark, surreal world of dissipation; comments on the ephemeral nature of success and the attraction of excess; branches out into romantic disappointment; and finally sketches a broad, pessimistic history of America that borders on nihilism. Of course, the lyrics kick in some time after one has appreciated the album's music, which marks a peak in the Eagles' playing. Early on, the group couldn't rock convincingly, but the rhythm section of Henley and Meisner has finally solidified, and the electric guitar work of Don Felder and Joe Walsh has arena-rock heft. In the early part of their career, the Eagles never seemed to get a sound big enough for their ambitions; after changes in producer and personnel, as well as a noticeable growth in creativity, *Hotel California* unveiled what seemed almost like a whole new band. It was a band that could be bombastic, but also one that made music worthy of the later tag of "classic rock," music appropriate for the arenas and stadiums the band was playing. The result was the Eagles' biggest-selling regular album release, and one of the most successful rock albums ever.

William Ruhlmann

The Long Run
September 1979, Asylum

Three years in the making (which was considered an eternity in the '70s), the Eagles' follow-up to the massively successful, critically acclaimed *Hotel California* was a major disappointment, even though it sold several million copies and threw off three hit singles. Those singles, in fact, provide some insight

into the record. "Heartache Tonight" was an old-fashioned rock & roll song sung by Glenn Frey, while "I Can't Tell You Why" was a delicate ballad by Timothy B. Schmit, the band's newest member. Only "The Long Run," a conventional pop/rock tune with a Stax Records R&B flavor, bore the stamp and vocal signature of Don Henley, who had largely taken the reins of the band on *Hotel California*. Henley also dominated *The Long Run*, getting co-writing credits on nine of the ten songs, singing five lead vocals, and sharing another two with Frey. This time around, however, Henley's contributions were for the most part painfully slight. Only "The Long Run" and the regret-filled closing song, "The Sad Café," showed any of his usual craftsmanship. The album was dominated by second-rank songs like "The Disco Strangler," "King of Hollywood," and "Teenage Jail" that sounded like they couldn't have taken three hours much less three years to come up with. (Joe Walsh's "In the City" was up to his usual standard, but it may not even have been an Eagles recording, having appeared months earlier on the soundtrack to *The Warriors*, where it was credited as a Walsh solo track.) Amazingly, *The Long Run* reportedly was planned as a double album before being truncated to a single disc. If these were the keepers, what could the rejects have sounded like?

William Ruhlmann

Dave Edmunds

The Anthology (1968-1990)
April 1993, Rhino

A double-disc set covering Dave Edmunds' entire career, the 41-song *Anthology (1968-1990)* does a fine job of capturing his musical evolution, even if it is not without its faults. To a certain extent, *Anthology* is a definitive compilation, since it begins with Love Sculpture's infamous "Sabre Dance" and runs through his early solo recordings ("I Hear You Knocking"), before hitting Rockpile ("Trouble Boys," "Deborah," "Girls Talk," "Crawling from the Wreckage," "Queen of Hearts") and Edmunds' overly synthesized recordings with Jeff Lynne, adding a couple of rarities like the excellent Carlene Carter duet "Baby Ride Easy" along the way. However, the track selection is uneven, including far too many Love Sculpture songs and Lynne collaborations, which tends to dilute the spirit of Edmunds' best music. Still, *Anthology* is the best overview of Edmunds' entire career, even if the single-disc *The Best of Dave Edmunds* may be a better, more consistent introduction for many listeners.

Stephen Thomas Erlewine

The Electric Flag

Old Glory: The Best of Electric Flag
October 1995, Columbia/Legacy

A perfect single-disc anthology of a band with what seemed

like unlimited potential, but in reality limited output and few quality studio recordings that accurately reflected its combined musicianship. Like its musical cousins, Blood, Sweat & Tears, Electric Flag was one of the first bands to combine rock with big-band jazz swagger. This concept and the fact that Electric Flag contained Michael Bloomfield on electric guitar was reason enough for the band to be one of the most anticipated aggregations of the era. Yet many of the recordings show off the band's limitations like a sore thumb. A certain over-baked production and arrangement feel permeates many of the fine songs from the band's debut (*A Long Time Comin'*, included in its entirety), such as "Groovin' Is Easy" and "She Should Have Just," rendering it somewhat top-heavy. Yet, despite these moments of excess, the band could also perform modern blues-rock like no other and, for these tracks alone, *Old Glory* is worth purchasing. "Texas" and "Goin' Down Slow" (an outtake from the first album sessions) combine the group's real strengths with a supple energy that is positively beguiling. Between Buddy Miles' drumming and vocals, Bloomfield's unparalleled skill on electric guitar, Barry Goldberg's keyboards, and Nick Gravenites' songwriting and vocals lay true magic. The fact that these moments are few and far between can make the disc a bit frustrating but, when the listener gets into cuts such as the aforementioned "Texas" and "You Don't Realize," it's well worth the wait. The five songs from the post-Bloomfield version of the group are nearly disposable, but a pair of earlier, live cuts from the band's debut at the Monterey Pop Festival (with Bloomfield) save the end of the collection. Although Electric Flag was troubled, chaotic, and disorganized, *Old Glory* proves that the band was important and had positively sterling moments, despite its foibles.

Matthew Greenwald

Electric Light Orchestra

Electric Light Orchestra
1971, Harvest

Although ELO quickly became Jeff Lynne's baby, it was launched as a collaboration between Lynne and his bandmates in the Move, multi-instrumentalist Roy Wood, and drummer Bev Bevan. Indeed, the label on ELO's first album reads "Move Enterprises Ltd. presents the services of the Electric Light Orchestra," and most histories claim that the initial idea for the spin-off group combining rock and classical music was Wood's, not Lynne's. Wood and Lynne split the songwriting duties on *Electric Light Orchestra*, much as they did on late-period Move albums, but it seems like their visions of what ELO was were widely divergent. Wood's songs are clearly more classically influenced, with the string and horn sections driving the songs rather than merely coloring them, as they do on Lynne's tunes. The difference between Wood's baroque "Look at Me Now" and Lynne's hard rocking "10538 Overture" is obvious, and Lynne never wrote anything as purely classical as Wood's "The Battle of Marston Moor (July 2nd, 1644)" in his entire career. (The Gershwin-like

piano jazz of "Manhattan Rumble (49th Street Massacre)" is Lynne's equivalent piece, and suggests an intriguing avenue he unfortunately never explored further.) This dichotomy makes *Electric Light Orchestra* in some ways much more interesting than later ELO albums. When Wood left to form Wizzard after the release of this album, the tension generated by that clear difference between his and Lynne's songwriting styles was gone. Later ELO albums were much more commercially successful, but they were also considerably more stylistically attenuated. As good as they are, all of the later ELO albums sound pretty much exactly alike. *Electric Light Orchestra* sounds like nothing either Jeff Lynne or Roy Wood did before or after, and therein lies its fascination.

Stewart Mason

No Answer
1972, Jet

Electric Light Orchestra's debut album is an astonishing creation in its own right, but neophyte listeners should be aware that it bears very little resemblance to the sound for which ELO would become known on its subsequent records. *No Answer*, as it ended up being called in America through a miscommunication with ELO's U.S. label, is a minimalist work by comparison with anything on the band's later albums. The core trio of Roy Wood, Jeff Lynne, and Bev Bevan, augmented by one horn player and a violinist, approaches the music alternately like a hard rock band attacking a song and a string ensemble playing a chamber piece. Filled with surprisingly loose playing and sounds throughout, and with a psychedelic aura hovering over most of the music, *No Answer* is unique in ELO's output. Written and sung by Lynne, "10538 Overture" is the opener and the best song on the album. Wood's "Look at Me Now," by comparison, plays like a sweet, melodic follow-up to "Beautiful Daughter" from the Move's *Shazam*, with some digressions on the oboe and a cello and violin subbing for the guitars. The rest moves from period-style popular songs to strangely cinematic conceptual pieces, on which the rock elements almost disappear in favor of quasi-classical playing by all concerned. A beautiful acoustic guitar workout by Wood, "1st Movement" also features the song's composer on the oboe, while "Mr. Radio," an exercise in 1920s nostalgia written and sung by Lynne, digresses for a moment into 1940s-style classical piano pyrotechnics. His "Whisper in the Night" ends the album with a lean and textured acoustic sound that, ironically, disappeared from ELO's repertory when he exited the lineup following these sessions.

Bruce Eder

On the Third Day
December 1973, Jet

Electric Light Orchestra's third album showed a marked advancement, with a fuller, more cohesive sound from the band as a whole and major improvements in Jeff Lynne's singing and songwriting. This is where the band took on its familiar sound, Lynne's voice suddenly showing an attractive expressiveness reminiscent of John Lennon in his early solo years, and also sporting a convincing white British soulful quality that was utterly lacking earlier. The group also plugged the holes that made its work seem so close to being ragged on those earlier records. "Showdown" and "Ma-Ma-Ma Belle" (the latter featuring Marc Bolan on double lead guitar with Lynne) became AM radio fixtures while "Daybreaker" became a concert opener for the group and, along with "In the Hall of the Mountain King," kept the group's FM/art rock credentials in order.

Bruce Eder

Eldorado
October 1974, Jet

This is the album where Jeff Lynne finally found the sound he'd wanted since co-founding Electric Light Orchestra three years earlier. Up to this point, most of the group's music had been self-contained—Lynne, Richard Tandy, et al., providing whatever was needed, vocally or instrumentally, even if it meant overdubbing their work layer upon layer. Lynne saw the limitations of this process, however, and opted for the presence of an orchestra—it was only 30 pieces, but the result was a much richer musical palette than the group had ever had to work with, and their most ambitious and successful record up to that time. Indeed, *Eldorado* was strongly reminiscent in some ways of *Sgt. Pepper's Lonely Hearts Club Band*. Not that it could ever have the same impact or be as distinctive, but it had its feet planted in so many richly melodic and varied musical traditions, yet made it all work in a rock context, that it did recall the Beatles classic. It was a very romantic work, especially on the opening "Eldorado Overture," which was steeped in a wistful 1920s/1930s notion of popular fantasy (embodied in movies and novels like James Hilton's *Lost Horizon* and Somerset Maugham's *The Razor's Edge*) about disillusioned seekers. It boasted Lynne's best single up to that time, "Can't Get It Out of My Head," which most radio listeners could never get out of their respective heads, either. The integration of the orchestra would become even more thorough on future albums, but *Eldorado* was notable for mixing the band and orchestra (and a choir) in ways that did no violence to the best elements of both.

Bruce Eder

Face the Music
October 1975, Jet

Electric Light Orchestra's more modest follow-up to *Eldorado* is a very solid album, if not as bold or unified. It was also their first recorded at Musicland in Munich, which became Jeff Lynne's preferred venue for cutting records. At the time, he was also generating songs at a breakneck pace and had perfected the majestic, quasi-Beatles-type style (sort of high-wattage *Magical Mystery Tour*) introduced two albums earlier. The sound is stripped down a bit on *Face the Music*, Louis Clark's orchestral contributions generally more subdued than on *Eldorado*, even when they compete with the band, as on "Strange Magic." The soulful "Evil Woman" was one of the most respectable chart hits of its era, and one of the best songs that Lynne ever wrote (reportedly in 30 minutes), while "Strange Magic" showed off his writing in a more ethereal vein. "One Summer Dream," which is written in a similar mode, also has a touchingly wistful mood about it but is a somewhat lackluster finale compared to the albums that preceded and followed this one. The requisite rock & roll number, "Poker," is a quicker tempo than anything previously heard from the band, the guitar is pumped up louder than ever. And "Down Home Town," an experiment in achieving a country & western sound, is fresh at this point and more interesting than the equivalent material of *Out of the Blue*.

Bruce Eder

A New World Record
November 1976, Jet

Jeff Lynne reportedly regards this album and its follow-up, *Out of the Blue*, as the high points in the band's history. One might be better off opting for *A New World Record* over its successor, however, as a more modest-sized creation chock full of superb songs that are produced even better. Opening with the opulently orchestrated "Tightrope," which heralds the perfect production found throughout this album,

A New World Record contains seven of the best songs ever to come out of the group. The Beatles influence is present, to be sure, but developed to a very high degree of sophistication and on Lynne's own terms, rather than being imitative of specific songs. "Telephone Line" might be the best Lennon-McCartney collaboration that never was, lyrical and soaring in a way that manages  to echo elements of *Revolver* and the Beatles without ever mimicking them. The original LP's second side opened with "So Fine," which seems like the perfect pop synthesis of guitar, percussion, and orchestral sounds, embodying precisely what Lynne had first set out to do with Roy Wood at the moment ELO was conceived. From there, the album soars through stomping rock numbers like "Livin' Thing" and "Do Ya," interspersed with lyrical pieces like "Above the Clouds" (which makes striking use of pizzicato bass strings).

Bruce Eder

Out of the Blue
November 1977, Jet

The last ELO album to make a major impact on popular music, *Out of the Blue* was of a piece with its lavishly produced predecessor, *A New World Record*, but it's a much more mixed bag as an album. For starters, it was a double LP, a format that has proved daunting to all but a handful of rock artists, and was no less so here. The songs were flowing fast and freely from Jeff Lynne at the time, however, and well more than half of what is here is very solid, at least as songs if not necessarily as recordings. "Sweet Talkin' Woman" and "Turn to Stone" are among the best songs in the group's output, and much of the rest is very entertaining. The heavy sound of the orchestra, however, as well as the layer upon layer of vocal overdubs, often seem out of place. All in all, the group was trying too hard to generate a substantial-sounding double LP, complete with a suite, "Concerto for a Rainy Day." The latter is the nadir of the album, an effort at conceptual rock that seemed archaic even in 1977. Another chunk is filled up with what might best be called art rock mood music ("The Whale"), before you finally get to the relief of a basic rocker like "Birmingham Blues." Even here, the group couldn't leave well enough alone—rather than ending it on that note, they had to finish the album with "Wild West Hero," a piece of ersatz movie music that adds nothing to what you've heard over the previous 65 minutes. In its defense, *Out of the Blue* was massively popular and did become the centerpiece of a huge worldwide tour that earned the group status as a major live attraction for a time. [*Out of the Blue* was reissued in 2007 as a *30th Anniversary Edition* with new photos, liner notes, and three bonus tracks, including "The Quick and the Daft," "Latitude 88 North," and a home demo of "Wild West Hero."]

Bruce Eder

Strange Magic: The Best of Electric Light Orchestra
April 1995, Epic Associated/Legacy

ELO's smart blend of pop and rock with modernly

orchestrated classical music flourished throughout the '70s and '80s, since their sound was one of a kind. Plush arrangements that drowned themselves in bright synthesizers and vibrant guitar gave way to a brand new type of music, giving the Electric Light Orchestra a distinguished setting atop the vast rock & roll mantle. *Strange Magic* is a two-CD set of their most illustrious songs from their lengthy career. Every one of their charted hits, except three, appear here, leaving out "I'm Alive," "All Over The World," and the famed "Xanadu" with Olivia Newton John. These deletions aside, this generous 29-song compilation is a splendid cross-section of the group. The first disc is highlighted by the eight-plus minutes of "Roll Over Beethoven," which combines their trademarked classical and rock sound, and the guitar driven allure of "Ma-Ma-Ma Belle" showcases their edginess. ELO's most gracious offering, the beautiful "Can't Get It Out of My Head," appears here as well, with its grandeur stemming from its exquisite string work. The synth-saturated "Strange Magic" is one of their most colorful songs, and "Evil Woman" has Jeff Lynne showing off his concealed yet masterful voice. The second disc begins to show their drift into disco, with the keyboards front and center on "Shine a Little Love" along with the computerized texture of both "Turn to Stone" and "Sweet Talkin' Woman." The wispy synthesized tinkle of "Confusion" is a nice addition, bringing their domination of electric music to its full capacity. ELO's glide into the '80s found them playing more rock-infused music, relying on the keyboards a little less. Songs like "Hold on Tight," with its slippery rhythm, and the '60s-tinged sound of "Rock 'n' Roll Is King" proved that Lynne could pump out amiable rock tunes that befriended radio in a new decade. *Strange Magic* sums up this innovative group's musical career with an abundant amount of hits, bettered only by the box set.

Mike DeGagne

Emerson, Lake & Palmer

Emerson, Lake & Palmer
1970, Rhino

Lively, ambitious, almost entirely successful debut album, made up of keyboard-dominatedinstrumentals ("The Barbarian," "Three Fates") and romantic ballads ("Lucky Man") showcasing all three members' very daunting talents. This album, which reached the Top 20 in America and got to number four in England, showcased the group at its least pretentious and most musically—with the exception of a few moments on "Three Fates" and perhaps "Take a Pebble," there isn't much excess, and there is a lot of impressive musicianship here. "Take a Pebble" might have passed for a Moody Blues track of the era but for the fact that none of the Moody Blues' keyboard men could solo like Keith Emerson. Even here, in a relatively balanced collection of material, the album shows the beginnings of a dark, savage, imposingly gothic edge that had scarcely been seen before in so-called "art rock," mostly courtesy of Emerson's larger-than-life organ and synthesizer attacks. Greg Lake's beautifully sung, deliberately archaic "Lucky Man" had a brush with success on FM radio, and

Carl Palmer became the idol of many thousands of would-be drummers based on this one album (especially for "Three Fates" and "Tank"), but Emerson emerged as the overpowering talent here for much of the public.

Bruce Eder

Tarkus
June 1971, Rhino

Emerson, Lake & Palmer's 1970 eponymous LP was only a rehearsal. It hit hard because of the novelty of the act (allegedly the first supergroup in rock history), but felt more like a collection of individual efforts and ideas than a collective work. All doubts were dissipated by the release of *Tarkus* in 1971. Side one of the original LP is occupied by the 21-minute title epic track, beating both Genesis' "Supper's Ready" and Yes' "Close to the Edge" by a year. Unlike the latter group's cut-and-paste technique to obtain long suites, "Tarkus" is a thoroughly written, focused piece of music. It remains among the Top Ten classic tracks in progressive rock history. Because of the strength of side one, the material on the album's second half has been quickly forgotten—with one good reason: it doesn't match the strength of its counterpart—but "Bitches Crystal" and "A Time and a Place" make two good prog rock tracks, the latter being particularly rocking. "Jeremy Bender" is the first in a series of honky tonk-spiced, Far-West-related songs. This one and the rock & roll closer "Are You Ready Eddy?" are the only two tracks worth throwing away. Otherwise *Tarkus* makes a very solid album, especially to the ears of prog rock fans—no Greg Lake acoustic ballads, no lengthy jazz interludes. More accomplished than the trio's first album, but not quite as polished as *Brain Salad Surgery*, *Tarkus* is nevertheless a must-have.

François Couture

Pictures at an Exhibition
January 1972, Rhino

Pictures at an Exhibition was one of the seminal documents of the progressive rock era, a record that made its way into the collections of millions of high-school kids who never heard of composer Modest Mussorgsky and knew nothing of Russia's Nationalist "Five" or artist/architect Victor Hartmann, whose work was the inspiration for Mussorgsky. Chronologically, it was Emerson, Lake & Palmer's third LP release (they didn't regard it as an "official" album, as it was comprised of only part of a longer live performance), but for a lot of teenagers who'd missed out on the trio's self-titled debut album or resisted the unfamiliarity of *Tarkus*, *Pictures*—which was budget-priced in its original LP release in England and America—with its bracing live ambience and blazing pyrotechnics, was the album that put the group over, and did it with exactly the same kids who turned Jethro Tull's *Aqualung* and *Thick as a Brick* and Yes' *Fragile* into standard-issue accouterments of teenage suburban life. And, indeed, like the Tull and Yes albums, it worked on several levels that allowed widely divergent audiences to embrace it—with the added stimulus of certain controlled substances, it teased the brain with its mix of melody and heavy rock, and for anyone with some musical knowledge, serious or casual, it was a sufficiently bold use of Mussorgsky's original to stimulate hours of delightful listening. It wasn't the first treatment of a classical piece in this manner by any means—Keith Emerson had done several previously with his earlier group the Nice—but it was the first to reach a mass audience or get heavy radio play (at least of excerpts), and introduced the notion of "classical rock" to millions of listeners, including the classical community, most of whose members regarded this record as something akin to an armed assault. Those with less hidebound sensibilities appreciated Emerson's rollicking and delightful

"Blues Variations"—which bridged the gap between *Tarkus* and *Trilogy*—and Greg Lake's lyrical adaptations of "Promenade," "The Sage," and "The Great Gates of Kiev." It does some violence to Mussorgsky in the process, but is also the most concise, energetic, and well-realized live release in ELP's catalog, the hall small enough to capture the finer nuances of the playing by all three members of the trio, and especially the muscular bass work by Lake that keeps pushing the performance forward. It was great fun (an element missing from a good deal of progressive rock) in 1972, and it's still fun in 2005. It also made a fairly compelling case for adapting classical pieces in this way—ELP would later succeed with adaptations of works by Aaron Copland and Alberto Ginastera, among others, but this would be the longest such work to find mass listenership, sufficient so that in the late '80s there would be a legitimate classical organ arrangement put out by the Dorian label that referred to ELP's rendition as its linear predecessor. The early-'70s live sound is a little crude by today's standards, but the various CD upgrades from Rhino, Sanctuary, and Japanese WEA have given the recording a close, powerful sound that captures the tightness of the playing (drummer Carl Palmer is especially good) and makes up for any sonic inadequacies. Emerson is the dominant musical personality here, but Lake (who also gets to play some classical guitar) and Palmer get the spotlight more than enough to prevent it from being a pure keyboard showcase.

Bruce Eder

Trilogy
July 1972, Rhino

After the heavily distorted bass and doomsday church organ of Emerson, Lake & Palmer's debut album, the exhilarating prog rock of epic proportions on *Tarkus*, and the violent removal of the sacred aura of classical tunes on *Pictures at an Exhibition*, *Trilogy*, ELP's fourth album, features the trio settling down in more crowd-pleasing pastures. Actually, the group was gaining in maturity what they lost in raw energy. Every track on this album has been carefully thought, arranged, and performed to perfection, a process that also included some form of sterilization. Greg Lake's acoustic ballad "From the Beginning" put the group on the charts for a second time. The adaptation of Aaron Copland's "Hoedown" also yielded a crowd-pleaser. Prog rock fans had to satisfy themselves with the three-part "The Endless Enigma" and "Trilogy," both very strong but paced compositions. By 1972, Eddie Offord's recording and producing techniques had reached a peak. He provided a lush, comfy finish to the album that made it particularly suited for living-room listening and the FM airwaves. Yet the material lacks a bit of excitement. *Trilogy* still belongs to ELP's classic period and should not be overlooked. For newcomers to prog rock it can even make a less-menacing point of entry.

François Couture

Brain Salad Surgery
November 1973, Atlantic

The trio's most successful and well-realized album (after their first), and their most ambitious as a group, as well as their loudest, is also their most electronic sounding one. The main focus, thanks to the three-part "Karn Evil 9," is sci-fi rock, approached with a volume and vengeance that stretched the art rock audience's tolerance to its outer limit, but also managed to appeal to the metal audience in ways that little of *Trilogy* did. Indeed, "Karn Evil 9" is the piece and the place where Emerson and his keyboards finally matched in both music and flamboyance the larger-than-life guitar sound of Jimi Hendrix. Pete Sinfield's lyrics, while not up to his best King Crimson-era standard, were better than anything

the group had to work with previously, and Lake pulled out all the stops on his heaviest singing voice in handling them, coming off a bit like Peter Gabriel in the process. The songs (except for the throwaway "Benny the Bouncer") are also among their best work—the group's arrangement of Sir Charles Hubert Parry's setting of William Blake's "Jerusalem" man-

ages to be reverent yet rocking, while Emerson's adaptation of Alberto Ginastera's music in "Tocatta" outstrips even "The Barbarian" and "Knife Edge" from the first album as a distinctive and rewarding reinterpretation of a piece of serious music. Lake's "Still...You Turn Me On" is his last great ballad with the group, possessing a melody and arrangement sufficiently pretty to forgive the presence of the rhyming triplet "everyday a little sadder/a little madder/someone get me a ladder." The Rhino CD is to be preferred over all other domestic reissues, as it features an improved remastering, an interview, and packaging with a very cool 3-D cover design.

Bruce Eder

Welcome Back My Friends to the Show That Never Ends
August 1974, Sanctuary

Upon its release, the 1973 LP *Brain Salad Surgery* had been hailed as Emerson, Lake & Palmer's masterpiece. A long tour ensued that left the trio flushed and begging for time off. Before disbanding for three years, they assembled a three-LP live set (something of a badge of achievement at the time, earned by Yes in 1973 with *Yessongs* and, somewhat more dubiously, Leon Russell with *Leon Live*). *Welcome Back My Friends to the Show That Never Ends* gives a very accurate representation of ELP's shows at the time, including their uncertain sound quality. It isn't that the group didn't try hard to give a good show; they did, but left to just his two hands, without the use of multi-tracking and overdubs to build layer-upon-layer of electronic keyboard sounds, Keith Emerson was at a singular disadvantage on some of the boldest material in the trio's repertory. And even allowing how far the art and science of recording rock concerts had advanced in the 1970s, there were still inherent problems in recording a fully exposed bass—Greg Lake's primary instrument—in an arena setting that couldn't be overcome here. Even the most recent remastered editions could not fix the feedback, the occasionally leakages, the echo, the seeming distance—the listener often gets the impression of being seated in the upper mezzanine of an arena. That said, the group still had a lot of fire, enthusiasm, and cohesion at this point in its history, and that does come through. And if they don't solve every problem with the sound, the remastered editions from Rhino, Japanese WEA, and Sanctuary do give Lake's voice and Emerson's piano their richest, fullest possible tone and a fighting chance in these surroundings, and bring Carl Palmer's drumming much more up close and personal than it ever was on the LP. On the down side, the division into two CDs (as opposed to three LPs) means that the 26-minute "Take a Pebble"/"Piano Improvisations"/"Take a Pebble" chain—complete with Lake's excellent acoustic guitar spot for "Still You Turn Me On" and "Lucky Man"—is broken up between the two discs. The song selection—if not quite the career-ranging array of repertory that *Yessongs* was for Yes—is stellar and features all the material from *Brain Salad Surgery* (with the exception of "Benny the Bouncer"), including a complete 36-minute rendition of "Karn Evil 9," which filled both sides of the third LP in the original set. The latter is thoroughly bracing, with a level of visceral energy that was lacking in some moments of the original studio version, and is also almost as good a showcase for Lake, whose singing and playing here are better than they were on the studio original, as it is for Emerson and Palmer. Add to that a 27-minute "Tarkus"—complete with one Pete Sinfield-authored verse from King Crimson's "Epitaph" (which they'd been adding to the piece in concert at least since the *Trilogy* tour)—and you now have three quarters of the music. Hearing any of those three pieces (and the stunning "Toccata") performed live, obviously without any overdubs, makes one realize how accomplished these musicians were, and how well they worked together when the going was good. This was the group's last successful and satisfying tour, as subsequent journeys on the road, in association with the *Works* album, were mired in acrimony about expenses, repertory, ego clashes, and the decision about going out with an orchestra (or not), or were motivated purely by contractual and financial obligations, whereas here they proved that even their most ambitious ideas could work musically, done by just the three of them. The sometimes disappointing sound quality should not be too much of a turnoff for fans, but newcomers should definitely start with the studio albums, and make this the third or fourth ELP album in their collection. And it should be listened to *loud*.

Francois Couture & Bruce Eder

The Faces

First Step
1970, Warner Bros.

The notorious sloppiness of the Faces was apparent on their debut, almost moreso on the cover than on the music, as the group was stilled billed as the Small Faces on this 1970 debut although without Steve Marriott in front, and with Rod

small faces

Stewart and Ron Wood in tow, they were no longer Small. They were now larger than life, or at least mythic, because it's hard to call an album that concludes with a riotous ode to a hand-me-down suit as larger than life. That was the charm of the Faces, a group that always seemed like the boys next door made good, no matter where next door was. Part of the reason they seemed so relatable was that legendary messiness—after all, it's hard not to love somebody if they so openly displayed their flaws—but on their debut, it was hard not to see the messiness as merely the result of the old Faces getting accustomed to the new guys. Fresh from their seminal work with Jeff Beck, Rod and Ron brings a healthy dose of Beck's powerful bastardized blues, bracingly heard on the opening cover of "Wicked Messenger," but there's a key difference here; without Beck's guitar genius, this roar doesn't sound quite so titanic, it hits in the gut. That can also be heard and Rod and Woody's "Around the Plynth," or "Three

Button Hand Me Down," which is ragged rocking at its finest. Combine that with Ronnie Lane and Ian McLagan finding their ways as songwriters in the wake of the Small Faces' mod implosion, and this goes in even more directions. Lane unveils his gentle, folky side on "Stone," McLagan kicks in "Looking Out the Window" and "Three Button Hand Me Down." All these are moments that are good, often great, but the record doesn't quite gel, yet that doesn't quite matter. The Faces are a band that proves that sometimes loose ends are as great as tidiness, that living in the moment is what's necessary, and this *First Step* is a record filled with individual moments, each one to be savored.

Stephen Thomas Erlewine

Long Player
1971, Warner Bros.

On their second album *Long Player*, the Faces truly gel—which isn't quite the same thing as having the band straighten up and fly right because in many ways this is album is even more ragged than their debut, with tracks that sound like they were recorded

through a shoebox thrown up against a couple of haphazardly placed live cuts. But if the album seems pieced together from a few different sources, the band itself all seems to be coming from the same place, turning into a ferocious rock & roll band who, on their best day, could wrestle the title of greatest rock & roll band away from the Stones. Certainly, the sheer force of the nine minute jam on Big Bill Broonzy's "I Feel So Good" proves that, but what's more remarkable is how the band are dovetailing as songwriters, complimenting and collaborating with very different styles, to the extent that it's hard to tell who wrote what; indeed, the ragged, heartbroken "Tell Everyone" sounds like a Stewart original, but it comes from the pen of Ronnie Lane. The key is that Stewart, Lane and Ron Wood (Ian MacLagan only co-write "Bad 'n' Ruin") are all coming from the same place, all celebrating a rock & roll that's ordinary in subject but not in sound. Take "Bad 'n' Ruin," the tale of a ne'er do well returning home with his tail between his legs, after the city didn't treat him well. It has its counterpart in "Had Me A Real Good Time," where a reveler insists that he has to leave, concluding that he was glad to come but also glad to get home. These are songs that celebrate home, from family to the neighborhood, and that big heart beats strong in the ballads, too, from the aching "Sweet Lady Mary" to the extraordinary reworking of Paul McCartney's "Maybe I'm Amazed," which soars in ways Macca's exceptional original never did. Then, there's there humor—the ramshackle "On the Beach," the throwaway lines from Rod on "Had Me A Real Good Time"—which give this a warm, cheerful heart that helps make *Long Player* a record as big, messy, and wonderful as life itself.

Stephen Thomas Erlewine

A Nod Is as Good as a Wink...to a Blind Horse
1971, Warner Bros.

The Faces' third album, *A Nod Is as Good as a Wink...to*

a Blind Horse, finally gave the group their long-awaited hit single in "Stay with Me," helping send the album into the *Billboard* Top Ten, which is certainly a testament to both the song and the album, but it's hard to separate its success from that of Rod Stewart's sudden solo stardom. In the mere months that separated *Long Player* and *A Nod*, Rod had a phenomenal hit with "Maggie May" and *Every Picture Tells a Story*, his third solo album, something that would soon irreparably damage the band, but at the time it was mere good fortune, helping bring them some collateral success that they deserved. Certainly, it didn't change the character of the album itself, which is the tightest record the band ever made. Granted that may be a relative term, since sloppiness is at the heart of the band, but this doesn't feel cobbled together (which the otherwise excellent *Long Player* did) and it serves up tremendous song after tremendous song, starting with the mean, propulsive "Miss Judy's Farm" and ending with the rampaging good times of "That's All You Need." In between, Ronnie Lane serves up dirty jokes (the exquisitely funny "You're So Rude") and heartbreaking ballads (the absolutely beautiful "Debris"), the band reworks a classic as their own (Chuck Berry's "Memphis") and generally serves up a non-stop party like *A Nod*—the slow moments are for slow dancing, and as soon as it's over, it's hard not to want to do it all over again. It's another classic—and when you consider that the band also had *Long Player* to their credit and had their hands all over *Every Picture* in 1971, it's hard to imagine another band or singer having a year more extraordinary as this.

Stephen Thomas Erlewine

Ooh La La
1973, Warner Bros.

It wasn't all over but the shouting, but the Faces sure weren't thriving when they released their last album, *Ooh La La*, in 1973. The problem, of course, was Rod Stewart, who had turned into a superstar, causing innumerable tensions within the band. He had yet to decamp to America, had yet to turn to pop instead of rock & roll, but he was on the cusp of that sea change. Nevertheless, on the record at least, it didn't seem like being with the Faces was a strain on him; it still seemed that he enjoyed a good night out with the boys, and *Ooh La La* is precisely that: a good night out, one that's blessed with some very memorable moments. If there's not quite as many as on the past two Faces platters, chalk that up to circumstance perhaps. On *Long Player* and *A Nod Is as Good as a Wink*, they were a well-oiled machine at the peak of their powers. Here they're trying to rev up—they get there, but it's possible to hear the effort, as some of the songs fall just a little bit short of memorable. But there are some extraordinary moments here, including Rod's "Silicone Grown" and the wonderful "Cindy Incidentally," a sweet, easy pop song. But the heart of this album really belongs to Ronnie Lane, who dominates the second side of the album, starting with the Stewart collaboration "If I'm on the Late Side" and running through the sweet, soft "Glad and Sorry" to "Just Another Honky" and, finally, to the raucous yet bittersweet "Ooh La La," as great a song as they ever recorded and an appropriate drawing of the curtain on this tremendous band.

Stephen Thomas Erlewine

Five Guys Walk into a Bar...
July 2004, Warner Bros./Rhino

There has never been a better box set than the Faces' *Five Guys Walk into a Bar....* There has never been a box that captures an artist so perfectly, nor has a box set taken advantage of unreleased and rare material, to the point where it seems as essential and vital as the released recordings.

Simply put, there's never been a box set as *necessary* as this, since it tells the band's entire tale and explains exactly what the fuss is all about. Unfortunately, some explanations are in order, since the Faces never made it big, resigned to cult status in America and Britain alike. Nevertheless, if you love rock & roll with an all-consuming passion, you may consider the Faces the greatest rock & roll band ever. And you'd be right. Other bands were certainly bigger and plenty wielded a stronger influence, but the Faces were something unique, an endearingly ragged quintet that played raw, big-hearted rock & roll as hard as the Rolling Stones, but with a warm, friendly vibe that would have sounded utterly foreign coming from the Stones. At the turn of the '60s, that warmth was unusual in rock & roll, since most of the big bands were larger than life; even the Kinks, the quaintest and quietest of the titans of the late '60s, had a theatrical bent that lent them a mystique.

In contrast, the Faces were utterly without mystique. They were unpretentious to a fault, coming across like the lovable lads from the neighborhood who were always out for a good time, whether it was before, during, or after a gig. They were unassuming and mischievous, with their raggedness camouflaging a sweetness that flowed throughout their music; they were charming rogues, so endearing that even the infamously cranky, trendsetting British DJ John Peel had a soft spot a mile wide for them. That raggedness resulted in exhilarating music, but also made the Faces inconsistent onstage and in the studio. At their peak, nobody could touch them, but even their greatest albums were sloppy, never maintaining their momentum. They would also throw away great songs on non-LP singles, and their live performances—including BBC sessions for Peel—often had a raucous energy not quite captured on their albums. All of these elements taken as a whole add up to a great band, but no single album, not even the first-rate 1999 compilation *Good Boys When They're Asleep*, captured each of these elements.

Five Guys Walk into a Bar... does. Produced and sequenced by their keyboardist, Ian McLagan, the set throws all conventional rules of box sets out the window. It's not assembled in a chronological order. A grand 43 of its 67 tracks are non-LP cuts and rarities, including a whopping 31 previously unreleased tracks. It has all the B-sides never released on CD. Several songs are repeated in alternate live or studio versions. Such a preponderance of rarities would usually mean that a box set is only for the devoted, but that's not the case here—these rarities are the very reason why *Five Guys Walk into a Bar...* succeeds in a way none of their original albums do, since they fill in the gaps left behind on their four studio albums. This does mean that it features several Rod Stewart solo cuts that worked their way into the Faces' repertoire (partially because the band backed him on his solo albums, too), but that was an important part of their history (plus, the BBC version of "You're My Girl [I Don't Want to Discuss It]" is blistering hot), and while this showcases Stewart at his best—he never was better than he was in the early '70s, whether it was fronting the Faces or on his solo records—he never overshadows his mates on this box.

The focus is on the band as a whole, which means that the spotlight is shone on the late, perpetually underappreciated Ronnie Lane numerous times on each of the four discs, and that Ronnie Wood has his turn at the microphone on a wonderful live "Take a Look at the Guy." McLagan's song sequencing may appear to have no logic behind it, since it doesn't group recordings together by either era or scarcity, yet his seemingly haphazard approach makes musical and emotional sense, flowing like a set list yet remarkably maintaining momentum through its four lengthy discs. While it may sound like hyperbole, there's never a bad moment here, not a bad track among these 67 songs—it's consistent in a way the Faces never were when they were together. It's a joyous, addictive listen, too. It sounds like a party, one where everybody's invited and where the music doesn't stop playing until the break of dawn. That makes a perfect tribute for a band that never got the respect they were due, and never made the great album they should have made. With *Five Guys Walk into a Bar...*, the Faces finally have that great album and not just that, they have a box set that's as infectious and satisfying as any classic rock & roll album and a box set that's quite possibly the greatest box set ever made. Plus, it's just one hell of a good time.

Stephen Thomas Erlewine

The Firm

The Firm
1985, Atlantic

Anticipation was quite high when it was announced in 1984 that Paul Rodgers, the past voice of Bad Company, and Jimmy Page, Led Zeppelin's former guitarist, were creating a "supergroup" called the Firm. Page and Rodgers had first tinkered with the idea of an

album after their successful collaboration on the ARMS benefit tour for Ronnie Lane in 1983. Based upon the fact that it had been over five years since Page's last band effort, and two years since Rodger's lackluster finale with the original Bad Company, pundits were more than eager to hear what new material the duo would unleash. However, when the band's self-titled debut was actually released in 1985, it received a critical drubbing and was all but ignored by the record-buying public. That's too bad, for the album is quite good and does nothing to taint the sterling reputations of either of its key players. Page and Rodgers were joined on *The Firm* by veteran drummer Chris Slade and Roy Harper-alum Tony Franklin. Slade's Bonham-esque sledgehammer attack on the skins, coupled with Franklin's fretless basslines, added dimension to Rodgers' smooth vocals and Page's layered guitar textures. Page's tone throughout is very reminiscent of the sound of his overdubs on *Coda*, as well as the sound he would subsequently employ on 1988's *Outrider*. Opening track "Closer" cleverly uses a subtle horn section to good effect, while "Someone to Love" represents all the good elements of the band in one number. Rodgers' "Radioactive" was actually a minor hit for the band, its quirkiness overcoming the goofiness of the lyrics. The album's best cut is "Satisfaction Guaranteed," a mid-tempo gem with a snaky and exotic Page riff and a heartfelt vocal performance by Rodgers. The only weak track on the record is the unnecessary cover of the Righteous Brothers' "You've Lost That Loving Feeling," which feels totally out of place. The album-closing "Midnight Moonlight" could have been the Firm's best song, but the underwhelming arrangement and superfluous backing vocals partially destroyed it. The fact that "Midnight Moonlight" was actually an unfinished Led Zeppelin cut entitled "Swansong," left over from the *Physical Graffiti* sessions, led some to believe that Page had run out of new ideas for the project. While it is true that this album isn't as uniformly excellent as Led Zeppelin's work, it is the best

from this short-lived band and turned out to be Page's most consistent effort from the entire decade of the '80s.

Brian Downing

Fleetwood Mac

Peter Green's Fleetwood Mac
February 1968, Blue Horizon

Fleetwood Mac's debut LP was a highlight of the late-'60s British blues boom. Green's always inspired playing, the capable (if erratic) songwriting, and the general panache of the band as a whole placed them leagues above the overcrowded field. Elmore James is a big influence on this set, particularly on the tunes fronted by Jeremy Spencer ("Shake Your Moneymaker," "Got to Move"). Spencer's bluster, however, was outshone by the budding singing and songwriting skills of Green. The guitarist balanced humor and vulnerability on cuts like "Looking for Somebody" and "Long Grey Mare," and with "If I Loved Another Woman," he offered a glimpse of the Latin-blues fusion that he would perfect with "Black Magic Woman." The album was an unexpected smash in the U.K., reaching number four on the British charts.

Richie Unterberger

Pious Bird of Good Omen
August 1969, Columbia

With songs taken from *Fleetwood Mac* and *Mr. Wonderful*, *Pious Bird of Good Omen* serves as a worthy 12-track compilation of the band's early Fleetwood days. Climbing to number 18 in the U.K., the album managed to catapult Fleetwood Mac's version of Little Willie John's "Need Your Love So Bad" into the English charts for the third time, resting at number 42. The album itself was released by Blue Horizon after the group's contract with them had expired, making it one of the best routes in which to explore their mingling of Chicago and British blues. "Albatross," "Black Magic Woman," and "I Believe My Time Ain't Long" are timeless Fleetwood Mac standards, representing some of the band's best pre-*Rumours* work. Anyone who isn't familiar with Fleetwood Mac's origins should use *Pious Bird of Good Omen* as a starting point in investigating the first wave of the band, which will almost certainly lead to further interests into albums such as *English Rose*, *Then Play On*, and *Kiln House*, and then into later albums like *Bare Trees* and *Penguin*, which reveal subtle yet effective changes in the band's blues sound. But even aside from its purpose as a collection, *Pious Bird of Good Omen* makes for a terrific laid-back stroll through some of the best British blues music ever made.

Mike DeGagne

Then Play On
October 1969, Reprise

This Peter Green-led edition of the Mac isn't just an important transition between their initial blues-based incarnation and the mega-pop band they became, it's also their most vital, exciting version. The addition of Danny Kirwan as second guitarist and songwriter foreshadows not only the soft-rock terrain of "Bare Trees" and "Kiln House" with Christine Perfect-McVie, but also predicts *Rumours*. That only pertains to roughly half of the also excellent material here, though; the rest is quintessential Green. The immortal "Oh Well," with its hard-edged, thickly layered guitars and chamber-like sections, is perhaps the band's most enduring progressive composition. "Rattlesnake Shake" is another familiar number, a down-and-dirty, even-paced funk, with clean, wall-of-sound guitars. Choogling drums and Green's fiery improvisations power "Searching for Madge," perhaps Mac's most inspired work save "Green Manalishi," and leads into an unlikely symphonic interlude and the similar, lighter boogie "Fighting for Madge." A hot Afro-Cuban rhythm with beautiful guitars from Kirwan and Green on "Coming Your Way" not only defines the Mac's sound, but the rock aesthetic of

the day. Of the songs with Kirwan's stamp on them, "Closing My Eyes" is a mysterious waltz love song; haunting guitars approach surf music on the instrumental "My Dream"; and "Although the Sun Is Shining" is the ultimate pre-*Rumours* number someone should revisit. Blues roots still crop up on the spatial, loose, Hendrix-tinged "Underway," the folky blues tale of a lesbian affair on "Like Crying," and the final outcry of the ever-poignant "Show Biz Blues," with Green moaning "do you really give a damn for me?" *Then Play On* is a reminder of how pervasive and powerful Green's influence was on Mac's originality and individual stance beyond his involvement. Still highly recommended and a must-buy after all these years, it remains their magnum opus.

Michael G. Nastos

Future Games
November 1971, Reprise

By the time of this album's release, Jeremy Spencer had been replaced by Bob Welch and Christine McVie had begun to assert herself more as a singer and songwriter. The result is a distinct move toward folk-rock and pop; *Future Games* sounds almost nothing like Peter Green's Fleetwood Mac. Welch's eight-minute title track has one of his characteristic haunting melodies, and with pruning and better editing, it could have been a hit. Christine McVie's "Show Me a Smile" is one of her loveliest ballads. Initial popular reaction was mixed: the album didn't sell as well as *Kiln House*, but it sold better than any of the band's first three albums in the U.S. In the U.K., where the original lineup had been more successful, *Future Games* didn't chart at all; the same fate that would befall the rest of its albums until the Lindsey Buckingham-Stevie Nicks era.

William Ruhlmann

Bare Trees
March 1972, Reprise

Arguably the first consistently strong album Fleetwood Mac ever recorded—all the way back into the Peter Green/Jeremy Spencer era, the Mac's albums had previously consisted of individual moments of brilliance in a sea of uninspired filler—1972's *Bare Trees* is also the album where the band finally defines its post-blues musical personality. Low-key but less narcoleptically mellow than 1971's sleepy *Future Games*, *Bare Trees* is a singer/songwriter album in the traditional early-'70s style, backed up with just enough musical muscle to keep from sounding like weedy soft rock in the manner of Bread or Cat Stevens. This is the one Fleetwood Mac album on which singer/guitarist Danny Kirwan is the dominant figure, writing five songs to Chistine McVie and Bob Welch's two apiece. Impressively, all three writers get off a small masterpiece on side two; McVie's "Spare Me a Little of Your

Love" sounds like a dry run for the string of hits she would start writing with 1975's *Fleetwood Mac*, and it's her first really good pop song. By comparison, Kirwan and Welch's best songs are all-time career highlights. Kirwan's "Dust" combines a gentle, gliding melody with resigned, melancholy lyrics and his most memorable chorus. Welch's "Sentimental Lady" was, of course, his first solo hit in its 1977 re-recorded version, but this original take is far superior, and one of the great lost pop songs of the early '70s. Outfitted with a terrific vocal melody, hooks galore, and an impressive tremolo guitar solo, "Sentimental Lady" is perhaps a little trite lyrically, but it's a heartfelt and lovable tune regardless, and the best thing Fleetwood Mac did in the years between "Albatross" and "Over My Head." The rest of the album is less magical, but the instrumental "Sunny Side of Heaven" and the downright funky "Danny's Chant" are impressive in their use of atmospheric arrangements and so point toward the subtle but effective production choices that would make *Fleetwood Mac* and *Rumours* among the most listenable albums of their time. *Bare Trees* isn't in that league, but it shows that after five years of false starts and failed experiments, Fleetwood Mac were finally on their way.

Stewart Mason

Mystery to Me
October 1973, Reprise

At this point, the band was best-known as a British blues unit. Slowly but surely the band was becoming more acclimated with a production style that was reminiscent of the California pop sound. With the majority of the blues and psychedelic behind

them, *Mystery to Me* finds Fleetwood Mac in a more ruminative vein. American guitarist Bob Welch established that path. Despite the all-encompassing ethos, Welch's songwriting skills made him walk a fine line between the mystical and the silly. But luckily most everything works here. The leadoff song, the laid-back "Emerald Eyes" matches Welch's spacey lyrics and vocals as Christine McVie provides great backing help. The album's best track, the gorgeous and lyrically strong "Hypnotized" has Welch matching an effortless, soothing croon with jazzy guitar riffs. Throughout *Mystery to Me* the amazing and almost telepathic drums and bass of Mick Fleetwood and John McVie give this effort more panache and muscle than was represented on this effort's predecessor, *Bare Trees*. The best Christine McVie offering, "Keep on Going," has a strong, soulful string arrangement and her customary sensual and poised vocals. The only weak spot is the ill-advised cover of "For Your Love" that's steeped in hackneyed, post-psychedelic style. *Mystery to Me*'s interesting sound is directly attributed to the fact that it was recorded on the Rolling Stones Mobile Unit. This effort is custom-made for those who like thoughtful offerings and is a valuable set in the scheme of the band.

Jason Elias

Heroes Are Hard to Find
September 1974, Reprise

Although this was Bob Welch's last album with the band he had worked with since 1971, it sounds like he's at his peak.

Pared down to a foursome for the first and (as of 2002) only time since the addition of Danny Kirwan, both Welch and Christine McVie contribute some of their finest songs. Bolstered by sympathetic self-production and imaginative, often aggressive arrangements that include brassy horns on the title track (a blatant but failed attempt at a hit single), the album is one of their most cohesive yet diverse. Welch continues his fascination with UFOs in a sort of follow-up to *Mystery to Me*'s "Hypnotized" called "Bermuda Triangle" and even heads into a spacy Hendrix "Third Stone From the Sun" groove on "Coming Home." Christine McVie is in wonderful voice on her own ballads like "Prove Your Love" but outdoes herself on the magnificent "Come a Little Bit Closer," a stunning track whose grandeur is heightened by strings and McVie's majestic piano. It's a hidden classic and pedal steel by the Flying Burrito Brothers' Sneaky Pete Kleinow is an unexpected and perfect addition to the album's most fully realized tune. Welch's folk-pop "She's Changing Me" is one of his most upbeat, memorable melodies, offset by the rocker "Silver Heels" and his closing "Safe Harbor," a knowing nod back to Peter Green's atmospheric work on "Albatross" and his contributions to *Then Play On*. McVie's haunting rocker "Bad Loser" is reinforced by the propulsive rhythm section of Mick Fleetwood and John McVie, both adding tense bite to even the most tender of ballads. Welch left soon after the album's release, and the group went on to bigger and better things, but *Heroes* is a minor gem that retains its effortless pop charms and contains some buried jewels in the extensive Fleetwood Mac catalog.

Hal Horowitz

Fleetwood Mac
July 1975, Sony

It's unfair to say that Fleetwood Mac had no pop pretensions prior to the addition of Lindsey Buckingham and Stevie Nicks to the lineup in 1975. When they were led by Bob Welch they often flirted with pop, even recording the first version of the unabashedly smooth and sappy "Sentimental Lady," which would later be one of the defining soft rock hits of the late '70s. Still, there's no denying that 1975's *Fleetwood Mac* represents not just the rebirth of the band, but in effect a second debut for the group—the introduction of a band that would dominate the sound of American and British mainstream pop for the next seven years. In fact, in retrospect, it's rather stunning how thoroughly Buckingham and Nicks, who had previously recorded as a duo and were romantically entangled in the past, overtook the British blues band. As soon as the Californian duo came onboard, Fleetwood Mac turned into a West Coast pop/rock band, transforming the very identity of the band and pushing the band's other songwriter, keyboardist Christine McVie, to a kindred soft rock sound. It could have all been too mellow if it weren't for the nervy, restless spirit of Buckingham, whose insistent opener, "Monday Morning," sets the tone for the rest of the album, as well the next few years of the group's career. Surging with a pushily melodic chorus and a breezy Californian feel, the song has little to do with anything the Mac had done before this, and it is a positively brilliant slice of pop songwriting, simultaneously urgent and timeless. After that barnstorming opener, Buckingham lies back a bit, contributing only two other songs—a cover of Richard Curtis' "Blue Letter," the second best up-tempo song here, and the closer, "I'm So Afraid"—while the rest of the album is given over to the wily spirits of Nicks and McVie, whose singles "Rhiannon," "Say You Love Me," and "Over My Head" deservedly made this into a blockbuster. But a bandmember's contribution can never be reduced to his own tracks, and Buckingham not only gives the production depth, he motivates the rest of the band, particularly Nicks and McVie, to do great work, not just on the hit singles but the album tracks that give this record depth. It was diverse without being forced, percolating with innovative ideas, all filtered through an accessible yet sophisticated sensibility. While *Rumours* had more hits and *Tusk* was an inspired work of mad genius, *Fleetwood Mac* wrote the blueprint for Californian soft rock of the late '70s and was the standard the rest were judged by.

Stephen Thomas Erlewine

Rumours
February 1977, Reprise

Rumours is the kind of album that transcends its origins and reputation, entering the realm of legend—it's an album that simply exists outside of criticism and outside of its time, even if it thoroughly captures its era. Prior to this LP, Fleetwood Mac were moderately successful, but here they turned into a full-fledged phenomenon, with *Rumours* becoming the biggest-selling pop album to date. While its chart success was historic, much of the legend surrounding the record is born from the group's internal turmoil. Unlike most bands, Fleetwood Mac in the mid-'70s were professionally and romantically intertwined, with no less than two couples in the band, but as their professional career took off, the personal side unraveled. Bassist John McVie and his keyboardist/singer wife Christine McVie filed for divorce as guitarist/vocalist Lindsey Buckingham and vocalist Stevie Nicks split, with Stevie running to drummer Mick Fleetwood, unbeknown to the rest of the band. These personal tensions fueled nearly every song on *Rumours*, which makes listening to the album a nearly voyeuristic experience. You're eavesdropping on the bandmates singing painful truths about each other, spreading nasty lies and rumors and wallowing in their grief, all in the presence of the person who caused the heartache. Everybody loves gawking at a good public breakup, but if that was all that it took to sell a record, Richard and Linda Thompson's *Shoot Out the Lights* would be multi-platinum. No, what made *Rumours* an unparalleled blockbuster is the quality of the music. Once again masterminded by producer/songwriter/guitarist Buckingham, *Rumours* is an exceptionally musical piece of work—he toughens Christine McVie and softens Nicks, adding weird turns to accessibly melodic works, which gives the universal themes of the songs haunting resonance. It also cloaks the raw emotion of the lyrics in deceptively palatable arrangements that made a tune as wrecked and tortured as "Go Your Own Way" an anthemic hit. But that's what makes *Rumours* such an enduring achievement—it turns private pain into something universal. Some of these songs may be too familiar, whether through their repeated exposure on FM radio or their use in presidential campaigns, but in the context of the album, each tune, each phrase regains its raw, immediate emotional power—which is why *Rumours* touched a nerve upon its 1977 release, and has since transcended its era to be one of the greatest, most compelling pop albums of all time.

Stephen Thomas Erlewine

Tusk
October 1979, Reprise

More than any other Fleetwood Mac album, *Tusk* is born of a particular time and place—it could only have been created in the aftermath of *Rumours*, which shattered sales records, which in turn gave the group a blank check for its next album. But if they were falling apart during the making of *Rumours*, they were officially broken and shattered during the making of *Tusk*, and that disconnect between bandmembers resulted in a sprawling, incoherent, and utterly brilliant 20-track double album. At the time of its release, it was a flop, never reaching the top of the charts and never spawning a true hit single, despite two well-received Top Ten hits. Coming after the monumental *Rumours*, this was a huge disappointment, but the truth of the matter is that Fleetwood Mac couldn't top that success no matter how hard they tried, so it was better for them to indulge themselves and come up with something as unique as *Tusk*. Lindsey Buckingham directed both *Fleetwood Mac* and *Rumours*, but he dominates here, composing nearly half the album, and giving Christine McVie's and Stevie Nicks' songs an ethereal, floating quality that turns them into welcome respites from the seriously twisted immersions into Buckingham's id. This is the ultimate cocaine album—it's mellow for long stretches, and then bursts wide open in manic, frantic explosions, such as the mounting tension on "The Ledge" or the rampaging "That's Enough for Me," or the marching band-driven paranoia of the title track, all of which are relieved by smooth, reflective work from all three songwriters. While McVie and Nicks contribute some excellent songs, Buckingham owns this record with his nervous energy and obsessive production, winding up with a fussily detailed yet wildly messy record unlike any other. This is mainstream madness, crazier than Buckingham's idol Brian Wilson and weirder than any number of cult classics. Of course, that's why it bombed upon its original release, but *Tusk* is a bracing, weirdly affecting work that may not be as universal or immediate as *Rumours*, but is every bit as classic. As a piece of pop art, it's peerless.

Stephen Thomas Erlewine

Tango in the Night
1987, Reprise

Artistically and commercially, the Stevie Nicks/Lindsey Buckingham/Mick Fleetwood/Christine and John McVie edition of Fleetwood Mac had been on a roll for over a decade when *Tango in the Night* was released in early 1987. This would, unfortunately, be Buckingham's last album with the pop/rock supergroup—and he definitely ended his association with the band on a creative high note. Serving as the album's main producer, Buckingham gives an edgy quality to everything from the haunting "Isn't It Midnight" to the poetic "Seven Wonders" to the dreamy "Everywhere." Though Buckingham doesn't over-produce, his thoughtful use of synthesizers is a major asset. Without question, "Family Man" and "Caroline" are among the best

songs ever written by Buckingham, who consistently brings out the best in his colleagues on this superb album.

Alex Henderson

The Flying Burrito Brothers

The Gilded Palace of Sin
February 1969, Edsel

By 1969, Gram Parsons had already built the foundation of the country-rock movement through his work with the International Submarine Band and the Byrds, but his first album with the Flying Burrito Brothers, *The Gilded Palace of Sin*, was where he revealed the full extent of his talents, and it ranks among the finest and most influential albums the genre would ever produce. As a songwriter, Parsons delivered some of his finest work on this set; "Hot Burrito No. 1" and "Hot Burrito No. 2" both blend the hurt of classic country weepers with a contemporary sense of anger, jealousy, and confusion, and "Sin City" can either be seen as a parody or a sincere meditation on a city gone mad, and it hits home in both contexts. Parsons was rarely as strong as a vocalist as he was here, and his covers of "Dark End of the Street" and "Do Right Woman" prove just how much he had been learning from R&B as well as C&W. And Parsons was fortunate enough to be working with a band who truly added to his vision, rather than simply backing him up; the distorted swoops of Sneaky Pete Kleinow's fuzztone steel guitar provides a perfect bridge between country and psychedelic rock, and Chris Hillman's strong and supportive harmony vocals blend flawlessly with Parsons' (and he also proved to be a valuable songwriting partner, collaborating on a number of great tunes with Gram). While *The Gilded Palace of Sin* barely registered on the pop culture radar in 1969, literally dozens of bands (the Eagles most notable among them) would find inspiration in this music and enjoy far greater success. But no one ever brought rock and country together quite like the Flying Burrito Brothers, and this album remains their greatest accomplishment.

Mark Deming

Burrito Deluxe
April 1970, Edsel

Gram Parsons had a habit of taking over whatever band he happened to be working with, and on the first three albums on which he appeared—the International Submarine Band's *Safe at Home*, the Byrds' *Sweetheart of the Rodeo*, and the Flying Burrito Brothers' *The Gilded Palace of Sin*—he became the focal point, regardless of the talent of his compatriots. *Burrito Deluxe*, the Burritos' second album, is unique in Parsons' repertoire in that it's the only album where he seems to have deliberately stepped back to make more room for others; whether this was due to Gram's disinterest in a band he was soon to leave, or if he was simply in an unusually democratic frame of mind is a matter of debate. But while it is hardly a bad album, it's not nearly as striking as *The Gilded Palace of Sin*. Parsons didn't deliver many noteworthy originals for this set, with "Cody, Cody" and "Older Guys" faring best but paling next to the highlights from the previous album (though he was able to wrangle the song "Wild Horses" away from his buddy Keith Richards and record it a year before the Rolling Stones' version would surface). And while the band sounds tight and they play with genuine enthusiasm, there's a certain lack of focus in these performances; the band's frontman sounds as if his thoughts are often elsewhere, and the other players can't quite compensate for him, though on tunes like "God's Own Singer" and a cover of Bob Dylan's "If You Gotta Go," they gamely give it the old college try. *Burrito Deluxe* is certainly a better than average country-rock album, but coming from the band who made the genre's most strongly defining music, it's something of a disappointment.

Mark Deming

Hot Burritos! The Flying Burrito Brothers Anthology 1969-1972
April 2000, A&M

There's little question that the double-disc collection *Hot Burritos! The Flying Burrito Brothers Anthology 1969-1972* is comprehensive, since it contains the entirety of the band's first three albums plus a bevy of rarities, including six songs from *Close Up the Honky-Tonks*, two cuts from *Sleepless Nights*, two tracks from *The Last of the Red Hot Burritos*, the non-LP single "The Train Song," and "Six Days on the Road," originally released on the 1988 collection *Farther Along: The Best of the Flying Burrito Brothers*. That pretty much covers *everything* they cut during those four years. Since the Burritos were truly great while Gram Parsons was in the band—once he left, they were still solid, thanks to Chris Hillman—this may border on overkill for some listeners, especially since the Parsons years are covered expertly by *Farther Along*, which contained all but one song from *The Gilded Palace of Sin*, plus the best songs from *Deluxe* and rarities and highlights from posthumous releases. For neophytes, that's a better bet, yet the converted will find this quite nice. Apart from "The Train Song," which rarely shows up on collections, there aren't any revelations or even new songs, but there are nice liner notes, great outtakes from the photo shoot for *Gilded Palace*, and exquisite remastered sound. And, for Parsons fanatics, the Hillman-led *Flying Burrito Brothers* may seem like a new record, too, since they may have previously overlooked it. So, diehards get all the Parsons material in one place, while neophytes with a serious attention span will be introduced to one of the great bands of the last 25 years of the 20th century—and, yes, that means it qualifies as definitive.

Stephen Thomas Erlewine

John Fogerty

John Fogerty
1975, Asylum

This one-man extravaganza finds John Fogerty plowing the same ground he worked with Creedence Clearwater Revival. This mix of originals and rock & roll classics finds him in fine voice, with the familiar vocal scream and hot guitars augmented in places by saxophones reminiscent of CCR's "Travelin' Band." Several of these songs rank with the top tier of Fogerty's Creedence material, particularly "The Wall," "Almost Saturday Night," and the anthemic "Rockin'

All Over the World." He also delivers satisfying versions of Jackie Wilson's "Lonely Teardrops" and Frankie Ford's "Sea Cruise" (written by Huey "Piano" Smith). The closer, "Flyin' Away," could have come off the Doobie Brothers' *Toulouse Street*. This underappreciated album is worth checking out.

Jim Newsom

Centerfield
January 1985, Warner Bros.

"Put me in coach, I'm ready to play." These are lines familiar to any baseball fan, for John Fogerty's "Centerfield" has become the unofficial song of our national pastime. Those lines also signaled Fogerty's return to the music business after a ten-year absence. The music is mighty familiar, as Fogerty works the same terrain he mined for gold with Creedence Clearwater Revival from 1968-1972. The riff of the opening track, "The Old Man Down the Road," sounds so much like the Creedence hit "Run Through the Jungle" that Fogerty was sued by his former record company for plagiarizing himself. (He won the suit, the court upholding a composer's right to sound like himself.) "Old Man" was a Top Ten single, and this album reached number one itself. "Big Train (From Memphis)" is a rockabilly salute to Elvis, while "I Saw It on TV" takes us on a trip through the '50s and '60s "from Hooter to Doodyville," via the boob tube. "Searchlight" recalls "Keep On Chooglin" and the other extended one-chord jams of the Creedence days. Fogerty also lashes out at his old nemesis Saul Zaentz, head of that former label, Fantasy Records, with whom he had battled (and lost) over rights to his own catalog of Creedence songs. On "Mr. Greed" and "Zanz Kant Danz" (renamed "Vanz Kant Danz" on later pressings due again to the threat of lawsuit), he vents his anger over these past legal battles and foretells the one to come over "Old Man." Fans hoped *Centerfield* would indeed mark the return of John Fogerty to the playing field, but after releasing the bitter *Eye of the Zombie* the following year, he disappeared again, not to return until 1997's *Blue Moon Swamp*.

Jim Newsom

Foghat

Fool for the City
1975, Bearsville

After building a solid core audience through relentless touring and a string of hard-rocking albums, Foghat finally hit the big time in 1975 with *Fool for the City*. It still stands out as the best album in the group's catalog because it matched their road-tested abilities as hard rockers to a consistent set of tunes that were both well-crafted and ambitious. The tone for the album is set by its title track: This hard-rocking gem not only pairs riff-driven verses with an effective shout-along chorus, but also throws in a few surprising moments where the guitars are taken out of the mix completely and Nick Jameson's bass is allowed to take the lead in a funky breakdown. *Fool for the City* also produced an enduring rock radio favorite in "Slow Ride," a stomping rock tune that transcends the inherent clichés of its "love is like a car ride" lyrics with a furious performance from the band and a clever arrangement that works in well-timed automotive sound effects during the verses and plays up the band's ability to work an R&B-styled groove into their hard-rocking sound (again, note the thumping bassline from Jameson). Further radio play was earned with "Take It or Leave It," an acoustic-based ballad that worked synthesizers into its subtle yet carefully layered arrangement to become one of the group's finest slow numbers. The album's other songs don't stand like the aforementioned selections, but they all flow together nicely thanks to a consistently inspired performance from the band and clever little arrangement frills that keep the group's boogie-oriented rock fresh (example: the witty spoken word bit at the end of "Drive Me Home"). All in all, *Fool for the City* is both Foghat's finest achievement in the studio and one the high points of 1970s hard rock.

Donald A. Guarisco

The Best of Foghat
1989, Rhino

Rhino's *The Best of Foghat* is an excellent 16-track collection featuring every one of the hard-rocking boogie band's best-known songs, from "Slow Ride" and "I Just Want to Make Love to You" to "Fool for the City," "Drivin' Wheel," and "Ride, Ride, Ride." In short, it's all the Foghat most fans will ever need.

Stephen Thomas Erlewine

Foreigner

Foreigner
1977, Atlantic

Although punk rock's furious revolution threatened to overthrow rock's old guard in 1977, bands like Foreigner came along and proved that there was plenty of room in the marketplace for both the violent, upstart minimalism of punk and the airbrushed slickness of what would be called "arena rock." Along with Boston, Journey, Heart, and others, Foreigner celebrated professionalism over raw emotion. And, looking back, it's easy to see why they sold millions; not everyone in the world was pissed off, dissatisfied with the economy, or even necessarily looking for a change. In fact, for most suburban American teens, *Foreigner's* immaculate rock sound was the perfect soundtrack for cruising through well-manicured neighborhoods in their Chevy Novas. The album spawned some of the biggest FM hits of 1977, including the anthemic "Feels Like the First Time" and "Cold as Ice," both of which were anchored—like most of Foreigner's songs—by the muscular but traditional riffing of guitarist Mick Jones, the soaring vocals of Lou Gramm, and the state-of-the-art rock production values of the day, which allowed the band to sound hard but

polished. As pure rock craftsmanship goes, Foreigner was as good as it got in the late '70s.

Andy Hinds

Double Vision
1978, Atlantic

Foreigner promptly followed up its blockbuster debut with the equally successful *Double Vision* LP in 1978, which featured the FM mega-hits "Hot Blooded" and the driving title track. Opting not to mess with a good formula, the band wisely sticks to the polished hard rock sound that made its first record such a hit. Aside from the big singles, other highlights include the swaggering "Love Has Taken Its Toll" and the more restrained "Blue Morning, Blue Day." As always, Lou Gramm's impeccable rock vocals lead the way, supported by Mick Jones' tasteful, arena-sized guitar riffs.

Andy Hinds

Head Games
1979, Atlantic

Foreigner continues its platinum winning streak on *Head Games*, the band's third album. By the time *Head Games* was released, FM radio had fully embraced bands like Foreigner, Journey, and Boston, whose slick hard rock was tough enough to appeal to suburban teens, but smooth enough to be non-threatening to their parents. Tailor-made for the airwaves, "Dirty White Boy" and "Head Games" kept Foreigner at the top of the arena rock heap as the decade came to a close; and the supergroup's successes would continue well into the '80s.

Andy Hinds

4
1981, Atlantic

Over the course of their first three, late-'70s albums, Foreigner had firmly established themselves (along with Journey and Styx) as one of the top AOR bands of the era. But the band was still looking for that grand slam of a record which would push them to the very top of the heap. 1981's *4* would be that album. In producer Robert John "Mutt" Lang—fresh off his massive success with AC/DC's *Back in Black*—guitarist and all-around mastermind Mick Jones found both the catalyst to achieve this and his perfect musical soul mate. Lang's legendary obsessive attention to detail and Jones' highly disciplined guitar heroics (which he never allowed to get in the way of a great song) resulted in a collaboration of unprecedented, sparkling efficiency where not a single note is wasted. "Nightlife" is only the first in a series ("Woman in Black," "Don't Let Go," the '50s-tinged "Luanne") of energetic, nearly flawless melodic rockers; and with "Juke Box Hero," the band somehow managed to create both a mainstream hit single and a highly unique-sounding track, alternating heavy metal guitar riffing, chorused vocals, and one of the ultimate "wanna be a rock star" lyrics. As for the mandatory power ballad, the band also reached unparalleled heights with "Waiting for a Girl Like You." One of the decade's most successful cross-genre tearjerkers, it has since become a staple of soft rock radio and completely eclipsed the album's other very lovely ballad, "Girl on the Moon," in the process. And last but not least, the surprisingly funky "Urgent" proved to be one of the band's most memorable and uncharacteristic smash hits thanks to Junior Walker's signature saxophone solo. Through it all, vocalist Lou Gramm does his part, delivering a dazzling performance which confirmed his status as one of the finest voices of his generation. Three years later, Foreigner would achieve even greater success on a pop level with the uneven *Agent Provocateur*, but by then Jones and Gramm were locked in an escalating war of egos which would soon lead to the band's demise. All things considered, *4* remains Foreigner's career peak.

Ed Rivadavia

Jukebox Heroes: The Foreigner Anthology
August 2000, Rhino

It's easy to say that Rhino's *Jukebox Heroes: The Foreigner Anthology* is the definitive Foreigner retrospective, simply because there's so much music here: 39 tracks over the course of two discs, including all the hits, the bulk of notable album tracks, solo cuts from Lou Gramm and Mick Jones, plus two tracks from Jones-era Spooky Tooth. Clearly, that does amount to a clearly comprehensive collection, but the question is, is this a clear-cut choice for most fans? Well, it all depends on a listener's needs. This will be too much Foreigner if you're just looking for nothing but hits, especially since the classic era (roughly defined as pre-*Agent Provocateur*) stops at the end of the first disc. But, anyone that truly enjoys Foreigner's big, glossy arena rock will find that this doesn't test their patience, even if it runs out of steam toward the end of the collection. *Anthology* keeps interest because of canny selection and sequencing. The addition of Gramm and Jones songs on the second disc works wonders, since it not only strengthens its value for consumers—it's terrific to be able to have all Foreigner and Foreigner-related songs in one place, especially since Gramm's peerless "Midnight Blue" is not just the best thing here, it's the last great single of the album-rock era—it accelerates the pace and keeps things interesting just as the band's output gets a little patchy. So, *Anthology* winds up more consistently entertaining than skeptics could have imagined. It still may not convert those skeptics, but it will prove to the listener with the curiosity to delve deeper than the hits that it's worth doing so.

Stephen Thomas Erlewine

Peter Frampton

Wind of Change
1972, A&M

Peter Frampton's solo debut after leaving Humble Pie (as they stood on the brink of stardom) spotlights Frampton's well-crafted, though lyrically lightweight, songwriting and his fine guitar playing. The songs on *Wind of Change* are built primarily around acoustic guitar foundations, but "It's a Plain Shame" and "All I Want to Be (Is by Your Side)" sound like they could have been lifted off Humble Pie's *Rock On*. The sound is crisp, the melodies catchy, and Frampton's distinctive, elliptical Gibson Les Paul guitar leads soar throughout. A comparison between this album and Humble Pie's post-Frampton turn to generic boogie-rock shows why Frampton left that group. Although

Humble Pie's *Smokin'* was much more successful, hitting the Top Ten in the spring of 1972, *Wind of Change* was far superior musically. With its mix of ballads and upbeat numbers with just enough of a rock edge, *Wind of Change* showed Frampton at his creative peak. The band here includes Ringo Starr, Billy Preston, and Klaus Voorman.

Jim Newsom

Frampton's Camel
1973, A&M

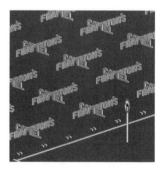

Named after Frampton's touring band at the time, *Frampton's Camel* has a harder-rocking feel than its predecessor *Wind of Change*, with Mick Gallagher's percussive electric piano and organ taking a prominent position in the mix and Frampton getting a harder sound from his electric guitars (though his acoustic playing is so lush and lyrical that it dominates the album here and there in its quiet way). The sound on this recording lays out the formula that Frampton would take to mega-success three years later with the release of *Frampton Comes Alive*. The songs are all first-rate or close to it—included here is the original studio version of the group composition "Do You Feel Like We Do," a quicker-tempo, extended (albeit less majestic) version of which appeared on the latter album and became a staple of classic-rock radio, but the Frampton-composed "I Got My Eyes on You" and "Don't Fade Away" and the Frampton-Gallagher "All Night Long" are also compelling examples of '70s hard rock at its commercial best. This album also includes a nice cover of Stevie Wonder's "I Believe (When I Fall in Love With You It Will Be Forever)," the power ballad "Lines on My Face," the rollicking "White Sugar," and Frampton's gorgeously lyrical, all acoustic "Just the Time of the Year." As on *Wind of Change*, Frampton's use of dynamics and mix of acoustic and electric guitars keeps the music from becoming one-dimensional. The October 2000 CD reissue, remastered in state-of-the-art sound, adds an even more expansive feel to this album and enhances its melodic richness.

Jim Newsom & Bruce Eder

Frampton
1974, A&M

Frampton exited Humble Pie because that group fell into a loud, hard rock groove that overwhelmed the technical skills he'd spent years working on as a guitarist; he poured a lot of that into this highly melodic mid-tempo rock album. In the days before it saturated the airwaves in the version from *Frampton Comes Alive*, "Show Me the Way" was just a nice, very pleasant love song that benefited from a mix of acoustic and electric guitar textures spun out over a great beat and some excruciatingly memorable hooks, vocal and instrumental. It was surrounded by a lot more like it, including "Baby, I Love Your Way" in its original studio form, "The Crying Clown," "Nowhere's Too Far (For My Baby)," and most of the rest, although apart from the two hits, the playing and singing is often better than the songs themselves. This prevents the Frampton album from being a true classic, but it is one of the better albums from its all-too-mellow era.

Bruce Eder

Frampton Comes Alive!
1976, A&M

At the time of its release, *Frampton Comes Alive!* was an anomaly, a multi-million-selling (mid-priced) double LP by an artist who had previously never burned up the charts with his long-players in any spectacular way. The biggest-selling live album of all time, it made Peter Frampton a household word and generated a monster hit single in "Show Me the Way." And the reason why is easy to hear: the Herd/Humble Pie graduate packed one hell of a punch on-stage—where he was obviously the most comfortable—and, in fact, the live versions of "Show Me the Way," "Do You Feel Like I Do," "Something's Happening," "Shine On," and other album rock staples are much more inspired, confident, and hard-hitting than the studio versions. [The 1999 reissue in A&M's "Remastered Classics" (31454-0930-2) series is a considerable improvement over the original double CD or double LP in terms of sound—the highs are significantly more lustrous, the guitars crunch and soar, and the bottom end really thunders, and so you get a genuine sense of the power of Frampton's live set, at least the heavier parts of his set, rather than the compressed and flat sonic profile of the old double-disc version. Frampton and the band sound significantly closer as well, even on the softer songs such as "Wind of Change," and the disc is impressive listening even a quarter century later. Of course, one must take this all with a grain of salt as a concert document—as was later revealed, there was considerable studio doctoring of the raw live tapes, a phenomenon that set the stage for such unofficial hybrid works as Bruce Springsteen's *Live/1975-85* and countless others.]

Bruce Eder

I'm in You
1977, A&M

It was almost inevitable that *I'm in You* would be thought of as a letdown no matter how good it was. Following up to one of the biggest selling albums of the decade, Peter Frampton faced a virtually impossible task, made even more difficult by the fact that in the two years since he'd cut any new material, he had evolved musically away from some of the sounds on *Frampton Comes Alive*. The result was mostly a surprisingly laid-back album steeped in lyricism and craftsmanship, particularly in its use of multiple overdubs even on the harder rocking numbers. From the opening bars of "I'm in You," dominated by the sound of the piano (played by Frampton) and an ARP synthesizer-generated string section, rather than a guitar, it was clear that Frampton was exploring new sides of his music. Cuts like "Won't You Be My Friend," a piece of white funk that might've been better at six minutes running time, seemed to be dangerously close to self-indulgence at eight minutes long. The high points also include the title track, "Don't Have to Worry," and a killer cover of Stevie Wonder's "Signed, Sealed Delivered (I'm Yours)"; a couple of solid rock numbers, "Tried to Love" and the crunching "(I'm A) Roadrunner" also work their way in here to pump up the tension and excitement. *I'm in You* was successful on its own terms, and had Frampton recorded it before the live album, it would probably be very fondly looked back on. As it was, many listeners were not impressed. The spring 2000 reissue in 20-bit audio recreates the original album artwork and notes and is the best way to appreciate the multi-layered sound (and the crunchier rock moments) on this album.

Bruce Eder

Free

Tons of Sobs
1968, A&M

Although Free was never destined to scrape the same skies as Led Zeppelin, when they first burst out of the traps in 1968, close to a year ahead of Jimmy Page and company, they set the world of British blues-rock firmly on its head, a blistering combination of youth, ambition, and, despite those tender years, experience that, across the course of their debut album, did indeed lay the groundwork for all that Zeppelin would embrace. That Free and Zeppelin were cut from the same cloth is immediately apparent, even before you start comparing the versions of "The Hunter" that highlight both bands' debut albums. Where Free streaks ahead, however, is in their refusal to compromise their own vision of the blues—even at its most commercial ("I'm a Mover" and "Worry"), *Tons of Sobs* has a density that makes Zeppelin and the rest of the era's rocky contemporaries sound like flyweights by comparison. The 2002 remaster of the album only amplifies the fledgling Free's achievements. With remastered sound that drives the record straight back to the studio master tapes, the sheer versatility of the players, and the unbridled imagination of producer Guy Stevens, rings crystal clear. Even without their visionary seer, however, Free impresses—three bonus tracks drawn from period BBC sessions are as loose as they are dynamic, and certainly make a case for a full Free-at-the-Beeb type collection. Of the other bonuses, two offer alternate versions of familiar album tracks, while "Guy Stevens Jam" is reprised from the *Songs of Yesterday* box set to further illustrate the band's improvisational abilities. As if they needed it.

Dave Thompson

Free
1969, A&M

Free's second album was recorded with the band itself in considerable turmoil as principle songwriters Paul Rodgers and Andy Fraser demanded strict discipline from their bandmates, and guitarist Paul Kossoff, in particular, equally demanded the spontaneity and freedom that had characterized the group's debut. It was an awkward period that saw both Kossoff and drummer Simon Kirke come close to quitting, an eventuality that only the intervention of label chief Chris Blackwell seems to have prevented. Few of these tensions are evident on the finished album—tribute, again, to Blackwell's powers of diplomacy. He replaced original producer Guy Stevens early into the sessions and, having reminded both warring parties where the band's strengths lie, proceeded to coax out an album that stands alongside its predecessor as a benchmark of British blues at the turn of the 1960s.

Dave Thompson

Fire and Water
1970, A&M

If Fleetwood Mac, Humble Pie, and Foghat were never formed, Free would be considered one of the greatest post-Beatles blues-rock bands to date, and *Fire and Water* shows why. Conceptually fresh, with a great, roots-oriented, Band-like feel, Free distinguished itself with the public like Black Sabbath and Deep Purple did (in terms of impact, only) in 1970. Free presented itself to the world as a complete band, in every sense of the word. From Paul Kossoff's exquisite and tasteful guitar work, to Paul Rodgers' soulful vocals, this was a group that was easily worthy of the mantle worn by Cream, Blind Faith, or Derek and the Dominos .

Matthew Greenwald

Highway
February 1971, A&M

The last and least of the original Free studio albums, *Highway* was recorded just three months after the band scored the career-redefining hit "Alright Now," with their profile at an career-topping high, but morale heading toward an all-time low. Guitarist Paul Kossoff was reeling from the death of friend Jimi Hendrix, a new single, "The Stealer"—the follow-up to The Hit—bellyflopped ignominiously and, when the album followed suit, the band itself was not far behind. Heavily influenced by their admiration of the Band, *Highway* has understandably been described as Free's answer to *Music From Big Pink*, sharing both the laid-back vibe and mellow looseness of that role model. Where it went awry, of course, was in the fact that Free was not cut out to be country-rock guitar-twangers, no matter how fiery their missionary zeal. Yet, the strutting rockers "The Stealer" and "Ride On Pony" alone shatter the brave new mood, while reflective romancers like "Love You So" and "Be My Friend" could well have been composed specifically to rid the band of the shadow of "Alright Now," and prove that underneath the coolest exterior, there beat a heart of the molten gold. Of course, Free had bathed in such waters before, and the closing "Soon I Will Be Gone" certainly bears comparison with any of their past ballads. Nevertheless, too much of *Highway* reacted to the pressures of the recent past, rather building upon the strengths that had made such events possible in the first place, and you reach the bonus tracks appended to the 2002 remaster despairing that they will ever rediscover that earlier flair. But the 1971 hit single "My Brother Jake" is a gorgeous knockabout clearly informed by the Faces' recent assault on Free's own throne, while a couple of BBC session tracks, sensibly highlighting both the best ("Ride On Pony") and the worst ("Be My Friend") of the album itself, pack a punch that was clearly absent in the studio. In fact, whatever your opinion of *Highway* itself, the bonus tracks comprise an entire new reason to pick up the album.

Dave Thompson

Heartbreaker
1973, Island

Free's return in 1972 was scarred by any number of traumas, not least of all the departure of bassist Andy Fraser and the virtual incapacity of guitarist Paul Kossoff—one-half of the original band, and the lion's share of its spirit as well. But did their erstwhile bandmates let it show? Not a jot. The hastily recruited Tetsu Yamauchi, and vocalist Paul Rodgers himself, filled the breach instrumentally, and probably 50 percent of the ensuing *Heartbreaker* ranks among Free's finest ever work. Of course, any record that can open with the sheer majesty of "Wishing Well," Rodgers' so-evocative

tribute to Kossoff, is immediately going to ascend to the halls of greatness, all the more so since Kossoff himself is in such fine form across both this cut and the next three—completing side one of the original vinyl, "Come Together in the Morning," "Travellin' in Style," and "Heartbreaker" add up to the band's most convincing sequence of songs since the days of *Fire and Water*. Further into the disc, two contributions from another new recruit, keyboard player John Bundrick, fall a little flat, a fate they share with the previously unreleased "Hand Me Down/Turn Me Round," one of the 2002 remaster's six bonus tracks. But a pair of solo Rodgers songs, "Easy on My Soul" and "Seven Angels," close the album with as much emotion as it opened on, and one could well argue that, after such a treat, the aforementioned bonus tracks are all but unnecessary, especially as the first few simply offer outtakes, alternates, and B-sides from the sessions themselves. As the CD wraps up, however, two final tracks reveal what happened once the album was completed, peeping into the band's rehearsal room on the eve of their summer tour of Japan to catch "Heartbreaker" and "Easy on My Soul" in such rough but eloquently heavenly form that this most emotionally weighted of Free's albums could demand no deeper coda.

Dave Thompson

Peter Gabriel

Peter Gabriel [1]
1977, Atco

Peter Gabriel tells why he left Genesis in "Solsbury Hill," the key track on his 1977 solo debut. Majestically opening with an acoustic guitar, the song finds Gabriel's talents gelling, as the words and music feed off each other, turning into true poetry. It stands out dramatically on this record, not because the music doesn't work, but because it brilliantly illustrates why Gabriel had to fly on his own. Though this is undeniably the work of the same man behind *The Lamb Lies Down on Broadway*, he's turned his artiness inward, making his music coiled, dense, vibrant. There is still some excess, naturally, yet it's the sound of a musician unleashed, finally able to bend the rules as he wishes. That means there are less atmospheric instrumental sections, as there were on his last few records with Genesis, but unhinged bizarreness in the arrangements, compositions, and productions, as the opener "Morbund the Burgermeister" vividly illustrates. He also has turned sleeker, sexier, capable of turning out a surging rocker of "Modern Love." If there is any problem with *Peter Gabriel*, it's that Gabriel is trying too hard to show the range of his talents, thereby stumbling occasionally with the doo wop-to-cabaret "Excuse Me" or the cocktail jazz of "Waiting for the Big One" (or, the lyric "you've got me cookin'/I'm a hard-boiled egg" on "Humdrum"). Still, much of the record teems with invigorating energy (as on "Slowburn," or the orchestral-disco pulse of "Down the Dolce Vita"), and the closer "Here Comes the Flood" burns with an anthemic intensity that would later become his signature in the '80s. Yes, it's an imperfect album, but that's a byproduct of Gabriel's welcome risk-taking—the very thing that makes the album work, overall.

Stephen Thomas Erlewine

Peter Gabriel [2]
1978, Atco

The pairing sounds ideal—the former front man of Genesis, as produced by the leading light of King Crimson. Unfortunately, Peter Gabriel's second album (like his first, eponymous) fails to meet those grandiose expectations, even though it seems to at first. "On the Air" and "D.I.Y." are stunning slices of modern rock circa 1978, bubbling with synths, insistent rhythms, and polished processed guitars, all enclosed in a streamlined production that nevertheless sounds as large as a stadium. Then, things begin to drift, at first in a pleasant way ("A Wonderful Day in a One-Way World" is surprisingly nimble), but by the end, it all seems a little formless. It's not that the music is overly challenging—it's that the record is unfocused. There are great moments scattered throughout the record, yet it never captivates, either through intoxicating, messy creativity (as he did on his debut) or through cohesion (the way the third *Peter Gabriel* album, two years later, would). Certain songs work well on their own—not just the opening numbers, but the mini-epic "White Shadow," the tight "Animal Magic," the tense yet catchy "Perspective," the reflective closer "Home Sweet Home"—yet for all the tracks that work, they never work well together. Ironically, it holds together a bit better than its predecessor, yet it never reaches the brilliant heights of that record. In short, it's a transitional effort that's well worth the time of serious listeners, even it's still somewhat unsatisfying.

Stephen Thomas Erlewine

Peter Gabriel [3]
1980, Geffen

Generally regarded as Peter Gabriel's finest record, his third eponymous album finds him coming into his own, crafting an album that's artier, stronger, more song oriented than before. Consider its ominous opener, the controlled menace of "Intruder." He's never found such a scary sound, yet it's a sexy scare, one that is undeniably alluring, and he keeps this going throughout the record. For an album so popular, it's remarkably bleak, chilly, and dark—even radio favorites like "I Don't Remember" and "Games Without Frontiers" are hardly cheerful, spiked with paranoia and suspicion, insulated in introspection. For the first time, Gabriel has found the sound to match with his themes, plus the songs to articulate his themes. Each aspect of the album works, feeding off each other, creating a romantically gloomy, appealingly arty masterpiece. It's the kind of record where you remember the details in the production as much as the hooks or the songs, which isn't to say that it's all surface—it's just that the surface means as much as the songs, since it articulates the emotions as well as Gabriel's cubist lyrics and impassioned voice. He wound up having albums that sold more, or generated bigger hits, but this third *Peter Gabriel* album remains his masterpiece.

Stephen Thomas Erlewine

Security
1982, Geffen

Security—which was titled *Peter Gabriel* everywhere outside of the U.S.—continues where the third Gabriel album left off, sharing some of the same dense production and sense of cohesion, yet lightening the atmosphere and expanding the sonic palette somewhat. The gloom that permeates the third album

has been alleviated and while this is still decidedly somber and serious music, it has a brighter feel, partially derived from Gabriel's dabbling in African and Latin rhythms. These are generally used as tonal coloring, enhancing the synthesizers that form the basic musical bed of the record, since much of this is mood music (for want of a better word). *Security* flows easily and enticingly, with certain songs—the eerie "San Jacinto," "I Have the Touch," "Shock the Monkey"—arising from the wash of sound. That's not to say that the rest of the album is bland easy listening—it's designed this way, to have certain songs deliver greater impact than the rest. As such, it demands close attention to appreciate tone poems like "The Family and the Fishing Net," "Lay Your Hands on Me," and "Wallflower"—and not all of them reward such intensive listening. Even with its faults, *Security* remains a powerful listen, one of the better records in Gabriel's catalog, proving that he is becoming a master of tone, style, and substance, and how each part of the record enhances the other.

Stephen Thomas Erlewine

So
1986, Geffen

Peter Gabriel introduced his fifth studio album *So* with "Sledgehammer," an Otis Redding-inspired soul-pop raver that was easily his catchiest, happiest single to date. Needless to say, it was also his most accessible, and, in that sense it was a good introduction to *So*, the catchiest, happiest record he ever cut. "Sledgehammer" propelled the record toward blockbuster status, and Gabriel had enough songs with single potential to keep it there. There was "Big Time," another colorful dance number; "Don't Give Up," a moving duet with Kate Bush; "Red Rain," a stately anthem popular on album rock radio; and "In Your Eyes," Gabriel's greatest love song which achieved genuine classic status after being featured in Cameron Crowe's classic, *Say Anything*. These all illustrated the strengths of the album: Gabriel's increased melodicism and ability to blend African music, jangly pop, and soul into his moody art rock. Apart from these singles, plus the urgent "That Voice Again," the rest of the record is as quiet as the album tracks of *Security*. The difference is, the singles on that record were part of the overall fabric; here, the singles *are* the fabric, which can make the album seem top-heavy (a fault of many blockbuster albums, particularly those of the mid-'80s). Even so, those songs are so strong, finding Gabriel in a newfound confidence and accessibility, that it's hard not to be won over by them, even if *So* doesn't develop the unity of its two predecessors.

Stephen Thomas Erlewine

The J. Geils Band

The J. Geils Band
1970, Atlantic

The J. Geils Band's self-titled debut serves notice that rock & roll wasn't dead in 1970 despite the best efforts of the singer/

songwriter brigade. Though it sounds a bit reserved in the light of the albums that followed, compared to the majority of bands on the scene, it was a nonstop blast of energy, fun, and sweat. Featuring the hipster jive of singer Peter Wolf, the amazing afro and harp chops of Magic Dick, the fret-burning work of J. Geils, and the jack of many trades Seth Justman (keys, compositions, backing vocals), the Geils Band rips through some classic blues by the likes of Otis Rush ("Homework"), Walter Price ("Pack Fair and Square"), and John Lee Hooker (a slow-burning "Serves You Right to Suffer"), old Motown gems ("First I Look at the Purse"), and originals that stand up well next to the covers ("Wait," "What's Your Hurry," and future live favorite "Hard Drivin' Man"). A nice mix of nostalgia, intensity, and bar band excitement, the album serves as fair warning that the Geils Band was on the scene and was ready to bring back the good-time spirit of the juke joint, the abandon of the early rock & roll scene, and the high energy of the late-'60s concert halls.

Tim Sendra

The Morning After
1971, Atlantic

The Morning After is a near perfect follow-up to the J. Geils Band's self-titled debut album. It's more of the same winning blend of rocked-out blues, jumped-up soul, and pure rock & roll wildness with enough attitude and energy to get a club full of people from zero to sweaty in less than 60 seconds. Featuring the original versions of songs that became radio staples in their live incarnations ("Looking for a Love," the Magic Dick showcase "Whammer Jammer"), a batch of covers of rare soul gems ("So Sharp," Don Covay's "The Usual Place," the aforementioned "Looking for a Love"), and some fine originals (the rip-roaring opener "I Don't Need You No More," the very funky "Gotta Have Your Love," and the heart-rending ballad "Cry One More Time," which was covered memorably by Gram Parsons on *G.P.*), *The Morning After* is definite proof that the J. Geils Band were well on their way to becoming one of the best rock & roll bands of any era.

Tim Sendra

"Live" Full House
1972, Atlantic

The J. Geils Band made many fine, sometimes great, studio albums but where they really captured their full, thrilling potential was on the concert stage. Most live albums tend to be a poor excuse for actually being at the show in question, but the Geils  Band's live albums jump out of the speakers with so much joy, fun, and unquenchable rock & roll spirit that you might as well be there. *"Live" Full House* was their first live record, and it is a blast from start to finish. Recorded in 1972 at Detroit's Cinderella Ballroom, the group runs through songs from their first two albums, *The J. Geils Band* and *The Morning After*, kicking out the jams on rockers like the Motown chestnut "First I Look at the Purse," Otis Rush's "Homework," and one of the group's first self-penned classics, "Hard Drivin' Man," as well as positively scorching through an incredible version of John Lee Hooker's dark and

evil blues "Serves You Right to Suffer." It's easy to overlook J. Geils himself on guitar when you have a magnetic frontman like Peter Wolf or the unstoppable force that is harp player Magic Dick (check "Whammer Jammer" for proof of his greatness), but his soloing on this track serves notice that he could tear off a ferocious solo with the best of them. *"Live" Full House* is a short, punchy shot of rock & roll genius by one of the great bands of the '70s and one of the best live albums ever recorded.

Tim Sendra

Bloodshot
1973, Atlantic

Bloodshot is the J. Geils Band's third studio album and their first Top Ten (and last until 1982's smash *Freeze Frame*). The band sounds tighter, meaner, and funkier than on their first two releases, frontman Peter Wolf is looser and wilder than ever, and J. Geils positively rips things up on guitar. This newfound power could be down to the band blanketing the country and honing their craft in sweaty bars and concert halls. The positive response to their raw and alive live album *Full House* may have helped too. Whatever the cause, *Bloodshot* fairly jumps through the speakers on flat-out rockers like their cover of obscure soul stomper "(Ain't Nothin But A) Houseparty," the lean and nasty "Back to Get Ya" (which features a classic Wolf aside, "Scramble my eggs, honey!"), and concert fave "Southside Shuffle." The band also shows their range with hokey but fun blues shuffle "Struttin' with My Baby," bopping jump blues ("Hold Your Loving"), and very convincing heartbroken balladry ("Start All Over Again"). The band also delivers their first self-penned classic, the reggae-influenced "Give It to Me," which starts off as a tight and tough reggae-influenced pop song and spreads out into a funky jam that equals anything similar the Stones ever attempted. Along with it being a hit, *Bloodshot* is the first Geils album to stake a claim on the major leagues of rock & roll.

Tim Sendra

Ladies Invited
1973, Atlantic

The J. Geils Band were coming off their biggest album yet (*Bloodshot*, which hit the Top Ten on the *Billboard* album charts) when *Ladies Invited* appeared in 1973. It didn't reach the same level of sale (peaking at number 51) and none of the songs became AOR staples. Despite this, the record is solidly entertaining Geils, full of jumping party tunes and heart-punching ballads all composed by the band itself. As usual the up-tempo songs are the best: "Did You No Wrong" is a dynamic rocker with some blistering J. Geils guitar work, "I Can't Go On" is a full-out funky jam, and "Lay Your Good Thing Down" is fine blue-eyed soul with slick hipster vocals from Peter Wolf. The ballads here show a level of emotion and commitment that you might not expect: "My Baby Don't Love Me" is a countrified, tear-in-your-beer weeper with aching harmony vocals from Seth Justman, "Chimes" is an atmospheric, paranoid tune with great dynamics and a vocal from Wolf that veers between intimate and over-the-top howling, and probably best of all is the laid-back, Stonesy "That's Why I'm Thinking of You." It is really a shock that none of these songs caught on with AOR programmers. The only one that got a few spins was "No Doubt About It," and it is the album's highlight, a low-down and nasty blues rocker featuring the one and only Magic Dick getting down on his lickin' stick. And that stuff like the driving "Take a Chance (On Romance)" and the corny but fun "Diddyboppin'" should have been blasting out of radios up and down the strip, in high-school parking lots, and on the beach—basically everywhere AOR sounds the best. Don't let anyone tell you that *Ladies Invited* is one of Geils' lesser works. It is just one of the band's overlooked works that deserve a second listen.

Tim Sendra

Hotline
1975, Atlantic

The J. Geils Band's sixth studio album, 1975's *Hotline*, didn't spawn any hits, didn't reach very high on the charts, and was very true to the band's formula (going back to a mix of originals and covers after two all-original albums). It is also one of their most cohesive, satisfying, and fun albums. Kicking off with one of their live favorites, a barn-burning cover of Harvey Scales & the Seven Sounds' obscure soul nugget "Love-Itis," the disc runs through hard-edged blues, funky soul, rip-roaring rock & roll, and a ballad or two. The bandmembers show no signs of letting down and sound as dedicated to their house-party ethic as ever. Along with "Love-Itis," at least half of the record would have sounded excellent blasting from AOR stations. Why none of them, like the driving "Easy Way Out," the peppy "Jealous Love," and the cold as ice "Mean Love," never got much airplay is a mystery. Elsewhere, the band shows nice restraint on the heartbroken ballad "Think It Over," exhibits blazing blues chops on John Brim's "Be Careful (What You Do)" and Eddie Burns' "Orange Driver," and get very funky on "Fancy Footwork." The one song that sounds like their hearts aren't all the way in it, the cover of the Impressions' "Believe In Me," is still a rollicking good time. This is one of the overlooked gems in the band's catalog, not as strong as their best work but certainly worth many listens.

Tim Sendra

Blow Your Face Out
1976, Rhino

Double-album live sets came into vogue in 1976 after Peter Frampton's sales went through the roof for A&M, Bob Seger found fame with *Live Bullet* on Capitol, and the J. Geils Band released its second in-concert document in four years, *Blow Your Face Out*. There is great power in these grooves recorded over two nights, November 15 and November 19, at the now deconstructed Boston Garden and in Detroit at Cobo Hall. Here's the beautiful dilemma with the Geils band: *Live: Full House*, recorded in Detroit in April of 1972, contains five songs that became J. Geils standards, and none of them overlap on the 1982 EMI single live disc, *Showtime*, chock-full of their latter-day classics. Can you believe there is absolutely no overlap from the first or third live album on this double disc, which came in between (except for "Looking for a Love," uncredited, which they slip into the intro of "Houseparty" on side two)? The Rhino CD contains Jeff Tamarkin's liner notes, while the original Atlantic album has an exquisite gatefold chock-full of photos, and inner sleeves with priceless band memo stuff à la Grand Funk's *Live Album*. Sides one and two are great, and three and four are even better. "Detroit Breakdown" rocks and grooves,

with tons of audience applause...Wolfy and the polished authority of his monologues are in command as the band oozes into "Chimes" from 1973's *Ladies Invited*. About three and a half minutes longer than the five-minute original, it is one of many highlights on this revealing pair of discs. A precursor to 1977's title track, "Monkey Island," "Chimes" gives this enigmatic band a chance to jam out slowly and lovingly over its groove. There is so much to this album: the Janis Joplin standard "Raise Your Hand" written by Eddie Floyd, Albert Collins' "Sno-Cone" from their first album, and "Truck Drivin' Man" beating Bachman-Turner Overdrive to the punch. B.B. King producer Bill Szymczyk does a masterful job bringing it all together, and the band photos on back look...roguish. "Must of Got Lost," "Where Did Our Love Go," and "Give It to Me" are here in all their glory, a different glory than the studio versions, on an album that should have done for Geils what *Live Bullet* and *Frampton Comes Alive* did for their respective artists. If only a legitimate release of their 1999 tour would be issued to stand next to this monster—during that tour they combined the best elements of all three of their previous live discs. The J. Geils Band is more important and influential than the boys have been given credit for. It will be the live documents that ensure they eventually get their due, and *Blow Your Face Out* is a very worthy component that can still frazzle speakers.

Joe Viglione

Monkey Island
1977, Atlantic

The J. Geils Band's chart profile had been steadily slipping since the Top Ten success of their third record, *Bloodshot*. Even the awe-inspiring live album *Blow Your Face Out*, the band's near-maniacal dedication to the live stage, and their nonstop presence on the FM dial couldn't get them a hit album. By the time of 1977's *Monkey Island* the band seemed a little confused by it all and maybe even a bit weary of the effort to make it on their own terms. In most cases this would make for an artistic disaster, but hearing Geils branch out and lie back makes for one of their more interesting and challenging, if not most coherent, releases. Ranging from the wall-shaking funk of "Surrender" to the soft rock sweetness of "You're the Only One" (which comes complete with Magic Dick impersonating Stevie Wonder at his most romantic), the bopping AM-friendly R&B of "I Do" (the album's only cover), and the roaring hard rock of "Somebody," the album covers a lot of territory. Add to that the epic-length and overblown "Monkey Island," the smooth ballad "I'm Falling," and the shockingly slick modern R&B confection "So Good," and the album becomes near schizophrenic. Luckily, despite all the soul searching, dead ends, and obvious commercial overtures, the album retains enough of the innate Geils Band charm (and a couple good tracks like "Surrender," "So Good," and the loose blues rocker "I'm Not Rough") to make it work to a certain extent. Not a classic by any means but worth hearing at least once if only to hear why *Sanctuary* (on which they figure out how to make a totally commercial record the Geils way) was such a stunning return to form.

Tim Sendra

Sanctuary
1978, EMI America

After the release of 1977's *Monkey Island*, the J. Geils Band severed ties with Atlantic and signed a fresh deal with EMI Records. The band's tenure with Atlantic only yielded a few successes, and on paper, teaming up with producer Joe Wissert, the man responsible for many of Earth, Wind & Fire's and Boz Scaggs' biggest hits, seemed like an odd choice. However, *Sanctuary* was a rebirth of sorts for the sextet: Wissert crystallized the band's attack, working off their leaner songwriting and simplifying their arrangements. Keeping their boogie-woogie bar band attack intact, Peter Wolf and Seth Justman delivered first-rate material, including the down and dirty opener "I Could Hurt You," the sublime title track and the lovely "One Last Kiss," which cracked the Top 40 in early 1978. The Stevie Wonder-ish "Take It Back," also a mild hit, predicted the commercial direction the band took on *Freeze Frame* three years later. The beautiful "Teresa," a heartbreaking ballad executed with help of a simple vocal/piano arrangement courtesy of the Wolf/Justman team, and "Wild Man," which sounds like a leftover from the Atlantic years, are also highlights. *Sanctuary*'s final song, the rollicking, Magic Dick-driven "Just Can't Stop Me," encapsulates everything magical (pun intended) and soulful about this band. With its effortless playing and a breakdown that'll have you on the edge of your seat, it served as the band's call into battle for the Freeze Frame tour. The Razor & Tie reissue features covers of "I Do" and "Land of a Thousand Dances" from the band's live record *Showtime*, recorded at the height of their *Freeze Frame* period. "Land of a Thousand Dances" in particular reminds you just how incredible these guys were live.

John Franck

Love Stinks
1980, Capitol

Released some two years after the band's EMI debut, *Sanctuary*, the *Love Stinks* project would see the J. Geils Band going in an even more commercial-leaning direction than its predecessor. Taking over the main production duties, keyboard player/main songwriter Seth Justman set out to better the band's gold-plus-selling *Sanctuary*. And to some degree, he wildly succeeded. Although not as consistent or diverse as *Sanctuary*, *Love Stinks* would feature one of the band's most recognizable FM songs ever—the album's infectious title track "Love Stinks." In a live setting, the track would often turn into a veritable *tour de force* only to be outdone by Peter Wolf's hilarious rap about "Adam and Eve in the Garden of Eden smoking weed together," which would introduce the song (often on a nightly basis). "Night Time" is another great, although somewhat typical "rave-on" type of J. Geils song; "No Anchovies Please" is a little strange; and closer "Till the Walls Come Tumblin' Down" is, as the song title hints, just that. Bolstered by "Just Can't Wait," another good album opener, *Love Stinks* turns out to be solid effort, but one that sounds a little outdated at times due to its acerbic, synth textures. Not one of the band's best overall records but one that would allow the band to outdo itself with the classic *Freeze Frame* a year later.

John Franck

Freeze Frame
1981, Capitol

Tempering their bar band R&B with a touch of new wave pop production, the J. Geils Band finally broke through into the big leagues with *Freeze Frame*. Fans of the hard-driving rock of the group's '70s albums will find the sleek sound of *Freeze Frame* slightly disorienting, but the production gives the album cohesion. Good-time rock & roll remains at the core of the group's music, but the sound of the record is glossier, shining with synthesizers and big pop hooks. With its singalong chorus, "Centerfold" exemplifies this trend, but it's merely the tip of the iceberg. "Freeze Frame" has a great stop-start chorus, "Flamethrower"

and "Piss on the Wall" rush along on hard-boogie riffs, and "Angel in Blue" is terrific neo-doo wop. There are still a handful of throwaways, but even the filler has a stylized, synthesized flair that makes it enjoyable, and the keepers are among the band's best.

Stephen Thomas Erlewine

Houseparty: Anthology
1992, Rhino

The superb two-disc anthology *Houseparty* concentrates on the rousing, full-throttle blues-boogie of their heyday, including a full album's worth of live material (ten songs from their three live albums). The pop success of "Love Stinks" and "Freeze Frame" makes sense in the context of the set, but the songs that cut the deepest are the blues-rock numbers on the first disc and the live songs. Thankfully, the compilers (*Trouser Press* editor Ira Robbins and bandmembers Peter Wolf and Seth Justman) end *Houseparty* with three songs from *Sanctuary*, helping secure the image of the J. Geils Band as one of America's top rock & roll groups.

Stephen Thomas Erlewine

Genesis

Nursery Cryme
November 1971, Atco

If Genesis truly established themselves as progressive rockers on *Trespass*, *Nursery Cryme* is where their signature persona was unveiled: true English eccentrics, one part Lewis Carroll and one part Syd Barrett, creating a fanciful world that emphasized the band's instrumental prowess as much as Peter Gabriel's theatricality. Which isn't to say that all of *Nursery Cryme* works. There are times when the whimsy is overwhelming, just as there are periods when there's too much instrumental indulgence, yet there's a charm to this indulgence, since the group is letting itself run wild. Even if they've yet to find the furthest reaches of their imagination, part of the charm is hearing them test out its limits, something that does result in genuine masterpieces, as on "The Musical Box" and "The Return of the Giant Hogweed," two epics that dominate the first side of the album and give it its foundation. If the second side isn't quite as compelling or quite as structured, it doesn't quite matter because these are the songs that showed what Genesis could do, and they still stand as pinnacles of what the band could achieve.

Stephen Thomas Erlewine

Foxtrot
October 1972, Atco

Foxtrot is where Genesis began to pull all of its varied inspirations into a cohesive sound—which doesn't necessarily mean that the album is streamlined, for this is a group that always was grandiose even when they were cohesive, or even when they rocked, which they truly do for the first time here. Indeed, the startling thing about the opening "Watcher of the Skies" is that it's the first time that Genesis attacked like a rock band, playing with a visceral power. There's might and majesty here, and it, along with "Get 'Em Out by Friday," is the truest sign that Genesis has grown muscle without abandoning the whimsy. Certainly, they've rarely sounded as fantastical or odd as they do on the epic 22-minute closer "Supper's Ready," a nearly side-long suite that remains one of the group's signature moments. It ebbs, flows, teases and taunts, see-sawing between coiled instrumental attacks and delicate pastoral fairy tales. If Peter Gabriel remained a rather inscrutable lyricist, his gift for imagery is abundantly, as there are passages throughout the album that are hauntingly evocative in their precious prose. But what impresses most about *Foxtrot* is how that precociousness is delivered with pure musical force. This is the rare art-rock album that excels at both the art and the rock, and it's a pinnacle of the genre (and decade) because of it.

Stephen Thomas Erlewine

Selling England by the Pound
November 1973, Atco

GENESIS

SELLING ENGLAND BY THE POUND

Genesis proved that they could rock on *Foxtrot* but on its follow-up *Selling England by the Pound* they didn't follow this route, they returned to the English eccentricity of their first records, which wasn't so much a retreat as a consolidation of powers. For even if this eight-track album has no one song that hits as hard as "Watcher of the Skies," Genesis hasn't sacrificed the newfound immediacy of *Foxtrot*: they've married it to their eccentricity, finding ways to infuse it into the delicate whimsy that's been their calling card since the beginning. This, combined with many overt literary allusions—the Tolkeinisms of the title of "The Battle of Epping Forest" only being the most apparent—gives this album a story book quality. It plays as a collection of short stories, fables and fairy tales, and it is also a rock record, which naturally makes it quite extraordinary as a collection, but also as a set of individual songs. Genesis has never been as direct as they've been on the fanciful yet hook-driven "I Know What I Like (In Your Wardrobe)"—apart from the fluttering flutes in the fade-out, it could easily be mistaken for a glam single—or as achingly fragile as on "More Fool Me," sung by Phil Collins. It's this delicate balance and how the album showcases the band's narrative force on a small scale as well as large that makes this their arguable high-water mark.

Stephen Thomas Erlewine

The Lamb Lies Down on Broadway
November 1974, Atco

GENESIS

Given all the overt literary references of *Selling England by the Pound*, along with their taste for epic suites such as "Supper's Ready," it was only a matter of time before Genesis attempted a full-fledged concept album, and 1974's *The Lamb Lies Down on Broadway* was a massive rock opera: the winding, wielding story of a Puerto Rican hustler name Rael making his way in New York City. Peter Gabriel made some tentative moves toward developing this story into a movie with William Friedkin but it never took off, perhaps it's just as well; even with the lengthy libretto included with the album, the story never makes sense. But just because the story is rather impenetrable doesn't mean that the *album* is as well, because it is a forceful, imaginative piece of work that showcases the original Genesis lineup at a peak. Even if the story is rather hard to piece together, the album is set up in a remarkable fashion, with the first LP being devoted to pop-oriented rock songs and the second being largely devoted to instrumentals. This means that *The Lamb Lies Down on Broadway* contains both Genesis' most immediate music to date and its most elliptical. Depending on a listener's taste, they may gravitate toward the first LP with its tight collection of ten rock songs, or the nightmarish landscapes of the second, where Rael descends into darkness and ultimately redemption (or so it would seem), but there's little question that the first album is far more direct than the second and it contains a number of masterpieces, from the opening fanfare of the title song, to the surging "In the Cage," from the frightening "Back in NYC" to the soothing conclusion "The Carpet Crawlers." In retrospect, this first LP plays a bit more like the first Gabriel solo album than the final Genesis album, but there's also little question that the band helps form and shape this music (with Brian Eno adding extra coloring on occasion), while Genesis shines as a group shines on the impressionistic second half. In every way, it's a considerable, lasting achievement and it's little wonder that Peter Gabriel had to leave the band after this record: they had gone as far as they could go together, and could never top this extraordinary album.

Stephen Thomas Erlewine

Trick of the Tail
February 1976, Atco

After Peter Gabriel departed for a solo career, Genesis embarked on a long journey to find a replacement, only to wind back around to their drummer, Phil Collins, as a replacement. With Collins as their new frontman, the band decided not to pursue the stylish, jagged postmodernism of *The Lamb Lies Down on Broadway*—a move that Gabriel would do in his solo career—and instead returned to the English eccentricity of *Selling England by the Pound* for its next effort, *A Trick of the Tail*. In almost every respect, this feels like a truer sequel to *Selling England by the Pound* than *Lamb*; after all, that double album was obsessed with modernity and nightmare, whereas this album returns the group to the fanciful fairy tale nature of its earlier records. Also, Genesis were moving away from the barbed pop of the first LP and returning to elastic numbers that showcased their instrumental prowess, and they sounded more forceful and unified as a band than they had since *Foxtrot*. Not that this album is quite as memorable as *Foxtrot* or *Selling England*, largely because its songs aren't as immediate or memorable: apart from "Dance on a Volcano," this is about the sound of the band playing, not individual songs, and it succeeds on that level quite wildly—to the extent that it proved to longtime fans that Genesis could possibly thrive without its former leader in tow.

Stephen Thomas Erlewine

Wind & Wuthering
December 1976, Atco

Wind & Wuthering followed quickly on the heels of *A Trick of the Tail* and they're very much cut from the same cloth, working the same English eccentric ground that was the group's stock in trade since *Trespass*. But if *A Trick of the Tail* played like Genesis' attempt at crafting a great Genesis record without Peter Gabriel, as a way of finding their footing as a quartet, *Wind & Wuthering* finds Genesis tentatively figuring out what their identity will be in this new phase of their career. The most obvious indication of this is Mike Rutherford's "Your Own Special Way," which is both the poppiest tune the group had cut and also the first that could qualify as a love song. It stands out on a record that is, apart from that, a standard Genesis record, but quite a good one in that regard.

Stephen Thomas Erlewine

And Then There Were Three
March 1978, Atlantic

And Then There Were Three, more than either of its immediate predecessors, feels like the beginning of the second phase of Genesis—in large part because the lineup had indeed dwindled down to Tony Banks, Mike Rutherford, and Phil Collins, a situation alluded to in the title. But it wasn't just a whittling of the lineup; the group's aesthetic was also shifting, moving away from the fantastical, literary landscapes that marked both the early Genesis LPs and the two transitional post-Gabriel outings, as the bandmembers turned their lyrical references to contemporary concerns and slowly worked pop into the mix, as heard on the closing "Follow You Follow Me," the band's first genuine pop hit. Its calm, insistent melody, layered with harmonies, is a perfect soft rock hook, although there's a glassy, almost eerie quality to the production that is also heard throughout the rest of the record. These chilly surfaces are an indication that Genesis don't quite want to abandon prog at this point, but the increasing emphasis on melody and tight song structures points the way toward the group's '80s work.

Stephen Thomas Erlewine

Duke
March 1980, Atlantic

If *And Then There Were Three* suggested that Genesis were moving toward pop, *Duke* is where they leaped into the fray. Not that it was exactly a head-first leap: the band may have peppered the album with pop songs, but there was still a heavy dose of prog, as the concluding "Duke" suite made clear. But even the artiest moments are distinguished by the approach of their new producer, Hugh Padgham. Under his direction, Genesis are slicker, punchier, and bigger than they were before, adding dimension and texture to the long instrumental passages by punching up the production and layering on Tony Banks' keyboards. This is modernist art rock,

quite dissimilar to the fragile, delicate *Selling England by the Pound*, and sometimes the precision of the attack can be a little bombastic. Nevertheless, this is a major leap forward in distinguishing the sound of Genesis, the band, and along with a new signature sound come pop songs, particularly in the guise of "Misunderstanding" and "Turn It on Again." The first is a light, nearly soulful, heartache song, the latter is a thunderous arena rocker, and both showcase the new version of Genesis at its absolute best. The rest of the record comes close to matching them.

Stephen Thomas Erlewine

Abacab
September 1981, Atlantic

Duke showcased a new Genesis—a sleek, hard, stylish trio that truly sounded like a different band from its first incarnation—but *Abacab* was where this new incarnation of the band came into its own. Working once again with producer Hugh Padgham, the group escalated the innovations of *Duke*, increasing the pop hooks, working them seamlessly into the artiest rock here. And even if the brash, glorious pop of "No Reply at All"—powered by the percolating horns of Earth, Wind & Fire, yet polished into a precise piece of nearly new wave pop by Padgham—suggests otherwise, this is still art rock at its core, or at least album-oriented rock, as the band works serious syncopations and instrumental forays into a sound that's as bright, bold, and jagged as the modernist artwork on the cover. They dabble in other genres, lacing "Me and Sarah Jane" with a reggae beat, for instance, which often adds dimension to their sound, as when "Dodo" rides a hard funk beat and greasy organ synths yet doesn't become obvious; it turns inward, requiring active listening. Truly, only "No Reply at All," the rampaging title track (possibly their hardest-rocking song to date), and the sleek and spooky "Man on the Corner" (which hides a real melancholy heart underneath its glistening surface) are immediate and accessible—although the Mockney jokes of "Who Dunnit?" could count, it's too much of a geeky novelty to be pop. The rest of *Abacab* is truly modern art rock, their last album that could bear that tag comfortably.

Stephen Thomas Erlewine

Genesis
October 1983, Atlantic

Moments of *Genesis* are as spooky and arty as those on *Abacab*—in particular, there's the tortured howl of "Mama," uncannily reminiscent of Phil Collins' *Face Value* and the two-part "Home By the Sea"—but this eponymous 1983 album is indeed a rebirth, as so many self-titled albums delivered in the thick of a band's career often are. Here, the art-rock functions as coloring to the pop songs, unlike on *Abacab* and *Duke* where the reverse is true. Some of this may be covering their bets—to ensure that the longtime fans didn't jump ship, they gave them a bit of art—some of it may be that the band just couldn't leave prog behind, but the end result is the same: as of this record, Genesis was now primarily a pop band. Anybody that paid attention to "Misunderstanding" and "No Reply at All" could tell that this was a good pop band, primarily thanks to the rapidly escalating confidence of Phil Collins, but *Genesis* illustrates just how good they could be by balancing such sleek, pulsating pop tunes as "That's All" with a new-found touch for aching ballads, as on "Taking it All Too Hard." They still rocked—"Just a Job To Do" has an almost nasty edge to its propulsion—and they could still get too silly as on "Illegal Alien," where Phil's Speedy Gonzalez accident is an outright embarrassment (although in some ways it's not all that far removed from his Artful

Dodger accent on the previous album's "Who Dunnit?"), and that's why the album doesn't quite gel. It has a little bit too much of everything—too much pop, too much art, too much silliness—so it doesn't pull together, but if taken individually, most of these moments are very strong, testaments to the increasing confidence and pop power of the trio, even if it's not quite what longtime fans might care to hear.

Stephen Thomas Erlewine

David Gilmour

About Face
February 1984, Columbia

David Gilmour released his second solo venture in 1984, following the apparent dissolution of Pink Floyd. He had released a record on his own in 1978, but *About Face* is much more accessible. Gilmour has a stellar band backing him, including Jeff Porcaro (drums), Pino Palladino (bass), and Anne Dudley (synthesizer). The songs on *About Face* show a pop sensibility that Pink Floyd rarely was concerned with achieving. Although the album didn't attract the attention of a Floyd release, several cuts did manage to get airplay. "Until We Sleep" is rife with shimmering synthesizers and cavernous drums, and "Blue Light" was a minor pop hit, with Gilmour's trademark delay-drenched guitar giving way to a driving, horn-laced rocker. Pete Townshend wrote two of the tracks: "Love on the Air" and the propulsive "All Lovers Are Deranged." Of course, there's more than enough of Gilmour's fluid guitar playing to satisfy, including the gorgeous "Murder," a gentle acoustic track that explodes with some fiery organ by Steve Winwood and concludes with a fierce coda. *About Face* is well-honed rock album that is riveting from beginning to end.

Tom Demalon

Grand Funk Railroad

Grand Funk
January 1970, Capitol

Grand Funk Railroad's 1970 somewhat eponymous album, their second for Capitol, is characteristic of the classic rock radio sound that would permeate the airwaves of the late 20th century. Grand Funk Railroad was a seminal force in giving the friendlier side of the heavy rock sound its charm and making it stick. Built on fuzzed-out blues riffs, simple lyrics, and at times seemingly unnecessary jamming, *Grand Funk*'s songs are mild in nature. Far less extreme than Black Sabbath, but slightly toothier than Foghat or Bad Company, Grand Funk's major influence is from the loose, blues-based power trio formula of bands such as Cream and the Jimi Hendrix Experience. *Grand Funk* combines rawness with radio-friendly melodies and vocal harmonies that would become their trademark

sound. Hordes of bands to come, from Foreigner to Bon Jovi, would emulate Grand Funk's sound and style, focusing on good-time rocking material while attempting a few token social commentary pieces. This is a good album as far as early hard rock goes, and as Grand Funk Railroad would move farther and farther away from the type of roughness and loose arrangements found here, it is well worth picking up as an example of one of their early efforts.

Jeff Schwachter

Closer to Home
June 1970, Capitol

This is the trio's fourth album and the record that really broke them through to a more commercially successful level of metal masters such as Led Zeppelin and Black Sabbath. Rather than rushing headlong back into their typical hard, heavy, and overamplified approach, Grand Funk Railroad began expanding their production values. Most evident is the inclusion of strings on the album's title track, the acoustic opening on the disc's leadoff cut, "Sins a Good Man's Brother," as well as the comparatively mellow "Mean Mistreater." But the boys had far from gone soft. The majority of *Closer to Home* is filled with the same straight-ahead rock & roll that had composed their previous efforts. The driving tempo of Mel Schacher's viscous lead basslines on "Aimless Lady" and "Nothing Is the Same" adds a depth when contrasted to the soul-stirring and somewhat anthem-like "Get It Together." The laid-back and slinky "I Don't Have to Sing the Blues" also continues the trend of over-the-top decibel-shredding; however, instead of the excess force of other bands, such as MC5, Grand Funk Railroad are able to retain the often-elusive melodic element to their heavy compositions.

Lindsay Planer

We're an American Band
November 1973, Collector's Pipeline

Having made several changes in their business and musical efforts in 1972, Grand Funk Railroad made even more extensive ones in 1973, beginning with their name, which was officially truncated to "Grand Funk." And keyboardist Craig Frost, credited as a sideman on *Phoenix*, the previous album, was now a full-fledged bandmember, filling out the musical arrangements. The most notable change, however, came with the hiring of Todd Rundgren to produce the band's eighth album. Rundgren, a pop/rock artist in his own right, was also known for his producing abilities, and he gave Grand Funk exactly what they were looking for: *We're an American Band* sounded nothing like its muddy, plodding predecessors. Sonically, the record was sharp and detailed and the band's playing was far tighter and more accomplished. Most important, someone, whether the band or Rundgren, decided that gruff-voiced drummer Don Brewer should be employed as a lead singer as often as guitarist Mark Farner. Brewer also contributed more as a songwriter, and the results were immediate. The album's title song, an autobiographical account of life on the road written and sung by Brewer, was released in advance of the album and became a gold-selling number one hit, Grand Funk's first really successful single. Despite the band's previous popularity, for many, it must have been the first Grand Funk record they either heard or bought. Elsewhere on the album, Farner contributed his usual wailing vocals and guitar, singing of his heartfelt, if simpleminded, political concerns. But *We're an American Band* really belonged to Brewer and Rundgren, and its success constituted a redefinition of Grand Funk that came just in time.

William Ruhlmann

Caught in the Act
1975, Capitol

By 1975, Grand Funk Railroad had reached a new level of fame and fortune thanks to pop-friendly albums like *We're an American Band* and *Shinin' On*. However, they had not dropped the turbo-charged rock & roll that built their early success and that fact is proven by this exciting double-live album. *Caught in the Act* covers all the highlights of their catalog up to that point, including both the major hits and a generous sampling of album-track favorites. All the songs benefit from the amped-up live atmosphere and several improve over the studio versions thanks to the consistent high level of energy that the band pours into each tune. The best example is the latter phenomenon one-two punch of the albums' opening tracks: "Footstompin' Music" leaps out of the speakers with a galloping beat and pulsing organ that effortlessly outstrips its album version, then the band smoothly segues into a barnstorming, revamped version of "Rock 'n' Roll Soul" that tacks an infectious "Nothin' but a party" chant onto the song's beginning. Even the hits add new frills that keep them feeling like rote run-throughs: "The Loco Motion" is soulfully fleshed out by the addition of female backing vocals and hard rock muscle applied to "Black Licorice" transforms it into a speedy, fist-pumping rocker. Another big highlight is the atmospheric version of "Closer to Home," which sports a tighter, more complex arrangement than its studio counterpart and makes an excellent showcase for Craig Frost's skills on a variety of keyboard (he nimbly recreates the song's orchestral coda with an elegant performance on the Mellotron). The end result is a live album that is the equal of the studio's best studio-recorded outings. Simply put, *Caught in the Act* is a necessity for Grand Funk Railroad fans and may even attract non-fans with its effective combination of energy and instrumental firepower.

Donald A. Guarisco

Greatest Hits
April 2006, Capitol

Grand Funk Railroad took their veiled Motown/Stax influences and grafted them onto a fuzz-drenched hard blues-rock template, and muffler dragging roared out of Flint, Michigan like the little engine that could, confounding the critics and building an impressive record sales portfolio in the 1970s by giving their ardent, blue-collar fans no more and no less than what was expected of them. Distilled into a 14-track greatest-hits set like this one, it's easy to see that Grand Funk (they dropped—then re-added—the "Railroad" part of their name as the juggernaut rolled on) was essentially a singles band (although their albums did phenomenally well back in the day) with not a whole lot to say but a knack for saying it really well, which, when you think about it, is usually a sure ticket into the Top 40. *Greatest Hits* has all the essential jukebox fare (lacking only their so-so cover of the Rolling Stones' "Gimme Shelter"), including the clichéd but emotionally right "Heartbreaker," everybody's favorite guilty pleasure, the mock epic "I'm Your Captain," and a pair of pop-soul gems, the group's cover of the Soul Brothers Six's "Some

Kind of Wonderful," and Mark Farner's best-ever song, the marvelous "Bad Time," which came complete with cellos and fuzz guitar. For most, this single-disc collection will be more than adequate, but listeners looking for the complete Grand Funk story should check out Capitol's three-disc *Thirty Years of Funk* from 1999, or the four-disc *Trunk of Funk*, also from Capitol, released in 2002. The very best is here, though.

Steve Leggett

The Grass Roots

Anthology: 1965–1975
July 1991, Rhino

It may be expensive, and two CDs of their work may seem like overkill, but this double-disc set is the one to get. Not only does it contain every hit and each single, and every B-side, from 1965's "Where Were You When I Needed You" through 1975's glorious "Mamacita," but the sound is extraordinary, far better than on any of the other hits compilations, and provides several revelations about the quality of their work. Highlights, in addition to the expected hits ("Let's Live for Today," "Midnight Confessions," "Two Divided by Love" etc.) include tracks like "Is It Any Wonder," with a chorus as radiant as anything the Mamas and the Papas ever recorded, and the seldom heard, vibrant "Mamacita." If you could never imagine listening to 120 minutes of Grass Roots material (this reviewer couldn't, either), this set will make you feel differently.

Bruce Eder

The Grateful Dead

The Grateful Dead
March 1967, Warner Bros.

The Grateful Dead's eponymously titled debut long-player was issued in mid-March of 1967. This gave rise to one immediate impediment—the difficulty in attempting to encapsulate/recreate the Dead's often improvised musical magic onto a single LP. Unfortunately, the sterile environs of the recording studio disregards the subtle and often not-so-subtle ebbs and zeniths that are so evident within a live experience. So, while this studio recording ultimately fails in accurately exhibiting the Grateful Dead's tremendous range, it's a valiant attempt to corral the group's hydra-headed psychedelic jug-band music on vinyl. Under the technical direction of Dave Hassinger—who had produced the Rolling Stones as well as the Jefferson Airplane—the Dead recorded the album in Los Angeles during a Ritalin-fuelled "long weekend" in early 1967. Rather than prepare all new material for the recording sessions, a vast majority of the disc is comprised of titles that the band had worked into their concurrent performance repertoire. This accounts for the unusually high ratio (seven:two) of folk and blues standards to original compositions. The entire group took credit for the slightly saccharine "Golden Road (To Unlimited Devotion)," while Jerry Garcia (guitar/vocals) is credited for the noir garage-flavored raver "Cream Puff War." Interestingly, both tracks were featured as the respective A- and B-sides of the only 45 rpm single derived from this album. The curious aggregate of cover tunes featured on the Dead's initial outing also demonstrates the band's wide-ranging musical roots and influences. These include Pigpen's greasy harp-fuelled take on Sonny Boy Williamson's "Good Morning Little School Girl" and the minstrel one-man-band folk of Jessie "the Lone Cat" Fuller's "Beat It On Down the Line." The apocalyptic Cold War folk anthem "Morning Dew" (aka "[Walk Me Out in The] Morning Dew") is likewise given a full-bodied electric workout as is the obscure jug-band stomper "Viola Lee Blues." Fittingly, the Dead would continue to play well over half of these tracks in concert for the next 27 years. [Due to the time limitations inherent within the medium, the original release included severely edited performances of "Good Morning Little School Girl," "Sitting on Top of the World," "Cream Puff War," "Morning Dew," and "New, New Minglewood Blues." These tracks were restored in 2001, when the Dead's Warner Brothers catalog was reassessed for the *Golden Road (1965-1973)* box set.]

Lindsay Planer

Anthem of the Sun
July 1968, Warner Bros.

As the second long-player by the Grateful Dead, *Anthem of the Sun* (1968) pushed the limits of both the music as well as the medium. General dissatisfaction with their self-titled debut necessitated the search for a methodology to seamlessly juxtapose the more inspired segments of their live performances with the necessary conventions of a single LP. Since issuing their first album, the Dead welcomed lyricist Robert Hunter into the fold—freeing the performing members to focus on the execution and taking the music to the next level. Another addition was second percussionist Mickey Hart, whose methodical timekeeping would become a staple in the Dead's ability to stop on the proverbial rhythmic dime. Likewise, Tom Constanten (keyboards) added an avant-garde twist to the proceedings with various sonic enhancements that were more akin to John Cage and Karlheinz Stockhausen than anything else coming from the burgeoning Bay Area music scene. Their extended family also began to incorporate folks like Dan Healy—whose non-musical contributions and innovations ranged from concert PA amplification to meeting the technical challenges that the band presented off the road as well. On this record Healy's involvement cannot be overstated, as the band were essentially given *carte blanche* and simultaneous on-the-job training with regards to the ins and outs of the still unfamiliar recording process. The idea to create an aural pastiche from numerous sources—often running simultaneously—was a radical concept that allowed consumers worldwide to experience a simulated Dead performance firsthand. One significant pattern which began developing saw the band continuing to refine the same material that they were concurrently playing live night after night prior to entering the studio. The extended "That's It for the Other One" suite is nothing short of a psychedelic roller coaster. The wild ride weaves what begins as a typical song into several divergent performances—taken from tapes of live shows—ultimately returning to the home base upon occasion, presumably as a built-in reality check. Lyrically, Bob Weir (guitar/vocals) includes references to their 1967 pot bust ("...the heat came 'round and busted me for smiling on a cloudy day") as well as the band's spiritual figurehead

Neal Cassidy ("...there was Cowboy Neal at the wheel on a bus to never ever land"). Although this version smokes from tip to smouldering tail, the piece truly developed a persona all its own and became a rip-roaring monster in concert. The tracks "New Potato Caboose" and Weir's admittedly autobiographically titled "Born Cross-Eyed" are fascinatingly intricate side trips that had developed organically during the extended work's on-stage performance life. "Alligator" is a no-nonsense Ron "Pigpen" McKernan workout that motors the second extended sonic collage on *Anthem of the Sun*. His straight-ahead driving blues ethos careens headlong into the Dead's innate improvisational psychedelia. The results are uniformly brilliant as the band thrash and churn behind his rock-solid lead vocals. Musically, the Dead's instrumental excursions wind in and out of the primary theme, ultimately ending up in the equally frenetic "Caution (Do Not Stop on Tracks)." Although the uninitiated might find the album unnervingly difficult to follow, it obliterated the pretension of the post-*Sgt. Pepper's* "concept album" while reinventing the musical parameters of the 12" LP medium. [The expanded and remastered edition included in the *Golden Road (1965-1973)* (2001) box set contains a live performance from August 23, 1968, at the Shrine in Los Angeles. This miniset features an incendiary medley of "Alligator" and "Caution (Do Not Stop on Tracks)" concluding with over four minutes of electronic feedback.]

Lindsay Planer

Aoxomoxoa
June 1969, Warner Bros.

The Grateful Dead's third studio effort was also the first that the band did without any Warner Bros. staff producers or engineers hampering their creative lifestyle and subsequent processes. As they had done with their previous release, *Anthem of the Sun*, the Dead were actively seeking new forays and pushing envelopes on several fronts simultaneously during *Aoxomoxoa* (1968)—which was created under the working title of "Earthquake Country." This was no doubt bolstered by the serendipitous technological revolution which essentially allowed the Dead to re-record the entire contents when given free reign at the appropriately named Pacific High Recording facility. As fate would have it, they gained virtually unlimited access to the newly acquired Ampex MM-1000—the very first 16-track tape machines ever produced—which was absolutely state of the art in late 1968. The band was also experiencing new directions artistically. This was primarily the net result of the budding relationship between primary (by default) melodic contributor Jerry Garcia (guitar/vocals) and Robert Hunter (lyrics), who began his nearly 30-year association with the Grateful Dead in earnest during these sessions. When the LP hit the racks in the early summer of 1969, Deadheads were greeted by some of the freshest and most innovative sounds to develop from the thriving Bay Area music scene. The disc includes seminal psychedelic rockers such as "St. Stephen," "China Cat Sunflower," and "Cosmic Charlie," as well as hints of the acoustic direction their music would take on the Baroque-influenced "Mountains of the Moon" and "Rosemary." The folky "Dupree's

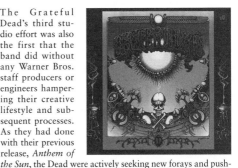

Diamond Blues"—which itself was loosely based on the traditional "Betty & Dupree"—would likewise foreshadow the sound of their next two studio long-players, *Workingman's Dead* (1969) and *American Beauty* (1970). The too-trippy-for-its-own-good "What's Become of the Baby" is buried beneath layers of over-indulgence. This is unfortunate, as Hunter's surreal lyrics and Garcia's understated vocals languish beneath the soupy sonics. In 1972, *Aoxomoxoa* was overhauled, and the original mix—which includes several significant differences such as an a cappella vocal tag at the tail end of "Doin' That Rag"—has yet to be reissued in any form. When the title was reworked for inclusion in the *Golden Road (1965-1973)* (2001) box set, three previously unreleased and incomplete studio instrumental jams—respectively titled "Clementine Jam," "Nobody's Spoonful Jam," and "The Eleven Jam"—as well as a live rendering of "Cosmic Charlie" from a January 1969 performance were added as "bonus material(s)."

Lindsay Planer

Live/Dead
November 1969, Warner Bros.

The Grateful Dead's fourth title was likewise their first extended concert recording. Spread over two LPs, *Live/Dead* (1969) finally was able to relay the intrinsic sonic magnificence of a Dead show in real time. Additionally, it unleashed several key entries into their repertoire, including the sidelong epic and Deadhead anthem "Dark Star" as well as wailing and otherwise electrified acidic covers of the Rev. Gary Davis blues standard "Death Don't Have No Mercy" and the R&B rave-up "(Turn on Your) Lovelight." Finally, the conundrum of how to bring a lengthy performance experience to the listener has been solved. The album's four sides provided the palette from which to replicate the natural ebb and flow of a typical Dead set circa early 1969. Tomes have been written about the profound impact of "Dark Star" on the Dead and their audience. It also became a cultural touchstone signifying that rock music was becoming increasingly experimental by casting aside the once-accepted demands of the short, self-contained pop song. This version was recorded on February 27, 1969, at the Fillmore West and is presented pretty much the way it went down at the show. The same is true of the seven remaining titles on *Live/Dead*. The rousing rendition of "St. Stephen" reinvents the *Aoxomoxoa* (1968) prototype with rip-roaring thunder and an extended ending which slams into an instrumental rhythmic excursion titled "The Eleven" after the jam's tricky time signature. The second LP began with a marathon cover of "(Turn on Your) Lovelight," which had significant success for both Bobby "Blue" Bland and Gene Chandler earlier in the decade. With Ron "Pigpen" McKernan at the throttle, the Dead barrel their way through the work, reproportioning and appointing it with fiery solos from Garcia and lead vocal raps courtesy of McKernan. "Death Don't Have No Mercy" is a languid noir interpretation of Rev. Gary Davis's distinct Piedmont blues. Garcia's fretwork smolders as his solos sear through the melody. Likewise notable is the criminally underrated keyboard work of Tom Constanten, whose airy counterpoint rises like a spirit from within the soul of the song. The final pairing of "Feedback"—which is what is sounds like it might be—with the "lowering down" funeral dirge "And We Bid You Goodnight" is true to the way that the band concluded a majority of their performances circa 1968-1969. They all join in on an a cappella derivative of Joseph Spence and the Pinder Family's traditional Bahamian distillation. Few recordings have ever represented the essence of an artist in performance as faithfully as *Live/Dead*. It

has become an aural snapshot of this zenith in the Grateful Dead's 30-year evolution and as such is highly recommended for all manner of enthusiasts. The 2001 remastered edition that was included in the *Golden Road (1965-1973)* (2001) box set tacks on the 45 rpm studio version of "Dark Star" as well as a vintage radio advert for the album.

Lindsay Planer

Workingman's Dead
June 1970, Warner Bros.

The Grateful Dead were already established as paragons of the free-form, improvisational San Francisco psychedelic sound when they abruptly shifted gears for the acoustic *Workingman's Dead*, a lovely exploration of American roots music illuminating the group's country, blues, and folk influences. The lilting "Uncle John's Band," their first radio hit, opens the record and perfectly summarizes its subtle, spare beauty; complete with a new focus on more concise songs and tighter arrangements, the approach works brilliantly. Despite its sharp contrast to the epic live space jams on which the group's legend primarily rests, *Workingman's Dead* nonetheless spotlights the Dead at their most engaging, stripped of all excess to reveal the true essence of their craft.

Jason Ankeny

American Beauty
November 1970, Warner Bros.

A companion piece to the luminous *Workingman's Dead*, *American Beauty* is an even stronger document of the Grateful Dead's return to their musical roots. Sporting a more full-bodied and intricate sound than its predecessor thanks to the addition of subtle electric textures, the record is also more representative of the group as a collective unit, allowing for stunning contributions from Phil Lesh (the poignant opener, "Box of Rain") and Bob Weir ("Sugar Magnolia"); at the top of his game as well is Jerry Garcia, who delivers the superb "Friend of the Devil," "Candyman," and "Ripple." Climaxing with the perennial "Truckin'," *American Beauty* remains the Dead's studio masterpiece—never again would they be so musically focused or so emotionally direct.

Jason Ankeny

Grateful Dead (Skull & Roses)
October 1971, Warner Bros.

The Grateful Dead's second live release was an eponymously titled double LP whose cover bears the striking skull-and-roses visual motif that would become instantly recognizable and an indelibly linked trademark of the band. As opposed to their debut concert recording, *Live/Dead* (1969), this hour and ten minutes concentrates on newer material, which consisted of shorter self-contained originals and covers. Coming off of the quantum-leap success of the studio country-rock efforts *Workingman's Dead* (1969) and *American Beauty*, *Grateful Dead* offers up a pair of new Jerry Garcia/Robert

Hunter compositions—"Bertha" and "Wharf Rat"—both of which garnered a permanent place within the band's live catalog. However, "The Other One"—joined in progress just as Billy Kreutzmann fires up a blazing percussion solo—sprawls as the album's centerpiece. The Dead also begin incorporating several traditional folk, blues, and R&B cover tunes, such as Merle Haggard's "Mama Tried," Kris Kristofferson's "Me & Bobby McGee," as well as a few that had been in their songbook for several years, including John Phillips' "Me & My Uncle" and "Big Boss Man," a blues standard popularized by Jimmy Reed. Their formidable improvisational chops have begun to take on new facets of lean intricacy as Mickey Hart (percussion) and Tom Constanten (keyboards) were no longer in the band. Additionally, the arrival of Keith Godchaux (organ) and his wife, Donna Godchaux (vocals), had yet to occur. As such, the Grateful Dead spent the spring and summer of 1971 in their original five-piece configuration—which is when these recordings were documented. The *Golden Road (1965-1973)* (2001) box set features a remastered version of *Grateful Dead* and includes two additional covers—Buddy Holly's "Oh, Boy!" as well as Leiber & Stoller's "(I'm A) Hog for You"—plus an unmarked vintage radio spot for the album. Enthusiasts should note that this era is likewise represented on the four-CD *Ladies and Gentlemen...The Grateful Dead* (2000) archival release.

Lindsay Planer

Europe '72
November 1972, Warner Bros.

The Grateful Dead commemorated their first extended European tour with an extravagant triple-LP set appropriately enough titled *Europe '72*. This collection is fashioned in much the same way as their previous release—which had also been a live multi-disc affair. The band mixes a bevy of new material—such as "Ramble on Rose," "Jack Straw," "Tennessee Jed," "Brown-Eyed Woman," and "He's Gone"—with revisitations of back-catalog favorites. Among them are "China Cat Sunflower"—which was now indelibly linked to the longtime Dead cover "I Know You Rider"—as well as "Cumberland Blues," "Truckin'," "Sugar Magnolia," and "Morning Dew." With the additional album the band was able to again incorporate some of their exceedingly stretched-out instrumental improvisations—titled "Epilogue" and "Prelude" here. Since their last outing, the group had expanded to include the husband-and-wife team of Keith Godchaux (keyboards) and Donna Jean Godchaux (vocals). Sadly, this European jaunt would be the last of its kind to include the formidable talents and soul of founding member Ron "Pigpen" McKernan (organ/mouth harp/vocals), who was in increasingly fragile health. Although few in number, his contributions to *Europe '72* are among the most commanding not only of this release, but of his career.

Lindsay Planer

Wake of the Flood
November 1973, Grateful Dead

After satisfying their nine-title/dozen-disc deal with Warner Brothers, the Dead began their own record labels: Grateful Dead Records (for group releases) and Round Records (for solo projects). *Wake of the Flood* was the first Dead disc issued entirely under the band's supervision—which also included manufacturing and marketing. Additionally, the personnel had been altered as Ron "Pigpen" McKernan had passed away. The keyboard responsibilities were now in the capable hands of Keith Godchaux—whose wife Donna Jean Godchaux also provided backing vocals. It had been nearly

three years since *American Beauty*—their previous and most successful studio album to date—and, as always, the Dead had been honing the material in concert. A majority of the tracks had been incorporated into their live sets—some for nearly six months—prior to entering the recording studio. This gave the band a unique perspective on the material, much of which remained for the next 20-plus years as staples of their concert performances. However, the inspiration and magic of the Grateful Dead's music has always been a challenge to capture in the non-reciprocal confines of a studio. Therefore, while *Wake of the Flood* was certainly as good—if not arguably better than—most of their previous non-live efforts, it falls far short of the incendiary performances the band was giving during this era. There are a few tracks that do tap into some of the Dead's jazzier and exceedingly improvisational nature. "Eyes of the World" contains some brilliant ensemble playing—although the time limitations inherent in the playback medium result in the track fading out just as the Dead start to really cook. Another highlight is Bob Weir's "Weather Report Suite," which foreshadows the epic proportions that the song would ultimately reach. In later years, the band dropped the opening instrumental "Prelude," as well as "Part One," choosing to pick it up for the extended "Let It Grow" section. The lilting Jerry Garcia ballad "Stella Blue" is another track that works well in this incarnation and remained in the Dead's rotating set list for the remainder of their touring careers.

Lindsay Planer

From the Mars Hotel
June 1974, Grateful Dead

The Grateful Dead made their reputation on the road with their live shows, and they always struggled to capture that magic in the studio. *From the Mars Hotel*, while not a classic, represents one of their better studio albums. Jerry Garcia sounds engaged throughout and takes the vocal reigns for most of the songs on the album—although he's not the most gifted vocalist, he proves himself able and versatile. He sings the rollicking opener, "U.S. Blues," with a tongue-in-cheek seriousness that gives the political song an edge, and he lends emotional sincerity to the atmospheric ballad "China Doll." Garcia shines on guitar during the funk workout "Scarlet Begonias," but the ensemble work is best displayed on the album's centerpiece, "Unbroken Chain." During this song, all the musicians are allowed to shine: Phil Lesh, the bassist and songwriter, provides tender vocals over a piano-based arrangement while the bridge allows the guitars and drums to stretch out in classic Grateful Dead style. This album is highly recommended for fans, but casual listeners should start with *American Beauty* or *Workingman's Dead*.

Vik Iyengar

Blues for Allah
September 1975, Grateful Dead

The Grateful Dead went into a state of latent activity in the fall of 1974 that lasted until the spring of the following year when the band reconvened at guitarist/vocalist Bob Weir's Ace Studios to record *Blues for Allah*. The disc was likewise the third to be issued on their own Grateful Dead Records label. When the LP hit shelves in September of 1975, the Dead were *still* not back on the road—although they had played a few gigs throughout San Francisco. Obviously, the time off had done the band worlds of good, as *Blues for Allah*—more than any past or future studio album—captures the Dead at their most natural and inspired. The opening combo of "Help on the Way," "Slipknot!," and "Franklin's Tower" is a multifaceted suite, owing as much to Miles Davis circa the *E.S.P.* album as to anything the Grateful Dead had been associated with. "Slipknot!" contains chord changes, progressions, and time signatures which become musical riddles for the band to solve—which they do in the form of "Franklin's Tower." Another highly evolved piece is the rarely performed "King Solomon's Marbles," an instrumental that spotlights, among other things, Keith Godchaux's tastefully unrestrained Fender Rhodes finger work displaying more than just a tinge of Herbie Hancock inspiration. These more aggressive works contrast the delicate musical and lyrical haiku on "Crazy Fingers" containing some of lyricist Robert Hunter's finest and most beautifully arranged verbal images for the band. Weir's guitar solo in "Sage & Spirit" is based on one of his warm-up fingering exercises. Without a doubt, this is one of Weir's finest moments. The light acoustic melody is tinged with an equally beautiful arrangement. While there is definite merit in *Blues for Allah*'s title suite, the subdued chant-like vocals and meandering melody seems incongruous when compared to the remainder of this thoroughly solid effort.

Lindsay Planer

In the Dark
July 1987, Arista

The Grateful Dead's last lineup returned intact for *In the Dark*, an album that ironically thrust the band back into the spotlight on the strength of the band's lone Top 40 single, "Touch of Grey." Fans had long mused that the Dead's studio albums lacked the easygoing energy and natural flow of their live performances, and *In the Dark* does come close to capturing that lightning in a bottle. Jerry Garcia, who apparently had to relearn the guitar after a near-fatal illness, approaches his instrument recharged, while his voice (a beneficiary of the extended hiatus?) shows some of its original smoothness. Of his four songwriting collaborations with long-standing lyricist Robert Hunter, "Touch of Grey" is far and away the best. "When Push Comes to Shove" and "West L.A. Fadeaway" use familiar blues-based riffs that lack the pair's often-contagious chemistry, and "Black Muddy River" has one foot firmly stuck in mawkish MOR terrain (although Garcia can be dealt a free pass here in light of the song's real-life implications as an attempt to make his peace with the world). What pushes *In the Dark* past the band's also-rans are two terrific songs from Bob Weir and John Barlow, the cheerfully cranky "Hell in a Bucket" (co-written with Brent Mydland) and the cautionary tale "Throwing Stones." Rarely have Weir's songs sounded so effortless; punctuated by Garcia's guitar, they have more in common with the upbeat, flavorful sound of past Garcia/Hunter compositions than the pair's own work this time out (a rare case of role reversal). In the middle of it all is a country-rock song from Mydland, "Tons of Steel," that sounds oddly out of place. Although the album is unmistakable as the work of the Dead, much of it recalls the punchy, pungent production of Dire Straits' recent work. It's not the second coming of the Dead, but a more entertaining epilogue you couldn't ask for.

Dave Connolly

Grin

The Very Best of Grin
June 1999, Spindizzy/Epic Associated/Legacy

The failure of Grin to sell large numbers of records in the early '70s is one of those mysteries of popular music. They seemed to have everything, all in the person of leader Nils Lofgren, an accomplished guitarist and songwriter with a connection to the CSNY axis who had played on Neil Young's *After the Gold Rush* when he was only 18-years-old. He was still under 21 when the first self-titled Grin album was released in 1971. Maybe his youth had something to do with the band's limited commercial success; he often let other band members take lead vocals on the songs he wrote, preferring a group context that sometimes hid his talents. Nevertheless, the band's albums garnered good reviews and the first three (of four) made the charts, with "White Lies" charting as a single. Those albums were stylistically diverse and somewhat uneven, but contained catchy pop/rock songs ("Like Rain," "Love or Else," "Sad Letter"), any one of which could have changed Grin's story with the right promotion. This well-chosen best-of (actually the second one, following a 1976 LP, despite a sticker on the CD proclaiming "1st-Ever GRIN 'Best-Of' Collection!"), containing a couple of previously unreleased tracks and a non-LP B-side, accurately portrays the band's pop-folk-rock-country sound, from "Everybody's Missin' the Sun" (which could have fit on *After the Gold Rush* easily) to "You're the Weight," from the band's 1973 swan song *Gone Crazy*, licensed from A&M Records. Lofgren, of course, went on to a more successful solo career from the mid-'70s to the mid-'80s before becoming "the most overqualified second guitarist in rock" in Bruce Springsteen's E Street Band, as Springsteen himself put it. But the work of Grin is more than juvenilia: In the early '70s, it was good enough to make fans frustrated that the band didn't get more of a hearing. And it sounds just as good more than 25 years later.

William Ruhlmann

The Guess Who

Wheatfield Soul
1968, RCA

Wheatfield Soul by the Guess Who has become a collectors item of sorts over the years, fetching various prices in fan circles, and it is an important "first" step for the reconstituted group which initially hit with "Shakin' All Over" when it was led by Chad Allan. The album is Jack Richardson's excellent production of Randy Bachman and Burton Cummings' music played by this particular four-piece unit, which Peter Clayton's liner notes claim were together "for three years when they cut this album in late 1968." The naïve sound of Cummings' voice on the album tracks is charming, but the hit "These Eyes" has that authority which the band would repeat on diverse chart songs like "No Time," "American Woman," and even "Star Baby" further down the road. "Pink Wine Sparkles in the Glass" is a precursor to "New Mother Nature," but the solo Cummings composition "I Found Her in a Star" is very nice Guess Who-style pop that their fans adore. "Friends of Mine" is a strange one, though, ten minutes and three seconds of Burton Cummings imitating Jim Morrison, not just Morrison, but the copping of his vocal riffs straight from "When the Music's Over." This is a band stretching and searching for direction, and rather than hit you with hard Randy Bachman assaults which were a welcome addition to future long-players by this group, as well as Bachman-Turner Overdrive, *Wheatfield Soul* concentrates on Brit-pop and experimental songs. Randy Bachman's "A Wednesday in Your Garden" is British rock meets jazz, and is one of the LP's most interesting numbers. The Chick Crumpacker and Don Wardell liner notes to *Ultimate Collection* note that "These Eyes" "was technically the 18th release by the band." The key is that it was the first from the quartet of Cummings, Bachman, Kale, and Peterson as produced by Jack Richardson. *Ultimate Collection* also notes that "Lightfoot" was written for "fellow Canadian Gordon Lightfoot." The notes go on to point out that "Maple Fudge" and "We're Coming to Dinner" were real oddities, but a style that would reappear over the band's long and illustrious catalog. Maybe that's what makes *Wheatfield Soul* so sought after, inventive themes that eventually found their way onto later albums like *Artificial Paradise* and *Rockin'*. Perhaps the tragedy is that they didn't get to work with Frank Zappa—the Guess Who's left-field musings would have been the perfect follow-up to Zappa's work with Grand Funk. Take two of "Lightfoot" appears on *Ultimate Collection*, which only utilized three songs from this important first album after the band was reborn. But for all the musical wandering, it is "These Eyes" which remains timeless, the song that stands out as the masterpiece on this creative adventure.

Joe Viglione

Canned Wheat
1969, Buddha

As far as late-'60s and early-'70s rock bands go, the Guess Who has been both blessed and cursed. Blessed because their songs are still played quite frequently on oldies radio stations, cursed because they're only remembered for those songs. Truth be told, the Guess Who was a darn good rock band: Burton Cummings's great rock & roll voice—similar in power to Bad Company's Paul Rodgers—keeps even the most overdone Guess Who songs fresh, and Randy Bachman's underrated guitar work always serves the song's needs. "Undun"'s wonderful, jazzy riff, which fits the song perfectly, is associated with the overall sound of the Guess Who, not Bachman. 1969's cleverly-titled *Canned Wheat* introduced several of the band's most remembered songs: "Laughing," "Undun," and "No Time." The album also has six other keepers, including the mellow "6 A.M. or Nearer," complete with jazzy guitar and flute, and the lovely ballad "Minstrel Boy." The original version of "No Time" is fun, even if it isn't radically different; little nuances, like the fade out, shake the listener out of the "I've heard this song a thousand times" syndrome. There are a couple of throwaway bonus tracks, "Species Hawk" and "Silver Bird," that are nice to have, even if they aren't up to the other material. The liner notes are helpful, and it's funny to learn that radio stations ordered copies of "Undun" for airplay, not realizing that it was the B-side of "Laughing." *Canned Wheat* still sounds incredibly fresh, a product from the heyday of classic rock. For those who want to dig beneath the band's "oldie" status to find the real thing, this album shouldn't be missed.

Ronnie Lankford, Jr.

American Woman
January 1970, Buddha

The Guess Who's most successful LP, reaching number nine in America (and charting for more than a year), has held up well and was as close to a defining album-length statement as the original group ever made. It's easy to forget that until "American Woman," the Guess Who's hits had been confined to softer, ballad-style numbers—that song (which originated as a spontaneous on-stage jam) highlighted by Randy Bachman's highly articulated fuzz-tone guitar, a relentless beat, and Burton Cummings moving into Robert Plant territory on the lead vocal, transformed their image. As an album opener, it was a natural, but the slow acoustic blues intro by Bachman heralded a brace of surprises in store for the listener. The presence of the melodic but highly electric hit version of "No Time" (which the band had cut earlier in a more ragged rendition) made the first ten minutes a hard rock one-two punch, but the group then veers into progressive rock territory with "Talisman." Side two was where the original album was weakest, though it started well enough with "969 (The Oldest Man)." "When Friends Fall Out," a remake of an early Canadian release by the group, attempted a heavy sound that just isn't sustainable, and "8:15" was a similar space filler, but "Proper Stranger" falls into good hard rock groove. In August of 2000, Buddha Records issued a remastered version of this album with a bonus track from a subsequent session, "Got to Find Another Way." Ironically, *American Woman* was the final testament of the original Guess Who—guitarist/singer Randy Bachman quit soon after the tour behind this album; the group did endure and even thrive (as did Bachman), but *American Woman* represented something of an ending as well as a triumph.

Bruce Eder

Share the Land
1970, Buddha

Recorded in the immediate aftermath of lead guitarist Randy Bachman's departure from the group, *Share the Land* was a better album than anyone could rightfully have expected, and it was the biggest selling original album in their entire output, appearing in the wake of "American Woman" and lofted into the Top 20 (with a lot of advance orders) with a pair of hits of its own. The music ranges from the catchy, anthem-like title tune to proto-metal excursions, with coherent digressions into blues and country ("Comin' Down Off the Money Bag"/"Song of the Dog"). Burton Cummings is in excellent voice on the lead vocals, and the other members provide some of the finest harmonies ever heard on a Guess Who album, on "Do You Miss Me Darlin'" and "Three More Days." The new double lead guitar team of Kurt Winter and Greg Leskiw gave the band a greater range than they'd ever had, moving freely in various rock and blues idioms, and the rhythm section was as solid as ever. That having been said, however, the music hasn't necessarily aged well (or, perhaps, those who've achieved a maturity level beyond age 18 have aged past it)—listening to details such as Winter's shouts of "Freedom!" and "Paint me a picture" on "Three More Days," one can't escape the thought that at least half of this album not only wasn't aimed at the overachieving end of the high school and college populations, but was aggressively *not* aimed at them. And from here on, beyond whatever virtuosity the members brought to their sound, it seemed as though the group was working from formula rather than inspiration. The fall 2000 reissue on the Buddha label features a high-resolution remastering, and includes a pair of very good lost numbers from the early sessions for the record, "Palmyra" and "The Answer," featuring Bachman on guitar.

Bruce Eder

Live at the Paramount
1972, Buddha

The August 2000 reissue of *Live at the Paramount* on the Buddha label has 13 songs, the whole 75 minutes of music from the first of two shows, and provides the best explanation of how the Guess Who endured as a major concert draw years after their biggest hits were behind them; when they were spot-on, as they were that night, they gave an exciting show. Remixed and remastered properly, this is now a killer concert album, showing off the double lead guitar attack that was a hallmark of their live sound in blazing glory, energizing even familiar songs like "New Mother Nature," and Burton Cummings near the peak of his form with the band as a singer. Surprisingly, the songs that were left off of the original LP included several hits, both vintage ("These Eyes," "No Time") and relatively recent ("Rain Dance," "Share the Land"), though the highlight is "Sour Suite," which is a dazzling showcase for Cummings as a singer and pianist. The remixing also helps the material that was on this album originally, pumping up the volume on the bluesy jam that opens "American Woman," which also sounds a lot better (and is worth hearing in the 15 minute jam version featured here). "Share the Land" comes off better here than its official version, set ablaze by Kurt Winter's and Don McDougal's guitars and a spirited vocal performance.

Bruce Eder

Greatest Hits
February 1999, RCA

There have been plenty of Guess Who collections on the market, from the original *Best of the Guess Who* to the multi-disc *Track Record*. Of all of these, the best is the 1999 collection *Greatest Hits*, which contains a generous 18 songs, including all but two of their charting American singles—not counting 1965's "Shakin' All Over," the missing songs are "Broken" (the B-side to "Albert Flasher") and "Runnin' Back to Saskatoon" (which barely scraped the charts). Although the Guess Who's albums are distinctive (more so than their reputation would lead you to believe), there's little question that they're best heard as a singles band, and this is the best place to hear them that way. After a spin of *Greatest Hits*, it's clear that the Guess Who made some of the best mainstream rock of their era—and while they never received much critical respect (apart from iconoclast Lester Bangs, of course), their music

holds up better than much of their peers', which means that the Guess Who deserves to have the last laugh.

Stephen Thomas Erlewine

Shakin' All Over!
September 2001, Sundazed

Sundazed's *Shakin' All Over!* is naturally a godsend for dedicated Guess Who fans, presenting a 24-track summary of the group's recordings between 1963 and 1967, all taken from the original master tapes for the first time. This alone, along with the originally unissued "Use Your Imagination" and "Just a Matter of Time" and John Einarson's liner notes make this a fine fan package, but what makes this more than just a for-fans-only release is that the music is quite good. It is true that some of it is a little generic in the sense that they were a North American band finding their voice by turning out British-styled pop/rock, both in the driving Animals sense and the melodic Merseybeat style. It's very clear at certain points they're still developing their style, including their taste in covers, but they generally sound very appealing, both when they rock hard and when they indulge in candy-coated melodies. In fact, they can rock pretty damn hard, not just on the title song, but on another Johnny Kidd cover called "Baby Feelin'," Johnny Otis' "Tuff E Nuff," Randy Bachman's great "Believe Me" (which sounds a bit like early MC5) and "It's My Pride," plus Burton Cummings' fine "If You Don't Want Me," while on the other end of the spectrum, Bachman's instrumental British Invasion tribute "Made in England' is pretty endearing, as is the sweet (albeit dippy) "Stop Teasing Me" and the pretty cover of Neil Young's "Flying on the Ground is Wrong." (Young, in the liner notes, claims Bachman was an early influence, and it's not only possible to hear that, he's absolutely right that Bachman was quite a guitarist.) In one sense, this is a specialist release, since it will only appeal to Guess Who freaks and '60s guitar band fanatics, but it will satisfy both camps equally.

Stephen Thomas Erlewine

Sammy Hagar

Standing Hampton
1981, Geffen

After releasing several competent but more or less undistinguished albums on Capitol, Sammy Hagar switched to Geffen in 1981 and released *Standing Hampton*, a polished but tough record that showed a surprising amount of pop songcraft. The added production gloss and improved melodic sense proved commercially successful—the album was his first million-seller and it cracked the Top 30—and artistically successful as well; the record was the most consistent and memorable album he had recorded to date, featuring the singles "I'll Fall in Love Again," "Baby's on Fire," and "There's Only One Way to Rock."

Stephen Thomas Erlewine

Three Lock Box
1983, Geffen

Continuing the sleek, driving pop-oriented sound of Hagar's breakthrough, *Standing Hampton*, *Three Lock Box* equals its predecessor, featuring such highlights as the double entendres of the title track and the hit single "Your Love Is Driving Me Crazy."

Stephen Thomas Erlewine

VOA
1984, Geffen

VOA was the last album Sammy Hagar recorded before he became the lead singer of Van Halen, and this effort shows why he was invited to join the band. With songs like "I Can't Drive 55," he adds a simple melody to the song which never distracts from the all-important, hard-driving riff. On "Two Sides of Love," he shows that he has the ability to pull off a power ballad, wrenching every bit of feeling out of the song. Like Hagar himself, *VOA* is never subtle, but in hard rock, that's a positive attribute.

Stephen Thomas Erlewine

George Harrison

All Things Must Pass
November 1970, Capitol

Without a doubt, Harrison's first solo recording, originally issued as a triple album, is his best. Drawing on his backlog of unused compositions from the late Beatles era, Harrison crafted material that managed the rare feat of conveying spiritual mysticism without sacrificing his gifts for melody and grand, sweeping arrangements. Enhanced by Phil Spector's lush orchestral production, and Harrison's own superb slide guitar, nearly every song is excellent: "Awaiting on You All," "Beware of Darkness," the Dylan collaboration "I'd Have You Anytime," "Isn't It a Pity," and the hit singles "My Sweet Lord" and "What Is Life" are just a few of the highlights. A very moving work, with a very significant flaw: the jams that comprise the final third of the album are entirely dispensable, and have probably only been played once or twice by most of the listeners that own this record.

Richie Unterberger

The Concert for Bangladesh
December 1971, Sony

Hands down, this epochal concert at New York's Madison Square Garden—first issued on three LPs in a handsome orange-colored box—was the crowning event of George Harrison's public life, a gesture of great goodwill that captured the moment in history and, not incidentally, produced some rousing music as a permanent legacy. Having been moved by his friend Ravi Shankar's appeal to help the homeless Bengali refugees of the 1971 India-Pakistan war, Harrison leaped into action, organizing on short notice what became a bellwether for the spectacular rock & roll benefits of the 1980s and beyond. The large, almost unwieldy band was loaded with rock luminaries—including Beatles alumnus Ringo Starr, Eric Clapton, Badfinger, and two who became stars as a result of their electric performances here, Leon Russell ("Jumpin' Jack Flash"/"Youngblood") and Billy Preston ("That's The Way God Planned It"). Yet Harrison is in confident command, running through highlights from his recent triumphant *All Things Must Pass* album in fine voice, secure enough to revisit his Beatles legacy from *Abbey Road* and the *White Album*. Though overlooked at the time by impatient rock fans eager to hear the hits, Shankar's

opening raga, "Bangla Dhun," is a masterwork on its own terms; the sitar virtuoso is in dazzling form even by his standards and, in retrospect, Shankar, Ali Akbar Khan, and Alla Rakha amount to an Indian supergroup themselves. The high point of the concert is the surprise appearance of Bob Dylan—at this reclusive time in his life, every Dylan sighting made headlines—and he read the tea leaves perfectly by performing five of his most powerful, meaningful songs from the '60s. Controversy swirled when the record was released; then-manager Alan Klein imposed a no-discount policy on this expensive set and there were questions as to whether all of the intended receipts reached the refugees. Also, in a deal to allow Dylan's participation, the set was released by Capitol on LP while Dylan's label Columbia handled the tape versions. Yet, in hindsight, the avarice pales beside the concert's magnanimous intentions, at a time when rock musicians truly thought they could help save the world.

Richard S. Ginell

Living in the Material World
May 1973, Capitol

How does an instant multimillion-selling album become underrated? George Harrison's follow-up to *All Things Must Pass* was necessarily a letdown for fans and critics, appearing after a two-and-a-half-year interval without the earlier album's backlog of excellent songs from which to draw. And it does seem like Harrison narrowed his sights and his vision on this record, which has neither the bold expansiveness nor the overwhelming confidence of its predecessor. And some of the most serious songs here, such as "The Light That Has Lighted the World," seem dirge-like. What *Living in the Material World* does show off far better than the earlier record, however, is Harrison's guitar work—he's the only axeman on *Material World*, and it does represent his solo playing and songwriting at something of a peak. Most notable are his blues stylings and slide playing, glimpsed on some of the later Beatles sessions but often overlooked by fans. "Don't Let Me Wait Too Long" is driven by a delectable acoustic rhythm guitar and has a great beat. The title track isn't great, but it does benefit from a tight, hard band sound, and "The Lord Loves the One (That Loves the Lord)," despite its title, is the high point of the record, a fast, rollicking, funky, bluesy jewel with a priceless guitar break (maybe the best of Harrison's solo career) that should have been at the heart of any of Harrison's concert set. Vocally, he isn't as self-consciously pretty or restrained here, but it is an honest performance, and his singing soars magnificently in his heartfelt performance on "The Day the World Gets Round." Perhaps a less serious title would have represented the album better, but nobody was looking for self-effacement from any ex-Beatle except Ringo (who's also here, natch) in those days.

Bruce Eder

Extra Texture
September 1975, Capitol

Despite George Harrison's reputation for solemn, lugubriously paced albums in the early '70s—and this one is mostly no exception—the jacket is full of jokes, from the eaten-away Apple logo (the Apple label would expire at year's end) to the punning title, the list of non-participants, and the mischievous grin of the ex-Beatle above the arch caption "OHNOTHIMAGEN" ("Oh, not him again!"). The record gets off to a great start with the instantly winning single "You"—a bit of which is then repeated to open side two. But here, the basic idea and instrumental track come from Feb. 1971, during George's most fertile period, dressed up with vocals and string synthesizer four years later. One of George's most beautifully harmonized, majestic, strangely underrated ballads "The Answer's at the End"—whose inspiring lyric was based upon an inscription on George's home by its builder, Sir Frank Crisp—comes next, followed by "This Guitar (Can't Keep From Crying)," an attractive sequel to "While My Guitar Gently Weeps." At this point, the devoted fan's hopes go up; could this be an unsung masterpiece? But George has fired off his best stuff first, and the record slowly and inexorably tails off, closing with a baffling salute to ex-Bonzo Dog Band member "Legs" Larry Smith. Yet despite its stretches of treadmill material, *Extra Texture* has worn better as a whole than its Apple neighbors *Dark Horse* and even much of *Living in the Material World*, for even the lesser tunes reveal a few musical blossoms upon re-listening and the front-loaded songs are among the best of his solo career.

Richard S. Ginell

George Harrison
February 1979, Dark Horse

George Harrison is, except for the overdubbed London strings, a painstakingly polished L.A.-made product—and not a particularly inspired one at that. It's an ordinary album from an extraordinary talent. "Love Comes to Everyone" leads it off on a depressing note, a treadmill tune with greeting-card verses, and there are too many other such halfhearted songs lurking here, although some are salvaged by a nice instrumental touch: a catchy recurring guitar riff on "Soft Touch" and some lovely slide guitar on "Your Love Is Forever." Compared to the original, tougher Beatles version that was left off the White Album, the remake of "Not Guilty" is an easy listening trifle, though it was a revelation when it came out (the original had to wait until 1996 and *Anthology 3* for an official release), and the succeeding "Here Comes the Moon" is a lazy retake on another Beatles song. "Blow Away" would be the record's most attractive new song—and a number 16 hit—but "Faster," a paean to Harrison's passion for Formula One auto racing, probably better reflected where his head was at this time. There are a few quirks: "Soft-Hearted Hana" is a strange, stream-of-consciousness Hawaiian hallucination and "Dark Sweet Lady" is a Latin-flavored tune written for his new wife, Olivia. Finally, the inevitable spiritual benediction "If You Believe" offers some thoughtful philosophy to ponder, if not an especially memorable tune.

Richard S. Ginell

Cloud Nine
November 1987, Dark Horse

Teaming with legendary Beatles obsessive Jeff Lynne, George Harrison crafted a remarkably consistent and polished comeback effort with *Cloud Nine*. Lynne adds a glossy production, reminiscent of ELO, but what is even more noticeable is that he's reined in Harrison's indulgences, keeping the focus on a set of 11 snappy pop/rock numbers. The consistency of the songs remains uneven, but the best moments—"Devil's Radio," "Cloud 9," "Just for Today," "Got My Mind Set on You," and the tongue-in-cheek Beatles pastiche "When We Was Fab"—make *Cloud Nine* one of his very best albums.

Stephen Thomas Erlewine

Heart

Dreamboat Annie
March 1976, Capitol

In the 1980s and '90s, numerous women recorded blistering rock, but things were quite different in 1976—when female singers tended to be pigeonholed as soft rockers and singer/songwriters and were encouraged to take after Carly Simon, Melissa Manchester, or Joni Mitchell rather than Led Zeppelin or Black Sabbath. Greatly influenced by Zep, Heart did its part to help open doors for ladies of loudness with the excellent *Dreamboat Annie* (reissued on a gold audiophile CD by DCC Compact Classics in 1995). Aggressive yet melodic rockers like "Sing Child," "White Lightning & Wine," and the rock radio staples "Magic Man" and "Crazy on You" led to the tag "the female Led Zeppelin." And in fact, Robert Plant did have a strong influence on Ann Wilson. But those numbers and caressing, folk-ish ballads like "How Deep It Goes" and the title song also make it clear that the Nancy and Ann Wilson had their own identity and vision early on.

Alex Henderson

Little Queen
May 1977, Portrait

After acquiring a substantial following with *Dreamboat Annie*, Heart solidified its niche in the hard rock and arena rock worlds with the equally impressive *Little Queen*. Once again, loud-and-proud, Led Zeppelin-influenced hard rock was the thing that brought Heart the most attention. But while "Barracuda" and "Kick It Out" are the type of sweaty rockers one thought of first when Heart's name was mentioned, hard rock by no means dominates this album. In fact, much of *Little Queen* consists of such folk-influenced, acoustic-oriented fare as "Treat Me Well" and "Cry to Me." Anyone doubting just how much Heart's ballads have changed over the years need only play "Dream of the Archer" next to a high-volume power ballad like "Waiting for an Answer" from 1990's *Brigade*.

Alex Henderson

Dog & Butterfly
September 1978, Portrait

Dog & Butterfly became Heart's fourth million-selling album and placed two songs of opposing styles in the Top 40. Like their *Magazine* album, *Dog & Butterfly* peaked at number 17 on the charts, but the material from it is much stronger from every standpoint, with Anne and Nancy Wilson involving themselves to a greater extent. The light, afternoon feel of the title track peaked at number 34, while the more resounding punch of "Straight On" went all the way to number 15 as the album's first single. With keyboard player Howard Leese making his presence felt, and the vocals and guitar work sounding fuller and more focused, the band seems to be rather comfortable once again. Average bridge-and-chorus efforts like "Cook with Fire" and "High Time" aren't spectacular, but they do emit some appeal as far as filler is concerned, while "Lighter Touch" may be the best of the uncharted material. After this album, guitarist Roger Fisher left the band, but Heart didn't let up. 1980's *Bebe le Strange* showed an even greater improvement, peaking at number five in April of that year.

Mike DeGagne

Heart
June 1985, Capitol

Heart was pretty much considered washed up when they released *Heart* in 1985. They learned a few important things while they had taken a short sabbatical—they knew that hooks were important and they knew they could play up their looks for MTV. So, they delivered both with *Heart*, giving their audience anthemic hooks and tightly corseted bosoms, leading to the most popular album they ever had. This doesn't mean it's the best, since its calculated mainstream bent may disarm some long-term fans, but it is true that they do this better than many of their peers, not just because they have good polished material from professional songwriters but because they can deliver this material professionally themselves. Yes, "These Dreams," "Never," and "What About Love" don't quite fit into the classic Heart mode, but they are good mid-'80s mainstream material, delivered as flawlessly as possible. There's still a lot of filler on this record, but the best moments are among the best mainstream AOR of its era.

Stephen Thomas Erlewine

Jimi Hendrix

Are You Experienced? [UK]
1967, MCA

One of the most stunning debuts in rock history, and one of the definitive albums of the psychedelic era. On *Are You Experienced?*, Jimi Hendrix synthesized various elements of the cutting edge of 1967 rock into music that sounded both futuristic and rooted in the

best traditions of rock, blues, pop, and soul. It was his mind-boggling guitar work, of course, that got most of the ink, building upon the experiments of British innovators like Jeff Beck and Pete Townshend to chart new sonic territories in feedback, distortion, and sheer volume. It wouldn't have meant much, however, without his excellent material, whether psychedelic frenzy ("Foxey Lady," "Manic Depression," "Purple Haze"), instrumental freak-out jams ("Third Stone From the Sun"), blues ("Red House," "Hey Joe"), or tender, poetic compositions ("The Wind Cries Mary") that demonstrated the breadth of his songwriting talents. Not to be underestimated were the contributions of drummer Mitch Mitchell and bassist Noel Redding, who gave the music a rhythmic pulse that fused parts of rock and improvised jazz. Many of these songs are among Hendrix's very finest; it may be true that he would continue to develop at a rapid pace throughout the rest of his brief career, but he would never surpass his first LP in terms of consistently high quality. The

British and American versions of the album differed substantially when they were initially released in 1967; MCA's 17-song CD reissue does everyone a favor by gathering all of the material from the two records in one place, adding a few B-sides from early singles, as well.

Richie Unterberger

Axis: Bold as Love
December 1967, MCA

Jimi Hendrix's second album followed up his groundbreaking debut effort with a solid collection of great tunes and great interactive playing between himself, Noel Redding, Mitch Mitchell, and the recording studio itself. Wisely choosing manager Chas

Chandler to record the album, since he was in the midst of a creative hot streak, Hendrix stretched further musically than the first album, but even more so as a songwriter. He was still quite capable of coming up with spacy rockers like "You Got Me Floating," "Up From the Skies," and "Little Miss Lover," radio-ready to follow on the commercial heels of "Foxey Lady" and "Purple Haze." But the beautiful, wistful ballads "Little Wing," "Castles Made of Sand," "One Rainy Wish," and the title track set closer show remarkable growth and depth as a tunesmith, harnessing Curtis Mayfield soul guitar to Dylanesque lyrical imagery and Fuzz Face hyperactivity to produce yet another side to his grand psychedelic musical vision. These are tempered with Jimi's most avant-garde tracks yet, "EXP" and the proto-fusion jazz blowout of "If 6 Was 9."

Cub Koda

Electric Ladyland
October 1968, MCA

Jimi Hendrix's third and final album with the original Experience found him taking his funk and psychedelic sounds to the absolute limit. The result was not only one of the best rock albums of the era, but also Hendrix's original musical vision at its absolute apex. When revisionist rock critics refer to him as the maker of a generation's mightiest dope music, *this* is the album they're referring to.

But *Electric Ladyland* is so much more than just background music for chemical intake. Kudos to engineer Eddie Kramer (who supervised the remastering of the original two-track stereo masters for this 1997 reissue on MCA) for taking Hendrix's visions of a soundscape behind his music and giving it all context, experimenting with odd mic techniques, echo, backward tape, flanging, and chorusing, all new techniques at the time, at least the way they're used here. What Hendrix sonically achieved on this record expanded the concept of what could be gotten out of a modern recording studio in much the same manner as Phil Spector had done a decade before with his Wall of Sound. As an album this influential (and as far as influencing a generation of players and beyond, this was his ultimate statement for many), the highlights speak for themselves: "Crosstown Traffic," his reinterpretation of Bob Dylan's "All Along the Watchtower," "Burning of the Midnight Lamp," the spacy "1983...(A Merman I Should Turn to Be)," and "Voodoo Chile (Slight Return)," a landmark in Hendrix's playing. With this double set (now on one compact disc), Hendrix once again pushed the concept album to new horizons.

Cub Koda

Smash Hits
July 1969, Reprise

One of the first hits compilations assembled of Jimi Hendrix's catalog, *Smash Hits* remains one of the best, since it keeps its focus narrow and never tries to extend its reach. Basically, this album contains the songs everybody knows from Hendrix, drawing heavily from *Are You Experienced?*, plus adding the non-LP "Red House," "51st Anniversary," and "Highway Chile." Those non-LP selections may still make this worth seeking out, even if they've appeared on subsequent hits collections, but the main strength of *Smash Hits* is that it contains the best-known, big-name songs in one place. Maybe not enough to make the collection essential, but still enough to make it a representative, accurate sampler.

Stephen Thomas Erlewine

Band of Gypsys
1970, Capitol

Band of Gypsys was the only live recording authorized by Jimi Hendrix before his death. It was recorded and released in order to get Hendrix out from under a contractual obligation that had been hanging over his head for a couple years. Helping him out were longtime friends Billy Cox on bass and Buddy Miles on the drums because the Experience had broken up in June of 1969, following a show in Denver. This rhythm section was vastly different from the Experience. Buddy Miles was an earthy, funky drummer in direct contrast to the busy, jazzy leanings of Mitch Mitchell. Noel Redding was not really a bass player at all but a converted guitar player who was hired in large part because Hendrix liked his hair! These new surroundings pushed Hendrix to new creative heights. Along with this new rhythm section, Hendrix took these shows as an opportunity to showcase much of the new material he had been working on. The music was a seamless melding of rock, funk, and R&B, and tunes like "Message to Love" and "Power to Love" showed a new lyrical direction as well. Although he could be an erratic live performer, for these shows, Hendrix was *on*—perhaps his finest performances. His playing was focused and precise. In fact, for most of the set, Hendrix stood motionless, a far cry from the stage antics that helped establish his reputation as a performer. Equipment problems had plagued him in past live shows as well, but everything was perfect for the Fillmore shows. His absolute mastery of his guitar and effects is even more amazing considering that this was the first time he used the Fuzz Face, wah-wah pedal, Univibe, *and* Octavia pedals on-stage together. The guitar tones he gets on "Who Knows" and "Power to Love" are powerful and intense, but nowhere is his absolute control more evident than on "Machine Gun," where Hendrix conjures bombs, guns, and other sounds of war from his guitar, all within the context of a coherent musical statement. The solo on "Machine Gun" totally rewrote the book on what a man could do with an electric guitar and is arguably the most groundbreaking and devastating guitar solo ever. These live versions of "Message to Love" and "Power to Love" are far better than the jigsaw puzzle studio versions that were released posthumously. Two Buddy Miles compositions are also included, but the show belongs to Jimi all the way. *Band of Gypsys* is not only an important part of the Hendrix legacy, but one of the greatest live albums ever.

Sean Westergaard

Blues
April 1994, MCA

While Jimi Hendrix remains most famous for his hard rock and psychedelic innovations, more than a third of his recordings were blues-oriented. This CD contains 11 blues originals and covers, eight of which were previously unreleased. Recorded between 1966 and 1970, they feature the master guitarist stretching the boundaries of electric blues in both live and studio settings. Besides several Hendrix blues-based originals, it includes covers of Albert King and Muddy Waters classics, as well as a 1967 acoustic version of his composition "Hear My Train a Comin'."

Richie Unterberger

First Rays of the New Rising Sun
April 1997, MCA

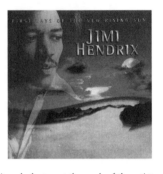

Posthumous reconstructions of unfinished works are inherently dangerous, principally because even the most capable scholar or producer can only make, at best, an educated guess as to how the work in question would have been completed. Indeed, in dealing with some such pieces, you're sometimes lucky to get the work of the artist claimed (the Mozart Symphony No. 37 is a case in point—it doesn't exist; the piece once labeled Symphony No. 37 and attributed to Mozart is now known to have been authored by Michael Haydn); and while there's no question that the songs on this CD were recorded by Jimi Hendrix, even the people who worked on the sides with him can't say which songs would have ended up on the finished version of *First Rays of the New Rising Sun* (assuming that he even ended up using that title for the album), or what embellishments he would have added to any of them in the course of completing them, or even if he might not have totally reconsidered such matters as tempo and approach to any of them. In the end, *First Rays of the New Rising Sun* is a little like any of the various "performing editions" of Gustav Mahler's never-completed Symphony No. 10, in that what's here is impressive, but may have little to do with what would finally have been heard by the public, had the artist lived to finish it—we don't know if Mahler would have scored a particular passage for horns or strings, or Hendrix would have put another, different lead guitar part, or a second (or third) guitar part on to any of these songs, or added choruses, or re-thought his vocal performance? Hendrix had gone so long between albums, seemingly adrift stylistically at various times, that there's no telling exactly what direction he was finally going to end up working toward. All of that said, this is a superb album, and a worthy if very different, earthier successor to *Electric Ladyland*'s psychedelic excursions—the later tracks, ironically enough, cut at that album's long promised and long-delayed studio namesake—and also show him working in some genuinely new directions. For starters, Hendrix's voice emerges here as a genuinely powerful instrument in its own right—his voice was never as exposed in the mix of his songs as it is here; partly this is because Hendrix and engineer Eddie Kramer never finished embellishing the songs, or completed the final mixes. But whatever the reasons, the change is refreshing—Hendrix's voice is not only powerful and expressive throughout, but a more melodic instrument than it seemed on his earlier releases; indeed, hearing these sides is a bit like listening to those middle-years Muddy Waters recordings when Chess Records had the Chicago blues legend abandon his guitar playing in favor of concentrating on his singing; the results might not be what all fans expected, but it sure sounds good, because it turns out that Hendrix had an expressive voice and was also moving his music into new areas that were stimulating him. A lot of the material here shows Hendrix, for the first time, moving his songs specifically into a black music idiom, embracing R&B and funk elements in his singing, playing, and overall sound; some of it could qualify as Hendrix's extension of his years playing with the Isley Brothers. Songs here such as "Freedom," "Izabella," "Angel," and "Dolly Dagger" show him finally acknowledging that musical world that he had largely by-passed, and the closer, "Belly Button Window," is one of his most successful traditional bluesy outings. The psychedelic workouts are more jam-like and experimental, and the ballads are prettier and even more dreamlike in their background soundscapes. "Astro Man" also captures a light moment for the artist, as he opens the guitar workout with a quote from the Mighty Mouse theme song, *sotto voce* beneath the guitar. And speaking of the guitar, despite the prominence of Hendrix's vocals on a lot of this album, the guitar playing is pretty much up to the standard that one would expect, if not necessarily the final versions of some of the songs. Most of the material on *First Rays of the New Rising Sun* surfaced among the various posthumous Hendrix LPs issued from the 1970s through the early 1990s, but a lot of it was tampered with, mostly in the form of posthumous overdubbed embellishments supervised by producer Alan Douglas—all of that has been stripped off and the multi-track masters retrieved and restored. What he would have eventually come up with and released as his next musical statement is anyone's guess, but this gets you as close to that answer—and that vision—as you're ever likely to get. It is the best representation of where the songs were at the point that he died, and it's fully competitive, in terms of merits and surprises, with his trio of completed studio albums.

Bruce Eder & Cub Koda

BBC Sessions
June 1998, MCA

These are the recordings that Jimi Hendrix made for BBC radio in the late '60s. As such, they're loose, informal, and off-the-top-of-his-head improvisational fun. These versions of the hits "Foxey Lady," "Fire," two versions of "Purple Haze," and "Hey Joe" stay surprisingly close to the studio versions, but the tone of Hendrix's guitar on these is positively blistering and worth the price of admission alone. There's also a lot of blues on this two-disc collection, and Hendrix's versions of "Hoochie Coochie Man" (with Alexis Korner on slide guitar), "Catfish Blues," "Killing Floor," and "Hear My Train A-Comin'" find him in excellent form. But perhaps the best example of how loosely conceived these sessions were are the oddball covers that Hendrix tackles, including Stevie Wonder's "I Was Made to Love Her" (featuring Wonder on drums), Dylan's "Can You Please Crawl out Your Window?," The Beatles' "Day Tripper," and, in recognition of his immediate competition, Cream's "Sunshine of Your Love." No lo-fi bootleg tapes here (everything's from the original masters and gone over by Eddie Kramer), the music and

sound are class-A all the way, making a worthwhile addition to anyone's Hendrix collection.

Cub Koda

Don Henley

I Can't Stand Still
1982, Warner Bros.

Don Henley's first solo album may still have had the ghost of the Eagles lingering in the corners, but for the most part it showcases his stalwart partnership with producer and songwriter Danny Kortchmar. Lyrically, Henley's songs are a tad weak, but for an inaugural album from a man who had spent most of his career surrounded by multi-talented musicians and writers, on the whole it fairs quite well. His material deals with the hardships of love, the fickleness of the media, and the declining state of education, all induced with a friendly pop sound. The title track, a trouble-in-paradise love song, has Henley pouring his heart out with sugary angst, but is helped along with some avid keyboard work. "Dirty Laundry" is Henley's attack on the shallowness of the network newsperson that peaked at number three on *Billboard*'s Top 40. Its bouncy chorus and contagious organ riffs proved that his role as a musician could conform to any style. His social commentary comes into fruition with "Johnny Can't Read," loosely based on the increasing amount of high-school dropouts at the time and helped bolster Henley's reputation as a musician with a concern for pressing issues. Numerous musicians help him out on this album as well, including former Eagles members Timothy B. Schmidt, Joe Walsh, and J.D. Souther; drummer Jeff Porcaro and guitarist Steve Lukather, both from Toto; and even Warren Zevon. Don Henley's adept combination of lyrical wit and thought-provoking staidness begins to materialize on *I Can't Stand Still*, paving the way for an extremely accomplished solo career.

Mike DeGagne

Building the Perfect Beast
1984, Geffen

After experimenting with synthesizers and a pop sound on his solo debut, Don Henley hits the mark on his sophomore release, *Building the Perfect Beast*. This album established Henley as an artist in his own right after many successful years with the Eagles, as it spawned numerous hits. While the songs seem crafted for pop radio, it's hard to fault him for choosing arrangements that would get his messages to the masses. Unlike most pop in the 1980s, however, Henley had deep intellectual themes layered beneath the synthesizer sounds and crisp production. In the opening song "Boys of Summer," he talks about trying to recapture the past while knowing that things will never be the same. Henley has a gift for writing about the heart and soul of America and for mixing his love for the country and small-town life ("Sunset Grill") with cynicism about government ("All She Wants to Do Is Dance") and modernization ("Month of Sundays"). Although the politics and the sound of the album make the decade of release easy to place, Henley's earnest delivery and universal messages give many of the tracks a timeless feel, which is no small feat. This is Henley's most consistent album, and it is the place to start for those wanting to sample his solo work.

Vik Iyengar

The Hollies

On a Carousel, 1963–1974: The Ultimate Hollies
October 2006, Raven

In the United States, the Hollies don't always get their due as one of the truly great acts of the British Invasion era, but while the Beatles, the Rolling Stones and the Kinks may have more hip cache, few bands consistently made better or more memorable singles, and this compilation proves the point with ease. Boasting 25 great tunes, *On a Carousel, 1963–1974: The Ultimate Hollies* features every song that the Hollies landed in the Top 20 in the United States and the United Kingdom, and the result is 78 minutes of pure pop bliss. The Hollies could rock the house when they were of a mind, as the cracking covers of "Stay" and "Just One Look" that open the set confirm, but it was when the group began following a more polished sound and Allan Clarke, Graham Nash and Tony Hicks locked their trademark harmonies into place that they established their identity as more than just another beat group. "Look Through Any Window," "Bus Stop," "On a Carousel," "Carrie Anne," "Stop Stop Stop," "Jennifer Eccles"—pop record making doesn't get much better than this, and crammed together on one disc this group's run of hits is a remarkable thing to witness. And while many like to give the post-Nash era of the group short shrift, in context, the latter period Hollies hits still sound impressive, proving Nash wasn't the only man of talent in this act. Warren Barnett's remastering sounds splendid, retaining the punchy original mono mixes on most of the tracks, and Ian McFarlane's liner notes do a fine job of tracing the group's history through these 11 years. *On a Carousel 1963-1974* is as good a single-disc Hollies collection as you're ever likely to find, collecting the biggest hits and best moments from their golden era, and while some fans might want more, this is a superb place to introduce yourself to a truly wonderful group.

Mark Deming

Hot Tuna

Hot Tuna
May 1970, RCA

When Hot Tuna's self-titled debut album was released in May 1970, it seemed like the perfect spin-off project for a major rock group, Jefferson Airplane's lead guitarist and bass player indulging in a genre exercise by playing a set of old folk-blues tunes in a Berkeley coffeehouse. The music seemed as far removed from the Airplane's acid rock roar as it did from commercial prospects, and thus, it allowed these sometimes overlooked bandmembers to blow off some steam musically without threatening their day jobs. In retrospect, however, it's easy to hear that something more was going on. Friends since their teens, Jorma Kaukonen and Jack Casady

had developed a musical rapport that anchored the Airplane sound but also existed independently of it, and shorn of the rock band arrangements and much of the electricity (Casady still played an electric bass), their interplay was all the more apparent. Kaukonen remained the accomplished fingerpicking stylist he had been before joining the Airplane, while Casady dispensed with the usual timekeeping duties of the bass in favor

of extensive contrapuntal soloing, creating a musical conversation that was unique. It was put at the service of a batch of songs by the likes of the Reverend Gary Davis and Jelly Roll Morton with the occasional Kaukonen original thrown in, making for a distinct style. Kaukonen's wry singing showed an intense identification with the material that kept it from seeming repetitious despite the essential similarities of the tunes. (Harmonica player Will Scarlett also contributed to the mood.) The result was less an indulgence than a new direction. [The 1996 CD reissue added five tracks from the same set of shows, increasing the disc's running time by more than 45 percent. "Belly Shadow" was a lost Kaukonen instrumental. The others would become familiar numbers in Hot Tuna's repertoire.]

William Ruhlmann

Burgers
1972, RCA

Burgers, Hot Tuna's third album, marked a crucial transition for the group. Until now, Hot Tuna had been viewed as a busman's holiday for Jefferson Airplane lead guitarist Jorma Kaukonen and bassist Jack Casady. Their first album was an acoustic set of folk-blues standards recorded in a coffeehouse, their second an electric version of the same that added violinist Papa John Creach (who also joined the Airplane) and drummer Sammy Piazza. Then the Airplane launched Grunt, its own vanity label, which encouraged all bandmembers to increase their participation in side projects. *Burgers*, originally released as the fourth Grunt album, sounded more like a full-fledged work than a satellite effort. It was Hot Tuna's first studio album, and Kaukonen wrote the bulk of the material, not all of it in the folk-blues style that had been the group's métier. "Sea Child," for example, employed his familiar acid rock sound and would have fit seamlessly onto an Airplane album. And "Water Song," one of his most accomplished instrumentals, had a crystalline acoustic guitar part that really suggested the sound of rippling water. On the material that did recall the earlier albums, Hot Tuna split the difference between its acoustic and electric selves, sometimes, as on "True Religion," beginning in folky fingerpicking style only to add a rock band sound after the introduction. The result was more restrained than the second album, but not as free as the first, with the drums imposing steady rhythms that often kept Casady from soloing as much, though Creach's violin made for plenty of improvisation within the basic blues structures. All of which is to say that, not surprisingly, on its third album in as many years, Hot Tuna had evolved its own sound and music, and seemed less a diversion than its members' new top priority.

William Ruhlmann

Humble Pie

Rock On
1971, A&M

On this, their second album, Humble Pie proved that they were not the "minor league Rolling Stones" as people often described them. Led by the soulful Steve Marriot, the Pie was a great *band* in every sense of the word. Although Peter Frampton elevated himself to superstar status in just a few years, this album proves what an excellent lead guitarist he was. The record has an undeniable live feel to it, due in part to Glyn Johns' humble yet precise recording, framing the group as if they were a boogie version of the Band. When all of these elements come together on songs such as "Sour Grain" and "Stone Cold Fever," it's an unbeatable combination.

Matthew Greenwald

Smokin'
1972, A&M

After a couple of years of relentless touring, Humble Pie capitalized on their loyal U.S. following to capture the market with this, their third album. Although lead guitarist Peter Frampton was replaced by Clem Clemson—an excellent player—the band remained es-

sentially the same. Led by singer/guitarist Steve Marriot's soulful wail, the group enjoyed a huge hit from this record, "30 Days in the Hole"—the track which defined the Pie's not-so-subtle appeal. The rest of the record is equally funky and intriguing. Stephen Stills guests on "Road Runner 'G' Jam," playing some nasty Hammond organ fills. In the end though, the group defined themselves as the undisputed leaders of the boogie movement in the early 1970s, as a *band*.

Matthew Greenwald

Natural Born Bugie: The Immediate Anthology
2000, Castle

Steve Marriott left the Small Faces behind because he wanted to boogie. He no longer wanted to deal with the precious minutia and English whimsy that proved to be the Small Faces' greatest legacy; he wanted to adopt American blues, rock, and folk for his own—a character trait not unique to Marriott, since not only his peers felt the same way, but also generations of British rockers who would decide to leave England behind for American roots music whenever they wanted to prove their authenticity. Humble Pie would later sink into heavy, obvious grandiosity, shooting for the cheap seats (and succeeding) in American stadiums, but the band's initial albums were fascinating amalgams of rustic folk, blues, and heavy rock with a slight progressive tinge, all underpinned by an earnest student's love for a form he doesn't quite intuitively understand. These were the records that Marriott made while Peter Frampton was still in the band, and the ex-Herd member proved to be pivotal to the group's success, since the

group had two solid songwriters who fed off each other's energies. Not that they were perfect—far from it, actually, since they were both too earnest and too eager to delve into directionless jams—but the end result was fascinating, as Castle's excellent double-disc anthology *Natural Born Bugie* proves. Spanning two discs, this contains everything Humble Pie recorded for Immediate, including the band's debut single, *As Safe As Yesterday Is*, and *Town and Country*, plus no less than nine unreleased tracks and two songs only available on a German CD. This set makes a convincing argument that the group had a lot to offer in its early years, when country blues and folk were as prominent as driving bloozy boogie. So, there might not be any radio hits here, but this collection is often effective (and, at its worst, interesting) and easily the best way to hear the band at its peak.

Stephen Thomas Erlewine

Ian Hunter

Ian Hunter
1975, Columbia

After leaving Mott the Hoople in early 1975, Ian Hunter quickly threw himself into recording this eponymous solo debut. Not surprisingly, it contains a lot of the glam rock charm of Hunter's old group: "The Truth, the Whole Truth, Nothing But the Truth" and "I Get So Excited" are fist-pumping tunes that combine punchy hard rock riffs with intelligent lyrics in a manner similar to Mott the Hoople's finest moments. However, Ian Hunter pulls off this grandiose sound without the overtly ornate production that defined the final Mott the Hoople albums because Mick Ronson's cleverly crafted arrangements manage to create a big wall of sound without utilizing a huge amount of instruments or overdubs. As a result, Ian Hunter's lyrics shine through in each song and show off his totally personalized mixture of attitude and intelligence: the legendary and oft-covered "Once Bitten, Twice Shy" is a cheeky, clever exploration of rock & roll's ability to corrupt the innocent, and "Boy" is a critique of a rocker who has allowed his pretensions to overpower his heart (many say this tune was aimed at fellow star and onetime Mott the Hoople producer David Bowie). Another highlight is "It Ain't Easy When You Fall," a moving tribute to a fallen friend that gracefully builds from delicate verses into a soaring chorus. The end result is a memorable debut album that gives listeners their hard rock fix and manages to engage their brains at the same time. Anyone interested in the finest moments of 1970s glam rock should give this classic a spin.

Donald A. Guarisco

All American Alien Boy
1976, Columbia

After the relative success of his debut, it would have been very easy for Ian Hunter to continue in the glam-inspired vein that made that album so successful. Instead, he twisted his sound in a jazz direction for *All American Alien Boy*, a partially successful attempt to open up his sound from its traditional rock & roll routes. Since Hunter couldn't utilize the producing and arranging skills of longtime cohort Mick Ronson because of a dispute with Ronson's manager, Hunter took the reins himself and invited a diverse cast of session musicians that included everyone from journeyman drummer Aynsley Dunbar to jazz bass wizard Jaco Pastorius. The resulting album mixture of conventional Mott the Hoople-style rock and sonic experiments never truly gels, but does contain some fine tracks. The experiments are hit and miss: the title track is a funky, sax-flavored exploration of Hunter's adjustment to life in America that works nicely, but the interesting lyrics of "Apathy 83" get buried in an uncharacteristically bland soft rock arrangement. The songs that work best are the more traditional-sounding numbers: "Irene Wilde" is a delicately crafted autobiographical ballad about the rejection that made Hunter decide to *ibe somebody, someday,î* and "God—Take 1" is a stirring, Dylan-styled rocker featuring witty lyrics that illustrate a conversation with a weary and down-to-earth version of God. However, the true gem of the album is "You Nearly Did Me In," an elegant and emotional ballad about the emptiness that follows a romantic breakup. It also notable for the stirring backing vocals from guest stars Queen on its chorus. In the end, *All-American Alien Boy* lacks the consistency to fully succeed as an album but still offers enough stellar moments to make it worthwhile for Ian Hunter's fans.

Donald A. Guarisco

You're Never Alone With a Schizophrenic
1979, Razor & Tie

This classic album from 1979 is considered by many to be the high point of Ian Hunter's solo career. Although its sales never matched up to the enthusiastic critical reaction it received, this polished hard rock gem has held up nicely through the years and is definitely deserving of its strong cult reputation. *You're Never Alone With a Schizophrenic* also marked the reunion of Hunter with his finest creative ally, Mick Ronson, who had been forced to sit out of Hunter's last few albums due to management problems. Together, the reunited duo put together an album that matches Hunter's literate lyrics to a set of catchy, finely crafted tunes brimming with rock & roll energy. Two of the finest tracks are "Cleveland Rocks," an affectionate, Mott the Hoople-styled tribute to an unsung rock & roll city that later became the theme for *The Drew Carey Show*, and "Ships," a heartrending ballad built on a spooky and ethereal keyboard-driven melody that was later covered with great success by Barry Manilow. Elsewhere, the album features plenty of tunes that soon became mainstays of Hunter's live show: "Just Another Night" is a rollicking rocker with an infectious, piano-pounding melody reminiscent of 1970s-era Rolling Stones, and "Bastard" is a pulsating rocker that features guest star John Cale contributing to its ominous hard rock atmosphere. However, the unsung gem of the album is "When the Daylight Comes," a beautifully crafted mid-tempo rocker that balances a soulful, organ-driven melody with rousing guitar riffs and surprisingly vulnerable lyrics about romance. It should also be noted that *You're Never Alone With a Schizophrenic* benefits from a sterling mix by Bob Clearmountain, who gives the sound a muscular quality that makes it leap out of the stereo speakers. In the end, *You're Never Alone With a Schizophrenic* is not only Ian Hunter's finest and most consistent album but one of the true gems of late-'70s rock & roll.

Donald A. Guarisco

The James Gang

Yer' Album
1969, One Way

The James Gang's debut LP, *Yer' Album*, was very much a first record and very much a record of its time. The heavy rock scene of the period was given to extensive jamming, and four tracks ran more than six minutes each. The group

had written some material, but they were still something of a cover band, and the disc included their extended workouts on Buffalo Springfield's "Bluebird" and the Yardbirds' "Lost Woman," the latter a nine-minute version complete with lengthy guitar, bass, and drum solos. But in addition to the blues rock there were also touches of pop and progressive rock, mostly from Walsh who displayed a nascent sense of melody, not to mention some of the taste for being a cutup that he would display in his solo career. Walsh's "Take a Look Around" must have made an impression on Pete Townshend during the period before the album's release when the James Gang was opening for the Who since Townshend borrowed it for the music he was writing for the abortive *Lifehouse* follow-up to *Tommy*. If "Wrapcity (i.e., Rhapsody) in English," a minute-long piano and strings interlude, seems incongruous in retrospect, recall that this was an eclectic era. But the otherwise promising "Fred," which followed, broke down into a pedestrian jazz routine, suggesting that the band was trying to cram too many influences onto one record and sometimes into one song. Nevertheless, they were talented improvisers, as the open-ended album closer—Jerry Ragavoy and Mort Shuman's "Stop," made clear. After ten minutes, Szymczyk faded the track out, but Walsh was still going strong. *Yer' Album* contained much to suggest that the James Gang, in particular its guitarist, had a great future, even if it was more an album of performances than compositions.

William Ruhlmann

Rides Again
1970, MCA

With their second album *Rides Again*, the James Gang came into their own. Under the direction of guitarist Joe Walsh, the group—now featuring bassist Dale Peters—began incorporating keyboards into their hard rock, which helped open up their musical horizons. For much of the first side of *Rides Again*, the group tear through a bunch of boogie numbers, most notably the heavy groove of "Funk #49." On the second side, the James Gang departs from their trademark sound, adding keyboard flourishes and elements of country-rock to their hard rock. Walsh's songwriting had improved, giving the band solid support for their stylistic experiments. What ties the two sides of the record together is the strength of the band's musicianship, which burns brightly and powerfully on the hardest rockers, as well as on the sensitive ballads.

Stephen Thomas Erlewine

Thirds
1971, MCA

The James Gang Rides Again set the stage for the group's third album to propel them to Top Ten, headliner status, but that didn't happen. The band was on its last legs, rent by dissension as Walsh became the focus of attention, and the ap-propriately titled

Thirds reflected the conflict. Among the nine original songs, four were contributed by Walsh, two each by bass player Dale Peters and drummer Jim Fox, and one was a group

composition. But it was Walsh's songs that stood out. His "Walk Away," was the first single, and it climbed into the Top 40 in at least one national chart, the group's only 45 to do that well. "Midnight Man," the follow-up single, was another Walsh tune, and it also made the charts. The Fox and Peters compositions were a step down in quality, particularly Peters'. But the problem wasn't just material, it was also musical approach. *James Gang Rides Again* had emphasized the band's hard rock sound, which was its strong suit. But they had never given up the idea of themselves as an eclectic unit, and *Thirds* was their most diverse effort yet, with pedal steel guitar, horn and string charts, and backup vocals by the Sweet Inspirations turning up on one track or another. At a time when Walsh was being hailed as a guitar hero to rank with the best rock had to offer, he was not only submerging himself in a group with inferiors, but also not playing much of the kind of lead guitar his supporters were raving about. As a result, though *Thirds* quickly earned a respectable chart position and eventually went gold, it was not the commercial breakthrough that might have been expected.

William Ruhlmann

Jefferson Airplane

Jefferson Airplane Takes Off
August 1966, RCA

The debut Jefferson Airplane album was dominated by singer Marty Balin, who wrote or co-wrote all the original material and sang most of the lead vocals in his heartbreaking tenor with Paul Kantner and Signe Anderson providing harmonies and backup. (Anderson's lead vocal on "Chauffeur Blues" indicated she was at least the equal of her successor, Grace Slick, as a belter.) The music consisted mostly of folk-rock love songs, the most memorable of which were "It's No Secret" and "Come up the Years." (There was also a striking version of Dino Valente's "Get Together" recorded years before the Youngbloods' hit version.) Jorma Kaukonen already displayed a talent for mixing country, folk, and blues riffs in a rock context, and Jack Casady already had a distinctive bass sound. But the Airplane of Balin-Kantner-Kaukonen-Anderson-Casady-Spence is to be distinguished from the Balin-Kantner-Kaukonen-Casady-Slick-Dryden version of the band that would emerge on record five months later, chiefly by Balin's dominance. Later, Grace Slick would become the group's vocal and visual focal point. On *Jefferson Airplane Takes Off*, the Airplane was Balin's group. This first pressing of the album, of which few copies were manufactured, differed from later ones. The track "Runnin' 'Round This World" contained here, was deleted from subsequent pressings because the line "The nights I've spent with you have been fantastic trips" was deemed objectionable as referring to sex and drugs. Also, this first pressing contains the original recordings of "Let Me In" and "Run Around," both of which were subsequently re-recorded to tone down the risqué lyrics, those re-recordings inserted into the most common third pressing of the LP. Decades after its release, record album price guides showed values for copies of the rare first pressing in the thousands of dollars.

William Ruhlmann

Surrealistic Pillow
February 1967, RCA

The second album by Jefferson Airplane, *Surrealistic Pillow* was a groundbreaking piece of folk-rock-based psychedelia,

and it hit—literally—like a shot heard round the world; where the later efforts from bands like the Grateful Dead, Quicksilver Messenger Service, and especially, the Charlatans, were initially not too much more than cult successes, *Surrealistic Pillow* rode the pop charts for most of 1967, soaring into that rarefied Top Five region occupied by the likes of the Beatles, the Rolling Stones, and so on, to which few American rock acts apart from the Byrds had been able to lay claim since 1964. And decades later the album still comes off as strong as any of those artists' best work. From the Top Ten singles "White Rabbit" and "Somebody to Love" to the sublime "Embryonic Journey," the sensibilities are fierce, the material manages to be both melodic and complex (and it rocks, too), and the performances, sparked by new member Grace Slick on most of the lead vocals, are inspired, helped along by Jerry Gar-

cia (serving as spiritual and musical advisor and sometimes guitarist). Every song is a perfectly cut diamond, too perfect in the eyes of the bandmembers, who felt that following the direction of producer Rick Jarrard and working within three- and four-minute running times, and delivering carefully sung accompaniments and succinct solos, resulted in a record that didn't represent their real sound. Regardless, they did wonderful things with the music within that framework, and the only pity is that RCA didn't record for official release any of the group's shows from the same era, when this material made up the bulk of their repertory. That way the live versions, with the band's creativity unrestricted, could be compared and contrasted with the record. The songwriting was spread around between Marty Balin, Slick, Paul Kantner, and Jorma Kaukonen, and Slick and Balin (who never had a prettier song than "Today," which he'd actually written for Tony Bennett) shared the vocals; the whole album was resplendent in a happy balance of all of these creative elements, before excessive experimentation (musical and chemical) began affecting the band's ability to do a straightforward song. The group never made a better album, and few artists from the era ever did.

[*Surrealistic Pillow* on CD has been problematic—actually, make that a real pain in the ass. It's been reissued numerous times on compact disc, in distinctly different editions—a plain 11-song disc from the 1980s that sounded wretched and was an embarrassment; a high-priced RCA-BMG gold-disc upgrade, with significantly better sound from the mid-'90s that encompassed the stereo and mono mixes of the album; a European version from 2000/2001 (with four bonus tracks but no mono mix or liner notes) that got into the U.S. as an import; a U.S.-issued 2001 upgrade, initially available in the bizarre four-CD box *Ignition*, which encompassed the stereo and mono mixes in a brighter, sharper, louder remastering than the 1996 version, but still—in some listeners' eyes—lacking the presence and the soaring sound of the original LP; and a 2003 reissue (on the BMG Heritage label), mastered by renowned reissue producer Bob Irwin (of Sundazed Records fame), including the mono single versions of "White Rabbit" and "Somebody to Love," along with the related bonus tracks "Come Back Baby," "In the Morning," "J.P.P. McStep B. Blues," and "Go to Her," which have previously been scattered around various anthologies and other expanded editions. Those tracks generally push Kaukonen even more to the fore and give the balance of the material a bluesier feel. And there's an uncredited "hidden" bonus cut, an instrumental of "D.C.B.A. - 25."]

Bruce Eder

After Bathing at Baxter's
December 1967, BMG

The Jefferson Airplane opened 1967 with *Surrealistic Pillow* and closed it with *After Bathing at Baxter's*, and what a difference ten months made. Bookending the year that psychedelia emerged in full bloom as a freestanding musical form, *After Bathing at Baxter's* was among the purest of rock's psychedelic albums, offering few concessions to popular taste and none to the needs of AM radio, which made it nowhere remotely as successful as its predecessor, but it was also a lot more daring. The album also showed a band in a state of ferment, as singer/guitarist Marty Balin largely surrendered much of his creative input in the band he'd founded, and let Paul Kantner and Grace Slick dominate the songwriting and singing on all but one cut ("Young Girl Sunday Blues"). The group had found the preceding album a little too perfect, and not fully representative of the musicians or what they were about, and they were determined to do the music their way on *Baxter's*; additionally, they'd begun to see how far they could take music (and music could take them) in concert, in terms of capturing variant states of consciousness.

Essentially, *After Bathing at Baxter's* was the group's attempt to create music that captured what the psychedelic experience sounded and felt like to them from the inside; on a psychic level, it was an introverted exercise in music-making and a complete reversal of the extroverted experience in putting together *Surrealistic Pillow*. Toward that end, they were working "without a net," for although Al Schmitt was the nominal producer, he gave the group the freedom to indulge in any experimentation they chose to attempt, effectively letting them produce themselves. They'd earned the privilege, after two huge hit singles and the Top Five success of the prior album, all of which had constituted RCA's first serious new rock success (and the label's first venture to the music's cutting edge) since Elvis Presley left the Army. The resulting record was startlingly different from their two prior LPs; there were still folk and blues elements present in the music, but these were mostly transmuted into something very far from what any folksinger or bluesman might recognize. Kantner, Jorma Kaukonen, and Jack Casady cranked up their instruments; Spencer Dryden hauled out an array of percussive devices that was at least twice as broad as anything used on the previous album; and everybody ignored the length of what they were writing and recording, or how well they sang, or how cleanly their voices meshed. The group emerged four months later with one of the rawest, most in-your-face records to come out of the psychedelic era, and also a maddeningly uneven record, exciting and challenging in long stretches, yet elsewhere very close to stultifyingly boring, delightful in its most fulfilling moments (which were many), but almost deliberately frustrating in its digressions, and amid all of that, very often beautiful.

The album's 11 songs formed five loosely constructed "suites," and it didn't ease listeners into those structures. Opening "The Ballad of You and Me and Pooneil" (a Kantner-authored tribute to Fred Neil) amid a cascading wash of feedback leading to a slashing guitar figure, the band's three singers struggle to meld their voices and keep up. A softer, almost folk-like interlude, highlighted by Slick's upper-register keening, breaks up the beat until the guitar, bass, and drums crash back in, with a bit of piano embellishment.

Then listeners get to the real break, an almost subdued interlude on the guitars, and a return to the song at a more frenzied pitch, the guitar part dividing and evolving into ever more brittle components until a crescendo and more feedback leads to "A Small Package of Value Will Come to You, Shortly." This brilliantly comical and clever percussion showcase co-authored by Spencer Dryden and the band's manager, Bill Thompson, is a million miles beyond any drummer's featured number in any popular band of that era, and it leads into Marty Balin's "Young Girl Sunday Blues," the most rhythmically consistent song here and one of a tiny handful of moments that seem to slightly resemble the band's past work. The aforementioned tracks comprise just the first suite, designated "Steetmasse."

"The War Is Over" suite opens with "Martha," the album's folk-style interlude, almost a throwback to the group's original sound, except that the listener suddenly finds himself in the midst of a psychedelic delirium, heralded by the dissonant accompaniment and a high-energy fuzztone guitar solo (spinning out sitar-like notes) coming out of nowhere and a speed change that slows the tempo to zero, as though the tape (or time, or the listener's perception of it) were stretching out, and the pounding, exuberant "Wild Tyme," a celebration of seemingly uninhibited joy. "Hymn to the Older Generation" is made up of Kaukonen's "The Last Wall of the Castle," an alternately slashing and chiming guitar pyrotechnic showcase that rivaled anything heard from Jimi Hendrix or the Who that year, and Grace Slick's gorgeous "Rejoyce," a hauntingly beautiful excursion into literary psychedelia, whose James Joyce allusions carry the Lewis Carroll literary allusions of the previous album's "White Rabbit" into startlingly new and wonderful (if discursive) directions and depths. "How Suite It Is" opens with the album's single, the lean, rhythmic "Watch Her Ride," whose pretty harmonies and gently psychedelic lyrics persuaded RCA that this was their best shot at AM airplay, and, true to form on an album filled with contradictions, it leads into "Spare Chaynge," the crunching, searing, sometimes dirge-like nine-minute jam by Kaukonen, Dryden, and Casady that wasn't ever going to get on AM radio—ever—and, indeed, might well initially repel any Airplane fan who only knew their hit singles. "Shizoforest Love Suite" closes the album with Slick's "Two Heads," with its vocal acrobatics and stop-and-go beat, and "Won't You Try"/"Saturday Afternoon," the latter Kantner's musical tribute to the first San Francisco "Be-In" (memorialized more conventionally by the Byrds on "Renaissance Fair"); it features many of the more subdued, relaxed, languid moments on the record, divided by a killer fuzz-laden guitar solo.

Needless to say, this is not the album by which one should start listening to this band—"Spare Chaynge" remains an acquired taste, a lot more aimless than, say, the extended jams left behind by the Quicksilver Messenger Service, though it did point the way toward what Kaukonen and Casady would aim for more successfully when they formed Hot Tuna. But most of the rest is indisputably among the more alluring musical experimentation of the period, and Kantner's "The Ballad of You and Me and Pooneil" and "Watch Her Ride," as well as Balin's "Young Girl Sunday Blues," proved that the group could still rock out with a beat, even if not so prettily or cleanly as before. [*After Bathing at Baxter's* was represented poorly on CD until 1996, when it was finally reissued in an upgraded edition, which was later deleted and was only available as part of the bizarre 2001-vintage *Ignition* box. It has since been remastered again, with very important, downright essential bonus tracks, as of 2003. Additionally, *After Bathing at Baxter's* was the last Jefferson Airplane album to appear in a mono version, which sounds very different than the more common stereo mix, and has yet to show up on CD.]

Bruce Eder

Crown of Creation
September 1968, RCA

The group's fourth album, appearing ten months following *After Bathing at Baxter's*, isn't the same kind of leap forward that *Baxter's* represented from *Surrealistic Pillow*. Indeed, in many ways, *Crown of Creation* is a more conservative album stylistically, opening with "Lather," a Grace Slick original that was one of the group's very last forays (and certainly their last prominent one) into a folk idiom. Much of what follows is a lot more based in electric rock, as well as steeped in elements of science fiction (specifically author John Wyndham's book *The Chrysalids*) in several places, but *Crown of Creation* was still deliberately more accessible musically than its predecessor, even as the playing became more bold and daring within more traditional song structures. Jack Casady by this time had developed one of the most prominent and distinctive bass sounds in American rock, as identifiable (if not quite as bracing) as John Entwistle's was with the Who, as demonstrated on "In Time," "Star Track," "Share a Little Joke," "If You Feel," (where he's practically a second lead instrument), and the title song, and Jorma Kaukonen's slashing, angular guitar attack was continually surprising as his snaking lead guitar parts wended their way through "Star Track" and "Share a Little Joke." The album also reflected the shifting landscape of West Coast music with its inclusion of "Triad," a David Crosby song that Crosby's own group, the Byrds, had refused to release—its presence (the only extant version of the song for a number of years) was a forerunner of the sound that would later be heard on Crosby's own debut solo album, *If I Could Only Remember My Name* (on which Slick, Paul Kantner, and Casady would appear). The overall album captured the group's rapidly evolving, very heavy live sound within the confines of some fairly traditional song structures, and left ample room for Slick and Marty Balin to express themselves vocally, with Balin turning in one of his most heartfelt and moving performances on "If You Feel." "Ice Cream Phoenix" pulses with energy and "Greasy Heart" became a concert standard for the group—the studio original of the latter is notable for Slick's most powerful vocal performance since "Somebody to Love." And the album's big finish, "The House at Pooneil Corners," seemed to fire on all cylinders, their amps cranked up to ten (maybe 11 for Casady), and Balin, Slick, and Kantner stretching out on the disjointed yet oddly compelling tune and lyrics. It didn't work 100 percent, but it made for a shattering finish to the album. *Crown of Creation* has been reissued on CD several times, including a Mobile Fidelity audiophile edition at the start of the '90s, but in 2003, RCA released a remastered edition with four bonus tracks from the same sessions including the mono single mix of "Share a Little Joke," the previously unreleased 8 minute "The Saga of Sydney Spacepig," Spencer Dryden's co-authored "Ribump Ba Bap Dum Dum," which is a spaced-out assembly of noises, effects, and pop-culture catch-phrases, and the more accessible "Would You Like a Snack?," an atonal piece of musical scatology featuring Grace Slick and co-authored by Slick and Frank Zappa.

Bruce Eder & Al Campbell

Bless Its Pointed Little Head
February 1969, RCA

Jefferson Airplane's first live album demonstrated the group's development as concert performers, taking a number of songs that had been performed in concise, pop-oriented versions on their early albums—"3/5's of a Mile in 10 Seconds," "Somebody to Love," "It's No Secret," "Plastic Fantastic Lover"—and rendering them in arrangements that were longer, harder rocking, and more densely textured, especially in terms of the guitar and basslines constructed by Jorma Kaukonen and Jack Casady. The group's three-part vocal harmonizing and dueling was on display during such songs as a nearly seven-minute version of Fred Neil's folk-blues standard "The Other Side of This Life," here transformed into a swirling rocker. The album emphasized the talents of Kaukonen and singer Marty Balin over the team of Paul Kantner and Grace Slick, who had tended to dominate recent records: the blues song "Rock Me Baby" was a dry run for Hot Tuna, the band Kaukonen and Casady would form in two years, and Balin turned in powerful vocal performances on several of his own compositions, notably "It's No Secret." Jefferson Airplane was still at its best in concise, driving numbers, rather than in the jams on Donovan's "Fat Angel" (running 7:35) or the group improv "Bear Melt" (11:21); they were just too intense to stretch out comfortably. But *Bless Its Pointed Little Head* served an important function in the group's discography, demonstrating that their live work had a distinctly different focus and flavor from their studio recordings.

William Ruhlmann

Volunteers
November 1969, BMG

Controversial at the time, delayed because of fights with the record company over lyrical content and the original title (*Volunteers of America*), *Volunteers* was a powerful release that neatly closed out and wrapped up the '60s. Here, the Jefferson Airplane presents itself in full revolutionary rhetoric, issuing a call to "tear down the walls" and "get it on together." "We Can Be Together" and "Volunteers" bookend the album, offering musical variations on the same chord progression and lyrical variations on the same theme. Between these politically charged rock anthems, the band offers a mix of words and music that reflect the competing ideals of simplicity and getting "back to the earth," and overthrowing greed and exploitation through political activism, adding a healthy dollop of psychedelic sci-fi for texture. Guitarist Jorma Kaukonen's beautiful arrangement of the traditional "Good Shepherd" is a standout here, and Jerry Garcia's pedal steel guitar gives "The Farm" an appropriately rural feel. The band's version of "Wooden Ships" is much more eerie than that released earlier in the year by Crosby, Stills & Nash. Oblique psychedelia is offered here via Grace Slick's "Hey Frederick" and ecologically tinged "Eskimo Blue Day." Drummer Spencer Dryden gives an inside look at the state of the band in the country singalong "A Song for All Seasons."

The musical arrangements here are quite potent. Nicky

Hopkins' distinctive piano highlights a number of tracks, and Kaukonen's razor-toned lead guitar is the recording's unifying force, blazing through the mix, giving the album its distinctive sound. Although the political bent of the lyrics may seem dated to some, listening to *Volunteers* is like opening a time capsule on the end of an era, a time when young people still believed music had the power to change the world. *Volunteers* was reissued in late 2001 by BMG Records' Spanish division in a crisply remastered edition containing 30 minutes of outtakes, which consist mostly of early versions, usually with very different lead guitar—often a lot louder—and vocal parts, of "Wooden Ships," "Volunteers," "We Can Be Together," "Turn My Life Down," "Good Shepherd," and "Hey Frederick." Some of these are very different from their official released versions and all are certain to please fans of Jorma Kaukonen, whose electric playing is heavily showcased on all of them.

Jim Newsom

Thirty Seconds Over Winterland
April 1973, BMG

By the summer of 1972, the Jefferson Airplane were on their final approach to the eventual evolution that would produce Jefferson Starship, arguably the most drastic difference being the absence of Jorma Kaukonen (guitar, vocals) and Jack Casady (bass), both of whom were several years into Hot Tuna, a project that began as a musical diversion for the pair and rapidly developed into a permanent roots rock unit. Released in 1973, *Thirty Seconds Over Winterland* (cleverly named after the Mervyn LeRoy-directed 1944 film *Thirty Seconds Over Tokyo*) would become the Airplane's swansong. Included were seven tracks taken from the band's last tour of the 1970s, specifically, August 24 and 25 at the Auditorium Theatre in Chicago and the last two gigs the Bay Area combo played in its native San Francisco on September 21 and 22, fittingly held at the band's longtime stomping grounds at the Winterland Arena. Only Kaukonen, Casady, and Paul Kantner (guitar, vocals) remained from the first lineup. They are joined by Grace Slick—who took over from Signe Anderson just prior to the recording of 1967's landmark *Surrealistic Pillow*—and violinist Papa John Creach. Former Turtles and Crosby, Stills, Nash & Young drummer Johnny Barbata had come aboard in the previous year, and the latest addition was Quicksilver Messenger Service co-founder David Freiberg, whose contributions at the time were primarily vocal. The bulk of the effort was drawn from 1971's *Bark* and 1972's *Long John Silver*. Although they were still performing "Somebody to Love," "Volunteers," and "Wooden Ships" in concert, a cursory stab at "Crown of Creation" is the earliest cut on this package that harks back to their acid rock persona. Despite some questionable intonations from Kaukonen on "Have You Seen the Saucers," the opener quickly establishes the Jefferson Airplane's harder edge. Kaukonen's "Feel So Good" is the jewel in this otherwise thorny rock & roll tiara. The tune stretches over ten minutes, spotlighting Casady's quake-inducing contributions and Creach's unmistakable fiddle. Speaking of Papa John, he shines on the propelling "Milk Train," featuring a seminal lead from Slick. An outtake of note from the September 22 show made its way onto the 1992 *Jefferson Airplane Loves You* box set. Marty Balin returned for the one-off, albeit incendiary, "You Wear Your Dresses Too Short."

Lindsay Planer

Red Octopus
1975, RCA

Technically speaking, *Red Octopus* was the first album credited to Jefferson Starship, though practically the same lineup made *Dragon Fly*, credited to Grace Slick/Paul Kantner/Jefferson Starship. The difference, however, was crucial: Marty Balin was once again a fully integrated band member, writing or co-writing five of the ten tracks. And there can be little doubt that it was Balin's irresistible ballad "Miracles," the biggest hit single in the Jefferson Whatever catalog, that propelled *Red Octopus* to the top of the charts, the only Jefferson album to chart that high and the best-

selling album in their collective lives. This must have been sweet vindication for Balin, who founded Jefferson Airplane but then drifted away from the group as it veered away from his musical vision. Now, the collective was incorporating his taste without quite integrating it—"Miracles," with its strings and sax solo by nonband member Irv Cox, was hardly a characteristic Airplane/Starship track. But then, neither exactly was Papa John Creach's showcase, "Git Fiddler," or bassist Pete Sears' instrumental "Sandalphon," which sounded like something from an early Procol Harum album. Slick has three strong songs, among them the second single "Play on Love." Like *Dragon Fly*, *Red Octopus* reflected a multiplicity of musical tastes; there were ten credited songwriters, seven of whom were in the band. If there is any consistency in this material, it is in subject matter (love songs). The album is more ballad-heavy and melodic than the Airplane albums, which made it more accessible to the broader audience it reached, though "Sweeter Than Honey" is as tough a rocker as the band ever played.

William Ruhlmann

Jethro Tull

This Was
1968, Chrysalis

Jethro Tull was very much a blues band on their debut album, vaguely reminiscent of the Graham Bond Organization only more cohesive, and with greater commercial sense. The revelations about the group's roots on *This Was*—which was recorded during the summer of 1968—can be astonishing, even 30 years after the fact. Original lead guitarist Mick Abrahams contributed to the songwriting and the singing, and his presence as a serious bluesman is felt throughout, often for the better: "Some Day the Sun Won't Shine for You," an Ian Anderson original that could just as easily be credited to Big Bill Broonzy or Robert Johnson; "Cat's Squirrel," Abrahams' big showcase, where he ventures into Eric Clapton territory; and "It's Breaking Me Up," which also features some pretty hot guitar from Abrahams. Roland Kirk's "Serenade to a Cuckoo" (the first song Anderson learned to play on flute), their jazziest track ever, is one of the best parts of the album. The drum solo on "Dharma for One" now seems like a mistake, but is understandable in the context of the time in which it was done. The one number here that everybody knows, "A Song for Jeffrey," almost pales amid these surroundings, but at the time it was a superb example of commercial psychedelic blues. This would be the last album of its kind by the group, as Abrahams' departure and the lure of more fertile inspiration tugged them toward English folk music. Curiously, the audio mix here is better than that on their second album, with a much stronger, harder group sound overall. In late 2001, *This Was* was reissued in a re-mastered edition with much crisper sound and three bonus tracks. The jazzy improvisation "One for John Gee" (a reference to the manager of the Marquee Club), the folky "Love Story" (which marked the end Mick Abrahams' tenure with the group), and the novelty piece "Christmas Song" have all been heard before but, more to the point, they're worth hearing again, especially in the fidelity they have here.

Bruce Eder

Stand Up
September 1969, Chrysalis

The group's second album, with Ian Anderson (vocals, flute, acoustic guitars, keyboards, balalaika), Martin Barre (electric guitar, flute), Clive Bunker (drums), and Glen Cornick (bass), solidified their sound. There are still elements of blues present in their music, but except for the opening track, "A New Day Yesterday," it is far more muted than on their first album—new lead guitarist Martin Barre had few of the blues stylings that characterized Mick Abrahams' playing. Rather, the influence of English folk music manifests itself on several cuts, including "Jeffrey Goes to Leicester Square" and "Look Into the Sun." The instrumental "Bouree," which could've passed for an early Blood, Sweat & Tears track, became a favorite concert number, with an excellent solo bit featuring Cornick's bass, although at this point Anderson's flute playing on-stage needed a lot of work. As a story-song with opaque lyrics, jarring tempo changes, and loud electric passages juxtaposed with soft acoustic-textured sections, "Back to the Family" is an early forerunner to *Thick As a Brick*. Similarly, "Reasons for Waiting," with its mix of closely miked acoustic guitar and string orchestra, all hung around a hauntingly beautiful folk-based melody, pointed in the direction of that conceptual piece and its follow-up, *A Passion Play*. The only major flaw in this album is the mix, which divides the electric and acoustic instruments and fails to find a solid center, but even that has been fixed on recent CD editions. The original LP had a gate-fold jacket that included a pop-up representation of the band that has been lost on all subsequent CD versions, except for the Mobile Fidelity audiophile release. In late 2001, *Stand Up* was re-released in a remastered edition with bonus tracks that boasted seriously improved sound. Anderson's singing comes off richer throughout, and the electric guitars on "Look Into the Sun" are very well-delineated in the mix, without any loss in the lyricism of the acoustic backing; the rhythm section on "Nothing Is Easy" has more presence, Bunker's drums and high-hat playing sounding much closer and sharper; the mandolin on "Fat Man" is practically in your lap; you can hear the action on the acoustic guitar on "Reasons for Waiting," even in the orchestrated passages; and the band sounds like it's in the room with you pounding away on "For a Thousand Mothers." Among the bonus tracks, recorded at around the same time, "Living in the Past," "Driving Song," and "Sweet Dreams" all have a richness and resonance that was implied but never heard before.

Bruce Eder

Aqualung
April 1971, Chrysalis

Released at a time when a lot of bands were embracing pop-Christianity (à la *Jesus Christ Superstar*), *Aqualung* was a bold statement for a rock group, a pro-God antichurch tract that probably got lots of teenagers wrestling with these ideas for the first time in their lives. This was the album that made Jethro Tull a fixture on FM radio, with riff-heavy songs like "My God," "Hymn 43," "Locomotive Breath," "Cross-Eyed Mary," "Wind Up," and the title track. And from there, they became a major arena act, and a fixture at the top of the record charts for most of the 1970s. Mixing hard rock and folk melodies with Ian Anderson's dour musings on faith and religion (mostly how organized religion had restricted man's relationship with God), the record was extremely profound for a number seven chart hit, one of the most cerebral albums ever to reach millions of rock listeners. Indeed, from this point on, Anderson and company were compelled to stretch the lyrical envelope right to the breaking point. As a compact disc, *Aqualung* has gone through numerous editions, mostly owing to problems finding an original master tape when the CD boom began. When the album was issued by Chrysalis through Columbia Records in the mid-'80s, the source tape was an LP production master, and the first release was criticized for thin, tinny sound; Columbia remastered it sometime around 1987 or 1988, in a version with better sound. Chrysalis later switched distribution to Capitol-EMI, and they released a decent sounding CD that is currently available. Chrysalis also issued a 25th anniversary edition in 1996.

Bruce Eder

Thick as a Brick
April 1972, Chrysalis

Jethro Tull's first LP-length epic is a masterpiece in the annals of progressive rock, and one of the few works of its kind that still holds up decades later. Mixing hard rock and English folk music with classical influences, set to stream-of-consciousness lyrics so dense with imagery that one might spend weeks pondering their meaning—assuming one feels the need to do so—the group created a dazzling *tour de force*, at once playful, profound, and challenging, without overwhelming the listener. The original LP was the best-sounding, best-engineered record Tull had ever released, easily capturing the shifting dynamics between the soft all-acoustic passages and the electric rock crescendos surrounding them.

Bruce Eder

Living in the Past
October 1972, Chrysalis

Listen to this collection, put together to capitalize on the explosive growth in the group's audience after *Aqualung*, and it's easy to understand just how fine a group Jethro Tull was in the early '70s. Most of the songs, apart from a few heavily played album tracks ("Song for Jeffrey," etc.) and a pair of live tracks from a 1970 Carnegie Hall show, came off of singles and EPs that, apart from the title song, were scarcely known in America, and it's all so solid that it needs no apology or explanation. Not only was Ian Anderson writing solid songs every time out, but the group's rhythm section was about the best in progressive rock's pop division. Along with any of the group's first five albums, this collection is seminal and essential to any Tull collection, and the only compilation by the group that is a must-own disc.

Bruce Eder

Minstrel in the Gallery
September 1975, Chrysalis

Minstrel in the Gallery was Tull's most artistically successful and elaborately produced album since *Thick As a Brick* and harkened back to that album with the inclusion of a 17-minute extended piece ("Baker Street Muse"). Although English folk elements abound, this is really a hard rock showcase on a par with—and perhaps even more aggressive than—anything on *Aqualung*. The title track is a superb showcase for the group, freely mixing folk melodies, lilting flute passages, and archaic, pre-Elizabethan feel, and the fiercest electric rock in the group's history—parts of it do recall phrases from *A Passion Play*, but all of it is more successful than anything on *War Child*. Martin Barre's attack on the guitar is as ferocious as anything in the band's history, and John Evan's organ matches him amp for amp, while Barriemore Barlow and Jeffrey Hammond-Hammond hold things together in a furious performance. Anderson's flair for drama and melody come to the fore in "Cold Wind to Valhalla," and "Requiem" is the loveliest acoustic number in Tull's repertory, featuring nothing but Anderson's singing and acoustic guitar, Glascock's bass, and a small string orchestra backing them. "Nothing at All" isn't far behind for sheer, unabashed beauty, but "Black Satin Dancer" is a little too cacophonous for its own good. "Baker Street Muse" recalls *Thick As a Brick* and *A Passion Play*, not only in its structure but a few passages; at slightly under 17 minutes, it's a tad more manageable than either of its conceptual predecessors, and it has all of their virtues, freely overlapping hard rock and folk material, classical arrangements (some of the most tasteful string playing on a Tull recording), surprising tempo shifts, and complex stream-of-consciousness lyrics (some of which clearly veer into self-parody) into a compelling whole.

Bruce Eder

Songs from the Wood
February 1977, Chrysalis

Far and away the prettiest record Jethro Tull released at least since *Thick as a Brick* and a special treat for anyone with a fondness for the group's more folk-oriented material. Ian Anderson had moved to the countryside sometime earlier, and it showed in his choice of source material. The band's aggressive rock interplay and Anderson's fascination with early British folk melodies produce a particularly appealing collection of songs—the seriousness with which the group took this effort can be discerned by the album's unofficial "full" title on the original LP: "Jethro Tull With Kitchen Prose, Gutter Rhymes, and Divers Songs from the Wood." The group's sound was never more carefully balanced between acoustic folk and

hard rock—the result is an album that sounds a great deal like the work of Tull's Chrysalis Records labelmates Steeleye Span (though Nigel Pegrum never attacked his cymbals—or his entire drum kit—with Barriemore Barlow's ferocity). The harmonizing on "Songs From the Wood" fulfills the promise shown in some of the singing on *Thick as a Brick*, and the delicacy of much of the rest, including "Ring Out, Solstice Bells" (where the group plays full out, but with wonderful elegance), "Hunting Girl," and "Velvet Green," set a new standard for the group's sound. "Pibroch (Cap in Hand)," which is dominated by Martin Barre's electric guitar—in a stunning array of overlapping flourishes at full volume—is the only concession to the group's usual hard rock rave-ups, and even it has some lovely singing to counterbalance the bulk of the song.

Bruce Eder

Jo Jo Gunne

Jo Jo Gunne
1972, Asylum

From the ashes of the multifaceted jazz/psych/rock combo Spirit rose Jo Jo Gunne. The band's personnel included Jay Ferguson (keyboards/lead vocals), Mark Andes (bass/vocals), his brother Matthew Andes (guitar/vocals), and Curly Smith (drums/vocals). Their self-titled debut would be the only release from this lineup as well as arguably the strongest of the four efforts to bear the Jo Jo Gunne moniker. Commencing with the upbeat pop of "Run Run Run," this album builds upon Ferguson's well-established melodic tradition, which is immeasurably enhanced by the power trio's aggressive instrumentation and arrangements. Sides such as "Shake That Fat," "I Make Love," and "99 Days" epitomize the heavy boogie rock of the early '70s. While Matthew Andes' contributions are a far cry from the flashy fretwork of Jimmy Page, he ably manages some solid leads and equally memorable riffs, such as the catchy introduction to "Babylon" or the laid-back "Flying Home"—which could be mistaken for a long-lost Outlaws or Lynyrd Skynyrd tune. The band's versatility is continually evident throughout, with the funky and soulful "Academy Award" suggesting the influence of Little Feat. The languid propulsion of "Take It Easy"—which shouldn't be confused with the Jackson Browne composition—develops nicely into a midtempo groover that is again driven by Andes' fluid guitar solos. Although Jo Jo Gunne would issue another three long-players, they would each feature a slightly different personnel, with Smith being the first to jump ship prior to the band's follow-up, *Bite Down Hard* (1973). In 2000 both LPs were compiled—along with a trio of previously unissued bonus tracks from the *Jo Jo Gunne* (1972) sessions, onto the *Asylum Recordings: Jo Jo Gunne + Bite Down Hard* (2000) single-CD two-fer. In 2003 both titles also became available (sans bonus tracks) separately from Collectors' Choice Music.

Lindsay Planer

So...Where's the Show?
1974, Asylum

After the erratic and self-consciously weird *Jumpin' the Gunne*, this album is a return to form. More than that, actually—the replacement of founding guitarist Matt Andes with John Stahely resulted in a tighter, more focused, and generally more interesting band than ever before. Jo Jo Gunne was originally formed to be, in Jay Ferguson's phrase, "a hard-ass rock band," and on *So...Where's the Show?* they finally were one. Ferguson responded to the harder edge by abandoning the synthesizer in favor of a jazzy piano sound, an inspired move under the circumstances. The combination enlivens even the dud songs; "I'm Your Shoe" starts as a pedestrian slow-grind, but has an incredible instrumental break in which the whole band rocks hard and fast, then drops out suddenly to let Ferguson take a wonderful and delicate piano solo. The element of surprise gets you the first time, the brilliant playing every time afterward. When the band actually takes on a song with a half-decent hook all the way through, the results are splendid. The title cut, "She Said Allright," and "Falling Angel" are all winners, and there isn't a single track that is actually a dud. If it was inevitable that Jo Jo Gunne was going to break up, at least they left one consistently good album behind.

Richard Foss

Billy Joel

Piano Man
November 1973, Columbia

Embittered by legal disputes with his label and an endless tour to support a debut that was dead in the water, Billy Joel hunkered down in his adopted hometown of Los Angeles, spending six months as a lounge singer at a club. He didn't abandon his dreams—he continued to write songs, including "Piano Man," a fictionalized account of his weeks as a lounge singer. Through a combination of touring and constant hustling, he landed a contract with Columbia and recorded his second album in 1973. Clearly inspired by Elton John's *Tumbleweed Connection*, not only musically but lyrically, as well as James Taylor, Joel expands the vision and sound of *Cold Spring Harbor*, abandoning introspective numbers (apart from "You're My Home," a love letter to his wife) for character sketches and epics. Even the title track, a breakthrough hit based on his weeks as a saloon singer, focuses on the colorful patrons, not the singer. If his narratives are occasionally awkward or incomplete, he compensates with music that gives the songs a sweeping sense of purpose—they *feel* complete, thanks to his indelible melodies and savvy stylistic repurposing. He may have borrowed his basic blueprint from *Tumbleweed Connection*, particularly with its Western imagery and bluesy gospel flourishes, but he makes it his own, largely due to his melodic flair, which is in greater evidence than on *Cold Spring Harbor*. *Piano Man* is where he suggests his potential as a musical craftsman. He may have weaknesses as a lyricist—such mishaps as the "instant pleasuredome" line in "You're My Home" illustrate that he doesn't have an ear for words—but *Piano Man* makes it clear that his skills as a melodicist can dazzle.

Stephen Thomas Erlewine

Streetlife Serenade
October 1974, Columbia

Billy Joel hit a bit of a slump with *Streetlife Serenade*, his third album. Stylistically, it was a reiteration of its predecessor's *Tumbleweed Connection* obsessions, spiked with, of all things, *Rockford Files* synthesizers and ragtimes pulled from *The Sting*. That isn't a facetious reference, either—it's no coincidence that the record's single and best song, "The Entertainer," shares a title with the Scott Joplin rag that provided *The Sting* with a main theme. Joel is attempting a grand Americana lyrical vision, stretching from the Wild West through the Depression to "Los Angelenos" and "The Great Suburban Showdown." It doesn't work, not only because of his shortcomings as a writer, but because he didn't have the time to pull it all together. There are no less than two instrumentals, and even if "Root Beer Rag" (yet another sign of *The Sting*'s influence) is admittedly enjoyable, they're undeniably fillers, as is much of the second side. Since he has skills, he's able to turn out a few winners—"Roberta," a love song in the vein of *Cold Spring Harbor*, the mournful "Streetlife Serenader," and the stomping "Los Angelenos"—but it was the astonishingly bitter "The Entertainer," where he not only disparages his own role but is filled with venom over "Piano Man" being released in a single edit, that made the subtext clear: he had enough with California, enough with the music industry, enough with being a sensitive singer-songwriter. It was time for Billy to say goodbye to Hollywood and head back home to New York.

Stephen Thomas Erlewine

Turnstiles
May 1976, Columbia

There's a reason *Turnstiles* begins with the Spector-esque epic "Say Goodbye to Hollywood." Shortly after *Streetlife Serenade*, Joel ditched California—and, by implication, sensitive Californian soft rock from sensitive singer/songwriters—for his hometown of New York. "Say Goodbye to Hollywood" was a celebration of his move, a repudiation of his past, a fanfare for a new beginning, which is exactly what *Turnstiles* was. He still was a singer/songwriter—indeed, "Summer, Highland Falls" was his best ballad to date, possibly his best ever—but he decided to run with his musical talents, turning the record into a whirlwind tour of pop styles, from Sinatra to Springsteen. There's little question that the cinematic sprawl of *Born to Run* had an effect on *Turnstiles*, since it has a similar widescreen feel, even if it clocks in at only eight songs. The key to the record's success is variety, the way the album whips from the bouncy, McCartney-esque "All You Wanna Do Is Dance" to the saloon song "New York State of Mind"; the way the bitterly cynical "Angry Young Man" gives way to the beautiful "I've Loved These Days" and the surrealistic apocalyptic fantasy "Miami 2017 (Seen the Lights Go Out on Broadway)." No matter how much stylistic ground Joel covers, he's kept on track by his backing group. He fought to have his touring band support him on *Turnstiles*, going to the lengths of firing his original producer, and it was clearly the right move, since they lend the album a cohesive feel. *Turnstiles* may not have been a hit, but it remains one of his most accomplished and satisfying records, clearly paving the way to his twin peaks of the late '70s, *The Stranger* and *52nd Street*.

Stephen Thomas Erlewine

The Stranger
September 1977, Columbia

Billy Joel teamed with Phil Ramone, a famed engineer who had just scored his first producing hits with Art Garfunkel's *Breakaway* and Paul Simon's *Still Crazy After All These Years* for *The Stranger*, his follow-up to *Turnstiles*. Joel still favored big, sweeping melodies, but Ramone convinced him to streamline his arrangements and clean up the production. The results aren't necessarily revelatory, since he covered so much ground on *Turnstiles*, but the commercialism of *The Stranger* is a bit of a surprise. None of his ballads have been as sweet or slick as "Just the Way You Are"; he never had created a rocker as bouncy or infectious as "Only the Good Die Young"; and the glossy production of "She's Always a Woman" disguises its latent misogynist streak. Joel balanced such radio-ready material with a series of New York vignettes, seemingly inspired by Springsteen's working-class fables and clearly intended to be the artistic centerpieces of the album. They do provide *The Stranger* with the feel of a concept album, yet there is no true thematic connection between the pieces, and his lyrics are often vague or mean-spirited. His lyrical shortcomings are overshadowed by his musical strengths. Even if his melodies sound more Broadway than Beatles—the epic suite "Scenes From an Italian Restaurant" feels like a show-stopping closer—there's no denying that the melodies of each song on *The Stranger* are memorable, so much so that they strengthen the weaker portions of the album. Joel rarely wrote a set of songs better than those on *The Stranger*, nor did he often deliver an album as consistently listenable.

Stephen Thomas Erlewine

52nd Street
October 1978, Columbia

Once *The Stranger* became a hit, Billy Joel quickly re-entered the studio with producer Phil Ramone to record the follow-up, *52nd Street*. Instead of breaking from the sound of *The Stranger*, Joel chose to expand it, making it more sophisticated and somewhat jazzy.

Often, his moves sounded as if they were responses to Steely Dan—indeed, his phrasing and melody for "Zanzibar" is a direct homage to Donald Fagen circa *The Royal Scam*, and it also boasts a solo from jazz great Freddie Hubbard à la Steely Dan—but since Joel is a working-class populist, not an elitist college boy, he never shies away from big gestures and melodies. Consequently, *52nd Street* unintentionally embellishes the Broadway overtones of its predecessor, not only on a centerpiece like "Stiletto," but when he's rocking out on "Big Shot." That isn't necessarily bad, since Joel's strong suit turns out to be showmanship—he dazzles with his melodic skills and his enthusiastic performances. He also knows how to make a record. Song for song, *52nd Street* might not be as strong as *The Stranger*, but there are no weak songs—indeed, "Honesty," "My Life," "Until the Night," and the three mentioned above are among his best—and they all flow together smoothly, thanks to Ramone's seamless production and Joel's melodic craftsmanship. It's remarkable to think that in a matter of three records, Joel had hit upon a workable, marketable formula—one that not only made him one of the biggest-selling artists of his era, but one of the most enjoyable mainstream hitmakers. *52nd Street* is a testament to that achievement.

Stephen Thomas Erlewine

Glass Houses
March 1980, Columbia

The back-to-back success of *The Stranger* and *52nd Street*

may have brought Billy Joel fame and fortune, even a certain amount of self-satisfaction, but it didn't bring him critical respect, and it didn't dull his anger. If anything, being classified as a mainstream rocker—a soft rocker—infuriated him, especially since a generation of punks and new wave kids were getting the praise that eluded him. He didn't take this lying down—he recorded *Glass Houses*. Comparatively a harder-rocking album than either of its predecessors, with a distinctly bitter edge, *Glass Houses* still displays the hallmarks of Billy Joel the pop craftsman and Phil Ramone the world-class hitmaker. Even its hardest songs—the terrifically paranoid "Sometimes a Fantasy," "Sleepin' With the Television On," "Close to the Borderline," the hit "You May Be Right"—have bold, direct melodies and clean arrangements, ideal for radio play. Instead of turning out to be a fiery rebuttal to his detractors, the album is a remarkable catalog of contemporary pop styles, from McCartney-esque whimsy ("Don't Ask Me Why") and arena rock ("All for Leyna") to soft rock ("C'etait Toi [You Were the One]") and stylish new wave pop ("It's Still Rock and Roll to Me," which ironically is closer to new wave pop than rock). That's not a detriment; that's the album's strength. *The Stranger* and *52nd Street* were fine albums in their own right, but it's nice to hear Joel scale back his showman tendencies and deliver a solid pop/rock record. It may not be punk—then again, it may be his concept of punk—but *Glass Houses* is the closest Joel ever got to a pure rock album.

Stephen Thomas Erlewine

The Nylon Curtain
September 1982, Columbia

Billy Joel hit back as hard as he could with *Glass Houses*, his bid to prove that he could rock as hard as any of those new wave punks. He might not have proven himself a punk—for all of his claims of being a hard rocker, his work inevitably is pop because of his fondness for melody—but he proved to himself that he could still rock, even if the critics didn't give him any credit for it. It was now time to mature, to move pop/rock into the middle age and, in the process, earn critical respect. In short, *The Nylon Curtain* is where Billy Joel went serious, consciously crafting a song cycle about Baby Boomers in the Reagan era. Since this was an album about Baby Boomers, he chose to base his music almost entirely on the Beatles, the pivotal rock band for his generation. Joel is naturally inclined to write big melodies like McCartney, and he idolizes Lennon, which makes *The Nylon Curtain* a fascinating cross between ear candy and social commentary. His desire to record a grand concept album is admirable, but his ever-present lyrical shortcomings mean that the songs paint a picture without arriving at any insights. He occasionally gets lost in his own ambition, as on the waterlogged second side, but the first half of the song suite—"Allentown," "Laura," "Pressure," "Goodnight Saigon," "She's Right on Time"—is layered, successful, mature pop that brings Joel tantalizingly close to his ultimate goal of sophisticated pop/rock for mature audiences.

Stephen Thomas Erlewine

An Innocent Man
August 1983, Columbia

Recording *The Nylon Curtain* exhausted Billy Joel, and even though it had a pair of major hits, it didn't rival its predecessors in terms of sales. Since he labored so hard at the record, he decided it was time for a break—it was time to record an album just for fun. And that's how his homage to pre-Beatles pop, *An Innocent Man*, was conceived: it was designed as a breezy romp through the music of his childhood. Joel's grasp on history isn't remarkably astute—the opener "Easy Money" is a slice of Stax/Volt pop-soul, via the Blues Brothers (quite possibly the inspiration for the album), and the label didn't break the pop charts until well after the British Invasion—but he's in top form as a craftsman throughout the record. Only once does he stumble on his own ambition ("This Night," which appropriates its chorus from Beethoven). For the rest of the record, he's effortlessly spinning out infectious, memorable melodies in a variety of styles, from the Four Seasons send-up "Uptown Girl" and the soulful "Tell Her About It" to a pair of doo wop tributes, "The Longest Time" and "Careless Talk." Joel has rarely sounded so carefree either in performance or writing, possibly due to "Christie Lee" Brinkley, a supermodel who became his new love prior to *An Innocent Man*. He can't stop writing about her throughout the album—only three songs, including the haunted title track, *aren't* about her in some form or fashion. That giddiness is infectious, helping make *An Innocent Man* an innocent delight that unwittingly closes Joel's classic period.

Stephen Thomas Erlewine

Elton John

Elton John
August 1970, Rocket/Island

Empty Sky was followed by *Elton John*, a more focused and realized record that deservedly became his first hit. John and Bernie Taupin's songwriting had become more immediate and successful; in particular, John's music had become sharper and more diverse, rescuing Taupin's frequently nebulous lyrics. "Take Me to the Pilot" might not make much sense lyrically, but John had the good sense to ground its willfully cryptic words with a catchy blues-based melody. Next to the increased sense of songcraft, the most noticeable change on *Elton John* is the addition of Paul Buckmaster's grandiose string arrangements. Buckmaster's orchestrations are never subtle, but they never overwhelm the vocalist, nor do they make the songs schmaltzy. Instead, they fit the ambitions of John and Taupin, as the instant standard "Your Song" illustrates. Even with the strings and choirs that dominate the sound of the album, John manages to rock out on a fair share of the record. Though there are a couple of underdeveloped songs, *Elton John* remains one of his best records. [The CD reissue includes the bonus tracks "Bad Side of the Moon," "Grey Seal," and "Rock n Roll Madonna."]

Stephen Thomas Erlewine

Tumbleweed Connection
1971, UNI

Instead of repeating the formula that made *Elton John* a success, John and Bernie Taupin attempted their most ambitious record to date for the follow-up to their breakthrough. A loose concept album about the American West, *Tumbleweed Connection* emphasized the pretensions that always lay beneath their songcraft. Half of the songs don't follow conventional pop song structures; instead, they flow between verses and vague choruses. These experiments are remarkably successful, primarily because Taupin's lyrics are evocative and John's melodic sense is at its best. As should be expected for a concept album about the Wild West, the music draws from country and blues in equal measures, ranging from the bluesy choruses of "Ballad of a Well-Known Gun" and the modified country of "Country Comfort" to the gospel-inflected "Burn Down the Mission" and the rolling, soulful "Amoreena." Paul Buckmaster manages to write dramatic but appropriate string arrangements that accentuate the cinematic feel of the album.

Stephen Thomas Erlewine

Madman Across the Water
November 1971, Rocket/Island

Trading the cinematic aspirations of *Tumbleweed Connection* for a tentative stab at prog rock, Elton John and Bernie Taupin delivered another excellent collection of songs with *Madman Across the Water*. Like its two predecessors, *Madman Across the Water* is driven by the sweeping string arrangements of Paul Buckmaster, who gives the songs here a richly dark and haunting edge. And these are songs that benefit from grandiose treatments. With most songs clocking in around five minutes, the record feels like a major work, and in many ways it is. While it's not as adventurous as *Tumbleweed Connection*, the overall quality of the record is very high, particularly on character sketches "Levon" and "Razor Face," as well as the melodramatic "Tiny Dancer" and the paranoid title track. *Madman Across the Water* begins to fall apart toward the end, but the record remains an ambitious and rewarding work, and John never attained its darkly introspective atmosphere again.

Stephen Thomas Erlewine

Honky Chateau
May 1972, MCA

Considerably lighter than *Madman Across the Water*, *Honky Chateau* is a rollicking collection of ballads, rockers, blues, country-rock, and soul songs. On paper, it reads like an eclectic mess, but it plays as the most focused and accomplished set of songs Elton John and Bernie Taupin ever wrote. The skittering boogie of "Honky Cat" and the light psychedelic pop of "Rocket Man" helped send *Honky Chateau* to the top of the charts, but what is truly impressive about the album is the depth of its material. From the surprisingly cynical and nasty "I Think I'm Gonna Kill Myself" to the moving ballad "Mona Lisas and Mad Hatters," John is at the top of his form, crafting immaculate pop songs with memorable melodies and powerful hooks. While Taupin's lyrics aren't much more comprehensible than before, John delivers them with skill and passion, making them feel more substantial than they are. But what makes *Honky Chateau* a classic is the songcraft, and the way John ties disparate strands of roots music into distinctive and idiosyncratic pop—it's one of the finest collections of mainstream singer/songwriter pop of the early '70s.

Stephen Thomas Erlewine

Don't Shoot Me I'm Only the Piano Player
January 1973, Rocket/Island

Elton John became a true superstar with 1972's *Honky Chateau*. He followed that album with *Don't Shoot Me I'm Only the Piano Player*, his most direct, pop-oriented album to date. Designed as a pastiche of classic and contemporary pop styles, the album almost sounds like an attempt to demonstrate the diversity of the John/Taupin team. Though the hits are remarkable—"Daniel" is a moving ballad and "Crocodile Rock" is a sly take on '50s rock & roll—the album is slightly uneven. Several of the album tracks, particularly the knowing "I'm Gonna Be a Teenage Idol" and the rocking "Elderberry Wine," are as strong as anything John had recorded, but there are too many melodies that simply don't catch hold. Nevertheless, the singles were strong enough to keep the album at the top of the charts, and at its best, it is a very enjoyable piece of well-crafted pop/rock. [The CD reissue includes the bonus tracks "Screw You (Young Man's Blues)," "Jack Rabbit," "Whenever You're Ready (We'll Go Steady Again)," and the piano version of "Skyline Pigeon."]
Stephen Thomas Erlewine

Goodbye Yellow Brick Road
October 1973, Rocket/Island

Goodbye Yellow Brick Road was where Elton John's personality began to gather more attention than his music, as it topped the American charts for eight straight weeks. In many ways, the double album was a recap of all the styles and sounds that made John a star. *Goodbye Yellow Brick Road* is all over the map, beginning with the prog rock epic "Funeral for a Friend (Love Lies Bleeding)" and immediately careening into the balladry of "Candle in the Wind." For the rest of the album, John leaps between popcraft ("Bennie and the Jets"), ballads ("Goodbye Yellow Brick Road"), hard rock ("Saturday Night's Alright for Fighting"), novelties ("Jamaica Jerk-Off"), Bernie Taupin's literary pretensions ("The Ballad of Danny Bailey"), and everything in between. Though its diversity is impressive, the album doesn't hold together very well. Even so, its individual moments are spectacular and the glitzy, crowd-pleasing showmanship that fuels the album pretty much defines what made Elton John a superstar in the early '70s.
Stephen Thomas Erlewine

Caribou
June 1974, MCA

Glitzy showmanship is what fuels *Caribou*, the least successful collection to be reissued in this batch of Elton John albums. Though the shiny surface of the album is alluring, only a few tracks rank among John's best work. "The Bitch Is Back" is one of his best hard rock cuts and "Don't Let the Sun Go Down on Me" is one of his classic ballads, but the album tracks tend to be ridiculous filler on the order of "Solar Prestige a Gammon" or competent genre exercises like "You're So Static." There are a couple of exceptions—"Pinky" is a fine ballad and "Dixie Lily" is an endearing stab at country—but on the whole, *Caribou* is

a disappointment. [The CD reissue includes the bonus tracks "Pinball Wizard," "Sick City," "Cold Highway," and "Step Into Christmas."]
Stephen Thomas Erlewine

Greatest Hits
November 1974, Polydor

Rarely has a greatest-hits collection been as effective as Elton John's first compilation of *Greatest Hits*. Released at the end of 1974, after *Goodbye Yellow Brick Road* and *Caribou* had effectively established him as a superstar, *Greatest Hits* is exactly what it says it is—it features every one of his Top Ten singles ("Your Song," "Rocket Man," "Honky Cat," "Crocodile Rock," "Daniel," "Goodbye Yellow Brick Road," "Bennie and the Jets," "Don't Let the Sun Go Down on Me"), plus the number 12 "Saturday Night's Alright for Fighting" and radio and concert favorites "Border Song" and "Candle in the Wind." Despite the exclusion of a couple of lesser hits from this era, most notably "Levon" and "Tiny Dancer," *Greatest Hits* is a nearly flawless collection, offering a perfect introduction to Elton John and providing casual fans with almost all the hits they need.
Stephen Thomas Erlewine

Captain Fantastic and the Brown Dirt Cowboy
May 1975, Rocket/Island

Sitting atop the charts in 1975, Elton John and Bernie Taupin recalled their rise to power in *Captain Fantastic and the Brown Dirt Cowboy*, their first explicitly conceptual effort since *Tumbleweed Connection*. It's no coincidence that it's their best album since then, showcasing each at the peak of his power, as John crafts supple, elastic, versatile pop and Taupin's inscrutable wordplay is evocative, even moving. What's best about the record is that it works best of a piece—although it entered the charts at number one, this only had one huge hit in "Someone Saved My Life Tonight," which sounds even better here, since it tidily fits into the musical and lyrical themes. And although the musical skill on display here is dazzling, as it bounces between country and hard rock within the same song, this is certainly a grower. The album needs time to reveal its treasures, but once it does, it rivals *Tumbleweed* in terms of sheer consistency and eclipses it in scope, capturing John and Taupin at a pinnacle. They collapsed in hubris and excess not long afterward—*Rock of the Westies*, which followed just months later is as scattered as this is focused—but this remains a testament to the strengths of their creative partnership.
Stephen Thomas Erlewine

Rock of the Westies
October 1975, Polydor

Less than four months after issuing the landmark and autobiographical *Captain Fantastic and the Brown Dirt Cowboy* (1975), Elton John re-emerged with a new band and a slightly modified sound. However, the departure of Dee Murray (bass) and Nigel Olsson (drums) would ultimately begin a deceleration in terms of John's success, which rivalled only the Beatles' and Elvis Presley's in terms of global acclaim. The revamped band grew to include new associates James Newton Howard (keyboards) and Kenny Passarelli (bass) as well as Roger Pope (drums) and Caleb Quaye (guitar), who had both performed with John as far back as his first long-player, *Empty Sky* (1968). He also retained the services of Davey Johnstone (guitar) and Ray Cooper (percussion) from the most recent lineup. Musically, *Rock* of the Westies (1975) maintains the balance of harder-edged material and effective ballads. In fact, one of the album's strongest suits is the wide spectrum of strong material. The ballsy no-nonsense "Street Kids" and the aggressive gringo rock of the ZZ Top sound-alike "Grown Some Funk of Your Own" contrast the poignant power balladry of "I Feel Like a Bullet (In the Gun of Robert Ford)" or the dark and brooding tale of addiction on "Feed Me." Perhaps inspired by the crossover R&B appeal of "Philadelphia Freedom," the uptempo "Island Girl" bears a distinct and danceable groove that lies somewhere between a slightly Jamaican vibe and disco. Perhaps more soulful in the traditional sense are the boogie-based "Hard Luck Story" or propulsive Bo Diddley beat that drives "Billy Bones and the White Bird." While the increasingly fickle public as well as lack of a strong follow-up to the chart-topping single "Island Girl" may have prevented *Rock of the Westies* from becoming the heir apparent to *Captain Fantastic and the Brown Dirt Cowboy*, in the wake of John's flawless predecessors it remains a strong and worthwhile entry that also sets the stage for its follow-up, *Blue Moves* (1976).

Lindsay Planer

Rickie Lee Jones

Rickie Lee Jones
March 1979, Warner Bros.

One of the most impressive debuts for a singer/songwriter ever, this infectious mixture of styles not only features a strong collection of original songs (the hits are "Chuck E's in Love" and "Young Blood, "but "Danny's All-Star Joint" and "Coolsville" are just as good) but also a singer with a savvy, distinctive voice that can be streetwise, childlike, and sophisticated, sometimes all in the same song.

William Ruhlmann

Janis Joplin

I Got Dem Ol' Kozmic Blues Again Mama!
1969, Columbia

Janis Joplin's solo debut was a letdown at the time of release, suffering in comparison with Big Brother's *Cheap Thrills* from the previous year, and shifting her style toward soul-rock in a way that disappointed some fans. Removed from that context, it sounds better today, though it's still flawed. Fronting the short-lived Kozmic Blues Band, the arrangements are horn heavy and the material soulful and bluesy. The band sounds a little stiff, though, and although Joplin's singing is good, she would sound more electrifying on various live versions of some of the songs that have come out over the years. The shortage of quality original compositions—indeed, there are only eight tracks total on the album—didn't help either, and the cover selections were

erratic, particularly the Bee Gees' "To Love Somebody." On the other hand, "Try" is one of her best soul outings, and the reading of Rodgers & Hart's "Little Girl Blue" is inspired. The 1999 CD reissue adds three bonus tracks: a cover of Bob Dylan's "Dear Landlord" from the *Kozmic Blues* sessions that was first heard on the *Janis* box set, and previously unreleased versions of "Summertime" and "Piece of My Heart" from the Woodstock Festival. "Summertime" is okay, but this "Piece of My Heart" really pales next to the Big Brother interpretation.

Richie Unterberger

Pearl
February 1971, Columbia/Legacy

Janis Joplin's second masterpiece (after *Cheap Thrills*), *Pearl* was designed as a showcase for her powerhouse vocals, stripping down the arrangements that had often previously cluttered her music or threatened to drown her out. Thanks also to a more consistent set of songs, the results are magnificent—given room to breathe, Joplin's trademark rasp conveys an aching, desperate passion on funked-up, bluesy rockers, ballads both dramatic and tender, and her signature song, the posthumous number one hit "Me and Bobby McGee." The unfinished "Buried Alive in the Blues" features no Joplin vocals—she was scheduled to record them on the day after she was found dead. Its incompleteness mirrors Joplin's career; *Pearl*'s power leaves the listener to wonder what else Joplin could have accomplished, but few artists could ask for a better final statement. [The 1999 CD reissue adds four previously unreleased live July 1970 recordings: "Tell Mama," "Little Girl Blue," "Try," and "Cry Baby."]

Steve Huey

Janis
November 1993, Columbia/Legacy

This three-CD box set is the most thorough and valuable retrospective of Janis Joplin's career. Besides including all of her most essential recordings with and without Big Brother & the Holding Company, this 49-song package features quite a few enticing rarities; 18 of the tracks were previously unissued. These include a 1962 home recording of the Joplin original "What Good Can Drinkin' Do," which marked the first time her singing was captured on tape; a pair of acoustic blues tunes from 1965 with backup guitar by future Jefferson Airplane star Jorma Kaukonen, an acoustic demo of "Me and Bobby McGee," a 1970 birthday song for John Lennon, and live performances from her appearance on *The Ed Sullivan Show* in 1969. The real showstopper is the previously unissued, eight-minute version of "Ball and Chain" from Big Brother's first set at the 1967 Monterey Pop Festival (the cut on the *Monterey Pop* box set is from their second set). The more forgettable tracks from her solo albums are wisely excised, as are the Big Brother songs which did not feature her vocals. This is the rare multi-disc set of a major artist that manages to cover all the official milestones and present a bounty of worthwhile rarities at the same time.

Richie Unterberger

Journey

Infinity
May 1978, Columbia

By 1977 Journey had reached a creative crossroads, with three underwhelming studio albums under their belt and little to show in the way of commercial success. At the prodding of manager Herbie Herbert, who felt a major shakeup was needed in order to reignite their spark, the band was convinced to audition and eventually recruit the services of former Alien Project vocalist Steve Perry. Sure enough, adding him to the band just prior to the sessions for *Infinity* proved to be a stroke of genius, and a move that undeniably altered the course of history for the fledging Bay Area act. Released in January of 1978, *Infinity* easily proved to be the band's most cohesive work to date. Dead and buried were the jazz fusion overtones of previous offerings, and with the new songwriting combo of Perry/Neal Schon leading the march, the band set out to completely redefine their sound. Traditional pop arrangements were now adopted, cutting out the unnecessary musical fat, and allowing each bandmember to play to his strength: Perry's soaring, whale of a voice, Schon's scorching fret work, and Gregg Rolie's subtle keyboard arrangements. Enlisting eccentric producer Roy Thomas Baker (already famous for guiding the likes of Queen and Nazareth to giant commercial triumphs of their own) also proved to be a rewarding move for the boys. With newfound confidence, Journey crafted a record that could finally land them on the radio. Loaded with future FM staples like "Wheel in the Sky" (which hit the Top 50 in April of 1978), "Lights" (which quietly peaked at number 68 that August), and "Anytime" (pretty much a flop, crawling to number 83 in July), *Infinity* introduced Journey to an entirely new audience. Even non-singles like "Patiently (the first tune Perry ever wrote with Schon) and "Somethin' to Hide" were leaps and bounds beyond the band's previous accomplishments. And, ultimately, though *Infinity* merely introduced the band to mainstream radio (it was the never-ending tour on which the band embarked on to support it that drove the disc past the platinum plateau), it effectively cemented their rep as one of America's most beloved (and sometimes hated) commercial rock/pop bands. With over 170 shows under their belts, Journey had just begin to hit their stride. [*Infinity* was reissued in 2006, housed in a fancy digipack with an expanded booklet.]

John Franck & Ed Rivadavia

Evolution
April 1979, Columbia

With the platinum triumph of *Infinity* still ringing in their ears like coins in a slot machine, Journey was now committed to completing their transformation from jazz fusion/prog rock mavens into arena rock superstars with their fifth album, 1979's *Evolution*. This transition (also clearly illustrated by the futuristic insect gracing each album cover henceforth) would not come without its growing pains, however, and while producer Roy Thomas Baker was back for a second go-round, original drummer Aynsley Dunbar would be the first casualty of the band's new direction. Thankfully, former Ronnie Montrose skin-beater Steve Smith soon brought his college-trained jazz fusion background to the table, and the band was ready to get back to work. If *Infinity* had defined a new songwriting formula for the act, *Evolution* only served to develop it and streamline it further, clearly qualifying as their strongest effort to date and endearing the band to millions of FM rock listeners in the process. With commercial rock ditties like "Lovin', Touchin', Squeezin'" (their first single to crack the Top 20), "Too Late"

(which reached number 70), and the powerful "Just the Same Way" (which peaked at number 58) leading the way to radio dominance, Journey had never sounded stronger or more determined. And with Steve Perry's tenor pipes now clearly driving the band's engine, and guitarist Neal Schon beginning to relish in his guitar hero persona, Journey could seemingly do no wrong. *Evolution* quickly became the band's biggest-selling album (moving over 800,000 units in less than three months), and Perry and co. soon embarked on yet another mammoth tour, which set many an attendance record, and set the stage for even greater triumph with 1980's *Departure*. [*Evolution* was reissued in 2006, housed in a fancy digipack with an expanded booklet.]

John Franck & Ed Rivadavia

Departure
March 1980, Columbia

The third and final album of what could be called Journey's cocoon phase (*Escape* would give birth to a fully formed butterfly and put the band through a different stratosphere), 1980's *Departure* would also be the quintet's last with keyboardist/vocalist Gregg Rolie. Produced by Geoff Workman and Kevin Elson (essentially both engineers turned producers), the album continued to build on the band's previous two recordings, but offered an added edge, arrangement-wise. This was likely due to the fact that the band had walked into Automatt Studios with 19 new tunes and proceeded to record most of them live, eventually trimming down to 11 songs. Catapulting all the way up to number eight on the Billboard Top 200, *Departure* was the band's highest charting album to date and got off to an explosive start with the driving riffs and chorused vocals of "Anyway You Want It" (another radio smash that would chart Top 25). Never sounding tighter, the quintet then launches into "Walks Like a Lady" (another future FM staple, which would climb to number 32) and a string of outstanding rockers, including future concert opener "Where Were You" and the stop-go-stop-go energy of "Line of Fire." On the other hand, elegant power ballads like "Good Morning" and "Stay Awhile" would foreshadow the band's future commercial triumphs on *Escape*. And even though it packs the occasional filler like "Someday Soon" and "Homemade Love" (a weak attempt to boogie that falls absolutely flat and, tellingly, was the only Gregg Rolie-sung tune here), *Departure* is a solid record all around. Soon, Rolie would be replaced by the greater pop-savvy songwriting muscle of former Babys keyboard man Jonathan Caine, and Journey would go from huge cult act to monster superstars.

John Franck & Ed Rivadavia

Escape
August 1981, Columbia

Escape was a groundbreaking album for San Francisco's Journey, charting three singles inside *Billboard*'s Top Ten, with "Don't Stop Believing" reaching number nine, "Who's Crying Now" number four, and "Open Arms" peaking at number two and  holding there for six weeks. *Escape* flung Journey steadfastly into the AOR arena, combining Neal Schon's grand yet palatable guitar playing with Jonathan Cain's blatant keyboards. All this was topped off by the passionate, wide-ranged vocals of Steve Perry, who is the true lifeblood of this album, and this band. The songs on *Escape* are more rock-flavored, with more hooks and a harder cadence compared to their former sound. "Who's Crying Now" spotlights the sweeping fervor of Perry's voice, whose theme about the ups and downs of a relationship was plentiful in Journey's repertoire. With "Don't Stop Believing," the whisper of Perry's ardor is crept up to with Schon's searing electric guitar work, making for a perfect rock song. One of rock's most beautiful ballads, "Open Arms," gleams with an honesty and feel only Steve Perry could muster. Outside of the singles, there is a certain electricity that circulates through the rest of the album. The songs are timeless, and as a whole, they have a way of rekindling the innocence of youthful romance and the rebelliousness of growing up, built from heartfelt songwriting and sturdy musicianship.

Mike DeGagne

Frontiers
February 1983, Columbia

Frontiers managed to give Journey four Top 40 hits, with "After the Fall" and "Send Her My Love" both reaching number 23, "Faithfully" at number 12, and "Separate Ways" peaking at number eight—the same amount that 1981's *Escape* brandished. While they tried to use the same musical recipe as *Escape*, *Frontiers* comes up a little short, mainly because the keyboards seem to overtake both Schon's guitar playing and Steve Perry's strong singing. An overabundance of Jonathan Cain's synth work cloaks the quicker tunes and seeps into the ballads, slightly widening the strong partnership of Perry and Schon. "Faithfully" tried to match the powerful beauty of "Open Arms," and while it's a gorgeous ballad, it just comes inches away from conjuring up the same soft magic. "Separate Ways" grabs attention right off the bat with stinging synthesizer and a catchy guitar riff, and "Send Her My Love" emphasizes Perry's keen ability to pour his heart out. The rest of the songs on the album lack the warmth that Journey is famous for, especially in their mix of fervor and intimacy shown on this album's predecessor.

Mike DeGagne

Greatest Hits
November 1988, Columbia

Greatest Hits is an excellent, thorough 14-track collection containing all of Journey's big hits, from 1978's "Wheel in the Sky" to 1986's "I'll Be Alright Without You." Although the songs aren't presented in chronological order and a handful of minor hits ("Suzanne," "Walks Like a Lady") aren't included, it doesn't matter, since every essential Journey single—"Only the Young," "Don't Stop Believin'," "Any Way You Want It," "Separate Ways," "Lovin', Touchin', Squeezin'," "Open Arms," "Send Her My Love"—is here, which means that it's all most casual fans will ever need.

Stephen Thomas Erlewine

Judas Priest

British Steel
1980, Columbia

With *Hell Bent for Leather*, Judas Priest had begun the task of developing their image for increased mainstream attention, reveling in leather-and-motorcycle trappings while beginning to simplify and streamline their sound. *British Steel*

brings that process full circle, offering the band's catchiest, most accessible set of tunes yet, while retaining the precision guitar assault and quasi-operatic vocals that had come to define their sound. It was the simplest music Priest had yet attempted, but thanks to the (mostly) top-notch songwriting and AC/DC-like willingness to allow the songs' grooves room to breathe, the record is a smashing success overall, with maybe one or two subpar tracks. There are a couple of trends beginning here that would take their toll later on—the lyrics are a bit more juvenile, and the music seems to prize commercialism over complexity—but in this context, neither really matters, as Priest display a real penchant for stadium-ready anthems. "Breaking the Law" and "Living After Midnight" became genuine hit singles in the U.K., and deservedly so, while the album became their first to reach the U.S. Top 40, going platinum in the process.

Steve Huey

Screaming for Vengeance
1982, Columbia

Following the underwritten, erratic *Point of Entry*, *Screaming for Vengeance* returned Judas Priest to the top of the metal heap, boasting a much more consistent set of songs, highlighted by the monumental "You've Got Another Thing Comin'." Some of the bluesier elements of *Point of Entry* are still here, but the heavier moments tend to dominate the album's flavor (particularly the title track); plus, there are arena-ready headbanging anthems like "Electric Eye," "Bloodstone," and, of course, "You've Got Another Thing Comin'," the latter two proof that the band really knew how to work a mid-tempo rock groove. Although the sound is commercial, *Screaming for Vengeance* doesn't feel like it's pandering as *Point of Entry* sometimes did; it's a catchy, accessible metal record in the best sense of the description, and it rivals *British Steel* as Priest's best album of the '80s.

Steve Huey

Kansas

Masque
October 1975, Columbia

Kansas' third album, *Masque*, is a lyrically dark effort courtesy of guitarist/keyboardist Kerry Livgren's brooding songwriting. Musically, *Masque* foreshadows the tight melodies and instrumental interplay on the next two albums, *Leftoverture* and *Point of Know Return*, which together serve as the peak of Kansas' vision. The band deserves more respect than it gets for incorporating British hard rock and progressive rock to become the only U.S. progressive rock band of note during the genre's 1970s heyday. Robbie Steinhardt's violin work certainly helped give Kansas a distinctive sound. The liner notes indicate *Masque* is a "concept album" thanks to the title's definition: "A disguise of reality created through a theatrical or musical performance." Vocalist/keyboardist Steve Walsh's "It Takes a Woman's Love (To Make a Man)" is the leadoff track, and it's atypical of the rest of the album. The song is a fairly basic yet groovy pop/rock tune about musicians' loneliness on the road, but it is spiced up with some saxophone lines. "Two Cents Worth" addresses guilt, misery, and spiritual longing—pretty heavy stuff for six guys who were only in their mid-twenties. In "Icarus—Borne on Wings of Steel," Kansas' prog rock ambitions show through the mythology-based lyrics and the densely arranged guitars and keyboards. Walsh and Steinhardt's "All the World" is largely a bleak examination of loneliness and death, although it does end with a glimmer of hope. "Child of Innocence" is a tough blast of hard rock with a soaring chorus. "Mysteries and Mayhem" rocks along, yet it's rich with haunting nightmare imagery and biblical references. The nine-and-a-half-minute epic "The Pinnacle" closes the album.

Bret Adams

Leftoverture
October 1976, Kirshner

For any art rock band, the fourth album means it's time for a self-styled masterpiece—if you need proof, look at *Selling England by the Pound* or *Fragile*. So, with Kansas, the most determinedly arty of all American art rock bands, they composed and recorded *Leftoverture*, an impenetrable conundrum of significance that's capped off by nothing less than a five-part suite, appropriately titled "Magnum Opus," and featuring such promising movement titles as "Father Padilla Meets the Perfect Gnat" and "Release the Beavers." Of course, there's no telling whether this closing opus relates to the opener, "Carry On Wayward Son," the greatest single Kansas ever cut—a song that manages to be pompous, powerful, ridiculous, and catchy all at once. That they never manage to rival it anywhere on this record is as much a testament to their crippling ambition as their lack of skills. And it's unfair to say Kansas are unskilled, since they are certainly instrumentally proficient and they can craft songs or, rather, compositions that appear rather ambitious. Except these compositions aren't particularly complex, rhythmically or harmonically, and are in their own way as ambling as boogie rock, which still feels to be their foundation. It's not really fair to attack Kansas for a concept album with an impenetrable concept—it's possible to listen to *Lamb Lies Down on Broadway* hundreds of times and not know what the hell Rael is up to—but there's neither hooks nor true grandiosity here to make it interesting. That said, this still may be Kansas' most consistent set, outside of *Point of Know Return*. Take that for what you will.

Stephen Thomas Erlewine

Point of Know Return
1977, Kirshner

This is the definitive Kansas recording and includes their most famous tune, "Dust in the Wind." The band is in peak form and also churned out the single "Point of Know Return," which is still played daily on classic rock stations. While their pop-oriented approach and standard rock guitar sound helped define the classic rock sound of the '70s, careful listening reveals that this band's talent goes beyond colleagues such as Bachman-Turner Overdrive and Boston. Their arrangements and time signatures more accurately reflect the music of Yes and Emerson, Lake & Palmer. "Paradox" and "The Spider" are both excellent examples of their progressive approach. Unfortunately, the band always struggled to maintain a healthy balance of progression combined with pop. That made for such awkward moments here as "Portrait (He Knew)" and "Lightning's Hand." Yet despite the minor inconsistencies and a dated sound, their interplay

and superior musicianship make this both an essential classic rock and progressive rock recording.

Robert Taylor

Paul Kantner & Jefferson Starship

Blows Against the Empire
1970, RCA

Paul Kantner's debut solo album actually was credited to "Paul Kantner/Jefferson Starship," the first use of the "Starship" billing, predating the formation of the group with that name by four years. Kantner used it, extrapolating on the name of his current band, Jefferson Airplane, to refer to *Blows*'s science fiction concept: A bunch of left-wing hippies closely resembling his San Francisco Bay Area compatriots hijack a government-built starship and head off to re-start the human race on another planet. Kantner had presaged this post-apocalyptic colonization idea on "Wooden Ships" on the last Airplane album, *Volunteers*, and here he expanded it out to album length with the help of members of The Airplane, the Grateful Dead, Quicksilver Messenger Service, and Crosby, Stills and Nash, plus assorted others, a shifting supergroup informally known as PERRO, The Planet Earth Rock And Roll Orchestra. (Kantner later would borrow that name for a subsequent solo album.) *Blows* actually was a little loose as concept albums go, seeming as concerned with the arrival of Kantner and Grace Slick's baby as with the departure of the starship. Kantner employed often dense instrumentation and complex arrangements, but there were enough hooks and harmonies to keep things interesting. *Blows* eventually went gold, and it was even nominated for a science fiction award usually reserved for novels.

William Ruhlmann

King Crimson

In the Court of the Crimson King
1969, EG

This reissue of King Crimson's debut, *In the Court of the Crimson King* (1969), renders all previous pressings obsolete. In the late '90s, Robert Fripp remastered the entire Crimson catalog for inclusion in a 30th anniversary edition. Nowhere was the upgrade more deserved (or necessary) than on this rock & roll cornerstone. Initially, King Crimson consisted of Robert Fripp (guitar), Ian McDonald (reeds/woodwind/vibes/keyboards/Mellotron/vocals), Greg Lake (bass/vocals), Michael Giles (drums/percussion/vocals), and Peter Sinfield (words/illuminations). As if somehow prophetic, King Crimson projected a darker and edgier brand of post-psychedelic rock. Likewise, they were inherently intelligent—a sort of thinking man's Pink Floyd. Fripp demonstrates his innate aptitude for contrasts and the value of silence within a performance, even as far back as "21st Century Schizoid Man." The song is nothing short of the aural antecedent to what would become the entire heavy alternative/grunge sound. Juxtaposed with that electric intensity is the ethereal noir ballad "I Talk to the Wind." The delicate vocal harmonies and McDonald's achingly poignant flute solo and melodic counterpoint remain unmatched on an emotive level. The surreal and opaque lyrics are likewise an insight to Peter Sinfield's masterful wordplay, which graced their next three releases. The original A-side concludes with the powerful sonic imagery of "Epitaph." The haunting Mellotron wails, and Fripp's acoustic—as well as electric—guitar counterpoints give the introduction an almost sacred feel, adding measurably to the overall sinister mood. Giles' percussion work provides a pungent kick during the kettle drum intro and to the aggressive palpitation-inducing rhythm in the chorus. "Moonchild" is an eerie love song that is creepy, bordering on uncomfortable. The melody is agile and ageless, while the instrumentation wafts like the wind through bare trees. Developing out of the song is an extended improvisation that dissolves into a non-structured section of free jazz, with brief guitar lines running parallel throughout. The title track, "In the Court of the Crimson King," completes the disc with another beautifully bombastic song. Here again, the foreboding featured in Sinfield's lyrics is instrumentally matched by the contrasting verbosity in the chorus and the delicate nature of the verses and concluding solos. Of course, this thumbnail appraisal pales in comparison to experiencing the actual recording. Thanks to Fripp and company's laborious efforts, this 30th anniversary edition sports sound as majestic as it has ever been within the digital domain. Frankly, the HDCD playback compatibility even bests the warmth and timbre of an original 1-A vinyl pressing. This is especially critical during the quieter passages throughout "Moonchild" and "I Talk to the Wind." Initial releases were housed in a limited-edition gatefold replica of the original LP packaging and were accompanied by an oversized 12-page memorabilia booklet with photos and press clippings from the era.

Lindsay Planer

In the Wake of Poseidon
1970, EG

King Crimson opened 1970 scarcely in existence as a band, having lost two key members (Ian McDonald and Michael Giles), with a third (Greg Lake) about to leave. Their second album—largely composed of Robert Fripp's songwriting and material salvaged from their stage repertory ("Pictures of a City" and "The Devil's Triangle")—is actually better produced and better sounding than their first. Surprisingly, Fripp's guitar is not the dominant instrument here: The Mellotron, taken over by Fripp after McDonald's departure—and played even better than before—still remains the band's signature. The record doesn't tread enough new ground to precisely rival *In the Court of the Crimson King*. Fripp, however, has made an impressive show of transmuting material that worked on stage ("Mars" aka "The Devil's Triangle") into viable studio creations, and "Cadence and Cascade" may be the prettiest song the group ever cut. "The Devil's Triangle," which is essentially

an unauthorized adaptation of "Mars, Bringer of War" from Gustav Holst's *The Planets*, was later used in an eerie Bermuda Triangle documentary of the same name. In March of 2000, Caroline and Virgin released a 24-bit digitally remastered job that puts the two Mellotrons, Michael Giles' drums, Peter Giles' bass, and even Fripp's acoustic guitar and Keith Tippett's acoustic piano practically in the lap of the listener.

Bruce Eder

Larks' Tongues in Aspic
1973, EG

King Crimson reborn yet again—the newly configured band makes its debut with a violin (courtesy of David Cross) sharing center stage with Robert Fripp's guitars and his Mellotron, which is pushed into the background. The music is the most experimental of Fripp's career up to this time—though some of it actually dated (in embryonic form) back to the tail end of the Boz Burrell-Ian Wallace-Mel Collins lineup. And John Wetton was the group's strongest singer/bassist since Greg Lake's departure three years earlier. What's more, this lineup quickly established itself as a powerful performing unit working in a more purely experimental, less jazz-oriented vein than its immediate predecessor. "*Outer Limits* music" was how one reviewer referred to it, mixing Cross' demonic fiddling with shrieking electronics, Bill Bruford's astounding dexterity at the drum kit, Jamie Muir's melodic and usually understated percussion, Wetton's thundering (yet melodic) bass, and Fripp's guitar, which generated sounds ranging from traditional classical and soft pop-jazz licks to hair-curling electric flourishes. The remastered edition, which appeared in the summer of 2000 in Europe and slightly later in America, features beautifully remastered sound—among other advantages, it moves the finger cymbals opening the first section of the title track into sharp focus, with minimal hiss or noise to obscure them, exposes the multiple percussion instruments used on the opening of "Easy Money," and gives far more clarity to "The Talking Drum." This version is superior to any prior CD release of *Larks' Tongues in Aspic*, and contains a booklet reprinting period press clippings, session information, and production background on the album.

Bruce Eder

Red
November 1974, EG

King Crimson falls apart once more, seemingly for the last time, as David Cross walks away during the making of this album. It became Robert Fripp's last thoughts on this version of the band, a bit noiser overall but with some surprising sounds featured, mostly out of the group's past—Mel Collins' and Ian McDonald's saxes, Marc Charig's cornet, and Robin Miller's oboe, thus providing a glimpse of what the 1972-era King Crimson might've sounded like handling the later group's repertory (which nearly happened). Indeed, Charig's cornet gets just about the best showcase it ever had on a King Crimson album, and the truth is that few intact groups could have gotten an album as good as *Red* together. The fact that it was put together by a band in its death throes makes it all the more impressive an achievement. Indeed, *Red* does improve in some respects on certain aspects of the previous album—including "Starless," a cousin to the prior album's title track—and only the lower quality of the vocal compositions keeps this from being as strongly recommended as its two predecessors. *Red* was reissued on CD in the summer of 2000 in a remastered edition that features killer sound and an excellent booklet, containing a good account of the circumstances surrounding the recording of this album.

Bruce Eder

Carole King

Tapestry
March 1971, Ode

Carole King brought the fledgling singer/songwriter phenomenon to the masses with *Tapestry*, one of the most successful albums in pop music history. A remarkably expressive and intimate record, it's a work of consummate craftsmanship. Always a superior pop composer, King reaches even greater heights as a performer; new songs like the hits "It's Too Late" and "I Feel the Earth Move" rank solidly with past glories, while chestnuts like "You've Got a Friend," "Will You Still Love Me Tomorrow," and "(You Make Me Feel Like) A Natural Woman" take on added resonance when delivered in her own warm, compelling voice. With its reliance on pianos and gentle drumming, *Tapestry* is a light and airy work on its surface, occasionally skirting the boundaries of jazz, but it's also an intensely emotional record, the songs confessional and direct; in its time it connected with listeners like few records before it, and it remains an illuminating experience decades later.

Jason Ankeny

The Kinks

The Kink Kontroversy
1965, PRT

The Kinks came into their own as album artists—and Ray Davies fully matured as a songwriter—with *The Kink Kontroversy*, which bridged their raw early British Invasion sound with more sophisticated lyrics and thoughtful production. There are still powerful ravers like the hit "Till the End of the Day" (utilizing yet another "You Really Got Me"-type riff) and the abrasive, Dave Davies-sung cover of "Milk Cow Blues," but tracks like the calypso pastiche "I'm on an Island," where Ray sings of isolation with a forlorn yet merry bite, were far more indicative of their future direction. Other great songs on this underrated album include the uneasy nostalgia of "Where Have All the Good Times Gone?," the plaintive, almost fatalistic ballads "Ring the Bells" and "The World Keeps Going Round," and the Dave Davies-sung declaration of independence "I Am Free." Some mediocre filler detracts from the disc's overall punch, though the CD reissue adds the great swinging London satire hit "Dedicated Follower of Fashion," as well as previously unissued alternate takes of "When I See That Girl of Mine" and "Dedicated Follower of Fashion."

Richie Unterberger

Face to Face
October 1966, Reprise

The Kink Kontroversy was a considerable leap forward in terms of quality, but it pales next to *Face to Face*, one of the finest collections of pop songs released during the '60s.

Conceived as a loose concept album, *Face to Face* sees Ray Davies' fascination with English class and social structures flourish, as he creates a number of vivid character portraits. Davies' growth as a lyricist has coincided with the Kinks' musical growth. *Face to Face* is filled with wonderful moments, whether it's the mocking Hawaiian guitars of the rocker "Holiday in Waikiki," the droning Eastern touches of "Fancy," the music hall shuffle of "Dandy," or the lazily rolling "Sunny Afternoon." And that only scratches the surface of the riches of *Face to Face*, which offers other classics like "Rosy Won't You Please Come Home," "Party Line," "Too Much on My Mind," "Rainy Day in June," and "Most Exclusive Residence for Sale," making the record one of the most distinctive and accomplished albums of its time. [The CD reissue of *Face to Face* included six bonus tracks: the singles and B-sides "I'm Not Like Everybody Else," "Dead End Street," "Big Black Smoke," "Mister Pleasant," and "This Is Where I Belong," plus the previously unreleased "Mr. Reporter" and backing track "Little Women."]

Stephen Thomas Erlewine

Something Else by the Kinks
1967, Reprise

Face to Face was a remarkable record, but its follow-up, *Something Else*, expands its accomplishments, offering 13 classic British pop songs. As Ray Davies' songwriting becomes more refined, he becomes more nostalgic and sentimental, retreating from the psychedelic and mod posturings that had dominated the rock world. Indeed, *Something Else* sounds like nothing else from 1967. The Kinks never rock very hard on the album, preferring acoustic ballads, music hall numbers, and tempered R&B to full-out guitar attacks. Part of the album's power lies in its calm music, since it provides an elegant support for Davies' character portraits and vignettes. From the martial stomp of "David Watts" to the lovely, shimmering "Waterloo Sunset," there's not a weak song on the record, and several—such as the allegorical "Two Sisters," the Noël Coward-esque "End of the Season," the rolling "Lazy Old Sun," and the wry "Situation Vacant"—are stunners. And just as impressive is the emergence of Dave Davies as a songwriter. His Dylanesque "Death of a Clown" and bluesy rocker "Love Me Till the Sun Shines" hold their own against Ray's masterpieces, and help make *Something Else* the endlessly fascinating album that it is.

Stephen Thomas Erlewine

The Village Green Preservation Society
November 1968, Reprise

Ray Davies' sentimental, nostalgic streak emerged on *Something Else*, but it developed into a manifesto on *The Village Green Preservation Society*, a concept album lamenting the passing of old-fashioned English traditions. As the opening title song says, the Kinks—meaning Ray himself, in this case—were for preserving "draught beer and virginity," and throughout the rest of the album, he creates a series of stories, sketches, and characters about a picturesque England that never really was. It's a lovely, gentle album, evoking a small British country town, and drawing the listener into its lazy rhythms and sensibilities. Although there is an undercurrent of regret running throughout the album, Davies' fondness for the past is warm, making the album feel like a sweet, hazy dream. And considering the subdued performances and the detailed instrumentations, it's not surprising that the record feels more like a Ray Davies solo project than a Kinks album. The bluesy shuffle of "Last of the Steam-Powered Trains" is the closest the album comes to rock & roll, and Dave Davies' cameo on the menacing "Wicked Annabella" comes as surprise, since the album is so calm. But calm doesn't mean tame or bland—there are endless layers of musical and lyrical innovation on *The Village Green Preservation Society*, and its defiantly British sensibilities became the foundation of generations of British guitar pop.

Stephen Thomas Erlewine

Arthur (Or the Decline and Fall of the British Empire)
October 1969, Castle

Arthur (Or the Decline and Fall of the British Empire) extends the British-oriented themes of *Village Green Preservation Society*, telling the story of a London man's decision to move to Australia during the aftermath of World War II. It's a detailed and loving song cycle, capturing the minutiae of suburban life, the numbing effect of bureaucracy, and the horrors of war. On paper, *Arthur* sounds like a pretentious mess, but Ray Davies' lyrics and insights have rarely been so graceful or deftly executed, and the music is remarkable. An edgier and harder-rocking affair than *Village Green*, *Arthur* is as multi-layered musically as it is lyrically. "Shangri-La" evolves from English folk to hard rock, "Drivin'" has a lazy grace, "Young and Innocent Days" is a lovely, wistful ballad, "Some Mother's Son" is one of the most uncompromising antiwar songs ever recorded, while "Victoria" and "Arthur" rock with simple glee. The music makes the words cut deeper, and the songs never stray too far from the album's subject, making *Arthur* one of the most effective concept albums in rock history, as well as one of the best and most influential British pop records of its era. [Castle's 1998 CD reissue of *Arthur* contained ten bonus tracks, including mono and stereo versions of the non-LP singles "Plastic Man," "Mindless Child of Motherhood," and "This Man He Weeps Tonight," mono versions of "Drivin'" and "She's Bought a Hat Like Princess Marina," the B-side "King Kong," and the previously unreleased "Mr. Shoemakers Daughter."]

Stephen Thomas Erlewine

Lola vs. the Powerman & the Money-Go-Round, Pt. 1
November 1970, Reprise

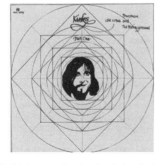

"Lola" gave the Kinks an unexpected hit and its crisp, muscular sound, pitched halfway between acoustic folk and hard rock, provided a new style for the band. However, the song only hinted at what its accompanying album *Lola vs. the Powerman & the Money-Go-Round, Pt. 1* was all about. It didn't matter that Ray Davies just had his first hit in years—he had suffered greatly at the hands of the music industry and he wanted to tell the story in song.

Hence, *Lola*—a loose concept album about Ray Davies' own psychosis and bitter feelings toward the music industry. Davies never really delivers a cohesive story, but the record holds together because it's one of his strongest set of songs. Dave Davies contributes the lovely "Strangers" and the appropriately paranoid "Rats," but this is truly Ray' show, as he lashes out at ex-managers (the boisterous vaudevillian "The Moneygoround"), publishers ("Denmark Street"), TV and music journalists (the hard-hitting "Top of the Pops"), label executives ("Powerman"), and, hell, just society in general ("Apeman," "Got to Be Free"). If his wit wasn't sharp, the entire project would be insufferable, but the album is as funny as it is angry. Furthermore, he balances his bile with three of his best melancholy ballads: "This Time Tomorrow," "A Long Way From Home," and the anti-welfare and union "Get Back in Line," which captures working-class angst better than any other rock song. These songs provide the spine for a wildly unfocused but nonetheless dazzling *tour de force* that reveals Ray's artistic strengths and endearing character flaws in equal measure.

Stephen Thomas Erlewine

Muswell Hillbillies
1971, Rhino

How did the Kinks respond to the fresh start afforded by *Lola*? By delivering a skewed, distinctly British, cabaret take on Americana, all pinned down by Ray Davies' loose autobiography and intense yearning to be anywhere else but here—or, as he says on the opening track, "I'm a 20th century man, but I don't want to be here." Unlike its predecessors, *Muswell Hillbillies* doesn't overtly seem like a concept album—there are no stories as there are on *Lola*—but each song undoubtedly shares a similar theme, namely the lives of the working class. Cleverly, the music is a blend of American and British roots music, veering from rowdy blues to boozy vaudeville. There's as much good humor in the performances as there are in Davies' songs, which are among his savviest and funniest. They're also quite affectionate, a fact underpinned by the heartbreaking "Oklahoma U.S.A.," one of the starkest numbers Davies ever penned, seeming all the sadder surrounded by the careening country-rock and music hall. That's the key to *Muswell Hillbillies*—it mirrors the messy flow of life itself, rolling from love letters and laments to jokes and family reunions. Throughout it all, Davies' songwriting is at a peak, as are the Kinks themselves. There are a lot of subtle shifts in mood and genre on the album, and the band pulls it off effortlessly and joyously—but it's hard not to hear Dave Davies' backing vocals and have it not sound joyous. Regardless of its commercial fate, *Muswell Hillbillies* stands as one of the Kinks' best albums.

Stephen Thomas Erlewine

The Kink Kronikles
1972, Reprise

Strictly speaking, the double-album compilation *The Kink Kronikles* isn't a greatest-hits collection. Covering the years 1966 through 1970, *The Kink Kronikles* may not be packed with hits—out of the album's 28 tracks, only nine were hits in the U.K. or the U.S.—yet it's a definitive overview of this era, which was one of Ray Davies' most productive (and influential) periods. Apart from the hits—the lazy, sardonic "Sunny Afternoon" and the gorgeous "Waterloo Sunset," and the 1970 comeback hits "Lola" and "Apeman"—there is a wealth of music that ranks among their very best material that isn't available on any other album. First off, non-LP British hit singles like the music hall raver "Dead End Street" and the wry "Autumn Almanac" are included, as are Dave Davies' two solo hits, "Death of a Clown" and "Suzannah's

Still Alive." Then there are the wealth of non-LP singles and B-sides that *didn't* make the British charts, plus worthy unreleased songs, obscurities like "This Is Where I Belong" and "She's Got Everything," and album tracks that demonstrate another side of the Kinks' musical versatility and Davies' abilities. The key to the success of *The Kink Kronikles* is how the singles and rarities complement each other and, taken together, present a full portrait. It's the rare compilation that is equally valuable to the collector and to the neophyte fan.

Stephen Thomas Erlewine

Sleepwalker
1977, Arista

Arista had made it clear they would not accept any concept albums from the Kinks, and *Sleepwalker*, their first effort for the label, makes good on the band's promise. Comprised entirely of glossy arena rockers and power ballads, the album is more of a stylistic exercise than a collection of first-rate songs. Ray Davies contributed a handful of fairly strong songs, highlighted by the exceptional "Juke Box Music," which sees him in a shockingly resigned frame of mind, claiming that rock & roll is just rock & roll, and nothing more. Unfortunately, he chose to illustrate that fact by loading the rest of *Sleepwalker* with competent but undistinguished mainstream rock. While that might have made the album a hit at the time, its processed sound and weak songs sound dated today, especially compared to the lively arena rock the Kinks later released.

Stephen Thomas Erlewine

Misfits
1978, Arista

The Kinks became arena rockers with *Sleepwalker*, and its follow-up, *Misfits*, follows in the same vein, but it's a considerable improvement on its predecessor. Ray Davies has learned how to write within the confines of the arena rock formula, and *Misfits* is one of rock & roll's great mid-life crisis albums, finding Davies considering whether he should even go on performing. "Misfits," a classic outsider rallying cry, and "Rock and Roll Fantasy" provide the two touchstones for the album—Davies admits that he and the Kinks will never be embraced by the rock & roll mainstream, but after Elvis' death, he's not even sure if rock & roll is something for mature adults to do. Over the course of *Misfits*, he finds answers to the question, both in his lyrics and through the band's muscular music. Eventually, he discovers that it is worth his time, but the search itself is superbly affecting—even songs like the musichall shuffle "Hay Fever," which appear as filler at first, have an idiosyncratic quirk that make them cut deeper. Although Ray would return to camp on their next album, *Misfits* is a moving record that manages to convey deep emotions while rocking hard. The Kinks hadn't made a record this good since *Muswell Hillbillies*.

Stephen Thomas Erlewine

Low Budget
July 1979, Arista

Low Budget doesn't have a narrative like *Preservation* or *Soap Opera*, but Ray Davies cleverly designed the album as a sly satire of the recession and oil crisis that gripped America in the late '70s—thereby satisfying his need to be a wry social commentator while giving American audiences a hook to identify with. It was a clever move that worked; not only did *Low Budget* become their highest-charting American album (not counting the 1966 *Greatest Hits* compilation), but it was also a fine set of arena rock, one of the better mainstream hard rock albums of its time. And it certainly was of its

time—so much so that many of the concerns and production techniques have dated quite a bit in the decades since its initial release. Nevertheless, that gives the album a certain charm, since it now plays like a time capsule, a snapshot of what hard rock sounded like at the close of the '70s. Perhaps not so coincidentally, Davies' songwriting fluctuates throughout the album, since it's dictated as much by commercial as artistic concerns, but the moments when he manages to balance the two impulses—as on the disco-fueled "(Wish I Could Fly Like) Superman," the vaudevillian "Low Budget," "A Gallon of Gas," the roaring "Attitude" (possibly their best hard rocker of the era, by the way), and "Catch Me Now I'm Falling," where Ray takes on the persona of America itself—are irresistible. *Low Budget* may not have the depth of, say, *Arthur* or *Village Green*, but it's a terrifically entertaining testament to their skills as a professional rock band and Davies' savvy as a commercial songwriter.

Stephen Thomas Erlewine

Greatest Hits, Vol. 1
1989, Rhino

Featuring a total of 18 highlights from the Kinks' early career, Rhino's *Greatest Hits* is the definitive compilation of the group's hit singles from the mid-'60s. Beginning with "You Really Got Me" and ending with "Sunny Afternoon," all of the  Kinks' essential garage rockers and British Invasion singles are here—"All Day and All of the Night," "Till the End of the Day," "Tired of Waiting for You," "A Well Respected Man," "Stop Your Sobbing," "Dedicated Follower of Fashion," "I'm Not Like Everybody Else," "Where Have All the Good Times Gone." Only the ambitious, Indian-tinged British hit "See My Friends" is missing, but it isn't a major oversight, especially since the disc distills the group's uneven early albums into manageable form for many fans. While *Kinkdom*, *Kink Kontroversy*, and *Face to Face* have many excellent album tracks in their own right, *Greatest Hits* remains a terrific summation of the group's earliest, hardest-rocking work.

Stephen Thomas Erlewine

Kiss

Kiss
April 1974, Casablanca

Kiss' 1974 self-titled debut is one of hard rock's all-time classic studio recordings. *Kiss* is chock full of their best and most renowned compositions, containing elements of Rolling Stones/New York Dolls party-hearty rock & roll, Beatles tunefulness, and Sabbath/Zep heavy metal, and wisely recorded primal and raw by producers Richie Wise and Kenny Kerner (of Gladys Knight fame). Main songwriters Stanley and Simmons each had a knack for coming up with killer melodies and riffs, as evidenced by "Nothin' to Lose" and "Deuce" (by Simmons), "Firehouse" and "Black Diamond" (by Stanley), as well as "Strutter" and "100,000 Years" (collaborations by the two). Also included is the Ace Frehley alcohol anthem "Cold Gin," "Let Me Know" (a song that Stanley played for Simmons upon their very first meeting, then titled "Sunday Driver"), and one of Kiss' few instrumentals: the groovy "Love Theme From Kiss" (penned by the entire band). The only weak track is a tacky cover of the 1959 Bobby Rydell hit "Kissin' Time," which was added to subsequent pressings of the album to tie in with a "Kissing Contest" promotion the band was involved in at the time. Along with 1976's *Destroyer*, Kiss' self-titled debut is their finest studio album, and has only improved over the years.

Greg Prato

Hotter Than Hell
November 1974, Casablanca

Although Kiss' self-titled debut performed respectably on the charts, it was not the blockbuster they had hoped for. With the album fading on the charts in the summer of 1974, Kiss was summoned back into the studio to work on a follow-up. Producers Richie Wise and Kenny Kerner were onboard again, and even though the sonics are muddier (and more filler is present composition-wise), *Hotter Than Hell* is another quintessential Kiss release. Many of the songs have been forgotten over the years (few are featured in concert anymore), but there are still more than a few gems to be found. It's unclear if the members of Kiss were having problems with their personal relationships at the time, but it's a common thread that runs through the songs. The plodding "Got to Choose" and the rapid-fire "Parasite" deal with love gone bad; the title track is about unobtainable love, while "Goin' Blind" is a disturbing tale of a 93 year old having an affair with a 16 year old. Also included are the early favorites "Let Me Go, Rock 'n' Roll" and "Watchin' You," as well as the original electric version of "Comin' Home" (an acoustic version was the opener of 1996's *MTV Unplugged*) and "Strange Ways," which contains one of Ace Frehley's best guitar solos. Even though *Hotter Than Hell* actually fared worse on the charts than the debut, it has become a revered album among Kiss fans over the years—and rightfully so.

Greg Prato

Dressed to Kill
April 1975, Casablanca

By the release of their third album, 1975's *Dressed to Kill*, Kiss were fast becoming America's top rock concert attraction, yet their record sales up to this point did not reflect their ticket sales. Casablanca label head Neil Bogart decided to take matters into his own hands, and produced the new record along with the band. The result is more vibrant sounding than its predecessor, 1974's sludgefest *Hotter Than Hell*, and the songs have more of an obvious pop edge to them. The best-known song on the album by far is the party anthem "Rock and Roll All Nite," but it was the track "C'Mon and Love Me" that became a regional hit in the Detroit area, giving the band their first taste of radio success. Since the band was on the road for a year straight, songs such as "Room Service" and "Ladies in Waiting" dealt with life on the road (i.e., groupies), and a pair of songs were reworked from Kiss' precursor band, Wicked Lester ("Love Her All I Can" and "She"). With *Dressed to Kill*'s Top 40 showing on the *Billboard* charts, the stage was now set for Kiss' big commercial breakthrough with their next release.

Greg Prato

Alive!
October 1975, Casablanca

Alive! was the album that catapulted Kiss from cult attraction to mega-superstars. It was their first Top Ten album,

remaining on the charts for 110 weeks and eventually going quadruple platinum. Culled from shows in Detroit, New Jersey, Iowa, and Cleveland on the *Dressed to Kill* tour, producer Eddie Kramer did a masterful job of capturing the band's live performance on record. The band's youthful energy is contagious, and with positively electric versions of their best early material, it's no mystery why *Alive!* is widely regarded as one of the greatest live hard rock recordings of all time. "Rock and

Roll All Nite" became a Top 20 smash and was the main reason for the album's success, but there are many other tracks that are just as strong—"Deuce," "Strutter," "Firehouse," "Parasite," "She," "100,000 Years," "Black Diamond," and "Cold Gin" all shine in a live setting. Although there's been some speculation of extensive overdubbing to correct mistakes, *Alive!* remains Kiss' greatest album ever. An essential addition to any rock collection.

Greg Prato

Destroyer
1976, Casablanca

The pressure was on Kiss for their fifth release, and the band knew it. Their breakthrough, *Alive!*, was going to be hard to top, so instead of trying to recreate a concert setting in the studio, they went the opposite route. *Destroyer* is one of Kiss' most experimental studio albums, but also one of their strongest and most interesting. Alice Cooper/Pink Floyd producer Bob Ezrin was on hand, and he strongly encouraged the band to experiment—there's extensive use of sound effects (the album's untitled closing track), the appearance of a boy's choir ("Great Expectations"), and an orchestra-laden, heartfelt ballad ("Beth"). But there's plenty of Kiss' heavy thunder rock to go around, such as the demonic "God of Thunder" and the sing-along anthems "Flaming Youth," "Shout It Out Loud," "King of the Night Time World," and "Detroit Rock City" (the latter a tale of a doomed concert-goer, complete with violent car-crash sound effects). But it was the aforementioned Peter Criss ballad, "Beth," that made *Destroyer* such a success; the song was a surprise Top Ten hit (it was originally released as a B-side to "Detroit Rock City"). Also included is a song that Nirvana would later cover ("Do You Love Me?"), as well as an ode to the pleasures of S&M, "Sweet Pain." *Destroyer* also marked the first time that a comic-book illustration of the band appeared on the cover, confirming that the band was transforming from hard rockers to superheroes.

Greg Prato

Alive II
November 1977, Casablanca

For Kiss' breakthrough 1975 release *Alive!*, the band had a total of three studio albums from which to select their in-concert repertoire. By mid-1977, Kiss had released another three studio recordings (*Destroyer*, *Rock and Roll Over*, and *Love Gun*), and with a new Kiss album needed for the holiday season, a second live album, *Alive II*, was assembled. Three sides were recorded live in concert at the Los Angeles Forum (with a few tracks recorded in Japan), while the fourth side featured five new studio recordings. Like its predecessor, there's been quite a lot of speculation concerning extensive overdubbing (the proof being that you can often hear several Paul Stanley voices singing backup simultaneously!), but *Alive II* shows that Kiss was still an exciting live band despite all the hype. Adrenaline-charged versions of "Detroit Rock City," "Love Gun," "Calling Dr. Love," "Shock Me," "God of Thunder," "I Want You," and "Shout It Out Loud" are all highlights. On the fourth side, Ace Frehley only plays on a single song (his self-penned classic "Rocket Ride") for reasons unknown, while Rick Derringer and session guitarist Bob Kulick filled in for the AWOL Frehley. Among the studio tracks is the made-for-the-stage anthem "Larger Than Life," which the band surprisingly never performed live.

Greg Prato

Double Platinum
1978, Casablanca

Double Platinum is a double-album, 20-track collection that gathers all of Kiss' biggest hits ("Rock and Roll All Nite," "Beth," "Detroit Rock City," "Love Gun"), but what makes it an essential retrospective and introduction is that it doesn't overlook key album tracks and concert favorites like "Cold Gin," "Deuce," "Black Diamond," and "She." If "Strutter" was represented by the original version, instead of a pointless 1978 remake—which was recorded only to entice collectors into buying an album of music they already owned—*Double Platinum* would have been a definitive collection, but as it stands, it's simply a very, very good overview.

Stephen Thomas Erlewine

Al Kooper

I Stand Alone
1968, Sony

Listening to *I Stand Alone* for the first time is a lot like first hearing the *Sgt. Pepper* album, except that this album challenges and rewards the listener in ways that the Beatles' psychedelic classic never tried to or could have. Al Kooper's first solo album is a dazzling, almost overpoweringly beautiful body of music, and nearly as sly at times in its humor as it is impressive in its musical sensibilities—specifically, the overture serves its function, and also pokes knowing, savagely piercing fun at the then-current vogue for sound collage-type pieces (most especially the Beatles' "Revolution #9"). Those looking for a reference point can think of *I Stand Alone* as a very, very distant cousin to the second Blood, Sweat & Tears album, as well as a much closer relative to the original group's *Child Is Father to the Man*, drawing on a few remnants from the tail end of his tenure with the group and a bunch of new songs and compositions by others that Kooper wanted to record—one beautiful element of his career, that helped distinguish him from a lot of other talented people of the period, is that unlike a lot of other musicians who were gifted songwriters Kooper never shied away from a good song written by someone else, especially if he could throw himself into it 100 percent or so; and he jumps in headfirst, as a stylist, singer, and musician, all over "I Stand Alone." Stylistically, it's a gloriously bold work, encompassing radiant soul, elements of jazz going back to the swing era, classical, pop, and even rockabilly—and freely (and masterfully) mixing all of them—into a phantasmagoric whole. The sources of inspiration (and, in some cases, songs) include Harry Nilsson ("One"), Bill Monroe (and who else, except maybe Elvis in a

really inspired moment, was even thinking of covering "Blue Moon of Kentucky" in 1969?), Sam & Dave ("Toe Hold"), Kenny Gamble and Leon Huff ("Hey, Western Union Man"), the Beatles, as well as Kooper himself—he delivers a lost classic in "Right Now for You" (which sounds like a really good lost cut from the Zombies' *Odessey & Oracle* album), and a hauntingly beautiful McCartney-esque nod to the Beatles in the "Eleanor Rigby"-like "Song and Dance for the Unborn Frightened Child." And, yet, for all of its diversity of sound and its free ranging repertory, and the unexpected edits and tempo changes, the album all holds together as a coherent body of work, a sort of more ambitious and personalized follow-up to *Child Is Father to the Man* that still leaves one kind of "whited out" (like the bleached irises of astronaut Dave Bowman's eyes at the end of his voyage through the stargate in *2001: A Space Odyssey*) at the end—not even *Sgt. Pepper* does that anymore. On the down side, the sound effects that Kooper dubbed in between (and sometimes during) the songs may seem strangely distracting today, but they were a product of their time—this was the tail end of the psychedelic era, after all, and even Simon & Garfunkel had succumbed to the temptation the previous year, though it's hard to imagine too many people in the business keeping a straight face about such production techniques after hearing the fun this album has at their expense. *I Stand Alone* was a musical trip worth taking in 1969—thanks to a 2003 Japanese reissue (in 24-bit sound, with the original jacket recreated), the ticket is still there for the asking, and the value of the journey is undiminished decades later.

Bruce Eder

Kooper Session: Super Session, Vol. 2
1970, Columbia

In 1969 producer/multi-instrumentalist and vocalist Al Kooper added talent scout to his already lengthy résumé on the follow-up to the highly successful Super Session disc which had been issued the previous year. One major difference between the two however is the relatively unknown cast featured on *Al Kooper Introduces Shuggie Otis*. Both albums again converge with the presentation of top-shelf musicianship and inspired performances. At only 15 years of age, Otis (guitar) is as potent a performer as Kooper (keyboards/ guitars). The duo are able to manifest an aggregate of material whose success leans as much on Kooper's experience as it does on Otis' sheer inspired youthful energy. The LP is divided between a side of shorter works [AKA "songs"] and a few extended instrumentals [AKA "blues"]. Kooper and Otis lead a house band which includes: Stu Woods (bass), Wells Kelly (drums) and Mark Klingman (piano). The tight arrangements aptly reveal Kooper's uncanny ability as a musical conduit. Tracks such as "Bury My Body"—a variation on "In My Time Of Dyin'"—has been reworked into a gospel rave-up and features Kooper on one of the album's only vocals. Conversely, "Double Or Nothing" is a spot-on recreation of a Booker T & the MGs track, which not only retains every Memphis-inspired intonation, but also shows off Shuggie's ability to cop Steve Cropper's guitar solo note-for-note. The blues instrumental jams are documented live and presented on this album the same way that they originally went down at the recording sessions. The descriptively-titled "Shuggie's Old Time Slide Boogie" is endowed with a nostalgic piano/bottleneck slide duet and even features the added production value of manufactured surface noise. Both "12:15 Slow Goonbash Blues" and "Shuggie's Shuffle" are certainly no less traditional allowing both Otis and Kooper the chance to stretch out and interact in real-time.

Lindsay Planer

Ronnie Lane & Slim Chance

Anymore for Anymore
1974, GM

Ronnie Lane certainly chose an apt name for his post-Faces combo, Slim Chance. He only enjoyed one solo hit—the rootsy yet boisterous "How Come," which made the U.K. Top Ten in 1974. "The Poacher" looked to become his second, if the BBC cameramen's union hadn't gone on strike when Lane and company had been booked to appear on *Top of the Pops*. Lane's brand of "hobobilly" reflected his life with an equal dash of hard luck and humor. He could pursue a folksier direction than he'd had room to explore in the Faces, and that side certainly shines on "Don't You Cry for Me"—bolstered by a strong Jimmy Jewell sax hook—as well as "The Poacher"'s rejection of personal power for its own sake. Lane didn't draw only on his rock & roll roots, however; "Amelia Earhardt" affectionately salutes the doomed '30s aviatrix with a musical nod to that period. He also showed a fascination for British music hall rooty-toot-toot ("Bird in a Gilded Cage"), gospel ("Bye & Bye [Gonna See the King]"), and simple folk (the Dillards' "Roll on Babe"). Of course, Lane's good-natured rowdiness meant that he couldn't resist a good knee-slapper when the temptation arose; "Chicken Wired" fits the bill aptly, with an infectious "chick-chick-chicken" chorus that'll stick to its listeners like the proverbial fly paper. (Lane evidently thought so, too; it appeared again on the *Mahoney's Last Stand* soundtrack.) Anyone who only casts him as a tragic figure needs to hear that song. New Millennium's reissue appends seven bonus tracks, such as acoustic takes of "How Come" and "The Poacher" and alternate tries of key tracks like "Amelia Earhardt." They're not especially revelatory, but do provide an interesting context for collectors. Ronnie Lane may not have meant much at the Top 40 box office, but his influence remains as broad as ever, and this album's a must-own blueprint.

Ralph Heibutzki

Ronnie Lane's Slim Chance
1974, A&M

The co-founder of the Small Faces turns in a low-key, easy-rolling gem even if he repackages some of his best material. "Stone," a whimsical ode to reincarnation, became "Evolution" when performed two years later with Pete Townshend on his debut solo album, *Who Came First*. A heart-tugging riff from *Slim Chance*'s "Give Me a Penny" shows up three years later on "Annie" from *Rough Mix*, another fine collaboration between Lane and Townshend. If you're going to get *Slim Chance* (and you should), pick the version that leads off with "The Poacher." Helped by Gallagher and Lyle, the song and its exquisite orchestration captures the spirit of the English countryside.

Mark Allan

Led Zeppelin

Led Zeppelin
January 1969, Atlantic

Led Zeppelin had a fully formed, distinctive sound from the outset, as their eponymous debut illustrates. Taking the heavy, distorted electric blues of Jimi Hendrix, Jeff Beck, and Cream to an extreme, Zeppelin created a majestic, powerful brand of guitar rock constructed around simple, memorable riffs and lumbering rhythms. But the key to the group's attack was subtlety: it wasn't just an onslaught of guitar noise, it was shaded and textured, filled with alternating dynamics and tempos. As *Led Zeppelin* proves, the group was capable of such multi-layered music from the start. Although the extended psychedelic blues of "Dazed and Confused," "You Shook Me," and "I Can't Quit You Baby" often gather the most attention, the remainder of the album is a better indication of what would come later. "Babe I'm Gonna Leave You" shifts from folky verses to pummeling choruses; "Good Times Bad Times" and "How Many More Times" have groovy, bluesy shuffles; "Your Time Is Gonna Come" is an anthemic hard rocker; "Black Mountain Side" is pure English folk; and "Communication Breakdown" is a frenzied rocker with a nearly punkish attack. Although the album isn't as varied as some of their later efforts, it nevertheless marked a significant turning point in the evolution of hard rock and heavy metal.

Stephen Thomas Erlewine

Led Zeppelin II
October 1969, Atlantic

Recorded quickly during Led Zeppelin's first American tours, *Led Zeppelin II* provided the blueprint for all the heavy metal bands that followed it. Since the group could only enter the studio for brief amounts of time, most of the songs that compose *II* are reworked blues and rock & roll standards that the band was performing on-stage at the time. Not only did the short amount of time result in a lack of original material, it made the sound more direct. Jimmy Page still provided layers of guitar overdubs, but the overall sound of the album is heavy and hard, brutal and direct. "Whole Lotta Love," "The Lemon Song," and "Bring It on Home" are all based on classic blues songs—only, the riffs are simpler and louder and each song has an extended section for instrumental solos. Of the remaining six songs, two sport light acoustic touches ("Thank You," "Ramble On"), but the other four are straight-ahead heavy rock that follows the formula of the revamped blues songs. While *Led Zeppelin II* doesn't have the eclecticism of the group's debut, it's arguably more influential. After all, nearly every one of the hundreds of Zeppelin imitators used this record, with its lack of dynamics and its pummeling riffs, as a blueprint.

Stephen Thomas Erlewine

Led Zeppelin III
October 1970, Atlantic

On their first two albums, Led Zeppelin unleashed a relentless barrage of heavy blues and rockabilly riffs, but *Led Zeppelin III* provided the band with the necessary room to grow musically. While there are still a handful of metallic rockers, *III* is built on a folky, acoustic foundation that gives the music extra depth. And even the rockers aren't as straightforward as before: the galloping "Immigrant Song" is powered by Robert Plant's banshee wail, "Celebration Day" turns blues-rock inside out with a warped slide guitar riff, and "Out on the Tiles" lumbers along with a tricky, multi-part riff. Nevertheless, the heart of the album lies on the second side, when the band delve deeply into English folk. "Gallows Pole" updates a traditional tune with a menacing flair, and "Bron-Y-Aur Stomp" is an infectious acoustic romp, while "That's the Way" and "Tangerine" are shimmering songs with graceful country flourishes. The band hasn't left the blues behind, but the twisted bottleneck blues of "Hats off to (Roy) Harper" actually outstrips the epic "Since I've Been Loving You," which is the only time Zeppelin sound a bit set in their ways.

Stephen Thomas Erlewine

Led Zeppelin IV
November 1971, Atlantic

Encompassing heavy metal, folk, pure rock & roll, and blues, Led Zeppelin's untitled fourth album is a monolithic record, defining not only Led Zeppelin but the sound and style of '70s hard rock. Expanding on the breakthroughs of *III*, Zeppelin fuse their majestic hard rock with a mystical, rural English folk that gives the record an epic scope. Even at its most basic—the muscular, traditionalist "Rock and Roll"—the album has a grand sense of drama, which is only deepened by Robert Plant's burgeoning obsession with mythology, religion, and the occult. Plant's mysticism comes to a head on the eerie folk ballad "The Battle of Evermore," a mandolin-driven song with haunting vocals from Sandy Denny, and on the epic "Stairway to Heaven." Of all of Zeppelin's songs, "Stairway to Heaven" is the most famous, and not unjustly. Building from a simple fingerpicked acoustic guitar to a storming torrent of guitar riffs and solos, it encapsulates the entire album in one song. Which, of course, isn't discounting the rest of the album. "Going to California" is the group's best folk song, and the rockers are endlessly inventive, whether it's the complex, multi-layered "Black Dog," the pounding hippie satire "Misty Mountain Hop," or the funky riffs of "Four Sticks." But the closer, "When the Levee Breaks," is the one song truly equal to "Stairway," helping give *IV* the feeling of an epic. An apocalyptic slice of urban blues, "When the Levee Breaks" is as forceful and frightening as Zeppelin ever got, and its seismic rhythms and layered dynamics illustrate why none of their imitators could ever equal them.

Stephen Thomas Erlewine

Houses of the Holy
March 1973, Atlantic

Houses of the Holy follows the same basic pattern as *Led Zeppelin IV*, but the approach is looser and more relaxed. Jimmy Page's riffs rely on ringing, folky hooks as much as they do on thundering blues-rock, giving the album a lighter, more open atmosphere. While the pseudo-reggae of "D'Yer Mak'er" and the affectionate James Brown send-up "The Crunge" suggest that the band was searching for material, they actually contribute to the musical diversity of the album. "The Rain Song" is one of Zep's finest moments, featuring a soaring string arrangement and a gentle, aching melody. "The Ocean" is just as good, starting with a heavy, funky guitar groove before slamming into an a cappella section and ending with a swinging, doo wop-flavored rave-up. With the exception of the rampaging opening number, "The Song Remains the Same," the rest of *Houses of the Holy* is fairly straightforward, ranging from the foreboding "No Quarter" and the strutting hard rock of "Dancing Days" to the epic folk/metal fusion "Over the Hills and Far Away."

Throughout the record, the band's playing is excellent, making the eclecticism of Page and Robert Plant's songwriting sound coherent and natural.

Stephen Thomas Erlewine

Physical Graffiti
February 1975, Swan Song

Led Zeppelin returned from a nearly two-year hiatus in 1975 with *Physical Graffiti*, a sprawling, ambitious double album. Zeppelin treat many of the songs on *Physical Graffiti* as forays into individual styles, only occasionally synthesizing sounds, notably on the tense, Eastern-influenced "Kashmir." With John Paul Jones' galloping keyboard, "Trampled Underfoot" ranks as their funkiest metallic grind, while "Houses of the Holy" is as effervescent as pre-Beatles pop and "Down by the Seaside" is the closest they've come to country. Even the heavier blues—the 11-minute "In My Time of Dying," the tightly wound "Custard Pie," and the monstrous epic "The Rover"—are subtly shaded, even if they're thunderously loud. Most of these heavy rockers are isolated on the first album, with the second half of *Physical Graffiti* sounding a little like a scrap heap of experiments, jams, acoustic workouts, and neo-covers. This may not be as consistent as the first platter, but its quirks are entirely welcome, not just because they encompass elements of the band's personality rarely showcased elsewhere—and even at its worst, *Physical Graffiti* towers above its hard rock peers of the mid-'70s.

Stephen Thomas Erlewine

Presence
1976, Swan Song

Presence scales back the size of *Physical Graffiti* to a single album, but it retains the grandiose scope of that double record. If anything, *Presence* has more majestic epics than its predecessor, opening with the surging, ten-minute "Achilles Last Stand" and closing with the meandering, nearly ten-minute "Tea for One." In between, Led Zeppelin add the lumbering blues workout "Nobody's Fault but Mine" and the terse, menacing "For Your Life," which is the best song on the album. These four tracks take up the bulk of the album, leaving three lighthearted throwaways to alleviate the foreboding atmosphere—and pretensions—of the epics. If all of the throwaways were as focused and funny as those on *Physical Graffiti* or *Houses of the Holy*, Zeppelin would have had another classic on their hands. However, the Crescent City love letter of "Royal Orleans" sags in the middle, and the ersatz rockabilly of "Candy Store Rock" doesn't muster up the loose, funky swagger of "Hots on for Nowhere," which it *should* in order to work. The three throwaways are also scattered haphazardly throughout the album, making it seem more ponderous than it actually is, and the result is the weakest album Zeppelin had yet recorded.

Stephen Thomas Erlewine

In Through the Out Door
1979, Swan Song

Somewhere between *Presence* and *In Through the Out Door*, disco, punk, and new wave had overtaken rock & roll, and Led Zeppelin chose to tentatively embrace these pop revolutions, adding synthesizers to the mix and emphasizing John Bonham's inherent way with a groove. The album's opening number, "In the Evening," with its stomping rhythms and heavy, staggered riffs, suggests that Zeppelin haven't deviated from their course, but by the time the rolling shuffle of "South Bound Suarez" kicks into gear, it's apparent that they've regained their sense of humor. After "South Bound Suarez," the group tries a variety of styles, whether it's an overdriven homage to Bakersfield county called "Hot Dog," the layered, Latin-tinged percussion and pianos of "Fool in the Rain," or the slickly seductive ballad "All My Love." "Carouselambra," a lurching, self-consciously ambitious synth-driven number, and the slow blues "I'm Gonna Crawl" aren't quite as impressive as the rest of the album, but the record was a graceful way to close to Zeppelin's career, even if it wasn't intended as the final chapter.

Stephen Thomas Erlewine

Coda
1982, Swan Song

An odds-and-sods collection assembled after John Bonham's death, *Coda* is predictably a hit-or-miss affair. The best material comes from later in Led Zeppelin's career, including the ringing folk stomp of "Poor Tom," the jacked-up '50s rock & roll of "Ozone Baby,"

and their response to punk rock, the savage "Wearing and Tearing." The rest of the album—sadly including the Bonham showcase "Bonzo's Montreux"—is average, despite the presence of some stellar playing, especially on the early blues-rock blitzkrieg "I Can't Quit You Baby" and "We're Gonna Groove."

Stephen Thomas Erlewine

BBC Sessions
November 1997, Atlantic

Led Zeppelin's BBC sessions were among the most popular bootleg items of the rock & roll era, appearing on a myriad of illegal records and CDs. They were all the more popular because of the lack of official Led Zeppelin live albums, especially since *The Song Remains the Same* failed to capture the essence of the band. For anyone who hadn't heard the recordings, the mystique of Zeppelin's BBC sessions was somewhat mystifying, but the official 1997 release of the double-disc *BBC Sessions* offered revelations for any fan who hadn't yet heard this music. While some collectors will be dismayed by the slight trimming on the "Whole Lotta Love Medley,"

almost all of the group's sessions are included here, and they prove why live Zeppelin was the stuff of legend. The 1969 sessions, recorded shortly after the release of the first album, are fiery and dynamic, outstripping the studio record for sheer power. Early versions of "You Shook Me," "Communication Breakdown," "What Is and What Should Never Be," and "Whole Lotta Love" hit harder than their recorded counterparts, while covers of Sleepy John Estes' "The Girl I Love She Got Long Black Wavy Hair," Robert Johnson's "Travelling Riverside Blues," and Eddie Cochran's "Something Else" are welcome additions to the Zeppelin catalog, confirming their folk, blues, and rockabilly roots as well as their sense of vision. Zeppelin's grand vision comes into sharper relief on the second disc, which is comprised of their 1971 sessions. They still have their primal energy, but they're more adventurous, branching out into folk, twisted psychedelia, and weird blues-funk. Certainly, *BBC Sessions* is the kind of album that will only appeal to fans, but anyone who's ever doubted Zeppelin's power or vision will be set straight with this record.

Stephen Thomas Erlewine

How the West Was Won
May 2003, Atlantic

For years, Led Zeppelin fans complained that there was one missing item in the group's catalog: a good live album. It's not that there weren't live albums to be had. *The Song Remains the Same*, of course, was a soundtrack of a live

performance, but it was a choppy, uneven performance, lacking the majesty of the group at its peak. *BBC Sessions* was an excellent, comprehensive double-disc set of their live radio sessions, necessary for any Zeppelin collection (particularly because it contained three songs, all covers, never recorded anywhere else), but some carped that the music suffered from not being taped in front of a large audience, which is how they built their legacy—or, in the parlance of this triple-disc collection of previously unreleased live recordings compiled by Jimmy Page, *How the West Was Won*. The West in this case is the West Coast of California, since this contains selections from two 1972 concerts in Los Angeles: a show at the LA Forum on June 25, and one two days later at Long Beach Arena. This is the first archival release of live recordings of Zeppelin at their peak and while the wait has been nigh on interminable, the end result is certainly worth the wait. Both of these shows have been heavily bootlegged for years and while those same bootleggers may be frustrated by the sequencing that swaps the two shows interchangeably (they always prefer full shows wherever possible), by picking the best of the two nights, Page has assembled a killer live album that captures the full, majestic sweep of Zeppelin at their glorious peak. And, make no mistake, he tries to shove everything into these three discs—tight, furious blasts of energy; gonzo freak-outs; blues; and rock, a sparkling acoustic set. Like always, the *very* long numbers—the 25-minute "Dazed and Confused," the 23-minute "Whole Lotta Love," the 19-minute "Moby Dick"—are alternately fascinating and indulgent, yet even when they meander, there is a real sense of grandeur, achieving a cinematic scale attempted by few of their peers (certainly no other hard rock or metal band could be this grand; only Queen or David Bowie truly attempted this). But the real power of the band comes through on the shorter songs, where their sound is distilled to its essence. In the studio, Zeppelin was all about subtle colors, textures, and shifts in the arrangement. Onstage, they were similarly epic, but they were looser, wilder, and hit harder; witness how "Black Dog" goes straight for the gut here, while the studio version escalates into a veritable guitar army—it's the same song, but the song has not remained the same. That's the case throughout *How the West Was Won*, where songs that have grown overly familiar through years of play seem fresh and new because of these vigorous, muscular performances. For those who never got to see Zeppelin live, this—or its accompanying two-DVD video set—is as close as they'll ever get. For those who did see them live, this is a priceless souvenir. For either group, this is absolutely essential, as it is for anybody who really loves hard rock & roll. It doesn't get much better than this.

Stephen Thomas Erlewine

John Lennon

John Lennon/Plastic Ono Band
December 1970, Capitol

The cliché about singer/songwriters is that they sing confessionals direct from their heart, but John Lennon exploded the myth behind that cliché, as well as many others, on his first official solo record, *John Lennon/Plastic Ono Band*. Inspired by his primal scream therapy with Dr. Walter Janov, Lennon created a harrowing set of unflinchingly personal songs, laying out all of his fears and angers for everyone to hear. It was a revolutionary record—never before had a record been so explicitly introspective, and very few records made absolutely no concession to the audience's expectations, daring the listeners to meet all the artist's demands. Which isn't to say that the record is unlistenable. Lennon's songs range from tough rock & rollers to piano-based ballads and spare folk songs, and his melodies remain strong and memorable, which actually intensifies the pain and rage of the songs. Not much about *Plastic Ono Band* is hidden. Lennon presents everything on the surface, and the song titles—"Mother," "I Found Out," "Working Class Hero," "Isolation," "God," "My Mummy's Dead"—illustrate what each song is about, and charts his loss of faith in his parents, country, friends, fans, and idols. It's an unflinching document of bare-bones despair and pain, but for all its nihilism, it is ultimately life-affirming; it is unique not only in Lennon's catalog, but in all of popular music. Few albums are ever as harrowing, difficult, and rewarding as *John Lennon/Plastic Ono Band*.

Stephen Thomas Erlewine

Imagine
September 1971, Capitol

After the harrowing *Plastic Ono Band*, John Lennon returned to calmer, more conventional territory with *Imagine*. While the album had a softer surface, it was only marginally less confessional than its predecessor. Underneath the sweet strings of "Jealous Guy" lies a broken and scared man, the jaunty "Crippled Inside" is a mocking assault at an acquaintance, and "Imagine" is a paean for peace in a world with no gods, possessions, or classes, where everyone is equal. And Lennon doesn't shy away from the hard rockers—"How Do You Sleep" is a scathing attack on Paul McCartney, "I Don't Want to Be a Soldier" is a hypnotic antiwar song, and "Give Me Some Truth" is bitter hard rock. If *Imagine* doesn't have the thematic sweep of *Plastic Ono Band*, it is nevertheless a remarkable collection of songs that Lennon would never be able to better again.

Stephen Thomas Erlewine

Mind Games
November 1973, Capitol

After the hostile reaction to the politically charged *Sometime in New York City*, John Lennon moved away from explicit protest songs and returned to introspective songwriting with *Mind Games*. Lennon didn't leave politics behind—he just tempered his opinions with humor on songs like "Bring on the Lucie (Freda Peeple)," which happened to undercut the intention of the song. It also indicated the confusion that lies at the heart of the album. Lennon doesn't know which way to go, so he tries everything. There are lovely ballads like "Out of the Blue" and "One Day (At a Time)," forced, ham-fisted rockers like "Meat City" and "Tight As," sweeping Spectoresque pop on "Mind Games," and many mid-tempo, indistinguishable pop/rockers. While the best numbers are among Lennon's finest, there's only a handful of them, and the remainder of the record is simply pleasant. But compared to *Sometime in New York City*, as well as the subsequent *Walls and Bridges*, *Mind Games* sounded like a return to form.

Stephen Thomas Erlewine

Walls and Bridges
September 1974, Capitol

Walls and Bridges was recorded during John Lennon's infamous "lost weekend," as he exiled himself in California during a separation from Yoko Ono. Lennon's personal life was scattered, so it isn't surprising that *Walls and Bridges* is a mess itself, containing equal amounts of brilliance and nonsense. Falling between the two extremes was the bouncy Elton John duet "Whatever Gets You Thru the Night," which was Lennon's first solo number one hit. Its bright, sunny surface was replicated throughout the record, particularly on middling rockers like "What You Got" but also on enjoyable pop songs like "Old Dirt Road." However, the best moments on *Walls and Bridges* come when Lennon is more open with his emotions, like on "Going Down on Love," "Steel and Glass," and the beautiful, soaring "#9 Dream." Even with such fine moments, the album is decidedly uneven, containing too much mediocre material like "Beef Jerky" and "Ya Ya," which are weighed down by weak melodies and heavy over-production. It wasn't a particularly graceful way to enter retirement.

Stephen Thomas Erlewine

Rock 'n' Roll
February 1975, Capitol

Although the chaotic sessions that spawned this album have passed into rock & roll legend and the recording's very genesis (as an out-of-court settlement between John Lennon and an aggrieved publisher) has often caused it to be slighted by many of the singer's biographers, *Rock 'n' Roll*, in fact, stands as a peak in his post-*Imagine* catalog: an album that catches him with nothing to prove and no need to try. Lennon could, after all, sing old rock & roll numbers with his mouth closed; he spent his entire career relaxing with off-the-cuff blasts through the music with which he grew up, and *Rock 'n' Roll* emerges the sound of him doing precisely that. Four songs survive from the fractious sessions with producer Phil Spector in late 1973 that ignited the album, and listeners to any of the posthumous compilations that also draw from those archives will know that the best tracks were left on the shelf—"Be My Baby" and "Angel Baby" among them. But a gorgeous run through Lloyd Price's "Just Because" wraps up the album in fine style, while a trip through "You Can't Catch Me" contrarily captures a playful side that Lennon rarely revealed on vinyl. The remainder of the album was cut a year later with Lennon alone at the helm, and the mood remains buoyant. It might not, on first glance, seem essential to hear him running through nuggets like "Be Bop A Lula," "Peggy Sue," and "Bring It on Home to Me," but, again, Lennon has seldom sounded so gleeful as he does on these numbers, while the absence of the Spector trademark Wall-of-Sound production is scarcely noticeable—as the object of one of Lennon's own productions, David Peel once pointed out, "John had the Wall of Sound down perfectly himself." Released in an age when both David Bowie and Bryan Ferry had already tracked back to musical times-gone-by (*Pin-Ups* and *These Foolish Things*, respectively), *Rock 'n' Roll* received short shrift from contemporary critics. As time passed, however, it has grown in stature, whereas those other albums have merely held their own. Today, *Rock 'n' Roll* sounds fresher than the rock & roll that inspired it in the first place. Imagine that.

Dave Thompson

Double Fantasy
November 1980, Capitol

The most distinctive thing about *Double Fantasy*, the last album John Lennon released during his lifetime, is the very thing that keeps it from being a graceful return to form from the singer/songwriter, returning to active duty after five years of self-imposed exile. As legend has it, Lennon spent those years in domestic bliss, being a husband, raising a baby, and, of course, baking bread. *Double Fantasy* was designed as a window into that bliss and, to that extent, he decided to make it a joint album with Yoko Ono, to illustrate how complete their union was. For her part, Ono decided to take a stab at pop and while these are relatively tuneful for her, they nevertheless disrupt the feel and flow of Lennon's material, which has a consistent tone and theme. He's surprisingly sentimental, not just when he's expressing love for his wife ("Dear Yoko," "Woman") and child ("Beautiful Boy [Darling Boy]"), but when he's coming to terms with their quiet years ("Watching the Wheels," "Cleanup Time") and his return to creative life. These are really nice tunes, and what's special about them is their niceness—it's a sweet acceptance of middle age, which, of course, makes his assassination all the sadder. For that alone, *Double Fantasy* is noteworthy, yet it's hard not to think that it's a bit of a missed opportunity—primarily because its themes would be stronger without the Ono songs, but also because the production is just a little bit too slick and constrained, sounding very much of its time. Ultimately, these complaints fall by the wayside because Lennon's best songs here cement the last part of his legend, capturing him at peace and in love. According to some reports, that perception was a bit of a fantasy, but sometimes the fantasy means more than the reality, and that's certainly the case here.

Stephen Thomas Erlewine

Working Class Hero: The Definitive Lennon
October 2005, Capitol

There sure hasn't been a shortage of John Lennon compilations over the years, but there hasn't been a new collection since 1997's *Lennon Legend* and there haven't been any two-CD sets covering his entire career—until 2005's *Working Class Hero: The Definitive Lennon*, that is. Released on October 4, 2005, this surely was intended as a tie-in to the Broadway show *Lennon: The Musical*, but it wound up appearing ten days after the musical concluded its disastrous run. Even if the show did tank, it provided the occasion for this strong collection. *Working Class Hero* may tread familiar territory—not only does it have all the usual suspects, from "Instant Karma" to "(Just Like) Starting Over," it has them in a sequencing that feels familiar, even it doesn't correspond to any specific previous release—but that's fine, because it provides a rather thorough overview of Lennon's best-known solo songs. In many cases, these are often his best, but there are surely some great songs missing here, particularly because the comp emphasizes material with a slight romantic bent or songs that play into the myth of St. John (meaning, mixed alongside the hits there are plenty of songs about Yoko and being a father, and rockers are given short shrift). But these are minor complaints: anybody who wants a succinct yet comprehensive compilation of most of Lennon's solo best should be satisfied with this.

Stephen Thomas Erlewine

David Lindley

El Rayo-X
1981, Asylum

By the time David Lindley made his move to a solo career, he was already a legend. Having toured and recorded with such names as Jackson Browne, Linda Ronstadt, and Crosby & Nash, his reputation as a multi-instrumentalist (on almost any stringed instrument) was awesome. Lindley scored a contract with Elektra Records and put together an excellent band that was able to keep up with his eclectic vision. Combining blues, rock & roll, Cajun, Zydeco, Middle Eastern music, and other elements, his debut album is an absolute joy. Lindley's version of "Mercury Blues" became an FM radio staple, and his slide guitar performances on this track alone are easily some of the finest of the decade. There are some wonderfully skewed originals on the record as well, making *El Rayo-X* one of the greatest rock music albums of its time. Fabulous.

Matthew Greenwald

Little Feat

Little Feat
1971, Warner Bros.

It sold poorly (around 11,000 copies) and the band never cut anything like it again, but Little Feat's eponymous debut isn't just one of their finest records, it's one of the great lost rock & roll albums. Even dedicated fans tend to overlook the album, largely because it's the polar opposite of the subtly intricate, funky rhythm & roll that made their reputation during the mid-'70s. *Little Feat* is a raw, hard-driving, funny and affectionate celebration of American weirdness, equal parts garage rock, roadhouse blues, post-Zappa bizarreness, post-Parsons country rock and slightly bent folk storytelling. Since it's grounded in roots rock, it feels familiar enough, but the vision of chief songwriter/guitarist/vocalist Lowell George is wholly unique and slightly off-center. He sees everything with a gently surreal sense of humor that remains affectionate, whether it's on an ode to a "Truck Stop Girl," the weary trucker's anthem "Willin'," or the goofy character sketch of the crusty old salt "Crazy Captain Gunboat Willie." That affection is balanced by gutsy slices of Americana like the careening travelogue "Strawberry Flats," the darkly humorous "Hamburger Midnight" and a jaw-dropping Howlin' Wolf medley guest-starring Ry Cooder, plus keyboardist Bill Payne's terrific opener "Snakes on Everything." The songwriting itself is remarkable enough, but the band is its equal—they're as loose, vibrant and alive as the Stones at their best. In most respects, this album has more in common with George's earlier band the Factory than the rest of the Little Feat catalog, but there's a deftness in the writing and performance that distinguishes it from either band's work, which makes it all the more remarkable. It's a pity that more people haven't heard the record, but that just means that anyone who owns it feels like they're in on a secret only they and a handful of others know.

Stephen Thomas Erlewine

Sailin' Shoes
1972, Warner Bros.

Little Feat's debut may have been a great album but it sold so poorly, they had to either broaden their audience or, in all likelihood, they'd be dropped from Warner. So, *Sailin' Shoes* is a consciously different record from its predecessor—less raw and bluesy, blessed with a varied production and catchier songs. That still doesn't make it a pop record, since Little Feat, particularly in its first incarnation, was simply too idiosyncratic, earthy and strange for that. It is, however, an utterly thrilling, individual blend of pop, rock, blues and country, due in no small part to a stellar set of songs from Lowell George. If anything, his quirks are all the more apparent here than they were on the debut, since Ted Templeman's production lends each song its own character, plus his pen was getting sharper. George truly finds his voice on this record, with each of his contributions sparkling with off-kilter humor, friendly surreal imagery and humanity, and he demonstrates he can authoritatively write anything from full-throttle rock & roll ("Teenage Nervous Breakdown"), sweet ballads ("Trouble," a sublimely reworked "Willin'"), skewered folk ("Sailin' Shoes"), paranoid rock ("Cold, Cold, Cold") and blues ("A Apolitical Blues") and, yes, even hooky mainstream rock ("Easy to Slip," which should have been the hit the band intended it to be). That's not to discount the contributions of the other members, particularly Bill Payne and Richie Hayward's "Tripe Face Boogie," which is justifiably one of the band's standards, but the thing that truly stuns on *Sailin' Shoes* is George's songwriting and how the band brings it to a full, colorful life. Nobody could master the twists and turns within George's songs better than Little Feat, and both the songwriter and his band are in prime form here.

Stephen Thomas Erlewine

Dixie Chicken
1973, Warner Bros.

Following Roy Estrada's departure during the supporting tour for *Sailin' Shoes*, Lowell George became infatuated with New Orleans R&B and mellow jamming, all of which came to a head on their third album, 1973's *Dixie Chicken*. Although George is firmly in charge—he dominates the record, writing or co-writing seven of the 10 songs—this is the point where Little Feat found its signature sound as a band, and no album they would cut from this point on was too different from this seductive, laid-back, funky record. But no album would be quite as good, either, since *Dixie Chicken* still had much of the charming lyrical eccentricities of the first two albums, plus what is arguably George's best-ever set of songs. Partially due to the New Orleans infatuation, the album holds together better than *Sailin' Shoes* and George takes full advantage of the band's increased musical palette, writing songs that sound easy but are quite sophisticated, such as the rolling "Two Trains," the gorgeous, shimmering "Juliette," the deeply soulful and funny "Fat Man in the Bathtub" and the country-funk of the title track, which was covered nearly as frequently as "Willin'." In addition to "Walkin' All Night," a loose bluesy jam by Barrere and Bill Payne, the band also hauls out two covers which fit George's vibe perfectly: Allan Toussaint's slow burner "On Your Way Down" and "Fool Yourself," which was written by Fred Tackett, who later joined a reunited Feat in the '80s. It all adds up to a nearly irresistible record, filled with great songwriting, sultry grooves, and virtuosic performances that never are flashy. Little Feat, along with many jam bands that followed, tried to top this album, but they never managed to make a record this understated, appealing and fine.

Stephen Thomas Erlewine

Feats Don't Fail Me Now
1974, Warner Bros.

If *Dixie Chicken* represented a pinnacle of Lowell George as a songwriter and band leader, its sequel *Feats Don't Fail Me Now* is the pinnacle of Little Feat as a group, showcasing each member at their finest. Not coincidentally, it's the moment where George begins to recede from the spotlight, leaving the band as a true democracy. These observations are only clear in hindsight, since if *Feats Don't Fail Me Now* is just taken as a record, it's nothing more than a damn good rock & roll record. That's not meant as a dismissal, either, since it's hard to make a rock & roll record as seemingly effortless and infectious as this. Though it effectively builds on the Southern-fried funkiness of *Dixie Chicken*, it's hardly as mellow as that record—there's a lot of grit, tougher rhythms, lots of guitar and organ. It's as supple as *Chicken*, though, which means that it's the sound of a touring band at their peak. As it happens, the band is on the top of their writing game as well, with Bill Payne contributing the rollicking "Oh Atlanta" and Paul Barrere turning in one of his best songs, the jazzy funk of "Skin it Back." Each has a co-writing credit with George—Payne on the unreleased *Little Feat*-era nugget "The Fan" and Barrere (plus Fred Martin) on the infectious title track—who also has a couple of classics with "Rock and Roll Doctor" and the great "Spanish Moon." *Feats* peters out toward the end, as the group delves into a 10-minute medley of two *Sailin' Shoes* songs, but that doesn't hurt one of the best albums Little Feat ever cut. It's so good, the group used it as the template for the rest of their career.

Stephen Thomas Erlewine

Waiting for Columbus
1978, Warner Bros.

Little Feat was one of the legendary live bands of the '70s, showered with praise by not only their small, fiercely dedicated cult of fans, but such fellow musicians as Bonnie Raitt, Robert Palmer, and Jimmy Page. Given all that acclaim, it only made sense for the group to cut a live album. Unfortunately, they waited until 1977, when the group had entered its decline, but as the double-album *Waiting for Columbus* proves, Little Feat in its decline was still pretty great. Certainly, the group is far more inspired on stage than they were in the studio after 1975—just compare "All That You Dream," "Oh Atlanta," "Old Folks' Boogie," "Time Loves a Hero," and "Mercenary Territory" here to the cuts on *The Last Record Album* and *Time Loves a Hero*. The versions on *Waiting* are full-bodied and fully-realized, putting the studio cuts to shame. Early classics like "Fat Man in the Bathtub" and "Tripe Face Boogie" aren't as revelatory, but it's still a pleasure to hear a great band run through their best songs, stretching them out and finding new quirks within them. If there are any flaws with *Waiting for Columbus*, it's that the Feat do a little bit too much stretching, veering toward excessive jamming on occasion—and that mildly fuzzy focus is really the only way you'd be able to tell that this is a great live band recorded slightly after their prime. Even so, there's much to savor on *Waiting for Columbus*, one of the great live albums of its era, thanks to rich performances that prove Little Feat were one of the great live bands of their time.

Stephen Thomas Erlewine

Hotcakes & Outtakes: 30 Years of Little Feat
September 2000, Rhino/Warner Archives

Rhino's four-disc box set *Hotcakes & Outtakes* treats all of Little Feat's incarnations with equal respect. This even-handed approach has advantages, even if Lowell George dominates the proceedings. How could he not? He was a musician of immense talents, shaping the band's core sound while building an impressive body of songs. This set reveals that the rest of the band, while not writers of George's ilk, still wrote their share of great songs and, best of all, their fusion of funk, blues, country, rock and jazz still sounded lively, even when they reunited a decade after his death. Yes,

it was missing his unique brilliance and vision, yet the re-united Feat still carried the torch well, which this set proves. Still, the best thing about the box is the fourth disc, devoted to "Studio Artifacts," all dating from George's heyday with the band. Actually, it goes a little further than that, beginning with cuts from George and Roy Estrada's mid-'60s band the Factory and pre-Warner Bros recordings, plus a generous selection of outtakes and demos, including selections from George's solo album, *Thanks I'll Eat It Here*. It's a treasure trove for any Little Feat fan, filled with amazing cuts like the barn-storming "Rat Faced Dog"—tracks so good, it's hard to believe they haven't been released before. The fourth disc is reason for any devoted fan to pick up this set, but is this worthwhile for the curious? Well, yes, since this offers a great summary of their fascinating career, even if it duplicates some songs at the expense of album tracks like "A Apolitical Blues" which really should be here. Even with that flaw, *Hotcakes & Outtakes* performs its job well, proving that Little Feat is an American rock & roll band like no other.

Stephen Thomas Erlewine

Nils Lofgren

Nils Lofgren
1975, Rykodisc

When Nils Lofgren released his first solo album in 1975, most fans were expecting a set confirming his guitar hero status, and more than a few listeners were vocally disappointed with the more laid-back and song-oriented disc Lofgren delivered. However, with the passage of time *Nils Lofgren* has come to be regarded as an overlooked classic, and with good reason—Lofgren has rarely been in better form on record as a songwriter, vocalist, musician, and bandleader. While Lofgren doesn't lay down a firestorm of guitar on each selection (with his piano unexpectedly high in the mix), when he does solo he makes it count, and the rough but tasty chordings and bluesy accents that fill out the frameworks of the songs give the performances plenty of sinew. Just as importantly, this is as good a set of songs as Lofgren has assembled on one disc, consistently passionate and forceful, from the cocky "If I Say It, It's So" and "The Sun Hasn't Set on This Boy Yet" to the lovelorn "I Don't Want to Know" and "Back It Up," while "Keith Don't Go (Ode to the Glimmer Twins)" comes from the heart of a true fan and "Rock and Roll Crook" suggests Lofgren had already learned plenty about the music business by this time. The production on *Nils Lofgren* is simple but simpatico, giving all the players plenty of room to shine, and Lofgren's rhythm section (Wornell Jones on bass and Aynsley Dunbar on drums) fits the album's funky but heartfelt vibe perfectly. Lofgren has made harder rocking and flashier albums since his debut, but he rarely hit the pocket with the same élan as he did on *Nils Lofgren*, and it remains the most satisfying studio album of his career.

Mark Deming

Love

Love
1966, Elektra

Love's debut is both their hardest-rocking early album and their most Byrds-influenced. Arthur Lee's songwriting muse hadn't fully developed at this stage, and in comparison with their second and third efforts, this is the least striking of the LPs featuring their classic lineup, with some similar-sounding folk-rock compositions and stock riffs. A few of the tracks are great, though: their punky rendition of Bacharach/David's "My Little Red Book" was a minor hit, "Signed D.C." and "Mushroom Clouds" were superbly moody ballads, and Bryan Maclean's "Softly to Me" served notice that Lee wasn't the only songwriter of note in the band.

Richie Unterberger

Da Capo
1967, Elektra

Love broadened their scope into psychedelia on their sophomore effort, Arthur Lee's achingly melodic songwriting gifts reaching full flower. The six songs that comprised the first side of this album when it was first issued are a truly classic body of work, highlighted by the atomic blast of pre-punk rock "Seven & Seven Is" (their only hit single), the manic jazz tempos of "Stephanie Knows Who," and the enchanting "She Comes in Colors," perhaps Lee's best composition (and reportedly the inspiration for the Rolling Stones' "She's a Rainbow"). It's only half a great album, though; the seventh and final track, "Revelation," is a tedious 19-minute jam that keeps *Da Capo* from attaining truly classic status.

Richie Unterberger

Forever Changes
1967, Elektra

It wasn't a hit, but *Forever Changes* continues to regularly appear on critics' lists of the top ten rock albums of all time, and it had an enormously far-reaching and durable influence that went way beyond chart listings. The best fusion of folk-rock and psychedelia, it features Arthur Lee's trembling vocals, beautiful melodies, haunting orchestral arrangements, and inscrutable but poetic lyrics, all of which sound nearly as fresh and intriguing upon repeated plays. One of rock's most organic, flowing masterpieces, every song has a lingering, shimmering beauty, including the two penned by the band's other talented songwriter/guitarist/singer, Bryan MacLean.

Richie Unterberger

Four Sail
1969, Elektra

From a retrospective point of view, this might be the first album in the career of singer and songwriter Arthur Lee that might have been received with more enthusiasm had it been released under his name, and not under the band name. Obviously, it must have been in his commercial best interests to retain the Love identity, but here Lee is the only member of the original band left. He is trying to recreate a Love-able identity with fewer players than he had before and a completely different sound. The old Love delivered material in a solidly folk-rock vein, meaning among other things an emphasis on combinations of acoustic and electric guitars. When the original group wanted something a little heavier, it would really put the hammer down. Records such as "My Little Red Book" and "Seven & Seven Is" were tough

enough to be rightly considered precursors of punk rock, which is a lot of mileage to get out of a Burt Bacharach tune. Lee's new lineup here does not have this kind of versatility. Guitarist Jay Donnellan plays a heavy lead guitar minus the impressive chops and gets lots of solo space in the arrangements. The rhythm section favors a more leaden sound as well, particularly drummer George Suranovich, who soaks the barbecue with Keith Moon and Mitch Mitchell licks. Lee fills in on several different instruments, but his real strength is the set of ten original songs he has provided. The tracks are deep in feeling and performed with an emotional fervor that sometimes approaches anguish. It is like going into a dark coffeehouse late at night and finding an electrically charged performer delivering messages about things familiar to one and all: love, memories, friendship, "Good Times," and even "Nothing." Lee's lyrics and performances have been compared to Jimi Hendrix, certainly a compliment. This album is such a good example of these strengths that it rises above the garage band sound to communicate a sense of time and place as well as some truly sincere feelings.

Eugene Chadbourne

Loverboy

Loverboy
1980, Columbia

Although their later albums produced better-known hits, this debut offering from Loverboy is one of their best albums. Despite their later reputation as AOR hitmakers, Loverboy was marketed as a new wave group early on and on this album makes it easy to see why: plenty of the songs feature the herky-jerky yet dance-friendly tempo associated with many new wave groups and sleek synthesizer textures form a central part of the group's sound. The most impressive songs are the ones that earned the band their early airplay: "The Kid Is Hot Tonite" is a radio-ready rocker that slickly balances mid-tempo guitar riffs with surging synthesizer lines, and "Turn Me Loose" is a clever multi-genre hybrid that blends hard rock guitar, a disco-ready beat, and new wave keyboard flourishes into a final product with across-the-board appeal. The remaining songs are just as interesting as the hits because they hop from genre to genre with style and energy: "Teenage Overdose" blends gritty heavy metal guitar riffs with snarling punk-style lyrics and a pop melody, while "Little Girl" filters rockabilly through new wave sonic techniques to create a retro-styled power pop tune worthy of Cheap Trick. These ambitious hybrids are performed with style and economy by the band, and special note should also be taken of Mike Reno's vocals: whether he's paying tribute to Elvis Presley on "Little Girl" or hitting the peak of his falsetto range in "Turn Me Loose," he tackles every number with energy and verve. The end result may be kitschy, but it is undeniably well crafted and makes perfect car stereo listening (the ultimate compliment for an AOR record). In short, *Loverboy* is a must for the group's fans and an excellent pick for anyone who enjoys the pop/rock of the 1980s.

Donald A. Guarisco

Get Lucky
1981, Columbia

After making a promising start with their self-titled debut, Loverboy hit the big time in 1981 with *Get Lucky*. This canny combination of AOR hooks and new wave production gloss boasts some memorable radio-ready tunes but isn't as solid an album as its success might lead one to believe. The best tunes on *Get Lucky* were the songs that became its hit singles: "Working for the Weekend" is a party anthem that blends some gutsy hard-rock guitar riffs with a synthesizer-drenched new wave rhythm arrangement to become a huge hit, while "The Lucky Ones" layers clever lyrics about the jealousy that success inspires in others over a song that mixes pomp rock grandeur with a punchy AOR arrangement full of gutsy yet slick guitar riffs. Loverboy got additional airplay with "When It's Over," a moody power ballad that boasts a show-stoppingly emotional vocal performance from Mike Reno, and "Take Me to the Top," a sleek mid-tempo piece built on a hypnotic syn-

thesizer arrangement. The rest of *Get Lucky* isn't as impressive as these hits because it relies on filler to pad the album out: "Gangs in the Street" is an overwrought song about street tensions whose lyrics are melodramatic to the point of being unintentionally funny, and "Emotional" is a sloppy bar band jam with annoyingly sexist lyrics and an awful vocal from Paul Dean. Due to this overabundance of less than stellar tracks, *Get Lucky* fails to be as consistent a listen as *Loverboy* or *Keep It Up*, but offers enough solid tracks to please the group's fans and AOR fanatics. Other listeners may want to check out the album's highlights on a compilation before picking it up.

Donald A. Guarisco

Keep It Up
1983, Columbia

After establishing themselves as a multi-platinum arena act with *Get Lucky*, Loverboy continued to crank out their unique new wave-tinged style of AOR on *Keep It Up*. Although this album's hits weren't as large or as indelible as those from *Get Lucky*, *Keep It Up* is actually a more consistent album. This time, the songs that hit the charts were "Hot Girls in Love" and "Queen of the Broken Hearts." The former is an up-tempo tune in the classic Loverboy style that dishes up a fist-pumping guitar rock tune fleshed out with slick synthesizer and organ textures. The latter song is a different, more complex animal: it's the surprisingly observant tale of a woman reluctant to fall in love that plays out over a hook-laden mid-tempo tune that plays off meditative guitar-laden verses against a synth-driven chorus that suddenly accelerates the tempo to a dance-pop level. Elsewhere, the album combines AOR hooks with lush instrumental treatments that approach prog rock: "Prime of Your Life" and "One Sided Love Affair" are built on stately, almost classical synthesizer riffs, while "Danger Zone" boasts a complex arrangement that alternates moody electronics with dramatic guitar bombast. "Meltdown" is another tune in this artsy vein: it's a slow rocker that combines the heaviest guitar riffs on the album with layered synth parts reminiscent of Rush. None of the other tunes on *Keep It Up* are as instantly accessible as its hits, but everything is arranged and performed with care. As a result, the album doesn't suffer from the inconsistent songs that marred *Get Lucky* and succeeds as a fully realized album of pop/rock. In short, *Keep It Up* is a

worthwhile listen for Loverboy fans and anyone who is into 1980s AOR.

Donald A. Guarisco

The Lovin' Spoonful

Greatest Hits
February 2000, Buddha

Although it sports the same amount of tracks (26) as Rhino's 1993 *Anthology*, up to now the last word in comprehensive Spoonful compilations, the 2000 issue of the umpteenth collection from this short-lived '60s band gets the nod over all others. Taken from the original first-generation masters, apparently for the first time, the sound quality—with a crispness and definition previously unheard—and even track selection, is the finest yet. "On the Road Again," "Wild About My Lovin'," and "Darlin' Companion," all excellent tunes representative of the Spoonful's good-time folksy/jugband style that were omitted from the Rhino set, are included, further reinforcing this as the last word in single-disc anthologies from this legendary band. What's startling is how many great songs the group recorded in such a short time span. The majority of the tracks were released within a two-year period from 1965–1967, almost all springing from the pen of John Sebastian who also took lead vocals on all the hits. The band was a textbook example of compressed quality, with only three tracks here breaking the three-minute barrier, and many clocking in at just under two. Which means there still could be an even more definitive compilation created by adding five more songs and extending the running time to the 77-minute CD maximum. Until then, this is the Lovin' Spoonful disc to own.

Hal Horowitz

Lynyrd Skynyrd

Pronounced Leh-Nerd Skin-Nerd
September 1973, MCA

The Allman Brothers came first, but Lynyrd Skynyrd epitomized Southern rock. The Allmans were exceptionally gifted musicians, as much bluesmen as rockers. Skynyrd was nothing but rockers, and they were Southern rockers to the bone. This didn't just mean that they were rednecks, but that they brought it all together—the blues, country, garage rock, Southern poetry—in a way that sounded more like the South than even the Allmans. And a large portion of that derives from their hard, lean edge, which was nowhere more apparent than on their debut album, *Pronounced Leh-Nerd Skin-Nerd*. Produced by Al Kooper, there are few records that sound this raw and uncompromising, especially records by debut bands. Then again, few bands sound this confident and fully formed with their first record. Perhaps the record is stronger because it's only eight songs, so there isn't a wasted moment, but that doesn't discount the sheer strength of each song. Consider the opening juxtaposition of the rollicking "I Ain't the One" with the heartbreaking "Tuesday's Gone." Two songs couldn't be more opposed, yet Skynyrd sounds equally convincing on both. If that's all the record did, it would still be fondly regarded, but it wouldn't have been influential. The genius of Skynyrd is that they unself-consciously blended album-oriented hard rock, blues, country, and garage rock, turning it all into a distinctive sound that sounds familiar but thoroughly unique. On top of that, there's the highly individual voice of Ronnie Van Zant, a songwriter who isn't afraid to be nakedly sentimental, spin tales of the South, or to twist macho conventions with humor. And, lest we forget, while he does this, the band rocks like a motherf*cker. It's the birth of a great band that birthed an entire genre with this album.

Stephen Thomas Erlewine

Second Helping
April 1974, MCA

Lynyrd Skynyrd wrote the book on Southern rock with their first album, so it only made sense that they followed it for their second album, aptly titled *Second Helping*. Sticking with producer Al Kooper (who, after all, discovered them), the group turned out a record that

replicated all the strengths of the original, but was a little tighter and a little more professional. It also revealed that the band, under the direction of songwriter Ronnie Van Zant, was developing a truly original voice. Of course, the band had already developed their own musical voice, but it was enhanced considerably by Van Zant's writing, which was at turns plainly poetic, surprisingly clever, and always revealing. Though *Second Helping* isn't as hard a rock record as *Pronounced*, it's the songs that make the record. "Sweet Home Alabama" became ubiquitous, yet it's rivaled by such terrific songs as the snide, punkish "Workin' for MCA," the Southern groove of "Don't Ask Me No Questions," the affecting "The Ballad of Curtis Loew," and "The Needle and the Spoon," a drug tale as affecting as their rival Neil Young's "Needle and the Damage Done," but much harder rocking. This is the part of Skynyrd that most people forget—they were a great band, but they were indelible because that was married to great writing. And nowhere was that more evident than on *Second Helping*.

Stephen Thomas Erlewine

Nuthin' Fancy
March 1975, MCA

Second Helping brought Lynyrd Skynyrd mass success and for the follow-up they offered *Nuthin' Fancy*. It was a self-deprecating title for a record that may have offered more of the same, at least on the surface, but was still nearly peerless as a Southern rock record. The biggest difference with this record is that the band, through touring, has become heavier and harder, fitting right in with the heavy album rock bands of the mid-'70s. The second notable difference is that Ronnie Van Zant may have been pressed for material, since there are several songs here that are just good generic rockers. But he and Skynyrd prove that what makes a great band great is how they treat generic material, and Skynyrd makes the whole of *Nuthin' Fancy* feel every bit as convincing as their first two records. For one, the record has a rawer edge than *Second Helping*, which helps make the slight preponderance of predictable (but not bad) material easy to accept, since it all sounds so good. Then there's the fact that many of these eight songs still showcase Van Zant at the top of his game, whether it's the storming opener "Saturday Night Special,"

"Railroad Song," "On the Hunt," or the rollicking "Whiskey Rock-a-Roller." Yes, this does pale in comparison with its predecessors, but most hard rock bands would give their left arm for a record that swaggers and hits as hard as *Nuthin' Fancy*.

Stephen Thomas Erlewine

Gimme Back My Bullets
February 1976, MCA

Lynyrd Skynyrd begins to show signs of wear on their third album, *Gimme Back My Bullets*. The band had switched producers, hiring Tom Dowd, the producer who served Atlantic's roster so well during the label's heyday. Unfortunately, he wasn't perfectly suited for Skynyrd, at least at this point in their history. The group had toured regularly since the release of their debut and it showed, not just in their performance, but in the songwriting of Ronnie Van Zant, who had been so consistent through their first three albums. Not to say that he was spent—the title track was defiant as "All I Can Do Is Write About It" was affecting, while "Searching" was a good ballad and "Double Trouble" was a good rocker. These songs, however, were surrounded by songs that leaned to the dull side of generic (unlike those on *Nuthin' Fancy*) and Dowd's production didn't inject energy into the group's performances. This doesn't mean *Gimme Back My Bullets* is a bad record, since the group was still in fairly good shape and they had some fine songs, but coming after three dynamite albums, it was undoubtedly a disappointment—so much so that it still sounds like a disappointment years later, even though it's one of only a handful of records by the original band.

Stephen Thomas Erlewine

One More from the Road
September 1976, MCA

Double live albums were commonplace during the '70s, even for bands that weren't particularly good in concert. As a travelin' band, Lynyrd Skynyrd made their fame and fortune by being good in concert, so it made sense that they released a double-live, entitled *One More from the Road*, in 1976, months after the release of their fourth album, *Gimme Back My Bullets*. That might have been rather quick for a live album—only three years separated this record from the group's debut—but it was enthusiastically embraced, entering the Top Ten (it would become one of their best-selling albums, as well). It's easy to see why it was welcomed, since this album demonstrates what a phenomenal catalog of songs Skynyrd accumulated. *Street Survivors*, which appeared the following year, added "That Smell" and "You Got That Right" to the canon, but this pretty much has everything else, sometimes extended into jams as long as those of the Allmans, but always much rawer, nearly dangerous. That catalog, as much as the strong performances, makes *One More from the Road* worth hearing. Heard here, on one record, the consistency of Skynyrd's work falls into relief, and they not only clearly tower above their peers based on what's here; the cover of "T for Texas" illustrates that they're carrying on the Southern tradition, not starting a new one. Like most live albums, this is not necessarily essential, but if you're a fan, it's damn hard to take this album off after it starts.

Stephen Thomas Erlewine

Street Survivors
October 1977, MCA

Street Survivors appeared in stores just days before Lynyrd Skynyrd's touring plane crashed, tragically killing many members of the band, including lead singer and songwriter

Ronnie Van Zant. Consequently, it's hard to see *Street Survivors* outside of the tragedy, especially since the best-known song here, "That Smell," reeks of death and foreboding. If the band had lived, however, *Street Survivors* would have been seen as an unqualified triumph, a record that firmly re-established Skynyrd's status as the great Southern rock band. As it stands, it's a triumph tinged with a hint of sadness, sadness that's projected onto it from listeners aware of what happened to the band after recording. Viewed as merely a record, it's a hell of an album. The band springs back to life with the addition of guitarist Steve Gaines, and Van Zant used the time off the road to write a strong set of songs, highlighted by "That Smell," "You Got That Right," and the relentless boogie "I Know a Little." It's tighter than any record since *Second Helping* and as raw as *Nuthin' Fancy*. If the original band was fated to leave after this record, at least they left with a record that serves as a testament to Skynyrd's unique greatness.

Stephen Thomas Erlewine

Skynyrd's First and...Last
September 1978, MCA

So named because this consists of Skynyrd's earliest recordings and was released after the tragic plane crash, thereby seeming to close the door on the band's career, *Skynyrd's First and...Last* is more than a simple historic curiosity, but not too much more. This music is more notable for being interesting—in how it's possible to hear Ronnie VanZant coming into his own as a writer, or hearing future Blackfoot leader Ricky Medlocke's early songs—than it is for being good, which it certainly is. Taken on its own, separated from the rest of the group's catalog, this would likely be seen as a great forgotten hard rock album from an obscure Southern outfit, but since Skynyrd went on to greater things, this winds up as a footnote—enjoyable, yes, but not quite necessary.

Stephen Thomas Erlewine

Manfred Mann

The Best of Manfred Mann: The Definitive Collection
June 1992, EMI America

This is one of nearly a dozen anthologies of Manfred Mann's music that cover their EMI period, and the 25 songs here make it the biggest of them. Additionally, there is an 11-minute interview with the band here, dating from December of 1964, that has never before appeared on record in the United States. The hits are all here, sometimes in more than one version, along with a cross-section of album tracks and B-sides, and it all sounds very good, though EMI's recent 24-bit remasterings of the band's original British LPs are much more impressive. But this CD misses being "definitive" because it leaves out some key B-sides to their early singles and overlooks the contents of several top-selling British EPs. The truth be told, no single CD, even one 73 minutes long, would be adequate to the task of defining this group's history or sound, even just covering the years 1963-66. As it is, the presence here of numbers like "She" and "The One in the Middle" (both written by Paul Jones) and their version of "My Little Red Book" (not a favorite of the band members, incidentally), makes it an essential part of any collection of the band's work, but one should also own *The Singles Plus* to get access to numbers like "Groovin'" and "Brother Jack," and the individual U.K. albums have enough merit to make them every bit as essential. In fairness, *The Definitive Collection* is the most thoroughly annotated compilation of the group's

work to surface as of the year 2000, and the group interview, though superficial and awkward, makes it unique.

Bruce Eder

The Best of Manfred Mann's Earth Band
1996, Warner Archives

Remakes can be atrocious wastes of wax: subpar carbon copy re-treads dressed up as calculated idolatry, or deconstructionist reconfigurations basking in the laziness of lyrics already written. However, two of the greatest rewrites in history belong to Manfred Mann's Earth Band. The treatments of Bruce Springsteen's "Blinded By the Light" and "For You" included here create a wholly unique variation on the stark, earthy originals by flipping the tracks and exposing the soft, white underbelly, then piling on excessive musical ornamentation like a master filmmaker visualizing a novel, blowing the inspiration at the nucleus into a bowdlerized paronomasia of sonic perfection. Pages have already been written about "Blinded By the Light," dissecting the rock critique jargon and roiling synthetic imagery. But it's the Earth Band classic that poured this bizarre stream-of-consciousness into the mainstream. Totally tubular and totally '70s, MMEB's "Blinded By the Light" is unquestionably one of the greatest left-field singles in history. Meanwhile, the awesome "For You," though more, like, totally '80s, comes across as nothing less of a masterwork. Hot licks and the always tasty voice of Chris Thompson make the whooping ELP keys bearable. "Spirit in the Night" is not as great a departure from the Springsteen standard, as "the Boss" himself began leaving his folk roots plane to reach a more bombastic base of inception (David Bowie performs a wild rendition of "It's Hard to Be a Saint in the City," all of the aforementioned from Springsteen's monolithic debut). Though consequently not as grand as the above epiphanies, "Spirit" nevertheless stands as a very strong piece. In fact, as the many glorious moments of MMEB pile on top of each other, one realizes what a discerning ear this African scion possessed, and what a wicked ensemble he surrounded himself with to realize these brilliantly blinding pastiches. Manfred Mann understood the nuances of Springsteen's Dylan discipleship, even as the band itself cleverly interpreted Robert Zimmerman's works. The distracting live read of "Quinn the Eskimo" goes on just too darn long, but "You Angel You" soars sublimely. "Davy's on the Road Again" and "Hollywood Town" also remain within the realm of enjoyableness, through expert over-embellishment. Sadly excluded is Randy Newman's "Living Without You," later reconstructed itself by Zebra. These erudite linear notes discuss too many other numbers not included (luckily, that annoying Olympic "Runner" song is omitted), still leaving a very listenable amalgam of tight prog (usually a contradiction) and a worthy addition to any personal library.

Doug Stone

All Manner of Menn: 1963–1969
August 2000, Raven

At first glance, this looks like a very enticing collection, and in many ways it is: 53 songs covering a lot of the highlights and rarities in the band's history from 1963 through 1969. There are a few flaws, however,

some of them minor and others potentially major, depending upon one's interests. For starters, it doesn't follow strict chronological order, opening with their biggest international hit, "Do Wah Diddy Diddy," from the summer of 1964, and then proceeding backward through October of 1963 and "Cock-A-Hoop" to July of 1963 and their jazzy debut, "Why Should We Not." That's not a huge problem; though for anyone who isn't familiar with the history, it's going to require a little sorting out. The EMI hits are all there on disc one, along with a few good album tracks, some superb B-sides, and compelling EP tracks ("With God on Our Side," "There's No Living Without Your Loving"). On the other hand, it's not as though most of that material isn't out somewhere already, and serious fans may feel cheated, in the sense that Raven could have (theoretically) raided EMI's vaults for an incredibly solid double-disc set of completely classic Manfred Mann up through mid-1966. They also might have then avoided the six Paul Jones solo tracks that close disc one, which, despite their chronological relationship to the group work, are the kind of commercial pop that doesn't mesh with anything here and does nothing but break the mood of this disc.

Disc two is devoted to the Mike d'Abo version of the band, which recorded successfully for Mercury Records but was never as musically ambitious as the earlier incarnation of the group; there's some good music among the 15 tracks on disc two, including rare B-sides and album cuts, such as "Box Office Draw" and "I Wanna Be Rich," as well as huge hits like "Quinn the Eskimo" and "Just Like a Woman," and it holds up well enough, though it's thoroughly less fascinating than the EMI material that preceded it. The last eight songs on the disc are drawn from various solo post-Manfred Mann projects by the individual members, including Mike d'Abo ("Little Miss Understood," "Belinda," "Free As a Bird"), Mike Hugg ("Blue Suede Shoes Again,") Mike Vickers ("On the Brink"), Manfred Mann and Mike Hugg ("Ski-Full of Fitness Theme"), and Tom McGuinness ("When I'm Dead and Gone," "Malt and Barley Blues," "Happy Birthday Ruthy Baby"). These tracks are more enlightening musically than the Manfreds' later tracks, and the Tom McGuinness material (all recordings by McGuinness–Flint) is good, solid, earthy rock & roll. The notes by McGuinness are extraordinarily detailed and revealing, in terms of correcting misconceptions and giving a humorous insider's perspective on the band.

Bruce Eder

The Marshall Tucker Band

The Marshall Tucker Band
1973, AJK

Taking a page from their Capricorn Records labelmates and Southern rock contemporaries the Allman Brothers, the Marshall Tucker Band issued a self-titled debut blending the long and winding psychedelic and jam band scene with an equally languid and otherwise laid-back country-rock flavor. Into the mix they also added a comparatively sophisticated jazz element—which is particularly prominent throughout their earliest efforts. The incipient septet featured the respective talents of Doug Gray (vocals), Toy Caldwell (guitar/vocals), his brother Tommy Caldwell (bass/vocals), George McCorkle (guitar), Paul Riddle (drums), and Jerry Eubanks (flute/sax/vocals). Their free-spirited brand of Southern rock was a direct contrast to the badass rebel image projected by the Outlaws or Lynyrd Skynyrd. This difference is reflected throughout the 1973 long-player *The Marshall Tucker Band*. The disc commences with one of the MTB's most revered works, the loose and limber traveling proto-jam "Take the Highway." The improvised instrumental section features some inspired interaction between Toy Caldwell and Eubanks. This also creates a unique synergy of musical styles that is most profoundly exhibited on the subsequent cut, "Can't You See." Caldwell's easygoing acoustic fretwork babbles like a brook against Eubanks lonesome airy flute lines. The remainder of the disc expounds on those themes, including the uptempo freewheelin' "Hillbilly Band." Unlike what the title suggests, the track is actually more akin to the Grateful Dead's "Eyes of the World" than anything from the traditional country or bluegrass genres. "Ramblin'" is an R&B rave-up that leans toward a Memphis style with some classy brass augmentations. The effort concludes on the opposite side of the spectrum with the tranquil gospel rocker "My Jesus Told Me So," offering up Caldwell's fluid guitar work with a sound comparable to that of Dickey Betts. "AB's Song" is an acoustic folk number that would not sound out of place being delivered by John Prine or Steve Goodman. This eponymous effort established the MTB's sound and initiated a five-year (1973-1978) and seven-title run with the definitive Southern rock label, Capricorn Records.

Lindsay Planer

A New Life
1974, Shout

Perhaps the only reason that *New Life* isn't quite as memorable as its self-titled predecessor is that the band's debut was just so startling when it appeared. By the time *New Life* was issued in 1974, to the band's credit, it seemed like the Marshall Tucker Band sound had always been a part of America's rock & roll scene. *New Life* is earthier than the first album, and country music is less layered over by the trappings of jam-band rock. "Blue Ridge Mountain Sky" is only eclipsed by Dickey Betts' "Ramblin' Man" as the ultimate road song from the period. Likewise, the pedal steel blues of "Too Stubborn" echo an earlier era altogether, as the ghost of Bob Wills comes into Toy Caldwell's songwriting. The whining guitars and lilting woodwinds of the title track bring the jazzier elements in the band's sound to the fore and wind them seamlessly into a swirling, pastoral country music. The Muscle Shoals horns lend a hand on the Allman Brothers' *Brothers and Sisters*-influenced "Another Cruel Love," and guest Charlie Daniels' fiddle cooks up a bluegrass stew on "24 Hours at a Time." The bonus track is a live version of "Another Cruel Love," sans horns, with mucho guitar and fiddle overdrive to compensate, and it smokes. The sound is fantastically balanced and warm, and like its predecessor, this album has dated very well.

Thom Jurek

Anthology: The First 30 Years
February 2005, Shout Factory

There's little question that Shout! Factory's double-disc compilation *The Marshall Tucker Band Anthology: The First 30 Years* is exhuastive. It spans 32 songs, sampling from 20 albums, running more or less in chronological order, and giving a good idea of the group's narrative. While that's a lot of ground, some charting singles are still missing—1975's "This Ol' Cowboy," 1978's "Dream Lover," 1980's "It Takes Time," 1983's "A Place I've Never Been," 1987's "Hangin' Out in Smoky Places," and 1993's "Walk Outside of the Lines" are all absent, which is kind of puzzling for a collection of this size, and will certainly be frustrating for listeners who know of MTB primarily from the radio. That said, for the serious fan who wants a thorough overview this is still a pretty good choice, since it does illustrate the arc of the group's career. For less dedicated fans, this will be a bit too much Marshall Tucker Band, and they may be better sticking with the group's definitive eponymous debut, since there is no good single-disc hits compilation on the market.

Stephen Thomas Erlewine

Dave Mason

Alone Together
1970, MCA

Dave Mason's first solo album was one of several recordings to come out of the Leon Russell/Delaney & Bonnie axis in 1970. (Other notables included Eric Clapton's solo debut and Joe Cocker's *Mad Dogs & Englishmen*.) *Alone Together* contains an excellent batch of melodically pleasing songs, built on a fat bed of strumming acoustic guitars with tasteful electric guitar accents and leads. Mason's vocals are embellished with harmonies from Rita Coolidge, Claudia Lennear, and Delaney & Bonnie. Besides the well-known semi-hit "Only You Know and I Know," and which was also a number 20 hit for Delaney & Bonnie, highlights include the bouncy gospel-inflected "Waitin' on You" and the banjo-bejeweled "Just a Song." "Look at You Look at Me" and the wonderfully wah-wahed "Shouldn't Have Took More Than You Gave" are reminiscent of Mason's former band, Traffic, whose drummer, Jim Capaldi is among the all-star cast assembled here. *Alone Together* represents Dave Mason at his peak. Later releases would betray lyrical shallowness, forced rhymes, and clichéd guitar licks. But here, everything comes together perfectly. The original vinyl release of *Alone Together* was also noteworthy for the marble grain of the record itself—as the record played on the turntable, the tone arm appeared to be floating through the clouds.

Jim Newsom

Ultimate Collection
September 1999, Hip-O

Even Dave Mason will tell you that his songs have been rehashed and repackaged more times than he can (or cares to) remember. "Feelin' Alright" alone has been covered nearly 50 times and has even been denigrated to the level of car commercials (Nissan, no less!). This latest, however, may in fact be the greatest. Though it only spans 20 years of Mason's self-taught and self-(mis)directed career, this "ultimate" Dave Mason collection includes most of his best-known songs and a number of rarer gems, giving a solid introduction to this oft-misunderstood musician. This compilation shows many sides of Mason: the opening hippie bounce of "You Can All Join In"; the grammatically questionable Delaney

and Bonnie-d roots chug of "Only You Know and I Know" (produced by Tommy Li Puma and featuring the likes of Leon Russell, Rita Coolidge, and fellow gridlocker Jim Capaldi); the easy dedication and advice of "Can't Stop Worrying, Can't Stop Loving," "Shouldn't Have Took More Than You Gave," and "To Be Free"; the rhythmic undertones of "Look at You Look at Me"; the cowbell-driven shuffle of "Let It Go, Let It Flow"; and the quick jangle of "Satin Red and Black Velvet Woman." Though licensing litigation probably prevented inclusion of Mason's collaborations with Eric Clapton, Carlos Santana, Bob Dylan, George Harrison, and Paul McCartney, the album does include the puzzlingly productive pairing with Cass Elliott ("Walk to the Point") and his 1987 bi-studio pop reunion with Steve Winwood ("Two Hearts"). And what Dave Mason compilation would be complete without his highest-charting hit, "We Just Disagree"? Certainly not this one. After all, it is the "ultimate."

Matthew Robinson

MC5

Kick Out the Jams
1969, Elektra

Rather than try to capture their legendary on-stage energy in a studio, MC5 opted to record their first album during a live concert at their home base, Detroit's Grande Ballroom, and while some folks who were there have quibbled that *Kick Out the Jams* isn't the most accurate representation of the band's sound, it's certainly the best of the band's three original albums, and easily beats the many semiauthorized live recordings of MC5 that have emerged in recent years, if only for the clarity of Bruce Botnick's recording. From Brother J.C. Crawford's rabble-rousing introduction to the final wash on feedback on "Starship," *Kick Out the Jams* is one of the most powerfully energetic live albums ever made; Wayne Kramer and Fred "Sonic" Smith were a lethal combination on tightly interlocked guitars, bassist Michael Davis and drummer Dennis Thompson were as strong a rhythm section as Detroit ever produced, and Rob Tyner's vocals could actually match the soulful firepower of the musicians, no small accomplishment. Even on the relatively subdued numbers (such as the blues workout "Motor City Is Burning"), the band sound like they're locked in tight and cooking with gas, while the full-blown rockers (pretty much all of side one) are as gloriously thunderous as anything ever committed to tape; this is an album that refuses to be played quietly. For many years, Detroit was considered the High Energy Rock & Roll Capital of the World, and *Kick Out the Jams* provided all the evidence anyone might need for the city to hold onto the title.

Mark Deming

Back in the USA
1970, Rhino

While lacking the monumental impact of *Kick Out the Jams*, the MC5's second album is in many regards their best and most influential, its lean, edgy sound anticipating the emergence of both the punk and

power pop movements to follow later in the decade. Book-ended by a pair of telling covers—Little Richard's "Tutti Frutti" and Chuck Berry's "Back in the U.S.A."—the disc is as much a look back at rock & roll's origins as it is a push forward into the music's future; given the Five's vaunted revolutionary leanings, for instance, it's both surprising and refreshing to discover the record's emotional centerpiece is a doo wop-inspired ballad, "Let Me Try," that's the most lovely and gentle song in their catalog. The recurring theme which drives *Back in the USA* is adolescence, its reminiscences alternately fond and embittered—while cuts like "Tonight," "Teenage Lust," "High School," and "Shakin' Street" celebrate youth in all its rebellious glory, others like "The American Ruse" and "The Human Being Lawnmower" condemn a system which eats its young, filling their heads with lies before sending them off to war. Equally gripping is the record's singular sound—produced by Jon Landau with an almost complete disregard for the bottom end, *Back in the USA* captures a live-wire intensity 180 degrees removed from the group's live sound yet perfectly suited to the material at hand, resulting in music which not only salutes the power of rock & roll but also reaffirms it.

Jason Ankeny

High Time
1971, Rhino

MC5 were nearing the end of their long and bumpy trail when they cut *High Time* in 1971, and it was widely ignored upon initial release. While it lacks the flame-thrower energy and "off the man!" politics of *Kick Out the Jams* or the frantic pace and "AM Radio of the People" sound of *Back in the USA*, heard in 2002 *High Time* sounds like MC5's relative equivalent to the Velvet Underground's *Loaded*, their last and most accessible album, but still highly idiosyncratic and full of well-written, solidly played tunes. Fred Smith's "Sister Anne" and "Skunk (Sonically Speaking)" bookend the album with a pair of smart, solidly performed hard rockers (bolstered by fine horn charts), and Wayne Kramer's "Poison" ranks with the best songs he brought to the band (he later revived it for his solo album *The Hard Stuff*). For a group that was apparently on the verge of collapse, MC5 approach this material with no small amount of skill and enthusiasm, and Geoffrey Haslam's production gives the band a big, punchy sound that suits them better than the lean, trebly tone of *Back in the USA*. It's interesting to imagine what MC5's history might have been like if *High Time* had been their first or second album rather than their last; while less stridently political than their other work, musically it's as uncompromising as anything they ever put to wax and would have given them much greater opportunities to subvert America's youth if the kids had ever had the chance to hear it.

Mark Deming

The Big Bang: The Best of the MC5
February 2000, Rhino

A best-of for a group that only made three albums might be considered an inessential addition to their discography, particularly as all three of those albums remain available on CD. However, if you only want one MC5 album, this compilation makes more sense than it might appear at first. It draws judiciously from each of the three records; adds three somewhat rare tracks from pre-*Kick Out the Jams* singles; and finishes with a live 1972 cut, "Thunder Express," recorded for French TV and previously available on a Skydog CD. In somewhat of a surprise, it leans most heavily on *Back in the U.S.A.* (with eight tracks), and not so much on the album that most would view as their most significant effort, *Kick*

Out the Jams (only four tracks). That decision works out better than you might think. The three tracks from 1967–1968 singles are fairly similar to the *Kick Out the Jams* vibe anyway, and if you don't own *Kick Out the Jams* already, you may well be ready for something a little cleaner-sounding and less assaultive by the time seven songs have gone by. It's unfortunate, nonetheless, that the two remaining pre-*Kick Out the Jams* tracks from non-LP 45s, "One of the Guys" and a different version of *Kick Out the Jams*' "Borderline," were not included. *Kick Out the Jams* itself would get most people's nod as the first and most essential MC5 purchase, but this is a close second, its value enhanced by detailed historical liner notes.

Richie Unterberger

Paul McCartney

McCartney
April 1970, Capitol

Paul McCartney retreated from the spotlight of the Beatles by recording his first solo album at his home studio, performing nearly all of the instruments himself. Appropriately, *McCartney* has an endearingly ragged, homemade quality that makes even its filler—and there is quite a bit of filler—rather ingratiating. Only a handful of songs rank as full-fledged McCartney classics, but those songs—the light folk-pop of "That Would Be Something," the sweet, gentle "Every Night," the ramshackle Beatles leftover "Teddy Boy," and the staggering "Maybe I'm Amazed" (not coincidentally the only rocker on the album)—are full of all the easy melodic charm that is McCartney's trademark. The rest of the album is charmingly slight, especially if it is read as a way to bring Paul back to earth after the heights of the Beatles. At the time the throwaway nature of much of the material was a shock, but it has become charming in retrospect. Unfortunately, in retrospect it also appears as a harbinger of the nagging mediocrity that would plague McCartney's entire solo career.

Stephen Thomas Erlewine

Ram
May 1971, Capitol

After the break-up, Beatles fans expected major statements from the three chief songwriters in the Fab Four. John and George fulfilled those expectations—Lennon with his lacerating, confessional *John Lennon/Plastic Ono Band*, Harrison with his triple-LP *All Things Must Pass*—but Paul McCartney certainly didn't, turning toward the modest charms of *McCartney*, and then crediting his wife Linda as a full-fledged collaborator on its 1971 follow-up, *Ram*. Where *McCartney* was homemade, sounding deliberately ragged in parts, *Ram* had a fuller production yet retained that ramshackle feel, sounding as if it were recorded in a shack out back, not far from the farm where the cover photo of Paul holding the ram by the horns was taken. It's filled with songs that feel tossed off, filled with songs that are cheerfully, incessantly melodic; it turns the monumental symphonic sweep of *Abbey Road* into a cheeky slice of whimsy on the two-part suite "Uncle Albert/Admiral Halsey." All this made *Ram* an object of scorn and derision upon its release (and for years afterward, in fact), but in retrospect it looks like nothing so much as the first indie pop album, a record that celebrates small pleasures with big melodies, a record that's guileless and unembarrassed to be cutesy. But McCartney never was quite the sap of his reputation, and even here, on possibly his most precious record, there's some ripping rock & roll in the mock-apocalyptic goof "Monkberry Moon Delight," the joyfully noisy "Smile Away," where his feet can be smelled a mile away, and "Eat at Home," a rollicking, winking sex song. All three of these are songs filled with good humor, and their foundation in old-time rock & roll makes it easy to overlook how inventive these productions are, but on the more obviously tuneful and gentle numbers—the ones that are more quintessentially McCartney-esque—it's plain to see how imaginative and gorgeous the arrangements are, especially on the sad, soaring finale, "Back of My Car," but even on its humble opposite, the sweet "Heart of the Country." These songs may not be self-styled major statements, but they are endearing and enduring, as is *Ram* itself, which seems like a more unique, exquisite pleasure with each passing year.

Stephen Thomas Erlewine

Red Rose Speedway
April 1973, Apple

All right, he's made a record with his wife and a record with his pickup band where democracy is allegedly the conceit even if it never sounds that way, so he returns to a solo effort, making the most disjointed album he ever cut. There's a certain fascination to its fragmented nature, not just because it's decidedly on the softer side of things, but because his desire for homegrown eccentricity has been fused with his inclination for bombastic art rock à la *Abbey Road*. Consequently, *Red Rose Speedway* winds up being a really strange record, one that veers toward the schmaltzy AOR MOR (especially on the hit single "My Love"), yet is thoroughly twisted in its own desire toward domestic art. As a result, this is every bit as insular as the lo-fi records of the early '90s, but considerably more artful, since it was, after all, designed by one of the great pop composers of the century. Yes, the greatest songs here are slight—"Big Barn Bed," "One More Kiss," and "When the Night"—but this is a deliberately slight record (slight in the way a snapshot album is important to a family yet glazes the eyes of any outside observer). Work your way into the inner circle, and McCartney's little flourishes are intoxicating—not just the melodies, but the facile production and offhand invention. If these are miniscule steps forward, consider this: if Brian Wilson can be praised for his half-assed ideas and execution, then why not McCartney, who has more character here than the Beach Boys did on their Brother records? Truthfully.

Stephen Thomas Erlewine

Band on the Run
December 1973, Capitol

Neither the dippy, rustic *Wild Life* nor the slick AOR flourishes of *Red Rose Speedway* earned Paul McCartney much respect, so he made the self-consciously ambitious *Band on the Run* to rebuke his critics. On the surface, *Band on the Run* appears to be constructed as a song cycle in the vein of *Abbey Road*, but subsequent listens reveal that the only similarities the two albums share are simply superficial. McCartney's talent for songcraft and nuanced arrangements is

in ample display throughout the record, which makes many of the songs—including the nonsensical title track—sound more substantial than they actually are. While a handful of the songs are excellent—the surging, inspired surrealism of "Jet" is by far one of his best solo recordings, "Bluebird" is sunny acoustic pop, and "Helen Wheels" captures McCartney rocking with abandon—most of the songs are more style than substance.

Yet McCartney's melodies are more consistent than any of his previous solo records, and there are no throwaways; the songs just happen to be not very good. Still, the record is enjoyable, whether it's the minor-key "Mrs. Vandebilt" or "Let Me Roll It," a silly response to John Lennon's "How Do You Sleep?," which does make *Band on the Run* one of McCartney's finest solo efforts. However, there's little of real substance on the record. No matter how elaborate the production is, or how cleverly his mini-suites are constructed, *Band on the Run* is nothing more than a triumph of showmanship.

Stephen Thomas Erlewine

Venus and Mars
May 1975, Capitol

Band on the Run was a commercial success, but even if it was billed as a Wings effort, it was primarily recorded by Paul, Linda, and Denny Laine. So, it was time to once again turn Wings into a genuine band, adding Joe English and Jimmy McCulloch to the lineup and even letting the latter contribute a song. This faux-democracy isn't what signals that this is a band effort—it's the attitude, construction, and pacing, which McCartney acknowledges as much, opening with an acoustic title track that's a salute to arena rock, leading to a genuine arena rock anthem, "Rock Show." From that, it's pretty much rocking pop tunes, paced with a couple of ballads and a little whimsy, all graced with a little of the production flair that distinguished *Band on the Run*. But where that record was clearly a studio creation and consciously elaborate, this is a straightforward affair where the sonic details are simply window dressing. McCartney doesn't really try anything new, but the songs are a little more varied than the uniform, glossy production would suggest; he dips into soft-shoe music hall shuffle on "You Gave Me the Answer," gets a little psychedelic with "Spirits of Ancient Egypt," kicks out a '50s rock & roll groove with "Magento and Titanium Man," and unveils a typically sweet and lovely melody on "Listen to What the Man Said." These are a slight shifts on an album that certainly feels like the overture for the arena rock tour that it was, which makes it one of McCartney's more consistent listens, even though it's possible to scan the song listing after several listens and not recognize any song outside of "Listen to What the Man Said" and the opening medley by title.

Stephen Thomas Erlewine

London Town
March 1978, Capitol

Reduced to the core trio of McCartney, McCartney, and Laine after the successful *Speed of Sound* tour, *London Town* finds

Wings dropping the band façade slightly, turning in their most song-oriented effort since *Band on the Run*—which, not coincidentally, was recorded with this very trio. And although its high points don't shine as brightly as those on its two immediate predecessors, it's certainly stronger than *Speed* and, in its own way, as satisfying as *Venus and Mars*. What *London Town* has in its favor is Wings' (or, more likely, McCartney's) decision to settle into slick soft rock, relying on glossy, synth-heavy productions as he ratchets up the melodic quotient. This gives the album a distinctly European flavor, a feeling that intensifies when the lyrics are taken into the equation, and this gives *London Town* a different flavor than almost any other record in his catalog. And if its best moments aren't as strong as McCartney at his best they, along with the album tracks, find him skillfully crafting engagingly light, tuneful songs that charm with their offhanded craft, domesticity, and unapologetic sweetness. McCartney's humor is in evidence here, too, with the terrific "Famous Groupies," which means there's a little of everything he does here, outside of flat-out rocking. It's a laid-back, almost effortless collection of professional pop and, as such, it's one of his strongest albums.

Stephen Thomas Erlewine

Tug of War
April 1982, Capitol

Reuniting with producer George Martin was a bit of a masterstroke on the part of Paul McCartney, since it guaranteed that *Tug of War* would receive a large, attentive audience. Martin does help McCartney focus, but it's hard to give all the credit to *Tug of War*, since McCartney was showing signs of creative rebirth on *McCartney II*, a homemade collection of synth-based tunes. This lush, ambitious, sprawling album couldn't be further from that record. That was deliberately experimental and intimate, while this is nothing less than a grand gesture, playing as McCartney's attempt to summarize everything he can do on one record. There's majestic balladry, folky guitars, unabashed whimsy, unashamed sentimentality, clever jokes, silliness, hints of reggae, a rockabilly duet with Carl Perkins, two collaborations with Stevie Wonder, and, of course, lots of great tunes. If anything, McCartney's trying a bit too hard here, and there are times that the music sags with its own ambition (or slightly dated production, as on the smash single "Ebony and Ivory"). But, at its best—the surging title track, the giddy "Take It Away," the vaudevillian stomp "Ballroom Dancing," the Lennon tribute "Here Today," the wonderful "Wanderlust"—it's as good as McCartney gets.

Stephen Thomas Erlewine

All the Best
1987, Capitol

Technically, *All the Best* was the first compilation of McCartney's solo material, since *Wings Greatest* covered songs released under the Wings aegis. Well, there is considerable overlap between the two records—no less than *ten* of that album's 12 songs are here, yet only the hard-rocking "Hi Hi Hi" is truly missed—although the seven new songs do give

this album a different character, for better or worse. With the U.S. version of *All the Best*, which has four different songs than its British counterpart, the balance shifts toward the positive, since it simply boasts a better selection of songs. Yes, "Once Upon a Long Ago," the single offered as bait on the British *All the Best*, isn't here, but it's not missed since two of the four songs exclusive to the American version are among McCartney's best solo singles ("Junior's Farm," "Uncle Albert/Admiral Halsey") and the other two are good adult contemporary easy listening (the previously non-LP "Goodnight Tonight," "With a Little Luck"). These songs add to the retrospective, although it's still not perfect—such highlights as "Maybe I'm Amazed" and "Take It Away" really should have been included. However, as a cross section of McCartney's solo singles, this is very, very good. It may be a little heavy on the schmaltz at times, yet this is still mainstream pop craft of the highest order.

Stephen Thomas Erlewine

Wingspan: Hits and History
May 2001, Capitol

Paul McCartney always got the short end of the stick when he was in the Beatles and again in the '70s, as he and his erstwhile partner John Lennon pursued solo careers. McCartney was attacked for his virtues—for his melodicism and his domesticity, along with his desire to form a real touring band following the Beatles. None of these were celebrated at the time, but he moved many, many records and sold countless concert tickets, which only hardened opposition toward him. But, in retrospect, McCartney's albums make for the most fascinating body of work among any of the ex-Beatles, and really among any of his peers. Yes, there were pitfalls among the heights, but that's part of what makes his career so fascinating—each record is distinctive, and even if the songs themselves are shallow, at least lyrically, the melodic skill and studio savvy behind each are hard not to admire. This may require a bit of conversion, and if you're not up to trudging through his individual works, even such masterworks as *Ram* (truly the roots of homemade pop), the double-disc set *Wingspan* is ideal. McCartney has had a number of career overviews before, including such seemingly comprehensive discs as *All the Best*, but those were plagued by vaguely haphazard sequencing. This is nearly perfectly executed, dividing McCartney's career between the "hits" and "history," with the latter being devoted to album tracks that are acknowledged classics, yet never were singles. Now, it's true that this isn't completely comprehensive—some will notice that superstar duets with Stevie Wonder and Michael Jackson are missing, and others will wonder where such terrific latter-day singles as "Press" are or why such charting hits as "So Bad" are bypassed, or why album tracks like "Ballroom Dancing" are absent—but nothing has come as close to capturing the quirky brilliance of McCartney's solo career, how it balanced whimsical pop with unabashedly sentimental romantic ballads, piledriving rockers, and anything in between. And what makes *Wingspan* so impressive is how the "History" disc fills in the gaps that "Hits" leaves, whether it's on the tremendous "Maybe I'm Amazed" (one of the very best songs he ever wrote), the charming "Junk," the clever "Take It Away," or such absolutely stunning miniatures as "Heart of the Country," an effortless folk-pop tune that ranks among his very best songs. That's why *Wingspan* isn't just a good hits collection—it's a convincing argument that McCartney's solo recordings are a rich, idiosyncratic body of work of their own merits. *Ram*, *Red Rose Speedway*, and *London Town* all have their merits, but if you need to be converted, this is where to start.

Stephen Thomas Erlewine

Don McLean

American Pie
October 1971, BGO

Don McLean's second album, *American Pie*, which was his first to gain recognition after the negligible initial sales of 1970's *Tapestry*, is necessarily dominated by its title track, a lengthy, allegorical history of rock & roll, because it became an unlikely hit, topping the singles chart and putting the LP at number one as well. "American Pie" has remained as much a cultural touchstone as a song, sung by everyone from Garth Brooks to Madonna, its title borrowed for a pair of smutty teen comedies, while the record itself has earned a registered three-million plays on U.S. radio stations. There may not be much more to note about it, then, except perhaps that even without a crib sheet to identify who's who, the song can still be enjoyed for its engaging melody and singable chorus, which may have more to do with its success than anything else. Of course, the album also included "Vincent," McLean's paean to Van Gogh, which has been played two-million times. Nothing else on the album is as effective as the hits, but the other eight original songs range from sensitive fare like "Till Tomorrow" to the sarcastic, uptempo "Everybody Loves Me, Baby." *American Pie*—the album—is very much a record of its time; it is imbued with the vague depression of the early '70s that infected the population and found expression in the works of singer/songwriters. "American Pie"—the song—is really a criticism of what happened in popular music in the '60s, and "Vincent" sympathizes with Van Gogh's suicide as a sane comment on an insane world. "Crossroads" and "Empty Chairs" are personal reflections full of regret and despondency, with the love song "Winterwood" providing the only respite. In the album's second half, the songs get more portentous, tracing society's ills into war and spiritual troubles in "The Grave" and "Sister Fatima." The songs are made all the more poignant by the stately folk-pop arrangements and McLean's clear, direct tenor. It was that voice, equally effective on remakes of pop oldies, that was his salvation when he proved unable to match the songwriting standard set on *Tapestry* and this collection. But then, the album has an overall elegiac quality that makes it sound like a final statement. After all, if the music has died, what else is there to say?

William Ruhlmann

Meat Loaf

Bat out of Hell
1977, Epic

There is no other album like *Bat out of Hell*, unless you want to count the sequel. This is Grand Guignol pop—epic, gothic, operatic, and silly, and it's appealing because of all of this. Jim Steinman was a composer without peer, simply because nobody else wanted

to make mini-epics like this. And there never could have been a singer more suited for his compositions than Meat Loaf, a singer partial to bombast, albeit shaded bombast. The compositions are staggeringly ridiculous, yet Meat Loaf finds the emotional core in each song, bringing true heartbreak to "Two out of Three Ain't Bad" and sly humor to "Paradise by the Dashboard Light." There's no discounting the production of Todd Rundgren, either, who gives Steinman's self-styled grandiosity a production that's staggeringly big but never overwhelming and always alluring. While the sentiments are deliberately adolescent and filled with jokes and exaggerated clichés, there's real (albeit silly) wit behind these compositions, not just in the lyrics but in the music, which is a savvy blend of oldies pastiche, show tunes, prog rock, Springsteen-esque narratives, and blistering hard rock (thereby sounding a bit like an extension of *Rocky Horror Picture Show*, which brought Meat Loaf to the national stage). It may be easy to dismiss this as ridiculous, but there's real style and craft here and its kitsch is intentional. It may elevate adolescent passion to operatic dimensions, and that's certainly silly, but it's hard not to marvel at the skill behind this grandly silly, irresistible album.

Stephen Thomas Erlewine

John Mellencamp

American Fool
1982, Mercury

John Cougar's first albums were so bereaved of strong material that the lean swagger of *American Fool* came as a shock. The difference is evident from the opening song, "Hurts So Good," a hard, Stonesy rocker with an irresistibly sleazy hook. Cougar never wrote anything as catchy as this before, nor had his romantic vision of small-town America resonated like it did on "Jack & Diane," a minor and remarkably affecting sketch of dead-end romance. These two songs are the only true keepers on *American Fool*, but the rest of the record works better than his previous material because his band is tighter than ever before, making his weaker moments convincing. Besides, songs like "Hand to Hold On To" and "China Girl," for all their faults, do indicate that his sense of craft is improving considerably.

Stephen Thomas Erlewine

Uh-Huh
1983, Mercury

Since *American Fool* illustrated that John Cougar was becoming an actual songwriter, it's only proper that he reclaimed his actual last name, Mellencamp, for the follow-up, *Uh-Huh*. After all, now that he had success, he wanted to be taken seriously, and *Uh-Huh* reflects that in its portraits of brokenhearted life in the Midwest and its rumbling undercurrent of despair. Although his lyrics still have the tendency to be a little too vague, they are more effective here than ever before, as is his music; he might not have changed his style at all—it's still a fusion of the Stones and Springsteen—except that he now knows how to make it his own. *Uh-Huh* runs out of steam toward the end, but the first half—with the dynamic rocker "Crumblin' Down," his best protest song, "Pink Houses," the punky "Authority Song," the melancholy "Warmer Place to Sleep," and the garage rocker "Play Guitar"—makes the record his first terrific album.

Stephen Thomas Erlewine

Scarecrow
November 1985, Mercury

Uh-Huh found John Mellencamp coming into his own, but he perfected his heartland rock with *Scarecrow*. A loose concept album about lost innocence and the crumbling of small-town America, *Scarecrow* says as much with its tough rock and gentle folk-rock as it does with its lyrics, which remain a weak point for Mellencamp. Nevertheless, his writing has never been more powerful: "Rain on the Scarecrow" and "Small Town" capture the hopes and fears of Middle America, while "Lonely Ol' Night" and "Rumbleseat" effortlessly convey the desperate loneliness of being stuck in a dead-end life. Those four songs form the core of the album, and while the rest of the album isn't quite as strong, that's only a relative term, since it's filled with lean hooks and powerful, economical playing that make *Scarecrow* one of the definitive blue-collar rock albums of the mid-'80s.

Stephen Thomas Erlewine

The Lonesome Jubilee
1987, Mercury

John Mellencamp's fascination with the American heartland came into full flower on *Scarecrow*, but with its follow-up, *The Lonesome Jubilee*, he began exploring American folk musics, adding fiddle, accordions, and acoustic guitars to his band, which allowed him to explore folk and country. The expansion of his band coincided with his continuing growth as a songwriter. Song for song, *The Lonesome Jubilee* is Mellencamp's strongest album, the record where he captured his romantic, if decidedly melancholy, vision of working-class America. He may recycle the same lyrical ideas as before, but he captures them better than ever, and his music is richer, which gives the album resonance. Again, there are a few moments where Mellencamp's reach exceeds his grasp, but "Paper in Fire," "Check It Out," "Cherry Bomb," "Empty Hands," and "Hard Times for an Honest Man" make the record his best.

Stephen Thomas Erlewine

Words & Music: John Mellencamp's Greatest Hits
October 2004, Utv

John Mellencamp has been in need of a thorough, career-spanning compilation for a while, and Island/UTV's 2004 release *Words & Music: John Mellencamp's Greatest Hits* finally fills that gap. His previous hits collection, 1997's *The Best That I Could Do*, was too short, since he had more hits than could fit on a brief 14-track disc. *Words & Music* doesn't have the problem of brevity. Spanning 37 songs over two discs, this has nearly all of his charting hits. Radio hits like "Justice and Independence '85" and "Rooty Toot Toot" may be absent, but they're not missed, since all the big hits are here, including "Pink Houses," "Lonely Ol' Night," "Paper in Fire," "Authority Song," "Crumblin' Down," "Small Town," "Hurts So Good," and "Jack & Diane," among many others (including two solid new songs). The biggest complaint that could be lodged against this collection is that

the sequencing is doggedly nonchronological, which may upset some listeners who would like to hear his career evolve, but this sequencing flows like a good concert and highlights the common threads in his music from 1978 to 2004. As such, it's not only a good collection of hits, but it's a good career summary and introduction, as well. [Initial pressings of *Words & Music* contained a bonus DVD containing videos for "Crumblin' Down," "R.O.C.K. in the U.S.A.," "Rain on the Scarecrow," "Check It Out (Live)," and "Key West Intermezzo (I Saw You First)."]

Stephen Thomas Erlewine

Steve Miller Band

Children of the Future
1968, Capitol

A psychedelic blues rock-out, 1968's *Children of the Future* marked Steve Miller's earliest attempt at the ascent that brought him supersonic superstardom. Recorded at Olympic Studios in London with storied producer Glyn Johns at the helm, the set played out as pure West Coast rock inflected with decade-of-love psychedelia but intriguingly cloaked in the misty pathos of the U.K. blues ethic. Though bandmate Boz Scaggs contributed a few songs, the bulk of the material was written by Miller while working as a janitor at a music studio in Texas earlier in the year. The best of his efforts resonate in a side one free-for-all that launches with the keys and swirls of the title track and segues smoothly through "Pushed Me Through It" and "In My First Mind," bound for the epic, hazy, lazy, organ-inflected "The Beauty of Time Is That It's Snowing," which ebbs and flows in ways that are continually surprising. The second half of the LP is cast in a different light—a clutch of songs that groove together but don't have the same sleepy flow. Though it has since attained classic status—Miller himself was still performing it eight years later—Scaggs' "Baby's Callin' Me Home" is a sparse, lightly instrumentalized piece of good old '60s San Francisco pop. His "Steppin' Stone," on the other hand, is a raucous, heavy-handed blues freakout with a low-riding bass and guitar breaks that angle out in all directions. And whether the title capitalized at all on the Monkees' similarly titled song, released a year earlier, is anybody's guess. *Children of the Future* was a brilliant debut. And while it is certainly a product of its era, it's still a vibrant reminder of just how the blues co-opted the mainstream to magnificent success.

Amy Hanson

Sailor
1968, Capitol

Most definitely a part of the late-'60s West Coast psychedelic blues revolution that was becoming hipper than hip, Steve Miller was also always acutely aware of both the British psychedelic movement that was swirling in tandem and of where the future lay, and how that would evolve into something even more remarkable. The result of all those ideas, of course, came together on 1968's magnificent *Sailor* LP. Speaking to *Goldmine* magazine in 2002, Miller reiterated that he was always aware of forward thinking: "It's amazing what the breakthroughs are, and the quality is absolutely better and you don't have the digital/analog argument anymore about what sounds the best. It's all new. And now anybody in the world can do what I wanted to do so badly when I got my deal with Capitol Records and got to finally go into a recording studio." What was begun on *Children of the Future* is more fully realized on *Sailor*, most notably on the opening "Song for Our Ancestors," which begins with a foghorn and only gets stranger from there. Indeed, the song precognizes Pink Floyd's 1971 opus "Echoes" to such an extent that one wonders how much the latter enjoyed Miller's own wild ride. Elsewhere, the beautiful, slow "Dear Mary" positively shimmers in a haze of declared love, while the heavy drumbeats and rock riffing guitar of "Living in the U.S.A." are a powerful reminder that the Steve Miller Band, no matter what other paths they meandered down, could rock out with the best of them. And, of course, this is the LP that introduced many to the Johnny "Guitar" Watson classic "Gangster of Love," a song that would become almost wholly Miller's own, giving the fans an alter ego to caress long before "The Joker" arose to show his hand. Rounding out Miller's love of the blues is an excellent rendering of Jimmy Reed's "You're So Fine." At their blues-loving best, *Sailor* is a classic Miller recording and a must-have—especially for the more contemporary fan, where it becomes an initiation into a past of mythic proportion.

Amy Hanson

Brave New World
1969, Capitol

Blasting out of stereo speakers in the summer of 1969, *Brave New World* was more fully realized, and rocked harder, than the Steve Miller Band's first two albums. From the opening storm of the uplifting title track to the final scorcher, "My Dark Hour," featuring Paul McCartney (credited as "Paul Ramon"), this recording was the strongest project before Miller's *Fly Like an Eagle* days. "Celebration Song" has a sliding bassline, while "LT's Midnight Dream" features Miller's slide guitar. "Can't You Hear Your Daddy's Heartbeat" sounds like it was lifted right off of Jimi Hendrix's *Are You Experienced*, and "Got Love 'Cause You Need It" also has a Hendrix-ian feel. "Kow Kow" is a wonderfully oblique song featuring Nicky Hopkins' distinctive piano style. Hopkins' piano coda on that song alone is worth the price of this album. "Space Cowboy," one of several songs co-written with Ben Sidran, defined one of Miller's many personas. "Seasons," another Sidran collaboration, is a beautifully atmospheric, slow-tempo piece. Steve Miller's guitar playing is the star of this album, blazing across the whole affair more prominently than on any other release in his lengthy career; many of the songs have a power trio feel. In addition to the fine guitar work, Miller's vocals are stronger here, and during this era in general, than they would be in his hitmaking days in the mid-'70s, when he was much more laid-back and overdubbed. Ever the borrower, adapter, and integrator, Steve Miller shapes the blues, psychedelia, sound effects, sweet multi-tracked vocal harmonies, and guitar-driven hard rock into one cohesive musical statement with this release.

Jim Newsom

Number 5
1970, Capitol

Released in the summer of 1970, *Number 5* was the fifth LP by the Steve Miller Band in just over two years. While it compares favorably to its immediate predecessor, *Your Saving Grace*, it is not quite up to the consistent excellence of the potent *Brave New World* from the previous summer. However, it does have a fair share of delights, especially the opening triumvirate of "Good Morning," "I Love You," and "Going to the Country." These selections, and all of side one, have a distinctly more rural feel than did previous recordings, due perhaps to the fact that the tracks were recorded in Nashville. Charlie McCoy contributes harmonica to several of these cuts, and Buddy Spicher plays fiddle on "Going to the Country," while Bobby Thompson adds banjo to "Tokin's." Side two is more uneven, with the lead-off mid-tempo rocker "Going to Mexico" serving as a conclusion to the first side's thematic coherence, and the closing "Never Kill Another Man" a string-laden ballad. Sandwiched between them are three experimental-sounding pieces, seasoned with sound effects, buried vocals, and semi-political themes. Although it couldn't have been predicted at the time, *Number 5* represented the end of an era for Steve Miller and bandmates, and subsequent albums would sound nothing like this first batch of great recordings.

Jim Newsom

The Joker
1973, Capitol

The Joker is, without question, the turning point in Steve Miller's career, the album where he infused his blues with a big, bright dose of pop and got exactly what he deserved: top ten hits and stardom. He also lost a lot of fans, the ones that dug his winding improvs, because those spacey jams were driven by chops and revealed new worlds. *The Joker* isn't mind-expanding, it's party music, filled with good vibes, never laying a heavy trip, always keeping things light, relaxed and easy-going. Sometimes, the vibes are interrupted, but not in a harsh way—the second side slows a bit, largely due to the sludgy "Come in My Kitchen" and "Evil," the two songs that were recorded live but lacking any kinetic energy—but for the most part, this is all bright and fun, occasionally truly silly, as on "Shu Ba Da Du Ma Ma Ma Ma." This silliness, of course, alienated old fans all the more, but that sense of fun is both the most appealing thing about *The Joker* and it set a touchstone for the rest of his career. Here, it's best heard on the terrific opener "Sugar Babe" and, of course, the timeless title track, which is sunny and ridiculous in equal measure. If nothing else quite up is to that standard in terms of songs—certainly, it's not as jammed-pack as its successor, *Fly Like An Eagle*—*The Joker* nevertheless maintains its good-time vibe so well that it's hard not to smile along...provided you're on the same wavelength as Miller, of course.

Stephen Thomas Erlewine

Fly Like an Eagle
1976, Capitol

Steve Miller had started to essay his classic sound with *The Joker*, but 1976's *Fly Like an Eagle* is where he took flight, creating his definitive slice of space blues. The key is focus, even on an album as stylishly, self-consciously trippy as this, since the focus brings about his strongest set of songs (both originals and covers), plus a detailed atmospheric production where everything fits. It still can sound fairly dated—those whooshing keyboards and cavernous echoes are certainly of their time—but its essence hasn't aged, as "Fly Like an Eagle" drifts like a cool breeze, while "Take the Money and Run" and "Rock'n Me" are fiendishly hooky, friendly rockers. The rest of the album may not be quite up to those standards, but there aren't any duds, either, as "Wild Mountain Honey" and "Mercury Blues" give this a comfortable backdrop, thanks to Miller's offhand, lazy charm. Though it may not quite transcend its time, it certainly is an album rock landmark of the mid-'70s and its best moments (namely, the aforementioned singles) are classics of the idiom.

Stephen Thomas Erlewine

Book of Dreams
1977, Eagle

Unless the Black Crowes dress up in NASA drag or Garth Brooks takes his glam-industrial doppelgänger Chris Gaines into Mothership terrain, Steve Miller should retain his monopoly on the "Space Cowboy" moniker for many years to come. And it is here, on this 1977 blockbuster, that Miller shored up his cosmic persona: from the winged horse on the album cover to a judicious smattering of synthesizers in the music, *Book of Dreams* bridged the gap between blues-rock and the indulgences of prog rock. Things do go awry when Renaissance Faire whimsy takes over clunkers like "Wish Upon a Star" and "Babes in the Wood," but luckily the balance of the record offers a satisfying blend of meaty blues and country riffs and tasteful atmospherics. The well-known suspects include "Swingtown," "Winter Time," and "Threshold," with relatively straightforward rock & boogie highlights coming by way of "True Fine Love," "Jet Airliner," and "Jungle Love." The non-hit cuts, "Sacrifice" and "My Own Space," do stand up to these FM favorites but fall short of making the album something the casual fan should consider with Miller's *Greatest Hits 1974-1978* in hand (that collection includes seven tracks off of *Book of Dreams*, plus all the hits from *The Joker* and *Fly Like an Eagle*). Still, this is a highlight of the '70s classic rock era and one of Miller's finest releases.

Stephen Cook

Young Hearts: Complete Greatest Hits
September 2003, Capitol

At his best, Steve Miller offered great rock & roll thrills—sleek, insidiously catchy, relentlessly propulsive, effervescent pop gems, songs that were possessed with their own cheerful momentum that proved irresistible and surprisingly enduring. At his best, he made rock & roll that evoked its time but transcended it since its song and studiocraft were precisely executed, and never running longer than needed; like all perfect pop or rock singles, they sound too short since you'd want them to last forever. Unfortunately, Miller at his very best is ten, maybe 12 (and if you're kind, *maybe* 14) songs, much shorter than the generous *Complete Greatest Hits*, which clocks in at 22 tracks. Strangely enough, that title is a bit disingenuous, since this does *not* contain all of Miller's charting singles, which, strangely enough, clock in at 20

tracks, if all the *Billboard* charts are used as a guideline. Of those 20 singles, a whole bunch are missing: "Your Cash Ain't Nothin' but Trash," "Going to the Country," "Heart Like a Wheel," "Circle of Love," "Give It Up," "Shangri-La," "Bongo Bongo," "Nobody but You Baby," and "Cool Magic." That's nine songs, nearly half of his charting singles. Then again, charting singles don't really tell the story of Miller and his band, since they were more popular on album-oriented radio than they were on the charts, which is why songs like "Space Cowboy," "Wild Mountain Honey," and "Dance Dance Dance" are better known than "Bongo Bongo." Nevertheless, if the compilers of this compilation were going to take its title seriously, these songs would be present (even if Miller seems to have disowned 1981's *Circle of Love*, since it's out of print and none of its singles are here), along with the cuts that remain staples of AOR to this day. Instead, it's a bit of a hodgepodge, containing all but three tracks from the classic *Greatest Hits 1974-1978*, plus the three other songs every listener wants: "Abracadabra," "Livin' in the U.S.A.," and "Space Cowboy." If those three tracks were substituted for those missing from *Greatest Hits 1974-1978*, this wouldn't be just the great Miller album; it would be one of the great rock guilty pleasures, the kind of records everybody would own but all serious rock geeks would be ashamed to have, even if they play it far more than *Trout Mask Replica*. But this collection meanders, adding a bunch of latter-day songs that are largely unknown. Some of them are good—1993's "Wide River," if given a better production, could be mistaken for the Steve Miller Band at its peak—but by and large, they slow this record down more than necessary. What makes this recommended—and, make no mistake, it is—is that it contains that core 12 to 14 songs that would make for one of the great rock albums. What keeps it from essential is the eight to ten songs that surround them, particularly since this starts off so strong, and then peters out, saving "Dance Dance Dance" for a last hurrah. Even so, this is the only place to go for all of Miller's hits (not counting the 1999 Australia collection, which has a similar feel but a slightly sharper track selection and a little leaner 20-track running time). But keep this in mind: if you want a party, you want *Greatest Hits 1974-1978*, since the feel and the groove is the same, and it clocks in at 14 tracks and 47 minutes—perfect length for repeated plays. At the end of the exhaustive *Complete Greatest Hits* you're pretty much exhausted—glad you have the key songs in your collection, wishing that the disc itself was as sleek and irresistible as the best tunes here.

Stephen Thomas Erlewine

Joni Mitchell

Ladies of the Canyon
April 1970, Reprise

This wonderfully varied release shows a number of new tendencies in Joni Mitchell's work, some of which would come to fuller fruition on subsequent albums. "The Arrangement," "Rainy Night House," and "Woodstock" contain lengthy instrumental sections, presaging the extensive non-vocal stretches in later selections such as "Down to You" from *Court and Spark*. Jazz elements are noticeable in the wind solos of "For Free" and "Conversation," exhibiting an important influence that would extend as late as *Mingus*. The unusually poignant desolation of "The Arrangement" would surface more strongly in *Blue*. A number of the selections here ("Willy" and "Blue Boy") use piano rather than guitar accompaniment; arrangements here are often more colorful and complex than before, utilizing cello, clarinet, flute, saxophone, and percussion. Mitchell sings more clearly and expressively than on prior albums, most strikingly so on "Woodstock," her celebration of the pivotal 1960s New York rock festival. This number, given a haunting electric piano accompaniment, is sung in a gutsy, raw, soulful manner; the selection proves amply that pop music anthems don't all have to be loud production numbers. Songs here take many moods, ranging from the sunny, easygoing "Morning Morgantown" (a charming small-town portrait) to the nervously energetic "Conversation" (about a love triangle in the making) to the cryptically spooky "The Priest" (presenting the speaker's love for a Spartan man) to the sweetly sentimental classic "The Circle Game" (denoting the passage of time in touching terms) to the bouncy and vibrant single "Big Yellow Taxi" (with humorous lyrics on ecological matters) to the plummy, sumptuous title track (a celebration of creativity in all its manifestations). This album is yet another essential listen in Mitchell's recorded canon.

David Cleary

Blue
June 1971, Reprise

Sad, spare, and beautiful, *Blue* is the quintessential confessional singer/songwriter album. Forthright and poetic, Joni Mitchell's songs are raw nerves, tales of love and loss (two words with relative meaning here) etched with stunning complexity; even tracks like "All I Want," "My Old Man," and "Carey"—the brightest, most hopeful moments on the record—are darkened by bittersweet moments of sorrow and loneliness. At the same time that songs like "Little Green" (about a child given up for adoption) and the title cut (a hymn to salvation supposedly penned for James Taylor) raise the stakes of confessional folk-pop to new levels of honesty and openness, Mitchell's music moves beyond the constraints of acoustic folk into more intricate and diverse territory, setting the stage for the experimentation of her later work. Unrivaled in its intensity and insight, *Blue* remains a watershed.

Jason Ankeny

For the Roses
November 1972, Asylum

On *For the Roses*, Joni Mitchell began to explore jazz and other influences in earnest. As one might expect from a transitional album, there is a lot of stylistic ground explored, including straight folk selections using guitar ("For the Roses") and piano ("Banquet," "See You Sometime," "Lesson in Survival"), overtly jazzy numbers ("Barangrill," "Cold Blue Steel and Sweet Fire"), and hybrids that cross the two ("Let the Wind Carry Me," "Electricity," "Woman of Heart and Mind," "Judgment of the Moon and Stars"). "Blonde in the Bleachers" grafts a rock & roll band coda onto a piano-based singer/songwriter main body. The hit single "You Turn Me on I'm a Radio" is an unusual essay into country-tinged pop, sporting a Dylanesque harmonica solo played by Graham Nash and lush backing vocals. Arrangements here build solidly upon the tentative expansion of scoring first seen in *Ladies of the Canyon*. "Judgment of the Moon and Stars" and "Let the Wind Carry Me" present lengthy instrumental interludes. The lyrics here are among Mitchell's best, continuing in the vein of gripping honesty and heartfelt depth exhibited on *Blue*. As always, there are selections about relationship problems, such as "Lesson in Survival," "See You Sometime," and perhaps the best of all her songs in this genre, "Woman of Heart and Mind." "Cold Blue Steel and Sweet Fire" presents a gritty inner-city survival scene, while "Barangrill" winsomely extols the uncomplicated virtues of a roadside truck stop. More than a bridge between great albums, this excellent disc is a top-notch listen in its own right.

David Cleary

Court and Spark
January 1974, Asylum

Joni Mitchell reached her commercial high point with *Court and Spark*, a remarkably deft fusion of folk, pop, and jazz which stands as her best-selling work to date. While as unified and insightful as *Blue*, the album—a concept record exploring the roles of honesty and trust in relationships, romantic and otherwise—moves away from confessional songwriting into evocative character studies: the hit "Free Man in Paris," written about David Geffen, is a not-so-subtle dig at the machinations of the music industry, while "Raised on Robbery" offers an acutely funny look at the predatory environment of the singles bar scene. Much of *Court and Spark* is devoted to wary love songs: both the title cut and "Help Me," the record's most successful single, carefully measure the risks of romance, while "People's Parties" and "The Same Situation" are fraught with worry and self-doubt (standing in direct opposition to the music, which is smart, smooth, and assured from the first note to the last).

Jason Ankeny

The Hissing of Summer Lawns
November 1975, Asylum

Joni Mitchell evolved from the smooth jazz-pop of *Court and Spark* to the radical *Hissing of Summer Lawns*, an adventurous work that remains among her most difficult records. After opening with the graceful "In France They Kiss on Main Street," the album veers sharply into "The Jungle Line," an odd, Moog-driven piece backed by the rhythms of the warrior drums of Burundi—a move into multiculturalism that beat the likes of Paul Simon, Peter Gabriel, and Sting to the punch by a decade. While not as prescient, songs like "Edith and the Kingpin" and "Harry's House—Centerpiece" are no less complex or idiosyncratic, employing minor-key melodies and richly detailed lyrics to arrive at a strange and beautiful fusion of jazz and shimmering avant pop.

Jason Ankeny

Hejira
November 1976, Asylum

Joni Mitchell's *Hejira* is the last in an astonishingly long run of top-notch studio albums dating back to her debut. Some vestiges of her old style remain here; "Song for Sharon" utilizes the static, pithy vocal harmonies from *Ladies of*

the Canyon's "Woodstock," "Refuge of the Roads" features woodwind touches reminiscent of those in "Barangrill" from *For the Roses*, and "Coyote" is a fast guitar-strummed number that has precedents as far back as *Clouds*' "Chelsea Morning." But by and large, this release is the most overtly jazz-oriented of her career up to this point—hip and cool, but never smug or icy. "Blue Motel Room" in particular is a prototypic slow jazz-club combo number, appropriately smooth, smoky, and languorous. "Coyote," "Black Crow," and the title track are by contrast energetically restless fast-tempo selections. The rest of the songs here cleverly explore variants on mid- to slow-tempo approaches. None of these cuts are traditionally tuneful in the manner of Mitchell's older folk efforts; the effect here is one of subtle rolls and ridges on a green meadow rather than the outgoing beauty of a flower garden. Mitchell's verses, many concerned with character portraits, are among the most polished of her career; the most striking of these studies are that of the decrepit Delta crooner of "Furry Sings the Blues" and the ambivalent speaker of "Song to Sharon," who has difficulty choosing between commitment and freedom. Arrangements are sparse, yet surprisingly varied, the most striking of which is the kaleidoscopically pointillistic one used on "Amelia." Performances are excellent, with special kudos reserved for Jaco Pastorius' melodic bass playing on "Refuge of the Roads" and the title cut. This excellent album is a rewarding listen.

David Cleary

Moby Grape

Moby Grape
June 1967, San Francisco Sound

Moby Grape's career was a long, sad series of minor disasters, in which nearly anything that could have gone wrong did (poor handling by their record company, a variety of legal problems, a truly regrettable deal with their manager, creative and personal differences among the band members, and the tragic breakdown of guitarist and songwriter Skip Spence), but their self-titled debut album was their one moment of unqualified triumph. *Moby Grape* is one of the finest (perhaps *the* finest) album to come out of the San Francisco psychedelic scene, brimming with great songs and fresh ideas while blessedly avoiding the pitfalls that pock marked the work of their contemporaries—no long, unfocused jams, no self-indulgent philosophy, and no attempts to sonically recreate the sound of an acid trip. Instead, Moby Grape built their sound around the brilliantly interwoven guitar work of Jerry Miller, Peter Lewis, and Skip Spence, and the clear, bright harmonies of all five members (drummer Don Stevenson and bassist Bob Mosely sang just as well as they held down the backbeat). As songwriters, the group blended straight-ahead rock & roll, smart pop, blues, country, and folk accents into a flavorful brew that was all their own, with a clever melodic sense that reflected the lysergic energy surrounding them without drowning in it. And producer David Rubinson got it all on tape in a manner

which captured the band's infectious energy and soaring melodies with uncluttered clarity, while subtly exploring the possibilities of the stereo mixing process. "Omaha," "Fall on You," "Hey Grandma," and "8:05" sound like obvious hits (and might have been if Columbia hadn't released them as singles all at once), but the truth is there isn't a dud track to be found here, and time has been extremely kind to this record. *Moby Grape* is as refreshing today as it was upon first release, and if fate prevented the group from making a follow-up that was as consistently strong, for one brief shining moment Moby Grape proved to the world they were one of America's great bands. While history remembers the Grateful Dead and Jefferson Airplane as being more important, the truth is neither group ever made an album quite this good.

Mark Deming

Molly Hatchet

Molly Hatchet
1978, Epic

Molly Hatchet comes out of the chute kicking and screaming on this, the band's debut effort. With obvious influences including fellow Floridians Lynyrd Skynyrd, as well as the Allman Brothers, Mountain, and any number of other hard rock bands, Hatchet didn't take long to catch on with what would become legions of fans. Songs like "Bounty Hunter" and the cover of the Allman Brothers Band's "Dreams I'll Never See" helped to build a solid base of fans who still hold tight to their Molly Hatchet rock & roll dreams. All in all, a splendid debut album from a band that, in true Southern fashion, has had its share of ups and downs. And Danny Joe Brown proves that he is a singer to be reckoned with.

Michael B. Smith

Flirtin' with Disaster
1979, Epic

With the release of its second album, Florida's Molly Hatchet dominated the airwaves in 1979 with the title track "Flirtin' With Disaster." Danny Joe Brown, the working man's musical hero, sings his butt off, accompanied by some impressive guitar work by Dave Hlubek. Other outstanding cuts include "Whiskey Man" and "Boogie No More."

Michael B. Smith

Eddie Money

Eddie Money
1977, Columbia

This strong debut benefits greatly from the expertise of veteran producer Bruce Botnick as well as the likes of former Steve Miller bassist Lonnie Turner and saxman Tom Scott. Guitarist Jimmy Lyon was to Money what Keith Scott was to Bryan

Adams. Money, son of a New York City cop, had a rock & roll epiphany en route to following his dad's career path. The debut album, long on craft but not without inspiration, deservedly shot radio-ready tunes "Two Tickets to Paradise" and "Baby Hold On" up the charts, the latter helped by former Elvin Bishop songmate Jo Baker. The key tune is the spirited "Wanna Be a Rock 'n' Roll Star," which spells out the game plan.

Mark Allan

The Essential Eddie Money
June 2003, Columbia

Eddie Money was never the flashiest rocker around. He looked like what he was, a regular guy who quit the N.Y.C. Police Academy to try to be a rock star. Take a look at the photos in the booklet of this career retrospective; when Money tried to look sexy, he simply ended up looking dorky. He didn't have the greatest voice either, sort of a regular Joe growl without much range. What he did have, however, were great songs and a tough, no-nonsense sound that made him an album rock radio fixture for much of the late '70s and early '80s. He also did the almost unthinkable for rock & roll and made a comeback. After a few weak albums in the mid-'80s that had people writing him off completely, he returned and hit the charts and airwaves even harder. This 15-track collection, *The Essential Eddie Money*, almost lives up to its title. It delivers one knockout blow after another, one AOR radio staple after another, until you are left shaking your head in wonderment. Beginning with the one-two punch of "Two Tickets to Paradise" and "Baby Hold On," continuing with the killer album rock radio hits of "Trinidad," the amazing "Shakin'," and the ultra-poppy "I Think I'm in Love," Money's best five songs of the late '70s/early '80s stand up admirably next to any other artist of the era and still sound vital and alive in today's rock climate. The songs that weren't hits, like the strutting "No Control" and the country-rock-styled "Gimme Some Water," are nowhere close to being filler and are quite enjoyable too. His comeback songs from 1986, "Take Me Home Tonight" and "I Wanna Go Back," add layers of studio gloss to Money's clean and unadorned sound and lean more toward the pop side of pop/rock, but don't suffer for the change in approach. And no one can argue that the moment when Ronnie Spector breaks in with part of "Be My Baby" on "Take Me Home Tonight" isn't one of the coolest, most heartwarming moments in recorded rock history. His last hit, "Walk on Water" from 1988, is a big synth-dominated rock ballad that had Money going out in style. The last three songs are best skipped over as they are extremely weak and, in the case of "There Will Never Be Another You" (featuring the always questionable Boney James on sax), downright cheesy. If you can ignore those last three songs, this is a perfect collection of one of the great unsung rockers of any era.

Tim Sendra

Montrose

Montrose
1973, Warner Bros.

The '70s gave us a slew of classic hard rock albums—the likes of which may never be equaled—and though it hasn't had the lasting influence of, say, Boston's or Ted Nugent's first albums, Montrose's eponymous debut proved equally influential and important in its day. Released in 1973, the record also introduced a young Sammy Hagar to the world,

but the explosive aggression of Ronnie Montrose's biting guitar left no doubt as to why it was his name gracing the cover. A rock-solid rhythm section featuring drummer Denny Carmassi and bassist Bill Church certainly didn't hurt, either, and unstoppable anthems such as "Rock the Nation" and "Good Rockin' Tonight" would lay the ground rules for an entire generation of late-'70s California bands, most notably Van Halen. Admittedly, tracks like "Make It Last" and "I Don't Want It" sound rather dated by today's sonic standards (no thanks to their ultra-silly lyrics), but no amount of time can dim the sheer euphoria of "Bad Motor Scooter," the adolescent nastiness of "Rock Candy," and the simply gargantuan main riff of the phenomenal "Space Station #5." A welcome addition to any respectable '70s hard rock collection.

Ed Rivadavia

The Very Best of Montrose
October 2000, Rhino

Except for a few ill-advised power ballads, Montrose was a hard-driving, head-butting, riff-rattling, non-stop rock machine whose best qualities—creative guitar playing, hooky melodies, and smart production—were argu-ably the blueprint  for Van Halen and any number of other similar crunch proto-metalers. As the only compilation of this under-recognized band, *The Very Best Of* captures 15 highlights from four Warner Bros. albums spanning 1973-1976, and tacks on three difficult to find cuts from 1987's reunion disc on Enigma. While Montrose was a fine fret shredder, there's little that's distinctive about his style. But the songs he applied his fiery six-string frenzy to remain timeless rock should-have-been classics, most of which have been unjustly neglected, and this comprehensive single disc compiles the best of them. With track by track annotation from the guitarist/songwriter/producer (and on one track, singer), remastered sound, well-documented liner notes, as well as full credits, there's little that Rhino could have improved on here. The absence of any Ronnie Montrose solo material, or his work with the band Gamma is understandable, since his style for those projects differed substantially from the hard-grinding groove he pounded out with his self-named band. Although the first eight tunes that cover the Sammy Hagar years (*Montrose* and *Paper Money*) are the best known, there's plenty of solid rocking on the other ten tracks. Singer Bob James (not the jazz-fusion pianist) wasn't nearly as magnetic as his better-known predecessor, but his Lou Gramm-styled range suited the material just fine, and the band, whose members changed on almost every album, were always solid, if unremarkable professionals. Tough pile drivers like "Rock Candy," "I Got the Fire," "Let's Go," and "Dancin' Feet," with their chunky, thunderous riffs and lighter-raising yet forgettable lyrics, can get any biker party started, and hearing them all together for the first time makes you wonder why Montrose isn't more highly regarded as an early influence on countless hot guitar rockers. No matter, because this is 76 minutes of undiluted, rugged guitar rock at its finest. Leave your brain cells at home and just enjoy.

Hal Horowitz

The Moody Blues

Days of Future Passed
1967, Polydor

This album marked the formal debut of the psychedelic-era Moody Blues; though they'd made a pair of singles featuring new (as of 1966) members Justin Hayward and John Lodge, *Days of Future Passed* was a lot bolder and more ambitious. What surprises first-time listeners—and delighted them at the time—is the degree to which the group shares the spotlight with the London Festival Orchestra without compromising their sound or getting lost in the lush mix of sounds. That's mostly because they came to this album with the strongest, most cohesive body of songs in their history, having spent the previous year working up a new stage act and a new body of material (and working the bugs out of it on-stage), the best of which ended up here. Decca Records had wanted a rock version of Dvorak's "New World Symphony" to showcase its enhanced stereo-sound technology, but at the behest of the band, producer Tony Clarke (with engineer Derek Varnals aiding and abetting) hijacked the project and instead cut the group's new repertory, with conductor/arranger Peter Knight adding the orchestral accompaniment and devising the bridge sections between the songs and the album's grandiose opening and closing sections. The record company didn't know what to do with the resulting album, which was neither classical nor pop, but following its release in December of 1967, audiences found their way to it as one of the first pieces of heavily orchestrated, album-length psychedelic rock to come out of England in the wake of the Beatles' *Sgt. Pepper* and *Magical Mystery Tour* albums. What's more, it was refreshingly original, rather than an attempt to mimic the Beatles; sandwiched among the playful lyricism of "Another Morning" and the mysticism of "The Sunset," songs like "Tuesday Afternoon" and "Twilight Time" (which remained in their concert repertory for three years) were pounding rockers within the British psychedelic milieu, and the harmony singing (another new attribute for the group) made the band's sound unique. With "Tuesday Afternoon" and "Nights In White Satin" to drive sales, *Days of Future Passed* became one of the defining documents of the blossoming psychedelic era, and one of the most enduringly popular albums of its era. On CD, its history was fairly spotty until 1997, when it was remastered by Polygram; that edition blows every prior CD release (apart from Mobile Fidelity's limited-edition disc) out of contention, though this record is likely due for another upgrade—and probably a format jump, perhaps to DVD-Audio—on or before its 40th anniversary in 2007.

Bruce Eder

In Search of the Lost Chord
1968, Polydor

In Search of the Lost Chord is the album on which the Moody Blues discovered drugs and mysticism as a basis for songwriting and came up with a compelling psychedelic creation, filled with songs about Timothy Leary and the astral plane and other psychedelic-era concerns. They dumped the orchestra this time out in favor of Mike Pinder's Mellotron, which was a more than adequate substitute, and the rest of the band joined in with flutes, sitar, tablas, and cellos, the playing of which was mostly learned on the spot. The whole album was one big experiment to see how far the group could go with any instruments they could find, thus making this album a rather close cousin to the Beatles' records of the same era. It is all beautiful and elegant, and "Legend of a Mind"'s chorus about "Timothy Leary's dead/Oh, no—he's outside, looking in" ended up anticipating reality; upon his death in 1996, Leary was cremated and launched into space on a privately owned satellite, with the remains of *Star Trek* creator Gene Roddenberry (another '60s pop culture icon) and other well-heeled clients.

Bruce Eder

On the Threshold of a Dream
1969, Polydor

On the Threshold of a Dream was the first album that the Moody Blues had a chance to record and prepare in a situation of relative calm, without juggling tour schedules and stealing time in the studio between gigs—indeed, it was a product of what were almost ideal circumstances, though it might not have seemed that way to some observers. The Moodies had mostly exhausted the best parts of the song bag from which their two preceding albums, *Days of Future Passed* and *In Search of the Lost Chord*, had been drawn, and as it turned out, even the leftover tracks from those sessions wouldn't pass muster for their next long-player project—but those albums had both been hits, and charted well in America as well as England, and had overlapped with a pair of hit singles, "Nights in White Satin" and "Tuesday Afternoon," on both sides of the Atlantic. Their success had earned them enough consideration from Decca Records that they could work at their leisure in the studio through all of January and most of February of 1969; what's more, with two LPs under their belt, they now had a much better idea of what they could accomplish in the studio, and write songs with that capability in mind. Equally important, they'd just come off of an extensive U.S. tour (opening for Cream) and had learned a lot in the course of concertizing over the previous year, achieving a much bolder yet tighter sound instrumentally as well as vocally, and they could now write to and for that sound as well. So this album is oozing with bright, splashy creative flourishes in two seemingly contradictory directions that somehow come together as a valid whole. On the original LP's first side (which was the more rock-oriented side), the songs "Lovely to See You," "Send Me No Wine," "To Share Our Love," and "So Deep Within You" all featured killer guitar hooks (electric and acoustic) and fills by Justin Hayward; beautiful, muscular bass from John Lodge; and vocal hooks everywhere. It's also a surprisingly hard-rocking album considering the amount of overdubbing that went into perfecting the songs, including cellos, wind and reed instruments, and lots of vocal layers—yet it even found room to display a pop-soul edge on "So Deep Within You" (a number that the Four Tops later recorded).

Side two was the more overtly ambitious of the two

halves—after a pair of songs dominated by acoustic guitar and heavy Mellotron, "Never Comes the Day" and "Lazy Day" (the latter a piece of social commentary showing that Ray Thomas, at least, still remembered his roots in Birmingham), the remainder of the record was devoted to the most challenging body of music in the group's history. Justin Hayward's deliberately archaic "Are You Sitting Comfortably?," a piece that sounds almost 400 years out of its own time, evokes images out of medieval and Renaissance history laced with magic and mysticism, all set to Hayward's acoustic guitar and Thomas' flute, leading into Graeme Edge's poetic contribution, "The Dream," accompanied by Mike Pinder's Mellotrons in their most exposed appearance to date on a record. And all of that flows into Pinder's three-part suite, "Have You Heard, Pt. 1"/"The Voyage"/"Have You Heard, Pt. 2," a *tour de force* for the band—check out Edge's and Lodge's rock-solid playing on "Have You Heard"—and for Pinder, whose Mellotrons, in conjunction with Thomas' flute and supported by some overdubbed orchestral instruments, push the group almost prematurely into the realm of progressive rock. This synthesis of psychedelia and classical music, including a section featuring Pinder on grand piano, may sound overblown and pretentious today, but in 1969 this was envelope-ripping, genre-busting music, scaling established boundaries into unknown territory, not only "outside the box" but outside of any musical box that had been conceived at that moment—perhaps it can be considered rock's flirtation with the territory covered by works such as Alexander Scriabin's *Mysterium*, and if it overreached (as did Scriabin), well, so did a lot of other people at the time, including Jimi Hendrix, the Doors, the Who, et al. To show the difference in the times, the Moodies even brought this extended suite successfully to their concert repertory, and audiences devoured it at the time (and evidently still did in 2005, as they brought part of it back to their set list that year). Amazingly, *On the Threshold of a Dream* was their first chart-topping LP in England, and remained on the charts for an astonishing 70 weeks, a feat made all the more remarkable by the fact that the accompanying single, "Never Comes the Day" b/w "So Deep Within You," never charted at all.

Bruce Eder

To Our Children's Children's Children
1969, Polydor

The 1997 remastering of this disc somewhat improves the sound on the band's most personal album, although the difference is less dramatic than on the other classic seven albums, and fans may miss the lyrics that were formerly included. Oddly enough, this was also the group's poorest-selling album of their psychedelic era, taking a lot longer to go gold—for all of their presumed connection to their audience, the band was perhaps stretching that link a little thinner than usual here. The material dwells mostly on time and what its passage means, and there is a peculiar feeling of loneliness and isolation to many of the songs. This was also the last of the group's big "studio" sound productions, built up in layer upon layer of overdubbed instruments—the sound is very lush and rich, but proved impossible to re-create properly on-stage, and after this they would restrict themselves to recording songs that the five of them could play in concert. There are no extended suites on this album, but Justin Hayward's "Watching and Waiting" and "Gypsy" have proved to be among the most popular songs in the group's history. The notes in the new edition also give a good account of how and why the Moody Blues founded their own Threshold label with *Children's Children* and their growing estrangement from Decca Records.

Bruce Eder

Question of Balance
1970, Atlantic

The Moody Blues' first real attempt at a harder rock sound still has some psychedelic elements, but they're achieved with an overall leaner studio sound. The group was trying to take stock of itself at this time, and came up with some surprisingly strong, lean numbers (Michael Pinder's Mellotron is surprisingly restrained until the final number, "The Balance"), which also embraced politics for the first time ("Question" seemed to display the dislocation that a lot of younger listeners were feeling during Vietnam). The surprisingly jagged opening track, "Question," recorded several months earlier, became a popular concert number as well as a number two (or number one, depending upon whose chart one looks at) single. Graeme Edge's "Don't You Feel Small" and Justin Hayward's "It's Up to You" both had a great beat, but the real highlight here is John Lodge's "Tortoise and the Hare," a fast-paced number that the band used to rip through in concert with some searing guitar solos by Hayward. Ray Thomas' "And the Tide Rushes In" (written in the wake of a fight with his wife) is one of the prettiest psychedelic songs ever written, a sweetly languid piece with some gorgeous shimmering instrumental effects. The 1997 remastered edition brings out the guitar sound with amazing force and clarity, and the notes tell a lot about the turmoil the band was starting to feel after three years of whirlwind success. The only loss is the absence of the lyrics included in earlier editions.

Bruce Eder

Every Good Boy Deserves Favour
1971, Polydor

Every Good Boy Deserves Favour is the best realized of the Moody Blues' classic albums. The lush melodies and the sound of Michael Pinder's Mellotron were never richer, and the guitar pyrotechnics on pieces like "The Story in Your Eyes" were never more vivid.  "Emily's Song," "Nice to Be Here," and "My Song" are among the best work the group ever did, and "The Story in Your Eyes" is the best rock number they ever cut, with a bracing beat and the kind of lyrical complexity one more expected out of George Harrison at the time.

Bruce Eder

Seventh Sojourn
1972, Polydor

Seventh Sojourn contains the Moody Blues' hardest-rocking body of songs, and shows the sudden emergence of John Lodge, who had never been a writing mainstay of the band before, as a major songwriter with "Isn't Life Strange" and "I'm Just a Singer (In a Rock and Roll Band)" (which reflected some of the strain of the group members), both of which became hits. Lodge and Graeme Edge's driving rhythm section comes through, as does the improved keyboard device called the Chamberlain, which supplanted the Mellotron here with a much stronger sound (especially on-stage). Justin

Hayward's "New Horizons" was the most romantic number since "Nights in White Satin."

Bruce Eder

Long Distance Voyager
1981, Polydor

Progressive rock bands stumbled into the '80s, some with the crutch of commercial concessions under one arm, which makes the Moody Blues' elegant entrance via *Long Distance Voyager* all the more impressive. Ironically enough, this was also the only album that the group ever got to record at their custom-designed Threshold Studio, given to them by Decca Records head Sir Edward Lewis in the early '70s and built to their specifications, but completed while they were on hiatus and never used by the band until *Long Distance Voyager* (the preceding album, *Octave*, having been recorded in California to accommodate Mike Pinder), before it was destroyed in the wake of Decca's sale to Polygram. In that connection, it was their best sounding album to date, and in just about every way is a happier listening experience than *Octave* was, much as it appears to have been a happier recording experience. While they may steal a page or two from the Electric Light Orchestra's recent playbook, the Moodies are careful to play their game: dreamy, intelligent songs at once sophisticated and simple. Many of these songs rank with the band's best: "The Voice" is a sweeping and majestic call to adventure, while the closing trio from Ray Thomas ("Painted Smile," "Reflective Smile," and "Veteran Cosmic Rocker") forms a skillfully wrought, if sometimes scathing, self-portrait. In between are winning numbers from John Lodge ("Talking Out of Turn," the pink-hued "Nervous") and Graeme Edge ("22,000 Days"), who tries his hand successfully in some philosophizing worthy of ex-member Mike Pinder. Apart from the opening track, Justin Hayward furnishes a pair of romantic ballads, the languid "In My World" (which benefits greatly from a beautiful chorus heavily featuring Ray Thomas' voice), which distantly recalls his *Seventh Sojourn* classic "New Horizons," and the more pop-oriented, beat-driven romantic ballad "Meanwhile." In typical Moodies fashion, these songs provide different perspectives of the same shared lives and observations. "Gemini Dream," which was a big hit in the U.S., does sound dated in today's post-*Xanadu* landscape, but never does the band lose the courage of their convictions. Although the title and the cover art reference the then-recent Voyager space probe (forever burned in the minds of anyone who slogged through the first *Star Trek* movie, but then there's never a brain-burrowing grub around when you need one), only half of the songs have a "voyager" connection if you apply it to touring on the road; apologetic love songs consume the other half. Still, not everything has to be a concept album, especially when the songs go down this smooth. This album should make anybody's short list of Moodies goodies. And, yes, that's Patrick Moraz who makes his debut here in place of original member Mike Pinder.

Dave Connolly & Bruce Eder

Van Morrison

Astral Weeks
November 1968, Warner Bros.

Astral Weeks is generally considered one of the best albums in pop music history. For all that renown, *Astral Weeks* is anything but an archetypal rock & roll album: in fact, it isn't a rock & roll album at all. Employing a mixture of folk,

blues, jazz, and classical music, Van Morrison spins out a series of extended ruminations on his Belfast upbringing, including the remarkable character "Madame George" and the climactic epiphany experienced on "Cyprus Avenue." Accompanying himself on acoustic guitar, Morrison sings in his elastic, bluesy voice, accompanied by a jazz rhythm section (Jay Berliner, guitar, Richard Davis, bass, Connie Kay, drums), plus reeds (John Payne) and vibes (Warren Smith, Jr.), with a string quartet over-

dubbed. An emotional outpouring cast in delicate musical structures, *Astral Weeks* has a unique musical power. Unlike any record before or since, it nevertheless encompasses the passion and tenderness that have always mixed in the best postwar popular music, easily justifying the critics' raves.

William Ruhlmann

Moondance
February 1970, Warner Bros.

The yang to *Astral Weeks*' yin, the brilliant *Moondance* is every bit as much a classic as its predecessor; Van Morrison's first commercially successful solo effort, it retains the previous album's deeply spiritual thrust but transcends its bleak, cathartic intensity to instead explore themes of renewal and redemption. Light, soulful, and jazzy, *Moondance* opens with the sweetly nostalgic "And It Stoned Me," the song's pastoral imagery establishing the dominant lyrical motif recurring throughout the album—virtually every track exults in natural wonder, whether it's the nocturnal magic celebrated by the title cut or the unlimited promise offered in "Brand New Day." At the heart of the record is "Caravan," an incantatory ode to the power of radio; equally stirring is the majestic "Into the Mystic," a song of such elemental beauty and grace as to stand as arguably the quintessential Morrison moment.

Jason Ankeny

His Band and the Street Choir
October 1970, Warner Bros.

After the brilliant one-two punch of *Astral Weeks* and *Moondance*, *His Band and the Street Choir* brings Van Morrison back down to earth, both literally and figuratively. While neither as innovative nor as edgy as its predecessors, *His Band and the Street Choir* also lacks their overt mysticism; at heart, the album is simply Morrison's valentine to the R&B that inspired him, resulting in the muscular and joyous tribute "Domino" as well as the bouncy "Blue Money" and "Call Me Up in Dreamland."

Jason Ankeny

Tupelo Honey
October 1971, Mercury

Tupelo Honey is typical of Van Morrison's early-'70s work in both sound and structure; after dispensing with the requisite hit—here, the buoyant, R&B-inflected "Wild Night"—he truly gets down to business, settling into a luminously pastoral drift typified by the nostalgic "Old Old Woodstock."

conveys just how heartbreaking rock & roll is for the average band. If that wasn't enough, he *trumps* that song with the closer "I Wish I Was Your Mother," a peerless breakup song that still surprises, even after it's familiar. It's a graceful, unexpected way to close a record that stands as one of the best of its era.

Stephen Thomas Erlewine

The Hoople
1974, Columbia

Mott was so good that the sequel, appropriately named *The Hoople*, has been unfairly dismissed as not living up to the group's promise. Yes, it doesn't compare to its predecessor, but most records don't. The bigger problem is that Mick Ralphs chose to leave during the supporting tour for *Mott*, leaving Ian Hunter as the undisputed leader of the group and subtly changing the character of the band's sound. Even with Hunter as the band's main songwriter, Ralphs helped shape their musical direction, so without a collaborator in hand, Hunter was left without a center. So, it isn't surprising that the record seems a little uneven, both in terms of songwriting and sound, but it's hardly without merit. "Roll Away the Stone," a leftover from *Mott*, is first-rate; "Crash Street Kidds" rocks viciously; "The Golden Age of Rock & Roll" is a pleasant spin on Bowie-esque nostalgia (think "Drive-In Saturday"); and Overend Watts follows through on that theme with "Born Late '58," a perfectly credible rocker. This all makes *The Hoople* an entertaining listen, even if it doesn't compare to Mott's earlier masterpieces.

Stephen Thomas Erlewine

Live
1974, Columbia

By 1974, Mott the Hoople was quite possibly the greatest concert band in the world, a blur of high-energy rock, high content poetics, and high camp costuming—Ian Hunter the tough guy in leather and shades; Ariel Bender the street kid, all satin hat flash; Overend Watts, the freakoid in skyscraper thigh boots; and a live show which out-dressed the lot of them. If any band deserved a live album, it was Mott. And if any live album failed to deliver, it was this one. Today, the album's deficiencies seem less severe. Though the band's Bender era remains considerably less well-documented than the earlier Mick Ralphs period, still live material has poured out from a variety of sources, from the *Shades of Ian Hunter* compilation to the *All the Young Dudes* box set, and onto the spring 2001 reissue of Bender's own *Floodgates* solo album (an excellent version of "Here Comes the Queen"). There's even a quasi-legal fan club release for the 1974 *King Biscuit* broadcast which remains the highpoint of the band's live career. *Live*, however, remains the only official document of the glory, and the problems commence on the back cover—a great shot of the band performing "Marionette" on a stage hung with puppets, when the song itself is nowhere in sight. Two shows recorded five months and two continents apart (London's Hammersmith Odeon in December 1973; New York's Uris Theater in May 1974) are highlighted by just seven songs and one medley. The hits "All the Young Dudes" and "All the Way From Memphis," of course, are present, but the remainder of the track list is bizarre to say the least—the ballads "Rest in Peace" and "Rose" were British B-sides only, while "Sucker," "Walking With a Mountain," and "Sweet Angeline" were never much more than filler on their own original albums (*Dudes*, *Mad Shadows*, and *Brain Capers*, respectively). The medley is mightier, spanning both

Mott's own history, and rock & roll's in general—who, after all, would deny the band their own exalted place in the lineage which stretches from "Whole Lotta Shakin'" to "Get Back" and beyond (the uncredited snatch of Bowie's "Jean Genie")? But even here, one cannot help but think more must have happened that night than a breakneck assault on a handful more cuts—and sure enough, it did. The Hammersmith show was the night when the management tried to halt the gig during the closing number, and wound up causing a riot. The liner notes remember it well, but the "Mountain" here was found in New York. It is a great album in its own way, the band are in terrific form, and Bender plays the guitar hero better than anyone else of his entire generation. But Mott gigs, like their albums, were about more than simple snapshots—that was what made the band so important, that's what made their music so memorable. And that's what the fearfully episodic *Live* completely overlooks.

Dave Thompson

Mountain

Climbing!
1970, Columbia/Legacy

Mountain was the combined forces of Leslie West, a gigantic guitarist/ vocalist who had played with New York garage-psych rockers the Vagrants, and Felix Pappalardi. Pappalardi had a slightly more impressive track record, coming from the modern East Coast folk-rock movement (the Youngbloods), before he applied his production skills to Cream. Through this, Felix never really stopped playing and eventually formed Mountain. Often billed as a junior-league version of Cream, *Climbing!*, Mountain's debut, had a lot of things going for it as well. Indeed, West was a changed man from the moment he saw Clapton play, and Pappalardi was able to help him achieve the exact same tone Clapton employed on *Disraeli Gears*. The hit off *Climbing!*, "Mississippi Queen" is a boogie classic, and it paved the way for countless imitators such as J. Geils Band, Foghat, and others. There are a lot of other great tracks here, such as "Never in My Life," which was an FM radio staple at the time.

Matthew Greenwald

Nantucket Sleighride
January 1971, Columbia

Following the success of *Climbing* and appearances at Woodstock and other outdoor festivals of the day, Mountain recorded more of the same for *Nantucket Sleighride*. The title track is a nice mixture of classical leaning intertwined with moderate rock; both "Don't Look Away" and "The Animal Trainer & the Toad" continue on the hard rock path so well worn by this band. Not groundbreaking, but it is well worth listening to.

James Chrispell

The Move

Message from the Country
1971, BGO

By 1971, it was clear that changes were in the offing for the Move. *Message from the Country* shows them carrying their sound, within the context of who they were, about as far as they could. One can hear them hit the limits of what guitars, bass, drums, and keyboards, with lots of harmony overdubs and ornate singing, could do. Indeed, parts of this record sound almost like a dry run from the first *Electric Light Orchestra* album, which was in the planning stages at the time. The influence of the Beatles runs through most of the songs stylistically. In Jeff Lynne's case, it was as though someone had programmed "Paperback Writer" and other chronologically related pop-psychedelic songs by the Beatles into their songwriting and arranging, but the album also shot for a range of sound akin to *The White Album* across the ten songs on this album—except that the members of the Move are obviously working much more closely together. Reduced to a trio and all but wiped out as a live act, they went ahead and generated what was, song for song, their most complex and challenging album. Heard today, it seems charmingly ornate in execution yet also simple in the listening, very basic rock & roll dressed up in the finest raiment that affordable studio time could provide. Despite the obvious jump from the post-psychedelic "Message from the Country" to the driving, delightful "Ella James" and the leap into airy pop-psychedelia on "No Time," not to mention the novelty interlude of "Don't Mess Me Up," there's a sense of unity here, the entire album somehow holding together as something powerful, bracing, and visceral, yet cheerfully trippy. In that sense, it goes *The White Album* one better. Based on its musical merits, it all should have sold the way some ELO albums later did, instead of getting lost in the transition between the histories of the two groups. And 35 years on and counting, it's still essential listening for fans of either the Move or ELO, as well as Roy Wood.

Bruce Eder

Graham Nash

Songs for Beginners
1971, Atlantic

This wonderful album, recorded with help from an all-star crew including David Crosby, Neil Young, Dave Mason, and Rita Coolidge, may not be the best solo record to come out of the CSNY orbit (Neil Young has it beat), but it is the most charming and genial. Like Graham Nash's "Marakesh Express" and "Teach Your Children," it inevitably brings a smile to anyone who hears it. From the soaring "I Used to Be a King" (almost a distant, mature, altered point-of-view sequel to "King Midas in Reverse") through the gossamer

"Simple Man" to the wah-wah-laden "Military Madness," the record is filled with gorgeous melodies, flawless singing, and lyrical complexities that hold up decades later. "Man in the Mirror" is almost Nash's answer to Young's "Nowadays Clancy Can't Even Sing," even containing similar tempo changes; only "Chicago," with its belated telling of one version of the tale of the 1968 Democratic National Convention, seems dated.

Bruce Eder

Nazareth

Razamanaz
1973, A&M

After pursuing a Rolling Stones-styled blend of rock and country elements on their first two albums, Nazareth segued into a harder rocking style with 1973's *Razamanaz*. The resulting album has a lot of energy and drive and much of this can be credited to Roger Glover's production, which tempers the group's tendency to experiment with different musical styles by imposing an overall sound that play's up the group's hard rock edge. The end result is an album that rocks consistently throughout but works in intriguing musical elements to keep things interesting. For instance, "Alcatraz" and "Night Woman" work a glam-styled tribal drum rhythm into the group's sound, and "Vigilante Man" starts out as a straight blues tune but soon mutates into a stomping slice of heavy metal. The most successful experiments come when the group works a country element into their rock attack: "Broken Down Angel" sounds like an early 1970s Rolling Stones track with heavier guitars, and "Bad Bad Boy" sounds like an old rockabilly tune as played by a 1970s hard rock band. Both tunes cleverly mix some effective pop hooks into their stew of hard rock and country elements and became hit singles in England as a result. Other *Razamanaz* highlights include the title track, a furious rocker that became a permanent part of the band's live set list, and "Woke Up This Morning," a heavy blues tune with darkly comic lyrics about a man with terminally bad luck. To sum up, *Razamanaz* is one of the finest albums in the Nazareth catalog and a gem of 1970s hard rock in general.

Donald A. Guarisco

Hair of the Dog
1975, A&M

After slowly but surely building a fanbase around the world with albums like *Razamanaz* and *Loud & Proud*, Nazareth finally hit the big time in 1975 with *Hair of the Dog*. The title track sets the mood for this stark album of hard rock with its combination of relentless guitar riffs, a throbbing, cowbell-driven beat, and an angry vocal from Dan McCafferty that denounces a "heart-breaker, soul-shaker." The end result is a memorably ferocious rocker that has become a staple of hard rock radio stations. The remainder of the album divides its time between similarly pulverizing hard rock fare and some intriguing experiments with the group's sound. In the rocker category, notable tracks include "Miss Misery," a bad romance lament driven by a doomy riff worthy of Black Sabbath, and "Changin' Times," a throbbing hard rock tune driven by a hypnotic, circular-sounding guitar riff. In the experimental category, the big highlight is "Please Don't Judas Me," an epic tune about paranoia that trades heavy metal riffs for a spooky, synthesizer-dominated atmosphere that is further enhanced by some light, Pink Floyd-styled slide guitar work. The American edition of this album also included a surprise hit for the group with their power ballad reinterpretation of the Everly Brothers classic "Love Hurts." However, the album's surprise highlight is a song that bridges the gap between the straight hard rock and experimental songs, "Beggars Day/Rose in Heather"; it starts out as a stomping rocker but smoothly transforms itself midway through into a gentle and spacey instrumental where soaring synthesizer lines support some moody guitar work. All in all, *Hair of the Dog* is the finest album in the Nazareth catalog. It is a necessity for both the group's fans and anyone who loves 1970s hard rock.

Donald A. Guarisco

The Nazz

Nazz
1968, Rhino

Though many of their American peers interpreted the sounds of the British Invasion in different ways, the Nazz's take on jangly guitar pop and nascent heavy psychedelia turned into a blueprint for the American Anglophile power pop guitar bands that followed in the '70s. Which is why the Nazz's eponymous debut album is still a fascinating listen, even if portions of the record haven't dated particularly well. Ironically, one of the songs that hasn't aged well is "Hello, It's Me," a ballad that Todd Rundgren later turned into a contemporary standard. It fails here because its dirgey arrangement meanders—something that can't be said for the rest of *Nazz*. That's not to say that the band knows exactly where they're going, since it often seems like they don't; they just like to try a lot of different styles, cross-breeding their favorite bands in a blatant act of fanboy worship. At their best, the results of this approach are flat-out stunning, as on the lead cut "Open My Eyes," which twists the Who's "I Can't Explain" around until it winds up in Roy Wood territory. While that may be the only undisputed classic on the record, almost everything else on the album will be interesting to listeners that are as obsessive about '60s Brit-rock as the Nazz themselves. It's great to hear Rundgren and lead vocalist Stewkey approximate the high-pitched harmonies of Cream on "Back of Your Mind," or hearing them swing through London on "See What You Can Be." It's possible that some pure pop fans will hear too much Cream and Hendrix on the record, but they're exceptional showpieces for Rundgren's fine guitar. And that's what shines through on *Nazz*—even when the record gets muddled, it's possible to hear the first flowering of Rundgren's talents.

Stephen Thomas Erlewine

Nazz Nazz
1969, Rhino

Originally intended as a double album titled *Fungo Bat*, *Nazz Nazz* is at once as equally diverse and more cohesive than the Nazz's eponymous debut. It's a weird trick, but the group pulls it off, largely due to the rapidly maturing talents of Todd Rundgren, their main songwriter and producer. Throughout the Nazz's first record, he proved that he was a gifted mimic and a savvy melodicist, yet he never quite landed upon a signature style outside of their debut single "Hello It's Me"/"Open My Eyes." Not coincidentally, these were the two songs on the record that the Nazz produced themselves, and they followed that lead on *Nazz Nazz*, fusing their sundry influences into a distinctive psych pop sound. Sonically, it's certainly more ambitious than its predecessor and, apart from the odd forays into soul and blues (filtered through Cream, naturally) on "Featherbedding Lover" and "Kiddie Boy," it's more consistent. In many ways, that makes *Nazz Nazz* a better listen than its predecessor, even if it doesn't have a knockout punch like "Open My Eyes." That's because Rundgren's songs exhibit a stronger sense of identity, as ballads like "Letters Don't Count" and snarky pop-rockers like "Hang On Paul" point the way toward his solo career. There are a few embarrassing detours, such as the hippie-dippy "Meridian Leeward," but the second Nazz record rivals the first because it offers a progression. It shows that the band, or at least Rundgren, have figured out how to blend their influences into something original. The Nazz may never have delivered a follow-up to this—*Nazz III* consists of the remaining sessions from the abandoned double album— but this is certainly ground zero for Rundgren's fascinating solo career.

Stephen Thomas Erlewine

Nazz III
1970, Rhino

Fungo Bat was scrapped for a variety of reasons, among them Todd Rundgren's insistence on singing lead vocals on his newer songs. *Nazz Nazz* was released instead, leaving the second half of the proposed LP temporarily in the vaults. Rundgren left the group before it was released. Taking hold of uncontested leadership of the group, lead vocalist Robert "Stewkey" Antoni erased Rundgren's lead vocals, replacing them with his own and releasing the entire project as *Nazz III*. This is, at the very least, sour grapes, but the situation is made all the more peculiar since most of the material finds Rundgren's songwriting moving toward the signature pop style that dominated his first solo records. Stewkey has publicly stated his distaste for Rundgren's Laura Nyro infatuation, so it's a little odd to hear him sing such finely crafted songs as "Only One Winner" and "Some People." That aside, *Nazz III* is an impressive effort that, if taken in conjunction, would have resulted in a very good double record. Sure, there's some clutter, but such detours as "Loosen Up," a po-faced parody of Archie Bell & the Drells' "Tighten Up," reveal the snotty side of Rundgren's humor. More importantly, the bulk of the record indicates how rapidly he was developing as a songwriter and a producer. Where he proved himself as a gifted mimic on *Nazz*, the group's second two albums found him assimilating those influences and developing a signature style. If anything, *Nazz III* demonstrates that better than its predecessor, which often seemed a little disjointed. There still isn't anything as immediate and indelible as "Open My Eyes," yet the best moments easily provide the road map for Rundgren's solo career. Even if he doesn't sing on it. [Originally released in 1970, *Nazz III* was reissued in 2006 and included bonus tracks.]

Stephen Thomas Erlewine

The New Riders of the Purple Sage

New Riders of the Purple Sage
1971, Columbia

Anyone who en-joyed the Grateful Dead's *Working-man's Dead* or *American Beauty* and wanted more, then or now, should get the New Riders of the Purple Sage's eponymous release and follow it with the Riders' next two albums. With Jerry Garcia and Mickey Hart in tow, and Jefferson Airplane's Spencer Dryden playing what drums Hart didn't, plus Commander Cody at the piano, *New Riders of the Purple Sage* is some of the most spaced-out country-rock of the period. Even ignoring the big names working with John Dawson, David Nelson, and Dave Torbert, however, this is a good record, crossing swords with the Byrds, the Burrito Brothers, and even Crosby, Stills, Nash & Young and holding its own. Maybe a few of the cuts (especially "Henry") are predictable at times, but mostly, *New Riders of the Purple Sage* was full of surprises then (the amazingly sweet, brittle guitars, in particular) and has tunes that have held up well: "Portland Woman," "Whatcha Gon-na Do," "I Don't Know You," and "Louisiana Lady," not to mention the eight leisurely paced minutes of acid-country found in "Dirty Business." There are no added notes, but they'd hardly be vital—the album is an open book.

Bruce Eder

New York Dolls

New York Dolls
1973, Mercury

There are hints of girl group pop and more than a hint of the Rolling Stones, but *The New York Dolls* doesn't really sound like anything that came before it. It's hard rock with a self-conscious wit, a celebration of camp and kitsch that retains a menacing, malevolent edge. The New York Dolls play as if they can barely keep the music from falling apart and David Johansen sings and screams like a man possessed. *The New York Dolls* is a noisy, reckless album that rocks and rolls with a vengeance. The Dolls rework old Chuck Berry and Stones riffs, playing them with a sloppy, violent glee. "Personality Crisis," "Looking for a Kiss," and "Trash" strut with confidence, while "Vietnamese Baby" and "Frankenstein" sound otherworldly, working the same frightening drone over and over again. *The New York Dolls* is the definitive proto-punk album, even more than anything the Stooges released. It plunders history while celebrating it, creating a sleazy urban mythology along the way.

Stephen Thomas Erlewine

Too Much Too Soon
1974, Mercury

After the clatter of their first album failed to bring them a wide audience, the New York Dolls hired producer Shadow Morton to work on the follow-up, *Too Much Too Soon*. The

differences are apparent right from the start of the ferocious opener, "Babylon." Not only are the guitars cleaner, but the mix is dominated by waves of studio sound effects and female backing vocals. Ironically, instead of making the Dolls sound safer, all the added frills emphasize their gleeful sleaziness and reckless sound. The Dolls sound on the verge of falling apart throughout the album, as Johnny Thunders and Syl Sylvain relentlessly trade buzz-saw riffs while David Johansen sings, shouts, and sashays on top of the racket. Band originals—including the bluesy raver "It's Too Late," the noisy girl-group pop of "Puss N' Boots," and the Thunders showcase "Chatterbox"—are rounded out by obscure R&B and rock & roll covers tailor-made for the group. Johansen vamps throughout Leiber & Stoller's "Bad Detective," Archie Bell's "(There's Gonna Be A) Showdown," the Cadets "Stranded in the Jungle," and Sonny Boy Williamson's "Don't Start Me Talkin'," yet it's with grit and affection—he really means it, man! The whole record collapses with the scathing "Human Being," on which a bunch of cross-dressing misfits defiantly declare that it's OK that they want too many things, 'cause they're human beings, just like you and me. Three years later, the Sex Pistols failed to come up with anything as musically visceral and dangerous. Perhaps that's why the Dolls never found their audience in the early '70s: Not only were they punk rock before punk rock was cool, but they remained weirder and more idiosyncratic than any of the bands that followed. And they rocked harder, too.

Stephen Thomas Erlewine

Randy Newman

12 Songs
1970, Reprise

On his debut al-bum, Randy New-man sounded as if he was still getting used to the notion of performing his own songs in the studio (despite years of cutting songwriting dem-os), but apparently he was a pretty quick study, and his second long-player, *12 Songs*, was a striking step forward for Newman as a recording artist. While much of *Randy Newman* was heavily orchestrated, *12 Songs* was cut with a small combo (Ry Cooder and Clarence White take turns on guitar), leaving a lot more room for Newman's Fats Domino-gone-cynical pia-no and the bluesier side of his vocal style, and Randy sounds far more confident and comfortable in this context. And Newman's second batch of songs were even stronger than his first (no small accomplishment), rocking more and grooving harder but losing none of their intelligence and careful craft in the process. "Have You Seen My Baby?" and "Mama Told Me Not to Come" are a pair of sly, updated New Orleans-style rockers (both of which would be much-covered in the coming years); "Let's Burn Down the Cornfield" and "Su-zanne" are subtly ominous tales of love and sex; "Yellow Man" was an early meditation on one of Newman's favorite themes, the absurdity of racial prejudice (which he would also glance at in his straight-but-twisted cover of "Under-neath the Harlem Moon"); and "My Old Kentucky Home" is a hilarious and quite uncharitable look at life in the deep

South (another theme that would pop up in his later work). Newman's humor started getting more acidic with *12 Songs*, but here even his most mordant character studies boast a recognizable humanity, which often make his subjects both pitiable and all the more loathsome. Superb material brilliantly executed, *12 Songs* was Randy Newman's first great album, and is still one of his finest moments on record.

Mark Deming

Sail Away
1972, Reprise

On his third studio album, Randy Newman found a middle ground between the heavily orchestrated pop of his debut and the more stripped-down, rock-oriented approach of *12 Songs*, and managed to bring new strength to both sides of his musical personality in the process. The title track, which Newman has described as a sort of commercial jingle written for slave traders looking to recruit naïve Africans, and "Old Man," in which an elderly man is rejected with feigned compassion by his son, were set to Newman's most evocative arrangements to date and rank with the most intelligent and effective use of a large ensemble by anyone in pop music. On the other end of the scale, "Last Night I Had a Dream" and "You Can Leave Your Hat On" are lean, potent mid-tempo rock tunes, the former featuring some slashing and ominous slide guitar from Ry Cooder, and the latter a witty and willfully perverse bit of erotic absurdity that later became a hit for Joe Cocker (who sounded as if he took the joke at face value). Elsewhere, Newman cynically ponders the perils of a stardom he would never achieve ("Lonely at the Top," originally written for Frank Sinatra), offers a broad and amusing bit of political satire ("Political Science"), and concludes with one of the most bitter rants against religion that anyone committed to vinyl prior to the punk era ("God's Song [That's Why I Love Mankind]"). Whether he's writing for three pieces or 30, Newman makes superb use of the sounds available to him, and his vocals are the model of making the most of a limited instrument. Overall, *Sail Away* is one of Newman's finest works, musically adventurous and displaying a lyrical subtlety that would begin to fade in his subsequent works.

Mark Deming

Good Old Boys
1974, Reprise

Randy Newman's songwriting often walks a narrow line between intelligent satire and willful cruelty, and that line was never finer than on the album *Good Old Boys*. Newman had long displayed a fascination with the American South, and *Good Old Boys* was a song cycle where he gave free reign to his most imaginative (and venomous) thoughts on the subject. The album's scabrous opening cut, "Rednecks," is guaranteed to offend practically anyone with its tale of a slow-witted, willfully (and proudly) ignorant Southerner obsessed with "keeping the n——s down." "A Wedding in Cherokee County" is more polite but hardly less mean-spirited, in which an impotent hick marries a circus freak; if the song's melody and arrangement weren't so skillful, it would be hard to imagine anyone bothering with this musical geek show. But elsewhere, *Good Old Boys* displays a very real compassion for the blighted history of the South, leavened with a knowing wit. "Birmingham" is a funny but humane tale of working-class Alabamians, "Louisiana 1927" and "Kingfish" are intelligent and powerfully evocative tales of the deep South in the depths of the Great Depression, and "Rollin'" is cheerful on the surface and troubling to anyone willing to look beneath it. Musically, Newman dives deep into his influences in Southern soul and also adds potent country accents (with the help of Al Perkins pedal-steel

guitar) while dressing up his songs in typically expert string and horn arrangements. And Newman assumes each character, either brave or foolish, with the skill of a gifted actor, giving even his most loathsome characters enough depth that they're human beings, despite their flaws. *Good Old Boys* is one of Newman's finest albums; it's also one of his most provocative and infuriating, and that's probably just the way he wanted it.

Mark Deming

Trouble in Paradise
1983, Reprise

Randy Newman began the slow process of transforming himself into a polished L.A. song-crafter on the album *Little Criminals*, and with *Trouble in Paradise* the metamorphosis was complete; by this time, Newman could make a record just as ear-pleasing as anything Paul Simon, Don Henley, or Lindsey Buckingham could come up with, and proved it by persuading all three to appear on the sessions. But no matter how polished the arrangements and smooth the production, Newman's songs don't sound like they're ready for radio, and he's too bright not to understand that songs about apartheid, self-pitying white bluesmen, and arrogant yuppies are poor prospects for the pop charts. *Trouble in Paradise* marked the high point of Newman's struggle between pop sheen and his satiric impulses, and the album is a significant improvement over *Little Criminals* and *Born Again*. The targets of Newman's satirical gaze are easy to skewer, and his pen is hardly subtle, but the overall tone is more respectful than on *Born Again* and the results are stronger. The bitter Afrikaner in "Christmas in Capetown" and the egocentric blowhard in "My Life Is Good" have at least *earned* Newman's disgust, and while many of the character studies ("Mikey," "I'm Different") and vignettes ("Miami," "Take Me Back") take a less than charitable view of their protagonists, like the losers and half-wits that populate *Good Old Boys*, they're human beings whose flaws reveal a hint of tragedy. And the closing number, "Song for the Dead," is a stunner in which a soldier explains to the bodies he's burying the purpose behind the war that took their lives. While too slick for Newman's core audience, *Trouble in Paradise* was his most intelligent and best realized work since *Good Old Boys*, and his finest album of the 1980s.

Mark Deming

The Nice

Nice
1969, Columbia

The Nice's third album was their first to break them into the star recording bracket in the U.K., where it reached number three on the charts. Though only measuring six songs in all, it covered a lot of territory, in a rich mixture of psychedelic  rock, jazz, and classical that did a lot to map the format for progressive rock. The extended pretension of some of the numbers, viewed less forgivingly, might also seem like an antecedent to pop/rock. But the studio side of the LP (in its pre-CD incarnation) included one of their best tracks, a cover of Tim Hardin's "Hang on to a Dream," with grand Keith Emerson classical lines and an angelic choir. It also included a reworking of the B-side of their first single in "Azrael Revisited," a slight throwback to the more playful psychedelia of their roots with "Diary of an Empty Day," and the nine-minute "For Example," in which Emerson stretched out his jazz-classical mutations to a fuller length, throwing in a quote from "Norwegian Wood" along the way. More attention was given to the second side of the LP, recorded live at the Fillmore East, with a berserk workout of a number from their debut album, "Rondo" and a 12-minute overhaul of Bob Dylan's "She Belongs to Me."

Richie Unterberger

Stevie Nicks

Bella Donna
1981, Modern

Stevie Nicks' solo career was off to an impressive, if over-due, start with *Bella Donna*, which left no doubt that she could function quite well without the input of her colleagues in Fleetwood Mac (a band she would remain a member of until 1993). The album yielded a number of hits that seemed omnipresent in the '80s, including the moving "Leather and Lace" (which unites Nicks with Don Henley), the poetic "Edge of Seventeen," and her rootsy duet with Tom Petty, "Stop Draggin' My Heart Around." But equally engaging are less exposed tracks like the haunting "After the Glitter Fades." Hit producer Jimmy Iovine wisely avoids over-producing, and keeps things sounding organic on this striking debut.

Alex Henderson

Crystal Visions: The Very Best of Stevie Nicks
March 2007, Reprise / Wea

The first American single-disc Stevie Nicks compilation since 1991's *Timespace*, Reprise's 2007 *Crystal Visions: The Very Best of Stevie Nicks* bests that previous set even if it falls just short of being truly definitive. The problem area lies in the place where it clearly attempts to distinguish itself from its predecessor: the inclusion of Fleetwood Mac songs. Where *Timespace* never attempted to explore this territory, *Crystal Visions* does, but with the exception of "Silver Springs," all of the Mac songs are re-recordings—"Dreams" is performed with Deep Dish, there's a live version of "Rhiannon," and a version of "Landslide" performed live with the Melbourne Symphony. None of these is necessarily bad, but it's hard not to wish that the original versions of these hits were alongside the original versions of "Edge of Seventeen," "I Can't Wait," "Stand Back," "Talk to Me," "Stop Draggin' My Heart Around," and "Leather and Lace," since that would have

resulted in a perfect Nicks retrospective. With the live versions, this merely becomes a near-perfect compilation, representing the scope and range of Nicks' career, as a solo artist, as a member of Fleetwood Mac, and as a duet partner. The big songs from all of her career are here, along with some sharply chosen lesser-known tunes—including a live version of Led Zeppelin's "Rock and Roll" and "Sorcerer"—that, along with good annotation by Nicks (and in the case of the deluxe edition, a DVD of 13 of her videos), help paint a full portrait of Nicks' career so well that it makes it all the more obvious that this compilation needs the originals of all the Mac songs to be perfect, but as it stands, *Crystal Visions* is very good (indeed, it's the best Nicks retrospective assembled to date).

Stephen Thomas Erlewine

Harry Nilsson

Nilsson Schmilsson
November 1971, RCA

Nilsson had a hit, a Grammy, and critical success, yet he still didn't have a genuine blockbuster to his name when it came time to finally deliver a full-fledged follow-up to *Nilsson Sings Newman*, so he decided it was time to make that unabashed, mainstream pop/rock album. Hiring Streisand's producer Richard Perry as a collaborator, Nilsson made a streamlined, slightly domesticated, unashamed set of mature pop/rock, with a slight twist. This is an album, after all, that begins by pining for the reckless days of youth, then segues into a snapshot of suburban disconnectedness before winding through a salute to and covers of old R&B tunes ("Early in the Morning" and "Let the Good Times Roll," respectively), druggie humor ("Coconut"), and surging hard rock ("Jump Into the Fire"). There are certainly hints of the Nilsson of old, particularly in his fondness for Tin Pan Alley and McCartney melodicism—as well as his impish wit—yet he hadn't made a record as cohesive as this since his first time out, nor had he ever made something as shiny and appealing as this. It may be more accessible than expected, yet it's anchored by his mischievous humor and wonderful idiosyncracies. Chances are that those lured in by the grandly melodramatic "Without You" will not be prepared for either the subtle charms of "The Moonbeam Song" or the off-kilter sensibility that makes even his breeziest pop slightly strange. In short, it's a near-perfect summary of everything Nilsson could do; he could be craftier and stranger, but never did he achieve the perfect balance as he did here.

Stephen Thomas Erlewine

Son of Schmilsson
July 1972, RCA

Emboldened by a huge hit and hanging with Lennon and Ringo, Harry Nilsson was ready to let it all go when it came time to record a follow-up to *Nilsson Schmilsson*. The very title of *Son of Schmilsson* implies that it's a de facto sequel to its smash predecessor but, as always with Nilsson, don't take everything at face value. Yes, he's back with producer Richard Perry and he's working from the same gleefully melodic, polished pop/rock territory as before, but this is an incredibly schizoid record, an album by an enormously gifted musician deciding that, since he's already going unhinged, he might as well *indulge* himself while he's at it. And, wow, are the results ever worth it. Opening with a song to a groupie—he sang his balls off, baby, he nearly broke the microphone—and ending with an ode to "The Most Beautiful World in the World," this record careens all over the place, bouncing from one idea to another, punctuated with B-horror movie sound effects, bizarre humor, profanity, and belches. There are song parodies, seemingly straight piano ballads, vulgar hard rock, lovely love songs, and a cheerful singalong with retirees at an old folks home who all proclaim, "I'd rather be dead than wet my bed." The sheer perversity of it all would be fascinating, yet if that's all it had to offer, it'd merely be a curiosity, the way his post-*Pussy Cats* records are. Instead, this is all married to a fantastic set of songs that illustrate what a skilled, versatile songsmith Nilsson was. No, it may not be the easiest album to warm to—and it's just about the weirdest record to reach number 12 and go gold—but if you appreciate Nilsson's musicality and weirdo humor, he never got any better.

Stephen Thomas Erlewine

Pussy Cats
August 1974, Buddha

The relationship between Harry Nilsson and John Lennon is legendary. They were notorious booze hounds and carousers, getting kicked out of clubs for misbehavior and generally terrorizing L.A. during Lennon's "lost weekend" of 1974. They wanted to make an album together—hell, anyone working at such a peak would—and the result was *Pussy Cats*, a Nilsson album produced by Lennon. Almost immediately, Nilsson got sick, resulting in a ruptured vocal cord. Not wanting Lennon to stop the sessions, Nilsson never told his friend, stubbornly working his way through the sessions until he lost his voice entirely. These are the sessions that make up *Pussy Cats*, an utterly bewildering record that's more baffling than entertaining. Like many superstar projects of its time, this is studded with contributions from friends and studio musicians, all intent on having a good time in the studio—which usually means hammering out rock & roll oldies. In this case, it meant both Dylan's "Subterranean Homesick Blues" and the children's song "Loop de Loop," which gives a good idea where Nilsson was at. Through its messiness, *Pussy Cats* winds up showing how he and Lennon violently careened between hedonism and self-loathing. Of the new songs, the inadvertently revealing "All My Life" is the strongest, followed by the sweet "Don't Forget Me," yet this is more about tone than substance. It's about hearing Nilsson's voice getting progressively harsher, as the backing remains appealingly professional and slick. It doesn't quite jibe, and it's certainly incoherent, but that's its charm. It may not be as wild as the lost weekend itself, but it couldn't have been recorded at any other time and remains a fascinating aural snapshot of the early days of 1974.

Stephen Thomas Erlewine

Greatest Hits
March 2002, RCA

Harry Nilsson was always a maverick artist, following his own sense of style down the byways of pop, turning out carefully crafted—even baffling—songs that shared no direct affinity with any other artist of his day. He drew heavily on American Tin Pan Alley traditions, using them to craft his own cracked and ironic view of the human condition, making him, in some ways, a singer stuck out of time. That he had hit records really seems more accidental and circumstantial than by any personal design, and maybe because of that, Nilsson never ended up being simply a musical commodity. This 21-song set has most of his key tracks, including the unique "1941," the deceptively wry "Cuddly Toy," his brilliant cover of Badfinger's "Without You," "One" (a massive hit for Three Dog Night), his wonderfully realized and slightly speeded up rendition of Fred Neil's "Everybody's Talkin'," the infectious "Coconut," and the screaming "Jump into the Fire," making this a perfect single-disc introduction to Nilsson's delicately fractured world.

Steve Leggett

Aldo Nova

Aldo Nova
1981, Portrait

Canadian rock singer/songwriter Aldo Nova doesn't get enough credit (some cynics would say blame) for helping invent the 1980s pop-metal genre, which focused equally on hard rocking anthems and soaring power ballads. *Aldo Nova* appeared in 1982 complete with irresistible melodies and choruses, explosive guitar licks, and huge-sounding drums. It was a full year or more before Def Leppard, Night Ranger, Bon Jovi, and others would latch on to this formula and rocket to stardom. Nova wrote, produced, arranged, and performed his double-platinum debut album by himself, except for drums and some bass guitar and piano parts. Nova is quite proficient on guitar, but his secret weapon is his keyboard and synthesizer prowess. The hit single (and early MTV favorite) "Fantasy" cannot be denied; it's loaded with guitar and keyboard hooks as well as a catchy chorus. "Foolin' Yourself" has a more straightforward pop feel and it was a minor hit. "Ball and Chain" is the best-known power ballad on *Aldo Nova*, but the hypnotic "You're My Love" is better. "Hot Love" is propelled by several guitar solo bursts. "Heart to Heart" and "See the Light" are fast, energetic songs with crisp guitar riffs and swirling synthesizer lines. *Aldo Nova* is a minor classic.

Bret Adams

NRBQ

NRBQ at Yankee Stadium
1978, Mercury

More than just NRBQ's best record, but one of the great records of the '70s (maybe ever!), this album contains the strongest batch of new Q songs on one record, many of them the best and most memorable songs in the band's long and storied career. From the opening track, Terry Adams' herky-jerky "Green Lights," to the rollicking "I Want You Bad," the band has rarely sounded better. The record's gem, however, is an Al Anderson song left over from their previous record (*All Hopped Up on Red Rooster*), "Ridin' in My Car." A song about lost love and blown chances, it has Anderson's characteristic wry sensibility and (non-fatal) heartache, all wrapped up in an ebullient pop package driven by Adams' melodic keyboard riffing and Tom Ardolino's amazingly assertive drumming. *Yankee Stadium* should have been a huge album, but Mercury booted it and never capitalized on the band's fanatical support base. Caveat emptor: when this record was issued by Mercury on CD, they inexplicably left off "Ridin' in My Car."

John Dougan

Kick Me Hard
1979, Rounder

NRBQ's short-lived alliance with Mercury Records resulted in one of the tightest and most consistently rockin' albums of their career, *NRBQ at Yankee Stadium*, but a year later they found themselves back on their own Red Rooster label, where the band relaxed and let their characteristic wit come to the forefront on 1979's *Kick Me Hard*. Opening with a musical look at America's drug laws as only NRBQ could interpret them ("Wacky Tobacky"), *Kick Me Hard* finds the Q indulging their fondness for goofiness on tunes like "It Was an Accident" (romance is complicated by unplanned pregnancy), "Things We Like to Do" (a rewrite of an old Ross Bagdasarian number in which the guys declare their fondness for miniskirts and the TV show *CHiPs*), and "Chores" (in which someone seems to enjoy doing their pig imitation just a bit *too much*). But as always, NRBQ also provides an equal amount of evidence that they're one of the most solid, soulful, and eclectic bands on the planet, running from barrelhouse R&B ("All Night Long"), rootsy rockabilly ("This Old House"), cool jazz ("Tenderly"), and other stuff that simply exists in a world all its own ("Electric Train"), with the band displaying sharp chops and tremendous charm throughout (especially guitarist Al Anderson and keyboard wizard Terry Adams). And as a bonus, you get perhaps the most remarkable version of "North to Alaska" ever captured by modern recording equipment! How can you go wrong? [The 1989 CD reissue of the album tacks on eight bonus cuts, including the free jazz workout "Welcome to Orlando" and "What Can I Say," later covered by Yo La Tengo.]

Mark Deming

Tiddlywinks
1980, Rounder

After being unceremoniously dumped by Mercury after *Yankee Stadium*, NRBQ returned to the warm embrace of Rounder and recorded a string of fine records that started with *Kick Me Hard*. This lineup was to remain intact for nearly 20 years, but here, fairly early on, the synchronicity among the quartet was apparent; it was if they'd been playing together forever, and the music excelled as a result. The songwriting was getting better too: Al, Terry, and Joey were dividing the chores but never losing the group's cohesiveness. At times, Terry's songs would be a little too goofy, and Joey's heartfelt pop might dip into saccharine sweetness now and again, but never so much that it becomes a huge problem. Of these two excellent records, *Kick Me Hard* lives up to its title, especially during the bluesy organ workout "Don't You Know" and the riff-happy "All Night Long" (great solo by Al). *Tiddlywinks* is carried by

"Me and the Boys" (later to be recorded by Bonnie Raitt) and Anderson's beautiful "Never Take the Place of You."

John Dougan

Ted Nugent

Free-for-All
1976, Epic

While Ted Nugent's second solo album, 1976's *Free-for-All*, was another raging slab of rock & roll, it wasn't quite as consistent as his self-titled debut. The main reason was due to singer/rhythm guitarist Derek St. Holmes' departure from the band just as recording of the album began (due to constant grappling with the Nuge about certain musical issues). To solve the problem, producer Tom Werman convinced a then-unknown singer by the name of Meat Loaf to handle the vocal chores on the songs Derek was going to sing. While it seems like a mismatch in theory, the results were not catastrophic—such rockers as "Writing on the Wall" (a virtual rewrite of "Stranglehold"), "Street Rats," and "Hammerdown" are classic Nuge stompers. But they would have been stronger with St. Holmes' contributions, as evidenced by a bonus outtake of "Street Rats" with St. Holmes on vocals and the turbo-charged "Turn It Up." But still, the title track is one of Ted's all-time best (featuring a downright vicious groove), as is the rocking tale about the 1967 Detroit riots, "Dog Eat Dog." Despite St. Holmes' absence (he would return in time for the album's subsequent tour), *Free-for-All* solidified Ted's commercial success, reaching the Top 25. [Note: As with Nugent's other 1999 reissues, an insightful essay on this Ted era by journalist Gary Graff is included, plus bonus tracks.]

Greg Prato

Cat Scratch Fever
1977, Epic

Despite becoming one of the rock's biggest concert attractions, Ted Nugent needed that one album and single that would break through in a big way, and the 1977 album and single of the same name, *Cat Scratch Fever*, did the trick. *Cat Scratch Fever* matched the focused ferocity of Nugent's excellent 1975 debut (due to singer Derek St. Holmes' re-entry into the band), featuring another first-rate set of brash hard rockers. While the title track is a certified classic anthem (the only solo Nugent single to crack the Top 30), other tracks are just as delightful, such as the oh so subtle "Wang Dang Sweet Poontang." Further standouts include such under-rated compositions as "Live It Up," "Workin' Hard, Playin' Hard," and "Out of Control," plus the exquisitely melodic instrumental "Home Bound," which the Beastie Boys would sample on their 1992 mega-hit album *Check Your Head* (the track "The Biz vs. the Nuge"). A Top 20 release, *Cat Scratch Fever* was the last Nugent release to feature his original solo band (St. Holmes, along with bassist Rob Grange, left for good in 1978). And while he enjoyed further chart success with such titles as *Weekend Warriors* and *Double Live Gonzo*, many consider *Cat Scratch Fever* to be Nugent's finest hour. [Note: As with Nugent's other 1999 reissues, an insightful essay on this Nugent era by journalist Gary Graff is included, plus bonus tracks.]

Greg Prato

Double Live Gonzo!
1978, Epic

As exciting as they were, Ted Nugent's first three albums

lacked the sonic punch in the gut of his outrageous live performances, something readily proved by 1978's classic *Double Live Gonzo!* Both Nugent and his band are in top form, yielding a fierce performance of their numerous mid-'70s classics. Mega-hit "Cat Scratch Fever" makes an obligatory appearance, but it's the songs from Nugent's self-titled debut which truly stand out. "Just What the Doctor Ordered" is damn near perfect, and the band really clicks on extended jams through "Motor City Madhouse" and the fantastic "Stranglehold." A consummate showman, Nugent also unleashes a number of hilarious, motormouth stage raps on "Baby Please Don't Go" and "Wang Dang Sweet Poontang" before offering the definitive version of his early classic "Great White Buffalo." In the year of the live album (1978), this one's about as good as they come.

Ed Rivadavia

Laura Nyro

Eli and the Thirteenth Confession
March 1968, Columbia

Nyro peaked early, and *Eli and the Thirteenth Confession*, just her second album, remains her best. It's not only because it contains the original versions of no less than three songs that were big hits for other artists: "Sweet Blindness" (covered by the 5th Dimension), "Stoned Soul Picnic" (also covered by the 5th Dimension), and "Eli's Comin'" (done by Three Dog Night). It's not even just because those three songs are so outstanding. It's because the album as a whole is so outstanding, with its invigorating blend of blue-eyed soul, New York pop, and early confessional singer/songwriting. Nyro sang of love, inscrutably enigmatic romantic daredevils, getting drunk, lonely women, and sensual desire with an infectious *joie de vivre*. The arrangements superbly complemented the material with lively brass, wailing counterpoint backup vocals, and Nyro's own ebullient piano. The 2002 CD reissue adds three previously unreleased demos, with no instrumental accompaniment save piano, of "Lu," "Stoned Soul Picnic," and "Emmie."

Richie Unterberger

Ozzy Osbourne

Blizzard of Ozz
1980, Jet

Ozzy Osbourne's 1981 solo debut *Blizzard of Ozz* was a masterpiece of neo-classical metal that, along with Van Halen's first album, became a cornerstone of '80s metal guitar. Upon its release, there was considerable doubt that Ozzy could become a viable solo attraction. *Blizzard of Ozz* demonstrated not only his ear for melody, but also an unfailing instinct for assembling top-notch backing bands. Onetime Quiet Riot

guitarist Randy Rhoads was a startling discovery, arriving here as a unique, fully formed talent. Rhoads was just as responsible as Osbourne—perhaps even more so—for the album's musical direction, and his application of classical-guitar techniques and scales rewrote the rulebook just as radically as Eddie Van Halen had. Rhoads could hold his own as a flashy soloist, but his detailed, ambitious compositions and arrangements revealed his true depth, as well as creating a sense of doomy, sinister elegance built on Ritchie Blackmore's minor-key innovations. All of this may seem to downplay the importance of Ozzy himself, which shouldn't be the case at all. The music is a thoroughly convincing match for his lyrical obsession with the dark side (which was never an embrace, as many conservative watchdogs assumed); so, despite its collaborative nature, it's unequivocally stamped with Ozzy's personality. What's more, the band is far more versatile and subtle than Sabbath, freeing Ozzy from his habit of singing in unison with the guitar (and proving that he had an excellent grasp of how to frame his limited voice). Nothing short of revelatory, *Blizzard of Ozz* deservedly made Ozzy a star, and it set new standards for musical virtuosity in the realm of heavy metal.

Steve Huey

Diary of a Madman
1981, Jet

The follow-up to the masterful *Blizzard of Ozz*, *Diary of a Madman* was rushed into existence by a band desperate to finish its next album before an upcoming tour. As a result, it doesn't feel quite as fully realized—a couple of the ballads are overly long and slow the momentum, and Randy Rhoads' guide solo on "Little Dolls" was never replaced with a version intended for the public. Yet despite the fact that some songs could have used a longer gestation period, there are numerous moments of brilliance on *Diary of a Madman*—at least half of it stands up to anything on *Blizzard*, and the title track is a jaw-droppingly intricate epic that represents the most classically influenced work of Rhoads' all-too-brief career. But even if parts of the album don't quite live up to the band's previous (and incredibly high) standards, they're by no means bad; moreover, the production is fuller, and the instruments better recorded this time around. It's not uncommon to find fans who prefer *Diary* to *Blizzard*, since it sets an even more mystical, eerie mood, and since Rhoads' playing is progressing to an even higher level. One can only wonder what the Osbourne/Rhoads collaboration might have produced in the future, had Rhoads not been killed in a bizarre and sadly avoidable plane crash.

Steve Huey

The Outlaws

Outlaws
1975, Arista

By the mid-'70s, Southern bands seemed be making a last stand for rock & roll, with two- and three-guitar lineups and not a keyboard in sight. The Outlaws' self-titled debut was released in 1975, a few years after the Allman Brothers Band's greatest glories and a couple of years before the untimely demise of the original Lynyrd Skynyrd. The Outlaws latched onto their Southern heritage by way of Florida, threw in some harmony by way of the Eagles, and then wrote a number of songs that played to their strengths. The result was—and is—a good classic rock & roll album. Several of the Outlaws' best songs are present here, including "There

Goes Another Love Song," "Green Grass and High Tides," and "Song for You." Hughie Thomasson only sings lead on these three songs, but since two of them were the best-known Outlaw songs, it is his voice that is most associated with the band. It's fun to hear cuts like "Song for You" and "Knoxville Girl," which never received a lot of radio play. "Keep Prayin'," sung by Henry Paul and Billy Jones, is a fine piece of Southern boogie with high soaring harmony on the chorus. Although "Green Grass and High Tides" has been played a million and six times on album-oriented rock stations, it nonetheless deserves mention. Created in the tradition of the Allman Brothers Band's "Dreams" and Lynyrd Skynyrd's "Free Bird," the song still sounds fresh in the context of the album, and doesn't feel long at its nearly ten-minute length. The Outlaws' debut blew a fresh blast of rock & roll onto a scene increasingly dominated by synthesizers and dance music. It will leave the listener singing along and dreaming about the good ol' days.

Ronnie Lankford Jr.

Ozark Mountain Daredevils

Time Warp: The Very Best of Ozark Mountain Daredevils
December 2000, A&M

Although it omits three songs from the far less comprehensive (and deleted) 1983 12-track *Best Of*, and doesn't include any live or post-A&M music, this 2000 release stands as the final word on the Ozark Mountain Daredevils' career. Cherry-picking 21 tunes from their five studio album stint circa 1974-1978—with the lion's share coming from their first three albums and only three selections from the final two—this is pretty much all you'll need from the under-recognized band that worked in the '70s country-rock shadows of Poco and Firefall, but weren't as dependable or pop savvy as either. In fact, their biggest hit, the Hall & Oates, blue-eyed soul-styled "Jackie Blue," was so atypical of the band's characteristically down-home approach that it ultimately may have been more damaging to their career than if they had clicked with a song more representative of their crisp, rural country pop/rock. As enjoyable and pleasantly organic as they were, the group lacked a distinctive vocalist, direction, and most importantly great songs. This collection focuses on their less commercially rocking, more rootsy side, and as such it's a consistently listenable, predominantly chronological compilation that is all any but the most die-hard fan will ever need. An extensive essay (including quotes from bandmembers) and rare photos in the disc's 16-page booklet sweeten the pot and make this as definitive an overview from a talented also-ran outfit as necessary. Like its closing title track, the Ozark Mountain Daredevils lived in a stylistic time warp, comfortable within its own limitations and unwilling—but not unable—to break free of them.

Hal Horowitz

Robert Palmer

Sneakin' Sally Through the Alley
1974, Island

Before becoming a slick, sharp-dressed pop star in the 1980s, Robert Palmer was a soul singer deeply rooted in R&B and funk. Those influences are on full display on his debut album *Sneakin' Sally Through the Alley*. With a backing band including members of Little Feat and the Meters, the music has a laid-back groove whether Palmer's covering New Orleans legend Allen Toussaint (the title track) or singing originals ("Hey Julia," "Get Outside"). While the music is tight and solid, it is Robert Palmer's voice that is revelatory—he sounds supremely confident among these talented musicians, and they seem to feed off his vocal intensity. Fans of the Meters or people who want to discover the funky side of Robert Palmer should check this one out.

Vik Iyengar

Pressure Drop
1976, Island

Palmer's own songs (especially the silky "Give Me an Inch" and "Work to Make It Work") and the backing of Little Feat help make this a worthy followup to *Sneakin' Sally Through the Alley*.

William Ruhlmann

Clues
1980, Island

After recording a series of albums that established him as a pop-minded interpreter of soul styles, Robert Palmer surprised fans in 1980 with the stylistic about-face of *Clues*. On this album, he brought his sound into the new wave era by playing up the rock edge to his music, stripping the high-production gloss from his sound, and incorporating synthesizers into the arrangements. The end result became a big hit in the U.K. and paved the way for later international successes like *Riptide* and *Heavy Nova*. *Clues* also produced two notable singles in "Looking for Clues," a clever slice of new wave pop that surprises the listener with an unexpected xylophone solo, and "Johnny and Mary," a moody synth-driven ballad with perceptive lyrics about a doomed romantic relationship. There is also an impressive cover of Gary Numan's "I Dream of Wires" that retains the chilly electronic grandeur of the original while successfully working in an earthier rhythm arrangement that makes the song dance-friendly. Elsewhere, Palmer shows he hasn't abandoned his penchant for soul and ethnic music: "Woke Up Laughing" filters an African-style, chant-like vocal melody through a minimalist electronic production style, and "Found You Now" effectively combines a reggae groove with a deadpan sense of cool that is very "new wave." The end result is a bit short (it clocks in at barely over a half hour), but it remains one of Robert Palmer's strongest and most consistent albums. In short, *Clues* is a must for Robert Palmer fans and worth a spin for anyone into new wave.

Donald A. Guarisco

Riptide
November 1985, Island

Coming on the heels of the massive success of the Power Station, *Riptide* packages Robert Palmer's voice and suave personality into a commercial series of mostly rocking songs that seem custom-tailored to be chart hits. The Power Station connection threatens to overpower Palmer's usually more eclectic musical interest, but with that band's producer/member Bernard Edwards handling production duties and members Andy Taylor and Tony Thompson contributing as well, stylistic similarities were inevitable. "Flesh Wound," though, sounds like a retread of "Some Like It Hot," with its squelching staccato guitars and tribal drums mimicking the hit single. "Hyperactive" adds a bit of a pop veneer to the formula, with its bright keyboards dating the song to the *Miami Vice* era; that's not to say it doesn't hold nostalgic charm. "Addicted to Love" shares some of the same punch, somewhat slowing down the Power Station's bombast into slinkier, blues territory, while maintaining a heavy rock crunch. The song skyrocketed to the top of the U.S. charts and sold more than a million copies as a single worldwide. A music video for the song, featuring sexy models gyrating blankly, no doubt helped sales and launched a new phase of Palmer's career, where music videos would nearly overshadow his songwriting. Equally catchy and almost as successful is the brilliant take on the Jimmy Jam/Terry Lewis song "I Didn't Mean to Turn You On." It is perhaps *Riptide*'s most daring track, with its fractured jittery notes, funky basslines, and pounding drums matching Palmer's bothered, sweaty vocals to create a yearning song that drips with passion. Also not to be missed is Earl King's "Trick Bag," which Palmer translates into a fun *Clues*-style minimalist modern blues song. Even if *Riptide* uses the Power Station as a blueprint, its only true faults reside in the cheesy album-opening and album-closing refrains of "Riptide," which seemingly satisfy Palmer's tropical proclivities. They might be relaxing and humorous as elevator music, but they are sharply at odds with the tone of the album and Palmer's usually impeccable musical taste. Cheesy opening and ending aside, *Riptide* has some truly addictive moments and it set him firmly on course, for better or worse, for the even harder-rocking *Heavy Nova*.

Tim DiGravina

Graham Parker

Howlin' Wind
July 1976, Mercury

For most intents and purposes, Graham Parker emerged fully formed on his debut album, *Howlin' Wind*. Sounding like the bastard offspring of Mick Jagger and Van Morrison, Parker sneers his way through a set of stunningly literate pub rockers. Instead of blindly sticking to the traditions of rock & roll, Parker invigorates them with cynicism and anger, turning his songs into distinctively original works. "Back to Schooldays" may be reconstituted rockabilly, "White Honey" may recall Morrison's white R&B bounce, and "Howlin' Wind" is a cross of Van's more mystical moments and the Band, but the songs themselves are original and terrific. Similarly, producer Nick Lowe gives the album a tough, spare feeling, which makes Parker and the Rumour sound like

one of the best bar bands you've ever heard. *Howlin' Wind* remains a thoroughly invigorating fusion of rock tradition, singer/songwriter skill, and punk spirit, making it one of the classic debuts of all time.

Stephen Thomas Erlewine

Stick to Me
October 1977, Mercury

Graham Parker and the Rumour's third new studio album to be released in 18 months finds the bandleader running short of top-flight material; "Thunder And Rain" and "Watch The Moon Come Down" are up to his usual standards, but songs like "The Heat In Harlem" find him dangerously out of his depth. As a result, although fiercely played, this star-crossed release (it had to be re-recorded when the first version suffered technical problems) is a cut below Parker's first two albums.

William Ruhlmann

Squeezing out Sparks
March 1979, Arista

Generally regarded as Graham Parker's finest album, *Squeezing out Sparks* is a masterful fusion of pub rock classicism, new wave pop, and pure vitriol that makes even his most conventional singer/songwriter numbers bristle with energy. Not only does Parker deliver his best, most consistent set of songs, but he offers more succinct hooks than before—"Local Girls" and "Discovering Japan" are powered by quirky hooks that make them new wave classics. But Parker's new pop inclinations are tempered by his anger, which seethes throughout the hard rockers and even his quieter numbers. Throughout *Squeezing out Sparks*, Graham spits out a litany of offenses that make him feel like an outsider, but he's not a liberal, he's a conservative. The record's two centerpieces—"Passion Is No Ordinary Word" and the anti-abortion "You Can't Be Too Strong"—indicate that his traditionalist musical tendencies are symptomatic of a larger conservative trend. But no one ever said conservatives made poor rock & rollers, and Parker's ruminations over a lost past give him the anger that fuels *Squeezing out Sparks*, one of the great rock records of the post-punk era.

Stephen Thomas Erlewine

The Alan Parsons Project

Tales of Mystery and Imagination
1975, Mercury

Tales of Mystery and Imagination is an extremely mesmerizing aural journey through some of Edgar Allan Poe's most renowned works. With the use of synthesizers, drums, guitar, and even a glockenspiel, Parsons' shivering effects make way for an eerie excursion into Poe's well-known classics. The instrumental "Dream

Within a Dream" has Orson Welles narrating in front of this wispy collaboration of guitars and keyboards. The EMI vocoder is used throughout "The Raven" with the Westminister City School Boys Choir mixed in to add a distinct flair to it's chamber-like sound. Parsons' expertise surrounds this album, from the slyness that prevails in "(The System Of) Doctor Tarr and Professor Feather" to the bodeful thumping of the drums that imitate a heartbeat on "The Tell-Tale Heart." "The Fall of the House of Usher" is a lengthy but dazzling array of musicianship that keeps the album's persona in tact, while enabling the listener to submerge into it's frightening atmosphere. With vocalists Terry Sylvester, John Miles, and Eric Woolfson stretched across each track, this variety of different singing styles adds color and design to the album's air. Without any underlying theme to be pondered upon, Alan Parsons instead paints a vivid picture of one of the most alluring literary figures in history by musically reciting his most famous works in expert fashion.

Mike DeGagne

I Robot
June 1977, Arista

Alan Parsons delivered a detailed blueprint for his Project on their 1975 debut, *Tales of Mystery and Imagination*, but it was on its 1977 follow-up, *I Robot*, that the outfit reached its true potential. Borrowing not just its title but concept from Isaac Asimov's classic sci-fi Robot trilogy, this album explores many of the philosophies regarding artificial intelligence—will it overtake man, what does it mean to be man, what responsibilities do mechanical beings have to their creators, and so on and so forth—with enough knotty intelligence to make it a seminal text of late-'70s geeks, and while it is also true that appreciating *I Robot* does require a love of either sci-fi or art rock, it is also true that sci-fi art rock never came any better than this. Compare it to Jeff Wayne's *War of the Worlds*, released just a year after this and demonstrating some clear influence from Parsons: that flirts voraciously with camp, but this, for all of its pomp and circumstance, for all of its overblown arrangements, this is music that's played deadly serious. Even when the vocal choirs pile up at the end of "Breakdown" or when the Project delves into some tight, glossy white funk on "The Voice," complete with punctuations from robotic voices and whining slide guitars, there isn't much sense of fun, but there is a sense of mystery and a sense of drama that can be very absorbing if you're prepared to give yourself over to it. The most fascinating thing about the album is that the music is restless, shifting from mood to mood within the course of a song, but unlike some art pop there is attention paid to hooks—most notably, of course, on the hit "I Wouldn't Want to Be Like You," a tense, paranoid neo-disco rocker that was the APP's breakthrough. It's also the closest thing to a concise pop song here—other tunes have plenty of hooks, but they change their tempo and feel quickly, which is what makes this an art rock album instead of a pop album. And while that may not snare in listeners who love the hit (they should turn to *Eye in the Sky* instead, the Project's one true pop album), that sense of melody when married to the artistic restlessness and geeky sensibility makes for a unique, compelling album

and the one record that truly captures mind and spirit of the Alan Parsons Project.

Stephen Thomas Erlewine

The Turn of a Friendly Card
November 1980, Arista

With two of the Alan Parsons Project's best songs, the lovely ballad "Time" and the wavy-sounding "Games People Play," *The Turn of a Friendly Card* remains one of this group's most enjoyable albums. Parsons' idea, the subject of the album's six tracks, centers around the age-old temptation of gambling and its stranglehold on the human psyche. On "Games People Play," vocalist Lenny Zakatek sounds compelling and focused, giving the song a seriousness that aids in realization of the album's concept. With "Time," it is Eric Woolfson who carries this luxurious-sounding ode to life's passing to a place above and beyond any of this band's other slower material. The breakdown of human willpower and our greedy tendencies are highlighted in the last track, entitled "The Turn of a Friendly Card," which is broken into five separate parts. "Snake Eyes," sung by Chris Rainbow, is the most compelling of the five pieces, and ties together the whole of the recording. As in every Parsons album, an instrumental is included, in this case an interesting number aptly titled "The Gold Bug." Like most of the band's instrumentals, its flow and rhythm simulate the overall tempo and concept of the album, acting as a welcome interlude. Although short, *The Turn of a Friendly Card* is to the point and doesn't let down when it comes to carrying out its idea.

Mike DeGagne

Eye in the Sky
June 1982, Arista

Eye in the Sky provided the Alan Parsons Project with their first Top Ten hit since 1977's *I Robot*, and it's hard not to feel that crossover success was one of the driving forces behind this album. The Project never shied away from hooks, whether it was on the tense white funk of "I Wouldn't Want to Be Like You" or the gleaming pop hooks of "Games People Play," but *Eye in the Sky* was soft and smooth, so smooth that it was easy to ignore that the narrator of the title track was an ominous omniscient who spied either on his lover or his populace, depending on how deeply you wanted to delve into the concepts of this album. And, unlike *I Robot* or *The Turn of a Friendly Card*, it is possible to listen to *Eye in the Sky* and not dwell on the larger themes, since they're used as a foundation, not pushed to center stage. What does dominate is the lushness of sound, the sweetness of melody: this is a soft rock album through and through, one that's about melodic hooks and texture. In the case of the spacy opening salvo "Sirius," later heard on sports talk shows across America, or "Mammagamma," it was all texture, as these instrumentals set the trippy yet warm mood that the pop songs sustained. And the real difference with *Eye in the Sky* is that, with the exception of those instrumentals and the galloping suite "Silence and I," all the artiness was part of the idea of this album was pushed into the lyrics, so the album plays as soft pop album—and a very, very good one at that. Perhaps nothing is quite as exquisite as the title song, yet "Children of the Moon" has a sprightly gait (not all that dissimilar from Kenny Loggins' "Heart to Heart"), "Psychobabble" has a bright propulsive edge (not all that dissimilar from 10cc), and "Gemini" is the project at its dreamiest. It all adds up to arguably the most consistent Alan Parsons Project album—perhaps not in terms of concept, but in terms of music they never were as satisfying as they were here.

Stephen Thomas Erlewine

Gram Parsons

G.P.
1972, Reprise

Given Gram Parsons' habit of taking control of the bands he played with (and his disinclination towards staying with them for very long), it was inevitable that he would eventually strike out on his own, and his first solo album, 1973's *G.P.*, is probably the best realized expression of his musical personality. Working with a crack band of L.A. and Nashville's finest (including James Burton on guitar, Ronnie Tutt on drums, Byron Berline on fiddle, and Glen D. Hardin on piano), he drew from them a sound that merged breezy confidence with deeply felt Southern soul, and he in turn pulled off some of his most subtle and finely detailed vocal performances; "She" and "A Song for You," in particular, are masterful examples of passion finding balance with understatement. Parsons also discovered that rare artist with whom he can be said to have genuinely collaborated (rather than played beside), Emmylou Harris; Gram and Harris' spot-on harmonies and exchanged verses on "We'll Sweep out the Ashes in the Morning" and "That's All It Took" are achingly beautiful and instantly established her as one country music's most gifted vocalists. On *G.P.*, Parsons' ambitious vision encompassed hard-country weepers, wistful ballads, up-tempo dance tunes, and even horn-driven rhythm and blues. He managed to make them all work, both as individual tunes and as a unified whole. If it falls just short of being his greatest work (an honor that goes to The Flying Burrito Bothers' *The Gilded Palace of Sin*) thanks to a couple songs that are a bit too oblique for their own good ("The New Soft Shoe" may be beautiful, but who knows just what it's supposed to be about), this album remains one that is hauntingly and has only gotten better with the passing years.

Mark Deming

Grievous Angel
1973, Reprise

Gram Parsons fondness for drugs and high living are said to have been catching up with him while he was recording *Grievous Angel*, and sadly he wouldn't live long enough to see it reach record stores, dying from a drug overdose in the fall of 1973. This album is a less ambitious and unified set than his solo debut, but that's to say that *G.P.* was a great album while *Grievous Angel* was instead a very, very good one. Much of the same band that played on his solo debut were brought back for this set, and they perform with the same effortless grace and authority (especially guitarist James Burton and fiddler Byron Berline). If Parsons was slowing down a bit as a songwriter, he still had plenty of gems on hand from more productive days, such as "Brass Buttons" and "Hickory Wind" (which wasn't *really* recorded live in Northern Quebec; that's just Gram and the band ripping it up live in the studio, with a handful of friends whooping it up to create honky-tonk atmosphere). He also proved to be a shrewd judge of other folks material as always; Tom T. Hall's "I Can't Dance" is a strong barroom rocker, and everyone

seems to be having a great time on The Louvin Brothers's "Cash on the Barrelhead." As a vocal duo, Parsons and Emmylou Harris only improved on this set, turning in a version of "Love Hurts" so quietly impassioned and delicately beautiful that it's enough to make you forget Roy Orbison ever recorded it. And while he didn't plan on it, Parsons could hardly have picked a better closing gesture than "In My Hour of Darkness." *Grievous Angel* may not have been the finest work of his career, but one would be hard pressed to name an artist who made an album this strong only a few weeks before their death—or at any time of their life, for that matter.

Mark Deming

Sacred Hearts and Fallen Angels: The Gram Parsons Anthology
May 2001, Rhino

Gram Parsons' legend is so great that it's easy for the neophyte to be skeptical about his music, wondering if it really is deserving of such effusive praise. Simply put, it is, and if you question the veracity of that statement, turn to Rhino's peerless double-disc set, *Sacred Hearts and Fallen Angels: The Gram Parsons Anthology*. This is the first truly comprehensive overview of Parsons' work, running from the International Submarine Band, through the Byrds, to the Flying Burrito Brothers and his two solo albums, scattering appropriate rarities or non-LP tracks along the way. This is no small feat, since it depends on extensive cross-licensing between record labels, plus concentration from the compilers, who won't allow personal biases to get in the way of telling the story. Miraculously, this happens, and the result is a lean, yet thorough, utterly addictive set that summarizes the brilliance of Gram Parsons, capturing his magnificent songwriting abilities and how he made country sound like rock & roll, while giving rock a sense of country's history. It's possible to complain about the handful of omissions— "Break My Mind" is one of the greatest recordings he did with the Byrds, the version of "Do You Know How It Feels" is better with the Burritos, the barroom anthems of his solo records ("Cry One More Time," "Big Mouth Blues," "I Can't Dance," "Cash on the Barrellhead") gave the weepers context—but this still hits every major point. After all, counting the early version of "Do You Know," only two songs are missing from *The Gilded Palace of Sin* and only four songs are missing from the two-fer of *GP*/*Grievous Angel*, *plus* this has the best of the ISB, Byrds, and songs that didn't make the solo album. So, even if there may be a personal favorite or two missing, *nothing* major is missing, which means this is a perfect, irresistible summation of Parsons' career, containing every great moment from all of his bands. His genius has never seemed purer than it does here, since it conveys the true scope of his talents and his career. If you are a fan of Parsons, this isn't necessary, even if it is an excellent listen (there's only one unreleased track, the ISB's "Knee Deep in the Blues"). If you haven't fallen in love with him, skip every other disc— this is what you need. Once you hear it, there's no way that you won't become a life-long fan.

Stephen Thomas Erlewine

Joe Perry Project

Let the Music Do the Talking
1980, Columbia

Joe Perry split from Aerosmith under less than favorable circumstances in 1979, directly assembling a solo band, the

Joe Perry Project (with Ralph Mormon [vocals], David Hull [bass], and Ronnie Stewart [drums]), which soon released its first album, 1980's *Let the Music Do the Talking*. Unlike his former band, which would now take excessive amounts of time to record albums that should have been cranked out quickly, *L.T.M.D.T.T.* recalled the brash and trashy appeal of early Aerosmith. Maybe because he wanted to show his former bandmates that he could succeed without them, the performances were extremely inspired, while the songwriting was sharp and focused. The anthemic title track was aimed at all the in-press bickering that was going on at the time between Aerosmith and Perry. While subsequent Perry Project albums didn't contain many Perry lead vocal spots, the singing on the debut is split 50/50 between Perry and Mormon. Tracks such as "Conflict of Interest," "Discount Dogs," "Shooting Star," and "Rocking Train" were all up-tempo highlights, and the instrumental "Break Song" showed off the fantastic interplay between the new band, while "The Mist Is Rising" was more low-key. A truly great and underrated record, *Let the Music Do the Talking* could have been a classic Aerosmith release if the drugs hadn't split the band apart.

Greg Prato

Tom Petty & the Heartbreakers

Tom Petty & the Heartbreakers
1976, Gone Gator/MCA

At the time Tom Petty & the Heartbreakers' debut was released in 1976, they were fresh enough to almost be considered punk. They weren't as reckless or visionary as the Ramones, but they shared a similar love for pure '60s rock and, for the Heartbreakers, that meant embracing the Byrds as much as the Stones. And that's pretty much what this album is—tuneful jangle balanced by a tough garage swagger. At times, the attitude and the sound override the songwriting, but that's alright, since the slight songs ("Anything That's Rock 'n' Roll," to pick a random example) are still infused with spirit and an appealing surface. Petty & the Heartbreakers feel underground on this album, at least to the extent that power pop was underground in 1976; with Dwight Twilley providing backing vocals for "Strangered in the Night," the similarities between the two bands (adherence to pop hooks and melodies, love of guitars) become apparent. Petty wound up eclipsing Twilley because he rocked harder, something that's evident throughout this record. Take that "American Girl"—it's a Byrds song by any other name, but he pushed the Heartbreakers to treat it as a rock & roll song, not as something delicate. There are times where the album starts to drift, especially on the second side, but the highlights—"Rockin' Around (With You)," "Hometown Blues," "The Wild One, Forever," the AOR staples "Breakdown" and "American Girl"—still illustrate how refreshing Petty & the Heartbreakers sounded in 1976.

Stephen Thomas Erlewine

You're Gonna Get It!
May 1978, Gone Gator/MCA

Tom Petty & the Heartbreakers didn't really knock out their second album—it was released two years after their debut—but it sure sounds as if they did. There are some wonderful moments on this record, but it often feels like leftovers from a strong debut, or an album written on the road, especially since the music is simply an extension of the first album. That said, when *You're Gonna Get It!* works, it devastates. That's not saying that "When the Time Comes" is a masterpiece, even if it's a fine opener, but it does mean that "I Need to Know" and the scathing "Listen to Her Heart" are testaments to how good this band could be when it was focused. If the rest of the album doesn't achieve this level of perfection, that's a signal that they were still finding their footing, but overall it's still a solid record, filled with good performances that are never quite as good as the songs. It's pretty good as it spins, but once it finishes, you remember those two songs at the heart of the record, maybe the opener and closer, which are stronger than the rest of the competent, enjoyable, yet unremarkable roots-rockers that surround them. Not necessarily a transitional effort—after all, it pretty much mirrors its predecessor—but a holding pattern that may not suggest the peaks of what's to come, but still delivers a good soundalike of the debut.

Stephen Thomas Erlewine

Damn the Torpedoes
November 1979, MCA

Not long after *You're Gonna Get It*, Tom Petty & the Heartbreakers' label, Shelter, was sold to MCA Records. Petty struggled to free himself from the major label, eventually sending himself into bankruptcy. He settled with MCA and set to work on his third album, digging out some old Mudcrutch numbers and quickly writing new songs. Amazingly, through all the frustration and anguish, Petty & the Heartbreakers delivered their breakthrough and arguably their masterpiece with *Damn the Torpedoes*. Musically, it follows through on the promise of their first two albums, offering a tough, streamlined fusion of the Stones and Byrds that, thanks to Jimmy Iovine's clean production, sounded utterly modern yet timeless. It helped that the Heartbreakers had turned into a tighter, muscular outfit, reminiscent of, well, the Stones in their prime—all of the parts combine into a powerful, distinctive sound capable of all sorts of subtle variations. Their musical suppleness helps bring out the soul in Petty's impressive set of songs. He had written a few classics before—"American Girl," "Listen to Her Heart"—but here his songwriting truly blossoms. Most of the songs have a deep melancholy undercurrent—the tough "Here Comes My Girl" and "Even the Losers" have tender hearts; the infectious "Don't Do Me Like That" masks a painful relationship; "Refugee" is a scornful, blistering rocker; "Louisiana Rain" is a tear-jerking ballad. Yet there are purpose and passion behind the performances that makes *Damn the Torpedoes* an invigorating listen all the same. Few mainstream rock albums of the late '70s and early '80s were quite as strong as this, and it still stands as one of the great records of the album rock era.

Stephen Thomas Erlewine

Hard Promises
May 1981, MCA

Damn the Torpedoes wasn't simply a culmination of Tom Petty's art; it happened to be a huge success, enabling him to call the shots on its successor, *Hard Promises*. Infamously, he used his first album as a star to challenge the record industry's practice of charging more for A-list artists, demanding that *Hard Promises* should be listed for less than most records by an artist of his stature, but if that was the only thing notable about the album, it would have disappeared like *Long After Dark*. Instead, it offered a reaffirmation that *Damn the Torpedoes* wasn't a fluke. There's not much new on the surface, since

it continues the sound of its predecessor, but it's filled with great songwriting, something that's as difficult to achieve as a distinctive sound. The opener, "The Waiting," became the best-known song on the record, but there's no discounting "A Woman in Love (It's Not Me)," "Nightwatchman," "Kings Road," "Insider," and "The Criminal Kind," album tracks that would become fan favorites. If *Hard Promises* doesn't have the sweep of *Damn the Torpedoes*, that's because its predecessor was blessed with good timing and an unusually strong set of songs. *Hard Promises* isn't quite so epochal, yet it has a tremendous set of songs and a unified sound that makes it one of Petty's finest records.

Stephen Thomas Erlewine

Long After Dark
November 1982, MCA

Riding high on the back-to-back Top Five, platinum hits *Damn the Torpedoes* and *Hard Promises*, Tom Petty quickly returned to the studio to record the Heartbreakers' fifth album, *Long After Dark*. Truth be told, there was about as long a gap between *Dark* and *Promises* as there was between *Promises* and *Torpedoes*, but there was a difference this time around—Petty & the Heartbreakers sounded tired. Even if there are a few new wave flourishes here and there, the band hasn't really changed its style at all—it's still Stonesy, Byrdsian heartland rock. As their first four albums illustrated, that isn't a problem in itself, since they've found numerous variations within their signature sound, providing they have the right songs. Unfortunately, Petty had a dry spell on *Long After Dark*. With its swirling, minor key guitars, "You Got Lucky" is a classic and "Change of Heart" comes close to matching those peaks, but the remaining songs rarely rise above agreeable filler. Since the Heartbreakers are a very good band, it means the record sounds pretty good as it's playing, but apart from those few highlights, nothing much is memorable once the album has finished. And coming on the heels of two excellent records, that's quite a disappointment.

Stephen Thomas Erlewine

Let Me Up (I've Had Enough)
April 1987, MCA

Tom Petty & the Heartbreakers spent much of 1986 on the road as Bob Dylan's backing band. Dylan's presence proved to be a huge influence on the Heartbreakers, turning them away from the well-intentioned but slick pretensions of *Southern Accents* and toward a loose, charmingly ramshackle roots rock that harked back to their roots yet exhibited the professional eclecticism they developed during the mid-'80s. All of this was on full display on *Let Me Up (I've Had Enough)*, their simplest and best album since *Hard Promises*. Not to say that *Let Me Up* is a perfect album—far from it, actually. Filled with loose ends, song fragments, and

unvarnished productions, it's a defiantly messy album, and it's all the better for it, especially arriving on the heels of the well-groomed *Accents*. Apart from the (slightly dated) rant "Jammin' Me'" (co-written by Dylan, but you can't tell), there aren't any standouts on the record, but there's no filler either—it's just simply a good collection of ballads ("Runaway Trains"), country-rockers ("The Damage You've Done"), pop/rock ("All Mixed Up," "Think About Me"), and hard rockers ("Let Me Up [I've Had Enough]"). While that might not be enough to qualify *Let Me Up* as one of Petty & the Heartbreakers' masterpieces, it is enough to qualify it as the most underrated record in their catalog.

Stephen Thomas Erlewine

Full Moon Fever
April 1989, MCA

Although *Let Me Up (I've Had Enough)* found the Heartbreakers regaining their strength as a band and discovering a newfound ease at songcraft, it just didn't sell that well. Perhaps that factor, along with road fatigue, led Tom Petty to record his first solo album, *Full Moon Fever*. Nevertheless, the distinction between "solo" and "Heartbreakers" is a fuzzy one because *Full Moon Fever* is essentially in the same style as the Heartbreakers albums; Mike Campbell co-wrote two songs and co-produced the record, and he, along with Benmont Tench and Howie Epstein, all play on the album. However, the album sounds different from any Heartbreakers record due to the presence of former Electric Light Orchestra leader Jeff Lynne. Petty co-wrote the lion's share of the album with Lynne, who also is the record's main producer. In his hands, Petty's roots rock becomes clean and glossy, layered with shimmering vocal harmonies, keyboards, and acoustic guitars. It's a friendly, radio-ready sound, and if it has dated somewhat over the years, the craft is still admirable and appealing. But the real reason *Full Moon Fever* became Petty's biggest hit is that it boasted a selection of songs that rivaled *Damn the Torpedoes*. *Full Moon Fever* didn't have a weak track; even if a few weren't quite as strong as others, the album was filled with highlights: "I Won't Back Down," the wistful "A Face in the Crowd," the rockabilly throwaways "Yer So Bad" and "A Mind With a Heart of Its Own," the Byrds cover "Feel a Whole Lot Better," the charging "Runnin' Down a Dream," and "Free Fallin'," a coming-of-age ballad that could be Petty's best song. *Full Moon Fever* might have been meant as an off-the-cuff detour, but it turned into a minor masterpiece.

Stephen Thomas Erlewine

Pink Floyd

The Piper at the Gates of Dawn
August 1967, Capitol

The title of Pink Floyd's debut album is taken from a chapter in Syd Barrett's favorite children's book, *The Wind in the Willows*, and the lyrical imagery of *The Piper at the Gates of Dawn* is indeed full of colorful, childlike, distinctly British whimsy, albeit filtered through the perceptive lens of LSD. Barrett's catchy, melodic acid pop songs are balanced with longer, more experimental pieces showcasing the group's instrumental freak-outs, often using themes of space travel as metaphors for hallucinogenic experiences—"Astronomy Domine" is a poppier number in this vein, but tracks like "Interstellar Overdrive" are some of the earliest forays into what has been tagged space rock. But even though Barrett's lyrics and melodies are mostly playful and humorous, the band's music doesn't always bear out those sentiments—in addition to Rick Wright's eerie organ work, dissonance, chromaticism, weird noises, and vocal sound effects are all employed at various instances, giving the impression of chaos and confusion lurking beneath the bright surface. *The Piper at the Gates of Dawn* successfully captures both sides of psychedelic experimentation—the pleasures of expanding one's mind and perception, and an underlying threat of mental disorder and even lunacy; this duality makes *Piper* all the more compelling in light of Barrett's subsequent breakdown, and ranks it as one of the best psychedelic albums of all time.

Steve Huey

A Saucerful of Secrets
June 1968, Capitol

A transitional album on which the band moved from Syd Barrett's relatively concise and vivid songs to spacy, ethereal material with lengthy instrumental passages. Barrett's influence is still felt (he actually did manage to contribute one track, the jovial "Jugband Blues"), and much of the material retains a gentle, fairy-tale ambience. "Remember a Day" and "See Saw" are highlights; on "Set the Controls for the Heart of the Sun," "Let There Be More Light," and the lengthy instrumental title track, the band begin to map out the dark and repetitive pulses that would characterize their next few records.

Richie Unterberger

Ummagumma
October 1969, Capitol

For many years, this double LP/CD was one of the most popular albums in Pink Floyd's pre-*Dark Side of the Moon* output, containing a live disc and a studio disc all for the price of one (in the LP version). The live set, recorded in Birmingham and Manchester in June 1969, is limited to four numbers, all drawn from the group's first two LPs or their then recent singles. Featuring the band's second lineup (i.e., no Syd Barrett), the set shows off a very potent group, their sound held together on-stage by Nick Mason's assertive drumming and Roger Waters' powerful bass work, which keep the proceedings moving no matter how spaced out the music gets; they also sound like they've got the amplifiers to make their music count, which is more than the early band had. "Astronomy Domine," "Careful With That Axe Eugene," "Set the Controls for the Heart of the Sun," and "A Saucerful of Secrets" are all superior here to their studio originals, done longer, louder, and harder, with a real edge to the playing. The studio disc was more experimental, each member getting a certain amount of space on the record to make his own music—Richard Wright's "Sysyphus" was a pure keyboard work, featuring various synthesizers, organs, and pianos; David Gilmour's "The Narrow Way" was a three-part instrumental for acoustic and electric guitars and electronic keyboards; and Nick Mason's "The Grand Vizier's Garden Party" made use of a vast range of acoustic and electric percussion devices. Roger Waters' "Grantchester Meadows" was a lyrical folk-like number unlike almost anything else the group ever did. In 1994 the album was remastered and reissued in a green

slipcase, in a version a lot louder and sharper (and cheaper) than the original CD release.

Bruce Eder

Atom Heart Mother
October 1970, Capitol

Appearing after the sprawling, unfocused double-album set *Ummagumma*, *Atom Heart Mother* may boast more focus, even a concept, yet that doesn't mean it's more accessible. If anything, this is the most impenetrable album Pink Floyd released while on Harvest, which also makes it one of the most interesting of the era. Still, it may be an acquired taste even for fans, especially since it kicks off with a side-long, 23-minute extended orchestral piece that may not seem to head anywhere, but is often intriguing, more in what it suggests than what it achieves. Then, on the second side, Roger Waters, David Gilmour, and Rick Wright have a song apiece, winding up with the group composition "Alan's Psychedelic Breakfast" wrapping it up. Of these, Waters begins developing the voice that made him the group's lead songwriter during their classic era with "If," while Wright has an appealingly mannered, very English psychedelic fantasia on "Summer 68," and Gilmour's "Fat Old Sun" meanders quietly before ending with a guitar workout that leaves no impression. "Alan's Psychedelic Breakfast," the 12-minute opus that ends the album, does the same thing, floating for several minutes before ending on a drawn-out jam that finally gets the piece moving. So, there are interesting moments scattered throughout the record, and the work that initially seems so impenetrable winds up being *Atom Heart Mother*'s strongest moment. That it lasts an entire side illustrates that Pink Floyd was getting better with the larger picture instead of the details, since the second side just winds up falling off the tracks, no matter how many good moments there are. This lack of focus means *Atom Heart Mother* will largely be for cultists, but its unevenness means there's also a lot to cherish here.

Stephen Thomas Erlewine

Relics
May 1971, Capitol

Since *Relics* is a compilation and not a regular studio album, it tends to be overlooked when thought of as one of Pink Floyd's better releases. It might not be regarded as a classic psychedelic masterpiece in the manner of *The Piper at the Gates of Dawn*, and it certainly won't ever achieve the multiple platinum status of *Dark Side of the Moon*, but it's a pretty good place to start with the band's early catalog. Originally issued in 1971, *Relics* culls from the band's first five singles (two A-sides and three B-sides, including the non-album pop classics "See Emily Play" and "Arnold Layne") and picks album material that capitalizes on the band's versatility while making it a thoroughly palatable listen. From *Piper*, you get the goofy childishness of "Bike" and the mesmerizing "Interstellar Overdrive," one of the band's trademark instrumental freak-outs; "The Nile Song," taken from the *More* soundtrack, is one of the heaviest songs the band recorded.

A little bit of everything that made early Pink Floyd can be found here. Without a doubt, the disc is an essential part of the band's discography, not to be disregarded in lieu of its overlap with studio album material.

Andy Kellman

Meddle
November 1971, Capitol

Atom Heart Mother, for all its glories, was an acquired taste, and Pink Floyd wisely decided to trim back its orchestral excesses for its follow-up, *Meddle*. Opening with a deliberately surging "One of These Days," *Meddle* spends most of its time with sonic textures and elongated compositions, most notably on its epic closer, "Echoes." If there aren't pop songs in the classic sense (even on the level of the group's contributions to *Ummagumma*), there is a uniform tone, ranging from the pastoral "A Pillow of Winds" to "Fearless," with its insistent refrain hinting at latter-day Floyd. Pink Floyd were nothing if not masters of texture, and *Meddle* is one of their greatest excursions into little details, pointing the way to the measured brilliance of *Dark Side of the Moon* and the entire Roger Waters era. Here, David Gilmour exerts a slightly larger influence, at least based on lead vocals, but it's not all sweetness and light—even if its lilting rhythms are welcome, "San Tropez" feels out of place with the rest of *Meddle*. Still, the album is one of the Floyd's most consistent explorations of mood, especially from their time at Harvest, and it stands as the strongest record they released between Syd's departure and *Dark Side*.

Stephen Thomas Erlewine

The Dark Side of the Moon
March 1973, Capitol

By condensing the sonic explorations of *Meddle* to actual songs and adding a lush, immaculate production to their trippiest instrumental sections, Pink Floyd inadvertently designed their commercial breakthrough with *Dark Side of the Moon*. The primary revelation of *Dark Side of the Moon* is what a little focus does for the band. Roger Waters wrote a series of songs about mundane, everyday details which aren't that impressive by themselves, but when given the sonic backdrop of Floyd's slow, atmospheric soundscapes and carefully placed sound effects, they achieve an emotional resonance. But what gives the album true power is the subtly textured music, which evolves from ponderous, neo-psychedelic art rock to jazz fusion and blues-rock before turning back to psychedelia. It's dense with detail, but leisurely paced, creating its own dark, haunting world. Pink Floyd may have better albums than *Dark Side of the Moon*, but no other record defines them quite as well as this one.

Stephen Thomas Erlewine

Wish You Were Here
September 1975, Capitol

Pink Floyd followed the commercial breakthrough of *Dark Side of the Moon* with *Wish You Were Here*, a loose concept album about and dedicated to their founding member Syd Barrett. The record unfolds gradually, as the jazzy textures of "Shine On You Crazy Diamond" reveal its melodic motif, and in its leisurely pace, the album shows itself to be a warmer record than its predecessor. Musically, it's arguably even more impressive, showcasing the group's interplay and David Gilmour's solos in particular. And while it's short on actual songs, the long, winding soundscapes are constantly enthralling.

Stephen Thomas Erlewine

Animals
January 1977, Capitol

Of all of the classic-era Pink Floyd albums, *Animals* is the strangest and darkest, a record that's hard to initially embrace yet winds up yielding as many rewards as its equally nihilistic successor, *The Wall*. It isn't that Roger Waters dismisses the human race as either pigs, dogs, or sheep, it's that he's constructed an album whose music is as bleak and bitter as that world view. Arriving after the warm-spirited (albeit melancholy) *Wish You Were Here*, the shift in tone comes as a bit of a surprise, and there are even less proper songs here than on either *Wish* or *Dark Side*. *Animals* is all extended pieces, yet it never drifts—it slowly, ominously works its way toward its destination. For an album that so clearly is Waters', David Gilmour's guitar dominates thoroughly, with Richard Wright's keyboards rarely rising above a mood-setting background (such as on the intro to "Sheep"). This gives the music, on occasion, immediacy and actually heightens the dark mood by giving it muscle. It also makes *Animals* as accessible as it possibly could be, since it surges with bold blues-rock guitar lines and hypnotic space rock textures. Through it all, though, the utter blackness of Waters' spirit holds true, and since there are no vocal hooks or melodies, everything rests on the mood, the near-nihilistic lyrics, and Gilmour's guitar. These are the kinds of things that satisfy cultists, and it will reward their attention—there's just no way in for casual listeners.

Stephen Thomas Erlewine

The Wall
November 1979, Capitol

Roger Waters constructed *The Wall*, a narcissistic, double-album rock opera about an emotionally crippled rock star who spits on an audience member daring to cheer during an acoustic song. Given its origins, it's little wonder  that *The Wall* paints such an unsympathetic portrait of the rock star, cleverly named "Pink," who blames everyone—particularly women—for his neuroses. Such lyrical and thematic shortcomings may have been forgivable if the album had a killer batch of songs, but Waters took his operatic inclinations to heart, constructing the album as a series of fragments that are held together by larger numbers like "Comfortably Numb" and "Hey You." Generally, the fully developed songs are among the finest of Pink Floyd's later work, but *The Wall* is primarily a triumph of production: its seamless surface, blending melodic fragments and sound effects, makes the musical shortcomings and questionable lyrics easy to ignore. But if *The Wall* is examined in depth, it falls apart, since it doesn't offer enough great songs to support its ambition, and its self-serving message and shiny production seem like relics of the late-'70s Me Generation.

Stephen Thomas Erlewine

The Final Cut
March 1983, Columbia

The Final Cut extends the autobiography of *The Wall*, concentrating on Roger Waters' pain when his father died in

World War II. Waters spins this off into a treatise on the futility of war, concentrating on the Falkland Islands, setting his blistering condemnations and scathing anger to impossibly subdued music that demands full attention. This is more like a novel than a record, requiring total concentration since shifts in dynamics, orchestration, and instrumentation are used as effect. This means that while this has the texture of classic Pink Floyd, somewhere between the brooding sections of *The Wall* and the monolithic menace of *Animals*, there are no songs or hooks to make these radio favorites. The even bent of the arrangements, where the music is used as texture, not music, means that *The Final Cut* purposely alienates all but the dedicated listener. Several of those listeners maintain that this is among Pink Floyd's finest efforts, and it certainly is an achievement of some kind—there's not only no other Floyd album quite like it, it has no close comparisons to anybody else's work (apart from Waters' own *The Pros and Cons of Hitch Hiking*, yet that had a stronger musical core). That doesn't make this easier to embrace, of course, and it's damn near impenetrable in many respects, but with its anger, emphasis on lyrics, and sonic textures, it's clear that it's the album that Waters intended it to be. And it's equally clear that Pink Floyd couldn't have continued in this direction—Waters had no interest in a group setting anymore, as this record, which is hardly a Floyd album in many respects, illustrates. Distinctive, to be sure, but not easy to love and, depending on your view, not even that easy to admire. [*The Final Cut* was reissued in a remastered edition in 2004. This edition added "When the Tigers Broke Free"—originally heard in the soundtrack to *The Wall*, but its moody, war-obsessed soundscape is better suited for *The Final Cut*—as the fourth track, inserted between "One of the Few" and "The Hero's Return," where it fits nicely into the album's narrative.]

Stephen Thomas Erlewine

Robert Plant

Pictures at Eleven
1982, Swan Song

For his debut solo album, Robert Plant doesn't exactly succumb to everyone's expectations. With a less-potent vocal style, Plant manages to carry out most of the songs in smooth, stylish fashion while rocking out rather convincingly on a couple of others. He gets some pretty good help from guitarist Robbie Blunt, who truly comes to life on "Worse Than Detroit," and both Phil Collins and Cozy Powell give Plant enough of a solid background to lean his sultry yet surging rock voice against. Plant channels his energy quite effectively through songs like "Pledge Pin" and "Moonlight in Samosa," while the single "Burning Down One Side" is a creditable one, even though it failed to crack the Top 50 in both the U.K. and the U.S. The most apparent characteristic about the album's eight tracks is the fact that Plant is able to escape most of his past and still sound motivated. Without depending too much on his Led Zeppelin days, he courses a new direction without changing or disguising his distinct vocal style whatsoever. *Pictures at Eleven* peaked within the Top Five on both sides of the Atlantic, successfully launching Plant's solo career.

Mike DeGagne

The Principle of Moments
1983, Es Paranza

Robert Plant's follow-up to *Pictures at Eleven* implements much of his debut's style and vocal meandering into a new and more exciting bunch of songs. The mysteriousness of

"Big Log," the album's first single, reached the Top 20 in the United States and in the U.K., while "In the Mood" is *The Principle of Moments'* finest offering, proving that Plant could roam freely with his voice and still have it work effectively. But Plant doesn't stop here, as he gives tracks like "Wreckless Love," "Stranger Here...Than Over There," and "Other Arms" an equal amount of curt abstractness and rock appeal. Because Plant's voice is so compelling in any state, the convolution of his writing tends to take a back seat to his singing in most of his solo work, which is definitely the case in most of the songs here. Plant went on tour with the Honeydrippers within the same year of *The Principle of Moments'* release, adding another facet to his already diverse solo repertoire.

Mike DeGagne

Shaken 'N Stirred
1985, Es Paranza

While some of *Shaken 'N Stirred's* makeup includes typical keyboard pop/rock, there's still plenty of variance, both vocally and otherwise, to keep the album from going under. The album cracked the Top 20 in the U.S. and in Britain thanks to the keen finesse of "Little by Little," which spreads out Plant's vocal puissance across an attractive rhythm. This time around, drummer Richard Hayward from Little Feat adds some percussive texture to a mixture of world beats, unconventional melodies and rhythms, and a number of other creative and colorful musical nuances. Some of the music sounds a little foreign and profound at first, but efforts like "Hip to Hoo" and "Kallalou" grow to be impressive, beyond-the-norm-styled numbers after a few listens. Plant's decision to create a non-commercial type of rock album proved that he could step outside his typical rock & roll roots and still make some appealing music, yet many fans found the album to be too dense and too experimental upon its initial release. Plant's voguish character is still ingrained throughout the tracks, and his tangents aren't so overwhelming that they throw his material in an altogether complete direction. If anything, the songs on *Shaken 'N Stirred* are an inspiring venture for Plant, as he manages to fulfill his slightly off-centered approach with some interesting and catchy results.

Mike DeGagne

Now & Zen
1988, Es Paranza

After years of trying to separate himself from his legendary status as Led Zeppelin's frontman, Robert Plant finally reconciles with his past on *Now & Zen*. He borrows a few Zeppelin riffs, and even enlists Jimmy Page to play guitar on his hit "Tall Cool One." This  album is also notable in that it marks his first collaboration with keyboardist Phil Johnstone, who would continue to play and write with Plant on subsequent albums. Musically, the album relies on standard rock arrangements except that the vocals and drums are at the forefront and keyboards instead of guitars are used to fill out the sound. Although most of the album is comprised of mid-tempo songs aimed at rock radio, Plant includes the lovely ballad "Ship of Fools," which demonstrates that he is more than capable of vocal subtlety. Plant, who often uses mysterious (and mystical) lyrics, writes some of his most direct songs, and the way in which the lyrics complement the melodic arrangements are partially responsible for the commercial success of *Now & Zen*. This is Robert Plant's best solo album, and a must-own for fans of Led Zeppelin.

Vik Iyengar

Sixty Six to Timbuktu
November 2003, Atlantic

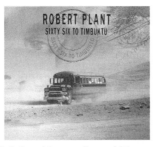

Sixty Six to Timbuktu has to be the icing on the cake for Robert Plant. After Led Zeppelin issued its second live album as well as a spectacular DVD in 2003, his career retrospective outside of the band is the new archetype for how they should be compiled. Containing two discs and 35 cuts, the set is divided with distinction. Disc one contains 16 tracks that cover Plant's post-Zep recording career via cuts from his eight solo albums. Along with the obvious weight of his former band's presence on cuts like "Tall Cool One," "Promised Land," and "Tie Dye on the Highway," there is also the flowering of the influence that Moroccan music in particular and Eastern music in general would have on him in readings of Tim Hardin's "If I Were a Carpenter," Jesse Colin Young's "Darkness, Darkness," and his own "29 Palms." There is also a healthy interest in technology being opened up on cuts from *Pictures at Eleven* and *Now & Zen*. The sequencing is creative, and the way one track seemingly foreshadows another is rather uncanny. But it is on disc two where the real treasures lie, and they are treasures. Of the 19 selections included, five are pre-Led Zeppelin. And these are no mere dead-dog files. Plant was revealing himself to be a jack-of-all-subgenres master: he drops a burning rendition of the Young Rascals' "You'd Better Run" circa 1966, and a wailing version of Billy Roberts' "Hey Joe" (recorded in 1967 and rivaling the emotional wallop of Jimi Hendrix's version recorded that same year). There's also the proto-blues moan and groan of "Operator" with British blues god Alexis Korner from 1968, which foreshadows the following year when he would join Zep. But Plant was not all raw raunch & roll. On Stephen Stills' "For What It's Worth," he lays out a paisley hippie sincerity that is downright stirring. And on "Our Song," he takes the example of crooners like Dion and sings a love song, so pure and true it might have come from screen rushes of *American Graffiti*. These tracks are worth their weight in gold for the integrity in their performances and their rough edges.

But these are just the beginning. What comes after the breakup of Led Zeppelin is a smorgasbord of exploratory music from a very restless and confident Plant. Here are outtakes, one-offs, loose ends, and covers that add up to 70 minutes of awesome music. There's the intense Zep sound-like skronk of "Road to the Sun," with Phil Collins on drums and Robbie Blunt doing his best Jimmy Page, and the shuffling rockabilly of Charlie Rich's "Philadelphia Baby," with Dave Edmunds, recorded at Sun Studios in Memphis for the *Porky's Revenge* soundtrack. On the roots tip there's also Plant's contribution of "Let's Have a Party" to *The Last Temptation of Elvis* compilation, as well as cuts he contributed to the Rainer, Skip Spence, and Arthur Alexander tribute

albums. There are B-sides such as "Naked if I Want To" from the U.S. release of "Calling to You," and "Hey Jayne," a limited bonus flip on the U.K. issue of the "I Believe" single from *Fate of Nations*, as well as a collaboration with the Afro-Celt Sound System on "Life Begin Again." This indulgence of modern technology began earlier than the 1990s, however, as the inclusion of Robin George's proto-electro "Red for Danger" attests—the track is previously unreleased. And this is only a smattering. There are cuts from his stint with the Jools Holland big band, the *Wayne's World* soundtrack, and many, many others. Once again, Plant's manner of sequencing is full of a crazy wisdom that is as witty as it is aesthetically sound. Finally, something has to be said about Plant's wonderfully informative, cocky, and delightfully humorous liner notes. Should he ever decide to give up music, he might become the next Lester Bangs. It all adds up to one hell of a package that provides the best surprise of the season and is a real candidate for reissue of the year.

Thom Jurek

Poco

Pickin' Up the Pieces
1969, Epic/Legacy

The group went into the studio with a sudden loss of one member (Randy Meisner), an engineer who didn't quite get what they were trying for, and a lot of pressure for a first album—and came up with this startlingly great record, as accomplished as any of Buffalo Springfield, and also reminiscent of the Beatles and the Byrds. *Pickin' Up the Pieces* is all the more amazing when one considers that Jim Messina and George Grantham were both covering for the departed Meisner in hastily learned capacities on bass and vocals, respectively. The title track is practically an anthem for the virtues of country-rock, with the kind of sweet harmonizing and tight interplay between the guitars that the Byrds, the Burritos, and others had to work awhile to achieve. The mix of good-time songs ("Consequently So Long," "Calico Lady"), fast-paced instrumentals ("Grand Junction"), and overall good feelings makes this a great introduction to the band, as well as a landmark in country-rock only slightly less important (and more enjoyable than) *Sweetheart of the Rodeo*.

Bruce Eder

Crazy Eyes
1973, Epic/Legacy

The third biggest-selling album in the group's history, *Crazy Eyes* is also the group's liveliest and most bracing work and contains some of their most soulful music. In short, it's the fruition of everything they'd been working toward for four years. Curiously, it's also one of a handful of examples of their use of outside help, including Chris Hillman on mandolin. The resulting sound is richer than anything found on any other Poco album, and the only tragedy is that the band reportedly cut enough tracks for two whole albums—one longs to hear the material that remained in the can. As it is, there's not a weak song, or even a wasted note anywhere on this album, and most bands would kill for a closing track as perfect as "Let's Dance Tonight."

Bruce Eder

The Forgotten Trail (1969-1974)
October 1990, Epic

This excellent two-disc collection captures Poco's finest moments from the days when they were laying down the template for all the country-rock music that was to follow. It's hard to remember, but when the Eagles first hit the scene, they were thought by many to be a Poco-wannabe band. Listen to this set and you'll hear why. *The Forgotten Trail (1969-1974)* culls tracks from Poco's first eight albums, as well as unreleased cuts and singles. From the classic anthem "Pickin' Up the Pieces," which kicks things off, through "You Better Think Twice," "C'mon," "Kind Woman," "From the Inside," "A Good Feelin' to Know," "Crazy Eyes," and on and on, this is wonderful music, ahead of its time in many ways. If Poco had arrived on the scene in the early '90s, they would have been kings of the country charts. Of course, without Poco, country music wouldn't have taken on the rock trappings that it did in the '80s and '90s. As it was, the band was considered too country for the Top 40 rock format of the time, and too rock & roll for country radio. This set is the place to start for an appreciation of the original Poco, when the group was considered to be Richie Furay's band. All the ingredients are here that made their music so delightful: the trademark high-vocal harmonies; Rusty Young's pedal steel guitar wizardry; Furay's patented juxtapositions of sad lyrics against bouncy, harmony-filled tunes; and their spirit of optimism and good feelings even in the face of hard luck and bad weather. The 36-page booklet does a fine job of telling the story in print, and the 38 songs speak volumes about the band's place and influence. Thanks to this compilation, Poco's trailblazing days need be forgotten no longer.

Jim Newsom

Iggy Pop

The Idiot
1977, Virgin

In 1976, the Stooges had been gone for two years, and Iggy Pop had developed a notorious reputation as one of rock & roll's most spectacular waste cases. After a self-imposed stay in a mental hospital, a significantly more functional Iggy was desperate to prove he could hold down a career in music, and he was given another chance by his longtime ally, David Bowie. Bowie co-wrote a batch of new songs with Iggy, put together a band, and produced *The Idiot*, which took Iggy in a new direction decidedly different from the guitar-fueled protopunk of the Stooges. Musically, *The Idiot* is of a piece with the impressionistic music of Bowie's "Berlin Period" (such as *Heroes* and *Low*), with it's fragmented guitar figures, ominous basslines, and discordant, high-relief keyboard parts. Iggy's new music was cerebral and inward-looking, where his early work had been a glorious call to the id, and Iggy was in more subdued form than with the Stooges, with his voice sinking into a world-weary baritone that was a decided contrast to the harsh, defiant cry heard on "Search and Destroy." Iggy was exploring new territory as a lyricist, and his songs on *The Idiot* are self-referential and poetic in a way that his work has rarely been in the past; for the most part the results are impressive, especially "Dum Dum Boys," a paean to the glory days of his former band, and "Nightclubbing," a call to the joys of decadence. *The Idiot* introduced the world to a very different Iggy Pop, and if the results surprised anyone expecting a replay of the assault of *Raw Power*, it also made it clear that Iggy was older, wiser, and still had plenty to say; it's a flawed but powerful and emotionally absorbing work.

Mark Deming

Lust for Life
1977, Virgin

On *The Idiot*, Iggy Pop looked deep inside himself, trying to figure out how his life and his art had gone wrong in the past. But on *Lust for Life*, released less than a year later, Iggy decided it was time to kick up his heels, as he traded in the mid-tempo introspection of his first album and began rocking hard again. Musically, *Lust for Life* is a more aggressive set than *The Idiot*, largely thanks to drummer Hunt Sales and his bassist brother Tony Sales. The Sales' proved they were a world class rhythm section, laying out power and spirit on the rollicking title cut, the tough groove of "Tonight," and the lean neo-punk assault of "Neighborhood Threat," and with guitarists Ricky Gardner and Carlos Alomar at their side, they made for a tough, wiry rock & roll band—a far cry from the primal stomp of the Stooges, but capable of kicking Iggy back into high gear. (David Bowie played piano and produced, as he had on *The Idiot*, but his presence is less clearly felt on this album.) As a lyricist and vocalist, Iggy Pop rose to the challenge of the material; if he was still obsessed with drugs ("Tonight"), decadence ("The Passenger"), and bad decisions ("Some Weird Sin"), the title cut suggested he could avoid a few of the temptations that crossed his path, and songs like "Success" displayed a cocky joy that confirmed Iggy was back at full strength. On *Lust for Life*, Iggy Pop managed to channel the aggressive power of his work with the Stooges with the intelligence and perception of *The Idiot*, and the result was the best of both worlds; smart, funny, edgy, and hard-rocking, *Lust for Life* is the best album of Iggy Pop's solo career.

Mark Deming

New Values
1979, Arista

From the time the Stooges first broke onto the music scene in 1967, Iggy Pop was rock's most remarkable one-man freak show, but by the mid-'70s, after the Stooges' messy collapse, Iggy found himself in need of a stable career. The rise of punk rock finally created a context in which Iggy's crash-and-burn theatrics seemed like inspired performance rather than some sort of cry for help, and in 1979, with everyone who was anyone name-checking Iggy as punk's Founding Father, he scored a deal with Arista Records, and *New Values* became his first recording since the new rock gained a foothold. These days, *New Values* sounds like Iggy Pop's new wave album; while former Stooges associates James Williamson and Scott Thurston worked on the album, the arrangements were dotted with synthesizer patches and electronic percussion accents that have not stood the test of time well at all, and the mix speaks of a more polite approach than the raw, raging rock of Iggy's best work. But the growth as a songwriter that David Bowie encouraged in Iggy on *The Idiot* and *Lust for Life* is very much in evidence here; "Tell Me a Story," "Billy Is a Runaway," and "How Do Ya Fix a Broken Part" are tough, unblinking meditations on Iggy's war with the persona he created for himself, and "I'm Bored" and "Five Foot One" proved rock's first great minimalist still had some worthy metaphors up his sleeve. If *New Values* wasn't a great Iggy Pop album, it was a very good one, and proved that he had a future without David Bowie's guidance, something that didn't seem so certain at the time.

Mark Deming

The Pretenders

Pretenders
January 1980, Sire

Few rock & roll re-cords rock as hard or with as much originality as the Pretenders' epony-mous debut album. A sleek, stylish fusion of Stonesy rock & roll, new wave pop, and pure punk aggres-sion, *Pretenders* is teeming with sharp hooks and a

viciously cool attitude. Although Chrissie Hynde establishes herself as a forceful and distinctively feminine songwriter, the record isn't a singer/songwriter's *tour de force*—it's a rock & roll album, powered by a unique and aggressive band. Guitarist James Honeyman-Scott never plays conventional riffs or leads, and his phased, treated guitar gives new di-mension to the pounding rhythms of "Precious," "Tattooed Love Boys," "Up the Neck," and "The Wait," as well as the more measured pop of "Kid," "Brass in Pocket," and "Mystery Achievement." He provides the perfect backing for Hynde and her tough, sexy swagger. Hynde doesn't fit into any conventional female rock stereotype, and neither do her songs, alternately displaying a steely exterior or a disarming emotional vulnerability. It's a deep, rewarding record, whose primary virtue is its sheer energy. *Pretenders* moves faster and harder than most rock records, delivering an endless series of melodies, hooks, and infectious rhythms in its 12 songs. Few albums, let alone debuts, are ever this astonish-ingly addictive.

Stephen Thomas Erlewine

Pretenders II
August 1981, Sire

The Pretenders' debut album was such a powerful, monu-mental record that its sequel was bound to be a bit of a disappointment, and *Pretenders II* is. Essentially, this album is an unabashed sequel, offering more of the same sound, attitude, and swagger, including titles that seem like rips on their predecessors and another Ray Davies cover. This gives the record a bit too much of a pat feeling, especially since the band seems to have a lost a bit of momentum—they don't rock as hard, Chrissie Hynde's songwriting isn't as consistent, James Honeyman-Scott isn't as inventive or clever. These all are disappointments, yet this first incarnation of the Pretenders was a tremendous band, and even if they of-fer diminished returns, it's still diminished returns on good material, and much of *Pretenders II* is quite enjoyable. Yes, it's a little slicker and more stylized than its predecessor, and, yes, there's a little bit of filler, yet any album where rockers as tough as "Message of Love" and "The Adultress" are bal-anced by a pop tune as lovely as "Talk of the Town" is hard to resist. And when you realize that this fantastic band only recorded two albums, you take that second album, warts and all, because the teaming of Hynde and Honeyman-Scott was one of the great pairs, and it's utterly thrilling to hear them together, even when the material isn't quite up to the high standards they set the first time around.

Stephen Thomas Erlewine

Learning to Crawl
January 1984, Sire

Chrissie Hynde and drummer Martin Chambers reassembled the Pretenders in 1982, following the death of James Honey-man-Scott and the departure of bassist Pete Farndon. *Learn-ing to Crawl*, appropriately, is the sound of a band coming to grips with loss and the responsibilities that come with ma-turity. Even though the subject matter is undeniably serious, the Pretenders rock with a vigorous energy that was missing on *Pretenders II*. It helps that Hynde's songs are among her best, of course. "Middle of the Road" encapsulates the con-tradictions in the album's main themes; "Back on the Chain Gang" is a moving tribute to Scott; "My City Was Gone" is a vicious attack on Reagan-era economic devastation; and the beautiful, ringing "2000 Miles" is one of the few rock & roll songs about Christmas to actually work. And while "Watching the Clothes" is a bit embarrassing, it isn't enough to stop *Learning to Crawl* from being one of the best rock & roll records of the early '80s.

Stephen Thomas Erlewine

Get Close
November 1986, Sire

In the first edition of the Pretenders, Chrissie Hynde was a smart and streetwise rock & roller with just enough maturity to make something of what life had shown her by her mid-twenties—and she had the rough-and-tumble band to match for her first

two albums. The second version of the group cast her as an unwitting but unbowed survivor, determined to move on and keep rocking despite the deaths of two of her bandmates, and the tough, no-nonsense approach of her new collaborators on *Learning to Crawl* reflected her attitude. 1986's *Get Close* marked the debut of the Pretenders' Mark Three, and on this album we're introduced to Chrissie Hynde, Mature Profes-sional Musician with a band to match. *Get Close* is never less than solid as a work of craft, and guitarist Robbie McIntosh, drummer Blair Cunningham, and bassist T.M. Stevens deliver tight and emphatic performances throughout, but they also sound like what they are—journeymen musicians who bring their chops to their projects while leaving their personalities at the door. While Hynde always dominated the Pretenders, by this time it was obvious that this was fully her show, and if she felt less like rocking and more like exploring her emo-tions and thoughts about parenthood on mid-tempo pop tunes, no one in the group was going to prod her into doing otherwise; the presence of a large number of additional ses-sion players further buffs away any of *Get Close*'s potential sharp edges. Despite all this, Hynde's voice is in great form throughout, and when she gets her dander up, she still has plenty to say and good ways to say it; "How Much Did You Get for Your Soul?" is a gleefully venomous attack on the musically unscrupulous; "Don't Get Me Wrong" is a superb pop tune and a deserved hit single; and the Motown-flavored "I Remember You" and the moody "Chill Factor" suggest she'd been learning a lot from her old soul singles. But after three great albums from the Pretenders, *Get Close* sounded good but not especially striking, and its hit-and-miss ap-proach, with a few great songs surrounded by lesser material, was something Hynde's fans would find themselves getting used to over the group's next few releases.

Mark Deming

The Pretty Things

S.F. Sorrow
1968, Original Masters

Who could ever have thought, going back to the Pretty Things' first recording session in 1965—which started out so disastrously that their original producer quit in frustration—that it would come to this? The Pretty Things' early history in the studio featured the band with its amps seemingly turned up to 11, but for much of *S.F. Sorrow* the band is turned down to 7 or 4, or even 2, or not amplified at all (except for Wally Allen's bass—natch); and they're doing all kinds of folkish things here that are still bluesy enough so you never forget who they are, amid weird little digressions on percussion and chorus, and harmony vocals that are spooky, trippy, strange, and delightful, and sitars included in the array of stringed instruments, plus an organ trying hard to sound like a Mellotron. Sometimes one gets an echo of Pink Floyd's *Piper at the Gates of Dawn* or *A Saucerful of Secrets*, and it all straddles the worlds of British blues and British psychedelia better than almost any record you can name. The album, for those unfamiliar, tells the story of "S.F. Sorrow," a sort of British Everyman—think of a working-class, luckless equivalent to the Kinks' *Arthur*, from cradle to grave. The tale and the songs are a bit downbeat and no amount of scrutiny can disguise the fact that the rock opera *S.F. Sorrow* is ultimately a bit of a confusing effort—these boys were musicians, not authors or dramatists. Although it may have helped inspire *Tommy*, it is, simply, not nearly as good. That said, it was first and has quite a few nifty ideas and production touches. And it does show a pathway between blues and psychedelia that the Rolling Stones, somewhere between *Satanic Majesties*, "We Love You," "Child of the Moon," and *Beggars Banquet*, missed entirely. [The CD reissue on Snapper adds four valuable songs from their 1967-1968 singles ("Defecting Grey," "Mr. Evasion," "Talkin' About the Good Times," and "Walking Through My Dreams"). This version of "Defecting Grey" is the original, long, uncut five-minute rendition, and not of trivial importance;] it's superior to the shorter one used on the official single.]

Bruce Eder & Richie Unterberger

Parachute
1970, Demon

If *S.F. Sorrow* is the Pretty Things' *Sgt. Pepper*, *Magical Mystery Tour*, and *Yellow Submarine* wrapped in one, then *Parachute* is their more succinct *White Album* and *Abbey Road*. It's not just a time line comparison. The Pretties made this fascinating LP in

the same studio as the Fab Four, London's *Abbey Road*, with Beatles engineer Norman Smith producing. "The Good Mr. Square" replicates the three-part harmony the Beatles

were so proud of on "Because." Two songs later, the group assembles a brief, interconnected three-song suite like the famous ones on side two of *Abbey Road*. Bassist Wally Allen's vocals on tracks such as "Sickle Clowns" have the same throaty, mad anguish that John Lennon exhibited on "Yer Blues" and "Happiness Is a Warm Gun." If *S.F. Sorrow* is hard rock grandeur, then *Parachute* is its more bitter twist, the dream dying and the witching hour upon us. Yet, if this isn't as much of a triumph, the creative neurons are still firing throughout a multi-varied, cohesive LP. Like *S.F. Sorrow*, it's a surprisingly palatable concept LP. This time the topic is a generation caught between the conflicting calls of (rural) peace, love, and boredom, and (urban) sophistication, sex, and squalor in a harsh world. Somehow the departure of the band's main creative force, Dick Taylor, didn't diminish the writing and inspired variety. Allen stepped up big time into the collaborator role with singer Phil May. The harmonies remain a strong point on an otherwise rock-inclined record, and the nasty edge of perfectly balanced bombast in the best songs have been a lost art ever since—it's not hard to see why *Rolling Stone* rated *Parachute* the best LP of 1970. (There are 18 minutes of good stuff tacked on the Snapper edition, taken from singles.)

Jack Rabid, The Big Takeover

Come See Me: The Very Best of the Pretty Things
April 2004, Shout! Factory

Come See Me: The Very Best of the Pretty Things is a lovingly packaged, mostly well-chosen collection of one of the best bands of the British Invasion that never quite managed to invade. Their lack of success in the States was certainly not due to a lack of great songs. The songs taken from the group's first three albums on Fontana bear this out. The stomping "Rosalyn," the mad take on Bo Diddley's "Roadrunner," the shuddering "Don't Bring Me Down," "Midnight to Six Man," and the snarling folk-rocker "You Don't Believe Me" are all beat group classics, revered by garage revivalists and lovers of tough R&B-influenced rock. The Pretty Things were tougher than the Stones, probably tougher than anyone in the U.K. In fact, stack up the murderously rough and tumble "Come See Me" or "Get the Picture" against any band that ever thought it was tough and you'll have a real fight on your hands. By its third album the group was showing signs of expanding its musical horizon. The string-laden pysch-pop ballad "The Sun" and acoustic guitar-based big pop tune "Death of a Socialite" bear this out. The collection gathers four songs from their post-Fontana period, which may be the creative high point of the group. "Deflecting Grey," "Walking Through My Dreams," "Talking About the Good Times," and "Mr. Evasion" all fully embrace the sonic possibilities of psychedelia without sacrificing any of the band's aggressiveness or ability to write big hooks. The collection sort of rushes through the rest of the band's career, only picking two songs (and not the strongest) from their excellent concept record *S.F. Sorrow*, one from their surprisingly solid hard rock album from 1970, *Parachute*, and two from their fairly dire 1974 effort *Silk Torpedo*, including the very Spinal Tap-ish "Singapore Silk Torpedo." Having songs from their hard rock period is not as bad an idea as some garage rock purists might imagine. The main problem is that the songs are poorly chosen. It would have been nice to include one or two songs the band recorded as Electric Banana in the late '60s. In fact Shout! Factory should look into a legit re-release of those recordings because they are some of the best work the band did. Still, this is the best Pretty Things collection of the CD era, and if it does anything to bring the Pretty Things to a wider audience, it has done well. Anyone who wants to know what the band was all about will be thoroughly educated and will most likely come away with a new favorite British Invasion band.

Tim Sendra

Procol Harum

Procol Harum
1967, Deram

Procol Harum's self-titled, debut album bombed in England, appearing six months after "A Whiter Shade of Pale" and "Homburg" with neither hit song on it. The LP was successful in America, where albums sold more easily, but especially since it *did* include "A Whiter Shade of Pale" and was reissued with a sticker emphasizing the presence of the original "Conquistador," a re-recording which became a hit in 1972. The music is an engaging meld of psychedelic rock, blues, and classical influences, filled with phantasmagorical lyrics, bold (but not flashy) organ by Matthew Fisher, and Robin Trower's most tasteful and restrained guitar. "Conquistador," "Kaleidoscope," "A Christmas Camel," and the Bach-influenced "Repent Walpurgis" are superb tracks, and "Good Captain Clack" is great, almost Kinks-like fun. Not everything here works, but it holds up better than most psychedelic or progressive rock.

Bruce Eder

Shine on Brightly
1968, Repertoire

After the multi-million selling "A Whiter Shade Of Pale," Procol Harum coalesced around a new line-up and cut a debut album in two days, the sales of which (because the hit song wasn't on it originally) were only fair, and a couple of new singles also failed to sell. Then they did *Shine On Brightly*, which initially drew on recordings going back to late 1967—in the course of preparing their first proper LP, the band junked an entire side of blues-based numbers in favor of the 18-minute suite "In Held 'Twas I," which rivaled anything yet heard from such established progressive rock outfits as the Nice or the Moody Blues in length and surpassed them in audacity, with an extensive spoken part surrounded by virtuoso classical and psychedelic passages (and even a featured spot for Dave Knights' bass). It all proved that they were more than a one-hit wonder and, released in late 1968, the album extended the definition of progressive rock, even as it kept much of the music rooted in established rock genres. "Skip Softly," for all of its grand piano pyrotechnics, was also a showcase for Robin Trower's bluesy, high-energy guitar attack, and "Wish Me Well" was an even better vehicle for his instrument, while "Magdalene (My Regal Zonophone)" was an interesting exercise in nostalgia highlighted by Matthew Fisher's organ.

Bruce Eder

A Salty Dog
March 1969, A&M

This album, the group's third, was where they showed just how far their talents extended across the musical landscape, from blues to R&B to classical rock. In contrast to their hastily recorded debut, or its successor, done to stretch their performance and composition range, *A Salty Dog* was recorded in a reasonable amount of time, giving the band a chance to fully develop their ideas. The title track is one of the finest songs ever to come from Procol Harum and one of the best pieces of progressive rock ever heard, and a very succinct example at that at under five minutes' running time—the lyric and the music combine to form a perfect mood piece, and the performance is bold and subtle at once, in the playing and the singing, respectively. The range of sounds on the rest includes "Juicy John Pink," a superb piece of pre-World War II-style country blues, while "Crucifiction Lane" is a killer Otis Redding-style soul piece, and "Pilgrim's Progress" is a virtuoso keyboard workout. *A Salty Dog* was reissued by Repertoire Records in 1997 with enhanced sound and the lost B-side "Long Gone Geek," a Robin Trower guitar workout par excellence.

Bruce Eder

Queen

Queen
September 1973, Elektra

Like any patchy but promising debut from a classic rock group, it's often easy to underrate Queen's eponymous 1973 debut, since it has no more than one well-known anthem and plays more like a collection of ideas than a cohesive album. But what ideas! Almost every one of Queen's signatures are already present, from Freddie Mercury's operatic harmonies to Brian May's rich, orchestral guitar overdubs, and the suite-like structures of "Great King Rat." That rich, florid feel could be characterized as glam, but even in these early days that appellation didn't quite fit Queen, since they were at once too heavy and arty to be glam and—ironically enough, their legendary excess—they were hardly *trashy* enough to be glam. But that only speaks to the originality of Queen: they may have traded in mystical sword-n-sorcerers like so many '70s prog bands, they may have hit as hard as Zeppelin (and Page's guitar army certainly was a forefather to May's overdubs), but they didn't sound anybody else, they were too *odd* in their theatricality to be mistaken for another band. That much was apparent on this debut, but one thing was crucially missing: songs that could coalesce their sound and present it in a memorable fashion. There is an exception to that rule— the wild, rampaging opener "Keep Yourself Alive," one of their very best songs—but too often the album plays like a succession of ideas instead of succinct songs, and the group's predilection for suites only highlights this, despite the occasional blast of fury like "Modern Times Rock & Roll." This can be quite appealing as sheer, visceral sound and, in that regard, *Queen* is kind of irresistible. It showcases the band in all their ornate splendor yet it's strangely lean and hard, revealing just how good the band was in their early days as a hard rock band. That might not quite make it an overlooked gem—it remains patchy on a song for song basis—but it sure makes for an interesting debut that provides a rough roadmap to their later work.

Stephen Thomas Erlewine

Queen II
April 1974, Elektra

In one regard, *Queen II* does indeed provide more of the same thing offer on the band's debut. Certainly, of all the other albums in Queen's catalog it bears the closest resemblance to its immediate predecessor, particularly in its lean, hard attack and in how it has only one song that is well-known to listeners outside of their hardcore cult: in this case, it's "Seven Seas of Rhye," which is itself more elliptical than "Keep Yourself Alive," the big song from the debut. But these similarities are superficial and *Queen II* is a very different beast than its predecessor, an album that is richer, darker, and weirder, an album that finds Queen growing as a band by leaps and bounds. There is still a surplus of ideas but their energies are better focused this time around, channeled into an over-inflated, pompous rock that could be called prog if it wasn't so heavy. Even with all the queens and ogres that populate *Queen II*, this never feels as fantastical as Genesis or Uriah Heep, and that's because Queen hits *hard* as a rock band here, where even the blasts of vocal harmonies feel like power chords, no matter how florid they are. Besides, these grandiose harmonies, along with the handful of wistful ballads here, are overshadowed by the onslaught of guitars and pummeling rhythms that give *Queen II* majesty and menace. Queen is coiled, tense and vicious here, delivering on their inherent sense of drama, and that gives *Queen II* real power as music, as well as a true cohesion. The one thing that is missing is any semblance of a pop sensibility, even when they flirt with a mock Phil Spector production on "Funny How Love Is." This hits like heavy metal but has an art-rock sensibility through and through, which also means that it has no true hook in for those that don't want to succumb to Queen's world. But that kind of insular drama is quite alluring its own right, which is why *Queen II* is one of the favorites of their hardcore fans. At the very least, it illustrates that Queen is starting to pull all their ambitions and influences into a signature sound, and it's quite powerful in that regard. [The 1991 reissue contains two remixes and the bonus track "See What A Fool I've Been," a slow crawl that's the closest Queen ever came to blues, even if it's somewhat tongue in cheek, it's still one of the best—and most song-oriented—things here.]

Stephen Thomas Erlewine

Sheer Heart Attack
November 1974, Elektra

Queen II was a breakthrough in terms of power and ambition, but Queen's third album *Sheer Heart Attack* was where the band started to gel. It followed quickly on the heels of the second record—just by a matter of months; it was the second album they released in 1974—but it feels like it had a longer incubation period, so great is the progress here. Which isn't quite to say that *Sheer Heart Attack* is flawless—it still has a tendency to meander, sometimes within a song itself, as when the killer opening "Brighton Rock" suddenly veers into long stretches of Brian May solo guitar—but all these detours do not distract from the overall album, they're in many ways the key to the record itself: it's the sound of Queen stretching their wings and as they learn how to soar to the clouds. There's a genuine excitement in hearing all the

elements to Queen's sound fall into place here, as the music grows grander and catchier without sacrificing their brutal, hard attack. One of the great strengths of the album is how all four members find their voice as songwriters, penning hooks that are big, bold, and insistent and crafting them in songs that work as cohesive entities instead of flourishes of ideas. This is evident not just in "Killer Queen"—the first, best flourishing of Freddie Mercury's vaudevillian camp—but also on the pummeling "Stone Cold Crazy," a frenzied piece of jagged metal that's all the more exciting because it has a real melodic hook. Those hooks are threaded throughout the record, on both the ballads and the other rockers, but it isn't just that this is poppier, it's that they're able to execute their drama with flair and style. There are still references to mystical worlds ("Lily of the Valley," "In the Lap of Gods") but there's not the fantasy does not overwhelm as it did on the first two records; the theatricality is now wielded on everyday affairs, which ironically makes them sound larger than life. And this sense of scale, combined with the heavy guitars, pop hooks and theatrical style, marks the true unveiling of Queen, making *Sheer Heart Attack* as the moment where they truly came into their own.

Stephen Thomas Erlewine

A Night at the Opera
December 1975, Elektra

Queen were straining at the boundaries of hard rock and heavy metal on *Sheer Heart Attack*, but they broke down all the barricades on *A Night at the Opera*, a self-consciously ridiculous and overblown hard rock masterpiece. Using the multi-layered guitars of its predecessor as a foundation, *A Night at the Opera* encompasses metal ("Death on Two Legs," "Sweet Lady"), pop (the lovely, shimmering "You're My Best Friend"), campy British music hall ("Lazing on a Sunday Afternoon," "Seaside Rendezvous"), and mystical prog rock ("'39," "The Prophet's Song"), eventually bringing it all together on the pseudo-operatic "Bohemian Rhapsody." In short, it's a lot like Queen's own version of *Led Zeppelin IV*, but where Zep find dark menace in bombast, Queen celebrate their own pomposity. No one in the band takes anything too seriously, otherwise the arrangements wouldn't be as ludicrously exaggerated as they are. But the appeal—and the influence—of *A Night at the Opera* is in its detailed, meticulous productions. It's prog rock with a sense of humor as well as dynamics, and Queen never bettered their approach anywhere else. [In 2005, Hollywood Records released a two-disc, remastered *30th Anniversary CD/DVD* of *A Night at the Opera* that included a DVD featuring original and new videos, as well as audio commentary from the band.]

Stephen Thomas Erlewine

A Day at the Races
December 1976, Hollywood

In every sense, *A Day at the Races* is an unapologetic sequel to *A Night at the Opera*, the 1975 breakthrough that established Queen as rock & roll royalty. The band never attempts to hide that the record is a sequel—the two albums boast the same variation on

the same cover art, the titles are both taken from old Marx Brothers films and serve as counterpoints to each other. But even the two albums *look* the same, they don't quite sound the same, *A Day at the Races* is a bit tighter than its predecessor, yet tighter doesn't necessarily mean better for a band as extravagant as Queen. One of the great things about *A Night at the Opera* is that the lingering elements of early Queen—the pastoral folk of "39," the metallic menace of "Death on Two Legs"—dovetailed with an indulgence of camp and a truly, well, operatic scale. Here, the eccentricities are trimmed back somewhat—they still bubble up on "The Millionaire Waltz," an example of the music-hall pop that dominated *Night*, the pro-Native American saga "White Man" is undercut somewhat by the cowboy-n-indians rhythms—in favor of a driving, purposeful hard-rock that still could have some slyly hidden perversities (or in the case of the opening "Tie Your Mother Down," some not-so-hidden perversity) but this is exquisitely detailed hard-rock, dense with detail but never lush or fussy. In a sense, it could even function as the bridge between *Sheer Heart Attack* and *Night at the Opera*—it's every bit as hard as the former and nearly as florid as the latter—but its sleek, streamlined finish is the biggest indication that Queen has entered a new phase, where they're globe-conquering titans instead of underdogs on the make.

Stephen Thomas Erlewine

News of the World
November 1977, Elektra

If *Day at the Races* was a sleek, streamlined album, its 1977 successor, *News of the World*, was its polar opposite, an explosion of styles that didn't seem to hold to any particular center. It's front-loaded with two of Queen's biggest anthems—the stomping, stadium-filling chant "We Will Rock You" and its triumphant companion, "We Are the Champions"—which are quickly followed by the ferocious "Sheer Heart Attack," a frenzied rocker that hits harder than anything on the album that shares its name, a remarkable achievement in itself. Three songs, three quick shifts in mood, but that's hardly the end of it. As the *News* rolls on, you're treated to the arch, campy crooning of "My Melancholy Blues," a shticky blues shuffle in "Sleeping on the Sidewalk," and breezy Latin rhythms on "Who Needs You." Then there's the neo-disco of "Fight from the Inside," which is eclipsed by the mechanical funk of "Get Down, Make Love," a dirty grind that's stripped of sensuality. That cold streak on "Get Down, Make Love" runs through the album as a whole. Despite the explosion of sounds and rhythms, this album doesn't add up to party thanks to that slightly distancing chilly vibe that hangs over the album. Nevertheless, many of these songs work well on their own as entities, so there is plenty to savor here, especially from Brian May. Whether he's doing the strangely subdued eccentric English pop "All Dead, All Dead" or especially the majestic yet nimble rocker "It's Late," he turns in work that gives this album some lightness, which it needs. And that's the reason *News of the World* was a monster hit despite its coldness—when it works, it's massive, earth-shaking rock & roll, the sound of a band beginning to revel in its superstardom.

Stephen Thomas Erlewine

Jazz
November 1978, Hollywood

Famously tagged as "fascist" in a *Rolling Stone* review printed at the time of its 1978 release, *Jazz* does indeed showcase a band that does thrive upon its power, thrilling upon the hold that it has on its audience. That confidence, that self-intoxication, was hinted at on *News of the World* but it takes full flower here, and that assurance acts as a cohesive device, turning this into one of Queen's sleekest albums. Like its patchwork predecessor, *Jazz* also dabbles in a bunch of different sounds—that's a perennial problem with Queen, where the four songwriters were often pulling in different directions—but it sounds bigger, heavier than *News*, thanks to the mountains of guitars Brian May has layered all over this record. If May has indulged himself, Freddie Mercury runs riot all over this album, infusing it with an absurdity that's hard to resist. This goofiness is apparent from the galloping overture "Mustapha," and things only get a lot sillier from that point out, as the group sings the praises of "Fat Bottomed Girls" and "Bicycle Races," as May and Mercury have an unspoken competition on who can overdub the most onto a particular track while Roger Taylor steers them toward their first disco song in the gloriously dumb "Fun It." But since over-the-top campiness has always been an attribute in Queen, this kind of grand-scale exaggeration gives *Jazz* a sense of ridiculousness that makes it more fun than many of their other albums.

Stephen Thomas Erlewine

The Game
June 1980, Hollywood

Queen had long been one of the biggest bands in the world by 1980's *The Game*, but this album was the first time they made a glossy, unabashed *pop* album, one that was designed to sound exactly like its time. They might be posed in leather jackets on the cover, but they hardly sound tough or menacing—they rarely *rock*, at least not in the gonzo fashion that's long been their trademark. Gone are the bombastic orchestras of guitars and with them the charging, relentless rhythms that kept Queen grounded even at their grandest moments. Now, when they rock, they'll haul out a clever rockabilly pastiche, as they do on the tremendous "Crazy Little Thing Called Love," a sly revival of old-time rock & roll that never sounds moldy, thanks in large part to Freddie Mercury's panache. But even that is an exception to the rule on *The Game*. Usually, when they want to rock here, they wind up sounding like Boston, as they do on John Deacon's "Need Your Loving Tonight," or they sound a bit like a new wave-conscious rocker like Billy Squier, as they do on the propulsive "Coming Soon." But even there are exceptions to the overall rule on *The Game*, since most of the album is devoted to disco-rock blends—best heard on the globe-conquering "Another One Bites the Dust," but also present in the unintentionally kitschy positivity anthem "Don't Try Suicide"—and the majestic power ballads that became their calling card in the '80s, as they reworked the surging "Save Me" and the elegant "Play the Game" numerous times, often with lesser results. So, *The Game* winds up as a mixed bag, as many Queen albums often do, but again the striking difference with this album is that it finds Queen turning decidedly, decisively pop, and it's a grand, state-of-the-art circa 1980 pop album that still stands as one of the band's most enjoyable records. But the very fact that it does showcase a band that's turned away from rock and toward pop means that for some Queen fans, it marks the end of the road, and despite the album's charms, it's easy to see why.

Stephen Thomas Erlewine

Greatest Hits
August 2004, Hollywood

Pay attention, because this gets tricky. Very tricky. The first Queen *Greatest Hits* released in America was a 14-track LP that hit the stores in 1981. Several years later, CDs overtook LPs as the leading format of recorded music, but due to various legal reasons, Queen's catalog didn't hit CD until 1991, and soon, CD compilations started to appear in bewildering configurations. In the U.K., where Queen remained on the charts throughout the '80s, a sequel to that 1981 *Greatest Hits* was released in 1991, chronicling such hits as "Under Pressure," "I Want to Break Free," and "Radio Ga Ga." In the U.S., Queen stopped having Top 40 hits after "Radio Ga Ga," so *Greatest Hits, Vol. 2* was filled with music largely unfamiliar to the American listener. Hollywood, the American label with the rights to the reissues, thus decided to slightly reconfigure that U.K. *Greatest Hits, Vol. 2* by dropping a few tracks and substituting such radio staples as "Tie Your Mother Down" and "Stone Cold Crazy," along with the hits "Under Pressure" and "Bohemian Rhapsody," which was a current hit in 1992 thanks to its exposure in the hit film *Wayne's World*. This reconfigured *Greatest Hits, Vol. 2* was called *Classic Queen* and it was a Top Ten hit, but surely listeners expecting Queen songs a little more classic than "Headlong" and "I'm Going Slightly Mad" were disappointed that, say, "We Will Rock You" and "Another One Bites the Dust" weren't on this new CD. So, six months after the March 1992 release of *Classic Queen*, Hollywood followed with *Greatest Hits*, which may have shared its name with the 1981 collection but essentially rounded up the tunes from that disc that didn't appear on *Classic Queen*, adding a few more tunes to bring it up to 17 tracks.

That's confusing enough, but it doesn't stop there. Since the 1981 collection had an expert track selection, it continued to be a big seller in the U.S. as an import CD, and then in 1994, Parolophone in the U.K. reworked the compilation to bring it up to 17 tracks—which appears to be the magic number for Queen compilations since that's what *Greatest Hits, Vol. 2*, *Classic Queen*, the 1992 *Greatest Hits*, and the subsequent 1999 *Greatest Hits, Vol. 3* all run. This reconfigured *Greatest Hits* was the best available hits compilation, but it was only available as an import in the States, *or* as part of the 1995 two-disc repackage of *Greatest Hits, Vols. 1 & 2*, *or* as part of the 2001 repackaging *The Platinum Collection*, which contained the British versions of the three *Greatest Hits* discs. These latter two were American releases that snuck out the preferred British version, because the British versions of the *Greatest Hits* always had the more logical track sequences; *Classic Queen* and the 1992 *Greatest Hits* were rush jobs. Despite that, those 1992 American compilations remained on the market, and *Classic Queen* remained the easiest way for a fan to get most, but not all, of Queen's hits as a single-disc collection.

Until this 2004 release, that is. Entitled *Greatest Hits: We Will Rock You Edition*, this is the long-awaited stand-alone reissue of the first Queen *Greatest Hits*, with the addition of three bonus tracks, plus an offer to save 20 percent on any package to see the Queen theatrical musical *We Will Rock*

You at Paris Las Vegas. So, it's a tie-in—and not just for the musical, because "I'm in Love With My Car" was used in commercial for Jaguar in 2004, so it's added as a bonus track (the other two bonus tracks are live versions of "Under Pressure" and "Tie Your Mother Down")—but who cares? This compilation is finally available on its own on CD in the U.S. and that's worth celebrating, even if at this point most fans who care will own the import or one of those repackages (or, frankly, could assemble the collection from the discs they already own). But for those listeners still looking for the perfect single-disc Queen collection, this is as close as you're going to get, and it's nice to have it available on the U.S. shores as a stand-alone domestic release.

Stephen Thomas Erlewine

Quicksilver Messenger Service

Quicksilver Messenger Service
May 1968, Capitol

Quicksilver Messenger Service's debut effort was a little more restrained and folky than some listeners had expected, given their reputation for stretching out in concert. While some prefer the mostly live *Happy Trails*, this self-titled collection is inarguably their strongest set of studio material, with the accent on melodic folk-rock. Highlights include their cover of folksinger Hamilton Camp's "Pride of Man," probably their best studio track; "Light Your Windows," probably the group's best original composition; and founding member Dino Valenti's "Dino's Song" (Valenti himself was in jail when the album was recorded). "Gold and Silver" is their best instrumental jam, and the 12-minute "The Fool" reflects some of the best and worst traits of the psychedelic era.

Richie Unterberger

Sons of Mercury (1968–1975)
July 1991, Rhino

When this two-CD set first appeared in the early '90s, it was among the only Quicksilver Messenger Service titles in the digital domain. It remained the closest thing to a definitive anthology of this seminal psychedelic Bay Area band. *Sons of Mercury*— a clever pun on the band's mythically derived name—begins with QMS's earliest released tracks, "Babe I'm Gonna Leave You" (not to be confused with the Joan Baez composition) and a cover of the Buffy Sainte-Marie classic "Codine." Both were featured in the '60s low-budget teensploitation flick *Revolution*, which preceded the band's self-titled debut by a few months in the early summer of 1968. The remainder of disc one contains a majority of QMS's self-titled debut long-player, as well as the previously unissued track "I Hear You Knockin' (It's Too Late)," recorded during the sessions for the first LP. This is followed by a large portion of their highly acclaimed follow-up, *Happy Trails*, which combined concert tapes with carefully incorporated studio enhancements. Disc two contains a sampling of material from the band's other six studio LPs. By the early '70s, the group had evolved beyond the original union of John Cipollina, Gary Duncan, David Freiberg, and Greg Elmore; the second lineup included Dino Valente and legendary British session keyboardist Nicky Hopkins. From this era, *Sons of Mercury* includes the FM radio hits "What About Me?" and "Fresh Air." Also incorporated are some of the later and much less representative works that QMS released sporadically through the mid-'70s, such as "Fire Brothers" and the largely forgettable "Gypsy Lights." It can be argued that, like Haight-Ashbury contemporaries the Grateful Dead, QMS was never aptly captured on vinyl—the band's expansive sonic explorations often extended beyond the time limits inherent in a typical album. Ironically, QMS never issued a retrospective concert recording during the group's active lifetime. One flaw here is including the diminutive 45-rpm edit of the "Who Do You Love?" suite from their second album. Granted, the full-length live version does take up an entire side of *Happy Trails*. However, no other single work in the QMS canon spotlighted each of the quartet in such an accurate way.

Lindsay Planer

Quicksilver
November 1971, One Way

One of the group's better albums, despite coming so late in their history that it was ignored by almost everyone. "Hope," "Fire Brothers," and "Don't Cry For My Lady Love" are among the best songs the group ever cut, and "I Found Love" is one of the prettiest, most upbeat songs ever to come from any classic San Francisco band. Some of the rest is self-indulgent, but that's what this era of music was about—the guitar pyrotechnics of "Song For Frisco" and "Play My Guitar" make them both more entertaining than their somewhat bland melodies; the latter song, in particular, sounds like a Marty Balin/Jefferson Airplane outtake that would have been right on target about four years before the release date of this album. The whole record feels that way, a throwback to the psychedelic era circa late 1967. It's also very much a folk-rock record, with a rich acoustic guitar texture on many of the songs. For the record, since the CD reissue has no personnel information, the band at this point was Dino Valenti (guitar, vocals), Greg Elmore (drums), Gary Duncan (vocals, guitar), Mark Ryan (bass), Mark Naftalin (keyboards), and Chuck Steaks (keyboards). If you ever wondered what the Airplane might have done as a follow-up to *Surrealistic Pillow* with Marty Balin still singing lead, this is it.

Bruce Eder

Rainbow

20th Century Masters—The Millennium Collection: The Best of Rainbow
October 2000, Polydor

The broad roster of artists under the Universal Music umbrella—thanks to record company merger mania—has enabled a slew of mid-line-priced *20th Century Masters—The Millennium Collection* titles. In some cases, such as Steve Winwood's, it's a unique volume. For others, such as Rainbow, it's a sensible purchase for budget-minded casual fans, but more complete one-CD retrospectives exist. Deep Purple hasn't truly received the widespread critical respect it deserves as a pioneering heavy metal band, so it's no surprise that guitarist Ritchie Blackmore's Rainbow isn't fully appreciated either. No consecutive studio albums bore the same lineup, so continuity can't be considered one of Rainbow's virtues. But from the progressive heavy metal, mid-'70s Ronnie James

Dio era to the calculated, radio-friendly, early-'80s Joe Lynn Turner era, the band created many excellent songs and foreshadowed the mid-'80s pop/metal boom. Rainbow's three best-known songs—"Since You Been Gone" (with Graham Bonnet's throat-bursting vocals), "Stone Cold," and "Street of Dreams"—are featured on *20th Century Masters—The Millennium Collection*. All three were modest hit singles, but only "Stone Cold" made the Top 40. "Man on the Silver Mountain" should also be recognizable to fans of "classic rock" radio. The beautifully hypnotic "Catch the Rainbow" and bombastic, strings-enriched epic "Stargazer" are other highlights. The menacing "Kill the King," supple "Rainbow Eyes," 13-minute live version of Deep Purple's blues showcase "Mistreated," and catchy "I Surrender" are treats too. ("Since You Been Gone" and "I Surrender" were both penned by Argent veteran Russ Ballard.) Although 1997's stunning *The Very Best of Rainbow* is the definitive compilation, the generous 11-song, 66-minute *20th Century Masters—The Millennium Collection* certainly has its own virtues.

Bret Adams

Bonnie Raitt

Bonnie Raitt
1971, Warner Bros.

The astounding thing about Bonnie Raitt's blues album isn't that it's the work of a preternaturally gifted blues woman, it's that Raitt doesn't choose to stick to the blues. She's decided to blend her love of classic folk blues with folk music, including new folk-rock tunes, along with a slight R&B, New Orleans, and jazz bent and a mellow Californian vibe. Surely, *Bonnie Raitt* is a record of its times, as much as Jackson Browne's first album is, but with this, she not only sketches out the blueprint for her future recordings, but for the roots music that would later be labeled as Americana. The reason that *Bonnie Raitt* works is that she is such a warm, subtle singer. She never oversells these songs, she lays back and sings them with heart and wonderfully textured reading. Her singing is complemented by her band, who is equally as warm, relaxed, and engaging. This is music that goes down so easy, it's only on the subsequent plays that you realize how fully realized and textured it is. A terrific debut that has only grown in stature since its release.

Stephen Thomas Erlewine

Give It Up
September 1972, Warner Bros.

Bonnie Raitt may have switched producers for her second album *Give It Up*, hiring Michael Cuscuna, but she hasn't switched her style, sticking with the thoroughly engaging blend of folk, blues, R&B, and Californian soft rock. If anything, she's strengthened her formula here, making the divisions between the genres nearly indistinguishable. Take the title track, for instance. It opens with a bluesy acoustic guitar before kicking into a New Orleans brass band about halfway through—and the great thing about it is that Raitt makes the switch sound natural, even inevitable, never forced. And that's just the tip of the iceberg here, since *Give It Up* is filled with great songs, delivered in familiar, yet always surprising, ways by Raitt and her skilled band. For those that want to pigeonhole her as a white blues singer, she delivers the lovely "Nothing Seems to Matter," a gentle mid-tempo number that's as mellow as Linda Ronstadt and far more seductive. That's the key to *Give It Up*: Yes, Raitt can be earthy and sexy, but she balances it with an inviting sensuality that makes the record glow. It's all delivered in a fantastic set of originals and covers performed so naturally it's hard to tell them apart and roots music so thoroughly fused that it all sounds original, even when it's possible to spot the individual elements or influences. Raitt would go on to greater chart successes, but she not only had trouble topping this record, generations of singers, from Sheryl Crow to Shelby Lynne, have used this as a touchstone. One of the great Southern California records.

Stephen Thomas Erlewine

Takin' My Time
1973, Warner Bros.

This album is an overlooked gem in the catalog of Bonnie Raitt. On *Takin' My Time*, she wears her influences proudly in an eclectic musical mix containing blues, jazz, folk, New Orleans R&B, and calypso. Although she did not write her own material for this album, she demonstrates an excellent ear for songs and chooses material from some of the best songwriters of the day. She is a great interpreter, and her renditions of Jackson Browne's "I Thought I Was a Child" and Randy Newman's "Guilty" from this album are the definitive versions of these songs. The highlights of this album are the romantic ballads "I Gave My Love a Candle" and "Cry Like a Rainstorm," where Raitt adds an emotional depth to the performance unusual for such a young woman. (Perhaps that's a result of her spending time with elder statesmen of the blues community such as Mississippi Fred McDowell and Sippie Wallace.) Although the faster-paced songs like the calypso "Wah She Go Do" seem a little out of place, the playful tune is welcome among an album filled with the heartache of the slower tunes. Despite being a relative newcomer, Raitt had already earned the respect of her mentors and her peers, as evidenced by the musical contributions of Taj Mahal, and Little Feat members Lowell George and Bill Payne on the album. This is the last consistent album she would make until her comeback in the mid-'80s.

Vik Iyengar

Streetlights
1974, Warner Bros.

Bonnie Raitt had delivered three stellar albums, but chart success wasn't forthcoming, even if good reviews and a cult following were. So, she teamed with producer Jerry Ragovoy for *Streetlights* and attempted to make the crossover record that Warner so desperately wished she'd release. Over the years, the concessions that she made here—particularly the middle-of-the road arrangements (as opposed to the appealingly laid-back sounds of her previous records), the occasional use of strings, but also some of the song selections—have consigned *Streetlights* to noble failure status. There's no denying that's essentially what *Streetlights* is, but that makes it out to seem worse than it really is. It winds up paling to the wonderful ease and warm sensuality of her first three albums—she only occasionally hits that balance—but it's still undeniably pleasant, and there are moments here where she really pulls off some terrific work, including the opening cover of Joni Mitchell's "That Song About the

Midway," a good version of John Prine's "Angel From Montgomery," and the much-touted take on Allen Toussaint's "What Is Success." It may be easy to lament the suppression of the laid-back sexiness and organic feel of Raitt's earlier records, but there's still enough here in that spirit to make this worthwhile.

Stephen Thomas Erlewine

Green Light
1982, Warner Bros.

Since 1975's *Homeplate*, Bonnie Raitt has veered closer to the mainstream than she has to the organic, sexy funk of her early-'70s records. This bothered many listeners, who chose to concentrate on the surface instead of the substance, but Raitt retained many of the same special qualities she demonstrated on those records into the '80s—namely, her excellent taste in material, fondness for blurring folk, blues, country, and rock, and her wonderfully subtle, always engaging, interpretations. *Green Lights* may suffer a bit from a production that clearly pegs it as a 1982 release, but strip away its production and it's yet another satisfying collection of roots-rockers and bluesy ballads from the always reliable Raitt. Producer Rob Fraboni's recording may be a little bit too mainstream, lacking the new wave spark of, say, Dave Edmunds' similar-sounding recordings of this era, but Raitt nevertheless rises above the limitations of the recording and delivers a tight, enjoyable collection of amiable mainstream rockers with just a hint of roots. This isn't nearly as sexy as even *Sweet Forgiveness*, and it doesn't have much grit, but it has spirit and is fun, and it's a nice, smooth ride for those that like the direction Raitt's going.

Stephen Thomas Erlewine

Nick of Time
March 1989, Capitol

Prior to *Nick of Time*, Bonnie Raitt had been a reliable cult artist, delivering a string of solid records that were moderate successes and usually musically satisfying. From her 1971 debut through 1982's *Green Light*, she had a solid streak, but 1986's *Nine Lives* snapped it,

falling far short of her usual potential. Therefore, it shouldn't have been a surprise when Raitt decided to craft its follow-up as a major comeback, collaborating with producer Don Was on *Nick of Time*. At the time, the pairing seemed a little odd, since he was primarily known for the weird hipster funk of Was (Not Was) and the B-52's' quirky eponymous debut, but the match turned out to be inspired. Was used Raitt's classic early-'70s records as a blueprint, choosing to update the sound with a smooth, professional production and a batch of excellent contemporary songs. In this context, Raitt flourishes; she never rocks too hard, but there is grit to her singing and playing, even when the surfaces are clean and inviting. And while she only has two original songs here, *Nick of Time* plays like autobiography, which is a testament to the power of the songs, performances, and productions. It was a great comeback album that made for a great story, but the record never would have been a blockbuster success if it wasn't for the music, which is among the finest Raitt ever made. She must have realized this, since *Nick of Time* served as the blueprint for the majority of her '90s albums.

Stephen Thomas Erlewine

The Rascals

All I Really Need: The Complete Atlantic Recordings, 1965–1971
October 2001, Rhino Handmade

If ever an American band went through a more startling transformation than the Rascals did during the six years the original band recorded for Atlantic, let them show their colors. Here was a young east group who from the jump had complete creative control over their recordings, publishing, production, and packaging—something unheard of then—and issued over 15 Top 40 singles, three Top Ten albums, and two more that cracked the Top 40, most of which were issued without critical acclaim at the time. This six-CD retrospective of the band's entire tenure on Atlantic (there were two more recordings afterwards, issued on Columbia with a splintered version of the band), documents their complete studio output of eight albums over four and a half discs, and devotes a disc and a half to singles, A- and B-sides, alternates, and different versions of hits. For those familiar with the hits, it's difficult to imagine that the Rascals ever rocked as hard as they did on their first two albums, *The Young Rascals* and *Collections*. On the debut, tracks like "Slow Down" and "Baby Let's Wait" have an urgency to put the needle in the red right from the jump. On their sophomore effort, with the singles "Come on Up," "Lonely Too Long," and "Love Is a Beautiful Thing," the Rascals were entrenched in the soul and R&B groove, but not enough to leave out screaming rockers such as "Land of a Thousand Dances" and "Mickey's Monkey." With *Once Upon a Dream*, the textured, layered psychedelic pop and soul continued with "Rainy Day," "Please Love Me," "My Hawaii," and "It's Wonderful," all intercut with random sound effects à la the Beach Boys, but more organic and less removed from the context of the music itself. The band's center of gravity began to shift with *Freedom Suite*, with its stunning single, "People Got to Be Free," which captured the spirit of the late '60s as well as—if not better than—any rock song. Here, placing it at the last half of disc three, after *Time Peace*, reveals the album as a narrative of hope and innocence without a shred of naïveté. Here was a band striving to integrate its music and politics (right about this time the band refused to perform on bills where there wasn't a perfect division of black and white acts) on songs such as "People Got to Be Free," "A Ray of Hope," "Any Dance'll Do," "Look Around," and others. While the pop hooks were plentiful, so was the experimentation and risk-taking with the mixes and instrumentation, with more making it into the mix—from accordions to pipe organs to brass bands and Indian instruments. With the issue of *See* in 1970 and *Search and Nearness* in 1971, the band was being pulled apart at the seams creatively, financially, and historically. Nonetheless, despite excesses on both albums, their fine, tight rock and pop songs still dominated the proceedings, especially on

See, where the band tried to capture their rock & roll roots. The longer tracks on *Search and Nearness* revealed that at the very end the band was traveling in a direction that took the R&B edge to groove jazz extremes, with circular moves and dense textures running through the middle of repetitive grooves and riffs. This is a long-overdue retrospective for a band who is enshrined in the Rock & Roll Hall of Fame and whose perfect marriage of rock, soul, and R&B has influenced more acts than anybody would ever care to admit. This set is a necessity to be sure for anyone obsessed with the history of rock & roll.

Thom Jurek

The Raspberries

Greatest
May 2005, Capitol

Your typical garden-variety rock historian says that Big Star never went over with American record buyers because the kids were more interested in hard rock or prog than smart power pop at the time—but that logic conveniently ignores the fact that the Raspberries were scoring hits and selling tickets all across the nation at the same time *Radio City* was dying on the vine. And while Eric Carmen may have lacked Alex Chilton's snazz as a freak-genius guitarist or songwriter, at their best the Raspberries were the band who succeeded where Big Star failed, crafting gloriously hooky but potently rockin' three-minute tunes that moved the British Invasion musical ethos ten years into the future. (And one could argue that Wally Bryson, Jim Bonfanti, and John Alleksic were a more potent backing band than Chilton had at the time, even if they lacked a visionary along the lines of Chris Bell.) *Greatest* covers most of the same territory that was charted out on previous Raspberries compilations (most notably the *Capitol Collectors Series* set from 1991), but the material has been remastered using 24-bit technology for greater punch and power, and the liner notes feature relevant commentary from Carmen, Bryson, and Bonfanti on the songs. From the glorious teenage lust anthem "Go All the Way" to "Overnight Sensation (Hit Record)," still the best song about the rush of hearing yourself on the radio, *Greatest* is an excellent one-stop shopping place for your Raspberries needs. You may not need this to replace any of the previous greatest-hits sets, but anyone looking for a great introduction to this great band can buy this with confidence.

Mark Deming

Lou Reed

Transformer
1972, RCA

David Bowie has never been shy about acknowledging his influences, and since the boho decadence and sexual ambiguity of the Velvet Underground's music had a major impact on Bowie's work, it was only fitting that as Ziggy Stardust mania was reaching its peak, Bowie would offer Lou Reed some much needed help with his career, which was stuck in neutral after his first solo album came and went. Musically, Reed's work didn't have too much in common with the sonic bombast of the glam scene, but at least it was a place where his eccentricities could find a comfortable home, and on *Transformer*, Bowie and his right-hand man, Mick Ronson, crafted a new sound for Reed that was better fitting (and more commercially astute) than the ambivalent tone of his first solo album. Ronson adds some guitar raunch to "Vicious" and "Hangin' Round" that's a lot flashier than what Reed cranked out with the Velvets, but still honors Lou's strengths in guitar-driven hard rock, while the imaginative arrangements Ronson cooked up for "Perfect Day," "Walk on the Wild Side," and "Goodnight Ladies" blend pop polish with musical thinking just as distinctive as Reed's lyrical conceits. And while Reed occasionally overplays his hand in writing stuff he figured the glam kids wanted ("Make Up" and "I'm So Free" being the most obvious examples), "Perfect Day," "Walk on the Wild Side," and "New York Telephone Conversation" proved he could still write about the demimonde with both perception and respect. The sound and style of *Transformer* would in many ways define Reed's career in the 1970s, and while it led him into a style that proved to be a dead end, you can't deny that Bowie and Ronson gave their hero a new lease on life—and a solid album in the bargain.

Mark Deming

Berlin
1973, RCA

Transformer and "Walk on the Wild Side" were both major hits in 1972, to the surprise of both Lou Reed and the music industry, and with Reed suddenly a hot commodity, he used his newly won clout to make the most ambitious album of his career, *Berlin*. *Berlin* was the musical equivalent of a drug-addled kid set loose in a candy store; the album's songs, which form a loose story line about a doomed romance between two chemically fueled bohemians, were fleshed out with a huge, boomy production (Bob Ezrin at his most grandiose) and arrangements overloaded with guitars, keyboards, horns, strings, and any other kitchen sink that was handy (the session band included Jack Bruce, Steve Winwood, Aynsley Dunbar, and Tony Levin). And while Reed had often been accused of focusing on the dark side of life, he and Ezrin approached *Berlin* as their opportunity to make The Most Depressing Album of All Time, and they hardly missed a trick. This all seemed a bit much for an artist who made such superb use of the two-guitars/bass/drums lineup with the Velvet Underground, especially since Reed doesn't even play electric guitar on the album; the sheer size of *Berlin* ultimately overpowers both Reed and his material. But if *Berlin* is largely a failure of ambition, that sets it apart from the vast majority of Reed's lesser works; Lou's vocals are both precise and impassioned, and though a few of the songs are little more than sketches, the best— "How Do You Think It Feels," "Oh, Jim," "The Kids," and "Sad Song"—are powerful, bitter stuff. It's hard not to be impressed by *Berlin*, given the sheer scope of the project, but while it earns an A for effort, the actual execution merits more of a B-.

Mark Deming

Rock N Roll Animal
1974, RCA

In 1974, after the commercial disaster of his album *Berlin*, Lou Reed needed a hit, and *Rock N Roll Animal* was a rare display of commercial acumen on his part, just the right album at just the right time. Recorded in concert with Reed's crack road band at the peak of their form, *Rock N Roll Animal* offered a set of his most anthemic songs (most dating from his days with the Velvet Underground) in arrangements that presented his lean, effective melodies and street-level lyrics in their most user-friendly form (or at least as user friendly as an album with a song called "Heroin" can get). Early-'70s arena rock bombast is often the order of the day, but guitarists Dick Wagner and Steve Hunter use their six-string muscle to lift these songs up, not weigh them down, and with Reed's passionate but controlled vocals riding over the top, "Sweet Jane," "White Light/White Heat," and "Rock 'n' Roll" finally sound like the radio hits they always should have been. Reed would rarely sound this commercial again, but *Rock N Roll Animal* proves he could please a crowd when he had to. The revised CD reissue of *Rock N Roll Animal* released in 2000 offers markedly better sound than the album's initial release, along with two bonus cuts that give a better idea of how this band approached the material from *Berlin* on-stage, as well as an amusing moment of Reed verbally sparring with a heckler.

Mark Deming

Coney Island Baby
February 1976, RCA

From 1972's *Transformer* onward, Lou Reed spent most of the '70s playing the druggy decadence card for all it was worth, with increasingly mixed results. But on 1976's *Coney Island Baby*, Reed's songwriting began to move into warmer, more compassionate territory, and the result was his most approachable album since *Loaded*. On most of the tracks, Reed stripped his band back down to guitar, bass, and drums, and the results were both leaner and a lot more comfortable than the leaden over-production of *Sally Can't Dance* or *Berlin*. "Crazy Feeling," "She's My Best Friend," and "Coney Island Baby" found Reed actually writing recognizable love songs for a change, and while Reed pursued his traditional interest in the underside of the hipster's life on "Charlie's Girl" and "Nobody's Business," he did so with a breezy, freewheeling air that was truly a relief after the lethargic tone of *Sally Can't Dance*. "Kicks" used an audio-tape collage to generate atmospheric tension that gave its tale of drugs and death a chilling quality that was far more effective than his usual blasé take on the subject, and "Coney Island Baby" was the polar opposite, a song about love and regret that was as sincere and heart-tugging as anything the man has ever recorded. *Coney Island Baby* sounds casual on the surface, but emotionally it's as compelling as anything Lou Reed released in the 1970s, and proved he could write about real people with recognizable emotions as well as anyone in rock music—something you might not have guessed from most of the solo albums that preceded it.

Mark Deming

Street Hassle
1978, Arista

The rise of the punk/new wave movement in the late '70s proved just how pervasive Lou Reed's influence had been through the past decade, but it also gave him some stiff competition, as suddenly Reed was no longer the only poet of the New York streets. 1978's *Street Hassle* was Reed's first album after punk had gained public currency, and Reed appeared to have taken the minimal approach of punk to heart. With the exception of *Metal Machine Music*, *Street Hassle* was Reed's rawest set of the 1970s; partly recorded live, with arrangements stripped to the bone, *Street Hassle* was dark, deep, and ominous, a 180-degree turn from the polished neo-glam of *Transformer*. Lyrically, *Street Hassle* found Reed looking deep into himself, and not liking what he saw. Opening with an uncharitable parody of "Sweet Jane," *Street Hassle* found Reed acknowledging just how much a self-parody he'd become in the 1970s, and just how much he hated himself for it, on songs like "Dirt" and "Shooting Star." *Street Hassle* was Reed's most creatively ambitious album since *Berlin*, and it sounded revelatory on first release in 1978. Sadly, time has magnified its flaws; the Lenny Bruce-inspired "I Wanna Be Black" sounds like a bad idea today, and the murk of the album's binaural mix isn't especially flattering to anyone. But the album's best moments are genuinely exciting, and the title cut, a three-movement poetic tone poem about life on the New York streets, is one of the most audacious and deeply moving moments of Reed's solo career. Raw, wounded, and unapologetically difficult, *Street Hassle* isn't the masterpiece Reed was shooting for, but it's still among the most powerful and compelling albums he released during the 1970s, and too personal and affecting to ignore.

Mark Deming

The Bells
1979, Buddha

After the harrowing triumph of *Street Hassle*, Lou Reed's *The Bells* sounded like a bit of a step back; it returned Reed to the more listener-friendly, keyboard-dominated sound of *Rock and Roll Heart*, the lyrics lacked the caustic self-loathing of songs like "Dirt" or "I Wanna Be Black," and it even featured a four-and-a-half-minute funk workout called "Disco Mystic" (hey, this was 1979). But lyrically, *The Bells* found Reed moving away from the boho decadence of most of his 1970s work and toward a more compassionate perspective on his characters; "Families" and "All Through the Night" display an empathy and emotional depth Reed didn't often allow himself as a solo artist, and "Stupid Man" and "Looking for Love" rocked hard while making the loneliness of their protagonists felt. And the title cut, with Reed experimenting with a guitar synthesizer and free jazz hero Don Cherry inviting the spirit on trumpet, is both a brave exploration of musical space and a lyrically touching sketch of loss and salvation. An album that's worn well over time, *The Bells* gains depth with each playing and now sounds like one of Reed's finest solo efforts of the 1970s.

Mark Deming

The Blue Mask
1982, RCA

In 1982, 12 years after he left the Velvet Underground, Lou Reed released *The Blue Mask*, the first album where he lived up to the potential he displayed in the most groundbreaking of all American rock bands. *The Blue Mask* was Reed's first album after he overcame a long-standing addiction to alcohol and drugs, and it reveals a renewed focus and dedication to craft—for the first time in years, Reed had written an entire album's worth of moving, compelling songs, and was performing them with keen skill and genuine emotional commitment. Reed was also playing electric guitar again, and with the edgy genius he summoned up on *White Light/White Heat*. Just as importantly, he brought Robert Quine on board as

his second guitarist, giving Reed a worthy foil who at once brought great musical ideas to the table, and encouraged the bandleader to make the most of his own guitar work. (Reed also got superb support from his rhythm section, bassist extraordinaire Fernando Saunders and ace drummer Doane Perry). As Reed stripped his band back to a muscular two-guitars/bass/drums format, he also shed the faux-decadent "Rock N Roll Animal" persona that had dominated his solo work and wrote clearly and fearlessly of his life, his thoughts, and his fears, performing the songs with supreme authority whether he was playing with quiet subtlety (such as the lovely "My House" or the unnerving "The Gun") or cranked-to-ten fury (the paranoid "Waves of Fear" and the emotionally devastating title cut). Intelligent, passionate, literate, mature, and thoroughly heartfelt, *The Blue Mask* was everything Reed's fans had been looking for in his work for years, and it's vivid proof that for some rockers, life can begin on the far side of 35.

Mark Deming

New Sensations
1984, RCA

Lou Reed never struck anyone as one of the happiest guys in rock & roll, so some fans were taken aback when his 1984 album *New Sensations* kicked off with "I Love You, Suzanne," a catchy up-tempo rocker that sounded a lot like a pop tune. After reaffirming his status as one of rock's greatest poets with *The Blue Mask* and *Legendary Hearts*, what was Reed doing here? Lou was having a great time, and his pleasure was infectious—*New Sensations* is a set of straight-ahead rock & roll that ranks with the most purely enjoyable albums of Lou's career. Reed opted not to work with guitarist Robert Quine this time out, instead overdubbing rhythm lines over his own leads, and if the guitars don't cut quite as deep, they're still wiry and in the pocket throughout, and the rhythm section of Fernando Saunders and Fred Maher rocks hard with a tough, sinewy groove. And while much of *New Sensations* finds Reed in a surprisingly optimistic mood, this isn't "Don't Worry, Be Happy" by any stretch of the imagination. On "Endlessly Jealous," "My Friend George," and "Fly Into the Sun," Reed makes it clear that happiness can be a hard-won commodity, and when Reed embraces life's pleasures on "Turn to Me" and "New Sensations," he does so with a fierce joy that's realistic, unblinking, and deeply felt, like a man whose signed on for the full ride and is going to enjoy the good times while they last. Like *Coney Island Baby*, *New Sensations* showed that Reed had a lot more warmth and humanity than he was given credit for, and made clear that he could "write happy" when he felt like, with all the impact of his "serious" material.

Mark Deming

REO Speedwagon

You Can Tune a Piano, But You Can't Tuna Fish
April 1978, Epic/Legacy

You Can Tune a Piano, But You Can't Tuna Fish was a break-through album for REO Speedwagon in a sense, gelling the guitar craft of Gary Richrath and the vocals of Kevin Cronin with songs that rambled and rolled and never stopped for air. Richrath's style rapidly formed some catchy hooks, and Cronin's songwriting is solid, while his voice sounds rejuvenated and downright fiery. "Roll With the Changes" and "Time for Me to Fly" only made it to number 58 and number 56 on the charts, but the album's sales trumped all of the chart statistics, giving REO its second platinum-selling album. Songs like "Do You Know Where Your Woman Is Tonight" and "Blazin' Your Own Trail Again" are well groomed around the edges, sounding smoother and more established than the band's earlier material. The harmonies on most of the songs stick to the guitar chords, and even the frantic "Unidentified Flying Tuna Trot," a wild and flighty guitar piece, is unraveled with tornado-like power. With the guitars sounding louder, the songs running quicker, and the culmination of both being well maintained, *Tuna Fish* proved that the members of REO Speedwagon could play rock & roll when they had to.

Mike DeGagne

Hi Infidelity
December 1980, Epic/Legacy

Many albums have scaled to the top of the American charts, many of them not so good, but few have been as widely forgotten and spurned as REO Speedwagon's *Hi Infidelity*. In a way, the group deserved this kind of success. They had been slogging it out in the arenas of the U.S., building up a sizeable audience because they could deliver live. And then, in 1980, they delivered a record that not just summarized their strengths, but captured everything that was good about arena rock. This is the sound of the stadiums in that netherworld between giants like Zeppelin and MTV's slick, video-ready anthems. This is unabashedly mainstream rock, but there's a real urgency to the songs and the performances that gives it a real emotional core, even if the production keeps it tied to the early, previsual '80s. And so what if it does, because this is *great* arena rock, filled with hooks as expansive as Three Rivers Stadium and as catchy as the flu. That, of course, applies to the record's two biggest hits—the power ballad "Keep on Loving You" and the surging "Take It on the Run"—which define their era, but what gives the album real staying power is that the rest of the record works equally well. That's most apparent on the Bo Diddley-inspired opener, "Don't Let Him Go," whose insistent beat sent it to the album rock charts, but also such great album tracks as "Follow My Heart," the sun-kissed '60s homage "In Your Letter," and "Tough Guys." What's really great about these songs is not just the sheen of professionalism that makes them addictive to listen to, but there's a real strain of pathos that runs through these songs—the album's title isn't just a clever pun, but a description of the tortured romantic relationships that populate this record's songs. This is really arena rock's *Blood on the Tracks*, albeit by a group of guys instead of a singular vision, but that makes it more affecting, as well as a killer slice of ear candy. It's easy to dismiss REO Speedwagon, since they weren't hip at the time, and no amount of historical revisionism will make them cool kitsch. And, let's face it, their records were usually hit-and-miss affairs. But they did get it right once, and it's on this glorious record—if you need proof why arena rock was giant, this is it. [In 2001, Epic/Legacy reissued *Hi Infidelity* with remastered sound and restored artwork.]

Stephen Thomas Erlewine

The Essential REO Speedwagon
August 2004, Epic/Legacy

REO Speedwagon reached the *Billboard* charts 24 times. Not all of those were big hits, of course. Some of the early singles barely qualified for the Hot 100, while some of the latter-day hits made no waves outside of the Mainstream Rock charts, which means that they are relatively unheard by the pop audience that loved *Hi Infidelity* and "Can't Fight This Feeling." In other words, all the big hits could have been assembled on a single-disc collection, but Epic/Legacy's 2004 release *The Essential REO Speedwagon* is a sprawling double-disc, 33-track history. There's a reason for that. The extra space gives plenty of room for the band—and Kevin Cronin was indeed a co-producer on this set—to show that they weren't just a power ballad powerhouse, that they also rocked hard and stretched out on occasion. Consequently, *The Essential* is more of a history than a standard hits collection. If anything, the hits take a back seat, with the first big anthem, "Roll With the Changes," not showing up until track 13 and *Hi Infidelity* not rearing its head until the second disc. If you just want the hits, the appropriately titled 1988 collection *The Hits* will serve those up, but *Essential* digs deeper, hitting nearly all of the key album tracks, concert staples, and fan favorites, drawing a picture of a band that was more muscular and complex than the hits, particularly power ballads like "Can't Fight This Feeling," would suggest. It's not for every listener, but for those fans who want more than the hits but don't want full-length albums, this is the perfect solution.

Stephen Thomas Erlewine

Keith Richards

Talk Is Cheap
1988, Virgin

In 1987, it was anyone's guess if the Stones would ever get back together. Sure, Mick Jagger and Keith Richards were well known for their public disagreements, but when Jagger decided to tour in support of his second solo album, *Primitive Cool*, Richards was disheartened and finally succumbed to the idea of recording without the Rolling Stones. Taking the band he had assembled to back up Chuck Berry for the *Hail! Hail! Rock 'n' Roll* documentary (along with longtime session player Waddy Wachtel), Richards put together an album that was straightforward, musical, and better than a good portion of the Stones' output in the first half of the '80s. The lead single "Take It So Hard," "Whip It Up," and "Struggle" are classic Richards riffology, and tracks like "Locked Away" are emotional without being maudlin and worldly but not sounding adult contemporary. The main point of *Talk Is Cheap* is the music, nothing more; Richards obviously didn't want to fret about anything but the groove. While Jagger's solo work sounded like Mick with some studio musicians, Keith had assembled a band, found a productive songwriting partner in Steve Jordan, and created a record that was free of frills. Simply put, Richards sounded like he was playing for himself, and playing with a certain sense of enjoyment. The new band, the X-pensive Winos, had a different work ethic than the Stones, forcing Richards to focus on the music. What resulted was a solid album built on fundamentals rather than style. It's hard not to see who the real musical force was in the Stones after hearing *Talk Is Cheap*.

Chris True

The Rolling Stones

The Rolling Stones (England's Newest Hitmakers) [US]
April 1964, London

The group's debut album was the most uncompromisingly blues/R&B-oriented full-length recording they would ever release. Mostly occupied with covers, this was as hardcore as British R&B ever got; it's raw and ready. But the Stones succeeded in establishing themselves as creative interpreters, putting '50s and early-'60s blues, rock, and soul classics (some quite obscure to white audiences) through a younger, more guitar-oriented filter. The record's highlighted by blistering versions of "Route 66," "Carol," the hypertempoed "I Just Want to Make Love to You," "I'm a King Bee," and "Walking the Dog." Their Bo Diddley-ized version of Buddy Holly's "Not Fade Away" gave them their first British Top Ten hit (and their first small American one). The acoustic ballad "Tell Me" was Jagger-Richards' first good original tune, but the other group-penned originals were little more than rehashed jams of blues clichés, keeping this album from reaching truly classic status.

[The Rolling Stones' London/ABKCO catalog was reissued in August of 2002, packaged in digipacks with restored album artwork, remastered, and released as hybrid discs that contain both CD and Super Audio CD layers. The remastering—performed with Direct Stream Digital (DSD) encoding—is a drastic improvement, leaping out of the speaker yet still sounding like the original albums. This is noticeable on the standard CD layer but is considerably more pronounced on the SACD layer, which is shockingly realistic in its detail and presence yet is still faithful to the original mixes; Keith Richards' revved-up acoustic guitar on "Street Fighting Man" still sends the machine into overdrive, for instance. It just sounds like he's in the room with you. Even if you've never considered yourself an audiophile, have never heard the differences between standard and gold-plated CDs, you *will* hear the difference with SACD, even on a cheap stereo system without a high-end amplifier or speakers. And you won't just hear the difference, you'll be an instant convert and wish, hope, and pray that other artists whose catalog hasn't been reissued since the early days of CD—Bob Dylan, Bruce Springsteen, Neil Young, *especially* the Beatles—are given the same treatment in the very near future. SACD and DSD are that good.]

Richie Unterberger

The Rolling Stones, Now!
April 1965, ABKCO

Although their third American album was patched together (in the usual British Invasion tradition) from a variety of sources, it's their best early R&B-oriented effort. Most of the Stones' early albums suffer from three or four very weak cuts; *Now!* is almost uniformly strong start-to-finish, the emphasis on some of their blackest material. The covers of "Down

Home Girl," Bo Diddley's vibrating "Mona," Otis Redding's "Pain in My Heart," and Barbara Lynn's "Oh Baby" are all among the group's best R&B interpretations. The best gem is "Little Red Rooster," a pure blues with wonderful slide guitar from Brian Jones (and a number one single in Britain, although it was only an album track in the U.S.). As songwriters, Jagger and Richards are still struggling, but they come up with one of their first winners (and an American Top 20 hit) with the yearning, soulful "Heart of Stone."

[The Rolling Stones' London/ABKCO catalog was reissued in August of 2002, packaged in digipacks with restored album artwork, remastered, and released as hybrid discs that contain both CD and Super Audio CD layers. The remastering—performed with Direct Stream Digital (DSD) encoding—is a drastic improvement, leaping out of the speaker yet still sounding like the original albums. This is noticeable on the standard CD layer but is considerably more pronounced on the SACD layer, which is shockingly realistic in its detail and presence yet is still faithful to the original mixes; Keith Richards' revved-up acoustic guitar on "Street Fighting Man" still sends the machine into overdrive, for instance. It just sounds like he's in the room with you. Even if you've never considered yourself an audiophile, have never heard the differences between standard and gold-plated CDs, you *will* hear the difference with SACD, even on a cheap stereo system without a high-end amplifier or speakers. And you won't just hear the difference, you'll be an instant convert and wish, hope, and pray that other artists whose catalog hasn't been reissued since the early days of CD—Bob Dylan, Bruce Springsteen, Neil Young, *especially* the Beatles—are given the same treatment in the very near future. SACD and DSD are that good.]

Richie Unterberger

Out of Our Heads
August 1965, ABKCO

In 1965, the Stones finally proved themselves capable of writing classic rock singles that mined their R&B/blues roots, but updated them into a more guitar-based, thoroughly contemporary context. The first enduring Jagger-Richards classics are here—"The Last Time," its menacing, folky B-side "Play With Fire," and the riff-driven "Satisfaction," which made them superstars in the States and defined their sound and rebellious attitude better than any other single song. On the rest of the album, they largely opted for mid-'60s soul covers, Marvin Gaye's "Hitch Hike," Otis Redding's "Cry to Me," and Sam Cooke's "Good Times" being particular standouts. "I'm All Right" (based on a Bo Diddley sound) showed their 1965 sound at its rawest, and there are a couple of fun, though derivative, bluesy originals in "The Spider and the Fly" and "The Under Assistant West Coast Promotion Man."

Richie Unterberger

December's Children (And Everybody's)
December 1965, ABKCO

The last Stones album in which cover material accounted for 50 percent of the content was thrown together from a variety of singles, British LP tracks, outtakes, and a cut from an early 1964 U.K. EP. Haphazard assembly aside, much of it's great, including the huge hit "Get Off of My Cloud" and the controversial, string-laden acoustic ballad "As Tears Go By" (a Top Ten item in America). Raiding the R&B closet for the last time, they also offered a breathless run-through of Larry Williams' "She Said Yeah," a sultry Chuck Berry cover ("Talkin' About You"), and exciting live versions of "Route 66" and Hank Snow's "I'm Moving On." More importantly,

Jagger-Richards' songwriting partnership had now developed to the extent that several non-A-side tracks were reasonably strong in their own right, such as "I'm Free" and "The Singer Not the Song." And the version of "You Better Move On" (which had been featured on a British EP at the beginning of 1964) was one of their best and most tender soul covers.

[The Rolling Stones' London/ABKCO catalog was reissued in August of 2002, packaged in digipacks with restored album artwork, remastered, and released as hybrid discs that contain both CD and Super Audio CD layers. The remastering—performed with Direct Stream Digital (DSD) encoding—is a drastic improvement, leaping out of the speaker yet still sounding like the original albums. This is noticeable on the standard CD layer but is considerably more pronounced on the SACD layer, which is shockingly realistic in its detail and presence yet is still faithful to the original mixes; Keith Richards' revved-up acoustic guitar on "Street Fighting Man" still sends the machine into overdrive, for instance. It just sounds like he's in the room with you. Even if you've never considered yourself an audiophile, have never heard the differences between standard and gold-plated CDs, you *will* hear the difference with SACD, even on a cheap stereo system without a high-end amplifier or speakers. And you won't just hear the difference, you'll be an instant convert and wish, hope, and pray that other artists whose catalog hasn't been reissued since the early days of CD—Bob Dylan, Bruce Springsteen, Neil Young, *especially* the Beatles—are given the same treatment in the very near future. SACD and DSD are that good.]

Richie Unterberger

Aftermath
June 1966, ABKCO

The Rolling Stones finally delivered a set of all-original material with this LP, which also did much to define the group as the bad boys of rock & roll with their sneering attitude toward the world in general and the female sex in particular. The borderline misogyny could get a bit juvenile in tunes like "Stupid Girl." But on the other hand the group began incorporating the influences of psychedelia and Dylan into their material with classics like "Paint It Black," an eerily insistent number one hit graced by some of the best use of sitar (played by Brian Jones) on a rock record. Other classics included the jazzy "Under My Thumb," where Jones added exotic accents with his vibes, and the delicate Elizabethan ballad "Lady Jane," where dulcimer can be heard. Some of the material is fairly ho-hum, to be honest, as Mick Jagger and Keith Richards were still prone to inconsistent songwriting; "Goin' Home," an 11-minute blues jam, was remarkable more for its barrier-crashing length than its content. Look out for an obscure gem, however, in the brooding, meditative "I Am Waiting."

[The Rolling Stones' London/ABKCO catalog was reissued in August of 2002, packaged in digipacks with restored album artwork, remastered, and released as hybrid discs that contain both CD and Super Audio CD layers. The remastering—performed with Direct Stream Digital (DSD) encoding—is a drastic improvement, leaping out of the speaker yet still sounding like the original albums. This is noticeable on the standard CD layer but is considerably more

pronounced on the SACD layer, which is shockingly realistic in its detail and presence yet is still faithful to the original mixes; Richards' revved-up acoustic guitar on "Street Fighting Man" still sends the machine into overdrive, for instance. It just sounds like he's in the room with you. Even if you've never considered yourself an audiophile, have never heard the differences between standard and gold-plated CDs, you *will* hear the difference with SACD, even on a cheap stereo system without a high-end amplifier or speakers. And you won't just hear the difference, you'll be an instant convert and wish, hope, and pray that other artists whose catalog hasn't been reissued since the early days of CD—Bob Dylan, Bruce Springsteen, Neil Young, *especially* the Beatles—are given the same treatment in the very near future. SACD and DSD are that good.]

Richie Unterberger

Flowers
June 1967, Abko

Dismissed as a rip-off of sorts by some critics as it took the patchwork bastardization of British releases for the American audience to extremes, gathering stray tracks from the U.K. versions of *Aftermath* and *Between the Buttons*, 1966-1967 singles (some of which had already been used on the U.S. editions of *Aftermath* and *Between the Buttons*), and a few outtakes. Judged solely by the music, though, it's rather great. "Lady Jane," "Ruby Tuesday," and "Let's Spend the Night Together" are all classics (although they had all been on an LP before); the 1966 single "Mother's Little Helper," a Top Ten hit, is also terrific; and "Have You Seen Your Mother Baby, Standing in the Shadow?" making its first album appearance, is the early Stones at their most surrealistic and angst-ridden. A lot of the rest of the cuts rate among their most outstanding 1966-1967 work. "Out of Time" is hit-worthy in its own right (and in fact topped the British charts in an inferior cover by Chris Farlowe); "Backstreet Girl," with its European waltz flavor, is one of *the* great underrated Stones songs. The same goes for the psychedelic Bo Diddley of "Please Go Home," and the acoustic, pensively sardonic "Sittin' on a Fence," with its strong Appalachian flavor. Almost every track is strong, so if you're serious about your Stones, don't pass this by just because a bunch of people slag it as an exploitative marketing trick (which it is). There's some outstanding material you can't get anywhere else, and the album as a whole plays very well from end to end.

[The Rolling Stones' London/ABKCO catalog was reissued in August of 2002, packaged in digipacks with restored album artwork, remastered, and released as hybrid discs that contain both CD and Super Audio CD layers. The remastering—performed with Direct Stream Digital (DSD) encoding—is a drastic improvement, leaping out of the speaker yet still sounding like the original albums. This is noticeable on the standard CD layer but is considerably more pronounced on the SACD layer, which is shockingly realistic in its detail and presence yet is still faithful to the original mixes; Keith Richards' revved-up acoustic guitar on "Street Fighting Man" still sends the machine into overdrive, for instance. It just sounds like he's in the room with you. Even if you've never considered yourself an audiophile, have never heard the differences between standard and gold-plated CDs, you *will* hear the difference with SACD, even on a cheap stereo system without a high-end amplifier or speakers. And you won't just hear the difference, you'll be an instant convert and wish, hope, and pray that other artists whose catalog hasn't been reissued since the early days of CD—Bob Dylan, Bruce Springsteen, Neil Young, *especially* the Beatles—are given the same treatment in the very near future. SACD and DSD are that good.]

Richie Unterberger

Their Satanic Majesties Request
November 1967, ABKCO

Without a doubt, no Rolling Stones album—and, indeed, very few rock albums from any era—split critical opinion as much as the Rolling Stones' psychedelic outing. Many dismiss the record as sub-*Sgt. Pepper* posturing; others confess, if only in private, to a fascination with the album's inventive arrangements, which incorporated some African rhythms, Mellotrons, and full orchestration. Never before or since did the Stones take so many chances in the studio. This writer, at least, feels that the record has been unfairly undervalued, partly because purists expect the Stones to constantly champion a blues 'n' raunch world view. About half the material is very strong, particularly the glorious "She's a Rainbow," with its beautiful harmonies, piano, and strings; the riff-driven "Citadel"; the hazy, dream-like "In Another Land," Bill Wyman's debut writing (and singing) credit on a Stones release; and the majestically dark and doomy cosmic rocker "2000 Light Years From Home," with some of the creepiest synthesizer effects (devised by Brian Jones) ever to grace a rock record. The downfall of the album was caused by some weak songwriting on the lesser tracks, particularly the interminable psychedelic jam "Sing This All Together (See What Happens)." It's a much better record than most people give it credit for being, though, with a strong current of creeping uneasiness that undercuts the gaudy psychedelic flourishes. In 1968, the Stones would go back to the basics, and never wander down these paths again, making this all the more of a fascinating anomaly in the group's discography.

[The Rolling Stones' London/ABKCO catalog was reissued in August of 2002, packaged in digipacks with restored album artwork, remastered, and released as hybrid discs that contain both CD and Super Audio CD layers. The remastering—performed with Direct Stream Digital (DSD) encoding—is a drastic improvement, leaping out of the speaker yet still sounding like the original albums. This is noticeable on the standard CD layer but is considerably more pronounced on the SACD layer, which is shockingly realistic in its detail and presence yet is still faithful to the original mixes; Keith Richards' revved-up acoustic guitar on "Street Fighting Man" still sends the machine into overdrive, for instance. It just sounds like he's in the room with you. Even if you've never considered yourself an audiophile, have never heard the differences between standard and gold-plated CDs, you *will* hear the difference with SACD, even on a cheap stereo system without a high-end amplifier or speakers. And you won't just hear the difference, you'll be an instant convert and wish, hope, and pray that other artists whose catalog hasn't been reissued since the early days of CD—Bob Dylan, Bruce Springsteen, Neil Young, *especially* the Beatles—are given the same treatment in the very near future. SACD and DSD are that good.]

Richie Unterberger

Beggars Banquet
November 1968, ABKCO

The Stones forsook psychedelic experimentation to return to their blues roots on this celebrated album, which was immediately acclaimed as one of their landmark achievements. A strong acoustic Delta blues flavor colors much of the material, particularly "Salt of the Earth" and "No Expectations," which features some beautiful slide guitar work. Basic rock & roll was not forgotten, however: "Street Fighting Man," a reflection of the political turbulence of 1968, was one of their most innovative singles, and "Sympathy for the Devil," with its fire-dancing guitar licks, leering Jagger vocals, African rhythms, and explicitly satanic lyrics, was an image-defining epic. On "Stray Cat Blues," Jagger and crew began to explore the kind of decadent sexual sleaze that they would take to the point of self-parody by the mid-'70s. At the time, though, the approach was still fresh, and the lyrical bite of most of the material ensured *Beggars Banquet*'s place as one of the top blues-based rock records of all time.

[The Rolling Stones' London/ABKCO catalog was reissued in August of 2002, packaged in digipacks with restored album artwork, remastered, and released as hybrid discs that contain both CD and Super Audio CD layers. The remastering—performed with Direct Stream Digital (DSD) encoding—is a drastic improvement, leaping out of the speaker yet still sounding like the original albums. This is noticeable on the standard CD layer but is considerably more pronounced on the SACD layer, which is shockingly realistic in its detail and presence yet is still faithful to the original mixes; Richards' revved-up acoustic guitar on "Street Fighting Man" still sends the machine into overdrive, for instance. It just sounds like he's in the room with you. Even if you've never considered yourself an audiophile, have never heard the differences between standard and gold-plated CDs, you *will* hear the difference with SACD, even on a cheap stereo system without a high-end amplifier or speakers. And you won't just hear the difference, you'll be an instant convert and wish, hope, and pray that other artists whose catalog hasn't been reissued since the early days of CD—Bob Dylan, Bruce Springsteen, Neil Young, *especially* the Beatles—are given the same treatment in the very near future. SACD and DSD are that good.]

Richie Unterberger

Let It Bleed
November 1969, ABKCO

Mostly recorded without Brian Jones—who died several months before its release (although he does play on two tracks) and was replaced by Mick Taylor (who also plays on just two songs)—this extends the rock and  blues feel of *Beggars Banquet* into slightly harder-rocking, more demonically sexual territory. The Stones were never as consistent on album as their main rivals, the Beatles, and *Let It Bleed* suffers from some rather perfunctory tracks, like "Monkey Man" and a countrified remake of the classic "Honky Tonk Woman" (here titled "Country Honk"). Yet some of the songs are among their very best, especially "Gimme Shelter," with its shimmering guitar lines and apocalyptic lyrics; the harmonica-driven "Midnight Rambler"; the druggy party ambience of the title track; and the stunning "You Can't Always Get What You Want," which was the Stones' "Hey Jude" of sorts, with its epic structure, horns, philosophical lyrics, and swelling choral vocals. "You Got the Silver" (Keith Richards' first lead vocal) and Robert Johnson's "Love in Vain," by contrast, were as close to the roots of acoustic down-home blues as the Stones ever got.

[The Rolling Stones' London/ABKCO catalog was re-issued in August of 2002, packaged in digipacks with restored album artwork, remastered, and released as hybrid discs that contain both CD and Super Audio CD layers. The remastering—performed with Direct Stream Digital (DSD) encoding—is a drastic improvement, leaping out of the speaker yet still sounding like the original albums. This is noticeable on the standard CD layer but is considerably more pronounced on the SACD layer, which is shockingly realistic in its detail and presence yet is still faithful to the original mixes; Keith Richards' revved-up acoustic guitar on "Street Fighting Man" still sends the machine into overdrive, for instance. It just sounds like he's in the room with you. Even if you've never considered yourself an audiophile, have never heard the differences between standard and gold-plated CDs, you *will* hear the difference with SACD, even on a cheap stereo system without a high-end amplifier or speakers. And you won't just hear the difference, you'll be an instant convert and wish, hope, and pray that other artists whose catalog hasn't been reissued since the early days of CD—Bob Dylan, Bruce Springsteen, Neil Young, *especially* the Beatles—are given the same treatment in the very near future. SACD and DSD are that good.]

Richie Unterberger

Get Yer Ya-Ya's Out!
September 1970, ABKCO

Recorded during their American tour in late 1969, and centered around their American tour in late 1969, and centered around material from the *Beggars Banquet-Let It Bleed* era. Often acclaimed as one of the top live rock albums of all time, its appeal has dimmed a little today. The live versions are reasonably different from the studio ones, but ultimately not as good, a notable exception being the long workout of "Midnight Rambler," with extended harmonica solos and the unforgettable section where the pace slows to a bump-and-grind crawl. Some Stones aficionados, in fact, prefer a bootleg from the same tour (*Liver Than You'll Ever Be*, to which this album was unleashed in response), or their amazing the-show-must-go-on performance in the jaws of hell at Altamont (preserved in the *Gimme Shelter* film). Fans that are unconcerned with picky comparisons such as these will still find *Ya-Ya's* an outstanding album, and it's certainly the Stones' best official live recording.

[The Rolling Stones' London/ABKCO catalog was re-issued in August of 2002, packaged in digipacks with restored album artwork, remastered, and released as hybrid discs that contain both CD and Super Audio CD layers. The remastering—performed with Direct Stream Digital (DSD) encoding—is a drastic improvement, leaping out of the speaker yet still sounding like the original albums. This is noticeable on the standard CD layer but is considerably more pronounced on the SACD layer, which is shockingly realistic in its detail and presence yet is still faithful to the original mixes; Keith Richards' revved-up acoustic guitar on "Street Fighting Man" still sends the machine into overdrive, for instance. It just sounds like he's in the room with you. Even if you've never considered yourself an audiophile, have never heard the differences between standard and gold-plated CDs, you *will* hear the difference with SACD, even on a cheap stereo system without a high-end amplifier or speakers. And you won't just hear the difference, you'll be an instant convert and wish, hope, and pray that other artists whose catalog hasn't been reissued since the early days of CD—Bob Dylan, Bruce Springsteen, Neil Young, *especially* the Beatles—are given the same treatment in the very near future. SACD and DSD are that good.]

Richie Unterberger

Sticky Fingers
April 1971, Virgin

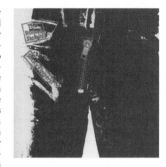

Pieced together from outtakes and much-labored-over songs, *Sticky Fingers* manages to have a loose, ram-shackle ambience that belies both its origins and the dark undercurrents of the songs. It's a weary, drug-laden album—well over half the songs explicitly mention drug use, while the others merely allude to it—that never fades away, but it barely keeps afloat. Apart from the classic opener, "Brown Sugar" (a gleeful tune about slavery, interracial sex, and lost virginity, not necessarily in that order), the long workout "Can't You Hear Me Knocking" and the mean-spirited "Bitch," *Sticky Fingers* is a slow, bluesy affair, with a few country touches thrown in for good measure. The laid-back tone of the album gives ample room for new lead guitarist Mick Taylor to stretch out, particularly on the extended coda of "Can't You Hear Me Knocking." But the key to the album isn't the instrumental interplay—although that is terrific—it's the utter weariness of the songs. "Wild Horses" is their first nonironic stab at a country song, and it is a beautiful, heart-tugging masterpiece. Similarly, "I Got the Blues" is a ravished, late-night classic that ranks among their very best blues. "Sister Morphine" is a horrifying overdose tale, and "Moonlight Mile," with Paul Buckmaster's grandiose strings, is a perfect closure: sad, yearning, drug-addled, and beautiful. With its offhand mixture of decadence, roots music, and outright malevolence, *Sticky Fingers* set the tone for the rest of the decade for the Stones.

Stephen Thomas Erlewine

Exile on Main St.
May 1972, Rolling Stones

Greeted with decidedly mixed reviews upon its original release, *Exile on Main St.* has become generally regarded as the Rolling Stones' finest album. Part of the reason why the record was initially greeted with hesitant reviews is that it takes a while to assimilate. A sprawling, weary double album encompassing rock & roll, blues, soul, and country, *Exile* doesn't try anything new on the surface, but the substance is new. Taking the bleakness that underpinned *Let It Bleed* and *Sticky Fingers* to an extreme, *Exile* is a weary record, and not just lyrically. Jagger's vocals are buried in the mix, and the music is a series of dark, dense jams, with Keith Richards and Mick Taylor spinning off incredible riffs and solos. And the songs continue the breakthroughs of their three previous albums. No longer does their country sound forced or kitschy—it's lived-in and complex, just like the group's forays into soul and gospel. While the songs, including the masterpieces "Rocks Off," "Tumbling Dice," "Torn and Frayed," "Happy," "Let It Loose," and "Shine a Light," are all terrific, they blend together, with only certain lyrics and guitar lines emerging from the murk. It's the kind of record that's gripping on the very first listen, but each subsequent listen reveals something new. Few other albums, let alone double albums, have been so rich and masterful as *Exile on Main St.*, and it stands not only as one of the Stones' best records, but sets a remarkably high standard for all of hard rock.

Stephen Thomas Erlewine

Goats Head Soup
August 1973, Virgin

Sliding out of perhaps the greatest winning streak in rock history, the Stones slipped into decadence and rock star excess with *Goats Head Soup*, their sequel to *Exile on Main St.* This is where the Stones' image began to eclipse their accomplishments, as Mick ascended to jet-setting celebrity and Keith slowly sunk deeper into addiction, and it's possible hearing them moving in both directions on *Goats Head Soup*, at times in the same song. As Jagger plays the devil (or, dances with Mr. D, as he likes to say), the sex and sleaze quotient is increased, all of it underpinned by some genuinely affecting heartbreak, highlighted by "Angie." This may not be as downright funky, freaky, and fantastic as *Exile*, yet the extra layer of gloss brings out the enunciated lyrics, added strings, wah-wah guitars, explicit sex, and violence, making it all seem trippily decadent. If it doesn't seem like there's a surplus of classics here, all the songs work well, illustrating just how far they've traveled in their songcraft, as well as their exceptional talent as a band—they make this all sound really easy and darkly alluring, even when the sex'n'satanism seems a little silly. To top it all of, they cap off this utterly excessive album with "Star Star," a nasty Chuck Berry rip that grooves on its own mean vulgarity—its real title is "Starf*cker," if you need any clarification, and even though they got nastier (the entirety of *Undercover*, for instance), they never again made something this dirty or nasty. And, it never feels more at home than it does at the end of this excessive record.

Stephen Thomas Erlewine

It's Only Rock 'N Roll
October 1974, Virgin

It's uneven, but at times *It's Only Rock 'n Roll* catches fire. The songs and performances are stronger than those on *Goats Head Soup*; the tossed-off numbers sound effortless, not careless. Throughout, the Stones wear their title as the "World's Greatest Rock & Roll Band" with a defiant smirk, which makes the bitter cynicism of "If You Can't Rock Me" and the title track all the more striking, and the reggae experimentation of "Luxury," the aching beauty of "Time Waits for No One," and the agreeable filler of "Dance Little Sister" and "Short and Curlies" all the more enjoyable.

Stephen Thomas Erlewine

Black and Blue
April 1976, Virgin

The Rolling Stones recorded *Black and Blue* while auditioning Mick Taylor's replacement, so it's unfair to criticize it, really, for being longer on grooves and jams than songs, especially since that's what's good about it. Yes, the two songs that are undeniable highlights are "Memory Motel" and "Fool to Cry," the album's two ballads and, therefore, the two that had to be written and arranged, not knocked out in the studio; they're also the ones that don't quite make as much sense, though they still work in the context of the record. No, this is all about groove and sound, as the Stones work Ron Wood into their fabric. And the remarkable thing is, apart from "Hand of Fate" and "Crazy Mama," there's little straight-

ahead rock & roll here. They play with reggae extensively, funk and disco less so, making both sound like integral parts of the Stones' lifeblood. Apart from the ballads, there might not be many memorable tunes, but there are times that you listen to the Stones just to hear them play, and this is one of them.

Stephen Thomas Erlewine

Some Girls
June 1978, Virgin

During the mid-'70s, the Rolling Stones remained massively popular, but their records suffered from Jagger's fascination with celebrity and Keith's worsening drug habit. By 1978, both punk and disco had swept the group off the front pages, and *Some Girls* was their fiery response to the younger generation. Opening with the disco-blues thump of "Miss You," *Some Girls* is a tough, focused, and exciting record, full of more hooks and energy than any Stones record since *Exile on Main St.* Even though the Stones make disco their own, they never quite take punk on their own ground. Instead, their rockers sound harder and nastier than they have in years. Using "Star Star" as a template, the Stones run through the seedy homosexual imagery of "When the Whip Comes Down," the bizarre, borderline-misogynistic vitriol of the title track, Keith's ultimate outlaw anthem, "Before They Make Me Run," and the decadent closer, "Shattered." In between, they deconstruct the Temptations' "(Just My) Imagination," unleash the devastatingly snide country parody "Far Away Eyes," and contribute "Beast of Burden," one of their very best ballads. *Some Girls* may not have the back-street aggression of their '60s records, or the majestic, drugged-out murk of their early-'70s work, but its brand of glitzy, decadent hard rock still makes it a definitive Stones album.

Stephen Thomas Erlewine

Tattoo You
August 1981, Virgin

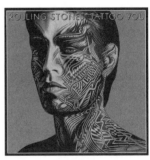

Like *Emotional Rescue* before it, *Tattoo You* was comprised primarily of leftovers, but unlike its predecessor, it never sounds that way. Instead, *Tattoo You* captures the Stones at their best as a professional stadium-rock band. Divided into a rock & roll side and a ballad side, the album delivers its share of thrills on the tight, dynamic first side. "Start Me Up" became the record's definitive Stonesy rocker, but the frenzied doo wop of "Hang Fire," the reggae jam of "Slave," the sleazy Chuck Berry rockers "Little T&A" and "Neighbours," and the hard blues of "Black Limousine" are all terrific. The ballad side suffers in comparison, especially since "Heaven" and "No Use in Crying" are faceless. But "Worried About You" and "Tops" are effortless, excellent ballads, and "Waiting on a Friend," with its Sonny Rollins sax solo, is an absolute masterpiece, with a moving lyric that captures Jagger in a shockingly reflective and affecting state of mind. "Waiting on a Friend" and the vigorous rock & roll of the first side make *Tattoo You* an essential latter-day Stones album, ranking just a few notches below *Some Girls*.

Stephen Thomas Erlewine

Undercover
November 1983, Virgin

As the Rolling Stones' most ambitious album since *Some Girls*, *Undercover* is a weird, wild mix of hard rock, new wave pop, reggae, dub, and soul. Even with all the careening musical eclecticism, what distinguishes *Undercover* is its bleak, nihilistic attitude—it's teeming with sickness, with violence, kinky sex, and loathing dripping from almost every song. "Undercover of the Night" slams with echoing guitars and rubbery basslines, as Jagger gives a feverish litany of sex, corruption, and suicide. It set the tone for the rest of the album, whether it's the runaway nymphomaniac of "She Was Hot" or the ridiculous slasher imagery of "Too Much Blood." Only Keith's "Wanna Hold You" offers a reprieve from the carnage, and its relentless bloodletting makes the album a singularly fascinating listen. For some observers, that mixture was nearly too difficult to stomach, but for others, it's a fascinating record, particularly since much of its nastiness feels as if the Stones, and Jagger and Richards in particular, are running out of patience with each other.

Stephen Thomas Erlewine

Linda Ronstadt

Heart Like a Wheel
1974, Capitol

Following the same formula as her early records, *Heart Like a Wheel* doesn't appear to be a great breakthrough on the surface. However, Ronstadt comes into her own on this mix of oldies and contemporary classics. Backed by a fleet of Los Angeles musicians, Ronstadt sings with vigor and passion, helping bring the music alive. But what really makes *Heart Like a Wheel* a breakthrough is the inventive arrangements that producer Peter Asher, Ronstadt, and the studio musicians have developed. Finding the right note for each song—whether it's the soulful reworking of "When Will I Be Loved," the hit "You're No Good," or the laid-back folk-rock of "Willing"—the musicians help turn *Heart Like a Wheel* into a veritable catalog of Californian soft rock, and it stands as a landmark of '70s mainstream pop/rock.

Stephen Thomas Erlewine

The Best of Linda Ronstadt: The Capitol Years
January 2006, Capitol

The title of Capitol's 2006 collection *The Best of Linda Ronstadt: The Capitol Years* is a little misleading: this isn't a mere single-disc overview of hits; this double-disc set is a virtual complete recorded works of Ronstadt's stint at Capitol between 1969-1974, encompassing the entirety of four albums—her 1969 solo debut, *Hand Sown...Home Grown*, its 1970 sequel, *Silk Purse*, 1972's self-titled third album, and its 1974 follow-up, *Heart Like a Wheel*, which brought her stardom—plus five bonus

tracks, two of them capturing her live at The Troubadour. Apart from *Heart Like a Wheel*, these LPs for Capitol were not hits, due partially to the fact that Ronstadt was still finding her footing as a record-maker during this time. It wasn't until her eponymous third album that everything began to click, thanks to her finally finding a sympathetic backing band (who would become Eagles not long after this record was cut), and then producer Peter Asher came in for *Heart Like a Wheel* and helped her find a slick, streamlined variation of her soft country-rock. And while it's true that her first two albums sometimes find her stumbling as she tries to blend country, pop, and folk while working with session musicians (some less-charitable listeners might find such period flair as fuzz-toned steel guitar as a detriment, too, although there's a certain undeniable charm to these dated sounds), they have aged remarkably well, warts and all, because they showcase a singer with excellent taste and restless ambition. Ronstadt was never a songwriter, but she had a terrific ear for good songs, choosing them primarily from the plethora of great singer/songwriters who cluttered the landscape in the late '60s and early '70s—not just Bob Dylan, Neil Young, Jackson Browne, and Randy Newman, but Fred Neil, Mickey Newbury, Paul Siebel, Gene Clark, Bernie Leadon, Livingston Taylor, Eric Andersen, John D. Loudermilk, Wayne Raney, and Lowell George, among others. Her interpretations, while not idiosyncratic, were energetic and impassioned, an appealing blend of laid-back Californian country-rock, folky songs, and pop attitude that was enjoyable even when it wasn't always entirely successful. Yet, in retrospect, especially in the context of this generous collection, the awkwardness of her first two albums no longer seems so pronounced. In fact, *Hand Sown...Home Grown* and *Silk Purse* look like flawed minor gems, while *Linda Ronstadt* and *Heart Like a Wheel* still stand as high-water marks of '70s Californian soft rock. And this double-disc set, boasting fine remastering and liner notes (which remain good even if there are no details about the bonus tracks and Lowell George is credited as "George Lowell"), is the definitive portrait of Ronstadt at her creative peak, when she was a vital part of Los Angeles' thriving music scene of the early '70s.

Stephen Thomas Erlewine

David Lee Roth

Eat 'Em and Smile
1986, Warner Bros.

Few would argue that David Lee Roth's first solo EP was a complete comedy send-up, albeit a very successful one that gained him enough favor with the MTV peanut gallery to solidify his potential as a solo artist. When threat became fact, however, Roth was smart enough to know that show tunes set to flashy videos weren't going to cut it and wisely proceeded to surround himself with musicians of impeccable pedigree. Thus armed, the "diamond" one set out to out-Van Halen Van Halen with his band's first effort, *Eat 'Em and Smile*, a more than adequate substitute for the overtly commercial tendencies of the "new and improved" original. Why mess with a winning recipe, indeed. Guitarist Steve Vai, bassist Billy Sheehan, and drummer Gregg Bissonette sound perfectly at home aping their boss' old cronies on such sizzling party anthems as "Shyboy" and "Elephant Gun." A fun-loving cover of "Tobacco Road" kicks off a very solid side two featuring the remarkably *Fair Warning-esque* "Big Trouble," and it doesn't get any better than first single, "Yankee Rose," where the squealing call and response between Roth and Vai reaches unparalleled comical heights. The glossy pump of "Goin' Crazy!" (originally conceived as the title track for Roth's botched movie project) hints at the pop excesses to come, and although two lounge pieces are knocked out for good measure, these are easily offset by the cool strut of "Ladies Nite in Buffalo?," arguably Roth's most legitimate piece of art ever.

Ed Rivadavia

Roxy Music

Roxy Music
1972, Virgin/

Falling halfway between musical primitivism and art rock ambition, Roxy Music's eponymous debut remains a startling redefinition of rock's boundaries. Simultaneously embracing kitschy glamour and avant-pop, *Roxy Music* shimmers with seductive style and pulsates with disturbing synthetic textures. Although no musician demonstrates much technical skill at this point, they are driven by boundless imagination—Brian Eno's synthesized "treatments" exploit electronic instruments as electronics, instead of trying to shoehorn them into conventional acoustic patterns. Similarly, Bryan Ferry finds that his vampiric croon is at its most effective when it twists conventional melodies, Phil Manzanera's guitar is terse and unpredictable, while Andy Mackay's saxophone subverts rock & roll clichés by alternating R&B honking with atonal flourishes. But what makes *Roxy Music* such a confident, astonishing debut is how these primitive avant-garde tendencies are married to full-fledged songs, whether it's the free-form, structure-bending "Remake/Remodel" or the sleek glam of "Virginia Plain," the debut single added to later editions of the album. That was the trick that elevated Roxy Music from an art school project to the most adventurous rock band of the early '70s.

Stephen Thomas Erlewine

For Your Pleasure
1973, Virgin

On Roxy Music's debut, the tensions between Brian Eno and Bryan Ferry propelled their music to great, unexpected heights, and for most of the group's second album, *For Your Pleasure*, the band equals, if not surpasses, those expectations. However, there are a handful of moments where those tensions become unbearable, as when Eno wants to move toward texture and Ferry wants to stay in more conventional rock territory; the nine-minute "The Bogus Man" captures such creative tensions perfectly, and it's easy to see why Eno left the group after the album was completed. Still, those differences result in yet another extraordinary record from Roxy Music, one that demonstrates even more clearly than the debut how avant-garde ideas can flourish in a pop setting. This is especially evident in the driving singles "Do the Strand" and "Editions of You," which pulsate with raw energy and jarring melodic structures. Roxy also illuminate the slower numbers, such as the eerie "In Every Dream Home a Heartache," with atonal, shimmering synthesizers, textures that were unexpected and innovative at the time of its release. Similarly, all of *For Your Pleasure* walks the tightrope between the experimental and the accessible, creating a new vocabulary for rock bands, and one that was exploited heavily in the ensuing decade.

Stephen Thomas Erlewine

Stranded
1973, Virgi

Without Brian Eno, Roxy Music immediately became less experimental, yet it remained adventurous, as *Stranded* illustrates. Under the direction of Bryan Ferry, Roxy moved toward relatively straightforward territory, adding greater layers of piano and heavy guitars. Even without the washes of Eno's synthesizers, Roxy's music remains unsettling on occasion, yet in this new incarnation, they favor more measured material, whether it's the reflective "A Song for Europe" or the shifting textures of "Psalm." Even the rockers, such as the surging "Street Life" and the segmented "Mother of Pearl," are distinguished by subtle songwriting that emphasizes both Ferry's tortured glamour and Roxy's increasingly impressive grasp of sonic detail.

Stephen Thomas Erlewine

Country Life
1974, Virgin

Continuing with the stylistic developments of *Stranded*, *Country Life* finds Roxy Music at the peak of their powers, alternating between majestic, unsettling art rock and glamorous, elegant pop/rock. At their best, Roxy combine these two extremes, like on the exhilarating opener "The Thrill of It All," but *Country Life* benefits considerably from the ebb and flow of the group's two extremes, since it showcases their deft instrumental execution and their textured, enthralling songwriting. And, in many ways, *Country Life* offers the greatest and most consistent set of Roxy Music songs, illustrating their startling depth. From the sleek rock of "All I Want Is You" and "Prairie Rose" to the elegant, string-laced pop of "A Really Good Time," *Country Life* is filled with thrilling songs, and Roxy Music rarely sounded as invigorating as they do here.

Stephen Thomas Erlewine

Siren
1975, Virgin

Abandoning the intoxicating blend of art rock and glam-pop that distinguished *Stranded* and *Country Life*, Roxy Music concentrates on Bryan Ferry's suave, charming crooner persona for the elegantly modern *Siren*. As the disco-fied opener "Love Is the Drug" makes clear, Roxy embraces dance and unabashed pop on *Siren*, weaving them into their sleek, arty sound. It does come at the expense of their artier inclinations, which is part of what distinguished Roxy, but the end result is captivating. Lacking the consistently amazing songs of its predecessor, *Siren* has a thematic consistency that works in its favor, and helps elevate its best songs—"Sentimental Fool," "Both Ends Burning," "Just Another High"—as well as the album itself into the realm of classics.

Stephen Thomas Erlewine

Avalon
1982, Virgin

Flesh + Blood suggested that Roxy Music were at the end of the line, but they regrouped and recorded the lovely *Avalon*, one of their finest albums. Certainly, the lush, elegant soundscapes of *Avalon* are far removed from the edgy avant-pop of their early records, yet it represents another landmark in their career. With its stylish, romantic washes of synthesizers and Bryan Ferry's elegant, seductive croon, *Avalon* simultaneously functioned as sophisticated make-out music for yuppies and as the maturation of synth pop. Ferry was never this romantic or seductive, either with Roxy or as a solo artist, and *Avalon* shimmers with elegance in both its music and its lyrics. "More Than This," "Take a Chance With Me," "While My Heart Is Still Beating," and the title track are immaculately crafted and subtle songs, where the shifting synthesizers and murmured vocals gradually reveal the melodies. It's a rich, textured album and a graceful way to end the band's career.

Stephen Thomas Erlewine

The Runaways

The Runaways
1976, Touchwood

When the Runaways debuted in 1976 with this self-titled LP, aggressive female rockers were the exception instead of the rule. Women had no problem becoming folk-rockers, singer/songwriters or Top 40 icons, but female artists who had more in common with Led Zeppelin and Aerosmith than Joni Mitchell were hardly the norm. With this album, the Runaways made it crystal clear that women (or specifically, adolescent girls) were more than capable of playing intense, forceful hard rock that went directly for the jugular. Lusty classics like "Cherry Bomb" and "You Drive Me Wild" made no attempt to conceal the fact that teenage girls could be every bit as sexual as the guys—a message that both men and women found intimidating. And on "Is It Day or Night," Cherie Currie sings about life in the fast lane with every bit as much conviction as Axl Rose would 11 years later. Currie and Joan Jett are equally riveting, and a 17-year-old Lita Ford was already an impressive guitarist. This LP was far from a commercial hit in the U.S., where timid rock radio programmers simply didn't know what to make of the Runaways. But interestingly, it did earn the band a strong following in the major rock market of Japan.

Alex Henderson

Queens of Noise
1977, Touchwood

The Runaways didn't compromise a bit on their outstanding sophomore effort, *Queens of Noise*. Melodic yet tough and aggressive, this is hard rock that pulls no punches either musically or lyrically. Classics like "Neon Angels (On the Road to Ruin)," "Take It or Leave It" and "I Love Playing With Fire" wouldn't have been shocking coming from Aerosmith or Kiss, but suburban adolescent girls singing openly and honestly about casual sex, intoxication, and wild, all-night parties was certainly radical for 1977. Joan Jett and Cherie Currie articulated the thoughts and feelings of the "bad girls" Kiss and countless others were describing, and they didn't hesitate to say that yes, women fantasized about sex. "Johnny Guitar" is a fine vehicle for guitarist/singer Lita Ford, who had solid chops before she was old enough to vote. *Queens of Noise* would be Currie's last album with the groundbreaking band.

Alex Henderson

Todd Rundgren

Runt
September 1970, Bearsville/Rhino

Reluctant to start a full-fledged solo career after leaving the Nazz, Todd Rundgren formed Runt, a band that was a front for what was in effect a solo project. Such isolationism lends *Runt* its unique atmosphere—it is the insular work of a fiercely talented artist finally given the opportunity to pursue his off-kilter musical vision. From the moment the slow, bluesy psychedelic grind of "Broke Down and Busted" starts the album, it's apparent that Rundgren could never have made *Runt* with the Nazz—and that's before the introspective ballads or the willfully strange stuff kicks in. Throughout the record, Rundgren reveals himself as a gifted synthesist, blending all manners of musical styles and quirks into a distinctive signature sound. He's as interested in sound as he is in song and while he would later pursue these tendencies to extremes, *Runt* finds him learning how to create an effective sound with the studio, which may be the reason why the album runs the gamut from hard rockers like "Who's That Man?" to ballads like "Once Burned." Although these songs are instantly appealing, the album really gets interesting when he reaches between those two extremes, whether it's in the classic pop medley "Baby Let's Swing," the bizarrely tongue-in-cheek "I'm in the Clique," or the equally impish "We Gotta Get You a Woman," which gave Rundgren his first hit. All the details buried within these songs—not only in the deceptively direct productions, but within the writing itself—confirm Rundgren's exceptional skill at songcraft. He occasionally slips on *Runt*, delivering tracks that rely on production instead of a blend of studiocraft and songcraft, but it remains a thoroughly impressive debut and one of his finest pop records.

Stephen Thomas Erlewine

Runt: The Ballad of Todd Rundgren
June 1971, Ampex

Upon its release, *Rolling Stone* called *The Ballad of Todd Rundgren* "the best album Paul McCartney" never made, and even if the album doesn't sound particularly McCartney-esque, it does share the homespun, melodic charm of the best of his early albums. Arguably, it's better than Paul's solo work, since it is focused and subtle, never drawing attention to Rundgren's considerable skills as a writer and producer. He tones down the hard rock and his impish wit, lending the album a sense of direction missing on *Runt*. That's not to say he abandoned his sense of humor—as if the cover shot of Rundgren sitting at a piano with a noose around his neck left any doubt. This time around, it takes some careful listening to hear the jokes, such as the opening Floyd Cramer piano lick on "Range War." On such clever in-jokes as "Chain Letter," as well as ballads like "Hope I'm Around," the artist reveals himself as an exceptional craftsman and songsmith. In fact, *Ballad* is considerably more song-oriented than its predecessor, with very little of the jams and instrumental sections that occasionally bogged down *Runt*. Here, even propulsive pop tunes such as "Bleeding" and "Long Flowing Robe," along with the hard rocker "Parole," are as much about the song as the performance, which is probably appropriate for an album called *The Ballad of Todd Rundgren*. Another thing about that title—it may be a joke, but the album inarguably offers a glimpse into Rundgren's inner world through a combination of introspective ballads, off-hand jokes, musical virtuosity, outright weirdness, and unabashed showmanship. And that's the charm of *The Ballad*—it's the slyly sardonic masterwork of a loner who may be sensitive, but is certainly not shy.

Stephen Thomas Erlewine

Something/Anything?
February 1972, Bearsville/Rhino

Others had recorded one-man albums before Todd Rundgren, most notably Stevie Wonder and Paul McCartney, but with *Something/Anything?* he captured the homemade ambience of *McCartney* with the visionary feel of *Music of My Mind*, adding an encyclopedic knowledge of pop music from Gilbert & Sullivan through Jimi Hendrix, plus the crazed zeal of a pioneer. Listening to *Something/Anything?* is a mind-altering trip in itself, no matter how many shamelessly accessible pop songs are scattered throughout the album, since each side of the double-record is a concept unto itself. The first is "a bouquet of ear-catching melodies"; side two is "the cerebral side"; on side three "the kid gets heavy"; side four is his mock pop operetta, recorded with a full band including the Sales Brothers. It gallops through everything—Carole King tributes ("I Saw the Light"), classic ballads ("Hello It's Me," "It Wouldn't Have Made Any Difference"), Motown ("Wolfman Jack"), blinding power pop ("Couldn't I Just Tell You"), psychedelic hard rock ("Black Maria"), pure weirdness ("I Went to the Mirror"), blue-eyed soul ("Dust in the Wind"), and scores of brilliant songs that don't fall into any particular style ("Cold Morning Light," "It Takes Two to Tango"). It's an amazing journey that's remarkably unpretentious. Rundgren peppers his writing with self-aware, self-deprecating asides, indulging his bizarre sense of humor with gross-outs ("Piss Aaron") and sheer quirkiness, such as an aural tour of the studio at the beginning of side two. There are a ton of loose ends throughout *Something/Anything?*, plenty of studio tricks, slight songs (but no filler), snippets of dialogue, and purposely botched beginnings, but all these

throwaways simply add context—they're what makes the album into a kaleidoscopic odyssey through the mind of an insanely gifted pop music obsessive.

Stephen Thomas Erlewine

A Wizard, a True Star
March 1973, Bearsville/Rhino

Something/Anything? proved that Todd Rundgren could write a pop classic as gracefully as any of his peers, but buried beneath the surface were signs that he would never be satisfied as merely a pop singer/songwriter. A close listen to the album reveals the eccentricities and restless spirit that surges to the forefront on its follow-up, *A Wizard, a True Star*. Anyone expecting the third record of *Something/Anything?*, filled with variations on "I Saw the Light" and "Hello It's Me," will be shocked by *A Wizard*. As much a mind-f*ck as an album, *A Wizard, a True Star* rarely breaks down to full-fledged songs, especially on the first side, where songs and melodies float in and out of a hazy post-psychedelic mist. Stylistically, there may not be much new—he touched on so many different bases on *Something/Anything?* that it's hard to expand to new territory—but it's all synthesized and assembled in fresh, strange ways. Often, it's a jarring, disturbing listen, especially since Rundgren's humor has turned bizarre and insular. It truly takes a concerted effort on the part of the listener to unravel the record, since Rundgren makes no concessions—not only does the soul medley jerk in unpredictable ways, but the anthemic closer, "Just One Victory," is layered with so many overdubs that it's hard to hear its moving melody unless you pay attention. And that's the key to understanding *A Wizard, a True Star*—it's one of those rare rock albums that demands full attention and, depending on your own vantage, it may even reward such close listening.

Stephen Thomas Erlewine

Todd
February 1974, Bearsville/Rhino

Maybe some listeners thought that the sonic trip *A Wizard, A True Star* was a necessary exercise in indulgence and that Todd Rundgren would return to the sweet pop of *Something/Anything?* for its follow-up. Not a chance. As it turned out, *A Wizard* was the launch pad for further dementia, and, depending on your point of view, indulgence. Its follow-up is *Todd*, an impenetrable double album filled with detours, side roads, collisions and the occasional pop tune. That those pop tunes are among his best may come as little consolation to the lightweight fan who has stumbled upon *Todd*. Conceptually, *A Wizard, A True Star* may be the wilder record, but *Todd* is a more difficult listen, thanks to the layers of guitar solos and blind synth prog tunes, such as "In and Out the Chakras We Go." Large stretches of the album are purely instrumental, foreshadowing the years of synth experiments with Utopia that were just around the corner. The murk subsides every so often, revealing either exquisite ballads ("A Dream Goes on Forever"), blistering rock ("Heavy Metal Kids") or, more murk and dementia (particularly with how Gilbert & Sullivan rear their heads not only on the requisite novelty "An Elpee's Worth of Tunes," but an honest-to-goodness cover of "Lord Chancellor's Nightmare Song"). These are some major additions to his catalog, but the experiments and the excesses are too tedious to make *Todd* a necessary listen for anyone but the devoted. But for those listeners, the gems make the rough riding worthwhile.

Stephen Thomas Erlewine

Faithful
April 1976, Bearsville/Rhino

Todd Rundgren considered 1966 the beginning of his professional musical career, largely because the Nazz formed around that time. As a celebration, he recorded *Faithful*. Presumably, *Faithful* celebrates the past and the future by juxtaposing a side of original pop material with a side of covers. Actually, "covers" isn't accurate—the six oldies that comprise the entirety of side one are re-creations, with Rundgren "faithfully" replicating the sound and feel of the Yardbirds ("Happenings Ten Years Time Ago"), Bob Dylan ("Most Likely You Go Your Way and I'll Go Mine"), Jimi Hendrix ("If Six Was Nine"), the Beach Boys ("Good Vibrations") and the Beatles ("Rain," "Strawberry Fields Forever"). All of this is entertaining, to a certain extent, especially since it's remarkable how close Rundgren comes to duplicating the very feel of the originals. Still, it's hard to see it as much more than a flamboyant throwaway, especially when compared with the glorious second side. For the first time since *Something/Anything?*, Rundgren allows himself to write and—more importantly—record straight-ahead pop songs. Certainly, *A Wizard, A True Star*, *Todd* and *Initiation* had their share of great songs, but they weren't delivered as pop songs; they were telegraphed as art. Here, Rundgren delivers pop and rock songs with ease, letting the melodies glide to the forefront. There are embellishments, of course, but the end result is a lushness that's apparent even on the hard rockers. If Rundgren had made all of *Faithful* originals, it would have been a pure pop masterpiece. As it stands, it's essential for the faithful—not only for hardcore Toddheads, but for devoted pop fans as well.

Stephen Thomas Erlewine

Hermit of Mink Hollow
April 1978, Bearsville/Rhino

Over the course of 1977, Todd Rundgren moved Utopia toward a more pop-oriented direction, winding up with the slick mainstream arena rock of *Oops! Wrong Planet*. With that in mind, it makes sense that *The Hermit of Mink Hollow*—his first full-fledged solo album since *Initiation*, if you discount the half-cover/half-original *Faithful*—finds Rundgren in his pop craftsman persona. The difference is, he's heartbroken. His relationship with Bebe Buell collapsed during 1977 and it's clear that the separation has pained him, since pain and melancholy underpin the album, whether it's on ballads ("Can We Still Be Friends") or on apparently joyous revelries, like "All the Children Sing." That said, this is a Rundgren solo album and he has not abandoned his trademarks, which means that the lush ballads are paired with novelties ("Onomatopoeia," which sounds exactly how you hope it does), ersatz soul ("You Cried Wolf"), and pure pop ("Hurting for You"). *Hermit* is also the first record Rundgren recorded completely alone since *Something/Anything?* Where that record sounded like the inner workings of a madman, with each song providing no indication what the next would sound like, *Hermit* is more cohesive. It also feels less brilliant, even if it is, in many ways, nearly as excellent as

Rundgren's masterwork, mainly because it doesn't have such a wide scope. Still, the reason *The Hermit of Mink Hollow* is such a milestone in Rundgren's career is because it's a small album, filled with details, and easily the most emotional record he made.

Stephen Thomas Erlewine

Healing
February 1981, Rhino

Healing is a subdued, reflective effort unlike anything else in Todd Rundgren's catalog. Certainly, there are some familiar elements throughout *Healing*, particularly on majestic ballads like "Compassion," but there are more new variations on his style since any album since *Initiation*. Not coincidentally, that record had hints of the spirituality that surges to the forefront on *Healing*, but it was nowhere near as musically focused as the latter record. Apart from "Compassion," there is a true lack of singles, which doesn't mean that there aren't standouts—since "Golden Goose" has a weird, jerky hook and the opener "Healer" is a terrific pop single—that stand on their own merit. Instead, the record works as a whole, flowing as seamlessly as *Something/Anything?* or *Hermit*. Unfortunately, it's not as strong as either of those records, largely because it's about texture and spirit, not individual songs. In a case like that, the music and ambience are as important as the actual songs, and while they're often very provocative, they tend to meander as well, particularly on the three-part "Healing" suite that comprises the last side of the record. On CD, its calming effect is dissipated because the bonus 7" single "Time Heals"/"Tiny Demons" is added at the end. Their presence makes it clear that *Healing* was intended as an album unto itself, without much in the way of singles, because each song—the former being excellent new wave pop, the other a fine ballad—could have been a single unto itself. In this context, they may deflate the lasting spiritual impression of the album, but they add musical weight, helping make the disc a fine effort.

Stephen Thomas Erlewine

The Ever Popular Tortured Artist Effect
January 1983, Rhino

As the early '80s continued to unfold, Todd Rundgren grew increasingly disenchanted with Bearsville, especially since the label wasn't supporting Utopia. He wrangled the band free in 1982, but he still had to deliver solo records to Bearsville. Not entirely pleased with the situation, Rundgren hammered out a collection of pop songs on his own, cynically titling the effort *The Ever Popular Tortured Artist Effect*. In later years, Rundgren disavowed the album, but it stands as one of his better collections of pop songs, even if it lacks a theme or a unifying sound. There are a fair share of throwaways, not only coming in the expected form of covers (a fine but pointless remake of the Small Faces' "Tin Soldier") and Gilbert & Sullivan parodies ("Emperor of the Highway"), but also in the monumentally silly "Bang the Drum All Day," which not only became a hit, but a hit that refused to die, lasting as a radio staple into the late '90s. These three songs are anomalies on *Tortured Artist*, which for the most part is pure pop and pop-soul, delivered with little fuss or pretention. There's also little deep meaning to the songs themselves, which is quite unusual for Rundgren, yet the best tunes—"Hideaway," "Influenza," "There Goes Your Baybay," "Drive," "Chant"—are indelible, irresistible pop confections that prove Rundgren can be quite involving, even when he's not trying his hardest.

Stephen Thomas Erlewine

Rush

2112
March 1976, Mercury

Whereas Rush's first two releases, their self-titled debut and *Fly By Night*, helped create a buzz among hard rock fans worldwide, the more progressive third release, *Caress of Steel*, confused many of their supporters. The band knew it was now or never with their fourth release, and they delivered just in time—1976's *2112* proved to be their much sought-after commercial breakthrough and remains one of their most popular albums. Instead of choosing between prog rock or heavy rock, both styles are merged together to create an interesting and original approach. The whole entire first side is comprised of the classic title track, which paints a chilling picture of a future world where technology is in control (Peart's lyrics for the piece being influenced by Ayn Rand). Comprised of seven "sections," the track proved that the trio was fast becoming rock's most accomplished instrumentalists. The second side contains shorter selections, such as the Middle Eastern-flavored "A Passage to Bangkok" and the album-closing rocker "Something for Nothing." *2112* is widely considered by Rush fans as their first true "classic" album, the first in a string of similarly high-quality albums.

Greg Prato

All the World's a Stage
September 1976, Mercury

The '70s may forever be remembered as the decade of the "live album," where many rock artists (Kiss, Peter Frampton, Cheap Trick, etc.) used the format for their commercial breakthrough. While Rush's *All the World's a Stage* is not as renowned as the aforementioned bands' live albums, it is still one of the better in-concert rock releases of the decade, and helped solidify the trio's stature as one of rock's fastest rising stars. Eventually, Rush would polish their live sound to sound almost like a studio record, but in the mid-'70s, they were still a raw and raging hard rock band, captured perfectly on *A.T.W.A.S.* Comprised almost entirely of their heavier material, the album packs quite a punch—"Bastille Day" and "Anthem" prove to be a killer opening combination, while over the top renditions of their extended epics "2112" and "By-Tor & the Snow Dog" prove to be standouts. Even their more tranquil studio material proves more explosive in concert ("Fly by Night," "Something for Nothing," "Lakeside Park," "In the End"). *All the World's a Stage* was a fitting way of closing the first chapter of Rush, as the liner notes state.

Greg Prato

A Farewell to Kings
September 1977, Mercury

On 1977's *A Farewell to Kings* it quickly becomes apparent that Rush had improved their songwriting and strengthened their focus and musical approach. Synthesizers also mark their first prominent appearance on a Rush album, a direction the band would continue to pursue on future releases. With the popular hit single "Closer to the Heart," the trio showed that they could compose concise and traditionally structured songs, while the 11-minute "Xanadu" remains an outstanding accomplishment all these years later (superb musicianship merged with vivid lyrics help create one of Rush's best all-time tracks). The album-opening title track begins with a tasty classical guitar/synth passage, before erupting into a powerful rocker. The underrated "Madrigal" proves to be a delicately beautiful composition, while "Cinderella Man" is one of Rush's few songs to include lyrics penned entirely by Geddy Lee. The ten-minute tale of a dangerous black hole, "Cygnus X-1," closes the album on an unpredictable note, slightly comparable to the two bizarre extended songs on 1975's *Caress of Steel*. *A Farewell to Kings* successfully built on the promise of their breakthrough *2112*, and helped broaden their audience.

Greg Prato

Hemispheres
October 1978, Mercury

While such albums as 1980's *Permanent Waves* and 1981's *Moving Pictures* are usually considered Rush's masterpieces (and with good reason), 1978's *Hemispheres* is just as deserving. Maybe the fact that the album consists of only four compositions (half are lengthy pieces) was a bit too intimidating for some, but the near 20-minute-long "Cygnus X-1 Book II—Hemispheres" is arguably the band's finest extended track. While the story line isn't as comprehensible as "2112" was, it's much more consistent musically, twisting and turning through five different sections which contrast heavy rock sections against more sedate pieces. Neil Peart had become one of rock's most accomplished lyricists by this point, as evidenced by "The Trees," which deals with racism and inequality in a unique way (set in a forest!). And as always, the trio prove to be experts at their instruments, this time on the complex instrumental "La Villa Strangiato." Geddy Lee's shrieking vocals on the otherwise solid "Circumstances" may border on the irritating, but *Hemispheres* remains one of Rush's greatest releases.

Greg Prato

Permanent Waves
January 1980, Mercury

Since Neil Peart joined the band in time for 1975's *Fly by Night*, Rush had been experimenting and growing musically with each successive release. By 1980's *Permanent Waves*, the modern sounds of new wave (the Police, Peter Gabriel, etc.) began to creep into Rush's sound, but the trio still kept their hard rock roots intact. The new approach paid off—two of their most popular songs, the "make a difference" anthem "Freewill," and a tribute to the Toronto radio station CFNY, "The Spirit of Radio" (the latter a U.K. Top 15 hit), are spectacular highlights. Also included were two "epics," the stormy "Jacob's Ladder" and the album-closing "Natural Science," which contains a middle section that contains elements of reggae. Geddy Lee also began singing in a slightly lower register around this time, which made their music more accessible to fans outside of the heavy prog rock circle. The album proved to be the final breakthrough Rush needed to become an arena headliner throughout the world, beginning a string of albums that would reach inside the Top Five of the U.S. *Billboard* album charts. *Permanent Waves* is an undisputed hard rock classic, but Rush would outdo themselves with their next release.

Greg Prato

Moving Pictures
February 1981, Mercury

Not only is 1981's *Moving Pictures* Rush's best album, it is undeniably one of the greatest hard rock albums of all time. The new wave meets hard rock approach of *Permanent Waves* is honed to perfection—all seven of the tracks are classics (four are still featured regularly in concert and on classic rock radio). While other hard rock bands at the time experimented unsuccessfully with other musical styles, Rush were one of the few to successfully cross over. The whole entire first side is perfect—their most renowned song, "Tom Sawyer," kicks things off, and is soon followed by the racing "Red Barchetta," the instrumental "YYZ," and a song that examines the pros and cons of stardom, "Limelight." And while the second side isn't as instantly striking as the first, it is ultimately rewarding. The long and winding "The Camera Eye" begins with a synth-driven piece before transforming into one of the band's more straight-ahead epics, while "Witch Hunt" and "Vital Signs" remain two of the trio's more underrated rock compositions. Rush proved with *Moving Pictures* that there was still uncharted territory to explore within the hard rock format, and were rewarded with their most enduring and popular album.

Greg Prato

Signals
September 1982, Mercury

Instead of playing it safe and writing *Moving Pictures, Pt. II*, Rush replaced their heavy rock of yesteryear with even more modern sounds for 1982's *Signals*. Synthesizers were now an integral part of the band's sound, and replaced electric guitars as the driving force for almost all the tracks. And more current and easier-to-grasp topics (teen peer pressure, repression, etc.) replaced their trusty old sci-fi-inspired lyrics. While other rock bands suddenly added keyboards to their sound to widen their appeal, Rush gradually merged electronics into their music over the years, so such tracks as the popular MTV video "Subdivisions" did not come as a shock to longtime fans. And Rush didn't forget how to rock out—"The Analog Kid" and "Digital Man" were some of their most up-tempo compositions in years. The surprise hit, "New World Man," and "Chemistry" combined reggae and rock (begun on 1980's *Permanent Waves*), "The Weapon" bordered on new wave, the placid "Losing It" featured Ben Mink on electric violin, while the epic closer "Countdown" painted a vivid picture of a space shuttle launch. *Signals*

proved that Rush were successfully adapting to the musical climate of the early '80s.

Greg Prato

Leon Russell

Leon Russell
May 1970, The Right Stuff

Leon Russell never quite hit all the right notes the way he did on his eponymous debut. He never again seemed as convincing in his grasp of Americana music and themes, never again seemed as individual, and never again did his limited, slurred bluesy voice seem as ingratiating. He never again topped his triptych of "A Song for You," "Hummingbird," and "Delta Lady," nor did his albums contain such fine tracks as "Dixie Lullaby." Throughout it all, what comes across is Russell's idiosyncratic vision, not only in his approach but in his very construction—none of the songs quite play out as expected, turning country, blues, and rock inside out, not only musically but lyrically. Yes, his voice is a bit of an acquired taste, but it's only appropriate for a songwriter with enough chutzpah to write songs of his own called "I Put a Spell on You" and "Give Peace a Chance." And if there ever was a place to acquire a taste for Russell, it's here.

Stephen Thomas Erlewine

Doug Sahm

Doug Sahm and Band
January 1973, Atlantic

Doug Sahm began his solo career in 1972, after the Sir Douglas Quintet finished its contract with Smash/Mercury and after Atlantic Records co-owner/producer Jerry Wexler convinced him to sign to his label. Wexler gave the Texas maverick the chance to cut a star-studded, big-budget album, shuffling him off to New York where Wexler and Arif Mardin helmed a series of sessions with an ever-revolving cast of musicians featuring Bob Dylan, Dr. John, David "Fathead" Newman, David Bromberg, and Flaco Jimenez, in addition to such Sir Doug stalwarts as Augie Meyers and the rhythm section of bassist Jack Barber and drummer George Rains (all but the latter were in the last incarnation of the Quintet, raising the question of whether the group was indeed finished or not, but such is the nature of Sahm's discography). This group cut a lot of material, which was whittled down to the 12-track album *Doug Sahm and Band*, released in early 1973. At the time, the record received a push from the label and was generally disparaged because of those very all-stars on whose back it was sold, but the years have been kind indeed to the album, and it stands among Sahm's best. Indeed, the heart of the album is not at all far removed from those latter-day Sir Douglas Quintet albums on Mercury, which isn't much of a stretch since Sahm never really strayed from his signature blend of rock & roll, blues, country, and Tejano, but the bigger band and bigger production give the music a different feel—one that's as loose as the best Quintet material, but off-handedly accomplished and slyly freewheeling. Original reviews noted that there was an overtly country direction on *And Band*, but that's not really true on an album that has Western swing and rambling country-rock like "Blues Stay Away from Me" and the anthemic "(Is Anybody Going To) San Antone" jutting up against pure blues in "Your Friends" and "Papa Ain't Salty," let alone loose-limbed rockers like "Dealer's Blues" and "I Get Off" or the skipping Tejano "Poison Love," fueled by Jimenez's addictive accordion.

These are all convincing arguments that the larger band allowed Sahm to indulge in all of his passions, to the extent of devoting full tracks to each of his favorite sounds—something that was a bit different than the Quintet records, which usually mixed it all up so it was impossible to tell where one influence ended and another began. That's still true on *And Band*—for instance, witness the brilliant cover of Willie Nelson's "Me and Paul," a country song goosed by soulful horns and delivered in a delirious drawl from Sir Doug—but much of the album finds that signature Sahm sprawl being punctuated by style-specific detours where Sahm seizes the opportunity to stretch out as much as his guests seize the opportunity to jam with this American musical visionary. These are all characteristics of a jam session, which these sessions essentially were—after all, on this album he only penned three out of the 12 songs—but relying on covers also points out how Doug Sahm sounds so much like himself, he makes other people's tunes sound as if he wrote them himself. Again, that's something that was true throughout his career, but here it is in sharper relief than most of his records due to the nature of the sessions. And while it's arguable whether this is better than latter-day Sir Douglas Quintet albums—or such mid-'70s records as *Groover's Paradise* or *Texas Rock for Country Rollers* for that matter—there's no question that this is music that is vividly, excitedly alive and captures Sahm at a peak. It's pretty much irresistible.

Stephen Thomas Erlewine

The Sir Douglas Band

Texas Tornado
October 1973, Atlantic

Doug Sahm recorded much of his second Atlantic album, *Texas Tornado*, around the release of his first, *Doug Sahm and Band*, and even used outtakes from those sessions to fill out this 11-track record, so it would seem that the two records would be nearly identical. But, as they say, appearances can be deceiving, and the two albums have fairly distinct characters, at least within the frame of Sahm's music, where all his music is instantly identifiable. The biggest difference between the two records is that a good eight of the 11 songs are Doug Sahm originals—an inversion of *And Band*, which relied on covers—and most of those are produced by Sahm himself, not Jerry Wexler and Arif Mardin, who helmed its predecessor, and he gives the record a feel that's considerably more streamlined than the cheerfully rambling *And Band*, while giving it a little grit by more or less concentrating on rock & roll. That the exceptions arrive early and are as disarming as the "Summer Wind"-styled, Sinatra-esque crooner "Someday" and lite bossa nova groover "Blue Horizon"—two detours that make more sense in the broader context of the complete Atlantic recordings showcased on Rhino Handmade's double-disc set *The Genuine Texas Groover* but

are bewildering here—gives the record an off-kilter feel that may cause some listeners to underrate what is not just a typically excellent Sahm set, but one of his strongest selections of songs. Apart from the barnstorming opener, "San Francisco FM Blues," perhaps the best attempt at shoehorning Sahm's untamed Texan feel to AOR, these all come on the dynamite second side that houses the anthemic title track, as perfect an encapsulation of his Tex-Mex fusion as they come, the rampaging roadhouse rocker "Juan Mendoza," one of his best salutes to Latin culture in the 2-step "Chicano," an excellent Sir Douglas-styled groover in "Hard Way," and the gloriously breezy "Nitty Gritty," one of his very best songs (not to mention one of his best performances, highlighted by his call to right-hand man Augie Meyers before his organ solo). Unlike *Doug Sahm and Band*, *Texas Tornado* is billed to the Sir Doug Band, which is not quite the Sir Douglas Quintet, but with all of his usual gang in place—not just Meyers but bassist Jack Barber, drummer George Rains, and saxophonist Rocky Morales, among others—it essentially is no different than a Sir Douglas Quintet album, but really that's splitting hairs since the album is simply first-rate Doug Sahm. It may be recorded toward the end of his peak period—after this, he turned out two other arguable classics before settling into a comfortably enjoyable groove that he rode out for the rest of his life—but it still captures him at an undeniable peak and it's undeniably irresistible.

Stephen Thomas Erlewine

Carlos Santana

Santana
August 1969, Columbia

Carlos Santana was originally in his own wing of the Latin Rock Hall of Fame, neither playing Afro-Cuban with rock guitar, as did Malo, nor flavoring mainstream rock with percussion, as did Chicago. His first record, as with the best fusion, created something a little different than just a mixture—a new style that, surprisingly remains all his own. Granted that Latin music has seeped into the mainstream since, but why aren't Van Halen and Metallica listening to this? Where they simmer, Santana boils over.

Carl Hoyt

Abraxas
September 1970, Columbia

The San Francisco Bay Area rock scene of the late '60s was one that encouraged radical experimentation and discouraged the type of mindless conformity that's often plagued corporate rock. When one considers just how different Santana, Jefferson Airplane, and the Grateful Dead sounded, it becomes obvious just how much it was encouraged. In the mid-'90s, an album as eclectic as *Abraxas* would be considered a marketing exec's worst nightmare. But at the dawn of the 1970s, this unorthodox mix of rock, jazz, salsa, and blues proved

quite successful. Whether adding rock elements to salsa king Tito Puente's "Oye Como Va," embracing instrumental jazz-rock on "Incident at Neshabur" and "Samba Pa Ti," or tackling moody blues-rock on Fleetwood Mac's "Black Magic Woman," the band keeps things unpredictable yet cohesive. Many of the Santana albums that came out in the '70s are worth acquiring, but for novices, *Abraxas* is an excellent place to start.

Alex Henderson

Santana III
September 1971, Columbia/Legacy

Santana III is an album that undeservingly stands in the shadows behind the towering legend that is the band's second album, *Abraxas*. This was also the album that brought guitarist Neal Schon—who was 17 years old—into the original core lineup of Santana. Percussionist Thomas "Coke" Escovedo was brought in to replace (temporarily) José Chepitó Areas, who had suffered a brain aneurysm, yet who recovered quickly and rejoined the band. The rest were Carlos, organist Gregg Rolie, drummer Michael Schrieve, bassist David Brown, and conguero Michael Carabello. "Batuka" is the powerful first evidence of something being very different. The band was rawer, darker, and more powerful with twin leads and Schon's harder, edgier rock & roll sound paired with Carlos' blend of ecstatic high notes and soulful fills. It cooks—funky, mean, and tough. "Batuka" immediately transforms itself into "No One to Depend On," by Escovedo, Carabello, and Rolie. The middle section is highlighted by frantic handclaps, call-and-response lines between Schon and Rolie, and Carlos joining the fray until the entire track explodes into a frenzied finale. And what's most remarkable is that the set just keeps on cooking, from the subtle slow burn of "Taboo" to the percussive jam workout that is "Toussaint l'Overture," a live staple in the band's set list recorded here for the first time (and featuring some cooking Rolie organ work at its beginning). "Everybody's Everything" is here, as is "Guajira" and "Jungle Strut"—tunes that are still part of Santana's live show. With acoustic guitars, gorgeous hand percussion, and Santana's fragile lead vocal, "Everything's Coming Our Way" is the only "feel good" track here, but it's a fitting way to begin winding the album down with its Schon and Santana guitar breaks. The album ends with a completely transformed reading of Tito Puente's "Para los Rumberos," complete with horns and frantic, almost insanely fast hand drumming and cowbell playing. It's an album that has aged extremely well due to its spare production (by Carlos and the band) and its live sound. This is essential Santana, a record that deserves to be reconsidered in light of its lasting abundance and vision.

Thom Jurek

Caravanserai
October 1972, Columbia

Drawing on rock, salsa, and jazz, Santana recorded one imaginative, unpredictable gem after another during the 1970s. But *Caravanserai* is daring even by Santana's high standards. Carlos Santana was obviously very hip to jazz fusion—something the innovative guitarist provides a generous dose of on the largely instrumental *Caravanserai*. Whether its approach is jazz-rock or simply rock, this album is consistently inspired and quite adventurous. Full of heartfelt, introspective guitar solos, it lacks the immediacy of *Santana* or *Abraxas*. Like the type of jazz that influenced it, this pearl (which marked the beginning of keyboardist/composer Tom Coster's highly beneficial membership in the band) requires a number of listenings in order to be absorbed and fully

appreciated. But make no mistake: this is one of Santana's finest accomplishments.

Alex Henderson

Love Devotion Surrender
1972, Columbia

A hopelessly misunderstood record in its time by Santana fans—they were still reeling from the radical direction shift toward jazz on *Caravanserai* and praying it was an aberration—it was greeted by Santana devotees with hostility, contrasted with kindness from major-league critics like Robert Palmer. To hear this recording in the context of not only Carlos Santana's development as a guitarist, but as the logical extension of the music of John Coltrane and Miles Davis influencing rock musicians—McLaughlin, of course, was a former Davis sideman—this extension makes perfect sense in the post-Sonic Youth, post-rock era. With the exception of Coltrane's "Naima" and McLaughlin's "Meditation," this album consists of merely three extended guitar jams played on the spiritual ecstasy tip—both men were devotees of guru Shri Chinmoy at the time. The assembled band included members of Santana's band and the Mahavishnu Orchestra in Michael Shrieve, Billy Cobham, Doug Rauch, Armando Peraza, Jan Hammer (playing drums!), and Don Alias. But it is the presence of the revolutionary jazz organist Larry Young—a colleague of McLaughlin's in Tony Williams' Lifetime band—that makes the entire project gel. He stands as the great communicator harmonically between the two very different guitarists whose ideas contrasted enough to complement one another in the context of Young's aggressive approach to keep the entire proceeding in the air. In the acknowledgement section of Coltrane's "A Love Supreme," which opens the album, Young creates a channel between Santana's riotous, transcendent, melodic runs and McLaughlin's rapid-fire machine-gun riffing. Young' double-handed striated chord voicings offered enough for both men to chew on, leaving free-ranging territory for percussive effects to drive the tracks from underneath. Check "Let Us Go Into the House of the Lord," which was musically inspired by Bobby Womack's "Breezing" and dynamically foreshadowed by Pharoah Sanders' read of it, or the insanely knotty yet intervallically transcendent "The Life Divine," for the manner in which Young's organ actually speaks both languages simultaneously. Young is the person who makes the room for the deep spirituality inherent in these sessions to be grasped for what it is: the interplay of two men who were not merely paying tribute to Coltrane, but trying to take his ideas about going beyond the realm of Western music to communicate with the language of the heart as it united with the cosmos. After three decades, *Love Devotion Surrender* still sounds completely radical and stunningly, movingly beautiful.

Thom Jurek

Lotus
May 1974, Columbia

Recorded in Japan in July 1973, this massive live album, originally on three LPs and now on two compact discs, was available outside the United States in 1974 but held back from domestic release until long into the CD age. It features the same "New Santana Band" that recorded *Welcome*, and combines that group's jazz and spiritual influences with performances of earlier Latin rock favorites like "Oye Como Va."

William Ruhlmann

Amigos
March 1976, Columbia

By the release of *Amigos*, the Santana band's seventh album, only Carlos Santana and David Brown remained from the band that conquered Woodstock, and only Carlos had been in the band continuously since. Meanwhile, the group had made some effort to arrest its commercial slide, hiring an outside producer, David Rubinson, and taking a tighter, more up-tempo, and more vocal approach to its music. The overt jazz influences were replaced by strains of R&B/funk and Mexican folk music. The result was an album more dynamic than any since *Santana III* in 1971. "Let It Shine" (number 77), an R&B-tinged tune, became the group's first chart single in four years, and the album returned Santana to Top Ten status.

William Ruhlmann

Savoy Brown

The Savoy Brown Collection (Chronicles Series)
July 1993, Polygram

With one of the smoothest and most compelling guitarists of the blues-rock style, Savoy Brown and the finger wizardry of Kim Simmonds unleashed some of the smoothest and most mesmerizing rock & roll of the 1970s. Their ingenious blend of contented blues and hard-edged rock resulted in some wholesome yet somewhat bypassed guitar music. *The Savoy Brown Collection* is a two-disc compilation that takes their best tunes from 14 different albums and presents the listener with a sufficient amount of material that never becomes tiresome. Some of the meatier material comes from 1971's *Street Corner Talking*, like the ultra-smooth "I Can't Get Next to You" and Willie Dixon's "Wang Dang Doodle." Equally impressive is the haunting "Poor Girl" or the desperate guitar cry of "Leavin' Again," both from the sensational *Looking In* album. The real treasures are the lone tunes taken from some of their lesser-known albums. "I'm Tired," from *A Step Further*, emanates pathos through instrumentation, while "Stranger Blues" is a startling example of prime guitar manipulation. Early material from albums like *Shake Down* and *Blue Matter* have former lead singer Chris Youlden at the helm, who departed before the *Looking In* album, replaced by Lonesome Dave Peverett who later formed Foghat. Overshadowed by bands like the Yardbirds and Led Zeppelin, Savoy Brown didn't get the acclaim they actually deserved. Rightfully so, the words "Featuring Kim Simmonds" are

underneath the title of this two CD set, since his craftsmanship is truly the heart of this talented band. Everything that is even the least bit important from this group is strewn across this compilation.

Mike DeGagne

Boz Scaggs

Boz Scaggs
1969, Atlantic

Departing from the Steve Miller Band after a two-album stint, Boz Scaggs found himself on his own but not without support. *Rolling Stone* publisher Jann Wenner, his friend, helped him sign with Atlantic Records and the label had him set up shop in Muscle Shoals, recording his debut album with that legendary set of studio musicians, known for their down-and-dirty backing work for Aretha Franklin and Wilson Pickett, among many other Southern soul legends. The Muscle Shoals rhythm section, occasionally augmented by guitarist Duane Allman, gives this music genuine grit, but this isn't necessarily a straight-up blue-eyed soul record, even if the opening "I'm Easy" and "I'll Be Long Gone" are certainly as deeply soulful as anything cut at Muscle Shoals. Even at this early stage Scaggs wasn't content to stay in one place, and he crafted a kind of Americana fantasia here, also dabbling in country and blues along with the soul and R&B that grounds this record. If the country shuffle "Now You're Gone" sounds just slightly a shade bit too vaudeville for its own good, it only stands out because the rest of the record is pitch-perfect, from the Jimmie Rodgers cover "Waiting for a Train" and the folky "Look What I Got!" to the extended 11-minute blues workout "Loan Me a Dime," which functions as much as a showcase for a blazing Duane Allman as it does for Boz. But even with that show-stealing turn, and even with the Muscle Shoals musicians giving this album its muscle and part of its soul, this album is still thoroughly a showcase for Boz Scaggs' musical vision, which even at this stage is wide and deep. It would grow smoother and more assured over the years, but the slight bit of raggedness suits the funky, down-home performances and helps make this not only a great debut, but also an enduring blue-eyed soul masterpiece.

Stephen Thomas Erlewine

Moments
March 1971, Columbia

"We Were Always Sweethearts" wasn't a huge hit single, but it was a good one, signaling that Boz Scaggs was a soul man of the first degree. *Moments* places him into a variety of settings, including soul, R&B, blues, country, and beautiful, string-drenched balladry. Side one of the LP is especially strong, the kind whose grooves were worn out by its listeners in the early '70s. The second half of the recording doesn't hold up as well, but the closer, "Can I Make It Last (Or Will It Just Be Over)," is a gorgeous, atmospheric instrumental that pulls at the heartstrings. Although Scaggs' big moment in the commercial spotlight was still a few years away, this recording provides many satisfying musical *Moments*.

Jim Newsom

Boz Scaggs & Band
November 1971, Columbia

Although most listeners know Boz Scaggs primarily for his 1976 disco-era, multi-million seller *Silk Degrees*, he produced several excellent recordings in the years leading up to that breakthrough. *Boz Scaggs & Band* is the middle release of a three-disc spurt which Scaggs produced in a two-year period, between 1971 and 1972. Although it is weaker than *Moments* and *My Time* which bookend it, this album still has much to offer. Sounding at times like the original average white band, and at other times like a bunch of Nashville cats, Boz and his eight-piece group traverse a wide terrain with great facility and much soul. "Here to Stay" is particularly appealing, hinting at things to come, and "Flames of Love" is an extended piece of smoking funk. "Monkey Time" and "Why Why" also turn up the funk. This album is well worth checking out.

Jim Newsom

My Time
1972, Columbia

Music critics of the early '70s kept predicting big things for Boz Scaggs, but his records of that period had trouble finding more than a cult audience. *My Time* continued with a mix similar to *Moments* from the previous year, with the opening "Dinah Flo," a great soul-drenched rocker that should have been a hit. In fact, the first three tracks present a powerful opening triumvirate which begs to be heard, with "Full-Lock Power Slide," an air guitarist's dream-come-true. Other high points are Scaggs' definitive cover of Allen Toussaint's "Freedom for the Stallion" and a take on Al Green's "Old Time Lovin'" that gives the original author a run for his money. Considering the success Van Morrison was having working the same territory, it's surprising that this album didn't achieve more in the commercial arena. Its blend of solid '60s soul and bluesy rock is very appealing. However, Boz Scaggs' time was still four years away. *My Time* is a rewarding listen nonetheless.

Jim Newsom

Slow Dancer
1974, Columbia

Featuring his would-be-soulman sound, *Slow Dancer* finds Boz Scaggs straddling the apparently fine line between Van Morrison and Isaac Hayes. While *Silk Degrees* is often touted as Scaggs' best '70s album—based largely upon the chart success of "Lowdown"—*Slow Dancer* features just as many catchy melodic tunes that meld a kind of boogie pub rock with an organic urban soul. Produced by Motown regular Johnny Bristol, Scaggs delivers some of his best performances on the Bristol-penned track "Pain of Love" and the Neil Young meets Marvin Gaye ballad "Sail on White Moon."

Matt Collar

Silk Degrees
February 1976, Columbia

Both artistically and commercially, Boz Scaggs had his greatest success with *Silk Degrees*. The laid-back singer hit the R&B charts in a big way with the addictive, sly "Lowdown" (which has been sampled by more than a few rappers and remains

a favorite among baby-boomer soul fans) and expressed his love of smooth soul music almost as well on the appealing "What Can I Say." But Scaggs was essentially a pop/rocker, and in that area he has a considerable amount of fun on "Lido Shuffle" (another major hit single), "What Do You Want the Girl to Do," and "Jump Street." Meanwhile, "We're All Alone" and "Harbor Lights" became staples on adult contemporary radio. Though not remarkable, the ballads have more heart than most of the bland material dominating that format.

Alex Henderson

Scorpions

Love at First Sting
1984, Mercury

Although the Scorpions had already achieved fame after 1982's *Blackout*, *Love at First Sting* brought them their biggest single of the decade, the slick anthem "Rock You Like a Hurricane," with some greatly underrated songs to back it up. The album opens with the hair-raising "Bad Boys Running Wild" and continues with songs such as the memorable "Big City Nights" and the half-ballad, half-powerhouse rocker "Coming Home." The record also contains what just may be the band's best ballad ever, the tear-jerking "Still Loving You." Considering the fact that it has some of their best-ever singles, *Love at First Sting* is definitely a must for all fans of the Scorpions.

Barry Weber

Bob Seger

Ramblin' Gamblin' Man
1968, Capitol

The Bob Seger System throw everything into *Ramblin' Gamblin' Man*, dabbling in folk, blues-rock, psychedelia, and piledriving rock & roll synonymous with Detroit. Typical of such a wide-ranging debut, not everything works. The System stumbles when they try psychedelic San Franciscan bands on their own turf. Trippy soundscapes like "Gone" drift into the ether, and the longer jams, "White Wall" and "Black Eyed Girl," meander. But the songs that do work are absolute monsters, highlighted by the title track, a thunderous bit of self-mythology driven by a relentless rhythm, wailing organ riff, and gospel chorus. It's a stunningly great record, and while nothing here quite equals it, the songs that come close (with the exception of "Train Man," the first inkling of Seger's knack for reflective, intimate ballads) are sterling examples of spare, bluesy, angry Michigan rock & roll. "Tales of Lucy Blue" has a spooky, menacing edge, "Ivory" is a great Motown-styled raver, and "Down Home" rides a manic riff and a simple blues harp to be one of the best rockers on the record. Then there's "2 +2 = ?," a ferocious antiwar song in the vein of Creedence Clearwater Revival's "Fortunate Son," but here Seger can't imagine why the nice guy in high school is now buried in the mud. It's a frightening, visceral song that stands among the best anti-Vietnam protests. Finally, the album closes with "The Last Song (Love Needs to Be Loved)," an unabashed peace, love, 'n' understanding anthem styled in the manner of West Coast hippie pop, particularly Love. It's atypical of anything on the album or anything Seger would ever do again, but in many ways, it's the perfect way to close an exciting, flawed debut that winds up being a symbol of its times by its very diversity.

Stephen Thomas Erlewine

Mongrel
August 1970, Capitol

Most artists that deliver a second record as shaky as *Noah* fold on their third album. Not Bob Seger. He reasserted control of the System, consigning Tom Neme to a fanboy's footnote, and returning the group to the piledriving rock that was his trademark. All of this was evident with his third album, the superb *Mongrel*. Never before, and never since, has Seger rocked as recklessly and viciously as he did here—after a spell in the wilderness, he's found his voice. He's so assured, he elevates his *Ramblin' Gamblin' Man* characters Lucy Blue and Chicago Green to mythic status in the pulverizing "Lucifer," perhaps the greatest song on this lean, muscular record. That assurance carries over not just through the ferocious rockers that dominate the album—"Evil Edna," "Highway Child," "Leanin on My Dream," and "Song to Rufus" all hit harder than latter-day MC5—but to quieter moments like "Big River," where he first hits upon the wistful, passionate ballad style later popularized with "Night Moves." The fact that the System connects on both illustrates that Seger is not just fronting an excellent band, but that he's developing into a first-class songwriter. Put it this way—the only time the System sounds ill at ease is when they tackle "River Deep—Mountain High," and that's not because they're ill-suited to the epic—it's because they find the lie in the song's artificial pretensions and deliver a performance that eclipses the song itself. That two-fisted punch of terrific performances and songs is unexpected, especially after an album as conflicted as *Noah*, but the truly remarkable thing is that *Mongrel* showcases a band so powerful and a songwriter so distinctive, that it still sounds white-hot decades after its release.

Stephen Thomas Erlewine

Smokin' O.P.'s
1972, Capitol

Bob Seger closed out his Capitol contract with *Brand New Morning*, a singer/songwriter album quite unlike anything he had yet released. Following its release he moved to the Detroit-based label Palladium and returned to hard-driving rock & roll with *Smokin' O.P.'s*, the polar opposite of *Brand New Morning*. According to legend, the title stands for "smoking other people's songs," which makes sense since this is a cover album that even covers Bob Seger & the Last Heard. In other words, it's nothing like the intimate, reflective, risky *Brand New Morning*, but that doesn't matter since it rocks so well and since it reveals that Seger isn't just a first-class bandleader and rock songwriter, but that he's a terrific interpreter of other writers' songs. Even well-worn tunes like "Bo Diddley" and "If I Were a Carpenter" get made fresh by internalizing the hooks, turning them into something fresh and original. That's also true of songs by such contemporaries as Stephen Stills ("Love the One You're With") and Leon Russell ("Humming Bird"), and he also breathes fire into blues and rock stalwarts like "Let It Rock," "Turn on Your Love

Light," and "Jesse James." *Smokin' O.P.'s* closes out with two originals, one new (the fine, but not especially noteworthy "Someday") and one old (the perennial "Heavy Music"). Neither change the essential character of the album, which is just a really fun, hard-rocking record that bought Seger some time while reasserting the fact that he could really rock. He could—and he could rock really well—which is why *Smokin' O.P.'s* remains a lot of fun, even if it's a relatively minor work in Seger's canon.

Stephen Thomas Erlewine

Back in '72
1973, Reprise

Returning to independent status, Bob Seger recorded *Back in '72*, not only the finest of his early-'70s albums but one of the great lost hard rock albums of its era. Seger didn't limit himself to self-penned songs on this excursion; borrowing an idea from *Smokin' O.P.'s*, he covers quite a few tunes, providing a balance to his own tunes. He makes "Midnight Rider" sound as if it were a Motor City raver instead of a sultry, late-afternoon Southern rocker, while casually tossing off "Rosalie," an irresistible ode to a local DJ that turned into a hard rock anthem when Thin Lizzy decided to record it later in the decade. That's the brilliance of *Back in '72*—there's no separation between the original and cover, it's all united in a celebration of rock & roll. That's why "Turn the Page," perhaps the weariest travelogue ever written, never feels self-pitying—that's just the facts, according to a first-rate Midwestern band that never got a break. All the same, *Back in '72* is a testament to great rock & roll, thanks to Seger's phenomenal songwriting and impassioned playing.

Stephen Thomas Erlewine

Seven
March 1974, Capitol

With his seventh album, appropriately titled *Seven*, Bob Seger delivered one of his strongest, hardest-hitting rock records—the toughest since the days of the Bob Seger System. Not to say that he ever abandoned rock & roll, since *Back in '72* was filled with fantastic rockers, but it was tempered with reflective singer/songwriter material. Not here. Even the slowest song, "20 Years From Now," is a steady mid-tempo ballad that showcases the band. Still, that's a rare moment of reflection on a record that opens with "Get out of Denver," the greatest Chuck Berry knockoff ever written, and never loses momentum. Great, raucous rockers pile up one after the other as Seger spins out barroom anthems ("Seen a Lot of Floors"), anti-establishment tirades ("Long Song Comin'," "Cross of Gold"), jokes ("U.M.C. [Upper Middle Class]"), bluesy rock ("All Your Love"), and simple garage rockers ("Need Ya," "School Teacher"). Only nine songs, lasting just over a half-hour, but it's one of the most infectious sets Seger ever cut, proving that he wasn't just a dynamite rocker, but he had the songs to match. And, again, it didn't have any success—it didn't even chart, actually. That doesn't change the fact that this is one of his very best albums.

Stephen Thomas Erlewine

Beautiful Loser
April 1975, Capitol

Beautiful Loser winds up sounding more like *Back in '72* than its immediate predecessor, *Seven*, largely because Bob Seger threaded reflective ballads and mid-tempo laments back into his hard-driving rock. He doesn't shy away from it, either, opening with the lovely title track. And why shouldn't he? These ballads were as much a part of his success as his storming rockers, since his sentimental streak seemed all the more genuine when contrasted with the rockers. If anything, *Beautiful Loser* might err a little bit in favor of reflection, with much of the album devoted to introspective, confessional mid-tempo cuts. There are a couple of exceptions to the rule, of course—"Katmandu" roars with humor, and his cover of "Nutbush City Limits" shames Tina Turner's original—but they are the only full-throttle rockers here, with "Black Night" coming in as a funky, swaggering cousin. It's the exact opposite of *Seven*, in other words, and in its own way, it's just as satisfying. Occasionally, it might be a little too sentimental for some tastes, but it's all heartfelt and he's written some terrific songs here, most notably the album's heart of "Jody Girl" and "Travelin' Man." Seger had started turning inward, searching his soul in a way he hadn't since the since-disowned *Brand New Morning*, and in doing so, he was setting the stage for his first genuine blockbuster.

Stephen Thomas Erlewine

Live Bullet
April 1976, Capitol

Live Bullet introduced Bob Seger to a wide audience, revealing a rocker of unbridled passion and a songwriter of considerable talent. Prior to its release, Seger had been toiling away, releasing seven albums and touring constantly ever since his debut scraped the national consciousness in 1968. The psychedelicized days of *Ramblin' Gamblin' Man* are long gone on *Live Bullet*, leaving behind a rocker who loved the Stones for their toughness, Dylan for his honesty, and Chuck Berry for his narrative—and one who found his own sound when the Silver Bullet Band came into its own through countless tours. *Live Bullet* was recorded live at Detroit's Cobo Hall, in front of a passionate, loving hometown audience spurring him into a great performance. The song selection relies heavily on *Beautiful Loser*, yet it dips into the previous albums enough to prove that Seger had been delivering consistently as a songwriter for years. But what really sold *Live Bullet* is how these terrific songs are delivered with a ferocious, committed intensity. This might not be much more than a simple rock & roll album, but it's one of the best of its kind, establishing Seger, in the eyes of skeptics, as a first-rate performer and writer. Here, "Heavy Music," "Get out of Denver," "Turn the Page," and "Ramblin' Gamblin' Man" all become hard rock classics, as does the band itself. It's a rare occasion when a double live album captures an artist at an absolute peak, while summarizing his talents, and that's exactly what *Live Bullet* does.

Stephen Thomas Erlewine

Night Moves
October 1976, Capitol

Bob Seger recorded the bulk of *Night Moves* before *Live Bullet* brought him his first genuine success, so it shouldn't come as a surprise that it's similar in spirit to the introspective *Beautiful Loser*, even if it rocks harder and longer. Throughout much of the album, he's coming to grips with being on the other side of 30 and still rocking. He floats back in time, turning in high-school memories, remembering when wandering down "Mainstreet" was the highlight of an evening, covering a rockabilly favorite in "Mary Lou." Stylistically, there's not much change since *Beautiful Loser*, but the difference is that Seger and his Silver Bullet Band—who turn in their first studio album here—sound intense and ferocious, and the songs are subtly varied. Yes, this is all hard rock, but the acoustic ballads reveal the influence of Dylan and Van Morrison, filtered through a Midwestern sensibility, and the rockers reveal more of Seger's personality than ever. Seger may have been this consistent before (on *Seven*, for example), but the mood had never been as successfully varied, nor had his songwriting been as consistent, intimate, and personal. Thankfully, this was delivered to a mass audience eager for Seger, and it not only became a hit, but one of the universally acknowledged high points of late-'70s rock & roll. And, because of his passion and craft, it remains a thoroughly terrific record years later.

Stephen Thomas Erlewine

Stranger in Town
May 1978, Capitol

Night Moves was in the pipeline when *Live Bullet* hit, and wound up eclipsing the double live set anyway, so *Stranger in Town* is really the record where Bob Seger started grasping the changes that happened when he became a star. It happened when he was old enough to have already formed his character. Even as celebrity creeps in, as on "Hollywood Nights," Seger remains a middle-class, Midwestern rocker, celebrating "Old Time Rock & Roll," realizing old flames are still the same, and still feeling like a number. Musically, it's as lively as *Night Moves*, rocking even harder in some places and being equally as introspective in the acoustic numbers. If it doesn't feel as revelatory as that record, in many ways it does feel like a stronger set of songs. Yes, musically, it doesn't offer any revelations, but it still feels impassioned, both in its performances and songs, and it's still one of the great rock records of its era.

Stephen Thomas Erlewine

Against the Wind
February 1980, Capitol

Though there are still some traces of the confessionals that underpinned *Beautiful Loser* through *Stranger in Town*, *Against the Wind* finds Bob Seger turning toward craft. Perhaps he had to, since *Against the Wind* arrived after three blockbuster albums and never-ending tours. Even so, this record winds up not feeling as immediate or soulful as its predecessors, especially since it begins with a tossed-off rocker called "The Horizontal Bop," possibly his most careless tune since "Noah." It's fun, but once it's done, the record really starts to kick into high gear with "You'll Accomp'ny Me," a ballad the equal of anything on its two predecessors. Throughout *Against the Wind*, Seger winds up performing better on the ballads than the rockers, which, while good, tend to sound a little formulaic. Still, Seger's formula is good and if "Her Strut" and "Betty Lou's Gettin' out Tonight" would have been second stringers on *Stranger in Town*, they offer a nice balance here, and the rest of the record alternates between similarly well-constructed rockers and introspective ballads like "Against the Wind" and "Fire Lake." Compared to its predecessors, this does feel a little weak, but compared with its peers, it's a strong, varied heartland rock album that finds Seger at a near peak.

Stephen Thomas Erlewine

The Distance
December 1982, Capitol

The Distance was hailed as a return to form upon the time of its release and, in many ways, might be a little stronger, a little more consistent than its predecessor, *Against the Wind*. Still, this album has the slickest production Bob Seger had yet granted, and the biggest hit single on *The Distance* wasn't written by him, it was a cover of Rodney Crowell's "Shame on the Moon." Now, this wasn't entirely unusual, since Seger had been an excellent interpreter of songs for years, but this, combined with the glossy sound, signaled that Seger may have been more concerned with his status as a popular, blue-collar rocker than his music. Not that there's much to fault with the music, since "Even Now" and "Roll Me Away" are easily two of his classics, and he turns out craftsmanlike rockers like "Makin' Thunderbirds" and "Boomtown Blues" with aplomb. For all its attributes, it feels like a mirror image of *Against the Wind*, an album where the rockers, on the whole, wind up being more convincing than the ballads. Now, that doesn't mean *The Distance* is a bad record, since it isn't—it's filled with first-rate heartland rockers—but Seger at his best could balance rockers with ballads, or if he concentrated on rockers, it would be more ferocious than this. This album is simply solid, a nice addition to his catalog, but not a knockout.

Stephen Thomas Erlewine

Simon & Garfunkel

Sounds of Silence
January 1966, Columbia

Simon & Garfunkel's second album was a radical departure from their first, owing to its being recorded in the wake of "The Sound of Silence," with its over-dubbed electric instrument backing, topping the charts. Paul Simon arrived with a large song-bag, enhanced by his stay in England over the previous year and his exposure to English folk music, and the duo rushed into the studio to come up with ten more songs that would fit into the folk-rock context of the single. The result was this, their most hurried and uncharacteristic album—Simon and Art Garfunkel had to sound like something they weren't, surrounded on many cuts by amplified folk-rock-style guitar, electric piano, and even horns. Much of the material came from *The Paul Simon Songbook*, an album that Simon had recorded for British CBS during his stay in England, some

parts of it more radically altered than others. The record was a rushed job overall, and apart from the title track, the most important songs here were also, oddly enough, among the least enduring, "I Am a Rock" and "Richard Cory"—the former for establishing the duo (and Simon as a songwriter) as confessional pop-poets, sensitive and alienated post-adolescents that endeared them to millions of college students going through what later came to be called an "identity crisis"; and the latter for endearing them to thousands of high-school English teachers with its adaptation of Edward Arlington Robinson's poem.

Bruce Eder

Parsley, Sage, Rosemary and Thyme
September 1966, Columbia

Simon & Garfunkel's first masterpiece, *Parsley, Sage, Rosemary and Thyme* was also the first album on which the duo, in tandem with engineer Roy Halee, exerted total control from beginning to end, right down to the mixing, and it is an achievement akin to the Beatles' *Revolver* or the Beach Boys' *Pet Sounds* album, and just as personal and pointed as either of those records at their respective bests. After the frantic rush to put together an LP in just three weeks that characterized the *Sounds of Silence* album early in 1966, *Parsley, Sage, Rosemary and Thyme* came together over a longer gestation period of about three months, an uncommonly extended period of recording in those days, but it gave the duo a chance to develop and shape the songs the way they wanted them. The album opens with one of the last vestiges of Paul Simon's stay in England, "Scarborough Fair/Canticle"—the latter was the duo's adaptation of a centuries-old English folk song in an arrangement that Simon had learned from Martin Carthy. The two transformed the song into a daunting achievement in the studio, however, incorporating myriad vocal overdubs and utilizing a harpsichord, among other instruments, to embellish it, and also wove into its structure Simon's "The Side of a Hill," a gentle antiwar song that he had previously recorded on *The Paul Simon Songbook* in England. The sonic results were startling on their face, a record that was every bit as challenging in its way as "Good Vibrations," but the subliminal effect was even more profound, mixing a hauntingly beautiful antique melody, and a song about love in a peaceful, domestic setting, with a message about war and death; Simon & Garfunkel were never as political as, say, Peter, Paul & Mary or Joan Baez, but on this record they did bring the Vietnam war home. The rest of the album was less imposing but just as beguiling—audiences could revel in the play of Simon's mind (and Simon & Garfunkel's arranging skills) and his sense of wonder (and frustration) on "Patterns," and appreciate the sneering rock & roll-based social commentary "The Big Bright Green Pleasure Machine." Two of the most beautiful songs ever written about the simple joys of living, the languid "Cloudy" and bouncy "The 59th Street Bridge Song (Feelin' Groovy)," were no less seductive, and the album also included "Homeward Bound," their Top Five hit follow-up to "The Sound of Silence," which had actually been recorded at the sessions for that LP. No Simon &

Garfunkel song elicits more difference of opinion than "The Dangling Conversation," making its LP debut here—one camp regards it as hopelessly pretentious and precious in its literary name-dropping and rich string orchestra accompaniment, while another holds it as a finely articulate account of a couple grown distant and disconnected through their intellectual pretentions; emotionally, it is definitely its precursor to the more highly regarded "Overs" off the next album, and it resonated well on college campuses at the time, evoking images of graduate school couples drifting apart, but for all the beauty of the singing and the arrangement, it also seemed far removed from the experience of teenagers or any listeners not living a life surrounded by literature ("couplets out of rhyme" indeed!), and understandably only made the Top 30 on AM radio. "For Emily, Whenever I May Find Her" was a romantic idyll that presented Art Garfunkel at his most vulnerable sounding, anticipating such solo releases of his as "All I Know," while "Flowers Never Bend With the Rainfall" was his most reflectively philosophical, dealing with age and its changes much as "Patterns" dealt with the struggle to change, with a dissonant note (literally) at the end that anticipated the style of the duo's next album. "A Simple Desultory Philippic," which also started life in England more than a year earlier, was the team's Dylanesque fuzz tone-laden jape at folk-rock, and a statement of who they weren't, and remains, alongside Peter, Paul & Mary's "I Dig Rock & Roll Music," one of the best satires of its kind. And the last of Simon's English-period songs, "A Poem on the Underground Wall," seemed to sum up the tightrope walk that the duo did at almost every turn on this record at this point in their career—built around a beautiful melody and gorgeous hooks, it was, nonetheless, a study in personal privation and desperation, the "sound of silence" heard from the inside out, a voice crying out. Brilliantly arranged in a sound that was as much rock as film music, but with the requisite acoustic guitars, and displaying a dazzling command and range of language, it could have ended the album. Instead, the duo offered "7 O'Clock News/Silent Night," a conceptual work that was a grim and ironic (and prophetic) comment on the state of the United States in 1966. In retrospect, it dated the album somewhat, but that final track, among the darkest album-closers of the 1960s, also proved that Simon & Garfunkel weren't afraid to get downbeat as well as serious for a purpose. Overall, *Parsley, Sage, Rosemary and Thyme* was the duo's album about youthful exuberance and alienation, and it proved perennially popular among older, more thoughtful high-school students and legions of college audiences across generations. [The August 2001 reissue offers not only the best sound ever heard on this album in any incarnation, but also a few bonuses—a slightly extended mastering of "Cloudy" that gives the listener a high-harmony surprise in its fade; and, as actual bonus tracks, Simon's solo demos of "Patterns" and "A Poem on the Underground Wall." Raw and personal, they're startling in their intimacy and their directness, and offer a more intimate view of Paul Simon, the artist, than ever seen.]

Bruce Eder

Bookends
March 1968, Columbia

Bookends is a literary album that contains the most minimal of openings with the theme, an acoustic guitar stating itself slowly and plaintively before erupting into the wash of synthesizers and dissonance that is "Save the Life of My Child." The classic "America" is next, a folk song with a lilting soprano saxophone in the refrain and a small pipe organ painting the acoustic guitars in the more poignant verses. The song relies on pop structures to carry its message of hope and

disillusionment as two people travel the American landscape searching for it until it dawns on them that everyone else on the freeway is doing the same thing. The final four tracks, "Mrs. Robinson," the theme song for the film *The Graduate*, "A Hazy Shade of Winter," and the album's final track, "At the Zoo," offer as tremblingly bleak a vision for the future as any thing done by the Velvet Underground, but rooted in the lives of everyday people, not in the decadent underground personages of New York's Factory studio. But the album is also a warning that to pay attention is to take as much control of one's fate as possible.

Thom Jurek

Bridge Over Troubled Water
February 1970, Columbia

Bridge Over Troubled Water was one of the biggest-selling albums of its decade, and it hasn't fallen too far down on the list in years since. Apart from the gospel-flavored title track, which took some evolution to get to what it finally became, however, much of *Bridge Over Troubled Water* also constitutes a stepping back from the music that Simon & Garfunkel had made on *Bookends*—this was mostly because the creative partnership that had formed the body and the motivation for the duo's four prior albums literally consumed itself in the making of *Bridge Over Troubled Water*. The overall effect was perhaps the most delicately textured album to close out the 1960s from any major rock act. *Bridge Over Troubled Water*, at its most ambitious and bold, on its title track, was a quietly reassuring album; at other times, it was personal yet soothing; and at other times, it was just plain fun. The public in 1970—a very unsettled time politically, socially, and culturally—embraced it; and whatever mood they captured, the songs matched the standard of craftsmanship that had been established on the duo's two prior albums. Between the record's overall quality and its four hits, the album held the number one position for two and a half months and spent years on the charts, racking up sales in excess of five million copies. The irony was that for all of the record's and the music's appeal, the duo's partnership ended in the course of creating and completing the album.

Bruce Eder

Carly Simon

Anthology
November 2002, Rhino

For Carly Simon fans looking for something a little more extensive than a single-disc greatest-hits collection, but not something so large and expensive as her *Clouds in My Coffee 1966-1996* box set, *Anthology* is a good deal. The two CDs include 40 songs from 1971 to 2000, among them nearly two dozen chart hits (though some of the later ones only made the adult contemporary charts). For the more cold-blooded fan who wants to zero in on her best and most popular work, there might well be more than she or he wants to hear, particularly on disc two, devoted entirely to post-1980 material, which reflects her move from tenuously folk-rock-related singer/songwriting to blander adult contemporary music. For those who see her early work as her best, *The Best of Carly Simon* remains about all you need; for those who appreciate her whole career, the lengthier single-disc anthology *The Very Best of Carly Simon: Nobody Does It Better* will likewise suffice. There's not much in rarities on *Anthology* either—nothing from her pre-Elektra recordings as part of the Simon Sisters, and nothing previously unreleased, though 1995's "Touched By the Sun" was only on the *Live at Grand Central* video, and four tracks are taken not from Simon albums but from film soundtracks (including, of course, her massive 1977 hit, "Nobody Does It Better"). All of this might be too much carping. This does, after all, gather material from more than half a dozen labels, presented respectfully with a 40-page booklet, though the liner notes are much heavier on fawning affection than historical details.

Richie Unterberger

Paul Simon

Paul Simon
January 1972, Warner Bros.

If any musical justification were needed for the breakup of Simon & Garfunkel, it could be found on this striking collection, Paul Simon's post-split debut. From the opening cut, "Mother and Child Reunion" (a Top Ten hit), Simon, who had snuck several subtle musical explorations into the generally conservative S&G sound, broke free, heralding the rise of reggae with an exuberant track recorded in Jamaica for a song about death. From there, it was off to Paris for a track in South American style and a rambling story of a fisherman's son, "Duncan" (which made the singles chart). But most of the album had a low-key feel, with Simon on acoustic guitar backed by only a few trusted associates (among them Joe Osborn, Larry Knechtel, David Spinozza, Mike Manieri, Ron Carter, and Hal Blaine, along with such guests as Stefan Grossman, Airto Moreira, and Stephane Grappelli), singing a group of informal, intimate, funny, and closely observed songs (among them the lively Top 40 hit "Me and Julio Down by the Schoolyard"). It was miles removed from the big, stately ballad style of *Bridge Over Troubled Water* and signaled that Simon was a versatile songwriter as well as an expressive singer with a much broader range of musical interests than he had previously demonstrated. You didn't miss Art Garfunkel on *Paul Simon*, not only because Simon didn't write Garfunkel-like showcases for himself, but because the songs he did write showed off his own, more varied musical strengths.

William Ruhlmann

There Goes Rhymin' Simon
May 1973, Warner Bros.

Retaining the buoyant musical feel of *Paul Simon*, but employing a more produced sound, *There Goes Rhymin' Simon* found Paul Simon writing and performing with assurance and venturing into soulful and R&B-oriented music. Simon returned to the kind of vocal pyrotechnics heard on the Simon & Garfunkel records by using gospel singers. On "Love Me Like a Rock" and "Tenderness" (which sounded as though it could have been written to Art Garfunkel), the Dixie Hummingbirds sang prominent backup vocals, and on "Take Me to the Mardi Gras," Reverend Claude Jeter contributed a falsetto part that Garfunkel could have handled, though not as warmly. For several tracks, Simon traveled to the Muscle Shoals Sound Studios to play with its house band,

getting a variety of styles, from the gospel of "Love Me Like a Rock" to the Dixieland of "Mardi Gras." Simon was so confident that he even included a major ballad statement of the kind he used to give Garfunkel to sing: "American Tune" was his musical State of the Union, circa 1973, but this time Simon was up to making his big statements in his own voice. Though that song spoke of "the age's most uncertain hour," otherwise *Rhymin' Simon* was a collection of largely positive, optimistic songs of faith, romance, and commitment, concluding, appropriately, with a lullaby ("St. Judy's Comet") and a declaration of maternal love ("Loves Me Like a Rock")—in other words, another mother-and-child reunion that made *Paul Simon* and *There Goes Rhymin' Simon* book-end masterpieces Simon would not improve upon (despite some valiant attempts) until *Graceland* in 1986.

William Ruhlmann

Still Crazy After All These Years
October 1975, Warner Bros.

The third new studio album of Paul Simon's post-Simon & Garfunkel career was a musical and lyrical change of pace from his first two, *Paul Simon* and *There Goes Rhymin' Simon*. Where Simon had taken an eclectic approach before, delving into a variety of musical  styles and recording all over the world, *Still Crazy* found him working for the most part with a group of jazz-pop New York session players, though he did do a couple of tracks ("My Little Town" and "Still Crazy After All These Years") with the Muscle Shoals rhythm section that had appeared on *Rhymin' Simon* and another ("Gone at Last") returned to the gospel style of earlier songs like "Loves Me Like a Rock." Of course, "My Little Town" also marked a return to working with Art Garfunkel, and another Top Ten entry for S&G. But the overall feel of *Still Crazy* was of a jazzy style subtly augmented with strings and horns. Perhaps more striking, however, was Simon's lyrical approach. Where *Rhymin' Simon* was the work of a confident family man, *Still Crazy* came off as a post-divorce album, its songs reeking of smug self-satisfaction and romantic disillusionment. At their best, such sentiments were undercut by humor and made palatable by musical hooks, as on "50 Ways to Leave Your Lover," which became the biggest solo hit of Simon's career. But elsewhere, as on "Have a Good Time" (written for but not used in the film *Shampoo* and perhaps intended to express the shallow feelings of the main character), the singer's cynicism seemed unearned. Still, as out of sorts as Simon may have been, he was never more in tune with his audience: *Still Crazy* topped the charts, spawned four Top 40 hits, and won Grammys for Song of the Year and Best Vocal Performance.

William Ruhlmann

One-Trick Pony
August 1980, Warner Bros.

Though it was released to coincide with the opening of the film *One-Trick Pony*, which Paul Simon wrote and starred in, the *One-Trick Pony* album is not a soundtrack, as it is sometimes categorized, at least, not exactly. If it were, it might contain the Paul Simon song "Soft Parachutes" and other non-Simon music featured in the movie. Instead, this is a studio album containing many of the movie songs, some of them in the same performances (two were cut live at the Agora Club in Cleveland). The record is not billed as a soundtrack, but a sleeve note reads, "The music on this Compact Disc was created for the Paul Simon Movie 'One-Trick Pony.'" Are we clear? Okay. Anyway, if Simon was in fact writing songs for Jonah, his movie character (as seems true of songs like "Jonah," "God Bless the Absentee," and "Long, Long Day"), he intended that character to take a somewhat less considered lyrical viewpoint than Paul Simon generally does, but to be even more enamored of light jazz fusion than Paul Simon had been on his last album, *Still Crazy After All These Years*. Tasty licks abound from the fretwork of Eric Gale, Hiram Bullock, and Hugh McCracken, and the rhythm section of Steve Gadd, Tony Levin, and Richard Tee is equally in the groove. This is the closest thing to a band album Simon ever made, and it contains some of his most rhythmic and energetic singing. But it is also his most uneven album, simply because the songwriting, with the exception of the title song and the ballads "How the Heart Approaches What It Yearns" and "Nobody," is not up to his usual standard. Maybe he was too busy writing his screenplay to polish these songs to the usual gloss. (It can't have been than Jonah wasn't supposed to be as talented as Paul Simon. Could it?) In any case, though the album spawned a Top Ten hit in "Late in the Evening" and may have sold more copies than the film did tickets, it remained a disappointment in both artistic and commercial terms.

William Ruhlmann

Hearts and Bones
October 1983, Warner Bros.

Hearts and Bones was a commercial disaster, the lowest-charting new studio album of Paul Simon's career. It is also his most personal collection of songs, one of his most ambitious, and one of his best. It retains a personal vision, one largely devoted to the challenges of middle-aged life, among them a renewed commitment to love; the title song was a notable testament to new romance, while "Train in the Distance" reflected on romantic discord. Elsewhere, "The Late Great Johnny Ace" was his meditation on John Lennon's murder and how it related to the mythology of pop music. Musically, Simon moved forward and backward simultaneously, taking off from the jazz fusion style of his last two albums into his old loves of doo wop and rock & roll while also incorporating current sounds with such new collaborators as dance music producer Nile Rodgers and minimalist composer Philip Glass. The result was Simon's most impressive collection in a decade and the most underrated album in his catalog.

William Ruhlmann

Graceland
August 1986, Warner Bros.

With *Graceland*, Paul Simon hit on the idea of combining his always perceptive songwriting with the little-heard mbaqanga music of South Africa, creating a fascinating hybrid that

re-enchanted his old audience and earned him a new one. It is true that the South African angle (including its controversial aspect during the apartheid days) was a powerful marketing tool and that the catchy music succeeded in presenting listeners with that magical combination: something they'd never heard before that nevertheless sounded familiar. As eclectic as any record Simon had made, it also delved into zydeco and conjunto-flavored rock & roll while marking a surprising new lyrical approach (presaged on some songs on *Hearts and Bones*); for the most part, Simon abandoned a linear, narrative approach to his words, instead drawing highly poetic ("Diamonds on the Soles of Her Shoes"), abstract ("The Boy in the Bubble"), and satiric ("I Know What I Know") portraits of modern life, often charged by striking images and turns of phrase torn from the headlines or overheard in contemporary speech. An enormously successful record, *Graceland* became the standard against which subsequent musical experiments by major artists were measured.

William Ruhlmann

The Sir Douglas Quintet

Mendocino
April 1969, Smash

Chart success for the title song led to a hurried release for this band's second album, although perhaps the most famous song, "She's About a Mover," originated a few years prior with another version. Listeners will probably be more familiar with the version heard here,

the one with the freaky feedback guitar solo and fake fade-out that oldies disc jockeys like to yabber over. This and "Mendocino" are only two of the many nearly perfect tracks on this record, some of which give off the illusion (perhaps an accurate one) that they were simply tossed off without a whole lot of preperation. "Texas Me" is genius on triple levels: there is the poetry of the lyrics, the soulful delivery from the singer, and finally the haunting recording flat with echoey, multitracked vocal and fiddle. When the listener reaches the end, "Baby It Just Don't Matter" it is as if one has strolled through an old neighborhood searching for a lost sound in the air, only to find a good, friendly rock band is jamming in a garage right down the block. The players are the classic Sir Douglas Quintet line-up including Augie Meyer.

Eugene Chadbourne

Together After Five
1970, Smash

A supreme example of the Doug Sahm sound and aesthetic is at work here in their third complete studio album. There is perhaps the best recorded version of the Augie Meyers "cheap organ" sound, a well from which many a garage rock organist hath drunken deep. And it is great the way this instrument emerges out of arrangements emphasizing stark interplay between acoustic guitar and drums. A real ringer but one of the highlights of the album is the instrumental "T-Bone Shuffle," which rivals the Art Ensemble of

Chicago for raucous boogie on the edge of lunacy. The songs include some of Sahm's best lyrics and most heartfelt singing, although he goes a bit overboard at times and threatens to come across like a burn-out overstaying his welcome on an open stage. This and a few strange errors in judgement such as the song "Dallas Alice"—imagine something that sounds too close to "Honey"for comfort and also has a flute solo— are the only things preventing this from being one of the best Sir Douglas Quintet albums.

Eugene Chadbourne

1+1+1=4
June 1970, Philips

The Sir Douglas Quintet delivered two excellent records back to back in *Mendocino* and *Together After Five*, but success was hard to come by, and it was hard to tell what path was the right one for a band as talented and fuzzily focused as this. Their fourth Mercury/Smash record, 1970's *1+1+1=4* didn't solve that puzzle and by trying to touch on a little of everything, it didn't provide any clear direction for the band to follow, nor did it showcase the band at its best. Even so, the Sir Douglas Quintet on a bad day were better and more interesting than many of their peers, and part of the fascination behind this record is to hear the group—or, more accurately, its leader Doug Sahm—try to craft an identity by adhering to the band's signature Tex-Mex while expanding in such disparate directions as pure country and horn-drenched progressive pop/rock. The country comes from sessions Sahm held with legendary producer Jerry Kennedy in Nashville; intended to be released as a solo single under the name Wayne Douglas, Sahm's laid-back Texas attitude never translated to the professional aesthetic of Nashville, and the results—"Be Real" and "Pretty Flower"—wind up being a fresh southern breeze on this typically loose-limbed, unfocused, freewheeling record. A large part of the charm of Sahm with the Sir Douglas Quintet is that he was undisciplined; he had no compunction in bringing in what engaged him at a particular time, tying it into his signature blend of rock & roll, R&B, and country. Here, he lays on a little bit too much of a guitar fed through a Leslie rotating speaker, a little bit too much of the punchy, jazzy horn-laced arrangements of such pop progressives as Blood, Sweat & Tears, and he panders a little bit too much to the album-oriented audience. It was all in vain, of course—no matter what he did, he couldn't erase the nature of his music, he couldn't remove the all-encompassing, all-Texan aesthetic, so it still sounded too idiosyncratic for its own good. That, of course, is what makes the music so rich and fascinating years after the fact, because even if Sahm tried different sounds, it still wound up sounding like him, and that's why it's aged much better than other records from that same year. It's a little too hazy and unfocused to be a true lost classic, but once you're hooked on the Sir Douglas sound, this is absolutely necessary. [The 2002 reissue on Acadia/Evangeline contains four bonus tracks: "I Wanna Be Your Mama Again (Nashville Version)," "I Don't Want to Go Home," "Leaving Kansas City," and "Colinda."]

Stephen Thomas Erlewine

The Return of Doug Saldaña
1971, Philips

Since the Sir Douglas Quintet's records were so consistently satisfying and worked such a similar territory—a loose-limbed, freewheeling eclecticism that encompassed rock & roll, blues, country, and R&B in unequal measures at varying times—it can be hard drawing distinctions between their records. Certainly, there was a leap in quality and consistency when they moved to Smash, particularly after their tremendous *Mendocino* record, but each followed similar

territory, with subtle shifts in either tone, subject, or music. Even so, their final Smash record, 1971's *The Return of Doug Saldaña*, is a special record that leapfrogs over the competition and arguably stands as their best record—the best representation of their musical aesthetic, their richest collection of music, their best collection of songs. Part of its appeal is that it stretches beyond the signature Tex-Mex sound they laid down with *Mendocino*; there is no song that captures that wild, wide-open sound, complete with the simple chord changes and careening organ. No, here the Sir Douglas quintet wind up emphasizing their musical roots—whether it's the roadhouse blues jam of "Papa Ain't Salty" or the '50s rock & roll pastiche of "She's Huggin' You, But She's Lookin' at Me," a cinematic pastiche that's the American equivalent of David Bowie's similarly romanticized "Drive-In Saturday"— while settling into the post-hippie hangover of the early '70s, as the dreams of the late '60s die. Witness how the raving opener, "Preach What You Live, Live What You Live," finds its counterpart in the sweetly resigned "Stoned Faces Don't Lie," and how it covers both spectrums of emotion, as Doug Sahm and his group embrace ideals while simultaneously finding them dwindling away. This is the subtext in an album that finds a surplus of great Texas music, from the breezy "Me and My Destiny" and a cover of "Wasted Days, Wasted Nights" to the folky narrative of "The Railpak Dun Done in the Del Monte" and the loose blues of "The Gypsy." No other record by the Sir Douglas Quintet has such a consistently great set of songs or captures their ambition and skill as well as this, which is why it is arguably not only their finest record, but also one of the great lost records of its era, holding its own with the best of such similarly minded groups as the Band. A fantastic record that's just waiting to be discovered. [The 2002 reissue on Acadia/Evangeline contains two bonus tracks, the typically wonderful "Michoacan" and "Westside Blues Again."]

Stephen Thomas Erlewine

Slade

Get Yer Boots On: The Best of Slade
March 2004, Shout Factory

While there has been an enormous number of Slade collections over the years, Shout Factory's 2004 release *Get Yer Boots On: The Best of Slade* is the first comprehensive U.S. compilation, containing both their '70s peak and their early-'80s comeback. If the track listing looks vaguely familiar to Slade-heads, that's because it does share numerous similarities to the 1994 British collection *Wall of Hits*, which also covered the band's entire career, extending it to their brief return to the U.K. charts in the early '90s. As a matter of fact, the track listing is *exactly* the same for the first nine tracks, then *Get Yer Boots On* inserts "Merry Xmas Everybody" to its proper chronological placing (*Wall of Hits* had it tacked onto the end), before resuming the *Wall of Hits* track listing for the next four songs, then skipping ahead to the '80s hits "Run Runaway" and "My Oh My," whose order is flipped from the 1994 comp. So, all

16 tracks on *Get Yer Boots On* are also on the 20-track *Wall of Hits* and pretty much in the same order to boot, but that's fine because not only is the Shout Factory release easier to find, it could be argued that the shorter running time results in a tighter, harder-rocking listen, particularly since it focuses on the group's mid-'70s peak, with none of the '90s tracks. The result is a terrific rock & roll record, full of big, dumb riffs, anthemic singalong choruses, and songs that are impossible to get out of your head. Because Slade's music was so deliberately dumb (and because it made no waves in America until Quiet Riot did note-for-note covers in the early '80s), they tend to be either forgotten (as they are in the U.S.) or dismissed (as they sometimes are in the U.K.), but *Get Yer Boots On* proves they made some of the most addictive, tuneful hard rock of the '70s—it's blue-collar glitter, as primal as AC/DC and catchy as bubblegum pop. Anybody who loves loud guitars and humongous hooks will find this irresistible, and this long-overdue U.S. compilation is the best place to discover how great this band really was.

Stephen Thomas Erlewine

The Small Faces

Small Faces [40th Anniversary Edition]
1966, Decca

What makes this fortieth anniversary edition of the Small Faces' self-titled 1966 debut album more worthwhile than other CD reissues of the same record—particularly the 1996 expanded edition on Dream, which offered five bonus tracks? Well, this 2006 upgrade, aside from bearing the obligatory "digitally remastered" sticker, offers *eleven* bonus tracks. These include all five of the bonus tracks from the 1996 expanded edition (those being alternate versions of "What'cha Gonna Do About It," "Come On Children," "Shake," and "E Too D" that showed up in the French EP format, as well as an extended version of "Own Up Time"). They also include all five of the 1965 and 1966 U.K. A-sides and B-sides from their first four singles that weren't included on the original *Small Faces* LP, as well as an alternate version of one of those A-sides, "Hey Girl" (source unspecified). Those A-sides and B-sides make great additions, as they all fit in well soundwise and style-wise with the tracks from the LP. The alternate versions are less essential, but still nifty for the die-hard Small Faces fan, which is whom this fortieth anniversary edition is targeted toward, after all. Also, the liner notes are a big improvement over the 1996 expanded edition, this time running to 20 pages of intensely detailed information about the group's early career and recordings by Andy Neill, with lots of photos and memorabilia reproductions. Yes, it's true that the big Small Faces fan is likely to already have all of these 23 tracks somewhere, so much has their catalog been reissued in various formats. This is likely to be unsurpassed, however, as the most thorough (and thoroughly annotated) collection of the material they released through the middle of 1966, when they were at their most raucous stage of their R&B-soaked mod rock sound. And, extra goodies and ribbons on the packaging aside, this is vital British Invasion music that at its best—the hits "What'cha Gonna Do About It," "Hey Girl," and "Sha La La La Lee," as well as the flop single "I've Got Mine," the single-worthy pop/rocker "Sorry She's Mine," and the Muddy Waters rave-up "You Need Loving" (which helped inspire Led Zeppelin's "Whole Lotta Love")—is mod rock at its best, though some of the other material here is energetic filler verging on generic R&B jams.

Richie Unterberger

Ogden's Nut Gone Flake
1968, Sony

There was no shortage of good psychedelic albums emerging from England in 1967-1968, but *Ogden's Nut Gone Flake* is special even within their ranks. The Small Faces had already shown a surprising adaptability to psychedelia with the single "Itchycoo Park" and much of their other 1967 output, but *Ogden's Nut Gone Flake* pretty much ripped the envelope. British bands had an unusual approach to psychedelia from the get-go, often preferring to assume different musical "personae" on their albums, either feigning actual "roles" in the context of a variety show (as on the Beatles' *Sgt. Pepper's Lonely Hearts Club Band* album), or simply as storytellers in the manner of the Pretty Things on *S.F. Sorrow*, or actor/performers as on the Who's *Tommy*. The Small Faces tried a little bit of all of these approaches on *Ogden's Nut Gone Flake*, but they never softened their sound. Side one's material, in particular, would not have been out of place on any other Small Faces release—"Afterglow (Of Your Love)" and "Rene" both have a pounding beat from Kenny Jones, and Ian McLagan's surging organ drives the former while his economical piano accompaniment embellishes the latter; and Steve Marriott's crunching guitar highlights "Song of a Baker." Marriott singing has him assuming two distinct "roles," neither unfamiliar—the Cockney upstart on "Rene" and "Lazy Sunday," and the diminutive soul shouter on "Afterglow (Of Your Love)" and "Song of a Baker." Some of side two's production is more elaborate, with overdubbed harps and light orchestration here and there, and an array of more ambitious songs, all linked by a narration by comic dialect expert Stanley Unwin, about a character called "Happiness Stan." The core of the sound, however, is found in the pounding "Rollin' Over," which became a highlight of the group's stage act during its final days—the song seems lean and mean with a mix in which Ronnie Lane's bass is louder than the overdubbed horns. Even "Mad John," which derives from folk influences, has a refreshingly muscular sound on its acoustic instruments. Overall, this was the ballsiest-sounding piece of full-length psychedelia to come out of England, and it rode the number one spot on the U.K. charts for six weeks in 1968, though not without some controversy surrounding advertisements by Immediate Records that parodied the Lord's Prayer. Still, *Ogden's* was the group's crowning achievement—it had even been Marriott's hope to do a stage presentation of *Ogden's Nut Gone Flake*, though a television special might've been more in order. As with most Immediate Records releases, it has gone through multiple reissue cycles on vinyl and CD; the original LP came in a circular sleeve in keeping with the design of the cover, and was reissued in a more convention jacket during the 1970s and early '80s. Most of the CD versions until the 1990s were, in keeping with the poor state of the Immediate Records tape library, substandard in sound, but since 1994 or so there has been a succession of good-sounding digital remasterings.

Bruce Eder

The Darlings of Wapping Wharf Launderette
May 2000, Immediate/Sequel

Here's the question for Small Faces fans: Is it better to own the original Immediate albums or to invest in the splendid double-disc set, *The Darlings of Wapping Wharf Launderette*? The question is a tricky one, since *Darlings* contains all of their Immediate recordings, meaning all of *Autumn Stone* (or *There Are But Four Small Faces*, as it's known in its American incarnation), plus all of the landmark *Ogden's Nut Gone Flake*. Granted, *Ogden's* is divided cleanly in half, with the first side appearing on disc one and the second on disc two, which may irritate listeners who like to hear the concept album uninterrupted. Nevertheless, it's hard not to view *Darlings* as a real bargain, since it gathers all the singles, albums, B-sides, plus some outtakes and alternate mixes and versions from the group's most creative period. And, hearing them in this setting, it's hard not to be stunned by the depth of the group's songwriting and restless musicality, which holds its own with peers like the Kinks and the Who. So, the question may indeed be an easy one, after all—if you want to be stunned by the Small Faces' peak, there's no better place to turn.

Stephen Thomas Erlewine

Southside Johnny & the Asbury Jukes

Hearts of Stone
1978, Epic

Hearts of Stone was the last record Southside Johnny & the Asbury Jukes cut for Epic. It was produced by Steven Van Zandt—who also wrote six of the set's nine tunes, sang backup, and played rhythm guitar (except on the title track.) E Street drummer Max Weinberg was also on hand for this set. This is easily the best of the band's three offerings for the label. Here, sophisticated arrangements, a huge band—with a five-piece horn section and a six-piece rock band with three guitarists (!)—and solid R&B songwriting merging with raucous, soulful barroom rock & roll are a marriage made in beer-drenched heaven. The title track, written by Bruce Springsteen, is a ballad as poignant as Tom Waits' "Jersey Girl," written in its own way to pay tribute to Springsteen. It's a broken love song that gets its fire from the depth and mournful force of the grain in Johnny Lyon's voice. He sings his ass off. Though he didn't, it's as if Springsteen wrote this song especially for Lyon. The Boss also wrote "Talk to Me" and co-wrote "Trapped Again" with Lyon and Van Zandt. While these three cuts are the ones audiences will purchase the LP for, they're hardly all that's here. Van Zandt's strength as a songwriter even at this early juncture is unmistakable. Songs such as "This Time Baby's Gone for Good" or the smoking "Take It Inside," are a perfect marriage of songcraft with arrangement and a vocalist who understands how to get inside lyric, melody, and on top of a wailing band to put the tune across with emotion, depth, and a truckload of street savvy. *Hearts of Stone* is more than a piece or rock curiosa at this juncture; it stands as an overlooked diamond in the fully realized rough, waiting to be rediscovered for the solid, timeless blend of R&B and rock that it is. [In late 2005, Beat Goes On reissued *Hearts of Stone* in England, in a very crisply remastered edition with strong, vivid sound and extensive notes by John Tobler, as well as complete lyrics. It's easily worth the higher list price, handily supplanting

the existing U.S. CD from Sony/Epic, which was mastered back in t the '80s—the drums, guitar, and bass on "Take It Inside" sound like they're in the room with you, and you can practically hear the action on the acoustic guitar on the latter number (and the action on Max Weinberg's drums on "Talk To Me"—the little details just flow off the disc), and all of the horns' voices are distinct and clear throughout. In short, it doesn't get much better than listening to this edition of the album.]

Thom Jurek & Bruce Eder

Spirit

Spirit
January 1968, Epic/Legacy

Spirit's debut unveiled a band that seemed determine to out-eclecticize everybody else on the California psychedelic scene, with its melange of rock, jazz, blues, folk-rock, and even a bit of classical and Indian music. Teenaged Randy California immediately established a signature sound with his humming, sustain-heavy tone; middle-aged drummer Ed Cassidy gave the group unusual versatility; and the songs tackled unusual lyrical themes, like "Fresh Garbage" and "Mechanical World." As is often the case in such hybrids, the sum fell somewhat short of the parts; they could play more styles than almost any other group, but couldn't play (or, more crucially, write) as well as the top acts in any given one of those styles. There's some interesting stuff here, nonetheless; "Uncle Jack" shows some solid psych-pop instincts, and it sounds like Led Zeppelin lifted the opening guitar lines of "Taurus" for their own much more famous "Stairway to Heaven."

Richie Unterberger

The Family That Plays Together
December 1968, Epic/Legacy

On this, the second Spirit album, the group put all of the elements together that made them the legendary (and underrated) band that they were. Jazz, rock & roll, and even classical elements combined to create one of the cleanest, most tasteful syntheses of its day. The group had also improved measurably from their fine debut album, especially in the area of vocals. The album's hit single, "I Got a Line on You," boasts especially strong harmonies as well as one of the greatest rock riffs of the period. The first side of this record is a wonderful and seamless suite, and taken in its entirety, one of the greatest sides on Los Angeles rock. The CD reissue also boasts some excellent bonus tracks. "So Little to Say" is one of Jay Ferguson's finest compositions ever, and the jazz-inspired instrumentals such as "Fog" and "Space Chile" showcase pianist John Locke as one of the most inspired and lyrical players in the rock idiom to date. All in all, a classic album and a true landmark.

Matthew Greenwald

Twelve Dreams of Dr. Sardonicus
1970, Epic/Legacy

Although *Twelve Dreams of Dr. Sardonicus* has the reputation of being Spirit's most far-out album, it actually contains the most disciplined songwriting and playing of the original lineup, cutting back on some of the drifting and offering some of their more melodic tunes. The lilting "Nature's Way" was the most endearing FM standard on the album, which also included some of Spirit's best songs in "Animal Zoo" and "Mr. Skin." [The 1996 CD reissue has four bonus tracks, though these are on the nonessential side: mono versions of "Animal Zoo" and "Morning Will Come," the 1970 single "Red Light Roll On," and the previously unissued "Rougher Road."]

Richie Unterberger

Time Circle (1968–1972)
July 1991, Epic/Legacy

From the opening riff of "Fresh Garbage," with its jazzy electric piano and fuzzy rock guitar, Spirit set out to carve a unique, eclectic niche in the music world of the late '60s. Though the band achieved only limited commercial success, the music they produced from 1968-1972 still sounds fresh decades later. *Time Circle* collects the bulk of their recorded output during this five-year period. The 41 tracks assembled here include nine from the group's eponymous debut, seven from the follow-up *The Family That Plays Together*, six from *Clear*, and nine-tenths of the classic *The Twelve Dreams of Dr. Sardonicus*. This set also includes unreleased tracks, singles, and B-sides to provide a complete look at this excellent quintet.

Jim Newsom

Spooky Tooth

Spooky Two
1969, A&M

Spooky Two is this British blues-rock band's *pièce de résistance*. All eight of the tracks compound free-styled rock and loose-fitting guitar playing that result in some fantastic raw music. With Gary Wright on keyboards and vocals and lead singer Mike Harrison behind the microphone, their smooth, relaxed tempos and riffs mirrored bands like Savoy Brown and, at times, even the Yardbirds. With some emphasis on keyboards, songs like "Lost in My Dream" and the nine-minute masterpiece "Evil Woman" present a cool, nonchalant air that grooves and slides along perfectly. "I've Got Enough Heartache" whines and grieves with some sharp bass playing from Greg Ridley, while "Better By You, Better By Me" is the catchiest of the songs, with it's clinging hooks and desperate-sounding chorus. The last song, "Hangman Hang My Shell on a Tree," is a splendid example of this group's ability to play off of one

another, mixing soulful lyrics with downtrodden instrumentation to conjure up the perfect melancholia. Although the band lasted about seven years, their other albums never really contained the same passion or talented collaborating by each individual musician as *Spooky Two*.

Mike DeGagne

Bruce Springsteen

Greetings from Asbury Park, N.J.
January 1973, Columbia

Bruce Springsteen's debut album found him squarely in the tradition of Bob Dylan: folk-based tunes arranged for an electric band featuring piano and organ (plus, in Springsteen's case, 1950s-style rock & roll tenor saxophone breaks), topped by acoustic guitar and a husky voice singing lyrics full of elaborate, even exaggerated imagery. But where Dylan had taken a world-weary, cynical tone, Springsteen was exuberant. His street scenes could be haunted and tragic, as they were in "Lost in the Flood," but they were still imbued with romanticism and a youthful energy. *Asbury Park* painted a portrait of teenagers cocksure of themselves, yet bowled over by their discovery of the world. It was saved from pretentiousness (if not preciousness) by its sense of humor and by the careful eye for detail that kept even the most high-flown language rooted. Like the lyrics, the arrangements were busy, but the melodies were well developed and the rhythms, pushed by drummer Vincent Lopez, were breakneck.

William Ruhlmann

The Wild, the Innocent & the E Street Shuffle
September 1973, Columbia

Bruce Springsteen expanded the folk-rock approach of his debut album, *Greetings From Asbury Park, N.J.*, to strains of jazz, among other styles, on its ambitious follow-up, released only eight months later. His chief musical lieutenant was keyboard player David Sancious, who lived on the E Street that gave the album and Springsteen's backup group its name. With his help, Springsteen created a street-life mosaic of suburban society that owed much in its outlook to Van Morrison's romanticization of Belfast in *Astral Weeks*. Though Springsteen expressed endless affection and much nostalgia, his message was clear: this was a goodbye-to-all-that from a man who was moving on. *The Wild, the Innocent & the E Street Shuffle* represented an astonishing advance even from the remarkable promise of *Greetings*; the unbanded three-song second side in particular was a flawless piece of music. Musically and lyrically, Springsteen had brought an unruly muse under control and used it to make a mature statement that synthesized popular musical styles into complicated, well-executed arrangements and absorbing suites; it evoked a world precisely even as that world seemed to disappear.

Following the personnel changes in the E Street Band in 1974, there is a conventional wisdom that this album is marred by production lapses and performance problems, specifically the drumming of Vini Lopez. None of that is true. Lopez's busy Keith Moon style is appropriate to the arrangements in a way his replacement, Max Weinberg, never could have been. The production is fine. And the album's songs contain the best realization of Springsteen's poetic vision, which soon enough would be tarnished by disillusionment. He would later make different albums, but he never made a better one. The truth is, *The Wild, the Innocent & the E Street Shuffle* is one of the greatest albums in the history of rock & roll.

William Ruhlmann

Born to Run
August 1975, Columbia

Bruce Springsteen's make-or-break third album represented a sonic leap from his first two, which had been made for modest sums at a suburban studio; *Born to Run* was cut on a superstar budget, mostly at the Record Plant in New York. Springsteen's backup band had changed, with his two virtuoso players, keyboardist David Sancious and drummer Vini Lopez, replaced by the professional but less flashy Roy Bittan and Max Weinberg. The result was a full, highly produced sound that contained elements of Phil Spector's melodramatic work of the 1960s. Layers of guitar, layers of echo on the vocals, lots of keyboards, thunderous drums—*Born to Run* had a big sound, and Springsteen wrote big songs to match it. The overall theme of the album was similar to that of *The E Street Shuffle*; Springsteen was describing, and saying farewell to, a romanticized teenage street life. But where he had been affectionate, even humorous before, he was becoming increasingly bitter. If Springsteen had celebrated his dead-end kids on his first album and viewed them nostalgically on his second, on his third he seemed to despise their failure, perhaps because he was beginning to fear he was trapped himself. Nevertheless, he now felt removed, composing an updated *West Side Story* with spectacular music that owed more to Bernstein than to Berry. To call *Born to Run* overblown is to miss the point; Springsteen's precise intention is to blow things up, both in the sense of expanding them to gargantuan size and of exploding them. If *The Wild, the Innocent & the E Street Shuffle* was an accidental miracle, *Born to Run* was an intentional masterpiece. It declared its own greatness with songs and a sound that lived up to Springsteen's promise, and though some thought it took itself too seriously, many found that exalting.

William Ruhlmann

Darkness on the Edge of Town
June 1978, Columbia

Coming three years and one extended court battle after *Born to Run*, *Darkness on the Edge of Town* was highly anticipated. Some attributed the album's embattled tone to Bruce Springsteen's legal troubles, but it carried on from *Born to Run*, in which Springsteen had first begun to view his colorful cast of characters as "losers." On *Darkness*, he began to see them as the working class: his characters, some of whom he inhabited and sang for in the first person, had little and were in danger of losing even that. Their only hope for redemption lay in working harder, and their only escape lay in driving. Springsteen presented these hard truths in hard rock settings, the tracks paced by powerful drumming and searing guitar solos. Though not as heavily produced as *Born to Run*, *Darkness* was given a full-bodied sound; Springsteen's stories were becoming less heroic, but his musical style remained

grand—the sound, and the conviction in his singing, added weight to songs like "Racing in the Street" and the title track, transforming the pathetic into the tragic. But despite the rock & roll fervor, *Darkness* was no easy listen, and it served notice that Springsteen was already willing to risk his popularity for his principles.

William Ruhlmann

The River
October 1980, Columbia

Imbedded within the double-disc running time of *The River* is a single-disc album that follows up on the themes and sound of *Darkness on the Edge of Town*—wide-screen, mid-tempo rock and stories of the disillusionment of working-class life and the conflicts within families. In these songs, which include the title track, "Independence Day," and "Point Blank," Bruce Springsteen's world view is just as dire as it had become on *Darkness*, but less judgmental. "Independence Day," for example, is a father-and-son ballad that has little of the anger of its hard rock counterpart on *Darkness*, "Adam Raised a Cain." Springsteen's heroes again seek to overcome their crushing troubles through defiance and by driving around, and though "The River" repeats the soured love theme of "Racing in the Street," he also posits romance as a possible escape, sometimes combining it with one of the other solutions, as on the eight-plus-minute "Drive All Night." But there is also another album lurking within *The River*, and it is a more lighthearted pop/rock collection of short, sometimes humorous songs like "Sherry Darling" and "I'm a Rocker." At times Springsteen combines elements of the two, as on "Out in the Street," perhaps the album's quintessential song, a catchy, up-tempo number that sounds like something from the early '60s and echoes the theme of the Vogues' 1966 hit "Five O' Clock World." "Hungry Heart," which became Springsteen's first Top Ten hit, combines a rollicking musical track with a more sober lyrical theme that emphasizes longing over disappointment. But a better guide to Springsteen's development are the songs "Stolen Car" and the album-closing "Wreck on the Highway," gentle, moody ballads imbued with a sense of hopelessness that anticipate his next record, *Nebraska*.

William Ruhlmann

Nebraska
September 1982, Columbia

There is an adage in the record business that a recording artist's demos of new songs often come off better than the more polished versions later worked up in a studio. But Bruce Springsteen was the first person to act on that theory, when he opted to release the demo versions of his latest songs, recorded with only acoustic or electric guitar, harmonica, and vocals, as his sixth album, *Nebraska*. It was really the content that dictated the approach, however. *Nebraska*'s ten songs marked a departure for Springsteen, even as they took him farther down a road he had been traveling previously. Gradually, his songs had become darker and more pessimistic, and those on *Nebraska* marked a new low. They also found him branching out into better developed stories. The title track was a first-person account of the killing spree of mass murderer Charlie Starkweather. (It can't have been coincidental that the same story was told in director Terrence Malick's 1973 film *Badlands*, also used as a Springsteen song title.) That song set the tone for a series of portraits of small-time criminals, desperate people, and those who loved them. Just as the recordings were unpolished, the songs themselves didn't seem quite finished; sometimes the same line turned up in two songs. But that only served to unify the album. Within the difficult times, however, there was hope, especially as the album went on. "Open All Night" was a Chuck Berry-style rocker, and the album closed with "Reason to Believe," a song whose hard-luck verses were belied by the chorus—even if the singer couldn't understand what it was, "people find some reason to believe." Still, *Nebraska* was one of the most challenging albums ever released by a major star on a major record label.

William Ruhlmann

Born in the U.S.A.
June 1984, Columbia

Bruce Springsteen had become increasingly downcast as a songwriter during his recording career, and his pessimism bottomed out with *Nebraska*. But *Born in the U.S.A.*, his popular triumph, which threw off seven Top Ten hits and became one of the best-selling albums of all time, trafficked in much the same struggle, albeit set to galloping rhythms and set off by chiming guitars. That the witless wonders of the Reagan regime attempted to co-opt the title track as an election-year campaign song wasn't so surprising: the verses described the disenfranchisement of a lower-class Vietnam vet, and the chorus was intended to be angry, but it came off as anthemic. Then, too, Springsteen had softened his message with nostalgia and sentimentality, and those are always crowd-pleasers. "Glory Days" may have employed Springsteen's trademark disaffection, yet it came across as a couch potato's drunken lament. But more than anything else, *Born in the U.S.A.* marked the first time that Springsteen's characters really seemed to relish the fight and to have something to fight for. They were not defeated ("No Surrender"), and they had friendship ("Bobby Jean") and family ("My Hometown") to defend. The restless hero of "Dancing in the Dark" even pledged himself in the face of futility, and for Springsteen, that was a step. The "romantic young boys" of his first two albums, chastened by "the working life" encountered on his third, fourth, and fifth albums and having faced the despair of his sixth, were still alive on this, his seventh, with their sense of humor and their determination intact. *Born in the U.S.A.* was their apotheosis, the place where they renewed their commitment and where Springsteen remembered that he was a rock & roll star, which is how a vastly increased public was happy to treat him.

William Ruhlmann

Live/1975–85
November 1986, Columbia

Long before he sold substantial numbers of records, Bruce Springsteen began to earn a reputation as the best live act in rock & roll. Fans had been clamoring for a live album for a long time, and with *Live/1975–85* they got what they wanted, at least in terms of bulk. His concerts were marathons, and this box set, including 40 tracks and running over three and a half hours, was about the average length of a show. In his brief liner notes, Springsteen spoke of the emergence of the album's "story" as he reviewed live tapes, and that story

seems nothing less than a history of his life, his concerns, and his career. The first cuts present the Springsteen of the early to mid-'70s; these performances, most of them drawn from a July 1978 show at the Roxy in Los Angeles, present the romantic, hopeful, earnest Springsteen. The second section begins with his first Top Ten hit, "Hungry Heart"—this is the Springsteen of the late '70s and early '80s, an arena rock star with working-class concerns. After an acoustic mini set given largely to material from *Nebraska*—songs of economic desperation and crime—comes a reshuffling of *Born in the U.S.A.*, songs in which the artist and his characters start to fight back and rock out. Finally, he brings it all back home to New Jersey, starting with the unofficial state anthem, "Born to Run." Fans could rejoice in the seven previously unreleased songs, but *Live/1975-85* wasn't as funny, moving, or exhilarating as a Springsteen show could be. Maybe no single album could have been, but where Springsteen impressed in concert because he tried so hard, here he seemed to have tried a little too hard to make a live album carry the freight of everything he had to say.

William Ruhlmann

Tunnel of Love
October 1987, Columbia

Just as he had followed his 1980 commercial breakthrough *The River* with the challenging *Nebraska*, Bruce Springsteen followed the most popular album of his career, *Born in the U.S.A.*, with another low-key, anguished effort, *Tunnel of Love*. Especially in their sound, several of the songs, "Cautious Man" and "Two Faces," for example, could have fit seamlessly onto *Nebraska*, though the arrangements overall were not as stripped-down and acoustic as on the earlier album. While *Nebraska* was filled with songs of economic desperation, however, *Tunnel of Love*, as its title suggested, was an album of romantic exploration. But the lovers were just as desperate in their way as *Nebraska*'s small-time criminals. In song after song, Springsteen questioned the trust and honesty on both sides in a romantic relationship, specifically a married relationship. Since Springsteen sounded more autobiographical than ever before ("Ain't Got You" referred to his popular success, while "Walk Like a Man" seemed another explicit message to his father), it was hard not to wonder about the state of his own two-and-a-half-year marriage, and it wasn't surprising when that marriage collapsed the following year. *Tunnel of Love* was not the album that the ten million fans who had bought *Born in the U.S.A.* as of 1987 were waiting for, and though it topped the charts, sold three million copies, and spawned three Top 40 hits, much of this was on career momentum. Springsteen was as much at a crossroads with his audience as he seemed to be in his work and in his personal life, though this was not immediately apparent.

William Ruhlmann

Billy Squier

Tale of the Tape/Don't Say No
August 2004, Beat Goes On

Before Billy Squier's career exploded (albeit briefly) with 1981's *Don't Say No*, the ex-Piper frontman issued an overlooked debut solo outing, 1980's *Tale of the Tape*, which has become increasingly hard to find over the years—especially on CD. But longtime fans have reason to rejoice, as Squier's first two solo releases were compiled together as a "two for one" deal in the U.K. (but easily obtainable in the U.S.

as an import)—*Tale of the Tape/Don't Say No*. Additionally, it also doesn't hurt that these two albums were Squier's best solo outings. While not as commercially successful or renowned as, say, *Emotions in Motion*, Squier's solo debut contained quite a few standouts that measure up well against his later hits—"Rich Kid," "You Should Be High Love," and "The Music's All Right"—and set the stage perfectly for his breakthrough sophomore effort. Undoubtedly his best solo effort, *Don't Say No* shows Squier going more for a heavy Led Zeppelin-esque sound on the hit title track and "Lonely Is the Night," but also manages to slip in quite a few melodic, pop-based tunes as well, especially the album opening "In the Dark" and "My Kinda Lover." As of 2004, *Tale of the Tape/Don't Say No* is the only way to get Squier's first release on CD, and with a fair list price, it's just about what you'd shell out for two separate CDs anyway.

Greg Prato

Ringo Starr

Ringo
November 1973, Capitol

With *Ringo*, Ringo Starr finally put his solo career in gear in 1973, after serving notice with back-to-back Top Ten singles in 1971 and 1972 that he had more to offer than his eccentric first two solo albums. *Ringo* was a big-budget pop album produced by Richard Perry and featuring Ringo's former Beatles bandmates as songwriters, singers, and instrumentalists. On no single track did all four appear, though George Harrison played the guitars on the John Lennon-penned leadoff track "I'm the Greatest," with Lennon playing piano and singing harmony. But it wasn't only the guests who made *Ringo* a success: Ringo advanced his own cause by co-writing two of the album's Top Ten singles, the number one "Photograph" and "Oh My My." The album's biggest hit was a second chart-topper, Ringo's cover of the old Johnny Burnette hit "You're Sixteen." Songs like "Have You Seen My Baby," a Randy Newman song with guitar by Marc Bolan, and Ringo and Vini Poncia's "Devil Woman" were just as good as the hits. Ringo's best and most consistent new studio album, *Ringo* represented both the drummer/singer's most dramatic comeback and his commercial peak. The original ten-track 1973 album got even better in 1991 as a 13-track CD reissue, the bonus tracks including the 1971 gold single "It Don't Come Easy" and its B-side, "Early 1970," a telling depiction of Ringo's perspective on the Beatles breakup.

William Ruhlmann

Goodnight Vienna
November 1974, Capitol

Goodnight Vienna was very much a follow-up to *Ringo*, on which Ringo Starr called upon his bevy of musical buddies. Most prominent among them was John Lennon, who again wrote the leadoff track, "(It's All Da-Da-Down To)

Goodnight Vienna," and played on three songs; also included are Elton John, who wrote and played on "Snookeroo," Dr. John, Billy Preston, Robbie Robertson, and Harry Nilsson. Richard Perry again produced, bringing his strong pop sensibility to the diverse material. The only real fall-off was in the songwriting; the album's Top Ten hits were "Only You," the old Platters song, and Hoyt Axton's novelty number "No No Song," which winked at intoxicants, but little else on the set stood out. *Goodnight Vienna* was another enjoyable Ringo record, but it lacked the star power and consistency of its predecessor. Still, compared to the rest of his '70s albums, it was a masterpiece.

William Ruhlmann

Steely Dan

Can't Buy a Thrill
1972, MCA

Walter Becker and Donald Fagen were remarkable craftsmen from the start, as Steely Dan's debut, *Can't Buy a Thrill*, illustrates. Each song is tightly constructed, with interlocking chords and gracefully interwoven melodies, buoyed by clever, cryptic lyrics. All of these are hallmarks of Steely Dan's signature sound, but what is most remarkable about the record is the way it differs from their later albums. Of course, one of the most notable differences is the presence of vocalist David Palmer, a professional blue-eyed soul vocalist who oversings the handful of tracks where he takes the lead. Palmer's very presence signals the one major flaw with the album—in an attempt to appeal to a wide audience, Becker and Fagen tempered their wildest impulses with mainstream pop techniques. Consequently, there are very few of the jazz flourishes that came to distinguish their albums—the breakthrough single, "Do It Again," does work an impressively tight Latin jazz beat, and "Reelin' in the Years" has jazzy guitar solos and harmonies—and the production is overly polished, conforming to all the conventions of early-'70s radio. Of course, that gives these decidedly twisted songs a subversive edge, but compositionally, these aren't as innovative as their later work. Even so, the best moments ("Dirty Work," "Kings," "Midnight Cruiser," "Turn That Heartbeat Over Again") are wonderful pop songs that subvert traditional conventions and more than foreshadow the paths Steely Dan would later take.

Stephen Thomas Erlewine

Countdown to Ecstasy
1973, MCA

Can't Buy a Thrill became an unexpected hit, and as a response, Donald Fagen became the group's full-time lead vocalist, and he and Walter Becker acted like Steely Dan was a rock & roll band for the group's second album, *Countdown to Ecstasy*. The loud guitars and pronounced backbeat of "Bodhisattva," "Show Biz Kids," and "My Old School" camouflage the fact that *Countdown* is a riskier album, musically speaking, than its predecessor. Each of its eight songs have sophisticated, jazz-inflected interludes, and apart from the bluesy vamps "Bodhisattva" and "Show Biz Kids," which sound like they were written for the stage, the songs are subtly textured. "Razor Boy," with its murmuring marimbas, and the hard bop tribute "Your Gold Teeth" reveal Becker and Fagen's jazz roots, while the country-flavored "Pearl of the Quarter" and the ominous, skittering "King of the World" are both overlooked gems. *Countdown to Ecstasy* is the only time Steely Dan played it relatively straight, and its eight songs are rich with either musical or lyrical detail that their album rock or art rock contemporaries couldn't hope to match.

Stephen Thomas Erlewine

Pretzel Logic
1974, MCA

Countdown to Ecstasy wasn't half the hit that *Can't Buy a Thrill* was, and Steely Dan responded by trimming the lengthy instrumental jams that were scattered across *Countdown* and concentrating on concise songs for *Pretzel Logic*. While the shorter songs usually indicate a tendency toward pop conventions, that's not the case with *Pretzel Logic*. Instead of relying on easy hooks, Walter Becker and Donald Fagen assembled their most complex and cynical set of songs to date. Dense with harmonics, countermelodies, and bop phrasing, *Pretzel Logic* is vibrant with unpredictable musical juxtapositions and snide, but very funny, wordplay. Listen to how the album's hit single, "Rikki Don't Lose That Number," opens with a syncopated piano line that evolves into a graceful pop melody, or how the title track winds from a blues to a jazzy chorus—Becker and Fagen's craft has become seamless while remaining idiosyncratic and thrillingly accessible. Since the songs are now paramount, it makes sense that *Pretzel Logic* is less of a band-oriented album than *Countdown to Ecstasy*, yet it is the richest album in their catalog, one where the backhanded Dylan tribute "Barrytown" can sit comfortably next to the gorgeous "Any Major Dude Will Tell You." Steely Dan made more accomplished albums than *Pretzel Logic*, but they never made a better one.

Stephen Thomas Erlewine

Katy Lied
1975, MCA

Building from the jazz fusion foundation of *Pretzel Logic*, Steely Dan created an alluringly sophisticated album of jazzy pop with *Katy Lied*. With this record, Walter Becker and Donald Fagen began relying solely on studio musicians, which is evident from the immaculate sound of the album. Usually, such a studied recording method would drain the life out of each song, but that's not the case with *Katy Lied*, which actually benefits from the duo's perfectionist tendencies. Each song is given a glossy sheen, one that accentuates not only the stronger pop hooks, but also the precise technical skill of the professional musicians drafted to play the solos. Essentially, *Katy Lied* is a smoother version of *Pretzel Logic*, featuring the same cross-section of jazz-pop and blues-rock. The lack of innovations doesn't hurt the record, since the songs are uniformly brilliant. Less overtly cynical than previous Dan albums, the album still has its share of lyrical stingers, but what's really notable are the melodies, from the seductive jazzy soul of "Doctor Wu" and the lazy blues of "Chain Lightning" to the terse "Black Friday" and mock calypso of "Everyone's Gone to the Movies." It's another excellent record in one of the most distinguished rock & roll catalogs of the '70s.

Stephen Thomas Erlewine

The Royal Scam
1976, MCA

The Royal Scam is the first Steely Dan record that doesn't exhibit significant musical progress from its predecessor, but that doesn't mean the album is any less interesting. The cynicism that was suppressed on *Katy Lied* comes roaring to the surface on *The Royal Scam*—not only are the lyrics bitter and snide, but the music is terse, broken, and weary. Not so coincidentally, the album is comprised of Walter Becker and Donald Fagen's weakest set of songs since *Can't Buy a Thrill*. Alternating between mean-spirited bluesy vamps like "Green Earrings" and "The Fez" and jazzy soft rock numbers like "The Caves of Altamira," there's nothing particularly bad on the album, yet there are fewer standouts than before. Nevertheless, the best songs on *The Royal Scam*, like the sneering "Kid Charlemagne" and "Sign in Stranger," rank as genuine Steely Dan classics.

Stephen Thomas Erlewine

Aja
1977, MCA

Steely Dan hadn't been a real working band since *Pretzel Logic*, but with *Aja*, Walter Becker and Donald Fagen's obsession with sonic detail and fascination with composition reached new heights. A coolly textured and immaculately produced collection of sophisticated jazz-rock, *Aja* has none of the overt cynicism or self-consciously challenging music that distinguished previous Steely Dan records. Instead, it's a measured and textured album, filled with subtle melodies and accomplished, jazzy solos that blend easily into the lush instrumental backdrops. But *Aja* isn't just about texture, since Becker and Fagen's songs are their most complex and musically rich set of songs—even the simplest song, the sunny pop of "Peg," has layers of jazzy vocal harmonies. In fact, Steely Dan ignores rock on *Aja*, preferring to fuse cool jazz, blues, and pop together in a seamless, seductive fashion. It's complex music delivered with ease, and although the duo's preoccupation with clean sound and self-consciously sophisticated arrangements would eventually lead to a dead end, *Aja* is a shining example of jazz-rock at its finest.

Stephen Thomas Erlewine

Gaucho
1980, MCA

Aja was cool, relaxed, and controlled; it sounded deceptively easy. Its follow-up, *Gaucho*, while sonically similar, is its polar opposite: a precise and studied record, where all of the seams show. *Gaucho* essentially replicates the smooth jazz-pop of *Aja*, but with none of that record's dark, seductive romance or elegant aura. Instead, it's meticulous and exacting; each performance has been rehearsed so many times that it no longer has any emotional resonance. Furthermore, Walter Becker and Donald Fagen's songs are generally labored, only occasionally reaching their past heights, like on the suave "Babylon Sisters," "Time Out of Mind," and "Hey Nineteen." Still, those three songs are barely enough to make the remainder of the album's glossy, meandering fusion worthwhile.

Stephen Thomas Erlewine

enlightenment for the uninitiated, and one that even casual fans should take seriously.

Bruce Eder

Steppenwolf

Born to Be Wild: A Retrospective
November 1991, MCA

Born To Be Wild: A Retrospective was the first attempt at a serious historical overview of Steppenwolf and founder/leader John Kay's career, and considering that the makers limited themselves to two CDs, they did an amazingly good job. A lot of listeners—even those who were around during the band's heyday—who think of Steppenwolf as nothing but successful purveyors of hard rock on the pop charts, may be surprised by what is here. Disc One reaches back to a pair of excellent tracks from the summer 1966 Columbia Records sessions by the Sparrow, the earlier band (featuring John Kay as lead singer) out of which Steppenwolf was formed. The array of Steppenwolf songs includes all of the expected hits and a lot more, which may be more than most casual fans will want. The latter will probably opt for the group's *20th Century Masters* single CD, but this set is not to be passed over lightly—as is quickly revealed on the first disc, Steppenwolf was one of the more prodigiously talented hard-rock acts of the late 1960's, easily able to go head-to-head with Iron Butterfly, Vanilla Fudge, or any other of the top American acts of the era and come out on top; they knew enough blues (and folk) licks, were good (and bold) enough with their instruments, and had a sufficiently charismatic lead singer in John Kay to generate six strong studio albums in five years—including three very consistent, challenging, and inventive LPs in 1968 and 1969—and a string of hit singles, This set doesn't give enough exposure to the group's somewhat underrated second album, but otherwise it's a very good cross-section of some of their most popular work interspersed with their more ambitious album cuts, their entire output represented except for the two live albums, *Early Steppenwolf* and *Steppenwolf Live*. This set was also the first updated digital transfer of the band's classic recordings, and what's here does sound richer and louder than the existing individual CDs from MCA (which, in fairness, were unusually good for middle/late '80s releases). The collection includes highlights of John Kay's early 70's solo sides and the mid-1970's incarnation of the group on Columbia Records, up thru the version of the group organized by Kay in the late 1980's. There are a few flaws in the package, to be sure, mostly in the annotation—Todd Everett's essay gets very sketchy about the music (especially their albums) after the first LP, and tend to focus more on personnel changes than on what they were actually releasing (which was still charting), and that's frustrating for anyone genuinely interested in the history of the music. But this is as good a survey of Steppenwolf and John Kay as we're likely to see, and the listening is a pleasure and a serious

Cat Stevens

Tea for the Tillerman
November 1970, A&M

Mona Bone Jakon only began Cat Stevens' comeback. Seven months later, he returned with *Tea for the Tillerman*, an album in the same chamber-group style, employing the same musicians and producer, but with a far more confident tone. *Mona Bone Jakon* had been full of references to death, but *Tea for the Tillerman* was not about dying; it was about living in the modern world while rejecting it in favor of spiritual fulfillment. It began with a statement of purpose, "Where Do the Children Play?," in which Stevens questioned the value of technology and progress. "Wild World" found the singer being dumped by a girl, but making the novel suggestion that she should stay with him because she was incapable of handling things without him. "Sad Lisa" might have been about the same girl after she tried and failed to make her way; now, she seemed depressed to the point of psychosis. The rest of the album veered between two themes: the conflict between the young and the old, and religion as an answer to life's questions. *Tea for the Tillerman* was the story of a young man's search for spiritual meaning in a soulless class society he found abhorrent. He hadn't yet reached his destination, but he was confident he was going in the right direction, traveling at his own, unhurried pace. The album's rejection of contemporary life and its yearning for something more struck a chord with listeners in an era in which traditional verities had been shaken. It didn't hurt, of course, that Stevens had lost none of his ability to craft a catchy pop melody; the album may have been full of angst, but it wasn't hard to sing along to. As a result, *Tea for the Tillerman* became a big seller and, for the second time in four years, its creator became a pop star.

William Ruhlmann

Teaser and the Firecat
October 1971, A&M

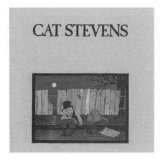

Even as a serious-minded singer/songwriter, Cat Stevens never stopped being a pop singer at heart, and with *Teaser and the Firecat* he reconciled his philosophical interests with his pop instincts. Basically, *Teaser*'s songs came in two modes: gentle ballads that usually found Stevens and second guitarist Alun Davies playing delicate lines over sensitive love lyrics, and up-tempo numbers on which the guitarists strummed away and thundering drums played in stop-start rhythms. There were also more exotic styles, such as the Greek-styled "Ruby-love," with its twin bouzoukis and a verse sung in Greek, and "Tuesday's Dead," with its Caribbean feel. Stevens seemed to have worked out some of his big questions, to the point of wanting to proselytize on songs like "Changes IV" and

"Peace Train," both stirring tunes in which he urged social and spiritual improvement. Meanwhile, his love songs had become simpler and more plaintive. And while there had always been a charming, childlike quality to some of his lyrics, there were songs here that worked as nursery rhymes, and these were among the album's most memorable tracks and its biggest hits: "Moonshadow" and "Morning Has Broken," the latter adapted from a hymn. The overall result was an album that was musically more interesting than ever, but lyrically dumbed-down. Stevens continued to look for satisfaction in romance, despite its disappointment, but he found more fulfillment in a still-unspecified religious pursuit that he was ready to tout to others. And they were at least nominally ready to listen: the album produced three hit singles and just missed topping the charts. *Tea for the Tillerman* may have been the more impressive effort, but *Teaser and the Firecat* was the Cat Stevens album that gave more surface pleasures to more people, which in pop music is the name of the game.

William Ruhlmann

Very Best of Cat Stevens
March 2000, A&M

It is impossible to compile a single-disc greatest-hits compilation for Cat Stevens that will come close to satisfying all of his admirers. *The Very Best of Cat Stevens* is the fifth major attempt to do so and, like its predecessors, it is challenged by its subject's success. *Remember Cat Stevens—The Ultimate Collection* is the longest of the five (24 tracks) and may be the most comprehensive. But *The Very Best of Cat Stevens*, released just a year later, has several advantages that make it more appealing. To begin with, it is the only compilation to sequence chronologically songs from every one of Stevens' albums, including the experimental *Foreigner*. It also contains the delightful folk creed "The Wind," which was a glaring omission from the so-called *Ultimate Collection*. Most significantly, it contains the previously unreleased "I've Got a Thing About Seeing My Grandson Grow Old." Stevens recorded a demo of the song during the *Mona Bone Jakon* sessions in 1970, but it never saw the light of day until it was remixed for this collection. Perhaps this was because it was considered too eccentric for public consumption, straddling the line between the hook-rich pop of Stevens' '60s records and the groundbreaking folk-rock of his '70s efforts. If so, the public was vastly underestimated. The song is a buried treasure that fits in perfectly in the company of Stevens' best work.

Evan Cater

Al Stewart

Year of the Cat
1976, Arista

Al Stewart had found his voice on *Past, Present & Future* and found his sound on *Modern Times*. He then perfected it all on 1976's *Year of the Cat*, arguably his masterpiece. There is no overarching theme here, as there was on its two immediate predecessors, but the impossible lushness of Alan Parsons' production and Stewart's evocative Continental narratives give the record a welcome feeling of cohesion that keeps the record enchanting as it moves from "Lord Grenville" to "Midas Shadow" to "Broadway Hotel," before it ends with the haunting title track. Along the way, Stewart doesn't dwell too deeply in any area, preferring to trace out mysteries with his evocative lyrical imagery and a spinning array of self-

consciously sophisticated music, songs that evoke American and European folk and pop with a deliberate grace. This could be unbearably precious if it didn't work so well. Stewart is detached from his music, but only in the sense that he gives this album a stylish elegance, and Parsons is his perfect foil, giving the music a rich, panoramic sweep that mimics Stewart's globe-trotting songs. The result is a tremendous example of how good self-conscious progressive pop can be, given the right producer and songwriter—and if you're a fan of either prog or pop and haven't given Al Stewart much thought, prepare to be enchanted.

Stephen Thomas Erlewine

Time Passages
1978, Arista

Year of the Cat brought Al Stewart a genuine worldwide smash with its title track, and for its successor, he did make a few concessions. These, however, were slight—just a slight increase of soft rock productions, an enhancement of the lushness that marked not only *Year of the Cat* but also *Modern Times*. These happened to be welcome adjustments to Stewart's sound, since they increased the dreamy continental elegance at the core of his work. And that's why *Time Passages* is the equal of *Year of the Cat*—it may be more streamlined, but the adjustments to his sound and the concessions to the mainstream just increase the soft grace of his eloquent historical pop epics. It's possible to view this as too precious, because it is pitched at an audience who believes the common-day concerns of pop are piffle, but this is exceptionally well-crafted, from Stewart's songs, where even three-minute songs seem like epics, to Alan Parsons' cinematic arrangements and productions. This added concentration on the texture of the recording, ensuring that it was clean, spacious, and gentle, with a welcoming surface. Of course, this means that *Time Passages* can work very well as background music, but it also reveals much upon concentrated listening—enough to make it stand proudly next to *Modern Times* and *Year of the Cat* as one of Al Stewart's very best albums.

Stephen Thomas Erlewine

Rod Stewart

The Rod Stewart Album
1969, Mercury

On his debut album (titled *An Old Raincoat Won't Ever Let You Down* in Britain, and *The Rod Stewart Album* in America, presumably because its original title was "too English" or cryptic for U.S. audiences), Rod Stewart essays a startlingly original blend of folk, blues, and rock & roll. The opening cover of the Stones' "Street Fighting Man" encapsulates his approach. Turning the driving acoustic guitars of the original inside out, the song works a laid-back, acoustic groove, bringing a whole new meaning to the song before escalating into a full-on rock & roll attack—without any distorted guitars, just bashing acoustics and thundering drums. Through this approach, Stewart establishes that rock can sound as rich and timeless as folk, and that folk can be as vigorous as rock. And he does this not only as an interpreter, breathing new life into Ewan MacColl's "Dirty Old Town" and defining Mike d'Abo's "Handbags & Gladrags," but also as a songwriter, writing songs as remarkable as "Blind Prayer," "An Old Raincoat Won't Ever Let You Down," and "Cindy's Lament." The music and the songs are so vivid and rich with detail that they reflect a whole way of life, and while Stewart would later flesh out this blueprint, it remains a stunningly original vision.

Stephen Thomas Erlewine

Gasoline Alley
1970, Mercury

Gasoline Alley follows the same formula of Rod Stewart's first album, intercutting contemporary covers with slightly older rock & roll and folk classics and originals written in the same vein. The difference is in execution. Stewart sounds more confident, claiming Elton John's "Country Comfort," the Small Faces' "My Way of Giving," and the Rolling Stones' version of "It's All Over Now" with a ragged, laddish charm. Like its predecessor, nearly all of *Gasoline Alley* is played on acoustic instruments—Stewart treats rock & roll songs like folk songs, reinterpreting them in individual, unpredictable ways. For instance, "It's All Over Now" becomes a shambling, loose-limbed ramble instead of a tight R&B/blues groove, and "Cut Across Shorty" is based around a howling, Mideastern violin instead of a rockabilly riff. Of course, being a rocker at heart, Stewart doesn't let these songs become limp acoustic numbers—these rock harder than any fuzz-guitar workout. The drums crash and bang, the acoustic guitars are pounded with a vengeance—it's a wild, careening sound that is positively joyous with its abandon. And on the slow songs, Stewart is nuanced and affecting—his interpretation of Bob Dylan's "Only a Hobo" is one of the finest Dylan covers, while the original title track is a vivid, loving tribute to his adolescence. And that spirit is carried throughout *Gasoline Alley*. It's an album that celebrates tradition while moving it into the present and never once does it disown the past.

Stephen Thomas Erlewine

Every Picture Tells a Story
1971, Mercury

Without greatly altering his approach, Rod Stewart perfected his blend of hard rock, folk, and blues on his masterpiece, *Every Picture Tells a Story*. Marginally a harder-rocking album than *Gasoline Alley*—the Faces blister on the Temptations cover "(I Know I'm) Losing You," and the acoustic title track goes into hyper-drive with Mick Waller's primitive drumming—the great triumph of *Every Picture Tells a Story* lies in its content. Every song on the album, whether it's a cover or original, is a gem, combining to form a romantic, earthy portrait of a young man joyously celebrating his young life. Of course, "Maggie May"—the ornate, ringing ode about a seduction from an older woman—is the centerpiece, but each song, whether it's the devilishly witty title track or the unbearably poignant "Mandolin Wind," has the same appeal. And the covers, including definitive readings of Bob Dylan's "Tomorrow Is Such a Long Time" and Tim Hardin's "Reason to Believe," as well as a rollicking "That's All Right," are equally terrific, bringing new dimension to the songs. It's a beautiful album, one that has the timeless qualities of the best folk, yet one that rocks harder than most pop music—few rock albums are quite this powerful or this rich.

Stephen Thomas Erlewine

Never a Dull Moment
1972, Mercury

Essentially a harder-rocking reprise of *Every Picture Tells a Story, Never a Dull Moment* never quite reaches the heights of its predecessor, but it's a wonderful, multifaceted record in its own right. Opening with the touching, autobiographical rocker "True Blue," which finds Rod Stewart trying to come to grips with his newfound stardom but concluding that he'd "rather be back home," the record is the last of Stewart's series of epic fusions of hard rock and folk. It's possible to hear Stewart go for superstardom with the hard-rocking kick and fat electric guitars of the album, but the songs still cut to the core. "You Wear It Well" is a "Maggie May" rewrite on the surface, but it develops into a touching song about being emotionally inarticulate. Similarly, "Lost Paraguayos" is funny, driving folk-rock, and it's hard not to be swept away when the Stonesy hard rocker "Italian Girls" soars into a mandolin-driven coda. The covers—whether a soulful reading of Jimi Hendrix's "Angel," an empathetic version of Dylan's "Mama, You Been on My Mind," or a stunning interpretation of Etta James' "I'd Rather Go Blind"—are equally effective, making *Never a Dull Moment* a masterful record. He never got quite this good ever again.

Stephen Thomas Erlewine

Atlantic Crossing
1975, Warner Bros.

Atlantic Crossing wasn't simply the moment when Rod Stewart left Britain for the greener pasture of America, it was the moment when he accepted his role as a full-fledged, jet-setting superstar. Stewart abandoned the formula of his first five solo records, as well as most of his folk-rock and hard rock undercurrents, trading them for a professionally polished, rock- and soul-inflected pop, courtesy of Muscle Shoals' musicians and producer Tom Dowd. The glossy production doesn't obscure or trivialize Stewart's talents—coming after the tired *Smiler*, the slickness actually accentuated his strength as an interpretive singer. "The Fast Half" suffers from a couple of weak tracks, but "Three Time Loser" and "Stone Cold Sober" catch fire, and "The Slow Half" is generally excellent, but Stewart's heart-wrenching rendition of Danny Whitten's "I Don't Want to Talk About It" ranks as one of his finest performances.

Stephen Thomas Erlewine

A Night on the Town
1976, Warner Bros.

After bouncing back to life with *Atlantic Crossing*, Rod Stewart crafted his most self-consciously ambitious record with *A Night on the Town*. The centerpiece of the album, "The Killing of Georgie, Pts. 1 & 2," was a long, winding Dylanesque tale of the murder of one of Stewart's gay friends and was one of his better songs of the mid-'70s. Even if "The Killing of Georgie" was the conscious artistic focal point of *A Night on the Town*, the true masterpiece of the album was an eloquent rendition of Cat Stevens' "The First Cut Is the Deepest." Apart from the flawed political platitudes of "Trade Winds," the rest of the album was filled with competent, professional pop/rock, highlighted by the number one hit "Tonight's the Night (Gonna Be Alright)," a ballad where the gallant Rod relieves a teenager of her virginity. And, again, the "Slow Half" was more convincing than the frequently perfunctory "Fast Half."

Stephen Thomas Erlewine

Blondes Have More Fun
1978, Warner Bros.

In its simplest terms, *Blondes Have More Fun* is Rod Stewart's disco album, filled with pulsating rhythms and slick, synthesized textures. It's also his trashiest, most disposable album, filled with cheap come-ons and bad double entendres. Of course, that makes *Blondes Have More Fun* one of his most enjoyable records, even if all the pleasures are guilty. With its swirling strings and nagging chorus, "Da Ya Think I'm Sexy?" was the reason the record hit number one, and decades later, the song stands as one of the best rock-disco fusions. The rest of the record isn't as engaging, but he throws out a handful of winning tracks in the same mold, including "Ain't Love a Bitch," "Attractive Female Wanted," and the title track.

Stephen Thomas Erlewine

Stephen Stills

Stephen Stills
1970, Atlantic

Talk about understatement—there's Stephen Stills on the cover, acoustic guitar in hand, promising a personal singer/songwriter-type statement. And there is some of that—even a lot of that personal music-making—on *Stephen Stills*, but it's all couched in astonishingly bold musical terms. *Stephen Stills* is top-heavy with 1970 sensibilities, to be sure, from the dedication to the memory of Jimi Hendrix to the now piggish-seeming message of "Love the One You're With." Yet, listening to this album three decades on, it's still a jaw-dropping experience, the musical equal to *Crosby, Stills & Nash* or *Déjà Vu*, and only a shade less important than either of them. The mix of folk, blues (acoustic and electric), hard rock, and gospel is seamless, and the musicianship and the singing are all so there, in your face, that it just burns your brain (in the nicest, most benevolent possible way) even decades later. Recorded amid the breakup of Crosby, Stills, Nash & Young, Stills' first solo album was his effort to put together his own sound and, not surprisingly, it's similar to a lot of stuff on the group's two albums. But it's also infinitely more personal, as well as harder and bluesier in many key spots; yet, it's every bit as soft and as lyrical as the group in other spots, and all laced with a degree of yearning and urgency that far outstrips virtually anything he did with the group. "Love the One You're With," which started life as

a phrase that Stills borrowed from Billy Preston at a party, is the song from this album that everybody knows, but it's actually one of the lesser cuts here—not much more than a riff and an upbeat lyric and mood, albeit all of it infectious. "Do for the Others," by contrast, is one of the prettiest and most moving pieces of music that Stills has ever been associated with, and "Church (Part of Someone)" showed him moving toward gospel and R&B (and good at it, too); and then there's "Old Times Good Times," musically as good a rock song as Stills has ever recorded (even if it borrows a bit from "Pre-Road Downs"), and featuring Jimi Hendrix on lead guitar. "Go Back Home" (which has Eric Clapton on guitar) is fine a piece of bluesy hard rock, while "Sit Yourself Down" features superb singing by Stills and a six-person backing chorus (that includes Cass Elliot, Graham Nash, and David Crosby) around a great tune. "To a Flame" is down-right ethereal, while the live "Black Queen" is a superb piece of acoustic blues. All of this is presented by Stills in the best singing voice of his career up to that point, bolder, more outgoing, and more powerful (a result of his contact with Doris Troy) than anything in his previous output. He also plays lots of instruments (à la *Crosby, Stills & Nash*, which is another reason it sounds so similar to the group in certain ways), though a bit more organ than guitar, thanks to the presence of Hendrix and Clapton on two cuts. If the album has a flaw, it's the finale, "We Are Not Helpless," which slightly overstays its welcome. But hey, this was still the late '60s, and excess was the rule, not the exception, and it's such modest excess.

Bruce Eder

Manassas
1972, Atlantic

A sprawling masterpiece, akin to the Beatles' *White Album*, the Stones' *Exile on Main St.*, or Wilco's *Being There* in its makeup, if not its sound. Rock, folk, blues, country, Latin, and bluegrass have all been styles touched on in Stephen Stills' career, and  the skilled, energetic musicians he had gathered in Manassas played them all on this album. What could have been a disorganized mess in other hands, though, here all gelled together and formed a cohesive musical statement. The songs are thematically grouped: part one (side one on the original vinyl release) is titled "The Raven," and is a composite of rock and Latin sounds that the group would often perform in full live. "The Wilderness" mainly centers on country and bluegrass (Chris Hillman's and Al Perkins' talents coming to the forefront), with the track "So Begins the Task" later covered by Stills' old flame Judy Collins. Part three, "Consider" is largely folk and folk-rock. "Johnny's Garden," reportedly for the caretaker at Stills' English manor house and not for John Lennon as is often thought, is a particular highlight. Two other notables from the "Consider" section are "It Doesn't Matter" (later redone with different lyrics by the song's uncredited co-writer Rick Roberts on the first Firefall album) and "Move Around," which features some of the first synthesizer used in a rock context. The closing section, titled "Rock & Roll Is Here to Stay," is a rock and blues set with one of the landmarks of Manassas' short life, the epic "The Treasure." A sort of Zen-like meditation on love and "oneness," enlivened by the band's most inspired recorded playing it evolves into a bluesy groove washed in Stills' fierce electric slide playing. The delineation lines of the four themed song groupings aren't cut in stone, though, and one of the strengths of the album is that there is a lot of overlap in styles throughout. The CD reissue's remastered sound is excellent, though missed is the foldout poster and handwritten lyrics from the original vinyl release. Unfortunately, the album has been somewhat overlooked over the years, even though Stills considers it some of the best work he has done. Bill Wyman (who guested on "The Love Gangster") has said he would have quit the Rolling Stones to join Manassas.

Rob Caldwell

The Stooges

The Stooges
1969, Elektra

While the Stooges had a few obvious points of influence—the swagger of the early Rolling Stones, the horny pound of the Troggs, the fuzztone sneer of a thousand teenage garage bands, and the Velvet Underground's experimental eagerness to leap into the void—they didn't really sound like anyone else around when their first album hit the streets in 1969. It's hard to say if Ron Asheton, Scott Asheton, Dave Alexander, and the man then known as Iggy Stooge were capable of making anything more sophisticated than this, but if they were, they weren't letting on, and the best moments of this record document the blithering inarticulate fury of the post-adolescent id. Ron Asheton's guitar runs (fortified with bracing use of fuzztone and wah-wah) are so brutal and concise they achieve a naïve genius, while Scott Asheton's proto-Bo Diddley drums and Dave Alexander's solid bass stomp these tunes into submission with a force that inspires awe. And Iggy's vividly blank vocals fill the "so what?" shrug of a thousand teenagers with a wealth of palpable arrogance and wondrous confusion. One of the problems with being a trailblazing pioneer is making yourself understood to others, and while John Cale seemed sympathetic to what the band was doing, he didn't appear to quite get it, and as a result he made a physically powerful band sound a bit sluggish on tape. But "1969," "I Wanna Be Your Dog," "Real Cool Time," "No Fun," and other classic rippers are on board, and one listen reveals why they became clarion calls in the punk rock revolution. Part of the fun of *The Stooges* is, then as now, the band managed the difficult feat of sounding ahead of their time and entirely *out* of their time, all at once.

Mark Deming

Fun House
1970, Elektra

The Stooges' first album was produced by a classically trained composer; their second was supervised by the former keyboard player with the Kingsmen, and if that didn't make all the difference, it at least indicates why *Fun House* was a step in the right direction. Producer Don Gallucci took the

approach that the Stooges were a powerhouse live band, and their best bet was to recreate the band's live set with as little fuss as possible. As a result, the production on *Fun House* bears some resemblance to the Kingsmen's version of "Louie Louie"—the sound is smeary and bleeds all over the place, but it packs the low-tech wallop of a concert pumped through a big PA, bursting with energy and immediacy. The Stooges were also a much stronger band this time out; Ron Asheton's blazing minimalist guitar gained little in the way of technique since *The Stooges*, but his confidence had grown by a quantum leap as he summoned forth the sounds that would make him the hero of proto-punk guitarists everywhere, and the brutal pound of drummer Scott Asheton and bassist Dave Alexander had grown to heavyweight champion status. And *Fun House* is where Iggy Pop's mad genius first reached its full flower; what was a sneer on the band's debut had grown into the roar of a caged animal desperate for release, and his rants were far more passionate and compelling than what he had served up before. *The Stooges* may have had more "hits," but *Fun House* has stronger songs, including the garage raver to end all garage ravers in "Loose," the primal scream of "1970," and the apocalyptic anarchy of "L.A. Blues." *Fun House* is the ideal document of the Stooges at their raw, sweaty, howling peak.

Mark Deming

Raw Power
1973, Columbia/Legacy

In 1972, the Stooges were near the point of collapse when David Bowie's management team, MainMan, took a chance on the band at Bowie's behest. By this point, guitarist Ron Asheton and bassist Dave Alexander had been edged out of the picture, and James Williamson had signed on as Iggy's new guitar mangler; Asheton rejoined the band shortly before recording commenced on *Raw Power*, but was forced to play second fiddle to Williamson as bassist. By most accounts, tensions were high during the recording of *Raw Power*, and the album sounds like the work of a band on its last legs—though rather than grinding to a halt, Iggy & the Stooges appeared ready to explode like an ammunition dump. From a technical standpoint, Williamson was a more gifted guitar player than Asheton (not that that was ever the point), but his sheets of metallic fuzz were still more basic (and punishing) than what anyone was used to in 1973, while Ron Asheton played his bass like a weapon of revenge, and his brother Scott Asheton remained a powerhouse behind the drums. But the most remarkable change came from the singer; *Raw Power* revealed Iggy as a howling, smirking, lunatic genius. Whether quietly brooding ("Gimme Danger") or inviting the apocalypse ("Search and Destroy"), Iggy had never sounded quite so focused as he did here, and his lyrics displayed an intensity that was more than a bit disquieting. In many ways, almost all *Raw Power* has in common with the two Stooges albums that preceded it is its primal sound, but while the Stooges once sounded like the wildest (and weirdest) gang in town, *Raw Power* found them heavily armed and ready to destroy the world—that is, if they didn't destroy themselves first.

Mark Deming

Styx

The Grand Illusion
July 1977, A&M

Other than being their first platinum-selling album, *The Grand Illusion* led Styx steadfastly into the domain of AOR rock. Built on the strengths of "Come Sail Away"'s ballad-to-rock metamorphosis, which gained them their second Top Ten hit, and on the high harmonies of newcomer Tommy Shaw throughout "Fooling Yourself," *The Grand Illusion* introduced Styx to the gates of commercial stardom. The pulverized growl of "Miss America" reveals the group's guitar-savvy approach to six-string rock, while De Young pretentiously struts his singing prowess throughout the title track. Shaw's induction into the band has clearly settled, and his guitar work, along with James Young's, is full and extremely sharp where it matters most. Even the songwriting is more effluent than *Crystal Ball*, which was released one year earlier, shedding their mystical song motifs for a more audience-pleasing lyric and chord counterpoise. Reaching number six on the album charts, *The Grand Illusion* was the first to display the gelled accomplishments of both Tommy Shaw and Dennis De Young as a tandem.

Mike DeGagne

Pieces of Eight
September 1978, A&M

Styx's feisty, straightforward brand of album rock is represented best by "Blue Collar Man" from 1978's *Pieces of Eight*, an invigorating keyboard and guitar rush—hard and heavy, yet curved by Tommy Shaw's emphasized vocals. Reaching number 21, with the frolicking romp of "Renegade" edging in at number 16 only six months later, *Pieces of Eight* maintained their strength as a front-running FM radio group. Even though these two tracks were both mainstream singles, the rest of the album includes tracks that rekindle some of Styx's early progressive rock sound, only cleaner. Tracks like "Sing for the Day," "Lords of the Ring," and "Aku-Aku" all contain slightly more complex instrumental foundations, and are lyrically reminiscent of the material from albums like *The Serpent Is Rising* or *Man of Miracles*, but not as intricate or instrumentally convoluted. While the writing may stray slightly from what Styx provided on *The Grand Illusion*, *Pieces of Eight* kept their established rock formula in tact quite firmly.

Mike DeGagne

Cornerstone
October 1979, A&M

Presenting radio with one of the best rock ballads ever, *Cornerstone* gave Chicago's Styx their big break with the number one single "Babe," which held that spot for two weeks in October of 1979. "Babe" is a smooth, keyboard-pampered love song that finally credited Dennis De Young's textured vocals. While this single helped the album climb all the way to the number two spot on the charts, the rest of the tracks from *Cornerstone* weren't nearly half as strong. "Why Me" made it to number 26, and both "Lights" and "Boat on the River" implement silky harmonies and welcoming choruses, yet failed to get off the ground. De Young's keyboards are effective without overly dominating the music, and the band's gritty rock & roll acerbity has been slightly

sanded down to compliment the commercial market. The songs aren't as tight or assertive as their last few albums, but Shaw's presence can be felt strongly on most of the tracks, especially where the writing is concerned. Outside of "Babe," *Cornerstone* tends to sound a tad weaker than one would expect.

Mike DeGagne

Paradise Theater
January 1981, A&M

After successfully establishing themselves as one of America's best commercial progressive rock bands of the late '70s with albums like *The Grand Illusion* and *Pieces of Eight*, Chicago's Styx had taken a dubious step towards pop overkill with singer Dennis DeYoung's ultra-schmaltzy ballad "Babe." The centerpiece of 1979's uneven *Cornerstone* album, the number one single would sew the seeds of disaster for the group by pitching DeYoung's increasingly mainstream ambitions against the group's more conservative songwriters, Tommy Shaw and James "JY" Young. Hence, what had once been a healthy competitive spirit within the band quickly deteriorated into bitter co-existence during the sessions for 1980's *Paradise Theater* (and all-out warfare by the time of 1983's infamous *Kilroy Was Here*). For the time being, however, *Paradise Theater* seemed to represent the best of both worlds, since its loose concept about the roaring '20s heyday and eventual decline of an imaginary theater (used as a metaphor for the American experience in general, etc., etc.) seemed to satisfy both of the band's camps with its return to complex hard rock (purists Shaw and JY) while sparing no amount of pomp and grandeur (DeYoung). The stage is set by the first track, "A.D. 1928," which features a lonely DeYoung on piano and vocals introducing the album's recurring musical theme before launching into Rockin' the Paradise"—a total team effort of wonderfully stripped down hard rock. From this point forward, DeYoung's compositions ("Nothing Ever Goes as Planned," "The Best of Times") continue to stick close to the overall storyline, while Shaw's ("Too Much Time on My Hands," "She Cares") try to resist thematic restrictions as best they can. Among these, "The Best of Times"—with its deliberate, marching rhythm—remains one of the more improbable Top Ten hits of the decade (somehow it just works), while "Too Much Time on My Hands" figures among Shaw's finest singles ever. As for JY, the band's third songwriter (and resident peacekeeper) is only slightly more cooperative with the *Paradise Theater* concept. His edgier compositions include the desolate tale of drug addiction, "Snowblind," and the rollicking opus "Half-Penny, Two-Penny," which infuses a graphic depiction of inner city decadence with a final, small glimmer of hope and redemption. The song also leads straight into the album's beautiful saxophone-led epilogue, "A.D. 1958," which once again reveals MC DeYoung alone at his piano. A resounding success, *Paradise Theater* would become Styx's greatest commercial triumph; and in retrospect, it remains one of the best examples of the convergence between progressive rock and AOR which typified the sound of the era's top groups (Journey, Kansas, etc.). For Styx, its success would spell both their temporary saving grace and ultimate doom, as the creative forces which had already been tearing at the band's core finally reached unbearable levels three years later. It is no wonder that when the band reunited after over a decade of bad blood, all the music released post-1980 was left on the cutting room floor—further proof that *Paradise Theater* was truly the best of times.

Ed Rivadavia

Come Sail Away: The Styx Anthology
May 2004, A&M

It seems that a double-disc collection of Styx would contain all their biggest hits, along with all of their key album tracks. *Come Sail Away: The Styx Anthology* comes close to fitting that description, but it falls short in a couple of noticeable ways. The compilers have made a conscious decision to emphasize the progressive hard rock side of the band, devoting most of the first disc of the 35-song collection to their '70s album-oriented rock radio staples. By the end of that disc, the hits start coming with "The Grand Illusion," "Fooling Yourself (The Angry Young Man)," and "Come Sail Away," and these spill over to the first part of the second disc, which covers their prime period of *Pieces of Eight*, *Cornerstone*, and *Paradise Theater*, including all the big hits. Around this time, the song selection, which had been excellent until now, starts to slip, missing minor hits like "Why Me" and "Nothing Ever Goes as Planned," and that inconsistency plagues the final stretch of the compilation. The most egregious omission is "Don't Let It End," the excellent power ballad from *Kilroy Was Here* that reached number six on the *Billboard* pop charts, and its absence is all the more notable with the inclusion of material from their late-'90s/early-2000s comeback efforts, which may bring the anthology up to date, but simply isn't as good as their prime period. This is a major omission and it hurts *Come Sail Away*, but not fatally since, apart from the missing "Don't Let It End" and the other mentioned minor singles, this does its job right, and provides a thorough and accurate summary of Styx's long career.

Stephen Thomas Erlewine

Supertramp

Crime of the Century
1974, A&M

Supertramp came into their own on their third album, 1974's *Crime of the Century*, as their lineup gelled but, more importantly, so did their sound. The group still betrayed a heavy Pink Floyd influence, particularly in its expansive art rock arrangements graced by saxo-phones, but Supertramp isn't nearly as spooky as Floyd—they're snarky collegiate elitists, an art rock variation on Steely Dan or perhaps a less difficult 10cc, filled with cutting

jokes and allusions, best heard on "Bloody Well Right." This streak would later flourish on *Breakfast in America*, but it's present enough to give them their own character. Also present is a slight sentimental streak and a heavy fondness for pop, heard on "Dreamer," a soaring piece of art pop that became their first big hit. That and "Bloody Well Right" are the concise pop moments on the record; the rest of *Crime of the Century* is atmospheric like *Dark Side of the Moon*, but with a lighter feel and a Beatles bent. At times the album floats off into its own world, with an effect more tedious than hypnotic, but it's still a huge leap forward for the group and their most consistent album outside of that 1979 master-work, *Breakfast in America*.

Stephen Thomas Erlewine

Crisis? What Crisis?
1975, A&M

Nestled between the accomplished *Crime of the Century* album and 1977's *Even in the Quietest Moments*, *Crisis? What Crisis?* may not have given the band any chart success, but it did help them capture a fan base that had no concern for Supertramp's commercial sound. With Rick Davies showing off his talent on the keyboards, and Roger Hodgson's vocals soaring on almost every track, they managed to win back their earlier progressive audience while gaining new fans at the same time. *Crisis* received extensive air play on FM stations, especially in Britain, and the album made it into the Top 20 there and fell just outside the Top 40 in the U.S. "Ain't Nobody But Me," "Easy Does It," and the beautiful "Sister Moonshine" highlight Supertramp's buoyant and brisk instrumental and vocal alliance, while John Helliwell's saxophone gives the album even greater width. The songwriting is sharp, attentive, and passionate, and the lyrics showcase Supertramp's ease at invoking emotion into their music, which would be taken to even greater heights in albums to come. Even simple tracks like "Lady" and "Just a Normal Day" blend in nicely with the album's warm personality and charmingly subtle mood. Although the tracks aren't overly contagious or hook laden, there's still a work-in-process type of appeal spread through the cuts, which do grow on you over time.

Mike DeGagne

Even in the Quietest Moments...
1977, A&M

The title of *Even in the Quietest Moments...* isn't much of an exaggeration—this 1977 album finds Supertramp indulging in some of their quietest moments, spending almost the album in a subdued mood. Actually, the cover photo picture of a snow-covered piano sitting on a mountain gives a good indication of what the album sounds like: it's elegant yet mildly absurd, witty but kind of obscure. It also feels more pop than it actually is, despite the opening single, "Give a Little Bit," their poppiest song to date, as well as their biggest hit. If the rest of the album doesn't boast another song as tight or concise as this—"Downstream" comes close but it doesn't have the same hook, while "Babaji," a pseudo-spiritual moment that falls from the pop mark; the other four tracks clock in well over six minutes, with the closer, "Fool's Overture," reaching nearly 11 minutes—it nevertheless places a greater emphasis on melody and gentle textures than any previous Supertramp release. So, it's a transitional album, bridging the gap between *Crime of the Century* and the forthcoming *Breakfast in America*, and even if it's not as full formed as either, it nevertheless has plenty of fine moments aside from "Give a Little Bit," including the music hall shuffle of

"Loverboy," the Euro-artiness of "From Now On," and the "Fool on a Hill" allusions on "Fool's Overture."

Stephen Thomas Erlewine

Breakfast in America
1979, A&M

With *Breakfast in America*, Supertramp had a genuine blockbuster hit, topping the charts for four weeks in the U.S. and selling millions of copies worldwide; by the 1990s, the album had sold over 18 million units across the world. Although their previous records had some popular success, they never even hinted at the massive sales of *Breakfast in America*. Then again, Supertramp's earlier records weren't as pop-oriented as *Breakfast*. The majority of the album consisted of tightly written, catchy, well-constructed pop songs, like the hits "The Logical Song," "Take the Long Way Home," and "Goodbye Stranger." Supertramp still had a tendency to indulge themselves occasionally, but *Breakfast in America* had very few weak moments. It was clearly their high-water mark.

Stephen Thomas Erlewine

Survivor

Ultimate Survivor
July 2004, Volcano

Appearing three years after Mercury's comprehensive collection *Fire in Your Eyes: Greatest Hits*, BMG Heritage's 2004 release *Ultimate Survivor* edges out that previous collection for the title of the best Survivor compilation yet assembled. Why? Because the song selection and sequencing are sharper, developing a real momentum over its 18 songs, and it's also better presented, with strong liner notes and muscular remastering. Where the Mercury collection sometimes felt padded toward its end, as it emphasized some latter-day material, this focuses on the group's '80s heyday so much that it includes the original version of "Rockin' into the Night," a song Survivor leader Frankie Sullivan and his songwriting partner, Jim Peterik, gave to .38 Special, and their version is every bit as good as that group of wild-eyed Southern boys. Little touches like these make *Ultimate Survivor* live up to its title.

Stephen Thomas Erlewine

Sweet

Desolation Boulevard
1974, Capitol

Sweet hit the peak of their powers on *Desolation Boulevard*, a wonderfully lightweight collection of fizzy melodies and big, dumb hooks. Essentially, the album consists of three dynamic singles buoyed by a bunch of filler, but those singles—"Ballroom Blitz," "The 6-Teens," and "Fox on the Run"—are addictive slices of bubblegum glam rock. And the

filler is ridiculously silly and enjoyable, with "Sweet F.A.," "I Wanna Be Committed," and "No You Don't" sounding like a kind of bizarre prototype for the Ramones' punky bubblegum (only without the irony, of course). Although the filler is relatively strong, there are a number of weak patches on *Desolation Boulevard*, but it remains an intoxicatingly fun record and one that sounds surprisingly fresh, even with all of its kitschy '70s production techniques.

Stephen Thomas Erlewine

The Best of Sweet
March 1993, Capitol

Recollections of Britain's arch-glam gods generally inspire two theories of their producers, Mike Chapman and his partner, Nicky Chinn. Either they knew just what they were doing and calculated accordingly, or blindly hit pay dirt, following toothless early singles like "Funny Funny" (none of which grace this disc). By this reckoning, Sweet was a '70s-era pinup band or a closeted hard rock quartet who only got their due after breaking the Chapman/Chinn combination. Actually, the truth lies in between; once the producers realized that fans wanted a tougher sound, they only needed the right song to burst the floodgates open, and stardom would beckon. That song turned out to be "Little Willy," which drew inspiration from late vocalist Brian Connolly's never-ending nightclubbing and sparked a remarkable run of 14 hit singles, including 11 that topped the British charts. Most of them are here, including "Wig Wam Bam," "Blockbuster," and the oft-covered "Ballroom Blitz," which provided a vivid, legitimate soundtrack to listeners' daily dreams and frustrations. The middle period following Chapman and Chinn's 1975 departure is well-represented by "The Lies in Your Eyes," the classic backhanded groupie putdown "Fox on the Run," "The 6-Teens," and the oft-covered "Action," a Top 20 U.S. hit in 1976. By then, the group's meld of high harmonies to a bullish, if somewhat slick, hard rock attack was well-established, extending Sweet's reach beyond their die-hard British turf. The group's last real Top Ten hit, 1978's "Love Is Like Oxygen," showed them toning down the decibels for lusher, more pop-oriented territory, as did "Mother Earth," an acoustic-based winner from *Cut Above the Rest*, the underrated 1979 album recorded following Connolly's departure for an unsuccessful solo career. The story essentially ended afterward, though the group kept recording into the '80s, while the '90s saw Connolly and Scott lead dueling versions of the band, with themselves being the only original member. This compilation does manage the tricky task of balancing hits and lesser-known songs, so it's a decent affair, but newcomers might still want to seek out *Desolation Boulevard* (1975) and *Give Us a Wink*, which remain the group's heaviest albums.

Ralph Heibutzki

T. Rex

T. Rex
1970, Castle

The fifth Tyrannosaurus Rex album was also the first T. Rex set, as Marc Bolan abbreviated the band name at the same time as enlarging everything else—most notably the group's sound. Transitional through and through, *T. Rex* is the obvious successor to *Beard of Stars*, but it's clearly looking toward *Electric Warrior*, a point proven when the band hit the tour and TV circuits early in 1971. But "Jewel," "Sun Eye," "Beltane Walk," and "One Inch Rock" are all bona fide Bolan classics and, if *T. Rex* itself was to be overshadowed by the simultaneous success of the "Ride a White Swan" single (pointedly not included on the album), then that only allowed Bolan more time in which to plan his next move. In many ways, this is the quintessential Bolan album, the last to be made before his entire life was swallowed up by super-stardom, but the first to begin imagining what that could be like. Certainly he has an awful lot of fun revisiting one of his earliest ever compositions, "The Wizard," while his ambition is writ large throughout the opening and closing snippets of "The Children of Rarn," excerpts from a full-fledged concept album that he was then contemplating. You also get "Is It Love?," one of his most contagiously underrated composi-tions ever, but really, there's not a sour moment to be found all album long. And it might just be the last Bolan album that you could say that about.

Dave Thompson

Electric Warrior
1971, Reprise

The album that essentially kick-started the U.K. glam rock craze, *Electric Warrior* completes T. Rex's transformation from hippie folk-rockers into flamboyant avatars of trashy rock & roll. There are a few vestiges of those early days re-maining in the acoustic-driven ballads, but *Electric Warrior* spends most of its time in a swinging, hip-shaking groove powered by Marc Bolan's warm electric guitar. The music recalls not just the catchy simplicity of early rock & roll, but also the implicit sexuality—except that here, Bolan gleefully hauls it to the surface, singing out loud what was once only communicated through the shimmying beat. He takes obvi-ous delight in turning teenage bubblegum rock into campy sleaze, not to mention filling it with pseudo-psychedelic hip-pie poetry. In fact, Bolan sounds just as obsessed with the heavens as he does with sex, whether he's singing about spiritual mysticism or begging a flying saucer to take him away. It's all done with the same theatrical flair, but Tony Visconti's spacious, echoing production makes it surprisingly convincing. Still, the real reason *Electric Warrior* stands the test of time so well—despite its intended disposability—is that it revels so freely in its own absurdity and willful lack of substance. Not taking himself at all seriously, Bolan is free to pursue whatever silly wordplay, cosmic fantasies, or non se-quitur imagery he feels like; his abandonment of any pretense to art becomes, ironically, a statement in itself. Bolan's lack of pomposity, back-to-basics songwriting, and elaborate theat-rics went on to influence everything from hard rock to punk to new wave. But in the end, it's that sense of playfulness, combined with a raft of irresistible hooks, that keeps *Electric Warrior* such an infectious, invigorating listen today.

Steve Huey

The Slider
July 1972, Mercury

Buoyed by two U.K. number one singles in "Tele-gram Sam" and "Metal Guru," *The Slider* became T. Rex's most pop-ular record on both sides of the Atlan-tic, despite the fact that it produced no hits in the U.S. *The Slider* essentially replicates all the virtues of *Electric Warrior*, crammed with effortless hooks and trashy fun. All of Bolan's signatures are here—mystical folk-tinged ballads, overt sexual come-ons

crooned over sleazy, bopping boogies, loopy nonsense po-etry, and a mastery of the three-minute pop song form. The main difference is that the trippy mix of *Electric Warrior* is replaced by a fuller, more immediate-sounding production. Bolan's guitar has a harder bite, the backing choruses are more up-front, and the arrangements are thicker-sounding, even introducing a string section on some cuts (both ballads and rockers). Even with the beefier production, T. Rex still doesn't sound nearly as heavy as many of the bands it influ-enced (and even a few of its glam contemporaries), but that's partly intentional—Bolan's love of a good groove takes pre-cedence over fast tempos or high-volume crunch. Lyrically, Bolan's flair for the sublimely ridiculous is fully intact, but he has way too much style for *The Slider* to sound truly stupid, especially given the playful, knowing wink in his delivery. It's nearly impossible not to get caught up in the irresistible rush of melodies and cheery good times. Even if it treads largely the same ground as *Electric Warrior*, *The Slider* is flawlessly executed, and every bit the classic that its predecessor is.

Steve Huey

Tanx
1973, Get Back

By 1973's *Tanx*, the T. Rex hit-making machine was begin-ning to show some wear and tear, but Marc Bolan still had more than a few winners up his sleeve. It was also admirable that Bolan was attempting to broaden the T. Rex sound—soulful backup singers and horns are heard throughout, a full two years before David Bowie used the same formula for his mega-seller *Young Americans*. However, *Tanx* did not contain any instantly recognizable hits, as their past couple of releases had, and the performances were not quite as vibrant, due to non-stop touring and drug use. Despite an era of transition looming on the horizon for the band, tracks such as "Rapids," "Highway Knees," "The Street & Babe Shadow," and "Born to Boogie" contain the expected classic T. Rex sound. The leadoff track, "Tenement Lady," is an interesting Beatlesque epic, while "Shock Rock" criticizes the early-'70s glam scene, which T. Rex played a prominent role in creating. Other highlights include one of Bolan's most gorgeous and heartfelt ballads, "Broken Hearted Blues," as well as the brief, explosive rocker "Country Honey." *Tanx* marked the close of what many consider T. Rex's golden era; unfortunately, the bandmembers would drift off one by one soon after, until Bolan was the only one remaining by the mid-'70s.

Greg Prato

Zinc Alloy and the Hidden Riders of Tomorrow
1974, TECI

By late 1973, Marc Bolan's star was waning fast. No longer gunning out those effortless classics which established him as the most important figure of the decade so far, he embarked instead on a voyage of musical discovery, which cast him so far adrift from the commercial pop mainstream that when his critics said he'd blown it, he didn't even bother answering them back. Or that's the way it appeared at the time, and today, too, it must be acknowledged that 1974's *Zinc Alloy & the Hidden Riders of Tomorrow* is not classic Bolan, even if one overlooks the transparency of its title. After all, hadn't Bowie already done the Fictional Someone & the Somethings From Somewhere routine? Indeed he had, as his fans kept remarking at the time, and when the knives began slashing *Zinc Alloy* to shreds, that was one of the fiercest wounds. Time, however, has healed almost all of them. Indeed, hind-sight proves that, far from losing his muse, Bolan's biggest sin was losing his once-impeccable sense of occasion. The world wasn't ready for this latest T. Rex, and the fact that it wasn't interested in the old T. Rex either is just another object lesson in the fabled fickleness of pop fans. How faulty was Bolan's timing, though? As it transpired, he was out by no more than a year, maybe less than six months. The era of disco was coming, and with it the wholesale transformation of a wealth of rocking talents. But while David Bowie was barely dreaming of young Americans' fame, and Bryan Ferry was still road testing the pharmaceutical properties of l'amour, Bolan was up to his neck in American radio, pulling out an album which exceeded his assumed capabilities no less than it shot right over the heads of the kids who once bought all his hits. "The Groover," the spring 1973 single which many regarded as the first sign of Bolan's fall from grace, marked the birth of this new fascination, a simple but solid slab of funk-inflected rock which did, indeed, groove. (The track is one of five bonus tracks appended to the album's Edsel reissue). The yearning, heavily orchestrated hit "Teenage Dream" hit notwithstanding, the heart of *Zinc Alloy*, then, simply followed in "The Groover"'s footsteps, an abandoned romp through the R&B influences which Bolan had always acknowledged, but never truly explored—the solid James Brown drive of "The Avengers (Superbad)," "Interstellar Soul," "Liquid Gang," and the implausibly slight, but impressively groove-ridden "You've Got to Jive to Stay Alive." Into the same bag, one can also throw the period b-sides "Satisfaction Pony" and "Sitting Here"—both of which have also been added to the album. Deeply soul-soaked songs like these aren't simply a new direction. They are the very signposts which would soon be guiding so many other English rock talents down some very unfamiliar alleyways. *Zinc Alloy* was released in March, 1974. Bowie began rehearsing his Philly Dogs tour in July. Yet, even with such credentials to uphold it, this isn't quite Bolan's soul album. Those demons would be exorcised on a second album cut with singer Sister Pat Hall and elsewhere in his collaborations with girlfriend Gloria Jones. Besides, the production here was just a little too cautious to truly convince the wary listener. Neither can it be neatly categorized in the same fashion as, say, Bowie's *Young Americans*—Bolan looked across the spectrum for his influences, but he never once went to Philadelphia. Rather, it straddles that same pop/rock, funky R&B landscape as early Funkadelic, Sly Stone and Co., neither fish nor fowl, dead fish nor foul, but something somewhere in between. Approach it with caution. But get in there regardless. [The 2001 Japanese re-release includes two songs not included on the original: "Truck On" and "Sitting Here."]

Dave Thompson

Bolan's Zip Gun
1975, Mercury

Having reinvented himself as a bionic soulboy across the course of 1974's *Zinc Alloy*, *Bolan's Zip Gun* was less a re-iteration of Marc Bolan's new direction than a confirmation of it. Much of the album returns to the understated romp he had always excelled at—the delightful knockabout "Precious Star," the unrepentant boogie of "Till Dawn" and the pounding title track all echo with the effortless lightheartedness which was Bolan at his most carelessly buoyant, while "Token of My Love" is equally incandescent, a playful blues which swiftly became a major in-concert favorite. But the essence of *Zip Gun* remains firmly in the funky pastures which characterized *Zinc Alloy*, with the only significant difference lying in the presentation. Out went the plush production which so diluted the earlier set, to be replaced by a sparser sound which emphasized the rhythms, heightened the backing vocals, and left rock convention far behind. "Light of Love," "Golden Belt" and the heavyweight ballad "I Really

Love You Babe" may not be Stax-sized attractions, but they have an earthy authenticity nevertheless, while bonus tracks on the Edsel remaster include single-only stabs at "Dock of the Bay" and "Do You Wanna Dance," further indications of just how seriously Bolan was taking his new role—and how far he'd moved from the bopping elf of three years earlier. The difference was, in 1972, Marc Bolan was a God. By 1975, he was barely even a minor deity. It was, of course, the old, old story. When he made records that sounded like the old ones, the kids all complained he'd stagnated and lost it. When he made records that didn't sound like them, then they moaned even louder that things just weren't the same. So he made ones that fell smack between the two poles, and that wasn't right either. And yet, played back to back alongside the "classics," there ain't much wrong with any of them. Whatever was the fuss all about, then? Decades on, each of Bolan's latter day albums retain a hint of their original controversy, but hindsight lends them an impact (and, for what it's worth, a credibility) which contemporary listeners could never have imagined. And *Zip Gun*, an album which scored the worst reviews of all, hits as hard as any of them.

Dave Thompson

Futuristic Dragon
1976, Mercury

The most blatantly, and brilliantly, portentous of Marc Bolan's albums since the transitional blurring of boundaries that was *Beard of Stars*, almost seven years prior, *Futuristic Dragon* opens on a wave of unrelenting feedback, guitars and bombast, setting an apocalyptic mood for the record which persists long after that brief (two minutes) overture is over. Indeed, even the quintessential bop of the succeeding "Jupiter Liar" is irrevocably flavored by what came before, dirty guitars churning beneath a classic Bolan melody, and the lyrics a spiteful masterpiece. While the oddly Barry White-influenced "Ride My Wheels" continues flirting with the neo-funk basics of 1975's *Bolan's Zip Gun*, the widescreen sonic majesty of *Futuristic Dragon* was, if anything, even more gratuitously ambitious than its predecessor. "Calling All Destroyers," "Sensation Boulevard" and the magnificent "Dawn Storm" all bristle with lyrical splendor, while "Casual Agent" revisits some older glories with its near-slavish re-creation of the old "Rip Off" vibe. But if the other tunes pursue Bolan's new-found fascination for pomp over pop with barely disguised glee, he wasn't above slipping the odd joke into the brew to remind us that he knew what he was doing. "Theme for a Dragon" is an all-but Wagnerian symphonic instrumental—with the sound of screaming teenyboppers as its backdrop, and the punch line lurking further afield among the handful of obvious hits which he also stirred in. The first of these, the big-budget ballad "Dreamy Lady," scored even before the rest of the album was complete. It was followed by the idiotically contagious "New York City," a piece of pure pop nonsense/genius which so effortlessly returned him to the British Top 20 that, for a few weeks through mid-1976, the idea of seeing "a woman coming out of New York City with a frog in her hand" really didn't seem as silly as it sounded. And when he followed that up with the rhythm'n'punk swagger of "I Love to Boogie," few people would deny that Bolan was on the way back up. That particular gem would be featured on his next album, 1977's *Dandy in the Underworld*; the Edsel remaster of *Futuristic Dragon* does, however, wrap up three further cuts from the era, the single sides "Laser Love," the languid "Life's an Elevator" and, best of all, "London Boys," a piece of undisguised childhood nostalgia which was allegedly written about David Bowie, one of Bolan's teenaged running mates. The song, incidentally, was drawn from a proposed concept album, ambitiously titled "London Opera" (one of two Bolan was then considering, the other was the sci-fi themed *Billy Super Duper*). The project was never completed, however—for something else was stirring in the capital's bowels, that snarling monster which emerged as punk. And the moment Bolan saw it, he knew precisely what it represented. He began work on a new album right away.

Dave Thompson

Dandy in the Underworld
1977, Mercury

Marc Bolan welcomed the advent of punk rock with the biggest smile he'd worn in years. The hippest young gunslingers could go on all night about the influence of the Velvet Underground, the Stooges, and the Ramones, but Bolan knew—and subsequent developments proved—that every single one of them had been nurtured in his arms, growing up with the ineffable stream of brilliant singles he slammed out between 1970-1972, and rehearsing their own stardom to the soundtrack he supplied. *Dandy in the Underworld*, released early in 1977, confirmed Bolan's punkoid pre-eminence. Still retaining its predecessors' demented soul revue edge, but packed solid with powerful pop, Bolan's personal predictions for the punk scene literally exploded out of the grooves. By the time the album wraps up with the rock'n'armageddon flavored "Teen Riot Structure," Bolan was not simply wearing the mantle of punk godfatherhood, he was happily sticking safety-pins through it and preparing his next move, the driving "Celebrate Summer" single, the greatest record he'd made in years. It was also his last—a month after its release, Marc Bolan was dead. Sorrow immediately imbibed *Dandy in the Underworld* with a dignity which, had Bolan lived, it probably wouldn't have otherwise deserved—it is not, overall, one of his strongest albums, and the demos and outtakes included on the later volumes of the *Unchained* series suggest that his proposed next album would have left it far behind. But conjecture, like hindsight, can be a dangerous gauge. At the time, *Dandy* not only seemed bloated with promise, it was pregnant with foreboding as well. Listen again to the lyrics of the title track—self-mythologizing autobiography and not a happy ending in sight. Just like real life.

Dave Thompson

20th Century Boy: The Ultimate Collection
August 2002, Hip-O

Given that the T. Rex/Marc Bolan catalog is cluttered with collections, all recycling much of the same material, it's easy to be suspicious of another hits compilation, such as Hip-O's 2002 release *20th Century Boy: The Ultimate Collection, especially* if it's billed as an "ultimate" retrospective. Against all odds,

this 23-track disc really is an "ultimate collection," or at least as close as it can possibly get, given the labyrinthine nature of Bolan's catalog. What this gets right is that it samples it all, from Tyrannosaurus Rex to *Dandy in the Underworld*, hitting all the big songs along the way—"Debora," "One Inch Rock," "Ride a White Swan," "Bang a Gong (Get It On)," "Cosmic Dancer," "Telegram Sam," "The Slider," "Children of the Revolution," "20th Century Boy"—which is the first time all of these have been on a collection so concise, succinct, and winning. Sure, some may complain about a missing single or album track, but this is a stellar, pitch-perfect compilation, balancing the aforementioned big hits with relatively lesser-known gems like "Raw Ramp" and a cover of "Summertime Blues," resulting in the only single-disc compilation to capture all sides of Marc Bolan and T. Rex. And that means it's not just a necessary introduction, it's also essential for those who already have a bunch of albums, because it puts his career in perspective.

Stephen Thomas Erlewine

James Taylor

Sweet Baby James
February 1970, Warner Bros.

The heart of James Taylor's appeal is that you can take him two ways. On the one hand, his music, including that warm voice, is soothing; its minor key melodies and restrained playing draw in the listener. On the other hand, his world view, especially on such songs as "Fire and Rain," reflects the pessimism and desperation of the 1960s hangover that was the early '70s. That may not be intentional: "Fire and Rain" was about the suicide of a fellow inmate of Taylor's at a mental institution, not the national malaise. But Taylor's sense of wounded hopelessness—"I'm all in pieces, you can have your own choice," he sings in "Country Road"—struck a chord with music fans, especially because of its attractive mixture of folk, country, gospel, and blues elements, all of them carefully understated and distanced. Taylor didn't break your heart; he understood that it was already broken, as was his own, and he offered comfort. As a result, *Sweet Baby James* sold millions of copies, spawned a Top Ten hit in "Fire and Rain" and a Top 40 hit in "Country Road," and launched not only Taylor's career as a pop superstar but also the entire singer/songwriter movement of the early '70s that included Joni Mitchell, Carole King, Jackson Browne, Cat Stevens, and others. A second legacy became clear two decades later, when country stars like Garth Brooks began to cite Taylor, with his use of steel guitar, references to Jesus, and rural and Western imagery on *Sweet Baby James*, as a major influence.

William Ruhlmann

Mud Slide Slim and the Blue Horizon
April 1971, Warner Bros.

James Taylor's commercial breakthrough in 1970 was predicated on the relationship between the private concerns expressed in his songs and the larger philosophical mood of his audience. He was going through depression, heartbreak, and addiction; they were recovering from the political and cultural storms of the '60s. On his follow-up to the landmark *Sweet Baby James*, Taylor brought his listeners up to date, wisely trying to step beyond the cultural, if not the personal, markers he had established. Despite affirming romance in songs like "Love Has Brought Me Around" and the moving "You Can Close Your Eyes" as well as companionship in "You've Got a Friend," the record still came as a defense against the world, not an embrace of it; Taylor was unable to forget the past or trust the present. The songs were full of references to the road and the highway, and he was uncomfortable with his new role as spokesman. The confessional songwriter was now, necessarily, writing about what it was like to be a confessional songwriter: *Mud Slide Slim and the Blue Horizon* served the valuable function of beginning to move James Taylor away from the genre he had defined, which ultimately would give him a more long-lasting appeal.

William Ruhlmann

JT
June 1977, Columbia/Legacy

On his last couple of Warner Brothers albums, *Gorilla* and *In the Pocket*, James Taylor seemed to be converting himself from the shrinking violet, too-sensitive-to-live "rainy day man" of his early records into a mainstream, easy-listening crooner with a sunny outlook. *JT*, his debut album for Columbia Records, was something of a defense of this conversion. Returning to the autobiographical, Taylor declared his love for Carly Simon ("There We Are"), but expressed some surprise at his domestic bliss. "Isn't it amazing a man like me can feel this way?" he sang in the opening song, "Your Smiling Face" (a Top 40 hit). At the same time, domesticity could have its temporary depressions ("Another Grey Morning"). The key track was "Secret O' Life," which Taylor revealed as "enjoying the passage of time." Working with his long-time backup band of Danny Kortchmar, Leland Sklar, and Russell Kunkel, and with Peter Asher back in the producer's chair, Taylor also enjoyed the playing of music, mixing his patented acoustic guitar-based folk sound with elements of rock, blues, and country. He even made the Country charts briefly with "Bartender's Blues," a genre exercise complete with steel guitar and references to "honky tonk angels" that he would later re-record with George Jones. The album's Top Ten hit was Taylor's winning remake of Jimmy Jones' "Handy Man," which replaced the grit of the original with his characteristic warmth. *JT* was James Taylor's best album since *Mud Slide Slim and the Blue Horizon* because it acknowledged the darkness of his earlier work while explaining the deliberate lightness of his current viewpoint, and because it was his most consistent collection in years. Fans responded: *JT* sold better than any Taylor album since *Sweet Baby James*.

William Ruhlmann

10cc

The Original Soundtrack
1975, Mercury

10cc's third album, *The Original Soundtrack*, finally scored them a major hit in the United States, and rightly so; "I'm Not in Love" walked a fine line between self-pity and self-parody with its weepy tale of a boy who isn't in love (really!), and the marvelously lush production and breathy vocals allowed the tune to work beautifully either as a sly joke or at face value. The album's opener, "Une Nuit a Paris," was nearly as marvelous; a sly and often hilarious extended parody of both

cinematic stereotypes of life and love in France and over-blown European pop. And side one's closer, "Blackmail," was a witty tale of sex and extortion gone wrong, with a superb guitar solo embroidering the ride-out. That's all on side one; side two, however, is a bit spottier, with two undistinguished tunes, "Brand New Day" and "Flying Junk," nearly dragging the proceedings to a halt before the band rallied the troops for a happy ending with the hilarious "The Film of Our Love." *The Original Soundtrack*'s best moments rank with the finest work 10cc ever released; however, at the same time it also displayed what was to become their Achilles' heel—the inability to make an entire album as strong and memorable as those moments.

Mark Deming

How Dare You!
1976, Mercury

After scoring their commercial breakthrough with "I'm Not in Love" from 1975's *The Original Soundtrack*, 10cc continued to build on their good fortune with *How Dare You*. It didn't spawn another massive hit like "I'm Not in Love," but it is a well-crafted album that shows off 10cc's eccentric humor and pop smarts in equal measure. This time, the hit singles were "I'm Mandy Fly Me" and "Art for Art's Sake." The first tune is the fanciful tale of a plane crash victim saved from death by the stewardess of his dreams that plays out a poppy mock-exotica musical backdrop while the second is a tongue-in-cheek parody of commercial-minded artists set to a rocking, cowbell-driven beat. Elsewhere, *How Dare You* pursues a similar mix of zany humor and pop hooks: "Iceberg" brings its tale of a frigid romantic partner to life with an incredibly intricate and jazzy vocal melody, and "I Wanna Rule the World" is a witty tale of a dictator-in-training with enough catchy riffs and vocal harmonies for two or three songs. *How Dare You* loses a bit of steam on its second side when the songs' tempos start to slow down, but "Rock 'n' Roll Lullaby" and "Don't Hang Up" keep the listener involved through a combination of melodic songwriting and typically well-crafted arrangements. In the end, *How Dare You* never hits the giddy heights of *The Original Soundtrack* but it remains a solid album of witty pop songs that will satisfy anyone with a yen for 10cc.

Donald A. Guarisco

Deceptive Bends
1977, Mercury

When Kevin Godley and Lol Creme left 10cc in 1976 to pursue a solo career, many thought it was the death knell for the group. However, Eric Stewart and Graham Gouldman kept the group alive as a duo (with the assistance of percussionist Paul Burgess) and turned in a surprisingly solid album with 1977's *Deceptive Bends*. It may lack the devil-may-care wackiness that popped up on previous 10cc albums, but it makes up for it by crafting a series of lush, catchy pop songs that are witty in their own right. *Deceptive Bends* also produced a pair of notable hits for the group: "Good Morning Judge" told the comical tale of a career criminal over a hook-laden, surprisingly funky pop backing while "The Things We Do for Love" was an irresistible Beatles pastiche that showcased 10cc's mastery of pop vocal harmonies. "People in Love," a surprisingly straightforward ballad built on a gorgeous string arrangement, also became a modest chart success. The remainder of the material doesn't stand out as sharply as these hits, but each of the tracks offers up plenty of naggingly catchy pop hooks, oodles of catchy riffs, and surprising twists in their arrangements. Highlights among the non-hit tracks include "Marriage Bureau Rendezvous," a satire of dating services set to a lilting soft rock melody, and "You've Got a Cold," a portrait of illness-influenced misery set to a percolating pop melody. The only place where *Deceptive Bends* slips is on "Feel the Benefit," the lengthy medley that closes the album. Its excessive length and hazy lyrics make it less satisfying than the album's shorter tunes, but it is kept afloat by a catchy, mock-Spanish midsection and some lovely string arrangements. All in all, *Deceptive Bends* is the finest achievement of 10cc's post-Godley and Creme lineup and well worth a spin for anyone who enjoyed *Sheet Music* or *The Original Soundtrack*.

Donald A. Guarisco

The Complete UK Recordings 1972–1974
March 2004, Varese

Varese's double-disc set *The Complete UK Recordings* is a welcome, even necessary, addition to 10cc's catalog, collecting everything the band recorded for Jonathan King's UK Records in the early '70s. That is, it contains the entirety of their first two albums—1973's *10cc* and 1974's *Sheet Music*—along with non-LP singles and B-sides, alternate versions, and single mixes. Given that these two records have floated in and out of print on CD over the years (including a version of the debut on Snapper that had the tracks sequenced as if it were on shuffle play), and have never had a full-fledged U.S. release, this is a valuable reissue, and the two records have never sounded this good, nor have they been presented with much care as they are here. While the alternate single mixes are largely of interest to dedicated fans (and they're the target audience for this, after all), the other non-LP material holds its own with *10cc* and *Sheet Music*, which are the band's two strangest and weirdly inventive records. While the albums that immediately followed *Sheet Music*—in particular *The Original Soundtrack* and *Deceptive Bends*—were more accessible, this pair of LPs prove that 10cc were fearless from the outset, willing to fall on their face and happy to indulge in pure ridiculousness. It's not for every taste, even for those who like the band's soft rock hits, but for those who like their pop progressive and spiked with silliness, these two 10cc albums are essential listening, and the best place to hear them is on this exemplary reissue.

Stephen Thomas Erlewine

Ten Years After

Cricklewood Green
April 1970, Chrysalis

Cricklewood Green provides the best example of Ten Years After's recorded sound. On this album, the band and engineer Andy Johns mix studio tricks and sound effects, blues-based song structures, a driving rhythm section, and Alvin Lee's signature lightning-fast guitar licks into a unified album that flows nicely from start to finish. *Cricklewood Green* opens with a pair of bluesy rockers, with "Working on the Road" propelled by a guitar and organ riff that holds the listener's attention through the use of tape manipulation as

the song develops. "50,000 Miles Beneath My Brain" and "Love Like a Man" are classics of TYA's jam genre, with lyrically meaningless verses setting up extended guitar workouts that build in intensity, rhythmically and sonically. The latter was an FM-radio staple in the early '70s. "Year 3000 Blues" is a country romp sprinkled with Lee's silly sci-fi lyrics, while "Me and My Baby" concisely showcases the band's jazz licks better than any other TYA studio track, and features a tasty piano solo by Chick Churchill. It has a feel similar to the extended pieces on side one of the live album *Undead*. "Circles" is a hippie-ish acoustic guitar piece, while "As the Sun Still Burns Away" closes the album by building on another classic guitar-organ riff and more sci-fi sound effects.

Jim Newsom

A Space in Time
1971, Chrysalis

A Space in Time was Ten Years After's best-selling album. This was due primarily to the strength of "I'd Love to Change the World," the band's only hit single, and one of the most ubiquitous AM and FM radio cuts of the summer of 1971. TYA's first album for Columbia, *A Space in Time* has more of a pop-oriented feel than any of their previous releases had. The individual cuts are shorter, and Alvin Lee displays a broader instrumental palette than before. In fact, six of the disc's ten songs are built around acoustic guitar riffs. However, there are still a couple of barn-burning jams. The leadoff track, "One of These Days," is a particularly scorching workout, featuring extended harmonica and guitar solos. After the opener, however, the album settles back into a more relaxed mood than one would have expected from Ten Years After. Many of the cuts make effective use of dynamic shifts, and the guitar solos are generally more understated than on previous outings. The production on *A Space in Time* is crisp and clean, a sound quite different from the denseness of its predecessors. Though not as consistent as *Cricklewood Green*, *A Space in Time* has its share of sparkling moments.

Jim Newsom

The Anthology 1967–1971
April 2002, Hip-O

Since Ten Years After's albums weren't stand-alone classics, this double CD of their prime years is the best bet for those who like the band but don't want to sit through some pretty mediocre and monotonous stuff to get to the  best bits. The 26 cuts are pretty well chosen, including naturally their most famed songs: "I'm Going Home" (the live Woodstock version), "I'd Love to Change the World," and the British hit "Love Like a Man." Even as it draws from the cream of their work, it can't quite make the argument for them as a major band, but it does show that they were a more versatile act than many would remember. There are some reasonable pop-and folk-rock-flavored songs from the pen of Alvin Lee; a fair amount of jazz influence from time to time, as on "Me and My Baby" and "Woman Trouble"; a song ("50,000 Miles Beneath My Brain") that borrows rather too liberally from the Rolling Stones, "Sympathy for My Devil"; and even a bit of Grateful Dead-like vocal harmony on "Hear Me Calling."

There's still, of course, quite a bit of blues-rock, flash guitar, and boogie, which sound better when broken up by more subdued and varied cuts and also benefit from the wise decision not to include too many covers. It's also nice that the collection includes both sides of two 1968 singles, although those were released on LP in the early '70s as part of *Alvin Lee & Company*.

Richie Unterberger

Them

Them Featuring Van Morrison
1987, London

Not to be confused with the identically titled Parrot Records release, which is a 20-track double-LP set, this is a 13-track single CD set and a U.S. reissue of the Decca U.K. LP from 1982. It would have been less confusing if they had called it "Them's Greatest Hits" since it is primarily a singles compilation. But then, only four of Them's singles were hits, either in the U.K. or the U.S.—"Baby, Please Don't Go," "Gloria," "Here Comes the Night," and "Mystic Eyes," all included here. Also featured are such non-charting singles as "Don't Start Crying Now," "One More Time," "(It Won't Hurt) Half as Much," and "Richard Cory." This is not the ideal Them compilation, but this is the one that contains Them's most familiar material.

William Ruhlmann

The Story of Them Featuring Van Morrison
1997, Deram

Them were a formidable, popular group in their own right before singer Van Morrison went on to even greater fame. This Belfast five only produced two LPs and a potful of 7" singles during its ascendance in the molten heat of the British Invasion. But they did manage two Top 40 hits in America in 1965 (the enduring number 24 "Here Comes the Night," later covered glam-style by David Bowie on *Pin Ups*, and number 33 "Mystic Eyes") and two Top Ten hits that same year in their native Britain ("Here Comes the Night" and a cover of Joe Williams' "Baby Please Don't Go"). And is there a single bar band in America that doesn't play "Gloria," shouting "G-L-O-R-I-A" just like the 19-year-old Morrison in 1964? Moreover, the group's West Coast U.S. tour of arenas like the Fillmore in the spring of 1966 had the Ulster youths commanding bills that included such admiring support groups as the Doors, Captain Beefheart & the Magic Band, the Grass Roots, and the Association. At one of them, Frank Zappa even joined them on-stage. Clearly, Them's tough, heavily American blues captivated, a direct result of the vicious voice of Morrison. It was even more a weapon on this tougher-sounding material than it's been since he became a solo star. Although the band chose songs to cover by John Lee Hooker, Jimmy Reed (twice), T-Bone Walker, Ray Charles, Screamin' Jay Hawkins, and Fats Domino, as seen here (as well as others by Bob Dylan, Simon & Garfunkel,

and Bobby Troup), the real precedent for the white-hot, gnashing growl in Morrison's teenage voice was Howlin' Wolf. Here's a red-throated snarl not even other great '60s English white soul singers—such as the Small Faces' Steve Marriott or the singer for the Action—could match, one even more unsettling than the Animals' Eric Burdon. Talk about making the hairs on your neck stand up! It's actually a pity, then, that Them relied so heavily on others' material (as did everyone else circa 1964), for the two dozen originals stand up well. In addition to "Gloria," Morrison was well on the road to his later genius when he penned "Could You, Would You" and "Hey Girl." True, his material could stand to rock & roll more, just as the Yardbirds held fast to Chicago blues but made their beat stomp. But still he comes on like some swamp-dwelling, moonshine-drinking, big man on the prowl. Them were raw and ready, and digitally brought back kicking and screaming from the original analogue master tapes, they are an eerie thing of bluesy beauty.

Jack Rabid, The Big Takeover

Thin Lizzy

Vagabonds of the Western World
1973, Deram

After achieving a reluctant Top Ten hit with a rock version of the traditional Irish pub ballad "Whiskey in the Jar," Thin Lizzy began work on *Vagabonds of the Western World*—their third, and ultimately last album for Decca Records. The single's surprise success gave the band bargaining power to demand more money and time to record, resulting in their first sonically satisfying album. The environmentally-conscious R&B of "Mama Nature Said" kicks things off with Eric Bell leading the way on slide guitar. The overblown "The Hero and the Madman" and the tepid "Slow Blues" threaten to derail the proceedings, but all is well again when the band break into their first bona fide classic "The Rocker." Brimming with attitude and dangerous swagger, Lynott sets the tone, as drummer Brian Downey explodes into life for the first time on vinyl. Thin Lizzy's Irish heritage permeates the title track, and the beautiful "Little Girl in Bloom" is absolutely flawless, featuring Lynott, the poet, in top form. In many ways, *Vagabonds...* actually rocks harder than Lizzy's next album, the soulful *Nightlife*—often considered the band's first "important" record. And with the inclusion of four non-LP singles, including the aforementioned "Whiskey in the Jar," this package becomes even more appealing.

Ed Rivadavia

Night Life
1974, Mercury

It's curious that *Night Life*—the first album Thin Lizzy recorded for Mercury, the first album to feature guitarists Scott Gorham and Brian Robertson, the album that in many ways kicked off their classic era—is in many ways a complete anomaly within their catalog. It's a subdued, soulful record, smooth in ways that Thin Lizzy never were before and rarely were afterwards. To be sure, the title *Night Life* is accurate but not in the sense of this providing a soundtrack for a night out on the town—quite the opposite actually. This is the soundtrack for an intimate night in, either alone or as a pair, since it has moments ideal for either contemplation or seduction. There are still some moments of tough, primal rock & roll—there's the funky workout of "It's Only Money" and the nasty "Sha-La-La," both excellent showcases for Gorham and Robertson—but they stick out among the jazzy, soulful whole, even if they never quite disrupt the mood. And its that mood that's so appealing about *Night Life*—it's a warm, soulful sound that resonates in ways Thin Lizzy's earlier records didn't. And it's not just because of the feel of the music, either, it's due to Phil Lynott's increasing growth as a songwriter. Much of this is quite sentimental—especially the closing "Dear Heart"—but it's never saccharine or sappy, it's big-hearted and effecting, best-heard on the gently propulsive, utterly addictive opener "She Knows" and the easy-rolling jazzy "Showdown." These may be the high watermarks on this album, but they're not the only highlights, they're just the most immediate, representative signs of the charms of this underrated gem of a record.

Stephen Thomas Erlewine

Fighting
1975, Mercury

It's hard not to interpret the "fighting my way back" chorus of the title track on Thin Lizzy's fifth album as the band's way of bouncing back from the uncommonly subdued *Night Life*. If that record was smooth and relaxed, *Fighting* is a tense, coiled, vicious rock & roll album, as hard as *Vagabonds*'s toughest moments but more accomplished, the sound of a band truly coming into its own. There are two key forces at work. First, there's the integration of guitarists Scott Gorham and Brian Robertson, who get to unleash furious playing on every track here. It's hard not to thrill at their harmonizing twin-lead interplay, which is enough to excuse the rather pedestrian nature of their original tunes here (Robertson penned the boogie "Silver Dollar," Gorham the closer "Ballad of a Hard Man"). That's especially true because of the other development here: the full flourishing of Phil Lynott as a rock & roll poet. Whether he's writing hard-charging rockers like "Wild One," jazzy Springsteen-isms of "For Those Who Love To Live" or combining both on "Freedom Song," his songs manage to be both mythic and commonplace, and when delivered by the vital, visceral lineup he has here, they're invigorating. Strangely enough, that leap forward as a writer is somewhat overshadowed by a triumph of the band, in how they completely steal Bob Seger's "Rosalie" turning it into their own anthem, but that again is a testament to the strength of this incarnation of Thin Lizzy, who truly begin their classic era with this dynamic LP.

Stephen Thomas Erlewine

Jailbreak
1976, Mercury

Thin Lizzy found their trademark twin-guitar sound on 1975's *Fighting*, but it was on its 1976 successor, *Jailbreak*, where the band truly took flight. Unlike the leap between *Night Life* and *Fighting*, there is not a great distance between *Jailbreak* and its predecessor. If anything, the album was more of a culmination of everything that came before, as Phil Lynott hit a peak as a songwriter just as guitarists Scott Gorham and Brian Robertson pioneered an intertwined, dual-lead guitar interplay that was one of the most distinctive sounds of '70s rock, and one of the most influential. Lynott no longer

let Gorham and Robertson contribute individual songs—they co-wrote, but had no individual credits—which helps tighten up the album, giving it a cohesive personality, namely Lynott's rough rebel with a heart of a poet. Lynott loves turning the commonplace into legend—or bringing myth into the modern world, as he does on "Cowboy Song" or, to a lesser extent, "Romeo and the Lonely Girl"—and this myth-making is married to an exceptional eye for details; when the boys are back in town, they don't just come back to a local bar, they're down at Dino's, picking up girls and driving the old men crazy. This gives his lovingly florid songs, crammed with specifics and overflowing with life, a universality that's hammered home by the vicious, primal, and precise attack of the band. Thin Lizzy is tough as rhino skin and as brutal as bandits, but it's leavened by Lynott's light touch as a singer, which is almost seductive in its croon. This gives *Jailbreak* a dimension of richness that sustains, but there's such kinetic energy to the band that it still sounds immediate no matter how many times it's played. Either one would make it a classic, but both qualities in one record makes it a truly exceptional album.

Stephen Thomas Erlewine

Johnny the Fox
1976, Mercury

Jailbreak was such a peak that it was inevitable that its follow-up would fall short in some fashion and *Johnny the Fox*, delivered the same year as its predecessor, did indeed pale in comparison. What's interesting about *Johnny the Fox* is that it's *interesting*, hardly a rote repetition of *Jailbreak* but instead an odd, fitfully successful evolution forward. All the same strengths are still here—the band still sounds as thunderous as a force of nature, Phil Lynott's writing is still graced with elegant turns of phrase, his singing is still soulful and seductive—but the group ramped up the inherent drama in Lynott's songs by pushing them toward an odd, half-baked concept album. There may be a story within *Johnny the Fox*—characters are introduced and brought back, at the very least—but it's impossible to tell. If the album only had an undercooked narrative and immediate songs, such digressions would be excusable, but the music is also a bit elliptical in spots, sometimes sounding theatrical, sometimes relying on narration. None of this falls flat, but it's never quite as gripping as *Jailbreak*—or the best moments here, for that matter, because when *Johnny the Fox* is good, it's great, as on the surging "Don't Believe a Word" or the elegiac "Borderline." These are the reasons why *Johnny the Fox* is worth the extra effort, because it does pay off even if it isn't quite as good as what came immediately before—or immediately afterward, for that matter.

Stephen Thomas Erlewine

Bad Reputation
1977, Mercury

If Thin Lizzy got a bit too grand and florid on *Johnny the Fox*, they quickly corrected themselves on its 1977 follow-up, *Bad Reputation*. Teaming up with the legendary producer Tony Visconti, Thin Lizzy managed to pull of a nifty trick of sounding leaner, tougher than they did on *Johnny*, yet they also had a broader sonic palette. Much of this is due, of course, to Visconti, who always had a flair for subtle dramatics that never called attention to themselves—witness *Ziggy Stardust*, which is layered with color but still sounds muscular—and he puts this to use in dramatic effect here, to the extent that Lizzy sounds stripped down to their bare bones, even when they have horns pushing them forward on "Dancing in the Moonlight" or when overdubbed vocals pile up on the title track. Of course, they *were* stripped down to a trio on this record, lacking guitarist Brian Robertson, but Scott Gorham's double duty makes his absence unnoticeable. Plus, this is pure visceral rock & roll, the hardest and heaviest that Thin Lizzy ever made, living up to the promise of the title track. And, as always, a lot of this has to do with Phil Lynott's writing, which is in top form whether he's romanticizing "Soldiers of Fortune" or heading down the "Opium Trail." It adds up to an album that rivals *Jailbreak* as their best studio album.

Stephen Thomas Erlewine

Live and Dangerous
1978, Warner Bros.

Released in 1978, just as the hot streak starting with 1975's *Fighting* and running through 1977's *Bad Reputation* came to an end, *Live and Dangerous* was a glorious way to celebrate Thin Lizzy's glory days and one of the best double live LPs of the 70s. Of course, this, like a lot of double-lives of that decade—Kiss' *Alive!* immediately springs to mind—isn't strictly live; it was overdubbed and colored in the studio (the very presence of studio whiz Tony Visconti as producer should have been an indication that some corrective steering may have been afoot). But even if there was some tweaking in the studio, *Live and Dangerous feels* live, containing more energy and power than the original LPs, which were already dynamic in their own right. It's this energy, combined with the expert song selection, that makes *Live and Dangerous* a true live classic.

Stephen Thomas Erlewine

Black Rose: A Rock Legend
1979, Warner Bros.

Black Rose: A Rock Legend would prove to be Thin Lizzy's last true classic album (and last produced by Tony Visconti). Guitarist Brian Robertson was replaced by Gary Moore prior to the album's recording. Moore had already been a member of the band in the early '70s and served as a tour fill-in for Robertson in 1977, and he fits in perfectly with Lizzy's heavy, dual-guitar attack. *Black Rose* also turned out to be the band's most musically varied, accomplished, and successful studio album, reaching number two on the U.K. album chart upon release. Lizzy leader Phil Lynott is again equipped with a fine set of originals, which the rest of the band shines on—the percussion-driven opener "Do Anything You Want To," the pop hit "Waiting for an Alibi," and a gentle song for Lynott's newly born daughter, "Sarah." Not all the material is as upbeat, such as the funky "S&M," as well two grim tales of street life and substance abuse—"Toughest Street in Town" and "Got to Give It Up" (the latter sadly prophetic for Lynott). *Black Rose* closes with the epic seven-minute title track, which includes an amazing, complex guitar solo by Moore that incorporates Celtic themes against a hard rock accompaniment. *Black Rose: A Rock Legend* is one of the '70s lost rock classics.

Greg Prato

Dedication: The Very Best of Thin Lizzy
April 1991, Mercury

Several Thin Lizzy best-of collections have surfaced over the years (such as 1981's *Adventures of Thin Lizzy* and 1984's *Lizzy Lives!*), but the best two are undeniably 1996's *Wild One* and 1991's *Dedication*. While not as extensive as *Wild One* (only one track is featured from their '80s work), *Dedication* contains more early selections than the other mentioned titles. But the real attraction for Lizzy buffs is the inclusion of the previously unreleased title track, which was completed by the other members years after Lynott's passing in 1986. Elsewhere, often-overlooked tracks like "She Knows," "Fighting My Way Back," and "Cowboy Song" get to share the spotlight with such familiar faves as "The Boys Are Back in Town," "Bad Reputation," "Jailbreak," "Waiting for an Alibi," "Dancing in the Moonlight," and "Don't Believe a Word." Also included is an essay in which Lynott is quoted as saying that he'd like Lizzy to be remembered as a great guitar band (in the tradition of the Yardbirds, etc.). After hearing the great tracks on *Dedication*, you'll be reminded that there was so much more to this legendary band.

Greg Prato

.38 Special

Wild-Eyed Southern Boys
1981, A&M

Building on the bandmembers' own personal accomplishments that came from the *Rockin' Into the Night* album, .38 Special released an even stronger bunch of songs a year later with *Wild-Eyed Southern Boys*. Focusing on the same Southern-based rock & roll formula, the efforts from *Southern Boys* contain a little more guitar zing while complementing the band's ability to produce marketable radio music. "Hold on Loosely," with its smooth vocal stride, managed to peak at number 27 in April of 1981, giving .38 Special its first Top 40 single, and the title track, "Honky Tonk Dancer," and "Back Alley Sally" keep a homespun flavor alive and well, indicating that the band's Southern roots haven't been dismissed completely. Even though the bulk of the tracks lean toward .38 Special's rootin'-tootin' good-time persona, tracks such as "Fantasy Girl" and "First Time Around" reveal a stronger regard for producing catchy and approachable rock & roll tunes. It's on *Wild-Eyed Southern Boys* that .38 Special seemed more confident, harnessing a distinct guitar rock sound that enabled the group to distinguish itself from other FM rock bands. Cracking the Top 20 on the album charts and eventually reaching platinum status, *Wild-Eyed Southern Boys* marked the onset of the band's success throughout the course of the decade.

Mike DeGagne

Special Forces
1982, A&M

Released in 1982, *Special Forces* contains .38 Special's best song in "Caught Up in You," a hook-filled, smoothly sung radio rock gem that gets its energy from the grace and power of its chorus. It's here that the guitar work of Don Barnes and Jeff Carlisi combine to give Donnie Van Zant's singing a slick ride, fluently shifting from soft-tempered to vocally blatant at the change of a chord. But the hooks and the well-proportioned rhythms don't stop there. "You Keep Runnin' Away" gave the album its second charted single, which peaked at number 38, and the borderline boogie rock dash of "Rough Housin'" is among *Special Forces*' best cuts. Even secondary efforts like "Chain Lightnin'" and "Breakin' Loose" fit in comfortably with the rest of the tracks, offering up a hearty dose of the group's early Southern rock taste. Wisely, .38 Special kept the musical recipe similar to its last couple of releases, with the only striking difference coming from an even greater ability to design a memorable and punchy lead single. Because *Special Forces* administers a solid mix of Top 40 polish and pure guitar rock, .38 Special gained a much larger fan base upon its release.

Mike DeGagne

The Very Best of the A&M Years (1977–1988)
April 2003, Interscope

Fans looking for a smart, economical, and sharp-sounding overview of radio-friendly Southern rockers .38 Special will find much to love in the *Very Best of the A&M Years (1977-1988)*. "Hold on Loosely," "Caught Up in You," "If I'd Been the One" and "Rockin' into the Night" are all present, as well as deeper cuts such as "Take Me Back" and "Wild-Eyed Southern Boys." Listeners who require more from their collections would be better off picking up Hip-O's monster, two-disc, 34-track *Anthology*.

James Christopher Monger

George Thorogood

Greatest Hits: 30 Years of Rock
May 2004, Capitol

Released to celebrate the 30th anniversary of George Thorogood & the Destroyers—their first album may not have come out until 1977, but they cut their first sessions in 1974—Capitol's *Greatest Hits: 30 Years of Rock* was designed to replace 1992's *The Baddest of George Thorogood and the Destroyers* as the band's definitive single-disc overview. Considering that the 1992 disc is out of print (as is the exhaustive and exhausting 1997 double-disc set *Anthology*), this does indeed stand as the best compilation currently in print, and even edges out *Baddest* by running a little bit longer and containing more of his late-'80s/early-'90s radio hits. Thing is, it doesn't contain all of his hits—"Treat Her Right," which was on the previous comp, is missing, as are several other charting songs: "Born to Be Bad," "Hello Little Girl," "I'm a Steady Rollin' Man," "Howlin' for My Baby," "Gone Dead Train," and "I Don't Trust Nobody." Chances are, most listeners won't notice that they are missing since not only are all of his big hits here—"Madison Blues," "One Bourbon, One Scotch, One Beer," "Move It on Over," "Who Do You Love," "Bad to the Bone," "I Drink Alone," "Gear Jammer," "Willie and the Hand Jive," "You Talk Too Much," "If You Don't Start Drinkin' (I'm Gonna Leave),"

"Get a Haircut"—but because all of his songs pretty much sound *exactly* the same, all in the same key with the same riffs, same guitar licks, same lunkheaded vocals. For anybody who is not a fan, this makes listening to George Thorogood a maddening experience, but fans will find this to be a satisfying overview, even if it falls just short of being complete.

Stephen Thomas Erlewine

Three Dog Night

The Complete Hit Singles
May 2004, Utv

Three Dog Night ran off a string of 21 Top 40 hits between 1968 and 1975, including three number ones: "Joy to the World," "Mama Told Me (Not to Come)," and "Black & White." Despite this, they are often written off as a lightweight band who couldn't write their own songs. Granted they were laid-back and very easygoing, but they had some heft. The vocals of Chuck Negron, Danny Hutton, and Cory Wells were surprisingly soulful and the band that backed them was solid, and even rocked pretty hard on occasion. They didn't write songs—it is true—but their genius was *picking* songs. Along with producer Richard Podolor, the group found songs by writers like Randy Newman, Harry Nilsson, Laura Nyro, Hoyt Axton, Paul Williams, and John Hiatt and turned them into hits. So the group had laudable credentials, but more importantly, the songs collected here play like the soundtrack to the '70s. If you were just a casual fan, listening to *Complete Hit Singles* provides moment after moment of "I didn't remember these guys did that song!" exclamations. The hits just keep coming one after the other: "Joy to the World," "Celebrate," "Shambala," "Liar," "An Old Fashioned Love Song," and "Let Me Serenade You." Never sappy, never overbearing, always settled into a low-key, hooky groove, these songs are about as good as early-'70s pop gets. Another impressive thing about Three Dog Night is that they never showed any signs of slowing down. 1974's "Play Something Sweet (Brickyard Blues)" is just as good as "Eli's Coming" from 1969. The only thing that stopped them was the inevitable bout of creative differences that split the band up in 1976. This collection basically supplants the excellent *Best of Three Dog Night* from 1983. It boasts improved sound and one more song, their last Top 40 hit, "Til the World Ends," from 1975.

Tim Sendra

Thunderclap Newman

Hollywood Dream
1969, Polydor

All these years, and all these accolades later, it still seems incredible that *Hollywood Dream* meant nothing at the time of its release; that America let it drift no higher than Number 161; that the U.K. did not even give it a hearing. Less than a year before, after all, "Something in the Air" was topping charts and readers' polls alike, and Thunderclap Newman were as close as Christmas to becoming the new Beatles. Instead, they weren't even the new Badfinger, and this exquisite LP withered on the vine. What a difference 20 years make. Reissued in 1991, *Hollywood Dream* had been utterly transformed by the admiration of so many subsequent listeners, to stand alongside *any* lost classic you could mention, among the finest albums of its psychedelic generation. "Something in the Air," of course, has never lost its hold on our hearts, but there was so much more to Thunderclap Newman and, across the 12-track original album, and half-a-dozen bonus tracks, the trio's genius is inescapable. For those "in the know," who had treasured their scratchy old Atlantic label vinyl, the real meat lay in the latter, as all three of Thunderclap Newman's original 45's joined their album brethren, together with their non-LP B-sides. "Something in the Air," fussed up for the LP, reverts to its original emphatic punch; "Accidents" is pruned from a shade under ten minutes to a little over three; and the piping "The Reason" (an odd choice for a single in the first place) sounds like a role model for every record Supertramp ever made. The real gem, however, is "Wilhemina," which sounds like a daft piece of rhyming doggerel set to a nursery tune, but also packs one of the most dramatic psych guitar solos this side of your favorite Who record. Producer Pete Townshend must have been astonished. As will you be, too, if all you've ever heard is the hit. So many bands have been hauled out of obscurity to be tagged the greatest secret you've never been told. Thunderclap Newman are one of the few who actually deserve that epithet.

Dave Thompson

Johnny Thunders

So Alone
1978, Real Music

Following the drug-fueled implosion of the Heartbreakers, Johnny Thunders bounced back with his first solo outing, *So Alone*. Featuring a veritable who's who of '70s punk and hard rock—Chrissie Hynde, Phil Lynott, Peter Perrett, Steve Marriott, Paul Cook, and Steve Jones, among others—the record was a testament to what the former New York Dolls guitarist could accomplish with a little focus. Much like Thunders' best work with the Dolls and Heartbreakers, *So Alone* is a gloriously sloppy amalgam of R&B, doo wop, and three-chord rock & roll. Despite the inevitable excesses that plagued every Thunders recording session, Steve Lillywhite's solid engineering job and a superb set of songs hold everything together. A cover of the Chantays' classic instrumental "Pipeline" leads things off, and is a teasing reminder of what a great guitarist Thunders could be when he put his mind to it. The record's indisputable masterpiece is "You Can't Put Your Arms Round a Memory," a wrenching, surprisingly literate ballad in which Thunders seems to acknowledge that his junkie lifestyle has doomed him to the abyss. Songs like "Leave Me Alone," "Hurtin'," and the chilling title track continue the theme of life inside the heroin balloon. Fortunately, all this back-alley gloom is leavened by some memorably animated moments. "London Boys" is a scathing reply to the Sex Pistols' indictment of the New York punk scene, "New York." The funky "Daddy Rolling Stone" features the inimitable Lynott on background vocals, while the rave-ups "Great Big Kiss" and "(She's So) Untouchable" are terrific

examples of Thunders' raunchy take on classic R&B. Sadly, Johnny Thunders never followed up on the promise of his solo debut. His subsequent records were a frustrating mix of drug-addled mediocrity and downright laziness. But for one brief moment, he seemed to put it all together. That moment is *So Alone*.

Andy Claps

Toto

Toto
October 1978, Columbia

It's as easy to see why radio listeners loved Toto as it is to see why critics hated them. Toto's rock-studio chops allowed them to play any current pop style at the drop of a hi-hat: one minute prog rock, the next hard rock, the next funky R&B. It all sounded great, but it also implied that music-making took craft rather than inspiration and that the musical barriers critics like to erect were arbitrary. Then, too, Toto's timing couldn't have been much worse. They rode in during the middle of punk/new wave with its D.I.Y. aesthetic, and their sheer competence was an affront. Of course, there's always been an alternate history of popular music not available to rock critics (it's written in record stores and concert halls and on the radio), and in that story, Toto was a smash. Singles like "I'll Supply the Love" and "Georgy Porgy" (featuring Cheryl Lynn) made the charts, and "Hold the Line" hit the Top Ten and went gold. The members of Toto had already influenced the course of '70s popular music by playing on half the albums that came out of L.A. All they were doing with this album was going public.

William Ruhlmann

Hydra
October 1979, Columbia

If Toto's musical advantage was that, since its members continued to play on many of the successful records made in L.A., its own music was popular almost by definition, its disadvantage was that it made little attempt to seek an individual musical signature—a particular style, say, or a distinctive singer (Bobby Kimball was not it) who could make its records immediately identifiable. "Hold the Line" had been a big hit, but who did it? Boston? Foreigner? As a result, Toto was less well positioned than most to come off a big debut album with the follow-up, and *Hydra* was unusually dependent on its leadoff single, "99." Maybe it was a tribute to the female lead on the old *Get Smart* TV show, but many listeners didn't get a song with a chorus that went, "Oh, 99, I love you," and the single stalled in the bottom half of the Top 40. The album went gold on momentum, but the songs, however well played, simply were not distinctive enough to consolidate the success Toto had achieved with its debut album.

William Ruhlmann

Toto IV
April 1982, Columbia

It was do or die for Toto on the group's fourth album, and they rose to the challenge. Largely dispensing with the anonymous studio rock that had characterized their first three releases, the band worked harder on its melodies, made sure its simple lyrics treated romantic subjects, augmented Bobby Kimball's vocals by having other group members sing, brought in ringers like Timothy B. Schmit, and slowed down the tempo to what came to be known as "power ballad" pace. Most of all, they wrote some hit songs: "Rosanna," the old story of a lovelorn lyric matched to a bouncy beat, was the gold, Top Ten comeback single accompanying the album release; "Make Believe" made the Top 30; and then, surprisingly, "Africa" hit number one ten months after the album's release. The members of Toto may have more relatives who are NARAS voters than any other group, but that still doesn't explain the sweep they achieved at the Grammys, winning six, including Album of the Year and Record of the Year (for "Rosanna"). Predictably, rock critics howled, but the Grammys helped set up the fourth single, "I Won't Hold You Back," another soft rock smash and Top Ten hit. As a result, *Toto IV* was both the group's comeback and its peak; it remains a definitive album of slick L.A. pop for the early '80s and Toto's best and most consistent record. Having made it, the members happily went back to sessions, where they helped write and record Michael Jackson's *Thriller*.

William Ruhlmann

Pete Townshend

Rough Mix
September 1977, Atco

Rough Mix, Pete Townshend's 1977 collaboration with former Small Faces and Faces songwriter and bass player Ronnie Lane, combines the loose, rollicking folk-rock of Lane's former band, Slim Chance, with touches of country, folk, and New Orleans rock & roll, along with Townshend's own trademark style. Lane's tunes, especially the beautiful "Annie," possess an understated charm, while Townshend, with songs such as "Misunderstood," the Meher Baba-inspired "Keep Me Turning," and the strange love song "My Baby Gives It Away," delivers some of the best material of his solo career. *Rough Mix* stands as a minor masterpiece and an overlooked gem in both artists' vast bodies of work. Eric Clapton, John Entwistle, and Charlie Watts guest.

Brett Hartenbach

Empty Glass
April 1980, Atco

Pete Townshend was heading toward collapse as the '70s turned into the '80s. He had battled a number of personal demons throughout the '70s, but he started spiraling downward after Keith Moon's death, questioning

more than ever why he did what he did (and this is a songwriter who always asked questions). Signs of that crept out on *Face Dances*, but he saved a full-blown exploration of his psyche for *Empty Glass*, his first solo album since *Who Came First*, a vanity project released to little notice around *Who's Next* (so limited in its distribution that *Empty Glass* seemed like his solo debut). Some of the songs on *Empty Glass* would have worked as Who songs, yet this is clearly a singer/songwriter album, the work of a writer determined to lay his emotions bare, whether on the plaintive "I Am an Animal" or the blistering punk love letter "Rough Boys." Since this is Townshend, it can be a little artier than it needs to be, as on the pseudo-Gilbert & Sullivan chorus of "Keep on Working," but the joy of *Empty Glass* is that his writing is sharp, his performances lively, his gift for pop hooks as apparent as his wit. Though it runs out of steam toward the end, *Empty Glass* remains one of the highlights of Townshend's catalog and is one of the most revealing records he cut, next to his other breakdown album, *Who By Numbers*.

Stephen Thomas Erlewine

All the Best Cowboys Have Chinese Eyes
June 1982, Atco

If *Empty Glass*, an album filled with songs that could have been performed by the Who, was a solo album because it was too revealing and personal, *All the Best Cowboys Have Chinese Eyes* was a solo record since it's impossible to hear anyone but Townshend wanting to indulge in this deliberately arty, awkwardly poetic bullsh*t. Where his other albums showed an inclination toward classical-influenced art rock, this is defiantly modern art, filled with stagey prose, synthesizers, drum machines, angular song structures, and a heavy debt to new wave—in short, Townshend's vision of what modern music should sound like in 1982. This kind of record taunts cynics and critics, being nearly impenetrable in its content even if the production and the music itself aren't all that inaccessible. The problem is, this is Arty with a capital A and Pretentious with a capital P, yet Townshend never seems embarrassed, never shies away from indulging himself in his own ego. While autobiographical to a certain extent (how else to read "Somebody Saved Me" or "Stardom in Acton," which drops the Who's home borough?), it's hard to tell exactly what he's on about. So it's easy to see why many listeners are exasperated instead of intrigued (or even admire its damn impenetrability), but it's also easy to get fascinated by the album's very obtuseness. This is very much of a piece and, apart from the gems "North Country Girl" and "Slit Skirts," it's hard to separate individual songs and see them as their own works. Indeed, separating *All the Best Cowboys* from its era is even difficult, since the album's surface glistens with new wave synths and guitars; this is clearly a record Townshend could only have made in 1982, emboldened by new wave, the reaction to *Empty Glass*, new sobriety, and general hubris. For these reasons, this is very much loved by a certain portion of Townshend's fan base—and for the same reasons many, many people despise it. And any record that fractures an audience so considerably is worth a spin.

Stephen Thomas Erlewine

White City
November 1985, Teichiku Japan

After the experimental *All the Best Cowboys Have Chinese Eyes*, Pete Townshend returned to a more traditional form of concept album with *White City*. Built around a loose narrative concerning urban despair, the album doesn't work very well conceptually, yet a handful of the individual songs are among his finest solo work, including the punchy "Face the Face" and the anthemic "Give Blood."

Stephen Thomas Erlewine

Traffic

Mr. Fantasy
December 1967, Island

Since Traffic's debut album, *Mr. Fantasy*, has been issued in different configurations over the years, a history of those differences is in order. In 1967, the British record industry considered albums and singles separate entities; thus, *Mr. Fantasy* did not contain the group's three previous Top Ten U.K. hits. Just as the album was being released in the U.K., Traffic split from Dave Mason. The album was changed drastically for U.S. release, both because American custom was that singles ought to appear on albums, and because the group sought to diminish Mason's presence; on the first pressing only, the title was changed to *Heaven Is in Your Mind*. In 2000, Island reissued *Mr. Fantasy* in its mono mix with the U.K. song list and five mono singles sides as bonus tracks; it also released *Heaven Is in Your Mind*, the American lineup in stereo with four bonus tracks. Naturally, the mono sound is punchier and more compressed, but it isn't ideal for the album, because Traffic was fashioned as an unusual rock band. Steve Winwood's primary instrument was organ, though he also played guitar; Chris Wood was a reed player, spending most of his time on flute; Mason played guitar, but he was also known to pick up the sitar, among other instruments. As such a mixture suggests, the band's musical approach was eclectic, combining their background in British pop with a taste for the comic and dance hall styles of *Sgt. Pepper*, Indian music, and blues-rock jamming. Songs in the last category have proven the most distinctive and long-lasting, but Mason's more pop-oriented contributions remain winning, as do more light-hearted efforts. Interest in the mono mix is likely to be restricted to longtime fans; anyone wishing to hear Traffic's first album for the first time is directed to *Heaven Is in Your Mind*.

William Ruhlmann

Traffic
February 1968, Island

After dispensing with his services in December 1967, the remaining members of Traffic reinstated Dave Mason in the group in the spring of 1968 as they struggled to write enough material for their impending second album. The result was a disc evenly divided between Mason's catchy folk-rock compositions and Steve Winwood's compelling rock jams. Mason's material was the most appealing both initially and eventually: the lead-off track, a jaunty effort called "You Can All Join In," became a European hit, and "Feelin' Alright?" turned out to be the only real standard to emerge from the album after it started earning cover versions from Joe Cocker and others in the 1970s. Winwood's efforts, with their haunting keyboard-based melodies augmented by Chris

Wood's reed work and Jim Capaldi's exotic rhythms, work better as musical efforts than lyrical ones. Primary lyricist Capaldi's words tend to be impressionistic reveries or vague psychological reflections; the most satisfying is the shaggy-dog story "Forty Thousand Headmen," which doesn't really make any sense as anything other than a dream. But the lyrics to Winwood/Capaldi compositions take a back seat to the playing and Winwood's soulful voice. As Mason's simpler, more direct performances alternate with the more complex Winwood tunes, the album is well-balanced. It's too bad that the musicians were not able to maintain that balance in person; for the second time in two albums, Mason found himself dismissed from the group just as an LP to which he'd made a major contribution hit the stores. Only a few months after that, the band itself split up, but not before scoring their second consecutive Top Ten ranking in the U.K.; the album also reached the Top 20 in the U.S., breaking the temporarily defunct group stateside.

William Ruhlmann

Last Exit
January 1969, Island

Since Traffic originally planned its self-titled second album as a double LP, the group had extra material left over, some of which saw release before the end of 1968 (there was a new, one-off single released in December, "Medicated Goo"/"Shanghai Noodle Factory"). In January 1969, Steve Winwood announced the group's breakup. That left Island Records, the band's label, in the lurch, since Traffic had built up a considerable following. As far as Island was concerned, it was no time to stop, and the label quickly set about assembling a new album. The non-LP B-side "Withering Tree," "Medicated Goo," and "Shanghai Noodle Factory" were pressed into service, along with "Just for You," the B-side of a solo single by on-again, off-again member Dave Mason that had been released originally in February 1968 and happened to feature the rest of the members of Traffic as sidemen; a short, previously unreleased instrumental; and two extended jams on cover songs from a 1968 live appearance at the Fillmore West. It all added up to more than half an hour of music, and that was enough to package it as the posthumous Traffic album *Last Exit*. Actually, *Last Exit* isn't bad as profit-taking products go. "Just for You" is one of Mason's elegant folk-pop songs, including attractive Indian percussion. "Medicated Goo" has proven to be one of Traffic's more memorable jam tunes, despite its nonsense lyrics, and the equally appealing "Shanghai Noodle Factory" is hard not to interpret as Winwood's explanation of the band's split. And while the cover material seems unlikely, the songs are used as platforms for the band to jam cohesively. So, Traffic's third album, thought at the time of its release to be the final one, has its isolated pleasures, even if it doesn't measure up to its two predecessors.

William Ruhlmann

John Barleycorn Must Die
July 1970, Island

At only 22 years old, Steve Winwood sat down in early 1970

to fulfill a contractual commitment by making his first solo album, on which he intended to play all the instruments himself. The record got as far as one backing track produced by Guy Stevens, "Stranger to Himself," before Winwood called his erstwhile partner from Traffic, Jim Capaldi, in to help out. The two completed a second track, "Every Mother's Son," then, with Winwood and Island Records chief Chris Blackwell moving to the production chores, brought in a third Traffic member, Chris Wood, to work on the sessions. Thus, Traffic, dead and buried for more than a year, was reborn. The band's new approach was closer to what it perhaps should have been back in 1967, basically a showcase for Winwood's voice and instrumental work, with Wood adding reed parts and Capaldi drumming and occasionally singing harmony vocals. If the original Traffic bowed to the perceived commercial necessity of crafting hit singles, the new Traffic was more interested in stretching out. Heretofore, no studio recording had run longer than the five-and-a-half minutes of "Dear Mr. Fantasy," but four of the six selections on *John Barleycorn Must Die* exceeded six minutes. Winwood and company used the time to play extended instrumental variations on compelling folk- and jazz-derived riffs. Five of the six songs had lyrics, and their tone of disaffection was typical of earlier Capaldi sentiments. But the vocal sections of the songs merely served as excuses for Winwood to exercise his expressive voice as punctuation to the extended instrumental sections. As such, *John Barleycorn Must Die* moved beyond the jamming that had characterized some of Traffic's 1968 work to approach the emerging field of jazz-rock. And that helped the band to achieve its commercial potential; this became Traffic's first gold album.

William Ruhlmann

Welcome to the Canteen
January 1971, Island

Following the success of *John Barleycorn Must Die*, Traffic planned a concert album for the fall of 1970, and it got as far as a test pressing before being canceled. A recording was necessary to satisfy the terms of British label Island records' licensing deal with American label United Artists, which had provided for five albums, of which four had been delivered. With Island starting to release its own albums in the U.S., the UA contract had to be completed, and hopefully not with the potentially lucrative studio follow-up to *John Barleycorn Must Die*. Thus, Traffic tried again to come up with a live album by recording shows on a British tour in July 1971. Joining for six dates of the tour was twice-dismissed Traffic singer/guitarist Dave Mason, who had subsequently scored a solo success with his *Alone Together* album. The resulting collection, *Welcome to the Canteen* (which was technically credited to the seven individual musicians, not to Traffic), proved how good a contractual obligation album could be. Sound quality was not the best (and it still isn't on the 2002 remastered CD reissue, though it's better), with the vocals under-recorded and stray sounds honing in, but the playing was exemplary, and the set list was an excellent mixture of old Traffic songs and recent Mason favorites. "Dear Mr. Fantasy" got an extended workout, and the capper was a rearranged version of Steve Winwood's old Spencer Davis Group hit "Gimme Some Lovin'." *Welcome to the Canteen*'s status as only a semi-legitimate offering was emphasized by the release, after a mere two months, of a new Traffic studio album on Island (*The Low Spark of High Heeled Boys*) that undercut its sales. But that doesn't make it any less appealing as a summing up of the Winwood/Mason/Traffic musical world.

William Ruhlmann

The Low Spark of High Heeled Boys
February 1971, Island

The Low Spark of High Heeled Boys marked the commercial and artistic apex of the second coming of Traffic, which had commenced in 1970 with *John Barleycorn Must Die*. The trio that made that album had been augmented by three others (Ric Grech, Jim Gordon, and "Reebop" Kwaku Baah) in the interim, though apparently the *Low Spark* sessions featured varying combinations of these musicians, plus some guests. But where their previous album had grown out of sessions for a Steve Winwood solo album and retained that focus, *Low Spark* pointedly contained changes of pace from his usual contributions of midtempo, introspective jam tunes. "Rock & Roll Stew" was an uptempo treatise on life on the road, while Jim Capaldi's "Light up or Leave Me Alone" was another more aggressive number with an unusually emphatic Capaldi vocal that perked things up on side two. The other four tracks were Winwood/Capaldi compositions more in the band's familiar style. "Hidden Treasure" and "Rainmaker" bookended the disc with acoustic treatments of nature themes that were particularly concerned with water, and "Many a Mile to Freedom" also employed water imagery. But the standout was the 12-minute title track, with its distinctive piano riff and its lyrics of weary disillusionment with the music business. The band had only just fulfilled a contractual commitment by releasing the live album *Welcome to the Canteen*, and they had in their past the embarrassing *Last Exit* album thrown together as a commercial stopgap during a temporary breakup in 1969. But that anger had proven inspirational, and "The Low Spark of High Heeled Boys" was one of Traffic's greatest songs as well as its longest so far. The result was an album that quickly went gold (and eventually platinum) in the U.S., where the group toured frequently.

William Ruhlmann

Shoot Out at the Fantasy Factory
January 1973, Island

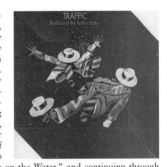

After two exemplary releases, *Shoot Out at the Fantasy Factory* marked a fall-off in quality for Traffic. The problems lay in both composition and performance. Beginning with the title track, based on a guitar riff reminiscent of the recent Deep Purple hit "Smoke on the Water," and continuing through the lengthy "Roll Right Stones," the folkish ballad "Evening Blue," reed player Chris Wood's instrumental "Tragic Magic," and the uncertain self-help song "(Sometimes I Feel So) Uninspired," the material was far from the group's best. Lyricist Jim Capaldi was co-credited with Steve Winwood as the album's producer, and he may have contributed to the cleaner mix that made his words easier to understand. Easier, that is, in the technical sense, since the musing about a sort of minor-league Stonehenge "Roll Right Stones" didn't do much with the image, and, though it struggled for a more positive outlook, "(Sometimes I Feel So) Uninspired" seemed to come out on the side of despair. Winwood's music seemed to recycle his own ideas when it didn't borrow from others. Meanwhile, the rhythm section had been replaced by Muscle Shoals studio aces David Hood and Roger Hawkins, who proved proficient but not as kinetic as their predecessors, so that the playing often seemed mechanical. Capaldi sang no songs here, and Wood's flute and saxophone, so often the flavoring of Traffic songs, were largely absent. What was left was a competent, if perfunctory effort in the band's familiar style. They had built up enough of a following through touring that the album was a commercial success, but it sounds like an imitation of earlier triumphs.

William Ruhlmann

Triumph

Classics
1989, MCA

Many people thought of Triumph as Rush Pt. 2, and from their first couple of albums, that comparison was not too far off. Another Canadian trio, the group had definite Rush-ish leanings. However, as time went on, they developed a more mainstream '80s metal approach. That somewhat generic style would see Triumph's star grow somewhat brighter than Rush's for a time, garnering them a lot of radio airplay and multiple hits. The lack of depth and individuality of that latter-era material also would see them burn out quite quickly, while Rush kept making a gradual building, both of musical competency and fame. So, while Rush is still in the limelight, Triumph has joined the ranks of the "where are they now?" club. This compilation showcases many of the facets of both sides of the band. It includes plenty of the more mindless and faceless hits while also showing that the group did have a penchant for creating considerably strong material as well. Among the high points are "Hold On," "Magic Power," "A World of Fantasy," and "Fight the Good Fight." The weaker material on show here includes "Tears In The Rain," "Live for the Weekend," and the .38 Special-ish "Follow Your Heart." Hits one and all, those tracks just don't stand up to the other material and really show their age, seeming quite trivial and worn out by now. To its credit, the CD includes a bonus cut in the form of "Rock and Roll Machine," a somewhat raw but inspired track from the first album. One can only regret that they didn't also choose to include "Blinding Light Show."

Gary Hill

Robin Trower

Twice Removed from Yesterday
1973, Chrysalis

Robin Trower's debut solo album was the first evidence that the Fender Stratocaster sound of Jimi Hendrix could be effectively replicated and even refabricated. And like Hendrix, Trower had paid his dues as a more-or-less backup musician, his former band Procol Harum having emphasized stately organ and piano rather than guitar. After leaving his old group, Trower experimented with different musicians and ideas for several years, which paid off when he finally released *Twice Removed From Yesterday*, a record that displayed the characteristics that would make him a guitar hero and stadium attraction of the mid-'70s. He de-emphasized the Hendrix fuzz, feedback, and distortion, and let the reverb from his Strat become his dominant tonal device. He wasn't as flamboyant as Hendrix, as earthy as Eric Clapton, or as unpredictable as Jeff Beck, but he played cleanly, emphasizing singular, effective notes, and he brought a melodicism and creativity to

the electric blues. His style is best suited for the slow, somber blues of songs like "Daydream" and "I Can't Wait Much Longer," where his solos are both carefully structured and melodic. The most intriguing tune on the album is the title track, a nugget of '70s-style psychedelic rock that showed Trower to be a pretty good songwriter. The best aspects of *Twice Removed* would come to full flowering on his next album, *Bridge of Sighs*, but this debut showed Trower to be an effective interpreter of the Hendrix sound, and not just what numerous others who came in his wake would prove to be: mere imitators.

Peter Kurtz

Bridge of Sighs
1974, Chrysalis

Guitarist Robin Trower's watershed sophomore solo disc remains his most stunning, representative, and consistent collection of tunes. This 24-bit digitally remastered 25th anniversary reissue, which tacks on five live tracks adding nearly 25 minutes to the original playing time, actually improves upon the original. Mixing obvious Hendrix influences with blues and psychedelia, then adding the immensely soulful vocals of James Dewer, Robin Trower pushed the often limited boundaries of the power trio concept into refreshing new waters. The concept gels best in the first track, "Day of the Eagle," where the opening riff rocking morphs into the dreamy washes of gooey guitar chords that characterize the album's distinctive title track that follows. At his best, Trower's gauzy sheets of oozing, wistful sound and subtle use of wah-wah combine with Dewer's whisky-soaked soul-drenched vocals to take a song like the wistful ballad "In This Place" into orbit. "Too Rolling Stoned," another highlight and one of the most covered tracks from this album, adds throbbing, subtle funk to the mix, changing tempos midway to a slow, forceful amble on top of which Trower lays his quicksilver guitar. The live tracks, although similar to the album versions, prove that even without overdubs and the safety of the studio, Trower and band easily convey the same feel, and add a slightly rougher edge, along with some low-key, crowd-pleasing flourishes. One of the few Trower albums without a weak cut, and in 2000, unfortunately one of the only ones still in print in the U.S., *Bridge of Sighs* holds up to repeated listenings as a timeless work, as well as the crown jewel in Robin Trower's extensive yet inconsistent catalog.

Hal Horowitz

The Tubes

Remote Control
1979, A&M

After stunning the rock world with their memorable debut in 1975, the Tubes ran into trouble. Although *Young And Rich* and *Now* had fine moments, they were uneven and left many rock pundits wondering if the Tubes had anything to offer besides shock value. They got their answer with the release of *Remote Control*, a cohesive and surprisingly thoughtful concept album. On this 1979 outing, the Tubes enlisted the services of wunderkind producer Todd Rundgren to create a concept album that skewers the television generation. The choice was a wise one—Rundgren helped the group harness their satirical bite and love of pomp-rock excess to create a sharp and engaging collection of songs. As they chronicle the life of an average joe whose life and dreams are swallowed by his television addiction, the Tubes lead the listener through a dazzling array of musical styles that include new-wave, lounge pop, reggae, and even full-throttle punk. Highlights include "Prime Time," a song that utilizes an effective combination of lounge-lizard atmosphere and new wave synthesizer textures to convey its portrait of television's seductiveness, and "Love's A Mystery (I Don't Understand)," a surprisingly straightforward ballad about romantic loss that features a truly heart-rending vocal from Fee Waybill. The group also gets a chance to show off their formidable instrumental chops on "Get-Overture," a tight instrumental that goes from atmospheric prog-rock to driving hard rock as it cleverly weaves together snippets of all the other songs' melodies. In short, *Remote Control* proves the Tubes were more than a bunch of musical jokesters. The end result is the band's finest hour and a treat for concept-album fanatics.

Donald A. Guarisco

The Completion Backward Principle
1981, Capitol

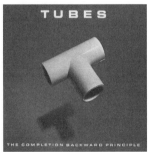

The Completion Backward Principle was the first release on EMI/Capitol by San Francisco-based the Tubes. It found the outrageous septet working with producer David Foster, who gives the record a high-gloss sheen. It's a pairing that, while possibly surprising to fans of the band's earlier releases, actually works quite nicely. The ballads (the Top 40 hit "Don't Want to Wait Anymore" and the Toto-esque "Amnesia") don't suit the band, but most everything else does. There's a pair of catchy new wavish rockers in "Talk to Ya Later" and "Think About Me," the wacky "Sushi Girl," and the R&B-flavored "A Matter of Pride." *The Completion Backward Principle* rightfully earned the Tubes new fans and set the table for their commercial breakthrough, *Outside/Inside*, two years later.

Tom Demalon

Outside Inside
1983, Capitol

Another bit of clever packaging outside (the record label featured an iris that appeared through a cutout on the sleeve) and inside, where producer David Foster and even more members of Toto help the Tubes punch up their new radio-ready sound with added energy. If their last record showed a newfound dancefloor sensibility, *Outside Inside* is absolutely funky. There are plenty of over-the-top arena pop numbers on here, including the hit "She's a Beauty," "No Not Again,"

and "Tip of My Tongue." Yet with so many cooks in the kitchen, the record is peppered with some strange entries, like "Wild Women of Wongo," "Drums," and "Outside Looking Inside." Maybe the Tubes were trying to exorcise their own artistic demons, the better to play a song like "Fantastic Delusion" or "The Monkey Time" with a clear conscience. *Outside Inside* is definitely a party record, which is fine, except that the Tubes were never a party band (after all, their most radio-friendly album to date, *The Completion Backward Principle*, was still pretty dark). The change in direction will probably alienate old fans, just as it clearly attracted new ones (the record reached the U.S. Top 20). If you enjoyed their hits from the '80s (e.g., "Talk to You Later," "She's a Beauty"), this is the album to own.

Dave Connolly

Goin' Down
1996, A&M

Although they are known to modern listeners as the band behind the new wave gem "She's a Beauty," the Tubes had an entirely different career during their mid-to-late 1970s tenure on the A&M label. Working with gifted producers like Al Kooper and Todd Rundgren, the group created a body of work that fused prog rock instrumental virtuosity, the sarcasm of new wave, and Frank Zappa-styled musical satire into a style all its own. Listeners get a great chance to sample the group's ambitious style on *Goin' Down*, a generous two-CD compilation that includes all the group's radio favorites, album tracks from each of their A&M releases (including the *Remote Control* album in its entirety), and most of the rarities that had previously appeared on *T.R.A.S.H. (Tubes Rarities and Smash Hits)*. The end result is one-stop shopping for any listener who wants to get all the highlights of the group's 1970s work without having to hunt down the their often-inconsistent albums. Songs like "What Do You Want From Life" and "Don't Touch Me There" sound as eccentrically witty as ever, but the real surprises are the album tracks: "My Head Is My Only House Unless It Rains" is a surprisingly subtle ballad full of hypnotic synthesizer textures, and "This Town" skewers big city life over a tune that recreates the vintage Frank Sinatra/Dean Martin lounge pop sound with surprising faithfulness. The package is rounded out by brief but informative liner notes and a selection of provocative pictures from the group's notorious 1970s stage shows. All in all, *Goin' Down* may be a little too much Tubes for the casual listener, but it remains the definitive portrait of the group's 1970s era for serious fans.

Donald A. Guarisco

Uriah Heep

Classic Heep: An Anthology
September 1998, Mercury

To irritate snobbish rock critics in the 1970s, all a band had to do was play heavy metal or progressive rock. Imagine their horror when Uriah Heep came along and consciously fused both styles. Uriah Heep was the subject of one vicious critic's infamous quote, "If this group makes it, I'll have to commit suicide." Well then, this critic is probably dead, because the British band did achieve widespread success. 1998's two-CD *Classic Heep: An Anthology* is a terrific compilation of Uriah Heep's 1970-1976 prime. The 30 songs are taken from nine studio albums: *Uriah Heep* (*Very 'Eavy, Very 'Umble* in the U.K.), *Salisbury*, *Look at Yourself*, *Demons and Wizards*,

229

The Magician's Birthday, *Sweet Freedom*, *Wonderworld*, *Return to Fantasy*, and *High and Mighty*. It surely won't inspire a serious critical re-examination of Uriah Heep, but it should. The band was aggressively experimental, and while not everything worked, during its peak years vocalist David Byron, guitarist Mick Box, keyboardist/guitarist Ken Hensley, bass guitarists Gary Thain and John Wetton, and drummer Lee Kerslake tried it all. Musically, Uriah Heep relied on Byron's dramatic vocals, Box's gritty guitar crunch, Hensley's rumbling keyboards, and Thain's (later Wetton's) busy bass licks, and the band's harmony vocals and background "aah"s and "ooh"s were unique. Of course, Uriah Heep's two most famous songs, "Stealin'" and "Easy Livin'," are included. "Stealin'," a staple of classic rock radio, is the band's best: a powerfully tight, explosive lament from a penitent, ashamed outlaw. "Easy Livin'," the band's only U.S. Top 40 hit, is a catchy, full-bore rocker. Other notable cuts are "Gypsy," "Bird of Prey," "Lady in Black," "Rainbow Demon," "Blind Eye," "Sweet Lorraine," "Wonderworld," "Return to Fantasy," "Weep in Silence," and the ambitious epics "July Morning," "Paradise/The Spell," and "The Magician's Birthday." The detailed liner notes include an insightful essay by Hensley.

Bret Adams

Utopia

Oops! Wrong Planet
September 1977, Bearsville/Rhino

Abandoning overt prog—thereby leaving behind the operas and extended instrumental sections, but not the organ solos—Utopia became a mainstream rock band with their fourth album, *Oops! Wrong Planet*. Since the group's first two albums were marginally listenable and *RA* flirted with outright parody, it comes as a shock to hear Utopia be outright accessible and listenable, two qualities virtually foreign to their previous work. The quartet has been revamped, redesigned as a mainstream arena rock band. And that means that the chores are spread a little more evenly—meaning, not only does everyone get to write, everyone gets to sing, occasionally on songs Todd wrote. Despite his efforts to democratize the group, Utopia still feels very much like Rundgren's baby, mainly because the only songs that really work are ones that he writes and sings. And since Utopia is now merely a hard rock band, Rundgren reserves his more ambitious ideas and complex songs for his solo records. The end result of all this is that *Oops! Wrong Planet* is more consistent than earlier Utopia records, but is not as sporadically brilliant or rewarding as Todd's solo albums. Even the bad moments, such as the very silly "Gangrene," aren't particularly unlistenable, yet there are simply too many average, undistinguished songs for the record to actually soar. Nevertheless, Rundgren turns in some fine moments—"Love in Action" is a terrific hard rocker, as is "Trapped," and "Love is the Answer" is an ideal stadium anthem—that make the record worthwhile for the

cult, even if it will sound like little more than a period piece to most listeners.

Stephen Thomas Erlewine

Adventures in Utopia
January 1980, Bearsville/Rhino

Oops! Wrong Planet wrote the blueprint for Utopia Mach II, but the group didn't deliver the polished, radio-ready follow-up *Adventures in Utopia* until two-and-a-half years later. Granted, leader Todd Rundgren kept busy in the interim, but it was an abnormally long time between records. As it turns out, the wait didn't matter, since Utopia delivered a record that was quintessentially 1980—a shiny, buffed album every bit as pop as *The Hermit of Mink Hollow*, but considerably less introspective and altogether ready for action. It's a bid for the big seats, and Utopia, surprisingly, achieved their goals, as the record climbed into the Top 40 and spawned a hit single with "Set Me Free," a song sung by Kasim Sulton. That fact alone indicates that *Adventures* is the closest Utopia had yet come to its band ideal. It's no surprise that Todd Rundgren still dominates the proceedings, but his presence is not omnipresent, which is to the benefit of the album. Like its predecessor, *Adventures* is consistent but a little bland, but the shiny pop surfaces are more appealing than the arena rock bluster of *Oops!*, which makes the fact that it has about the same number of memorable songs—"You Make Me Crazy," "Second Nature," "Set Me Free," and "The Very Last Time" (again, all top-loaded)—not quite as noticeable. It keeps things moving as the record is playing, and if the album as a whole isn't entirely memorable, at least the half that does take hold still sounds as if it was state-of-the-art pop/rock for 1980.

Stephen Thomas Erlewine

Deface the Music
October 1980, Bearsville/Rhino

Having just scored their first big hits with *Adventures in Utopia*, Utopia inexplicably took a step into arcana with its follow-up, *Deface the Music*. Foregoing the radio-ready style of *Adventures*, Utopia delves deeply into Beatlemania, creating a swift, brutally funny and insanely catchy send-up of the Fab Four's entire career. Clearly, the high (nearly arty) concept makes *Deface the Music* the first Utopia album since *Another Live* to sound like it is solely the work of Todd Rundgren. The music is so savvy, it's clear that these songs are primarily the work of Todd, even if they're credited to Utopia. Rundgren is able to write songs that evoke specific eras of the Beatles' career and have them be funny without being a slave to parody. Like the Rutles, this music works well on its own merits and, unlike the Rutles, Rundgren is as credible with "Penny Lane" psychedelia ("Hoi Poloi") or "Eleanor Rigby" chamber-pop ("Life Goes On") as he is with Merseybeat ("I Just Want to Touch You," "Crystal Ball"). Unlike the Rutles, it sounds like it was recorded in 1980, not the '60s, which intensifies the feeling that *Deface the Music* is merely a curiosity or an exercise for Rundgren, but since the entire thing is finished in just over a half hour, it feels more like a burst of cynical joy that is damn near impossible to resist.

Stephen Thomas Erlewine

Swing to the Right
March 1982, Bearsville/Rhino

Utopia wandered into the wilderness with *Deface the Music*, losing much of the audience they won with *Adventures in Utopia*. If its follow-up *Swing to the Right* is any indication, the band didn't really care, since they doggedly pursue a weird fusion of new wave pop, arena rock, and soul, all spiked with social commentary. According to some reports, Bearsville didn't want to release the album, relenting only after considerable pressure from Rundgren, who defended it as the group effort it certainly is. In fact, *Swing to the Right* marks the beginning of Utopia Mach III, when each member pulled equal weight as composers and frontmen—at times, it's hard to tell who contributed what, or even who takes lead vocals. Admittedly, Rundgren's efforts are the strongest—"Lysistrata" condenses a Greek play into a three-minute pop gem, and "One World," a silly but catchy "love is all you need" chant. Both songs accentuate the anti-Reagan theme of *Swing to the Right*, which is clearly telegraphed by the album's title. True, the message can be a little fuzzy, yet each song has a loose anti-conservative theme, including their cover of the O'Jays' "For the Love of Money," which also provides a musical keynote for this new wave-soul-inflected record. Unfortunately, this all reads better than it plays. Apart from the aforementioned Rundgren numbers and (possibly) the title track, no songs make a lasting impression, as Utopia's pop instincts fail them for the first time since *Oops! Wrong Planet*. As a Reagan-era curiosity, however, it's intermittently fascinating.

Stephen Thomas Erlewine

Utopia
September 1982, Unidisc

Utopia followed *Swing to the Right*, their first album for Elektra subsidiary Network, a mere six months after, dubbing the new album *Utopia*. Presumably, an eponymous release signaled a new beginning for the group, which is true to a certain extent. Utopia finally became a true collective here, with each member's contributions sounding remarkably similar, in performance and composition. Very few tunes bear an unmistakable Rundgren stamp, and even when they do, it's been processed into a signature Utopia sound—the first time they could truly be said to have a sound of their own. Strangely, this happens on an album where the group makes a self-conscious effort to sound contemporary, dressing in new wave gear for the cover shoot while molding the music after synthesized new wave pop. Granted, that quirkiness masks a fairly traditional set of Utopia arena pop, yet these songs wind up as the most consistent album in the group's catalog—which is saying a lot, considering that the album spreads over three sides. *Utopia* rarely sags in momentum, and even the weaker songs aren't far removed from the stronger material, highlighted by "Bad Little Actress," "Hammer in My Heart," "Princess of the Universe," and the excellent single "Feet Don't Fail Me Now." They had their moments before, but *Utopia* is where the band finally made a thoroughly enjoyable record; too bad they couldn't extend it through their final two records.

Stephen Thomas Erlewine

Anthology (1974–1985)
May 1989, Rhino

For all their many attributes, Utopia was notoriously uneven on record. They were just as capable of turning out great pop tunes as they were to wander into meandering jams or directionless hard rock—and this applies not only to their earliest art rock records, but also to their mainstream pop/rock albums. That's what makes Rhino's *Anthology (1974-1985)* such a welcome addition to their catalog. There may be a few great songs missing ("Hammer in My Heart," for example) and the three prog rock songs that appear toward the end of the album are a bit of a downer, but the remaining 13 tracks capture Utopia at their absolute best. The group may have attempted to cover more ground in their early prog rock incarnation, but often those records meandered, which meant that the songs only made sense on the original albums. Once they gave themselves over to pop/rock with 1977's *Oops! Wrong Planet*, they were still uneven, but uneven pop/rock albums can be distilled into one dynamic collection. And that's what happens here. "Crybaby," "The Very Last Time," "Set Me Free," "Love in Action," "Love Is the Answer," "You Make Me Crazy," "Lysistrata," "Feet Don't Fail Me Now" and "I Just Want to Touch You" were undisputed highlights on their respective albums, and hearing them all in a row is a sheer delight. Taken together, they argue that Utopia's records were better and more consistent than they actually were, but the fact is, *Anthology (1974-1985)* is "the definitive Utopia album," as Bud Scoppa writes in the liner notes. For Rundgren fans who love his solo records but never quite "got" Utopia, this is the only Utopia record they need.

Stephen Thomas Erlewine

Van Halen

Van Halen
February 1978, Warner Bros.

Among revolutionary rock albums, Van Halen's debut often gets short shrift. Although it altered perceptions of what the guitar could do, it is not spoken of in the same reverential tones as *Are You Experienced?* and although it set the template for how 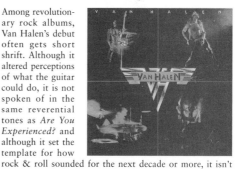 rock & roll sounded for the next decade or more, it isn't seen as an epochal generational shift, like *Led Zeppelin*, *The Ramones*, *The Rolling Stones*, or *Never Mind the Bollocks Here's the Sex Pistols*, which was released just the year before. But make no mistake, *Van Halen* is as monumental, as seismic as those records, but part of the reason it's never given the same due is that there's no pretension, nothing self-conscious about it. In the best sense, it is an artless record, in the sense that it doesn't seem contrived, but it's also a great work of art because it's an effortless, guileless expression of what the band is all about, and what it would continue to be over the years. The band did get better, tighter, over the years—peaking with their sleek masterpiece *1984*, where there was no fat, nothing untidy—but everything was in place here, from the robotic pulse of Michael Anthony and Alex Van Halen, to the gonzo shtick of David Lee Roth to the astonishing guitar of Eddie Van Halen. There may have been antecedents to this sound—perhaps you could trace Diamond Dave's shuck-n-jive to Black Oak Arkansas' Jim Dandy, the slippery blues-less riffs hearken back to Aerosmith—but *Van Halen*, to this day, sounds utterly unprecedented, as if it was a dispatch from a distant star. Some of the history behind the record has become rock lore: Eddie may have slowed down Cream records to a crawl to learn how Clapton played "Crossroads"—the very stuff legends are made of—but it's hard to *hear* Clapton here. It's hard to hear anybody else really, even with the traces of their influences, or the cover of "You Really Got Me," which doesn't seem as if it were chosen because of any great love of the Kinks, but rather because that riff got the crowd going. And that's true of all 11 songs here: they're songs designed to get a rise out of the audience, designed to get them to have a good time, and the album still crackles with energy because of it.

Sheer visceral force is one thing, but originality is another, and the still-amazing thing about *Van Halen* is how it sounds like it has no fathers. Plenty other bands followed this template in the '80s, but like all great originals *Van Halen* doesn't seem to belong to the past and it still sounds like little else, despite generations of copycats. Listen to how "Runnin' with the Devil" opens the record with its mammoth, confident riff and realize that there was no other band that sounded this way—maybe Montrose or Kiss were this far removed from the blues, but they didn't have the down-and-dirty hedonistic vibe that Van Halen did; Aerosmith certainly had that, but they were fueled by blooze and boogie, concepts that seem alien here. Everything about Van Halen is oversized: the rhythms are primal, often simple, but that gives Dave and Eddie room to run *wild*, and they do. They are larger than life, whether it's Dave strutting, slyly spinning dirty jokes and come-ons, or Eddie throwing out mind-melting guitar riffs with a smile. And of course, this record belongs to Eddie, just like the band's very name does. There was nothing, *nothing* like his furious flurry of notes on his solos, showcased on "Eruption," a startling fanfare for his gifts: Steve Howe may have tapped before, but nothing like Eddie's fluid, lightning runs. He makes sounds that were unimagined before this album, and they still sound nearly inconceivable. But, at least at this point, these songs were never vehicles for Van Halen's playing; they were true blue, bone-crunching rockers, not just great riffs but full-fledged anthems, like "Jamie's Cryin'," "Atomic Punk," and "Ain't Talkin' 'Bout Love," songs that changed rock & roll and still are monolithic slabs of rock to this day. They still sound vital, surprising, and ultimately fun—and really revolutionary, because no other band rocked like this before Van Halen, and it's still a giddy thrill to hear them discover a new way to rock on this stellar, seminal debut.

Stephen Thomas Erlewine

Van Halen II
March 1979, Warner Bros.

It's called *Van Halen II* not just because it's the band's second album but because it's virtually a carbon copy of their 1978 debut, right down to how the band showcases their prowess via covers and how Eddie Van Halen gets a brief, shining moment to showcase his guitar genius. This time, he does his thing on acoustic guitars on the remarkable "Spanish Fly," but that temporary shift from electrics to acoustics is the only true notable difference in attack here; in every other way, *Van Halen II* feels like its predecessor, even if there are subtle differences. First, there's only one cover this time

around—Betty Everett's "You're No Good," surely learned from Linda Ronstadt—and this feels both heavier and lighter than the debut. Heavier in that this sounds *big* and powerful, driven by mastodon riffs that aim straight at the gut. Lighter in that there's a nimbleness to the attack, in that there are pop hooks to the best songs, in that the group sounds emboldened by their success so they're swaggering with a confidence that's alluring. If the classic ratio is slightly lighter than on the debut, there are no bad songs and the best moments here—two bona fide party anthems in "Dance the Night Away" and "Beautiful Girls," songs that embody everything the band was about—are lighter, funnier than anything on the debut, showcases for both Diamond Dave's knowing shuck and jive and Eddie's phenomenal gift, so natural it seems to just flow out of him. At this point, it's hard not to marvel at these two frontmen, and hard not to be sucked into the vortex of some of the grandest hard rock ever made.

Stephen Thomas Erlewine

Women and Children First
March 1980, Warner Bros.

After two pure party albums, the inevitable had to happen: it was time for Van Halen to mature, or at least get a little serious. And so, *Women and Children First*, a record where the group started to get heavier, both sonically and, to a lesser extent, thematically, changing the feel of the band ever so slightly. Where the first two records were nothing but nonstop parties, there's a bit of a dark heart beating on this record, most evident on the breakneck metal of "Romeo Delight," but also the pair of opening party anthems, "And the Cradle Will Rock" and "Everybody Wants Some!!," which don't fly quite as high as "Dance the Night Away" or "Runnin' with the Devil" because of the tense, roiling undercurrents in Eddie's riffs, especially the thudding, circular keyboard riff propelling "And the Cradle Will Rock." The very fact that a keyboard drives this song, not a guitar, is a signal of Eddie's burgeoning ambition (which would soon become inseparable from his desire for respectability), and there are already some conflicts between this somber musicality and David Lee Roth's irrepressible hunger for fun. Where that tension would eventually tear the band apart, here it just makes for compelling music, adding richness and depth to this half-hour blast of rock & roll. This is the first Van Halen album to consist entirely of original material and there's some significant growth here to the writing, evident in the winding, cynical neo-boogie "Fools" and also in the manic "Loss of Control," which gallops by with the ferocity of hardcore punk. These, along with all previously mentioned songs, are the heaviest music Van Halen has made (or would ever make), but as the album rushes toward the end Diamond Dave pulls them toward his country-blues jive fixation with "Take Your Whiskey Home" and the all-acoustic "Could This Be Magic?" giving the album a dose of levity that is welcome if not necessarily needed. Then, before the album comes a close, the band unleashes its first stab at a power ballad with "In a Simple Rhyme," where the group's attempts at melodic grace are undercut by their compulsion to rock. This may not make for a full-fledged power ballad, but this tension between the two extremes—by their increasing songcraft and their unhinged rock & roll—makes for dynamic music, and captures all the contrasting glories of the album in one song.

Stephen Thomas Erlewine

Fair Warning
April 1981, Warner Bros.

Of all the early Van Halen records, *Fair Warning* often gets overlooked—partially because it's a dark, strange beast, partially because it lacks any song as purely fun as the hits from the first three records. Because of that, there were no hits from *Fair Warning* that turned into radio anthems; only "Unchained" and, to a lesser extent, the grinding opener, "Mean Street," rank among the group's best-known songs, and they're not as monumental as "And the Cradle Will Rock," from the preceding album, *Women and Children First*. There's a reason for that: this album ain't a whole lotta fun. *Fair Warning* is the first Van Halen album that doesn't feel like a party. This may be a reflection of the band's relentless work schedule, it may be a reflection of the increasing tension between Eddie Van Halen and David Lee Roth—the cause isn't important, because whatever the reason, *Fair Warning* winds up as a dark, dirty, nasty piece of work. Gloomy it may be, but dull it is not and *Fair Warning* contains some of the fiercest, hardest music that Van Halen ever made. There's little question that Eddie Van Halen won whatever internal skirmishes they had, since his guitar dominates this record, even with the lack of a single dedicated instrumental showcase (the first time he lacked one on a VH album). Eddie sounds restless here, pushing and pulling the group toward different rhythms and textures, from the disco beat that pulsates on "Push Comes to Shove" to the swinging rhythms on "So This Is Love?" and, especially, the murky synths that comprise the instrumental "Sunday Afternoon in the Park" and the grimy, gunky closing rocker, "One Foot Out the Door." Either inspired or spurred on by the gloomy rock Eddie cranked out, David Lee Roth casts his net far wider than his usual litany of girls and good times. He spits and swears, swaggering without his usual *joie de vivre*, with even his sex songs feeling weary and nasty. Whatever spawned it, that nastiness is the defining characteristic of *Fair Warning*, which certainly doesn't make it bunches of fun, but it showcases the coiled power of Van Halen better than any other album, which makes it worth visiting on occasion.

Stephen Thomas Erlewine

Diver Down
April 1982, Warner Bros.

Fair Warning was such a dark, intense record that Van Halen almost had no choice but to lighten up on their next album, and 1982's *Diver Down* is indeed *much* lighter than its predecessor. In many ways, it's a return to the early albums, heavy on covers and party anthems, but where those records were rough and exuberant—they felt like the work of the world's best bar band just made good, which is, of course, kind of what they were—this is undoubtedly the work of a finely honed band who has only grown tighter and heavier since their debut. As a band, they might be tight, but *Diver Down* is anything but tight. It's a downright mess, barely clocking in at 31 minutes, cobbled together out of five covers, two minute-long instrumentals, and five new songs. By most measures, this should be the kind of slop that's difficult to muddle through, but it's not: it's one of Van Halen's best records, one that's just pure joy to hear. Like the debut, it's a

great showcase for all the group's strengths, from Eddie Van Halen's always thrilling guitar to the bedrock foundation of Alex Van Halen and Michael Anthony's throbbing pulse to, of course, David Lee Roth's strut. Each member gets places to shine and, in a way, covers showcase their skills in a way none of the originals does, since they get to twist "Oh, Pretty Woman," "Dancing in the Street," and "Where Have All the Good Times Gone" inside out, all the better to make them their own. But this isn't complacent; Van Halen is stretching out in different ways, funneling the menace of *Fair Warning* into the ominous instrumental "Intruder," playing with the whiplash fury of a punk band on "Hang 'Em High," and honing their pop skills on the bright, new wavey rock of "Little Guitars" and the sweet "Secrets," which displays the lightest touch they've ever had on record. Combine that with the full-throttle attack on the covers, along with Dave's vaudevillian song and dance on "Big Bad Bill (Is Sweet William Now)"—a shtick that's electrified on the equally fun "The Full Bug"—and the result is a record that's nothing but fun, the polar opposite of its predecessor.

Stephen Thomas Erlewine

1984
January 1984, Warner Bros.

At the time of its release, much of the fuss surrounding *1984* involved Van Halen's adoption of synthesizers on this, their sixth album—a hoopla that was a bit of a red herring since the band had been layering in synths since their third album, *Women and Children First*.

Those synths were either buried beneath guitars or used as texture, even on instrumentals where they were the main instrument, but here they were pushed to the forefront on "Jump," the album's first single and one of the chief reasons this became a blockbuster, crossing over to pop audiences Van Halen had flirted with before but had never quite won over. Of course, the mere addition of a synth wasn't enough to rope in fair-weather fans—they needed pop hooks and pop songs, which *1984* had, most gloriously on the exuberant, timeless "Jump." There, the synths played a circular riff that wouldn't have sounded as overpowering on guitar, but the band didn't dispense with their signature monolithic, pulsating rock. Alex Van Halen and Michael Anthony grounded the song, keeping it from floating to pop, and David Lee Roth simply exploded with boundless energy, making this seem rock & roll no matter how close it got to pop. And "Jump" was about as close as *1984* got to pop, as the other seven songs—with the exception of "I'll Wait," which rides along on a synth riff as chilly as "Jump" is warm—are heavy rock, capturing the same fiery band that's been performing with a brutal intensity since *Women and Children First*. But where those albums placed an emphasis on the band's attack, this places an emphasis on the songs, and they're uniformly terrific, the best set of original tunes Van Halen ever had. Surely, the anthems "Panama" and "Hot for Teacher" grab center stage—how could they not, when the former is the band's signature sound elevated to performance art, with the latter being as lean and giddy, their one anthem that could be credibly covered by garage rockers?—but "Top Jimmy," "Drop Dead Legs," and the dense yet funky closer, "House of Pain," are full-fledged songs, with great riffs and hooks in the guitars and vocals. It's the best showcase of Van Halen's instrumental prowess as a band, the best showcase for Diamond Dave's glorious shtick, the best showcase for their songwriting, just their flat-out best album overall. It's a shame that Roth left after this album, but maybe it's for the best, since there's no way Van Halen could have bettered this album with Dave around (and they didn't better it once Sammy joined, either).

Stephen Thomas Erlewine

5150
March 1986, Warner Bros.

The power struggle within Van Halen was often painted as David Lee Roth's ego running out of control—a theory that was easy enough to believe given his outsized charisma—but in retrospect, it seems evident that Eddie Van Halen wanted respect to go along with his gargantuan fame, and Roth wasn't willing to play. Bizarrely enough, Sammy Hagar—the former Montrose lead singer who had carved out a successful solo career—was ready to play, possibly because the Red Rocker was never afraid of being earnest, nor was he afraid of synthesizers, for that matter. There was always the lingering suspicion that, yes, Sammy truly couldn't drive 55, and that's why he wrote the song, and that kind of forthright rocking is evident on the strident anthems of *5150*. From the moment the album opens with the crashing "Good Enough," it's clearly the work of the same band—it's hard to mistake Eddie's guitars, just as it's hard to mistake Alex and Michael Anthony's pulse, or Michael's harmonies—but the music feels decidedly different. Where Diamond Dave would have strutted through the song with his tongue firmly in cheek, Hagar plays it right down the middle, never winking, never joking. Even when he takes a stab at humor on the closing "Inside"—joshing around about why the guys chose him as a replacement—it never feels *funny*, probably because, unlike Dave, he's not a born comedian. Then again, *5150* wasn't really intended to be funny; it was intended to be a serious album, spiked by a few relentless metallic rockers like "Get Up," but functioning more as a vehicle to showcase Van Halen's—particularly the guitarist's—increasing growth and maturity. There are plenty of power ballads, in "Why Can't This Be Love" and "Love Walks In," there's a soaring anthem of inspiration in "Dreams," and even the straight-up rocker "Best of Both Worlds" is tighter and leaner than the gonzo excursions of "Panama" and "Hot for Teacher." And that's where Hagar comes in: Diamond Dave didn't have much patience for plainspoken lyrics or crafting songs, but Sammy does and he brings a previously unheard sense of discipline to the writing on *5150*. Not that Hagar is a craftsman like Randy Newman, but he's helped push Van Halen into a dedication on writing full-fledged songs, something that often seemed an afterthought in the original lineup. And so Van Hagar was a bit of an odd mix—a party band and a party guy, slowly veering into a bourgeois concept of respectability, something that eventually sunk the band—but on *5150* it worked because they had the songs and the desire to party, so those good intentions and slow tunes don't slow the album down; they give it variety and help make the album a pretty impressive opening act for Van Halen Mach II.

Stephen Thomas Erlewine

OU812
May 1988, Warner Bros.

The somber black and white cover could have been a knowing allusion to *Meet the Beatles!*, but it's really a signal that Van Halen is playing it for keeps on *OU812*, their second record with Sammy Hagar. Indeed, the striking thing about *OU812* is that all its humor is distilled into a silly punny title, because even the party tunes here—and there are many—are performed with a dogged, determined vibe. When David Lee Roth fronted the band, almost everything that Van Halen did seemed easy—as big, boisterous, and raucous as an actual party—but Van Hagar makes good times seem like tough work here. Apart from a few cuts—the countryish hook on "Finish What Ya Started," the slow, bluesy strut "Black and Blue"—the riffs are complicated, not catchy, the rhythms plod, they don't rock, and Sammy strains to inject some good times by singing too hard. It gives *OU812* a bit of a dour feel, not entirely dissimilar to *Fair Warning*, but unlike that early unheralded gem, this isn't a descent into darkness; it's merely a very inward rock record, as Eddie Van Halen pushes the band toward interesting musical territory. Often, this takes the form of jazzy chord changes or harmonies—most evidently on the sleek opener, "Mine All Mine," but also on the otherwise metallic boogie "Source of Infection"—but there's also "Cabo Wabo," the longest jam they've laid down on record to date, and a cover of Little Feat's "A Apolitical Blues" (which could have been a salute to producer Ted Templeman's early glories as much as a chance to do some down-n-dirty blues rock). Of course, there's also a pair of power ballads here, both poppier than the ones on *5150*—"When It's Love" is pure balladry, "Feels So Good" rides along on a gurgling synth—but really, they're red herrings on a record that's the hardest, darkest rock Van Halen has made since *Fair Warning*. And if it isn't as good as that record (even if it's nearly not as much fun), it's nevertheless the best showcase of the instrumental abilities of Van Hagar.

Stephen Thomas Erlewine

Vanilla Fudge

Vanilla Fudge
1967, Atco

In a debut consisting of covers, nobody could accuse Vanilla Fudge of bad taste in their repertoire; with stoned-out, slowed-down versions of such then-recent classics as "Ticket to Ride," "Eleanor Rigby," and "People Get Ready," they were setting the bar  rather high for themselves. Even the one suspect choice—Sonny Bono's "Bang Bang"—turns out to be rivaled only by Mott the Hoople's version of "Laugh at Me" in putting Bono's songwriting in the kindest possible light. Most of the tracks here share a common structure of a disjointed warm-up jam, a Hammond-heavy dirge of harmonized vocals at the center, and a final flat-out jam. Still, some succeed better than others: "You Keep Me Hanging On" has a wonderfully hammered-out drum part, and "She's Not There" boasts some truly groovy organ jams. While the pattern can sound repetitive today, each song still works as a time capsule of American psychedelia.

Paul Collins

The Velvet Underground

The Velvet Underground & Nico
January 1967, Verve

One would be hard pressed to name a rock album whose influence has been as broad and pervasive as *The Velvet Underground and Nico*. While it reportedly took over a decade for the album's sales to crack six figures, glam, punk, new wave, goth, noise, and nearly every other left-of-center rock movement owes an audible debt to this set. While The Velvet Underground had as distinctive a sound as any band, what's most surprising about this album is its diversity. Here, the Velvets dipped their toes into dreamy pop ("Sunday Morning"), tough garage rock ("Waiting for the Man"), stripped-down R&B ("There She Goes Again"), and understated love songs ("I'll Be Your Mirror") when they weren't busy creating sounds without pop precedent. Lou Reed's lyrical exploration of drugs and kinky sex (then risky stuff in film and literature, let alone "teen music") always received the most press attention, but the music Reed, John Cale, Sterling Morrison, and Maureen Tucker played was as radical as the words they accompanied. The bracing discord of "European Son," the troubling beauty of "All Tomorrow's Parties," and the expressive dynamics of "Heroin," all remain as compelling as the day they were recorded. While the significance of Nico's contributions have been debated over the years, she meshes with the band's outlook in that she hardly sounds like a typical rock vocalist, and if Andy Warhol's presence as producer was primarily a matter of signing the checks, his notoriety allowed The Velvet Underground to record their material without compromise, which would have been impossible under most other circumstances. Few rock albums are as important as *The Velvet Underground and Nico*, and fewer still have lost so little of their power to surprise and intrigue more than 30 years after first hitting the racks.

Mark Deming

White Light/White Heat
November 1967, Verve

The world of pop music was hardly ready for The Velvet Underground's first album when it appeared in the spring of 1967, but while *The Velvet Underground and Nico* sounded like an open challenge to conventional notions of what rock music could sound like (or what it could discuss), 1968's *White Light/White Heat* was a no-holds-barred frontal assault on cultural and aesthetic propriety. Recorded without the input of either Nico or Andy Warhol, *White Light/White Heat* was the purest and rawest document of the key Velvets lineup of Lou Reed, John Cale, Sterling Morrison, and Maureen Tucker, capturing the group at their toughest and most abrasive. The album opens with an open and enthusiastic endorsement of amphetamines (startling even from this group of noted drug enthusiasts), and side one continues with an amusing shaggy-dog story set to a slab of lurching mutant R&B ("The Gift"), a perverse variation on an old folktale ("Lady Godiva's Operation"), and the album's sole "pretty" song, the mildly disquieting "Here She Comes Now." While side one was a good bit darker in tone than the Velvets' first album, side two was where they truly threw down the gauntlet with the manic, free-jazz implosion of "I Heard Her Call My Name" (featuring Reed's guitar work at its most gloriously fractured), and the epic noise jam "Sister Ray," 17 minutes of sex, drugs, violence, and other non-wholesome fun with the loudest rock group in the history of Western Civilization as the house band. *White Light/White Heat* is easily the least accessible of The Velvet Underground's studio albums, but anyone wanting to hear their guitar-mauling tribal frenzy straight with no chaser will love it, and those benighted souls who think of the Velvets as some sort of folk-rock band are advised to crank their stereo up to ten and give side two a spin.

Mark Deming

The Velvet Underground
1969, Verve

Upon first release, The Velvet Underground's self-titled third album must have surprised their fans nearly as much as their first two albums shocked the few mainstream music fans who heard them. After testing the limits of how musically and thematically challenging rock could be on *The Velvet Underground and Nico* and *White Light/White Heat*, this 1969 release sounded spare, quiet, and contemplative, as if the previous albums documented some manic speed-fueled party and this was the subdued morning after. (The album's relative calm has often been attributed to the departure of the band's most committed avant-gardist, John Cale, in the fall of 1968; the arrival of new bassist Doug Yule; and the theft of the band's amplifiers shortly before they began recording.) But Lou Reed's lyrical exploration of the demimonde is as keen here as on any album he ever made, while displaying a warmth and compassion he sometimes denied his characters. "Candy Says," "Pale Blue Eyes," and "I'm Set Free" may be more muted in approach than what the band had done in the past, but "What Goes On" and "Beginning to See the Light" made it clear the VU still loved rock & roll, and "The Murder Mystery" (which mixes and matches four separate poetic narratives) is as brave and uncompromising as anything on *White Light/White Heat*. This album sounds less like The Velvet Underground than any of their studio albums, but it's as personal, honest, and moving as anything Lou Reed ever committed to tape.

Mark Deming

Loaded
1970, Warner Bros.

After The Velvet Underground cut three albums for the jazz-oriented Verve label that earned them lots of notoriety but negligible sales, the group signed with industry powerhouse Atlantic Records in 1970; label head Ahmet Ertegun supposedly asked Lou Reed to avoid sex and drugs in his songs, and instead focus on making an album "loaded with hits." *Loaded* was the result, and with appropriate irony it turned out to be the first VU album that made any noticeable impact on commercial radio—and also their swan song, with Reed leaving the group shortly before its release. With John Cale long gone from the band, Doug Yule highly prominent (he sings lead on four of the ten tracks), and Maureen Tucker absent on maternity leave, this is hardly a purist's Velvet Underground album. But while Lou Reed always wrote great rock & roll songs with killer hooks, on *Loaded* his tunes were at last given a polished but intelligent production that made them sound like the hits they should have been, and there's no arguing that "Sweet Jane" and "Rock and Roll" are as joyously anthemic as anything he's ever recorded. And if this release generally maintains a tight focus on the sunny side of the VU's personality (or would that be Reed's personality?), "New Age" and "Oh! Sweet Nuthin'" prove he had hardly abandoned his contemplative side, and "Train Around the Bend" is a subtle but revealing metaphor for his weariness with the music business. Sterling Morrison once said of *Loaded*, "It showed that we could have, all along, made truly commercial sounding records," but just as importantly, it proved they could do so without entirely abandoning their musical personality in the process. It's a pity that notion hadn't occurred to anyone a few years earlier.

Mark Deming

Rick Wakeman

The Six Wives of Henry VIII
1973, A&M

Not only did this album help pave the way for progressive rock, but it also introduced the unbridled energy and overall effectiveness of the synthesizer as a bona fide instrument. *Six Wives* gave Wakeman his chance to break away from the other instrumental complexities that made up Yes and allowed him to prove what a driving force the keyboard could truly be, especially in full album form. More than just synthesized wandering, Wakeman astoundingly conjures up a separate musical persona by way of an instrumental ode to each of Henry VIII's wives through his dazzling use of the Mellotron, Moog, and Hammond C3 organ. For example, Wakeman's fiery runs and fortissimo thwarting of the synthesizer throughout "Anne Boleyn" is a tribute to her feisty temper and valiant courage that she maintained while standing up to her husband. With "Jane Seymour," on the other hand, Wakeman's playing is somewhat subdued and gentile, which coincides with her legendary meekness and frailty, as well as her willingness to cater to Henry VIII. Wakeman's masterful use of his synthesizers is not only instrumentally stunning, but his talent of magically shaping the notes to represent behavioral idiosyncrasies of his characters is itself bewildering. Yes bassist Chris Squire lends a hand on "Catherine of Aragon," while guitarist Steve Howe and drummer Bill Bruford appear on a few tracks as well, as does former Strawbs member Dave Cousins, playing the electric banjo. *The Six Wives of Henry VIII* unleashes the unyielding power of the keyboard as a dominant instrument, but also displays Wakeman at the beginning of an extremely resplendent career as a solo musician.

Mike DeGagne

Journey to the Centre of the Earth
January 1974, Mobile Fidelity

Journey to the Centre of the Earth is one of progressive rock's crowning achievements. With the help of the London Symphony Orchestra and the English Chamber Choir, Wakeman turns this classic Jules Verne tale into an exciting and suspenseful instrumental narrative. The story is told by David Hemmings in between the use of Wakeman's keyboards, especially the powerful Hammond organ and the innovative

Moog synthesizer, and when coupled with the prestigious sound of the orchestra, creates the album's fairytale-like climate. Recorded at London's Royal Festival Hall, the tale of a group of explorers who wander into the fantastic living world that exists in the Earth's core is told musically through Wakeman's synthesized theatrics and enriched by the haunting vocals of a chamber choir. Broken into four parts, the album's most riveting piece entitled "The Battle" involves Wakeman's most furious synthesized attack, churning and swirling the keyboards into a mass instrumental hysteria. With both "The Journey" and "The Forest," it's the effective use of the strings and percussion section of the London Symphony Orchestra that causes the elements of fantasy and myth to emerge from the album's depths. The gorgeous voice of Ashley Holt is effectively prominent, and some interesting guitar work via Mike Egan arises occasionally but meritoriously in amongst the keyboard fervor. The whole of *Journey to the Center of the Earth* still stands as one of the most interesting conglomerations of orchestral and synthesized music, and it is truly one of Wakeman's most flamboyant projects.

Mike DeGagne

Myths and Legends of King Arthur and the Knights of the Round Table
1975, A&M

Rick Wakeman's third solo album is among his best, as he employs his vast array of keyboards to their full extent, musically describing the characters pertaining to the days of King Arthur's reign. With orchestra and choir included, although a little less prevalent than on *Journey*, he musically addresses the importance and distinguishing characteristics of each figure through the use of multiple synthesizers and accompanying instruments. "Lady of the Lake" is given a mystical, enchanted feel, perpetrated by a more subtle use of piano and synthesizer, while the battle of "Sir Lancelot and the Black Knight" is made up of a barrage of feuding keyboard runs and staccato riffs, musically recounting the intensity of the duel. But it's on "Merlin the Magician" where Wakeman truly shines, as the whimsy and peculiarity of this fabled figure is wonderfully conjured up through the frenzy of the synthesizer. As one of Wakeman's most famous pieces, it is here that his astounding musicianship is laid out for all to hear, a marvelous bisque of keyboard artistry. The album's entirety is a sensational execution of Wakeman's adroitness, and with vocals from Ashley Holt and Gary Pickford Hopkins, it still stands along with *Journey to the Center of the Earth* and *The Six Wives of Henry VIII* as one of his most astute pieces.

Mike DeGagne

Joe Walsh

Barnstorm
1972, Mobile Fidelity

Barnstorm, Joe Walsh's first solo album after leaving the

James Gang, garnered him fame not only as a guitarist but also as a songwriter. While it's true that Walsh established himself as a late-'60s/early-'70s guitar hero on the Gang's more boogie-oriented rock numbers, it's Walsh's love of lushly textured production and spacy, open-ended songs featuring both acoustic and electric guitars that is showcased here on this wildly adventurous and forgotten unqualified masterpiece. Recorded at the Caribou Ranch in Nederland, CO, *Barnstorm* reflects the big sky and wide open spaces. Accompanied by bassist Kenny Passarelli and drummer Joe Vitale, Walsh freely indulges himself with fat guitars and keyboards, beautiful choruses, country tinges, and pastoral pop hooks, as evidenced by the glorious opener, "Here We Go." This segues, via the sound of a spooky lonesome wind, into the hauntingly beautiful psychedelic country tune "Midnight Visitor," with elegantly woven acoustic guitars, fat carnival organ sounds, and—of course—the sound of the wind before it slips out the back door. And so it goes with the nearly Baroque psychedelic suite of "One and One," which slides seamlessly into "Giant Bohemoth" (sic) and the rollicking "Mother Says." Everywhere on the album's front half, reverie and American mythological archetypes and history weave together, displacing the listener from the here and now. The openly pastoral country-tinged rock of the album's second half signifies Walsh's considerable gifts as a songwriter who uses his guitar as a dreamy, mercurial narrative device, as signified by the masterpiece "Birdcall Morning"—one of the greatest rock & roll love songs of the early '70s. It is actually mirrored by the sadness and organic bluesy quality of "Home" and the unabashed pop/rock romanticism of "I'll Tell the World," complete with glorious four-part backing harmonies and a crunching guitar crescendo. Speaking of crunch, *Barnstorm* was also the first place that Walsh's classic "Turn to Stone" nugget ever appeared. In its original version, its guitars have far more edge, sinew, and raw power than on its subsequent re-recording. Rather than let it end there, Walsh tips the scales one more time back to the mysterious in the acoustic guitar and harmonica moment "Comin' Down." It's another love song, which evokes the notion of the past as a way of creating a hopeful present. And it just whispers to a close, leaving the listener literally stunned at what has just transpired in the space of 35 minutes.

Thom Jurek

The Smoker You Drink, the Player You Get
1973, MCA

The Smoker You Drink, the Player You Get, Walsh's second solo studio album, continues the heavy and light rock mix of tracks found on his previous release *Barnstorm*. Indeed, the opening two tracks bear this out. The first, perhaps Joe Walsh's most recognized track, "Rocky Mountain Way", comes replete with overly distorted guitars and the obligatory solo. The next song, "Bookends", is a tuneful ode to happy memories. Walsh's ability to swing wildly from one end of the rock scale to the other is unparalleled and makes for an album to suit many tastes.

Joe Vitale (drums, flute, backing vocals, keyboards, and synthesisers — a talented man) and Kenny Passarelli (bass and backing vocals) are once again employed, and once again prove themselves adept at handling Walsh's various styles. The album sees an addition to the backing band in the form of Rocke Grace on keyboards and vocals. The legendary Bill Szymczyk works along with Walsh to handle the production, and takes care of the mixing. Szymczyk's work on this area is as always astounding.

The Smoker You Drink, the Player You Get features some of the most remembered Joe Walsh tracks, but it's not just these that made the album the success it was. Each of the

nine tracks is a song to be proud of. This is a superb album by anyone's standards.

Ben Davies

But Seriously Folks
1978, Asylum

As far as studio albums go, *But Seriously Folks* is Joe Walsh's most insightful and melodic. *But Seriously Folks*, released in 1978, was the album the Eagles should have made rather than the mediocre *The Long Run*. It captures a reflective song cycle along the same thematic lines of *Pet Sounds*, only for the '70s. The album's introspective outlook glides through rejuvenation ("Tomorrow," "Over and Over"), recapturing the simple pleasures of the past ("Indian Summer"), mid-career indecision ("At the Station," "Second Hand Store"), and a melancholy instrumental ("Theme From Boat Weirdos"). The disc's finale, "Life's Been Good," is a sarcastic and bittersweet ode to Walsh's "rock star-party guy" persona which reached the Top 10 on the pop charts and became a staple of FM rock radio. The only way *But Seriously Folks* could have been improved, was to include "In the City," essentially solo Walsh, which unfortunately ended up on *The Long Run* instead.

Al Campbell

There Goes the Neighborhood
1981, Asylum

Joe Walsh's long and varied career has had its ups and downs, to say the least. Here, you see Walsh in good old rock form. The opening track, "Things," pretty much defines it all: drum beat intro, a simple riff kicks in, a few synths, and then Walsh's lead—it's this simple formula that gives the album its charm. This is early '80s rock in its most entertaining and fun form. Walsh's lead guitar is, as always, breathtaking. The rock legend's trademark sound is prominently featured throughout the album, and undoubtedly here he performs some of his finest solos. The only qualm that one can pick is that the whole album is in a much-similar vein. This is classic rock, though: once you start, you want more. *There Goes the Neighborhood* is by far one of Joe Walsh's greatest works, particularly from this era. Indeed, after the three-year absence in solo releases, Walsh proved himself ready and able to adapt to the sound of the time with shocking ability.

Ben Davies

Roger Waters

The Pros and Cons of Hitch Hiking
1984, Columbia

When dissected carefully, *The Pros and Cons of Hitch Hiking* becomes a fascinating conceptual voyage into the workings of the human psyche. As an abstract peering into the intricate functions of the subconscious, Waters' first solo album involves numerous dream sequences that both figuratively and symbolically unravel his struggle with marriage, fidelity, commitment, and age at the height of a midlife crisis. While the songs (titled by the times in which Waters experiences each dream) seem to lack in musical fluidity at certain points, they make up for it with ingenious symbolism and his brilliant use of stream of consciousness within a subconscious realm. Outside from the deep but sometimes patchy narrative framework, the music slightly lacks in rhythm or hooks, except for the title track that includes some attractive guitar playing via Eric Clapton. David Sanborn's saxophone is another attribute, adding some life to "Go Fishing" and "The Pros and Cons of Hitch Hiking." But it's truly the imagery and the visual design of the album that is front and center, since the importance lies in what Waters is trying to get across to the audience, decorated somewhat casually by his singing and the music. With Pink Floyd, the marriage of Waters' concepts and ideas with the talented musicianship of the rest of the band presented a complete masterpiece in both thought and music, while his solo efforts lean more toward the conceptual aspects of his work. With this in mind, *The Pros and Cons of Hitch Hiking* continues to showcase Waters' unprecedented knack of addressing his darkest thoughts and conceptions in a most extraordinary fashion.

Mike DeGagne

West, Bruce & Laing

Mountain
1969, Columbia/Legacy

Frequently classified as the first album by the group Mountain, which was named after it, Leslie West's initial solo album featured bass/keyboard player Felix Pappalardi, who also produced it and co-wrote eight of its 11 songs, and drummer N.D. Smart II. (This trio did, indeed, tour under the name Mountain shortly after the album's release, even performing at Woodstock, though Smart was replaced by Corky Laing and Steve Knight was added as keyboard player for the formal recording debut of the group, *Mountain Climbing!*, released in February 1970.) Pappalardi had been Cream's producer, and that power trio, as well as the Jimi Hendrix Experience, were the models for this rock set, which was dominated by West's throaty roar of a voice and inventive blues-rock guitar playing. Though West had led the Vagrants for years and cut a handful of singles with them, this was his first album release, and it made for an auspicious debut, instantly establishing him as a guitar hero and setting the style of Mountain's subsequent recordings. [Originally released in July 1969 as Windfall 4500, *Mountain* was reissued on CD on April 16, 1996, as Columbia/Legacy 66439.]

William Ruhlmann

Whatever Turns You On
1973, Windfall

Adding a bit of Procol Harum's sound to the mix is exactly what the doctor ordered for this superior second outing from the decision by Jack Bruce and Leslie West to merge their talents. "Shifting Sands" and the Peter Brown co-written "November Song" are amazing expressions for these artists, who break out of what people expected from them to create something important. Bruce does his best Neil Young in this "Helpless" takeoff, and West's guitar adds the bite that was not part of Buffalo Springfield, but the album jacket is just plain terrible, like the Guess Who's *Road Food* taken to an extreme. Had this album found its way into the sublime cover to their first effort, *Why Dontcha*, they might've been

taken more seriously by the critical elite of the day. The underground comic art by Joe Petagno is not the beautiful stuff he has produced since, and is not the eye-catching Robert Crumb work that made Big Brother's *Cheap Thrills* so inviting. Perhaps you can't tell a book by its cover, but that's what marketing departments are for, and the debacle that is the packaging on *Whatever Turns You On* disguises the on-target music finally starting to jell. "Rock & Roll Machine" is West finding a groove and, yes, Mountain keyboard player Steve Knight could have improved this very good song and brought it to another level. Andy Johns' production is a bit smoother, but he still lacks the finesse of a Denny Cordell or a George Martin. There's none of the sparkle that the Beatles' "Revolution" contained, an element that made hard rock radio-friendly. Jack Bruce, on the other hand, is delivering solid music tracks—the Brown/Bruce/West/Laing composition "Scotch Crotch" could've fit nicely on *Disraeli Gears* or *Wheels of Fire*, but not as one of those discs' 45 RPMs. And that's the same problem faced by the *Why Dontcha* album—great musicians jamming out, but failing to find their way around the maze, failing to write a "Can't Find My Way Home" or a "Tales of Brave Ulysses." "Slow Blues" is a fluid West/Bruce vocal combo with piano and slide guitar—superb fun for these guys, but not expanding beyond what they've given in the past. And while this album may be superior to the first, there's also a complacency, and maybe a feeling by the band that the world owed these journeymen something. For fans, it is a nice addition to the collection and great to listen to for a change of pace. For their careers, it sounds like men with a lot to give treading water. The nature of the record industry—executives wanting three million units out of the box and artists wanting to record on their own terms—wasn't the environment to allow a West, Bruce & Laing five or six more discs to catch a wave. It's too bad, because there was something there.

Joe Viglione

Wet Willie

Drippin' Wet
1973, Capricorn

This is the album to start with on Wet Willie, and their real best-of, a surging, forceful concert recording of white Southern soul and blues-rock at its best. The band holds its own alongside outfits like the Allman Brothers—no, this isn't the kind of history-making set  that *At Fillmore East* by the latter band constituted, but it is a great show presenting this group and its members at their very best. The playing is hard and muscular, the singing rich and expressive, and they have serious fun with numbers like "Red Hot Chicken" (stretched to ten minutes) and do a nice, laidback "Macon Hambone Blues," surrounded by crunchy renditions of pieces like "Airport." What's more, they switch effortlessly from a lean, guitar-centered blues-rock to a much funkier, sax-driven sound—maybe it was that diversity that prevented Wet Willie from really breaking big outside of the Southeast. The vibes they were picking up from the audience on New Year's Eve at the Warehouse in New Orleans make this a compelling concert document.

Bruce Eder

Keep on Smilin'
1974, Capricorn

The definitive Wet Willie studio album, bluesier than a lot of their other work, and much of it also somewhat more laidback. Beginning with "Country Side of Life," athe band sounds tight, tuned, and in top form. Their playing is clean and crisp, and the vocals exude a bold confidence. The hit title track is a compelling reggae-country meld that's one of the more interesting and long-wearing country-rock hits of its period. It's surrounded by gospel-flavored material and also one of the neater Stax-influenced tracks ever put down by a white band, "Soul Sister," which is also a great showcase for the Williettes. Other highlights include the acoustic country ballad "Alabama," a major change of pace for this band with some clever lyrical conceits; the ultra-funky "Soul Jones" (which manages to work in a quote from the Allman Brothers), and the soulful rocker "Lucy Was In Trouble," which became a key part of the group's concert sets. The only drawback is that the group didn't quite have enough material to cover a whole album here, and also is a little too loose compared with their live performances, as on *Drippin' Wet*. The 1998 Capricorn remastering has an especially full sound, improving significantly on the original LP.

Bruce Eder

The Who

The Who Sings My Generation
1965, MCA

An explosive debut, and the hardest mod pop recorded by anyone. At the time of its release, it also had the most ferociously powerful guitars and drums yet captured on a rock record. Pete Townshend's exhilarating chord crunches and guitar distortions threaten to leap off the grooves on "My Generation" and "Out in the Street"; Keith Moon attacks the drums with a lightning, ruthless finesse throughout. Some "Maximum R&B" influence lingered in the two James Brown covers, but much of Townshend's original material fused Beatlesque hooks and power chords with anthemic mod lyrics, with "The Good's Gone," "Much Too Much," "La La La Lies," and especially "The Kids Are Alright" being highlights. "A Legal Matter" hinted at more ambitious lyrical concerns, and "The Ox" was instrumental mayhem that pushed the envelope of 1965 amplification with its guitar feedback and nonstop crashing drum rolls. While the execution was sometimes crude, and the songwriting not as sophisticated as it would shortly become, the Who never surpassed the pure energy level of this record.

Richie Unterberger

A Quick One (Happy Jack)
1966, Reaction

The Who's second album is a less impressive outing than their debut, primarily because, at the urging of their managers, all four members penned original material (though Pete Townshend wrote more than anyone else). The pure adrenaline of *My Generation* also subsided somewhat as the band began to grapple with more complex melodic and lyrical themes, especially on the erratic mini-opera "A Quick One While He's Away." Still, there's some great madness on Keith Moon's instrumental "Cobwebs and Strange," and Townshend delivered some solid mod pop with "Run Run Run" and "So Sad About Us." John Entwistle was also revealed to be a writer of considerable talent (and a morbid bent) on "Whiskey Man" and "Boris the Spider."

Richie Unterberger

The Who Sell Out
1967, MCA

Pete Townshend originally planned *The Who Sell Out* as a concept album of sorts that would simultaneously mock and pay tribute to pirate radio stations, complete with fake jingles and commercials linking the tracks. For reasons that remain somewhat ill defined, the concept wasn't quite driven to completion, breaking down around the middle of side two (on the original vinyl configuration). Nonetheless, on strictly musical merits, it's a terrific set of songs that ultimately stands as one of the group's greatest achievements. "I Can See for Miles" (a Top Ten hit) is the Who at their most thunderous; tinges of psychedelia add a rush to "Armenia City in the Sky" and "Relax"; "I Can't Reach You" finds Townshend beginning to stretch himself into quasi-spiritual territory; and "Tattoo" and the acoustic "Sunrise" show introspective, vulnerable sides to the singer/songwriter that had previously been hidden. "Rael" was another mini-opera, with musical motifs that reappeared in *Tommy*. The album is as perfect a balance between melodic mod pop and powerful instrumentation as the Who (or any other group) would achieve; psychedelic pop was never as jubilant, not to say funny (the fake commercials and jingles interspersed between the songs are a hoot). The 1995 CD reissue has over half a dozen interesting outtakes from the time of the sessions, as well as unused commercials, the B-side "Someone's Coming," and an alternate version of "Mary Anne With the Shaky Hand."

Richie Unterberger

Tommy
1969, MCA

The full-blown rock opera about a deaf, dumb, and blind boy that launched the band to international superstardom, written almost entirely by Pete Townshend. Hailed as a breakthrough upon its release, its critical standing has diminished somewhat in the  ensuing decades because of the occasional pretensions of the concept and because of the insubstantial nature of some of the songs that functioned as little more than devices to advance the rather sketchy plot. Nonetheless, the double album has many excellent songs, including "I'm Free," "Pinball Wizard," "Sensation," "Christmas," "We're Not Gonna Take It," and the dramatic ten-minute instrumental "Underture." Though the album was slightly flawed, Townshend's ability to construct a lengthy conceptual narrative brought new possibilities to rock music. Despite the complexity of the project, he and the Who never lost sight of solid pop melodies, harmonies, and forceful instrumentation, imbuing the material with a suitably powerful grace.

Richie Unterberger

Live at Leeds
1970, MCA

Rushed out in 1970 as a way to bide time as the Who toiled away on their sequel to *Tommy*, *Live at Leeds* wasn't intended to be the definitive Who live album and many collectors maintain that the band had better shows only available on bootlegs. But those shows weren't easily available whereas *Live at Leeds* was, and even if this show may not have been the absolute best, it's so damn close to it that it would be impossible for anybody but aficionados to argue. Throughout the '70s the album was seen as one of the gold standards in live rock & roll, and certainly it had a fury that no proper Who studio album achieved. Here, they sound vicious—as heavy as Led Zeppelin but twice as volatile as they careened through early classics with the confidence of a band that finally achieved acclaim but had yet to become preoccupied with making art. There is no better record of how this band was a volcano of violence on-stage, how they teetered on the edge of chaos but never blew apart. This was most true on the original LP, which was a trim six tracks, three of them covers ("Young Man Blues," "Summertime Blues," "Shakin' All Over") and three originals from the mid-'60s ("Substitute," "My Generation," "Magic Bus"), none of them bearing a trace of its mod roots. This pure distilled power, all the better for its brevity, but as the CD reissue boom exploded in the '90s *Live at Leeds* was expanded twice, first as a 14-track expanded single disc containing excerpts of their *Tommy* performance from that February 14, 1970, gig along with all the non-*Tommy* cuts and then, in 2001, as a double-disc deluxe edition containing the entirety of the show. It's a treat to hear more (or all, depending on the edition) of this great performance, all in remastered sound, but there's something to be said for the original LP, which packed a lethal, lean punch quite unlike any other Who album.

Stephen Thomas Erlewine

Meaty Beaty Big and Bouncy
1971, MCA

Meaty Beaty Big and Bouncy has the distinction of being the first in a long line of Who compilations. It also has the distinction of being the best. Part of the reason why it is so successful is that it has an actual purpose. *Meaty* was designed as a collection of the group's singles, many of which never appeared on albums. The Who recorded their share of great albums during the '60s, but condensing their highlights to just the singles is an electrifying experience. "The Kids Are Alright" follows "I Can't Explain," "I Can See for Miles" bleeds into "Pictures of Lily" and "My Generation," "Magic Bus" gives way to "Substitute" and "I'm a Boy"—it's an extraordinary lineup, and each song builds on its predecessor's power. Since it was released prior to *Who's Next*, it contains none of the group's album rock hits, but that's for the best—their '60s singles have a kinetic, frenzied power that the louder, harder AOR cuts simply couldn't touch. Also, there is such a distinct change in sound with *Who's Next* that the two eras don't quite sound right on one greatest-hits collection, as *My Generation* and *Who's Better, Who's Best* proved. By concentrating on the early years—when the Who were fresh and Pete Townshend was developing his own songwriting identity—*Meaty Beaty Big and Bouncy* is musically unified

and incredibly powerful. *This* is what the Who sounded like when they were a great band.

Stephen Thomas Erlewine

Who's Next
1971, MCA

Much of *Who's Next* derives from *Lifehouse*, an ambitious sci-fi rock opera Pete Townshend abandoned after suffering a nervous breakdown, caused in part from working on the sequel to *Tommy*. There's no discernable theme behind these songs, yet this album is stronger than *Tommy*, falling just behind *Who Sell Out* as the finest record the Who ever cut. Townshend developed an infatuation with synthesizers during the recording of the album, and they're all over this album, adding texture where needed and amplifying the force, which is already at a fever pitch. Apart from *Live at Leeds*, the Who have never sounded as LOUD and unhinged as they do here, yet that's balanced by ballads, both lovely ("The Song Is Over") and scathing ("Behind Blue Eyes"). That's the key to *Who's Next*—there's anger and sorrow, humor and regret, passion and tumult, all wrapped up in a blistering package where the rage is as affecting as the heartbreak. This is a retreat from the '60s, as Townshend declares the "Song Is Over," scorns the teenage wasteland, and bitterly declares that we "Won't Get Fooled Again." For all the sorrow and heartbreak that runs beneath the surface, this is an invigorating record, not just because Keith Moon runs rampant or because Roger Daltrey has never sung better or because John Entwistle spins out manic basslines that are as captivating as his "My Wife" is funny. This is invigorating because it has all of that, plus Townshend laying his soul bare in ways that are funny, painful, and utterly life-affirming. That is what the Who was about, not the rock operas, and that's why *Who's Next* is truer than *Tommy* or the abandoned *Lifehouse*. Those were art—this, even with its pretensions, is rock & roll.

Stephen Thomas Erlewine

Quadrophenia
1973, MCA

Pete Townshend revisited the rock opera concept with another double-album opus, this time built around the story of a young mod's struggle to come of age in the mid-'60s. If anything, this was a more ambitious project than *Tommy*, given added weight by the fact that the Who weren't devising some fantasy but were re-examining the roots of their own birth in mod culture. In the end, there may have been *too* much weight, as Townshend tried to combine the story of a mixed-up mod named Jimmy with the examination of a four-way split personality (hence the title *Quadrophenia*), in turn meant to reflect the four conflicting personas at work within the Who itself. The concept might have ultimately been too obscure and confusing for a mass audience. But there's plenty of great music anyway, especially on "The Real Me," "The Punk Meets the Godfather," "I'm One," "Bell Boy," and "Love, Reign o'er Me." Some of

Townshend's most direct, heartfelt writing is contained here, and production-wise it's a *tour de force*, with some of the most imaginative use of synthesizers on a rock record. Various members of the band griped endlessly about flaws in the mix, but really these will bug very few listeners, who in general will find this to be one of the Who's most powerful statements.

Richie Unterberger

Odds & Sods
1974, MCA

Odds & Sods, a compilation of outtakes and rarities from the Who's first decade, is a rather jumpy listen that harbors few songs that could be termed top of the line. Also, since its 1974 release, several of the tracks have been issued on other compilations, or as bonus tracks to CD reissues of legitimate Who albums. Setting your expectations at the appropriate level, however, you'll find much of this worthwhile. "Pure and Easy," "Naked Eye," and "Long Live Rock" were all concert favorites of the group in the '70s; "Glow Girl" introduced some riffs that would resurface in *Tommy*; and "Postcard," John Entwistle's tale of rock life on the road, was one of his better compositions. This also has their very first single, "I'm the Face," recorded in 1964 when the group were known as the High Numbers. The 1998 CD reissue is a must-have even if you've got the original LP, as it doubles the album size with a dozen bonus tracks, most previously unreleased. These include some really interesting items: the Motown covers "Leaving Here" and "Baby Don't You Do It" are taken from demos circa late 1964, the latter track featuring some early guitar distortion freak-out in the solo; "Mary Anne with the Shaky Hand" is the rare U.S. B-side version; there are late-'60s studio versions of *Live at Leeds* faves "Summertime Blues" and "Young Man Blues"; the Rolling Stones' cover "Under My Thumb" and "Water" are B-sides that weren't on an album for a long time; and there are less exciting alternates and outtakes from *Tommy*, *Who's Next* and *Quadrophenia*.

Richie Unterberger

The Who by Numbers
1975, MCA

The Who by Numbers functions as Pete Townshend's confessional singer/songwriter album, as he chronicles his problems with alcohol ("However Much I Booze"), women ("Dreaming From the Waist" and "They Are All in Love"), and life in general. However, his introspective musings are rendered ineffective by Roger Daltrey's bluster and the cloying, lightweight filler of "Squeeze Box." In addition, Townshend's songs tend to be underdeveloped, relying on verbosity instead of melodicism, with only the simple power of "Slip Kid," the grace of "Blue Red and Grey," and John Entwistle's heavy rocker "Success Story" making much of an impact. [The 1996 CD reissue adds three live tracks from a 1976 concert.]

Stephen Thomas Erlewine

Who Are You
1978, MCA

On the Who's final album with Keith Moon, their trademark honest power started to get diluted by fatigue and a sense that the group's collective vision was beginning to fade. As instrumentalists, their skills were intact. More problematic was the erratic quality of the material, which seemed torn between blustery attempts at contemporary relevance ("Sister Disco,"

"New Song," "Music Must Change") and bittersweet insecurity ("Love Is Coming Down"). Most problematic of all were the arrangements, heavy on the symphonic synthesizers and strings, which make the record sound cluttered and overanxious. Roger Daltrey's operatic tough-guy braggadocio in particular was beginning to sound annoying on several cuts. Yet Pete Townshend's better tunes—"Music Must Change," "Love Is Coming Down," and the anthemic title track—continued to explore the contradictions of aging rockers in interesting, effective ways. Whether due to Moon's death or not, it was the last reasonably interesting Who record. The 1996 CD reissue adds five previously unreleased alternate takes and demos.

Richie Unterberger

The Kids Are Alright
1979, MCA

Like the film itself, the soundtrack to the Who's *Kids Are Alright* documentary is frustrating even as it pleases, since it falls short of being definitive. If the film was supposed to explain the excitement and history of the Who, tracing their evolution from mod superstars to arena rock gods, it somehow failed by just not quite gelling together. Similarly, the soundtrack attempts to gather a bunch of live rarities, thereby capturing the band at the peak of their powers, but it falls a little bit short of the mark by hopping all over the place chronologically, adding a couple of studio cuts (including live-in-the-studio tracks) along the way. So, you can view this as a missed opportunity or treasure what's here—and, really, the latter is the preferred method of listening to this album, since there is a lot to treasure here. There's the epochal performance of "My Generation" from the 1967 *Smothers Brothers* show, three performances from Woodstock, terrific television performances of "Magic Bus" and "Anyway, Anyhow, Anywhere," a blistering "Young Man Blues," and the definitive performance of "A Quick One, While He's Away," the version they played at the Rolling Stones' *Rock & Roll Circus*—a performance so good that, according to legend, it's the reason why the Stones shelved the show for 20 years, since the Who just left them in the dust (even if it's not true, it sure sounds plausible, based on this performance). Then, there are some really fine latter-day versions of "My Wife," "Baba O'Riley," and "Won't Get Fooled Again," along with a medley of "Join Together/Roadrunner/My Generation Blues" from 1975, that may not be era-defining, like those mentioned above, but they're pretty damn great all the same (as is "Long Live Rock," Townshend's best Chuck Berry homage and one of the few songs to capture what rock was all about in the '70s and beyond). So, it's a bit too haphazard to really be definitive, but the Who were always a bit haphazard, and if you love them, that's something you love about them. And, in turn, it's hard not to love this album, if you love them. (At the very least, you have to love the cover, which is not just the best portrait of the Who, it's one of the iconic images of rock history.)

Stephen Thomas Erlewine

The BBC Sessions
February 2000, MCA

A fine compilation of 1965-73 BBC performances, the majority of the tracks hailing from 1965-67, although some are drawn from 1970 and 1973. As one of the best live bands ever, the Who as expected come through pretty well in the live-in-the-studio environment, although the arrangements usually stick close to the records. Most of the songs were done by the group for studio releases as well, but there are a few covers that they never put on their albums or singles at the time, making this essential for the fan. Those numbers include the obscure James Brown tune "Just You and Me, Darling," "Dancing in the Street," "Good Lovin'," and "Leaving Here" (although a mid-1960s studio version of that last song was eventually released). Of the other tracks, particularly worthwhile are "Anyway, Anyhow, Anywhere," with its extensive feedback solo, quite a challenge to do live in May 1965; "The Good's Gone," which has a fuzz solo not on the studio version; and the 1970 performance of "Shakin' All Over," which might be the best rendition of that concert staple that they ever did. This does not have a few BBC songs that have shown up on bootlegs; particularly unfortunate exclusions are "So Sad About Us," "Summertime Blues," and their 1966 cover of the Everly Brothers' "Man with Money."

Richie Unterberger

Edgar Winter

Collection
1986, Rhino

Much more than the usual greatest-hits package, *Collection* is a well-thought-out compilation of the very best tracks of Edgar Winter's career. Obviously, his radio hits are here. "Frankenstein," "Free Ride," and "Hangin' Around" were all staples of mid-'70s AM radio. But Rhino Records doesn't kick this set off with any of the "hits," choosing to rock things up with a track from *Edgar Winter's White Trash*, "Give It Everything You've Got," before moving into the mellow blues of "Easy Street," highlighted by Winter's jazzy saxophone work. Also included are the excellent antiwar ballad "Dying to Live" and the melodic and catchy "Diamond Eyes" and "Round and Around." All in all, this is a definitive buffet of Winter, but don't let that stop you from sampling the original platters.

Michael B. Smith

Johnny Winter

Johnny Winter
1969, Columbia

Winter's debut album for Columbia was also arguably his bluesiest and best. Straight out of Texas with a hot trio,

Winter made blues-rock music for the angels, tearing up a cheap Fender guitar with total abandon on tracks like "I'm Yours and I'm Hers," "Leland Mississippi Blues," and perhaps the slow blues moment to die for on this set, B.B. King's "Be Careful With a Fool." Winter's playing and vocals have yet to become mannered or clichéd on this session, and if you've ever wondered what the fuss is all about, here's the best place to check out his true legacy.

Cub Koda

Second Winter
1969, Columbia

Johnny's second Columbia album shows an artist in transition. He's still obviously a Texas bluesman, recording in the same trio format that he left Dallas with. But his music is moving toward the more rock & roll sounds he would go on to create. The opener, "Memory Pain," moves him into psychedelic blues-rock territory, while old-time rockers like "Johnny B. Goode," "Miss Ann," and "Slippin' and Slidin'" provide him with familiar landscapes on which to spray his patented licks. His reworking of Dylan's "Highway 61 Revisited" is the high spot of the record, a career-defining track that's still a major component of his modern-day set list. This was originally released back in the day as a three-sided vinyl double album, by the way.

Cub Koda

Johnny Winter And
1970, DCC

Winter puts together a new band and takes on the assistance of Rick Derringer, who coproduces and provides such great songs as "Rock and Roll, Hoochie Koo."

William Ruhlmann

Steve Winwood

Arc of a Diver
January 1981, Island

Utterly unencumbered by the baggage of his long years in the music business, Winwood reinvents himself as a completely contemporary artist on this outstanding album, leading off with his best solo song, "While You See a Chance." Winwood also plays all the instruments.

William Ruhlmann

Back in the High Life
June 1986, Island

Turning to involved percussion tracks and horns, Winwood turns another musical corner on this sophisticated album, which contains echoes of everything from gospel to Caribbean music. Contains the number one hit "Higher Love."

William Ruhlmann

Wishbone Ash

Pilgrimage
1971, MCA

Wishbone Ash's sophomore release, *Pilgrimage*, unveiled their creative genius after a debut that merely presented them as a boogie- and blues-based rock outfit. The opening track, "Vas Dis," with its jazz bassline, slicing rhythm guitar, and gibberish vocals was their answer to "Hocus Pocus" by Focus (or vice versa as both were released in 1971). "No Water in the Well" is one of the great rock instrumentals of the early '70s as it accentuates the dual lead guitar acumen of Andy Powell and Ted Turner. "Jail Bait" has gone on to become a Wishbone Ash staple as well as possessing one of the more memorable guitar riffs of '70s rock & roll. A conscientious effort seemed to be in place for this band to write and perform material better suited to their gentler vocal tendencies. Where *Wishbone Ash* essentially went full tilt throughout, *Pilgrimage* is a moodier affair that includes beautiful, slower melodies like the brief instrumentals "Alone" and "Lullaby" along with the chilling "Valediction," which should have been an Ash classic but is rarely represented on live and hits collections. Even though this band toned it down a bit for this album, their impressive guitar playing was heightened due to the variance in their songwriting. Next to *Argus* this is the Wishbone Ash album to judge all other Ash albums by.

Dave Sleger

Argus
May 1972, MCA

If Wishbone Ash can be considered a group who dabbled in the main strains of early-'70s British rock without ever settling on one (were they a prog rock outfit like Yes, a space rock unit like Pink Floyd, a heavy metal ensemble like Led Zeppelin, or just a boogie band like Ten Years After?), the confusion compounded by their relative facelessness and the generic nature of their compositions, *Argus*, their third album, was the one on which they looked like they finally were going to forge their own unique amalgamation of all those styles into a sound of their own. The album boasted extended compositions, some of them ("Time Was," "Sometime World") actually medleys of different tunes, played with assurance and developing into imaginative explorations of new musical territory and group interaction. The lyrics touched on medieval themes ("The King Will Come," "Warrior") always popular with British rock bands, adding a majestic tone to the music, but it was the arrangements, with their twin lead guitar parts and open spaces for jamming, that made the songs work so well. *Argus* was a bigger hit in the U.K., where it reached the Top Five, than in the U.S., where it set up the commercial breakthrough enjoyed by the band's next album, *Wishbone Four*, but over the years it came to be seen as the quintessential Wishbone Ash recording, the one that best realized the group's complex vision.

William Ruhlmann

Ron Wood

Ronnie Wood Anthology: The Essential Crossexion
July 2006, Virgin

Most people don't think of Rolling Stones' guitarist Ronnie Wood as a solo artist. His career in pop music has been a long one and is entering its fifth decade. Like his former Faces' bandmate Rod Stewart, Wood has always been a supreme collaborator, even on his own projects. Finally, Virgin Records has issued *Ronnie Wood Anthology: The Essential Crossexion*, a double-disc of Wood's recordings as both a solo artist and as a member of bands like the Creation and the Birds (the U.K. group, not the California one), as bassist for the Jeff Beck Group, lead guitarist with the Faces, on Rod Stewart's early solo records, and, of course, with the Rolling Stones. For the most part, the compilers at Virgin have done an excellent job here. Wood fans could argue over track selections forever, but what you get is a single-disc overview of his solo albums, and another single-disc overview of his work with the aforementioned bands.

Wood's first solo outing, *I've Got My Own Album to Do*, was released in 1974 and it was a shade of things to come, as the first two cuts here "I Can Feel the Fire" and "Cancel Everything" show him working with Mick Jagger and Keith Richards respectively. The former cut also features David Bowie on backing vocals, but it's "Cancel Everything" that offers the real magic: just listen to the guitar interplay between Richards and Wood. Also on the first disc is a live version of "Seven More Days," written by Bob Dylan and recorded at Dylan's *30th Anniversary Concert Celebration*, where Wood was backed by Booker T. & the MG's. Other standouts include his read of George Harrison's "Far East Man," Bobby Womack's "If You Don't Want My Love," and the funky Brit-soul of "Fountain of Love," with horns and Anita Pointer on the backing vocals. The ballads "Always Wanted More" and "Breathe on Me" showcase two sides of Wood's sensitivity. But it's the funkiness of "Somebody Else Might" (with Bernard Fowler) immediately preceding the rowdy rocker "Josephine" that offers a wonderfully and wildly contrasting sonic picture of Wood's range. There is an unreleased track here as well called "You Strum and I'll Sing" with Rod Stewart and Kelly Jones.

Disc two is fascinating more for the cuts from the Birds and the Creation than for the better-known, later material. It's raw and yet derivative of a lot of stuff out at the time. Wood admits that "You're on My Mind," the first song he ever wrote, was inspired by the Yardbirds (no kidding) and recorded with the Birds (who have two singles' worth of material here)—the tune is no great shakes but it's pretty wondrous for its adventurousness within the 45 rpm format of the era. "How Can It Be" has tons of guitar, drum, and even harmonica effects. In his liner notes, Wood comments on the more psychedelic Creation material by simply saying: "Hovering on the verge of something good." OK. But the two Creation cuts here are really a mess, as though nobody knew what to leave out. There are three tracks from *Beck-Ola*, and one from *Truth*; they're earthy with wild guitar effects and a woolly savagery in the rhythm tracks that serves to focus on Rod the Mod's singing style and of course, Jeff Beck's guitartistry. Wood keeps them all from going off the rails while adding some imaginative effects all his own.

There are a whopping eight songs here that represent what must have been a beautiful time in Wood's life, when he was with the Faces and with Rod Stewart (who was always backed by the Faces in the early days, he just emerged as a killer frontman). These cuts include Ronnie Lane's "Ooh La La" and titles from "Every Picture Tells a Story" to "Gasoline Alley." There are only two cuts from the Rolling Stones and they're both from 1981 (when Wood's son Jesse was born); he co-wrote both with Jagger and Richards. The slide workout that occurs on "Black Limousine" is a fine set-ender; it's all rowdy and strutting, but it's really "Everything Is Turning to Gold," that takes the day. It's spooky, funky, and slippery. The raw energy and Charlie Watts' in-the-pocket beat, which everyone else plays all around, is amazing. Ultimately, this *Essential Crossexion* is a treat, a wonder ever revealing the sheer range and depth that Wood has displayed since the beginning. We don't hear often enough about the man, but we should. Highly recommended.

Thom Jurek

The Yardbirds

Five Live Yardbirds
December 1964, JVC Japan

Five Live Yardbirds was the first important—indeed, essential—live album to come out of the 1960s British rock & roll boom. In terms of the performance captured and the recording quality, it was also the best such live record of the entire middle of the decade. Cut at a Marquee Club show in 1964 , *Five Live Yardbirds* was a popular album, especially once Eric Clapton's fame began to spread after leaving the band. Although the album didn't appear officially in the United States until its CD release by Rhino in the late 1980s, four of its tracks—"Smokestack Lightning," "Respectable," "I'm a Man," and "Here 'Tis"—made up one side of their classic U.S. album *Having a Rave Up*, and the British EMI LP became a very popular import during the early 1970s as a showcase for both the band and the playing of Eric Clapton. That album had astonishingly good sound, which was not the case with any of the reissues that followed, on vinyl or CD—even Rhino's compact disc suffered from blurry textures and noise, though it was an improvement over any release since the original EMI LP. The 1999 Repertoire Records reissue is the first CD that matches the clarity and sharpness of the original LP, and along with that improvement, their original concert has been very sensibly expanded with a half-dozen live cuts from roughly the same period, recorded at the Crawdaddy Club. Among them is a killer live version of the Billy Boy Arnold classic "I Wish You Would." There's also a pair of live tracks from German television in 1967—"I'm a Man" and "Shapes of Things"; the two, in a flash, make up for what they lack in perfect fidelity.

Bruce Eder

Having a Rave Up
November 1965, Epic

In its original U.S. vinyl release, this album, comprised of several singles and B-sides plus excerpts off of *Five Live Yardbirds*, was one of the best LPs of the entire British invasion, ranking on a par with the greatest mid-1960s work of the Beatles and the Rolling Stones; it was also just a step away from being a best-of the Yardbirds as well. The contents have reappeared numerous times in many different configurations, but no collection has ever outdone the sheer compactness and high quality of *Having a Rave Up*. One major problem since the 1960s, as with all of the Yardbirds material owned by Charly Records, has been the sound—for years, Charly only had substandard master materials to offer. That situation

improved significantly in the mid- to late 1990s, and Repertoire Records is working from sources that are the cleanest and most impressive to have surfaced on these tracks during the CD era; one suspects that there might still be room for improvement, but not nearly as much as was previously the case—a quick comparison of tracks between this and the contents of *Train Kept A-Rollin'* reveals somewhat superior sound here. The Repertoire reissue also adds 11 songs that cut across the group's history: principally outtakes from later in their careers and some odd studio sides from much earlier, plus the B-side "New York City Blues" (a rewrite of "Five Long Years"), the single "Shapes of Things, and their featured number from the Antonioni movie *Blow Up*, the "Train Kept A-Rollin'" rewrite "Stroll On," featuring Jeff Beck and Jimmy Page in the lineup. There are new notes by Chris Welch that, although structured somewhat haphazardly, give a good account of the history of the varied (and overall stunning) contents of this CD.

Bruce Eder

Roger the Engineer
July 1966, Edsel

Once Jeff Beck joined the Yardbirds, the group began to explore uncharted territory, expanding their blues-rock into wild sonic permutations of psychedelia, Indian music, and avant-garde white noise. Each subsequent single displayed a new direction, one that expanded on the ideas of the previous single, so it would seem that *Roger the Engineer*—Beck's first full album with the group and the band's first album of all-original material—would have offered them the opportunity to fully explore their adventurous inclinations. Despite a handful of brilliant moments, *Roger the Engineer* falls short of expectations, partially because the band is reluctant to leave their blues roots behind and partially because they simply can't write a consistent set of songs. At their best on *Roger*, the Yardbirds strike a kinetic balance of blues-rock form and explosive psychedelia ("Lost Woman," "Over, Under Sideways, Down," "The Nazz Are Blue," "He's Always There," "Psycho Daisies"), but they can also bog down in silly Eastern drones (although "Happenings Ten Years Time Ago" is a classic piece of menacing psychedelia) or blues tradition ("Jeff's Boogie" is a pointless guitar workout that doesn't even showcase Beck at his most imaginative). The result is an unfocused record that careens between the great and the merely adequate, but the Yardbirds always had a problem with consistency—none of their early albums had the impact of the singles, and *Roger the Engineer* suffers from the same problem. Nevertheless, it is the Yardbirds' best individual studio album, offering some of their very best psychedelia, even if it doesn't rank among the great albums of its era.

Stephen Thomas Erlewine

Little Games
1967, EMI

If almost any group other than the Yardbirds had released *Little Games*, it would be considered a flawed but prime late-

'60s psychedelic/hard rock artifact instead of a serious step backward, and even a disappointment. Not that it's a bad album—it just lacks the cohesion and polish of the group's preceding album, *The Yardbirds* (aka *Over Under Sideways Down* aka *Roger the Engineer*). And well it should—although they were nominally the same group they'd been a year earlier, in reality the Yardbirds had undergone a massive shift in personnel since the release of *The Yardbirds*. The departure of original bassist Paul Samwell-Smith in June of 1966 set off a sequence of personnel shifts, bringing guitarist Jimmy Page into the lineup, first on bass and then on lead guitar in tandem with Jeff Beck (while rhythm guitarist Chris Dreja switched to bass), until Beck's exit in November 1966 for a solo career left Page as their lone guitarist. At the same time, the band was forced—by the failure of its single "Happenings Ten Years Time Ago"—to accept a new producer in the guise of Mickie Most, who was currently enjoying huge success with Donovan and had a formidable string of hit singles to his credit with Herman's Hermits, the Animals, et al. The Yardbirds' blues roots and progressive tendencies clashed with Most's pop/rock preferences, and the two sides never did reconcile, much less mesh for more than a few minutes on the finished album. To top it off, the bandmembers were finally seeing some serious money for their live performances (ironically, just as they were hanging on by their fingertips to a recording contract), courtesy of their new manager, Peter Grant, and so were committed to lots of stage work. The overall result was a hastily done and uneven LP with flashes of brilliance. Apart from the title single—one of the better compromises between where the group had been and where Most wanted to take them—the two best cuts were "White Summer" and "Drinking Muddy Water," excellent showcases for the experimental and bluesy sides of the band, respectively; both, curiously, were also virtually thefts, "White Summer" lifted from Davy Graham's arrangement of the 300-year-old "She Moves Through the Fair" and "Drinking Muddy Water" a rewrite of "Rollin' and Tumblin'," a blues standard usually attributed to McKinley Morganfield (aka Muddy Waters). The best of the rest included "Only the Black Rose," a strangely beautiful, moody acoustic psychedelic piece; "Stealing, Stealing," an unusual (for this band) pre-World War II-style acoustic blues complete with kazoo; and "Smile on Me," a hard, bluesy number that could have come from any part of the group's history. The attempt at a catchy rocker, "No Excess Baggage," however, needed more work and better involvement from vocalist Keith Relf; the power chord-laden "Tinker, Tailor, Soldier, Sailor" was a great piece of psychedelic pyrotechnics, but it also sounded more like the Who than the Yardbirds, though it did introduce Jimmy Page's violin bow discourses on the guitar; and "Little Soldier Boy" was a silly psychedelic pop piece more appropriate to the Monkees than the Yardbirds. The album was unintentionally revealing, in hindsight, of the growing schism within the band, as Relf and drummer Jim McCarty's growing embrace of flower power and hallucinogenic drugs came to be reflected in the trippier numbers such as "Glimpses," whereas Jimmy Page was starting to take his blues slower and flashier, and into wholly new territory with that violin bow. One more album or a proper concert might've sealed the deal for the Yardbirds, but instead one more tour sealed the fate of the band. *Little Games* has been reissued in vastly expanded form several times, starting in 1992.

Bruce Eder

Ultimate!
July 2001, Rhino

It had to happen sometime, and after about 30 years of piecemeal Yardbirds compilations, here it is: a lengthy best-

of anthology that manages to cross-license material from the Clapton, Beck, and Page eras. The result is a two-CD, 52-song anthology that includes all of their big hits, most of their outstanding albums tracks and non-hit singles, and a few rarities. If you're looking for one Yardbirds compilation, either as a starter or a summary, this is it. Previous anthologies almost always had to be divided in early 1966 after the "Shapes of Things" single for licensing reasons, but finally you can hear early blues-derived Clapton sides, 1965 ini-

tial British Invasion hit singles, "Shapes of Things," "Over Under Sideways Down," "Happenings Ten Years Time Ago," and the (comparatively slight) highlights of the 1967-1968 Page lineup all in one place. As quite minor quibbles, one could argue that some of the album tracks that were passed over—like "Respectable," "Ever Since the World Began," and "Glimpses"—would have been better choices than some of the cuts that did make it. A few relatively obscure items are included—the late 1963 recording "Boom Boom"/"Honey in Your Hips," the 1965 B-side "Steeled Blues," the 1966 B-side "Psycho Daises," the *Blow-Up* soundtrack item "Stroll On," the weird Italian pop single "Questa Volta"/"Pafff...Bum," and particularly the three pop-folky 1966 songs from Keith Relf's solo singles. Some of those lesser rarities are at cross-purposes with the overall tone of a set largely selected on the basis of quality, rather than collectability. Still, with fine liner notes and packaging, overall it gives the music of one of the greatest rock bands the respectful, high-class presentation it deserves.

Richie Unterberger

Yes

Yes
October 1969, Atlantic

Yes' debut album is surprisingly strong, given the inexperience of all those involved at the time. In an era when psychedelic meanderings were the order of the day, Yes delivered a surprisingly focused and exciting record that covered lots of bases (perhaps too many) in presenting their sound. The album opens boldly, with the fervor of a metal band of the era playing full tilt on "Beyond and Before," but it is with the second number, a cover of the Byrds' "I See You," that they show some of their real range. The song is highlighted by an extraordinary jazz workout from lead guitarist Peter Banks and drummer Bill Bruford that runs circles around the original by Roger McGuinn and company. "Harold Land" was the first song on which Chris Squire's bass playing could be heard in anything resembling the prominence it would eventually assume in their sound and anticipates in its structure the multi-part suites the group would later record, with its extended introduction and its myriad shifts in texture, timbre, and volume. And then there is "Every Little Thing," the most daring Beatles cover ever to appear on an English record, with an apocalyptic introduction and extraordinary shifts in tempo and dynamics, Banks' guitar and Bruford's drums so animated that they seem to be playing several songs at once. This song also hosts an astonishingly charismatic performance by Jon Anderson. There were numerous problems in recording this album, owing to the inexperience of the group, the producer, and the engineer, in addition to the unusual nature of their sound. Many of the numbers give unusual prominence to the guitar and drums, thus making it the most uncharacteristic of all the group's albums. Its first decent-sounding edition anywhere came with the 1997 remastering by Atlantic.

Bruce Eder

The Yes Album
March 1971, Atlantic

The album that first gave shape to the established Yes sound, build around science-fiction concepts, folk melodies, and soaring organ, guitar, and vocal showpieces. "Your Move" actually made the U.S. charts as a single, and "Starship Trooper," "Perpetual Change," and "Yours Is No Disgrace" became much-loved parts of the band's concert repertory for many tours to come. Remastered in 1995, with significantly improved sound.

Bruce Eder

Fragile
January 1972, Atlantic

The band's break-through album, dominated by science-fiction and fantasy elements and new member Rick Wakeman, whose organ, synthesizers, Mellotrons, and other keyboard exotica added a larger-than-life element to the proceedings. Ironically, the album was a patchwork job, hastily assembled in order to cover the cost of Wakeman's array of instruments. But the group built effectively on the groundwork left by *The Yes Album*, and the group had an AM-radio sucker-punch, aimed at all of those other progressive bands who eschewed the notion of hit singles, in the form of "Roundabout," the edited version (sort of "highlights" of the album version) of which pulled in millions of young kids who'd never heard them before. The single clicked, most album-buyers liked the long version and all of the rest of what they found, and the band was made. Remastered in much improved sound and graphics in 1995, look for the version of this CD with a reference to "digital remastering" across the top back of the jewel case.

Bruce Eder

Close to the Edge
September 1972, Atlantic

With 1971's *Fragile* having left Yes poised quivering on the brink of what friend and foe acknowledged was the peak of the band's achievement, *Close to the Edge* was never going to be an easy album to make. Drummer Bill Bruford was already shifting restlessly against Jon Anderson's increasingly mystic/mystifying lyricism, while contemporary reports of the recording sessions depicted bandmate Rick Wakeman, too, as little more than an observer to the vast tapestry that

Anderson, Steve Howe, and Chris Squire were creating. For it was vast. *Close to the Edge* comprised just three tracks, the epic "And You and I" and "Siberian Khatru," plus a side-long title track that represented the musical, lyrical, and sonic culmination of all that Yes had worked toward over the past five years. *Close to the Edge* would make the Top Five on both sides of the Atlantic, dispatch Yes on the longest tour of its career so far and, if hindsight be the guide, launch the band on a downward swing that only disintegration, rebuilding, and a savage change of direction would cure. The latter, however, was still to come. In 1972, *Close to the Edge* was a flawless masterpiece.

Dave Thompson

Tales from Topographic Oceans
January 1974, Atlantic

Either the finest record or the most overblown album in Yes' output. When it was released, critics called it one of the worst examples of progressive rock's overindulgent nature. Jon Anderson's fascination with Eastern religions never manifested itself more clearly or broadly, but one needn't understand any of that to appreciate the many sublimely beautiful moments on this album, some of the most gorgeous passages ever recorded by the band.

Bruce Eder

Relayer
December 1974, Atlantic/WEA

Yes had fallen out of critical favor with *Tales From Topographic Oceans*, a two-record set of four songs that reviewers found indulgent. But they had not fallen out of the Top Ten, and so they had little incentive to curb their musical ambitiousness. *Relayer*, released 11 months after *Tales*, was a single-disc, two-song album, its music organized into suites that alternated abrasive, rhythmically dense instrumental sections featuring solos for the various instruments with delicate vocal and choral sections featuring poetic lyrics devoted to spiritual imagery. Such compositions seemed intended to provide an interesting musical landscape over which the listener might travel, and enough Yes fans did that to make *Relayer* a Top Ten, gold-selling hit, though critics continued to complain about the lack of concise, coherent song structures.

William Ruhlmann

Going for the One
July 1977, Atlantic

Going for the One is perhaps the most overlooked item in the Yes catalog. It marked Rick Wakeman's return to the band after a three-year absence, and also a return to shorter song forms after the experimentalism of *Close to the Edge*, *Tales From Topographic Oceans*, and *Relayer*. In many ways, this disc could be seen as the follow-up to *Fragile*. Its five tracks still retain mystical, abstract lyrical images, and the music is grand and melodic, the vocal harmonies perfectly balanced by the stinging guitar work of Steve Howe, Wakeman's keyboards, and the solid rhythms of Alan White and Chris Squire. The title track features Howe on steel guitar (he's the only prog rocker who bothers with the instrument). "Turn of the Century" and the album's single, "Wonderous Stories," are lovely ballads the way only Yes can do them. "Parallels" is the album's big, pompous song, so well done that in later years the band opened concerts with it. Wakeman's stately church organ, recorded at St. Martin's Church, Vevey, Switzerland, sets the tone for this "Roundabout"-ish track. The concluding "Awaken" is the album's nod to the extended suite. Again, the lyrics are spacy in the extreme, but Jon Anderson and Squire are dead-on vocally, and the addition of Anderson's harp and White's tuned percussion round out this evocative track.

Ross Boissoneau

Drama
August 1980, Atlantic

For this one album, ex-Buggles Geoffrey Downes and Trevor Horn were drafted in to replace Jon Anderson and Rick Wakeman. It rocks harder than other Yes albums, and for classically inclined fans, it was a jarring departure; but it was a harbinger of Yes and Asia albums to come. A newly emboldened Chris Squire lays down aggressive rhythms with Alan White, and Steve Howe eschews his usual acoustic rags and flamenco licks for a more metallic approach, opting for sheets of electric sound. Prime cuts include the doom-laden "Machine Messiah" and the manic ska inflections of "Tempus Fugit." Despite the promise of this new material, the band soon fell apart; Horn went into production, Howe and Downes joined Asia, and Squire and White toyed and then gave up on a pair-up with Robert Plant and Jimmy Page, which was to be titled XYZ (i.e., Ex-Yes and Zeppelin).

Paul Collins

90125
November 1983, Atco

A stunning self-reinvention by a band that many had given up for dead, *90125* is the album that introduced a whole new generation of listeners to Yes. Begun as Cinema, a new band by Chris Squire and Alan White, the project grew to include the slick production

of Trevor Horn, the new blood (and distinctly '80s guitar sound) of Trevor Rabin, and eventually the trademark vocals of returning founder Jon Anderson. His late entry insured that Rabin and Horn had a major influence on the sound. The album also marked the return of prodigal keyboardist Tony Kaye, whose crisp synth work on "Changes" marked the band's definitive break with its art rock roots. "Owner of a Lonely Heart" was a huge crossover hit, and its orchestral break has been relentlessly sampled by rappers ever since. The vocal harmonies of "Leave It" and the beautifully sprawling "Hearts" are additional high points, but there's nary a duff track on the album.

Paul Collins

Neil Young

Neil Young
January 1969, Reprise

On his songs for Buffalo Springfield, Neil Young had demonstrated an eclecticism that ranged from the rock of "Mr. Soul" to the complicated, multi-part arrangement of "Broken Arrow." On his debut solo album, he continued to work with composer/arranger Jack Nitzsche, with whom he had made "Expecting to Fly" on the *Buffalo Springfield Again* album, and together the two recorded a restrained effort on which the folk-rock instrumentation, most of which was by Young, overdubbing himself, was augmented by discreet string parts. The country & western elements that had tinged the Springfield's sound were also present, notably on the leadoff track, "The Emperor of Wyoming," an instrumental that recalled the Springfield song "A Child's Claim to Fame." Still unsure of his voice, Young sang in a becalmed high tenor that could be haunting as often as it was listless and whining. He was at his least appealing on the nine-and-a-half-minute closing track, "The Last Trip to Tulsa," on which he accompanied himself with acoustic guitar, singing an impressionistic set of lyrics seemingly derived from Bob Dylan's *Highway 61 Revisited*. But double-tracking and the addition of a female backup chorus improved the singing elsewhere, and on "The Loner," the album's most memorable track, Young displayed some of the noisy electric guitar work that would characterize his recordings with Crazy Horse and reminded listeners of his ability to turn a phrase. Still, *Neil Young* made for an uneven, low-key introduction to Young's solo career, and when released it was a commercial flop, his only album not to make the charts. (Several months after the album's release, Young remixed it to bring out his vocals more and added some overdubs. This second version replaced the first in the U.S. from then on, though the original mix remained available overseas.)

William Ruhlmann

After the Gold Rush
August 1970, Reprise

In the 15 months between the release of *Everybody Knows This Is Nowhere* and *After the Gold Rush*, Neil Young issued a series of recordings in different styles that could have prepared his listeners for the differences between the two LPs. His two compositions on the Crosby, Stills, Nash & Young album *Déjà Vu*, "Helpless" and "Country Girl," returned him to the folk and country styles he had pursued before delving into the hard rock of *Everybody Knows*; two other singles, "Sugar Mountain" and "Oh, Lonesome Me," also emphasized those roots. But "Ohio," a CSNY single, rocked as hard as anything on the second album. *After the Gold Rush* was recorded with the aid of Nils Lofgren, a 17-year-old unknown whose piano was a major instrument, turning one of the few real rockers, "Southern Man" (which had unsparing protest lyrics typical of Phil Ochs), into a more stately effort than anything on the previous album and giving a classic tone to the title track, a mystical ballad that featured some of Young's most imaginative lyrics and became one of his most memorable songs. But much of *After the Gold Rush* consisted of country-folk love songs, which consolidated the audience Young had earned through his tours and recordings with CSNY; its dark yet hopeful tone matched the tenor of the times in 1970, making it one of the definitive singer/songwriter albums, and it has remained among Young's major achievements.

William Ruhlmann

Harvest
February 1972, Reprise

Neil Young's most popular album, *Harvest* employs a number of jarringly different styles. Much of it is country-tinged, although there is also an acoustic track, a couple of electric guitar-drenched rock performances, and two songs on which Young is ac-

companied by the London Symphony Orchestra. But the album does have an overall mood and an overall lyric content, and they conflict with each other: the mood is melancholic, but the songs mostly describe the longing for and fulfillment of new love. Young's concerns are perhaps most explicit on the controversial "A Man Needs a Maid," which contrasts the fears of committing to a relationship with simply living alone and hiring help. Over and over, he sings of the need for love in such songs as "Out on the Weekend," "Heart of Gold," and "Old Man," and the songs are unusually melodic and accessible; the rock numbers "Are You Ready for the Country" and "Alabama" are in Young's familiar style and unremarkable, and "There's a World" and "Words (Between the Lines of Age)" are ponderous and overdone. But the love songs and the harrowing portrait of a friend's descent into heroin addiction, "The Needle and the Damage Done," remain among Young's most affecting and memorable songs.

William Ruhlmann

Time Fades Away
October 1973, Reprise

Anyone who has followed Neil Young's career knows enough not to expect a simple evening of mellow good times when they see him in concert, but in 1973, when Young hit the road after *Harvest* had confirmed his status as a first-echelon rock star, that knowledge wasn't nearly as common as it is today. Young's natural inclinations to travel against the current of audience expectations were amplified by a stormy relationship between himself and his touring band, as well as the devastating death of guitarist Danny Whitten, who died of a drug overdose shortly after being given his pink slip during the first phase of tour rehearsals. The shows that followed turned into a nightly exorcism of Young's rage and guilt, as well as a battle between himself and an audience who, expecting to hear "Old Man" and "Heart of Gold," didn't know what to make of the electric assault they witnessed. All the more remarkably, Young brought along a mobile recording truck to capture the tour on tape for a live album and the result, *Time Fades Away*, was a ragged musical parade of bad karma and road craziness, opening with Young bellowing "14 junkies, too weak to work" on the title cut, and closing with "Last Dance," in which he tells his fans "you can live your own life" with all the optimism of a man on the deck of a sinking ship. While critics and fans were not kind to *Time Fades Away* upon first release, decades later it sounds very much of a piece with *Tonight's the Night* and *On the Beach*, albums that explored the troubled zeitgeist of America in the mid-'70s in a way few rockers had the courage to face. If the performances are often loose and ragged, they're also brimming with emotional force, and despite the dashed hopes of "Yonder Stands the Sinner" and "Last Dance," "Don't Be Denied" is a moving remembrance of

Young's childhood and what music has meant to him, and it's one of the most powerful performances Young ever committed to vinyl. Few rockers have been as willing as Young to lay themselves bare before their audience, and *Time Fades Away* ranks with the bravest and most painfully honest albums of his career—like the tequila Young was drinking on that tour, it isn't for everyone, but you may be surprised by its powerful effects.

Mark Deming

On the Beach
July 1974, Reprise

Following the 1973 *Time Fades Away* tour, Neil Young wrote and recorded an Irish wake of a record called *Tonight's the Night* and went on the road drunkenly playing its songs to uncomprehending listeners and hostile reviewers. Reprise rejected the record, and Young went right back and made *On the Beach*, which shares some of the ragged style of its two predecessors. But where *Time* was embattled and *Tonight* mournful, *On the Beach* was savage and, ultimately, triumphant. "I'm a vampire, babe," Young sang, and he proceeded to take bites out of various subjects: threatening the lives of the stars who lived in L.A.'s Laurel Canyon ("Revolution Blues"); answering back to Lynyrd Skynyrd, whose "Sweet Home Alabama" had taken him to task for his criticisms of the South in "Southern Man" and "Alabama" ("Walk On"); and rejecting the critics ("Ambulance Blues"). But the barbs were mixed with humor and even affection, as Young seemed to be emerging from the grief and self-abuse that had plagued him for two years. But the album was so spare and under-produced, its lyrics so harrowing, that it was easy to miss Young's conclusion: he was saying goodbye to despair, not being overwhelmed by it.

William Ruhlmann

Tonight's the Night
June 1975, Reprise

Written and recorded in 1973 shortly after the death of roadie Bruce Berry, Neil Young's second close associate to die of a heroin overdose in six months (the first was Crazy Horse guitarist Danny Whitten), *Tonight's the Night*

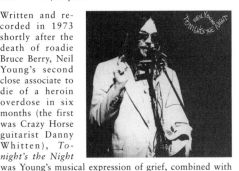

was Young's musical expression of grief, combined with his rejection of the stardom he had achieved in the late '60s and early '70s. The title track, performed twice, was a direct narrative about Berry: "Bruce Berry was a working man/ He used to load that Econoline van." Whitten was heard singing "Come On Baby Let's Go Downtown," a live track recorded years earlier. Elsewhere, Young frequently referred to drug use and used phrases that might have described his friends, such as the chorus of "Tired Eyes," "He tried to do his best, but he could not." Performing with the remains of Crazy Horse, bassist Billy Talbot and drummer Ralph Molina, along with Nils Lofgren (guitar and piano) and Ben Keith (steel guitar), Young performed in the ragged manner familiar from *Time Fades Away*—his voice was often hoarse and he strained to reach high notes, while the playing was loose, with mistakes and shifting tempos. But the style worked perfectly for the material, emphasizing the emotional tone of Young's mourning and contrasting with the polished sound of CSNY and *Harvest* that Young also disparaged. He remained unimpressed with his commercial success, noting in "World on a String," "The world on a string/Doesn't mean anything." In "Roll Another Number," he said he was "a million miles away/From that helicopter day" when he and CSN had played Woodstock. And in "Albuquerque," he said he had been "starvin' to be alone/Independent from the scene that I've known" and spoke of his desire to "find somewhere where they don't care who I am." Songs like "Speakin' Out" and "New Mama" seemed to find some hope in family life, but *Tonight's the Night* did not offer solutions to the personal and professional problems it posed. It was the work of a man trying to turn his torment into art and doing so unflinchingly. Depending on which story you believe, Reprise Records rejected it or Young withdrew it from its scheduled release at the start of 1974 after touring with the material in the U.S. and Europe. In 1975, after a massive CSNY tour, Young at the last minute dumped a newly recorded album and finally put *Tonight's the Night* out instead. Though it did not become one of his bigger commercial successes, the album immediately was recognized as a unique masterpiece by critics, and it has continued to be ranked as one of the greatest rock & roll albums ever made.

William Ruhlmann

Decade
November 1977, Reprise

Given the quirkiness of Neil Young's recording career, with its frequent cancellations of releases and last-minute rearrangements of material, it is a relief to report that this two-disc compilation is so conventional and so satisfying. A 35-track selection of the best of Young's work between 1966 and 1976, it includes songs performed by Buffalo Springfield, Crosby, Stills, Nash & Young, and the Stills-Young Band, as well as solo work. In addition to five unreleased songs, *Decade* offers such key tracks as the Springfield's "Mr. Soul," "Broken Arrow," and "I Am a Child"; "Sugar Mountain," a song that had appeared only as a single before; "Cinnamon Girl," "Down by the River," and "Cowgirl in the Sand" from *Everybody Knows This Is Nowhere*; "Southern Man" and the title track from *After the Gold Rush*; and "Old Man" and the chart-topping "Heart of Gold" from *Harvest*. This is the material that built Young's reputation between 1966 and 1972, although he is more idiosyncratic with the later material, including the blockbusters "Like a Hurricane" and "Cortez the Killer" but mixing in more unreleased recordings as the set draws to a close. He seems intent on making the album a listenable one that will appeal to a broad base of fans, and he succeeds despite the exclusion of much of the harrowing work of 1973-1975. Nevertheless, the album is an ideal sampler for new listeners, and since there is no one-disc Young compilation covering any significant portion of his career, this lengthy chronicle is the place to start.

William Ruhlmann

Comes a Time
October 1978, Reprise

Six and a half years later, *Comes a Time* finally was the Neil Young album for the millions of fans who had loved *Harvest*, an acoustic-based record with country overtones and romantic, autobiographical lyrics, and many of those fans returned to the fold, enough to make *Comes a Time* Young's first Top Ten album since *Harvest*. He signaled the album's direction with the leadoff track, "Goin' Back," and its retrospective theme augmented with an orchestral backup and the deliberate beat familiar from his number one hit "Heart of Gold."

Of course, Young remained sly about this retrenchment. "I feel like goin' back," he sang, but added, "back where there's nowhere to stay." Doubtless he had no intention of staying with this style, but for the length of the album, melodies, love lyrics, lush arrangements, and steel guitar solos dominated, and Young's vocals were made more accessible by being paired with Nicolette Larson's harmonies. Larson's own version of Young's "Lotta Love," released shortly after the one heard here, became a Top Ten hit single. Other highlights included the reflective "Already One," which treats the unusual subject of the nature of a divorced family, the ironic "Field of Opportunity," and a cover of Ian Tyson's folk standard "Four Strong Winds" (a country Top Ten hit for Bobby Bare in 1965).

William Ruhlmann

Rust Never Sleeps
July 1979, Reprise

Rust Never Sleeps, its aphoristic title drawn from an intended advertising slogan, was an album of new songs, some of them recorded on Neil Young's 1978 concert tour. His strongest collection since *Tonight's the Night*, its obvious antecedent was  Bob Dylan's *Bringing It All Back Home*, and, as Dylan did, Young divided his record into acoustic and electric sides while filling his songs with wildly imaginative imagery. The leadoff track, "My My, Hey Hey (Out of the Blue)" (repeated in an electric version at album's end as "Hey Hey, My My [Into the Black]" with slightly altered lyrics), is the most concise and knowing description of the entertainment industry ever written; it was followed by "Thrasher," which describes Young's parallel artistic quest in an extended metaphor that also reflected the album's overall theme—the inevitability of deterioration and the challenge of overcoming it. Young then spent the rest of the album demonstrating that his chief weapons against rusting were his imagination and his daring, creating an archetypal album that encapsulated his many styles on a single disc with great songs—in particular the remarkable "Powderfinger"—unlike any he had written before.

William Ruhlmann

Live Rust
November 1979, Reprise

All the kudos Neil Young earned for *Rust Never Sleeps* he lost for *Live Rust*, the double-LP live album released four months later. *Live Rust* was the soundtrack to Young's concert film *Rust Never Sleeps* (he had wanted to give it that title, but Reprise vetoed the idea, fearing confusion with the earlier album), and likewise was recorded October 22, 1978, at the Cow Palace in San Francisco. But much of the *Rust Never Sleeps* album had been recorded on the same tour, and *Live Rust* repeated four songs from that disc; besides, since Young had released the career retrospective *Decade* in 1977, critics felt he was unfairly recycling his older material and repeating his new material. In retrospect, however, *Live Rust*, now a single 74-minute CD, comes off as an excellent Neil Young live album and career summary, starting with the early song "Sugar Mountain" and running through then-new songs like "My My, Hey Hey (Out of the Blue)" and

"Powderfinger." Young is effective in both his acoustic folk-singer and hard-rocking Crazy Horse bandleader modes. The various distractions of the concert itself and the film, such as the pretentious props and cowled roadies, are absent, and what's left is a terrific Neil Young concert recording.

William Ruhlmann

Freedom
October 1989, Reprise

Neil Young is famous for scrapping completed albums and substituting hastily recorded ones in radically different styles. *Freedom*, which was a major critical and commercial comeback after a decade that had confused reviewers and fans, seemed to be a selection of the best tracks from several different unissued Young projects. First and foremost was a hard rock album like the material heard on Young's recent EP, *Eldorado* (released only in the Far East), several of whose tracks were repeated on *Freedom*. On these songs—especially "Don't Cry," which sounded like a song about divorce, and a cover of the old Drifters hit "On Broadway" that he concluded by raving about crack—Young played distorted electric guitar over a rhythm section in an even more raucous fashion than that heard on his Crazy Horse records. Second was a follow-up to Young's previous album, *This Note's for You*, which had featured a six-piece horn section. They were back on "Crime in the City" and "Someday," though these lengthy songs, each of which contained a series of seemingly unrelated, mood-setting verses, were more reminiscent of songs like Bob Dylan's "All Along the Watchtower" than of the soul standards that inspired the earlier album. Third, there were tracks that harked back to acoustic-based, country-tinged albums like *Harvest* and *Comes a Time*, including "Hangin' on a Limb" and "The Ways of Love," two songs on which Young dueted with Linda Ronstadt. There was even a trunk (or, more precisely, a drunk) song, "Too Far Gone," which dated from Young's inebriated *Stars 'n Bars* period in the '70s. While one might argue that this variety meant few Young fans would be completely pleased with the album, what made it all work was that Young had once again written a great bunch of songs. The romantic numbers were carefully and sincerely written. The long imagistic songs were evocative without being obvious. And bookending the album were acoustic and electric versions of one of Young's great anthems, "Rockin' in the Free World," a song that went a long way toward restoring his political reputation (which had been badly damaged when he praised President Reagan's foreign policy) by taking on hopelessness with a sense of moral outrage and explicitly condemning President Bush's domestic policy. *Freedom* was the album Neil Young fans knew he was capable of making, but feared he would never make again.

William Ruhlmann

Ragged Glory
October 1990, Reprise

Having re-established his reputation with the musically varied, lyrically enraged *Freedom*, Neil Young returned to being the lead guitarist of Crazy Horse for the musically homogenous, lyrically hopeful *Ragged Glory*. The album's dominant sound was made by Young's noisy guitar, which bordered on and sometimes slipped over into distortion, while Crazy Horse kept up the songs' bright tempos. Despite the volume, the tunes were catchy, with strong melodies and good choruses, and they were given over to love, humor, and warm reminiscence. They were also platforms for often extended guitar excursions: "Love to Burn" and "Love and Only Love" ran over ten minutes each, and the album as a whole lasted nearly 63 minutes with only ten songs. Much about the record had a retrospective feel—the first two tracks, "Country Home" and "White Line," were newly recorded versions of songs Young had played with Crazy Horse but never released in the '70s; "Mansion on the Hill," the album's most accessible track, celebrated a place where "psychedelic music fills the air" and "peace and love live there still"; there was a cover of the Premiers' garage rock oldie "Farmer John"; and "Days That Used to Be," in addition to its backward-looking theme, borrowed the melody from Bob Dylan's "My Back Pages" (by way of the Byrds' arrangement), while "Mother Earth (Natural Anthem)" was the folk standard "The Water Is Wide" with new, environmentally aware lyrics. Young was not generally known as an artist who evoked the past this much, but if he could extend his creative rebirth with music this exhilarating, no one was likely to complain.

William Ruhlmann

The Youngbloods

Get Together: The Essential Youngbloods
2002, RCA

Not quite as comprehensive a compilation of the Youngbloods' early years as Raven's *Euphoria 1965-1969*, which starts a few years earlier and has four more tracks, this 2002 release is still the best American collection from the seminal '60s folk/rock/jug band group's formative and most artistically vibrant period. It follows the quartet through their nascent days of the dated, whimsical psychedelic pop of "Merry-Go-Round" and the Jefferson Airplane rock of "Four in the Morning" (complete with a guitar solo that's a ringer for Jorma Kaukonen's style) to their final, mellower period as original member Jerry Corbitt's exit transferred the creative reins to Jesse Colin Young. Seven tracks are selected from each of their three RCA albums, with the only rarity being the previously mentioned "Merry-Go-Round," the B-side to "Foolin' Around (The Waltz)." Even with Corbitt in the band, it was Young's tender, yearning voice, exemplified best on "Get Together," that gave them their identity. Without that song and his singing, they would have likely faded into the mists of history as another '60s combo trying their hands at a moderately successful combination of folk, jazz, and jug band; a wannabe Lovin' Spoonful without a songwriter as memorable as John Sebastian. The Youngbloods' sound never really gelled until their third release, *Elephant Mountain*, not coincidentally the first album without Corbitt. Here, Young's songs like the ominous "Darkness, Darkness"—arguably the band's finest moment—the lovely "Sunlight," "Quicksand," and the beautiful "Ride the Wind" showed the melodic promise only hinted at on their first few discs. The group moved on to Warner Brothers, where they never fulfilled the promise *Elephant Mountain* hinted at, and they disbanded for good in 1972.

Hal Horowitz

Frank Zappa

Freak Out!
July 1966, Rykodisc

One of the most ambitious debuts in rock history, *Freak Out!* was a seminal concept album that somehow foreshadowed both art rock and punk at the same time. Its four LP sides deconstruct rock conventions right and left, eventually pushing into territory inspired by avant-garde classical composers. Yet the album is sequenced in an accessibly logical progression; the first half is dedicated to catchy, satirical pop/rock songs that question assumptions about pop music, setting the tone for the radical new directions of the second half. Opening with the nonconformist call to arms "Hungry Freaks, Daddy," *Freak Out!* quickly posits the Mothers of Invention as the antithesis of teen-idol bands, often with sneering mockeries of the teen-romance songs that had long been rock's commercial stock-in-trade. Despite his genuine emotional alienation and dissatisfaction with pop conventions, though, Frank Zappa was actually a skilled pop composer; even with the raw performances and his stinging guitar work, there's a subtle sophistication apparent in his unorthodox arrangements and tight, unpredictable melodicism. After returning to social criticism on the first song of the second half, the perceptive Watts riot protest "Trouble Every Day," Zappa exchanges pop song structure for experiments with musique concrÈte, amelodic dissonance, shifting time signatures, and studio effects. It's the first salvo in his career-long project of synthesizing popular and art music, high and low culture; while these pieces can meander, they virtually explode the limits of what can appear on a rock album, and effectively illustrate *Freak Out!*'s underlying principles: acceptance of differences and free individual expression. Zappa would spend much of his career developing and exploring ideas—both musical and conceptual—first put forth here; while his myriad directions often produced more sophisticated work, *Freak Out!* contains at least the rudiments of almost everything that followed, and few of Zappa's records can match its excitement over its own sense of possibility.

Steve Huey

Absolutely Free
May 1967, Rykodisc

Frank Zappa's liner notes for *Freak Out!* name-checked an enormous breadth of musical and intellectual influences, and he seemingly attempts to cover them all on the second Mothers of Invention album, *Absolutely Free*. Leaping from style to style without warning, the album has a freewheeling, almost schizophrenic quality, encompassing everything from complex mutations of "Louie, Louie" to jazz improvisations and quotes from Stravinsky's *The Rite of Spring*.

It's made possible not only by expanded instrumentation, but also Zappa's experiments with tape manipulation and abrupt editing, culminating in an orchestrated mini-rock opera ("Brown Shoes Don't Make It") whose musical style shifts every few lines, often in accordance with the lyrical content. In general, the lyrics here are more given over to absurdity and non sequiturs, with the sense that they're often part of some private framework of satirical symbols. But elsewhere, Zappa's satire also grows more explicitly social, ranting against commercial consumer culture and related themes of artificiality and conformity.

By turns hilarious, inscrutable, and virtuosically complex, *Absolutely Free* is more difficult to make sense of than *Freak Out!*, partly because it lacks that album's careful pacing and conceptual focus. But even if it isn't quite fully realized, *Absolutely Free* is still a fabulously inventive record, bursting at the seams with ideas that would coalesce into a masterpiece with Zappa's next project.

Steve Huey

We're Only in It for the Money
September 1968, Rykodisc

From the beginning, Frank Zappa cultivated a role as voice of the freaks—imaginative outsiders who didn't fit comfortably into any group. *We're Only in It for the Money* is the ultimate expression of that sensibility, a satirical masterpiece that simultaneously skewered the hippies and the straights as prisoners of the same narrow-minded, superficial phoniness. Zappa's barbs were vicious and perceptive, and not just humorously so: his seemingly paranoid vision of authoritarian violence against the counterculture was borne out two years later by the Kent State killings. Like *Freak Out*, *We're Only in It for the Money* essentially devotes its first half to satire, and its second half to presenting alternatives. Despite some specific references, the first-half suite is still wickedly funny, since its targets remain immediately recognizable. The second half shows where his sympathies lie, with character sketches of Zappa's real-life freak acquaintances, a carefree utopia in "Take Your Clothes Off When You Dance," and the strident, unironic protest "Mother People." Regardless of how dark the subject matter, there's a pervasively surreal, whimsical flavor to the music, sort of like *Sgt. Pepper* as a creepy nightmare. Some of the instruments and most of the vocals have been manipulated to produce odd textures and cartoonish voices; most songs are abbreviated, segue into others through edited snippets of music and dialogue, or are broken into fragments by more snippets, consistently interrupting the album's continuity. Compositionally, though, the music reveals itself as exceptionally strong, and Zappa's politics and satirical instinct have rarely been so focused and relevant, making *We're Only in It for the Money* quite probably his greatest achievement. [Rykodisc's 1987 reissue restored passages censored on the LP, but included re-recorded rhythm tracks and sounded quite different. Their 1995 re-reissue contains both the original music and content edits.]

Steve Huey

Uncle Meat
June 1969, Rykodisc

Just three years into their recording career, the Mothers of Invention released their second double album, *Uncle Meat*, which began life as the largely instrumental soundtrack to an unfinished film. It's essentially a transitional work, but it's a fascinating one, showcasing Frank Zappa's ever-increasing compositional dexterity and the Mothers' emerging instrumental prowess. It was potentially easy to overlook Zappa's melodic gifts on albums past, but on *Uncle Meat*, he thrusts them firmly into the spotlight; what few lyrics there are, Zappa says in the liner notes, are in-jokes relevant only to the band. Thus, *Uncle Meat* became the point at which Zappa began to establish himself as a composer and he would return to many of these pieces repeatedly over the course of his career. Taken as a whole, *Uncle Meat* comes off as a hodgepodge, with centerpieces scattered between variations on previous pieces, short concert excerpts, less-realized experiments, doo wop tunes, and comedy bits; the programming often feels as random as the abrupt transitions and tape experiments held over from Zappa's last few projects. But despite the absence of a conceptual framework, the unfocused sprawl of *Uncle Meat* is actually a big part of its appeal. It's exciting to hear one of the most creatively fertile minds in rock pushing restlessly into new territory, even if he isn't always quite sure where he's going. However, several tracks hint at the jazz-rock fusion soon to come, especially the extended album closer "King Kong"; it's his first unequivocal success in that area, with its odd time signature helping turn it into a rhythmically kinetic blowing vehicle. Though some might miss the gleeful satire of Zappa's previous work with the Mothers, *Uncle Meat*'s continued abundance of musical ideas places it among his most intriguing works.

Steve Huey

Hot Rats
October 1969, Rykodisc

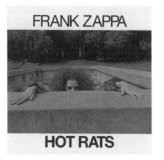

Aside from the experimental side project *Lumpy Gravy*, *Hot Rats* was the first album Frank Zappa recorded as a solo artist sans the Mothers, though he continued to employ previous musical collaborators, most notably multi-instrumentalist Ian Underwood. Other than another side project—the doo wop tribute *Cruising With Ruben and the Jets*—*Hot Rats* was also the first time Zappa focused his efforts in one general area, namely jazz-rock. The result is a classic of the genre. *Hot Rats*' genius lies in the way it fuses the compositional sophistication of jazz with rock's down-and-dirty attitude—there's a real looseness and grit to the three lengthy jams, and a surprising, wry elegance to the three shorter, tightly arranged numbers (particularly the sumptuous "Peaches en Regalia"). Perhaps the biggest revelation isn't the straightforward presentation, or the intricately shifting instrumental voices in Zappa's arrangements—it's his own virtuosity on the electric guitar, recorded during extended improvisational workouts for the first time here. His wonderfully scuzzy, distorted tone is an especially good fit on "Willie the Pimp," with its greasy blues riffs and guest vocalist Captain Beefheart's Howlin' Wolf theatrics. Elsewhere, his skill as a melodist was in full flower, whether dominating an entire piece or providing a memorable theme as a jumping-off point. In addition to Underwood, the backing band featured contributions from Jean-Luc Ponty, Lowell George, and Don "Sugarcane" Harris, among others; still, Zappa is unquestionably the star of the show. *Hot Rats* still sizzles; few albums originating on the rock side of jazz-rock fusion flowed so freely between both sides of the equation, or achieved such unwavering excitement and energy.

Steve Huey

Weasels Ripped My Flesh
August 1970, Rykodisc

A fascinating collection of mostly instrumental live and studio material recorded by the original Mothers of Invention, complete with horn section, from 1967-1969, *Weasels Ripped My Flesh* segues unpredictably between arty experimentation and traditional song structures. Highlights of the former category include the classical avant-garde elements of "Didja Get Any Onya," which blends odd rhythmic accents and time signatures with dissonance and wordless vocal noises; these pop up again in "Prelude to the Afternoon of a Sexually Aroused Gas Mask" and "Toads of the Short Forest." The latter and "The Eric Dolphy Memorial Barbecue" also show Frank Zappa's willingness to embrace the avant-garde jazz of the period. Yet, interspersed are straightforward tunes like a cover of Little Richard's "Directly From My Heart to You," with great violin from Don "Sugarcane" Harris; the stinging Zappa-sung rocker "My Guitar Wants to Kill Your Mama," and "Oh No," a familiar Broadway-esque Zappa melody (it turned up on *Lumpy Gravy*) fitted with lyrics and sung by Ray Collins. Thus, *Weasels* can make for difficult, incoherent listening, especially at first. But there is a certain logic behind the band's accomplished genre-bending and Zappa's gleefully abrupt veering between musical extremes; without pretension, Zappa blurs the normally sharp line between intellectual concept music and the visceral immediacy of rock and R&B. Zappa's anything-goes approach and the distance between his extremes are what make *Weasels Ripped My Flesh* ultimately invigorating; they also even make the closing title track—a minute and a half of squalling feedback, followed by applause—perfectly logical in the album's context.

Steve Huey

Over-Nite Sensation
September 1973, Rykodisc

Love it or hate it, *Over-Nite Sensation* was a watershed album for Frank Zappa, the point where his post-'60s aesthetic was truly established; it became his first gold album, and most of these songs became staples of his live shows for years to come. Whereas the Flo and Eddie years were dominated by rambling, off-color comedy routines, *Over-Nite Sensation* tightened up the song structures and tucked sexual and social humor into melodic, technically accomplished heavy guitar rock with jazzy chord changes and funky rhythms; meanwhile, Zappa's growling new post-accident voice takes over the storytelling. While the music is some of Zappa's most accessible, the apparent callousness and/or stunning sexual explicitness of "Camarillo Brillo," "Dirty Love," and especially "Dinah-Moe Humm" leave him on shaky aesthetic ground. Zappa often protested that the charges of misogyny leveled at such material missed out on the implicit satire of male stupidity, and also confirmed intellectuals' self-conscious reticence about indulging in dumb fun; however, the glee in his voice as he spins his adolescent fantasies can undermine his point. Indeed, that enjoyment, also evident in the silly wordplay, suggests that Zappa is throwing his juvenile crassness in the face of critical expectation, asserting his right to follow his muse even if it leads him into blatant stupidity (ironic or otherwise). One can read this motif into the absurd shaggy-dog story of a dental floss rancher in "Montana," the album's indisputable highlight, which features amazing, uncredited vocal backing from Tina Turner and the Ikettes. As with much of Zappa's best '70s and '80s material, *Over-Nite Sensation* could be perceived as ideologically problematic (if you haven't got the constitution for FZ's humor), but musically, it's terrific.

Steve Huey

Apostrophe (')
March 1974, Rykodisc

The musically similar follow-up to the commercial breakthrough of *Over-Nite Sensation*, *Apostrophe* became Frank Zappa's second gold and only Top Ten album with the help of the "doggy wee-wee" jokes of "Don't Eat the Yellow Snow," Zappa's first chart single (a longer, edited version that used portions of other songs on the LP). The first half of the album is full of nonsensical shaggy-dog story songs that segue into one another without seeming to finish themselves first; their dirty jokes are generally more subtle and veiled than the more notorious cuts on *Over-Nite Sensation*. The second half contains the instrumental title cut, featuring Jack Bruce on bass; "Uncle Remus," an update of Zappa's critique of racial discord on "Trouble Every Day"; and a return to the album's earlier silliness in "Stink-Foot." *Apostrophe* has the narrative feel of a concept album, but aside from its willful absurdity, the concept is difficult to decipher; even so, that doesn't detract from its entertainment value.

Steve Huey

Joe's Garage: Acts I, II & III
November 1979, Rykodisc

Joe's Garage was originally released in 1979 in two separate parts; *Act I* came first, followed by a two-record set containing *Acts II & III*. Rykodisc's reissue puts all three acts together on two CDs. *Joe's Garage* is generally regarded as one of Zappa's finest post-'60s conceptual works, a sprawling, satirical rock opera about a totalitarian future in which music is outlawed to control the population. The narrative is long, winding, and occasionally loses focus; it was improvised in a weekend, some of it around previously existing songs, but Zappa manages to make most of it hang together. *Acts II & III* give off much the same feel, as Zappa relies heavily on what he termed "xenochrony"—previously recorded guitar solos transferred onto new, rhythmically different backing tracks to produce random musical coincidences. Such an approach is guaranteed to produce some slow moments as well, but critics latched onto the work more for its conceptual substance. *Joe's Garage* satirizes social control mechanisms, consumerism, corporate abuses, gender politics, religion, and the rock & roll lifestyle; all these forces conspire against the title protagonist, an average young man who simply wants to play guitar and enjoy himself. Even though Zappa himself hated punk rock and even says so on the album, his ideas seemed to support punk's do-it-yourself challenge to the record industry and to social norms in general. Since this is 1979-era Zappa, there are liberal applications of his trademark scatological humor (the titles of "Catholic Girls," "Crew Slut," "Why Does It Hurt When I Pee?," and "Keep It Greasey" are self-explanatory). Still, in spite of its flaws, *Joe's Garage* has enough substance to make it one of Zappa's most important '70s works and overall political statements, even

if it's not focused enough to rank with his earliest Mothers of Invention masterpieces.

Steve Huey

Warren Zevon

Warren Zevon
1976, Asylum

Warren Zevon was a ten-year music industry veteran who had written songs for the Turtles, backed up Phil Everly, done years of session work, and been befriended by Jackson Browne by the time he cut his self-titled album in 1976 (which wasn't his debut, though the less said about 1969's misbegotten *Wanted Dead or Alive* the better). Even though *Warren Zevon* was on good terms with L.A.'s Mellow Mafia, he sure didn't think (or write) like any of his pals in the Eagles or Fleetwood Mac; Zevon's music was full of blood, bile, and mean-spirited irony, and the glossy surfaces of Jackson Browne's production failed to disguise the bitter heart of the songs on *Warren Zevon*. The album opened with a jaunty celebration of a pair of Old West thieves and gunfighters ("Frank and Jesse James"), and went on to tell remarkable, slightly unnerving tales of ambitious pimps ("The French Inhaler"), lonesome junkies ("Carmelita"), wired, hard-living lunatics ("I'll Sleep When I'm Dead"), and truly dastardly womanizers ("Poor Poor Pitiful Me"), and even Zevon's celebrations of life in Los Angeles, long a staple of the soft rock genre, had both a menace and an epic sweep his contemporaries could never match ("Join Me in L.A." and "Desperados Under the Eaves"). But for all their darkness, Zevon's songs also possessed a steely intelligence, a winning wit, and an unusually sophisticated melodic sense, and he certainly made the most of the high-priced help who backed him on the album. *Warren Zevon* may not have been the songwriter's debut, but it was the album that confirmed he was a major talent, and it remains a black-hearted pop delight.

Mark Deming

Excitable Boy
1978, Asylum

Warren Zevon's self-titled 1976 album announced he was one of the most striking talents to emerge from the Los Angeles soft rock singer/songwriter community, and Linda Ronstadt (a shrewd judge of talent if a sometimes questionable interpreter) recorded three of its songs on two of her biggest-selling albums, which doubtlessly earned Zevon bigger royalty checks than the album itself ever did. But if *Warren Zevon* was an impressive calling card, the follow-up, *Excitable Boy*, was an actual hit, scoring one major hit single, "Werewolves of London," and a trio of turntable hits ("Roland the Headless Thompson Gunner," "Lawyers, Guns and Money," and the title track). But while *Excitable Boy* won Zevon the larger audience his music certainly deserved, the truth is it was a markedly inferior album; while it had all the bile of *Warren Zevon*, and significantly raised Zevon's dark-humor factor, it was often obvious where his previous album had been subtle, and while all 11 tracks on *Warren Zevon* were strong and compelling, two of the nine tunes on *Excitable Boy*—"Johnny Strike Up the Band" and "Nighttime in the Switching Yard"—sound like they're just taking up space. Musically, most of *Excitable Boy* is stuck in a polished but unexceptional FM pop groove, and only "Veracruz" hints at the artful intelligence of *Warren Zevon*'s finest moments. It's hard to say if Zevon was feeling uninspired or just dumbing himself down when he made *Excitable Boy*, but while it made him famous, it lacks the smarts and substance of his best work.

Mark Deming

Bad Luck Streak in Dancing School
1980, Elektra

Excitable Boy earned Warren Zevon a hit single ("Werewolves of London") and the mainstream success he richly deserved, but his new fame came with a price; the hard-living Zevon did not react well to the temptations that come with rock stardom, and in the wake of *Excitable Boy* he had developed a severe drinking problem. *Bad Luck Streak in Dancing School* was cut as Zevon was working hard to stay clean and sober and put his career back on track, and it projects an ambition and strength of focus that was decidedly absent from *Excitable Boy*. The album's rockers hit harder and cut deeper than any of his previous work, especially the twisted Southern gothic of "Play It All Night Long" and the mercenary's anthem "Jungle Work," while "Bed of Coals" and "Wild Age" found Zevon bravely addressing his own failings and expressing his need for a greater maturity in his life. While the album was still short on subtlety compared to 1976's *Warren Zevon*, "Empty Handed Heart" proved Zevon could still write a straightforward song about love (not a happy one), but no one expected that from him anyway), and the two interludes for orchestra gave credence to Zevon's claims that he planned to write a symphony some day (and that it might even be worth hearing). And if "Gorilla You're a Desperado" was a throwaway, it was a better waste of time than "Night Time in the Switching Yard" on *Excitable Boy*. While *Bad Luck Streak in Dancing School* didn't quite return Zevon to the top of his game, it made clear that the quality of *Warren Zevon* was no fluke, and is a stronger effort than *Excitable Boy* in nearly every respect.

Mark Deming

Stand in the Fire
1981, Asylum

After the release of Warren Zevon's fourth album, *Bad Luck Streak in Dancing School*, he was clean and sober for the first time in years, and on-stage he was determined to make the most of his newfound strength and self-control. While his songs long had a dark and frantic undercurrent, Zevon was now capable of playing a no-holds-barred rock show where he could bring the sharper edges of his music to the forefront. Anyone who saw Zevon on what he called "The Dog Ate the Part We Didn't Like Tour" can attest to the fact he was in superb form, playing music that rocked hard while displaying intelligence, passion, and a sharply corrosive wit, and *Stand in the Fire*, recorded during a five-night stand at L.A.'s Roxy near the end of the tour, captures Zevon and his band at their peak. The musicians (anchored by flashy lead guitarist David Landau) pour out these tunes with plenty of fire, and the songs rock a lot harder than anything Zevon had summoned in the studio at that point. And the artist proved he was a superb rock & roll frontman on this tour, singing with mean-spirited glee (for a change, "Werewolves

of London" and "I'll Sleep When I'm Dead" sound just as menacing as they were meant to be) and spewing hilarious bile at every turn (his ad-libbed "the Ayatollah has his problems, too" on "Mohammed's Radio" alone is worth the price of admission). The set list is dominated by Zevon's better-known tunes of the period, though there are two otherwise unrecorded originals (the OK title cut and the blazing "The Sin"), and a rave-up encore on "Bo Diddley's a Gunslinger" that revels in the joyous surrealism of the lyrics, and if one might have hoped for a more imaginative selection of material, these guys nail everything on deck. No one argues that Warren Zevon is a gifted singer and songwriter, but *Stand in the Fire* proves that, when he wants to, he can also rock with the best of 'em.

Mark Deming

The Envoy
1982, Asylum

While moderation was never Warren Zevon's strong suit, his efforts to clean himself up in the early '80s resulted in two of his finest albums, 1980's literate but corrosive *Bad Luck Streak in Dancing School* and the following year's explosive live set *Stand in the Fire*. It seemed as if the wired chaos of Zevon's personal life had been channeled into his art on those LPs, but after another bout with the bottle and another attempt at sobriety, Zevon tried another approach at merging his music and his life on 1982's *The Envoy*. On *The Envoy*'s best songs, Zevon tackles his dangerous appetites head on; "Charlie's Medicine" is a chilling requiem for a drug dealer who used to sell him dope, "Jesus Mentioned" is a spare but curiously moving meditation on the death of Elvis Presley, who "went walking on the water with his pills," and the ragged but right "Ain't That Pretty at All" is an unlikely but powerful recovery anthem in which he howls "I'd rather feel bad than not feel anything at all." When Zevon confronts his own demons on *The Envoy*, the album is intense and compelling stuff, but unfortunately there aren't enough of these moments to prop up the rest of the set, which is smart and literate but not especially exciting. Novelist Thomas McGuane co-wrote "The Overdraft," a hard-charging rocker that unfortunately doesn't make much sense, while the languid "The Hula Hula Boys" plays like a joke in which the punch line got lost, and the two love songs, "Let Nothing Come Between You" and "Looking for the Next Best Thing," manage to sound at once heartfelt and like lesser variations on themes he'd covered with greater strength before. *The Envoy* would prove to be Zevon's last album for five years after he took another stumble into addiction, but while it's an often brave and ambitious disc, the high points don't quite redeem its weaknesses.

Mark Deming

Sentimental Hygiene
1987, Virgin

After a rather well-publicized fall off the wagon following the release of *The Envoy*, Warren Zevon went five years without releasing an album, but his time in the woodshed seemed to have done him good, as *Sentimental Hygiene* was his strongest album since *Warren Zevon* in 1976. While a few members of the L.A. Mellow Mafia (David Lindley, Waddy Wachtel, Don Henley) made cameo appearances on the album, for most of the sessions Zevon worked with Peter Buck, Mike Mills, and Bill Berry of R.E.M., who were about a year away from their mainstream commercial breakthrough; they made for a solid, no-nonsense rhythm section, and gave the music a passionate, forceful backbone that was largely absent from *The Envoy* (not to mention rocking harder than one might expect from the kings of jangle pop). Zevon put his newly muscular sound to good use; the songs on *Sentimental Hygiene* are Warren Zevon at his flintiest, as he indulges in his usual obsessions with machismo ("Boom Boom Mancini") and bad love (the title cut) while also exploring the media's skewed perspective on his addiction problems ("Detox Mansion," "Trouble Waiting to Happen"), his disgust with the music business ("Even a Dog Can Shake Hands"), and errors in both personal and political judgement ("Bad Karma," "Leave My Monkey Alone"). And Zevon scored three inspired musical guest shots on the album—Neil Young, whose jagged guitar runs embroider the title cut; Bob Dylan, whose howling harmonica is the ideal punctuation for the Springsteen-gone-psychotic "The Factory"; and George Clinton, who adds a bed of menacing funk to "Leave My Monkey Alone." *Sentimental Hygiene* proved that Warren Zevon was still an artist to be reckoned with, and that which didn't kill him had only made him stronger (and more bitterly funny).

Mark Deming

The Zombies

Odessey and Oracle
1968, CBS

Odessey and Oracle was one of the flukiest (and best) albums of the 1960s, and one of the most enduring long-players to come out of the entire British psychedelic boom, mixing trippy melodies, ornate choruses, and lush Mellotron sounds with a solid hard rock base. But it was overlooked completely in England and barely got out in America (with a big push by Al Kooper, who was then a Columbia Records producer); and it was neglected in the U.S. until the single "Time of the Season," culled from the album, topped the charts nearly two years after it was recorded, by which time the group was long disbanded. Ironically, at the time of its recording in the summer of 1967, permanency was not much on the minds of the bandmembers. *Odessey and Oracle* was intended as a final statement, a bold last hurrah, having worked hard for three years only to see the quality of their gigs decline as the hits stopped coming. The results are consistently pleasing, surprising, and challenging: "Hung Up on a Dream" and "Changes" are some of the most powerful psychedelic pop/rock ever heard out of England, with a solid rhythm section, a hot Mellotron sound, and chiming, hard guitar, as well as highly melodic piano. "Changes" also benefits from radiant singing. "This Will Be Our Year" makes use of trumpets (one of the very few instances of real

overdubbing) in a manner reminiscent of "Penny Lane"; and then there's "Time of the Season," the most well-known song in their output and a white soul classic. Not all of the album is that inspired, but it's all consistently interesting and very good listening, and superior to most other psychedelic albums this side of the Beatles' best and Pink Floyd's early work. Indeed, the only complaint one might have about the original LP is its relatively short running time, barely over 30 minutes, but even that's refreshing in an era where most musicians took their time making their point, and most of the CD reissues have bonus tracks to fill out the space available.

Bruce Eder

Zombie Heaven
November 1997, Big Beat

Sometimes boxed sets are just handy to have around, just to get all of the tracks that count (or all of a group's recordings) together in one place. Other times, however, they're a scintillating musical and educational experience even for longtime fans, and that's the case with *Zombie Heaven*. The group is mostly known here for their three major hits, although reissues showcasing different aspects of their history have been available for years. But even for this longtime fan, hearing their Brit-beat R&B stylings all in one place was a near-revelation, showcasing performing talent that was a good match for anyone in the Beatles' line-up and composers, in Rod Argent and, to a lesser degree, Chris White (who sounds like he's slipping into a Dylan thing on "I Don't Want To Know"), that could generate the occasional classic. They were far more than a three-song band, as just about every second of the 280 minutes of this box keeps reminding us. The set is broken down into four distinct parts, the first disc profiling the group's singles and B-sides, and their one Decca-release album, *Begin Here*, all in the best sound they've ever had or likely ever will have; Disc Two comprises their *Odessey & Oracle* album (sounding much better here than it does on the Rhino CD), and the surviving tracks of various post-Zombies and Zombies-in-name-only projects put together in the wake of "Time of the Season's" success, and one lost group classic, Rod Argent's "If It Don't Work Out," which became much better known in the hands of Dusty Springfield; Disc Three is made up of various outtakes, work-in-progress, and alternate versions of their songs and demos, some of them sounding really raw and hard, as well as one radio promo for the movie *Bunny Lake Is Missing*, in which the group was featured in a small part (blink and you may miss them); and Disc Four, maybe the most rewarding of all, featuring their complete BBC appearances, parts of which (but not the 29 tracks here) turned up on a Rhino LP some 17 years ago. Some tracks are better than others—their cover of "You Really Got A Hold On Me/Bring It On Home To Me" is one of the better British homages to Motown, lagging behind the Beatles' version on emotional wattage but winning points for subtlety—but except for a few of the late '60s outtakes, there's not a seconde-rate song here, and the sound puts all prior versions of this material to shame. And the notes will keep fans busy reading for weeks.

Bruce Eder

Absolutely the Best
July 1999, Fuel 2000

At the time of its release, *Absolutely the Best* was, indeed, absolutely the best single-disc Zombies collection available in the U.S. Of course the big hits "She's Not There," "Tell Her No," and "Time of the Season" were included, along with the group's minor U.S. chart entries "She's Coming Home," "I Want You Back Again," "Just out of Reach," and "Imagine the Swan," and some good album tracks. With 16 cuts in just over 40 minutes, this is not a comprehensive compilation, but for most fans who know only the three big hits and would welcome some similar sounding material, it's plenty.

William Ruhlmann

ZZ Top

Rio Grande Mud
1972, Warner Bros.

With their second album, *Rio Grande Mud*, ZZ Top uses the sound they sketched out on their debut as a blueprint, yet they tweak it in slight but important ways. The first difference is the heavier, more powerful sound, turning the boogie guitars into a locomotive force. There are slight production flares that date this as a 1972 record, but for the most part, this is a straight-ahead, dirty blues-rock difference. Essentially like the first album, then. That's where the second difference comes in—they have a much better set of songs this time around, highlighted by the swaggering shuffle "Just Got Paid," the pile-driving boogie "Bar-B-Q," the slide guitar workout "Apologies to Pearly," and two Dusty Hill-sung numbers, "Francine" and "Chevrolet." There are still a couple of tracks that don't quite gel and their fuzz-blues still can sound a little one-dimensional at times, but *Rio Grande Mud* is the first flowering of ZZ Top as a great, down-n-dirty blooze rock band.

Stephen Thomas Erlewine

Tres Hombres
1973, Warner Bros.

Tres Hombres is the record that brought ZZ Top their first Top Ten record, making them stars in the process. It couldn't have happened to a better record. ZZ Top finally got their low-down, cheerfully sleazy blooze-n-boogie right on this, their third album. As their sound gelled, producer Bill Ham discovered how to record the trio so simply that they sound indestructible, and the group brought the best set of songs they'd ever have to the table. On the surface, there's nothing really special about the record, since it's just a driving blues-rock album from a Texas bar band, but that's what's special about it. It has a filthy groove and an infectious feel, thanks to Billy Gibbons' growling guitars and the steady propulsion of Dusty Hill and Frank Beard's rhythm section. They get the blend of bluesy shuffles, gut-bucket rocking, and off-beat humor just right. ZZ Top's very identity comes from this earthy sound and songs as utterly infectious as "Waitin' for the Bus," "Jesus Just Left Chicago," "Move Me on Down the Line," and the John Lee Hooker boogie "La Grange." In a sense, they kept trying to remake this record from this point on—what is *Eliminator* if not *Tres Hombres* with sequencers and synthesizers?—but they never got it better than they did here.

Stephen Thomas Erlewine

Fandango!
1975, Warner Bros.

Blessed with their first full-fledged hit album, ZZ Top followed it up with *Fandango!*, a record split between a side of live tracks and a side of new studio cuts. In a way, this might have made sense, since they were a kick-ass live band, and they do sound good here, but it's hard not to see this as a bit of a wasted opportunity in retrospect. Why? Because the studio side is a worthy successor to the all-fine *Tres Hombres*, driven by "Tush" and "Heard It on the X," two of their greatest songs that build on that album by consolidating their sound and amplifying their humor. If they had sustained this energy and quality throughout a full studio album, it would have been their greatest, but instead the mood is broken by the live cuts. Now, these are really good live cuts—and "Backdoor Medley" and "Jailhouse Rock" were fine interpretations, making familiar songs sound utterly comfortable in their signature sound—and *Fandango!* remains one of their better albums, but it's hard not to think that it could have been even better.

Stephen Thomas Erlewine

Degüello
1979, Warner Bros.

ZZ Top returned after an extended layoff in late 1979 with *Degüello*, their best album since 1973's *Tres Hombres*. During their time off, ZZ Top didn't change much—hell, their sound never really changed during their entire career—but it did harden, in a way. The grooves became harder, sleeker, and their off-kilter sensibility and humor began to dominate, as "Cheap Sunglasses" and "Fool for Your Stockings" illustrate. Ironically, this, their wildest album lyrically, doesn't have the unhinged rawness of their early blooze rockers, but the streamlined production makes it feel sleazier all the same, since its slickness lets the perversity slide forth. And, forget not, the trio is in fine shape here, knocking out a great set of rockers and sounding stylish all the time. Undoubtedly one of their strong suits.

Stephen Thomas Erlewine

Eliminator
1983, Warner Bros.

ZZ Top had reached the top of the charts before, but that didn't make their sudden popularity in 1983 any more predictable. It wasn't that they were just popular—they were *hip*, for God's sake, since they were one of the only AOR favorites to figure out how to harness the stylish, synthesized grooves of new wave, and then figure out how to sell it on MTV. Of course, it helped that they had songs that deserved to be hits. With "Gimme All Your Lovin'," "Sharp Dressed Man," and "Legs," they had their greatest set of singles since the heady days of *Tres Hombres*, and the songs that surrounded them weren't bad either—they would have been singles on *El Loco*, as a matter of fact. The songs alone would have made *Eliminator* one of ZZ Top's three greatest albums, but their embrace of synths and sequencers made it a blockbuster hit, since it was the sound of the times. Years later, the sound of the times winds up sounding a bit stiff. It's still an excellent ZZ Top album, one of their best, yet it sounds like a mechanized ZZ Top thanks to the unflaggingly accurate grooves. Then again, that's part of the album's charm—this is new wave blues-rock, glossed up for the video, looking as good as the omnipresent convertible on the cover and sounding as irresistible as Reaganomics. Not the sort the old-school fans or blues-rock purists will love, but ZZ Top never sounded as much like a band of its time as they did here.

Stephen Thomas Erlewine

Chrome, Smoke & BBQ: The ZZ Top Box
October 2003, Warner Bros.

Prior to 2003's *Chrome, Smoke & BBQ*, ZZ Top's catalog was crying out for a comprehensive retrospective. Not that the band hadn't been anthologized before: they had two hits collections, with notably different track listings, and in 1987's *Six Pack*, they even had a makeshift box set, but all three of these were hampered by limited focus and haphazard execution. *Chrome, Smoke & BBQ* addresses both of these concerns by focusing on the trio's 20 years at Warner—from 1970's *ZZ Top's First Album* to 1990's *Recycler*—picking the best 70 or so songs from these ten albums and spreading them over the course of a lavish four-disc, 80-track box set. This is the first logical approach to ZZ Top's career yet, and while it isn't a perfect collection, it comes tantalizingly close to that ideal. The primary problem is that by the time the fourth disc rolls around, the collection has lost considerable momentum—and that's without even touching any material from the forgettable albums the band waxed for RCA in the '90s. With its robotic beats and flattened production, *Recycler* pointed the way toward those RCA records, yet it did have some excellent songs—"Give It Up," "My Head's in Mississippi," and "Doubleback"—that harked back to the group's strengths, something that would have been more apparent if these songs appeared at the end of disc three, after the *Afterburner* material. Instead, they're stranded on the fourth disc, along with four other songs from *Recycler*, for a grand total of seven of ten songs from that album, to which are added six "Medium

Rare" tracks—the obligatory obscurities that are included on each box set, this time being a pretty cool Spanish version of "Francene," an OK live take on "Cheap Sunglasses" from a 1980 promo single, and four 12" remixes, none of which are very good. This disc is required listening only for diehards. Fortunately, the other three discs are damn near perfect, containing six to seven songs from each of their albums except their debut (nearly all of those records had a mere ten tracks, making this a very generous sampling) along with three tracks from guitarist/vocalist Billy Gibbons' first band, the Moving Sidewalks, and a single, "Miller's Farm"/"Salt Lick," from the "embryonic" ZZ Top, before bassist Dusty Hill or drummer Frank Beard joined forces with Gibbons. All the hits and classic rock radio staples are here, of course, along with a wealth of album tracks that illustrate that even if the band didn't have much range—whether the production was raw and greasy as it was on "La Grange" or clean and sleek, like the Police playing the Rolling Stones, as on "Pearl Necklace," they rarely strayed from either fast blues boogie or slow blues—they did have strong songwriting chops, witnessed by such buried treasures as the raucous "Brown Sugar" and "Just Got Paid," the monster groove of "I'm Bad, I'm Nationwide," the sweet "Leila," the crawling "Blue Jean Blues," and the unspeakable sleaze of the oozing "Mexican Blackbird" and smirking "I Got the Six." All this and more (including a radio commercial for *Deguello*) spread out over three addictive discs that truly do condense ZZ Top's records to their very best. It would be nice to have the good *Recycler* songs sandwiched onto the third disc and top the set off at three discs—it would have been a nice symmetry, with one disc for each band member—but it's easy enough to ignore the last disc and revel in how good the rest of the set is. Basically, *Chrome, Smoke & BBQ* is all the ZZ Top you'd ever need. [*Chrome, Smoke & BBQ* was released in two editions, both containing a terrific book, filled with great photos—including early shots of Gibbons in the Moving Sidewalks, without the beard—testimonials by the likes of Billy Bob Thornton, Dwight Yoakam, Ann Richards, and of all people, David Lynch (who immortally proclaims "ZZ Top = the fast track to cool"), an excellent history by Tom Vickers, and track-by-track notes by Gibbons, Hill, and Beard, as told to Bob Merlis. The limited edition is quite fancy in its own right, encased in a mock roadhouse shack and containing a booklet shaped as a menu, a sheet of ZZ Top paper dolls (no perforations, however; this is for display purposes only), and a flipbook that finds the trio doing their signature twirling guitars and hand gestures. It's a little elaborate, but it's fun, particularly because the four discs are in jewel cases and can be transported while this sits on the set, next to the other impractical, oversized box sets, such as that Charley Patton box designed as a fake album of 78s, in your collection.]

Stephen Thomas Erlewine

MUSIC MAPS

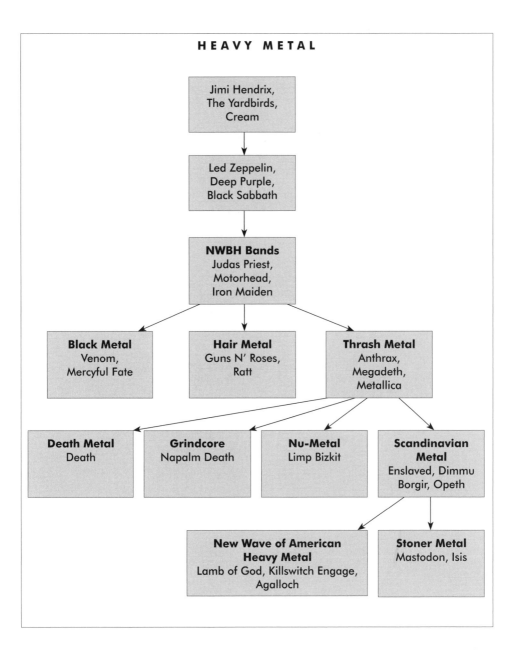

HEAVY METAL

Jimi Hendrix, The Yardbirds, Cream

Led Zeppelin, Deep Purple, Black Sabbath

NWBH Bands
Judas Priest, Motorhead, Iron Maiden

Black Metal
Venom, Mercyful Fate

Hair Metal
Guns N' Roses, Ratt

Thrash Metal
Anthrax, Megadeth, Metallica

Death Metal
Death

Grindcore
Napalm Death

Nu-Metal
Limp Bizkit

Scandinavian Metal
Enslaved, Dimmu Borgir, Opeth

New Wave of American Heavy Metal
Lamb of God, Killswitch Engage, Agalloch

Stoner Metal
Mastodon, Isis

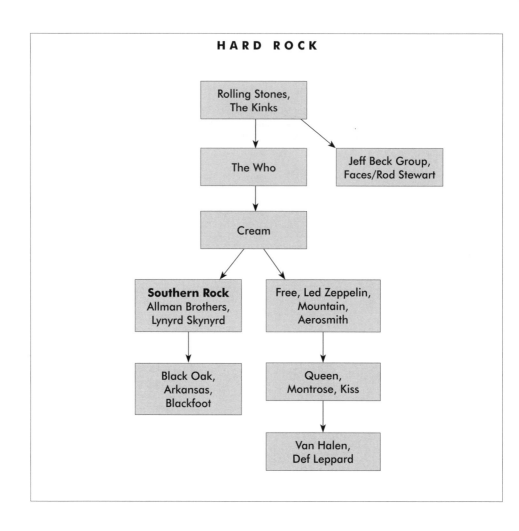

HARD ROCK

Rolling Stones, The Kinks

The Who

Jeff Beck Group, Faces/Rod Stewart

Cream

Southern Rock
Allman Brothers, Lynyrd Skynyrd

Free, Led Zeppelin, Mountain, Aerosmith

Black Oak, Arkansas, Blackfoot

Queen, Montrose, Kiss

Van Halen, Def Leppard

GUITAR HEROES

No instrument in rock & roll is as mythic as the guitar. Other instruments were there at the outset—most notably, the piano and the saxophone—and it's hard to imagine the music without the driving force of drums and bass, but the guitar was the center of the music, possessing a near-mystical aura. There's a reason why Eric Clapton was nicknamed God, a reason why Jimi Hendrix and Jimmy Page are still worshipped decades after they reigned—and there's a reason why a video game where contestants compete at miming guitar licks is one of the most popular games of the 2000s: the guitar symbolizes rock & roll. The name of that game is Guitar Hero, which is what the best guitarists always were. But who were the original guitar heroes, and where did they come from? This list traces the history, taking it into the end of the classic rock era.

Blues Guitar Heroes

BB King
Albert King
Freddie King
Hubert Sumlin
Magic Sam
T-Bone Walker
Clarence Gatemouth Brown
Otis Rush
Albert Collins
Ike Turner
Elmore James
Son House
Mississippi John Hurt

Jazz Guitar Heroes

Wes Montgomery
Kenny Burrell
Charlie Christian
Les Paul
Django Reinhardt
Eddie Lang
Lonnie Johnson
Grant Green
Joe Pass
Jim Hall
Freddie Green
John Scofield
Joe Pass
Tal Farlow

Country Guitar Heroes

Merle Travis
Chet Atkins
Roy Nichols
Don Rich
Roy Clark
Willie Nelson
Glen Campbell
Clarence White
Speedy West
Jimmy Bryant

Joe Maphis
Doc Watson
Tony Rice
Jerry Reed

Early Rock & Roll Guitar Heroes

Chuck Berry
Bo Diddley
James Burton
Scotty Moore
Link Wray
Carl Perkins
Eddie Cochran
Lonnie Mack
Duane Eddy
Cliff Gallup
Buddy Holly
Johnny Burnette
Hank Marvin
Lowman Pauling
Mickey Baker
Travis Wammack

British Invasion Heroes

George Harrison
Dave Davies
Pete Townshend
Alan Price
Hilton Valentine
Jeff Beck
Eric Clapton
Dick Taylor
Eddie Phillips

Folk Rock Heroes

Roger McGuinn
Neil Young
Stephen Stills
John Martyn
Richard Thompson
Bert Jansch

Blues Rock Heroes

Mike Bloomfield
Mick Abrahams
Peter Green
Jeremey Spence
Alvin Lee
Roy Buchanan
Lonnie Mack
Blind Al Wilson

The Birth of the Guitar Hero

Eric Clapton
Jeff Beck
Keith Richards
Jimmy Page
Jimi Hendrix
Pete Townshend
Alin Lee

Psychedelic Heroes

Jorma Kaukonen
Jerry Garcia
Bob Weir
Alvin Lee
Robbie Krieger
Randy California
Jon Cipollina

Jazz Rock Heroes

Carlos Santana
Terry Kath
Sonny Sharrock
John McLaughlin
Frank Zappa
Harvey Mandel
Larry Coryell
Al DiMeola

Underground Rock Heroes

Frank Zappa
Lou Reed
Sterling Morrison
Fred Sonic Smith
Wayne Kramer
Ron Asheton
Manuel Gottsching
Michael Rother

70s Titans

Brian May
David Gilmour
Jeff Beck
Jimmy Page
Joe Walsh
Neil Young
Duane Allman
Eddie Van Halen
Joe Perry & Brad Whitford
Eddie Hazel
Ted Nugent

70s Art Rock Heroes

Steve Howe
Steve Hackett
David Gilmour
Adrian Belew
Allan Holdsworth
John McLaughlin
Robert Fripp
Martin Barre
Alex Lifeson
Bill Nelson
Phil Miller
Phil Manzanera

Glam Rock Heroes

Mick Ronson
Marc Bolan
Punky Meadows
Noddy Holder

70s Hard Rock Heroes

Mick Ralphs
Paul Kossoff
Ron Wood
Tommy Bolin
Leslie West
Brian Robertson
Scott Gorham
Dick Wagner & Steve Hunter
Donald "Buck Dharma" Roeser
Nils Lofgren
Tommy Shaw
Ronnie Montrose
Ted Nugent
Randy Bachman
Thom Scholz
Pat Travers
Frank Marino
Joe Perry

70s Heavy Metal Heroes

Tony Iommi
Angus Young & Malcolm Young
Ritchie Blackmore
Ace Frehely
Randy Rhoads
Michael Schenker
Uli John Roth

70s Southern Rock Heroes

Duane Allman
Dickey Betts
Lowell George
Allen Collins
Gary Rossington
Ed King
Alvin Bishop

70s Session Masters

Steve Lukather
Ry Cooder
Denny Diaz
Jeff "Skunk" Baxter
Rick Derringer
Larry Carlton
Waddy Wachtel

70s Blues Rock

Johnny Winter
J. Geils
Steve Miller
Billy Gibbons
Mick Taylor
Rory Gallagher
Robin Trower

70s Pop Heroes

Lindsey Buckingham
Peter Frampton
George Harrison
Todd Rundgren
Rick Nielsen
Neal Schon
Mark Knopfler
Tom Scholz

TIMELINE: DEBUTS

Some debut albums have an immediate impact the year they're released, others fade into the background, with the band proving their staying power years later. Whether they're instant hits or nothing more than training wheels, it's fascinating to look at when classic rock bands released their first albums: it provides a snapshot of each year, and the progression—and peaks—of the classic rock era.

1963

The Beatles: *Please Please Me*

1964

The Rolling Stones: *The Rolling Stones (England's Newest Hitmakers)*
The Kinks: *The Kinks*

1965

Yardbirds: *Having a Rave Up*
Byrds: *Mr. Tambourine Man*
The Who: *Sing My Generation*

1966

Love: *Love*
Buffalo Springfield: *Buffalo Springfield*
Cream: *Fresh Cream*
The Mothers of Invention: *Freak Out!*
Jefferson Airplane: *Takes Off*

1967

The Jimi Hendrix Experience: *Are you Experienced?*
Moody Blues: *Days of Future Passed*
Velvet Underground: *The Velvet Underground & Nico*
Doors: *The Doors*
Grateful Dead: *Grateful Dead*
Pink Floyd: *The Piper at the Gates of Dawn*
Traffic: *Mr. Fantasy*

1968

Dr. John: *Gris-Gris*
Blood, Sweat & Tears: *Child Is Father to the Man*
Creedence Clearwater Revival: *Creedence Clearwater Revival*
The Band: *Music from Big Pink*
Van Morrison: *Astral Weeks*
Big Brother & the Holding Company: *Cheap Thrills*
Free: *Tons of Sobs*
Jeff Beck: *Truth*
Jethro Tull: *This Was*
The Bob Seger System: *Ramblin' Gamblin' Man*
Fleetwood Mac: *Peter Green's Fleetwood Mac*
Steve Miller Band: *Children of the Future*

1969

James Gang: *Yer Album*
King Crimson: *In the Court of the Crimson King*
Free: *Free*
Mott the Hoople: *Mott the Hoople*
MC5: *Kick Out the Jams*
Allman Brothers Band: *The Allman Brothers Band*
Rod Stewart: *The Rod Stewart Album*
Johnny Winter: *Johnny Winter*
Led Zeppelin: *Led Zeppelin*
Flying Burrito Brothers: *The Gilded Palace of Sin*
Chicago: *Chicago Transit Authority*
Crosby, Stills & Nash: *Crosby, Stills & Nash*
Blind Faith: *Blind Faith*
Santana: *Santana*
Yes: *Yes*
The Stooges: *The Stooges*
Neil Young: *Neil Young*
Genesis: *From Genesis to Revelation*
Elton John: *Empty Sky*

1970

The Faces: *First Step*
Mountain: *Climbing*
Stephen Stills: *Stephen Stills*
Black Sabbath: *Black Sabbath*
Paul McCartney: *McCartney*
Eric Clapton: *Eric Clapton*
Todd Rundgren: *Runt*
George Harrison: *All Things Must Pass*
John Lennon: *John Lennon/Plastic Ono Band*
ZZ Top: *ZZ Top's First Album*
Supertramp: *Supertramp*
J. Geils Band: *J. Geils Band*

1971

Electric Light Orchestra: *Electric Light Orchestra*
Carole King: *Tapestry*
Thin Lizzy: *Thin Lizzy*
Billy Joel: *Cold Spring Harbor*
Doobie Brothers: *The Doobie Brothers*
REO Speedwagon: *REO Speedwagon*

1972

Steely Dan: *Can't Buy a Thrill*
Roxy Music: *Roxy Music*
Gram Parsons: *G.P.*
Joe Walsh: *Barnstorm*
Blue Öyster Cult: *Blue Öyster Cult*
Jackson Browne: *Jackson Browne*
Paul Simon: *Paul Simon*
Eagles: *Eagles*
Styx: *Styx*

1973

New York Dolls: *New York Dolls*
Montrose: *Montrose*
Bruce Springsteen: *Greetings From Asbury Park, N.J.*
Aerosmith: *Aerosmith*
Queen: *Queen*
10cc: *10cc*

1974

Kiss: *Kiss*
Rush: *Rush*
Kansas: *Kansas*

1975

Ian Hunter: *Ian Hunter*
Jefferson Starship: *Red Octopus*
John Fogerty: *John Fogerty*
Journey: *Journey*
Ted Nugent: *Ted Nugent*

1976

Warren Zevon: *Warren Zevon*
Tom Petty: *Tom Petty & the Heartbreakers*
Boston: *Boston*
AC/DC: *High Voltage*
Heart: *Dreamboat Annie*
John Mellencamp: *Chestnut Street Incident*

1977

Iggy Pop: *Idiot*
Meat Loaf: *Bat Out of Hell*
Cheap Trick: *Cheap Trick*
Peter Gabriel: *Peter Gabriel* [1]
Foreigner: *Foreigner*

1978

Van Halen: *Van Halen*
Cars: *The Cars*
Dire Straits: *Dire Straits*
Toto: *Toto*

1979

Rickie Lee Jones: *Rickie Lee Jones*

1980

Loverboy: *Loverboy*
Pretenders: *The Pretenders*

DOUBLE ALBUMS

Above all, classic rock was an era built on albums—and maybe no albums carried greater mythic weight than the double album. Each double album provided so much music to get lost in, but it was more than just the music in the grooves—it was the entire package, the pull of the artwork, the way the gatefold spread open to reveal itself. The double album provided a full universe, one that's retained its mystique into the CD era, and even into the MP3 years. Here are some of the most memorable double albums (and a handful of triple albums, too) of the classic rock era.

1966

Bob Dylan: *Blonde on Blonde*
The Mothers of Invention: *Freak Out!*

1968

The Beatles: *The Beatles* [White Album]
Cream: *Wheels of Fire*
Jimi Hendrix: *Electric Ladyland*

1969

The Who: *Tommy*
Pink Floyd: *Ummagumma*

1970

Joe Cocker: *Mad Dogs & Englishmen*
Derek & the Dominos: *Layla*
George Harrison: *All Things Must Pass*

1971

Allman Brothers: *At the Fillmore East*
George Harrison: *The Concert for Bangledesh*

1972

Allman Brothers: *Eat a Peach*
Todd Rundgren: *Something/Anything?*
Rolling Stones: *Exile on Main St.*

1973

The Who: *Quadrophenia*
Elton John: *Goodbye Yellow Brick Road*
Yes: *Yessongs*

1974

Van Morrison: *It's Too Late to Stop Now*
Yes: *Tales from Topographic Oceans*
Todd Rundgren: *Todd*
Santana: *Lotus*
Bob Dylan and the Band: *Before the Flood*
Emerson, Lake & Palmer: *Welcome Back My Friends to the Show That Never Ends*
Electric Light Orchestra: *Eldorado*
Genesis: *Lamb Lies Down on Broadway*

1975

Led Zeppelin: *Physical Graffiti*
Bob Dylan and the Band: *Basement Tapes*
Kiss: *Alive!*

1976

J. Geils Band: *Blow Your Face Out*
Peter Frampton: *Frampton Comes Alive*
Paul McCartney: *Wings Over America*
Lynyrd Skynyrd: *One More from the Road*
Bob Seger: *Live Bullet*

1978

Thin Lizzy: *Live and Dangerous*
Little Feat: *Waiting for Columbus*

1979

Fleetwood Mac: *Tusk*
Pink Floyd: *The Wall*
Frank Zappa: *Joe's Garage*

1980

Bruce Springsteen: *The River*

LIVE ALBUMS

Prior to the classic rock era, live albums weren't common in rock & roll. There were a few exceptions to the rule, like Bo Diddley's 1963 LP *Bo Diddley's Beach Party*, but it wasn't until bands started to improvise—and when the industry shifted from singles to LPs in the wake of *Sgt. Pepper*—that live albums became a staple in rock & roll. From the beginning, there were two kinds of live albums: one that captures the kinetic energy of a band in concert and one that captures the instrumental virtuosity of the group. Classic rock started with the simple, exciting LPs of the Rolling Stones' *Got Live If You Want It!* and the Kinks' *Live at Kelvin Hall*, but in 1968, Cream stretched out on the second half of *Wheels of Fire* and Ten Years After unleashed *Undead*, and then there was no holding bands back. Soon, it became standard for classic rockers to release live albums, and almost all of them did. The best of these showcased a band and documented its growth and strength in a way the studio records never did, often bringing the group greater acclaim and a bigger audience. Examples are Kiss's *Alive!*, Bob Seger's *Live Bullet*, Cheap Trick's *At Budokan,* and, of course, Peter Frampton's era-defining double-LP blockbuster *Frampton Comes Alive*. Here's a listing of some of the most crucial live platters that mattered in the classic rock era.

1966

Rolling Stones: *Got Live If You Want It!*

1968

Kinks: *Live at Kelvin Hall*
Cream: *Wheels of Fire*
TenYears After: *Undead*

1969

John Lennon: *Live Peace in Toronto*
MC5: *Kick Out the Jams*

1970

Jimi Hendrix: *Band of Gypsys*
The Who: *Live at Leeds*
Joe Cocker: *Mad Dogs & Englishmen*
Rolling Stones: *Get Yer Ya-Ya's Out!*
Cream: *Live Cream*

1971

Traffic: *Welcome to the Canteen*
Allman Brothers: *At the Fillmore East*
George Harrison: *The Concert for Bangledesh*

1972

J. Geils Band: *Live Full House*
Guess Who: *Live at the Paramount*
Allman Brothers: *Eat a Peach*
Grateful Dead: *Europe '72*
Emerson, Lake & Palmer: *Pictures at an Exhibition*
Cream: *Live Cream, Vol. 2*
The Band: *Rock of Ages*
Deep Purple: *Made in Japan*

1973

Black Oak Arkansas: *Raunch 'n' Roll Live*
Neil Young: *Time Fades Away*
Yes: *Yessongs*
Traffic: *On the Road*

1974

Mott the Hoople: *Live*
Lou Reed: *Rock N Roll Animal*
Van Morrison: *It's Too Late to Stop Now*
Bob Dylan: *Before the Flood*
Santana: *Lotus*
David Bowie: *David Live*
Frank Zappa: *Roxy & Elsewhere*

1975

Kiss: *Alive!*

1976

Paul McCartney: *Wings Over America*
Led Zeppelin: *The Song Remains the Same*
Lynyrd Skynyrd: *One More for the Road*
J. Geils Band: *Blow Your Face Out*
Peter Frampton: *Frampton Comes Alive!*
Bob Seger: *Live Bullet*
Rush: *All the World's a Stage*

1977

Jackson Browne: *Running on Empty*
Kiss: *Alive II*
Genesis: *Seconds Out*
REO Speedwagon: *Live: You Get What You Play For*
Rolling Stones: *Love You Live*
Foghat: *Foghat Live*

Live Albums

1978

AC/DC: *If You Want Blood You've Got It*
Todd Rundgren: *Back to the Bars*
Thin Lizzy: *Live and Dangerous*
The Band: *The Last Waltz*
Little Feat: *Waiting for Columbus*

1979

Cheap Trick: *At Budokan*
Neil Young: *Live Rust*
Queen: *Live Killers*
The Who: *The Kids Are Alright*

1980

Eric Clapton: *Just One Night*

1981

Warren Zevon: *Stand in the Fire*
Billy Joel: *Songs in the Attic*
Rush: *Exit...Stage Left*

1982

Genesis: *Three Sides Live*

PLAYLISTS

Classic rock was certainly an album-oriented format, but it nevertheless was driven by songs, songs that were hit singles even if only on the radio. After all, the very term "classic rock" was popularized by radio, giving a good indication of the power of individual songs to the era itself. Some of these songs may have been played to death, some still retain their power after countless spins, some are memorable for their instrumentation, some are memorable for their riffs. Here, we divide many of those songs into playlists—whether you choose to load them into your MP3 player or not is entirely up to you.

Classic Rock Songs That You're Not Sick Of

The Byrds: "Eight Miles High"
The Chambers Brothers: "Time Has Come Today"
Creedence Clearwater Revival: "Green River"
Crosby, Stills & Nash: Suite: "Judy Blue Eyes"
Carole King: "I Feel the Earth Move"
Roxy Music: "Love Is the Drug"
Todd Rundgren: "Hello It's Me"
Bob Seger: "Heavy Music"
Rod Stewart: "Maggie May"
The Who: "Baba O'Riley"
The Band: "The Weight"
Bob Dylan: "Tangled Up in Blue"
Mott the Hoople: "All the Young Dudes"
The Faces: "Stay with Me"
Fleetwood Mac: "Go Your Own Way"
AC/DC: "You Shook Me All Night Long"
The Doobie Brothers: "Black Water"
Queen: "Killer Queen"
Gerry Rafferty: "Baker Street"
Journey: "Don't Stop Believing"
The Guess Who: "No Sugar Tonight/New Mother Nature"
Blue Öyster Cult: "(Don't Fear) The Reaper"
Billy Squier: "The Stroke"
The Doors: "Roadhouse Blues"
Van Halen: "Panama"
Steve Miller Band: "Jet Airliner"
The Rolling Stones: "Jumpin' Jack Flash"
Thin Lizzy: "The Boys Are Back in Town"
Led Zeppelin: "Hey Hey What Can I Do"
Alice Cooper: Be My Lover
Brownsville Station: "Smokin' in the Boys Room"
Billy Joel: "Scenes from an Italian Restaurant "

Classic Rock Songs That Need Not Be Played Again

Bad Company: "Feel Like Makin' Love"
Big Brother & the Holding Company: "Piece of My Heart"
Buffalo Springfield: "For What It's Worth"
The Byrds: "Turn! Turn! Turn!"
Joe Cocker: "With a Little Help from My Friends"
Eagles: "Hotel California"
Peter Frampton: "Baby, I Love Your Way"

Jethro Tull: "Aqualung"
Kansas: "Dust in the Wind"
Led Zeppelin: "Stairway to Heaven"
Steve Miller Band: "The Joker"
Pink Floyd: "Another Brick in the Wall, Pt. 2"
Procol Harum: "A Whiter Shade of Pale"
Lou Reed: "Walk on the Wild Side"
Steppenwolf: "Born to Be Wild"
Rod Stewart: "Hot Legs"
Elton John: "Crocodile Rock"
The Who: "Squeezebox"
Derek & The Dominos: "Layla"
Lynyrd Skynyd: "Sweet Home Alabama"
The Grateful Dead: "Truckin'"
The Doors: "L.A. Woman"
Bachman Turner Overdrive: "Takin' Care of Business"
Guess Who: "American Woman"
Billy Joel: "Piano Man"
Eric Clapton: "Wonderful Tonight"
Neil Young: "Hey Hey, My My (Into the Black)"
Queen: "Bohemian Rhapsody"
John Lennon: "Imagine"
Lynyrd Skynyrd: "Freebird"
Don McLean: "American Pie"
The Doors: "Light My Fire"
Creedence Clearwater Revival: "Proud Mary"
Van Morrison: "Brown Eyed Girl"
Bob Seger: "Old Time Rock & Roll"

Classic Rock Love Songs

Van Halen: "So This Is Love"
Foreigner: "Feels Like the First Time"
Nazareth: "Love Hurts"
Beach Boys: "Don't Worry Baby"
Queen: "Somebody to Love"
Harry Nilsson: "Don't Forget Me"
Pete Townshend: "Let My Love Open the Door"
Jimi Hendrix: "Little Wing"
Thin Lizzy: "Sarah"
Kiss: "Beth"
Roxy Music: "Mother of Pearl"
Bob Dylan: "Love Minus Zero/No Limit"
Moody Blues: "Nights in White Satin"
Bob Welch: "Sentimental Lady"
Paul McCartney: "Maybe I'm Amazed"

Blue Oyster Cult: "Burnin' for You"
Eric Clapton: "Wonderful Tonight"
Journey: "Open Arms"
Meat Loaf: "Two Out of Three Ain't Bad"
Rolling Stones: "Beast of Burden"

Classic Riffs

Cream: "Sunshine of Your Love"
Heart: "Barracuda"
Jimi Hendrix: "Purple Haze"
Led Zeppelin: "Heartbreaker"
Neil Young: "Cinnamon Girl"
Dire Straits: "Money for Nothing"
David Bowie: "Ziggy Stardust"
Van Halen: "Ain't Talkin' Love"
Van Halen: "Runnin' With the Devil"
The Kinks: "You Really Got Me"
The Rolling Stones: "(I Can't Get No) Satisfaction"
Jethro Tull: "Aqualung"
Creedence Clearwater Revival: "Up Around the Bend"
Led Zeppelin: "Immigrant Song"
Led Zeppelin: "The Ocean"
Led Zeppelin: "Whole Lotta Love"
Led Zeppelin: "Black Dog"
The Nazz: "Open Your Eyes"
The Who: "I Can't Explain"
Ozzy Osbourne: "Crazy Train"
Black Sabbath: "Iron Man"
Deep Purple: "Smoke on the Water"
AC/DC: "Back in Black"
AC/DC: "Highway to Hell"
T. Rex: "Get It On (Bang a Gong)"
Chuck Berry: "Johnny B. Goode"
ZZ Top: "La Grange"
George Thorogood: "Bad to the Bone"
Thin Lizzy: "Jailbreak"
Aerosmith: "Walk This Way"
Aerosmith: "Sweet Emotion"
Aerosmith: "Back in the Saddle"
Bad Company: "Feel Like Makin' Love"
The Rolling Stones: "Start Me Up"
The Rolling Stones: "Brown Sugar"
Free: "All Right Now"
The Beatles: "Daytripper"
Jimi Hendrix: "Voodoo Chile (Slight Return)"
Heart: "Crazy on You"
The Troggs: "Wild Thing"
David Bowie: "Rebel Rebel"
Motorhead: "Ace of Spades"
James Gang: "Funk #49"
Boston: "More Than a Feeling"

Classic Guitar Solos

The Rolling Stones: "Sympathy for the Devil"
Traffic: "Dear Mr. Fantasy"
Pink Floyd: "Comfortably Numb"
Pink Floyd: "Shine on You Crazy Diamond"
Pink Floyd: "Time"

Queen: "Keep Yourself Alive"
Queen: "Killer Queen"
Queen: "We Will Rock You"
Van Halen: "Hot for Teacher"
Led Zeppelin: "Heart Breaker"
Led Zeppelin: "Stairway to Heaven"
Santana: "Samba Pa Ti"
Blue Oyster Cult: "(Don't Fear) The Reaper"
Funkadelic: "Maggot Brain"
Van Halen: "Eruption"
Cream: "Crossroads"
Cream: "White Room"
Jeff Beck: "Beck's Bolerao"
Neil Young: "Cinnamon Girl"
Lynyrd Skynyrd: "Freebird"
Derek & the Dominoes: "Layla"
Jimi Hendrix: "All Along the Watchtower"
Jimi Hendrix: "Star Spangled Banner"
Jimi Hendrix: "Wind Cries Mary"
Allman Brothers: "Whipping Post"
The Beatles: "While My Guitar Gently Weeps"
Dire Straits: "Sultans of Swing"

Classic Drum Solos

Iron Butterfly: "In-a-Gadda-da-Vida"
The Beatles: "The End"
Cream: "Toad"
Led Zeppelin: "Bonzo's Montreux"
Grand Funk Railroad: "T.N.U.C."
Santana: "Soul Persuasion"
Jimi Hendrix: "Machine Gun"
Rush: "Rhythm Method"
Led Zeppelin: "Moby Dick"
Grateful Dead: "Drums"
The Sufaris: "Wipe Out"
The Who: "My Generation"
Rush: "Villa Strangiato"
Steely Dan: "Aja"
Jimi Hendrix: "Fire"
Yes: "Heart of the Sunrise"
Deep Purple: "Space Truckin'"

Classic Rock Anthems

The Animals: "We Gotta Get Out of This Place"
Argent: "Hold Your Head Up"
The Who: "My Generation"
Nazareth: "Hair of the Dog"
AC/DC: "Highway to Hell"
Grand Funk Railroad: "We're an American Band"
Journey: "Don't Stop Beliving"
Foreigner: "Juke Box Hero"
Aerosmith: "Sweet Emotion"
Mott the Hoople: "All the Young Dudes"
Black Sabbath: "War Pigs"
Rolling Stones: "Sympathy for the Devil"
Bruce Springsteen: "Born to Run"
Lynyrd Skynyrd: "Free Bird"
Molly Hatchet: "Flirtin' with Disaster"
Steppenwolf: "Born to Be Wild"

Kingsmen: "Louie, Louie"
Alice Cooper: "School's Out"
Thin Lizzy: "Boys Are Back in Town"
Queen: "We Are the Champions"
Slade: "Cum on Feel the Noize"
Survivor: "Eye of the Tiger"
MC5: "Kick Out the Jams"
Brownsville Station: "Smokin' in the Boys' Room"

Long Live Rock: Classic Rock Songs About Rock 'n' Roll

Joan Jett: "I Love Rock 'n' Roll"
Queen: "We Will Rock You"
Led Zeppelin: "Rock 'n' Roll"
Kiss: "Rock 'n' Roll All Nite"
The Who: "Long Live Rock"
The Rolling Stones: "It's Only Rock 'n' Roll"
Neil Young: "Rockin' in the Free World"
38 Special: "Rockin' into the Night"
AC/DC: "For Those About to Rock"
Rick Derringer: "Rock 'n' Roll Hoochie Coo"
Scorpions: "Rock You Like a Hurricane"
Bob Seger: "Old Time Rock 'n' Roll"
AC/DC: "It's a Long Way To The Top (If You Wanna Rock 'n' Roll)"
AC/DC: "Rock 'n' Roll Singer"

Classic Rock Instrumentals

Traffic: "Glad"
Jeff Beck: "Freeway Jam"
The Tornadoes: "Telstar"
Electric Light Orchestra: "Fire on High"
Van Halen: "Eruption"
Edgar Winter Group: "Frankenstein"
Queen: "God Save the Queen"
Mason Williams: "Classical Gas"
Booker T. & the MGs: "Green Onions"
Grateful Dead: "Dark Star"
Ventures: "Walk, Don't Run"
Yardbirds: "Beck's Bolero"
Jeff Beck: "Goin' Down"
Rush: "XXY"
Frank Zappa: "Peaches en Regalia"
Focus: "Hocus Pocus"
Love Sculpture: "Sabre Dance"
The Nice: "America"
Jeff Beck: "Cause We've Ended as Lovers"
Allman Brothers: "Jessica"

Gary Glitter: "Rock 'n' Roll, Pt. 2"
Doobie Brothers: "Steamer Lane Breakdown"
Paul Simon: "Anji"
Deep Purple: "Wring That Neck"
Van Halen: "Sunday Afternoon in the Park"
The Champs: "Tequila"
Pink Floyd: "Careful with That Axe, Eugene"
Funkadelic: "Maggot Brain"
Pink Floyd: "One of These Days"

20 Songs with More Cowbell

Grand Funk Railroad: "We're an American Band"
Bachman-Turner Overdrive: "Ain't Seen Nothin' Yet"
Mountain: "Mississippi Queen"
Kiss: "Rock 'n' Roll All Night"
Foghat: "Fool for the City"
Nazareth: "Hair of the Dog"
War: "Low Rider"
Free: "All Right Now"
Cheap Trick: "Dream Police"
Hugh Masekela: "Grazing in the Grass"
Rolling Stones: "Honkey Tonk Women"
Three Dog Night: "Black and White"
Creedence Clearwater Revival: "Down on the Corner"
Jimi Hendrix: "Stone Free"
Blue Öyster Cult: "(Don't Fear) the Reaper"
Beatles: "Drive My Car"
Strawberry Alarm Clock: "Incense and Peppermints"
Santana: "Oye Como Va"
David Bowie: "Diamond Dogs"
James Gang: "Funk #49"

This Guitar Can't Stop Talking

Peter Frampton: "Do You Feel Like We Do (live)"
Zapp and Roger: "More Bounce to the Ounce (or Computer Love)"
Aerosmith: "Sweet Emotion"
Rufus: "Tell Me Something Good"
The Doors: "Cars Hiss by My Window"
Joe Walsh: "Rocky Mountain Way"
Johnny Guitar Watson: "A Real Mother for Ya"
Steely Dan: "Haitian Divorce"
Steve Miller Band: "Joker"
Queen: "Delilah"
Pink Floyd: "Keep Talking"
The Eagles: "Those Shoes"